THE YOUNGHUSBAND EXPEDITION (TO LHASA)
An Interpretation

Simla
May 21. 03

My dear Father

There is a really magnificent business that I have dropped in for. Lord Curzon's original idea of sending an imposing mission — like Malcolm's to Persia, & Burnes' to Kabul in old days — to Lhasa has not been sanctioned; and I am not to go to Lhasa itself as far as is present settled, but only just inside Tibet. Still what I have to do is as important. I have to

From Simla, to 'My dear Father' dated May 21. 1903

THE YOUNGHUSBAND EXPEDITION (TO LHASA)

An Interpretation

*Second Edition
with a new chapter
"A Hundred Years On"*

PARSHOTAM MEHRA

Foreword by
SIR OLAF CAROE

GYAN PUBLISHING HOUSE
NEW DELHI-110002

The Younghusband Expedition (to Lhasa)—An Interpretation

Rs. 890

ISBN: 81-212-0843-2

Published in 2005 in India by
Gyan Publishing House
5, Ansari Road, Darya Ganj, New Delhi-110002
Phones : 23282060, 23261060, Fax : (011) 23285914
E-mail : gyanbook@vsnl.com
Website : http://www.gyanbooks.com

Laser Typesetting at : Shree Vaishnavi Creations, New Delhi
Printed at : Delux Offset Press, Delhi

To
Kamla
and
Isrun

Contents

Illustrations and Maps

Foreword

As one who has had some experience of the Tibetan question in its bearing on the defence of India, both before and after 1947, I am proud to have been asked to introduce Dr. Mehra to his English-reading public, now perhaps more conscious than in the days of the Raj of Tibet's importance in the balance of power in Asia. No student of contemporary events on the Himalaya can afford to be without the background given by an accurate and unbiased appraisal of the causes, the course, and the results of the expedition which went with Sir Francis Younghusband to Lhasa in 1904. Others have written on this subject. But, to my knowledge, none has subjected a dramatic theme to so close and painstaking an analysis as the author of the volume now presented.

Parshotam Lal Mehra is a Panjabi. Born in Amritsar, he graduated from the Panjab University with Honours in 1940, and remained as a history teacher there until 1951, when he joined the staff of the Indian Military Academy, at Dehra Dun. After wide-spaced travel, during which he was admitted to the degree of Ph.D. at Johns Hopkins, Baltimore, he became successively Research Officer in the Indian Ministry of Defence, and Reader in History at the transferred Panjab University which has arisen at the new capital of that state at Chandigarh. Of Dr. Mehra it may truly be said that his approach to historical material is far more solid and much less fantastic than the aery pinnacles of Corbusier against the foothills of the Himalaya.

The author writes with remarkable fairness and objectivity, apportioning balanced criticism or commendation where these are due, recognizing the strength and weaknesses of the character of the chief actors, whether in council or in the field, including British, Indian, Tibetan, Nepalese, Chinese or Russian. He is aware that, though Younghusband forced his way with an army to Lhasa, his personality was such that he left behind for his countrymen, and indeed for India, as it were, a pleasant odour, an impression due to the Tibetan recognition of him as a man of honour, thoughtful, gallant, very human and, as they could see, one to whom spiritual values were all-important. Younghusband's presence in Lhasa was indeed the beginning of the understanding, later developed by others, between the rulers of Tibet on the one hand and Britain and India on the other. Before his time there was a temporal and a spiritual barrier, set by the Himalaya and the then stagnation of Tibet, a barrier not overpassed by the inspirations of Buddhism. The fact that India is now doing all she can to ensure that the new Tibetan spirit shall live on owes at least something to those far-off initiatives in 1904.

Dr. Mehra puts all this to us in memorable words. And from records now available he gives us admirable documentation of the complicated springs of policy operating in Curzon's mind, and forced by him on an unwilling and moribund Conservative administration in Britain, a policy which eventually led to the Mission's taking the field. This analysis is followed by a fascinating narrative of the slow progress of the Mission in the field, leaving the reader with the conviction that, had not its leader been a man of the finest calibre, the whole expedition must have ended in military and political disaster. As one reads, it is impossible to withhold sympathy from the unfortunate man on the spot, with uncertain and often contradictory instructions, hampered by a mulish subordinate, surrounded by a hostile population, and required to keep his nerve and his temper at an altitude of 15,000 feet. It was a prodigious effort and it succeeded, leaving good-will behind. The smallness of the men who wished to censure Younghusband on his return is astonishing and it is fully brought out.

Today, no doubt, the Chinese, and others blind to their own record, would scorn all this as old-fashioned imperialism. To such a view Dr. Mehra's account is an admirable corrective. While he does not spare the arrogance of Curzon, the uneasy littleness of Brodrick and others, he is able to turn our eyes to the long-term importance of Tibet on the international stage—a fact now fully realized by the India of Mr. Nehru and Mr. Shastri. On one point I find the author's analysis not conclusive—the degree to which Curzon was justified in assigning Russian-inspired intrigue in Lhasa as the main ground for despatching the Mission, in other words, 'the Russian bogey'. On this issue it is probable that more evidence might have been available on a diligent perusal of the reports forwarded to Curzon by the Nepal Government, originating with their Agent in Lhasa.

Dr. Mehra writes a limpid and arresting English prose which is a pleasure to read. His pages are many, but they are enlivened by a humorous touch. Younghusband would have enjoyed the verdict of the Tibetans on the British character, cited from Charles Bell's writings and comparing us with the Chinese : 'When one has known the scorpion, one looks on the frog as divine.'

The frog has a proud look and a way of jumping unpredictably. But he is never fierce or vindictive.

Newham House   Olaf Caroe
Steyning (Sussex)

Preface to the Second Edition

In the course of a long tête-à-tête with my old friend Dr Alastair Lamb at the History of Tibet Conference in Edinburgh (September 2001), he impressed upon me the desirability of bringing out a new edition of my earlier work on the Younghusband expedition to Lhasa. Mounted in 1903-4, this would broadly synchronise with the centenary of the British invasion. Later, in the course of interaction with other friends both at home and abroad, Dr Lamb's views found wide endorsement. To be sure, before long I was grappling with the shape and form of the old-new book.

There was a broad consensus that the earlier edition stood as an integral whole; that it should not be tampered with either in terms of its contents or in revising/recasting the text. In deference, as the reader would no doubt discover, the old book remains virtually unchanged. All that has been done is to take note of new research in terms of an impressive array of periodical literature as well as detailed works that have made an appearance in the course of the forty odd years that separate the two editions. In the event, a new chapter, 'A Hundred Years On' took shape and form and is designed to comprehend all that was deemed relevant to the subject in the course of a fresh, hard scrutiny.

A number of friends helped. During my visit to St Petersburg (June 2002), Professor Alexandre Andreyev was gracious enough to loan to me a copy of his work which a year later was to appear in book form, *Soviet Russia and Tibet*, Leiden, 2003. I found his introductory chapters most useful in terms of Russian involvement with the Buryat Mongol high priest, Agvan Dorjief, the 13th Dalai Lama's roving ambassador who played such a crucial role in precipitating British intervention in Tibet's affairs. Dr David H Schimmelpenninck van der Oyer, a Canadian academic whom I met in St Petersburg was good enough to draw my attention to his own work on the subject which I found to be quite helpful.

Dr Isrun Engelhar, a distinguished academic whose scholarship and research relates principally to the well-known German traveller Ernest Schaefer's Tibet expedition (1938-39) and whom I had met both at St Andrews and later Vienna was most helpful in making me aware of Wilhelm Filchner's role in writing his *Sturm uber Asien* (1924), a half fictional account of Russian involvement in Tibet's affairs. More, she helped me acquire a copy of Dorjief' s *Memoirs.*

Dr Carole MacGranhan who teaches at Boulder, Colorado proved to be a stimulating interlocutor and was gracious enough to acquire for me photocopy of a recent doctoral dissertation, Julia Bronson Trott's " 'One turn of pitch and toss' : Curzon, Younghusband and the Gamble for Lhasa" (2000) at the University of Hawaii. A very well researched piece it should, hopefully, appear in print before long.

Dr Alastair Lamb not only drew my attention to Scott Berry's important work on Japanese travellers-*Monks, Spies and A Soldier of Fortune, 1995*- to Tibet with special reference to the half-monk, half-spy, Ekai Kawaguchi. More, he was good enough to gift me a copy of the book.

Nearer home, I was able to dig up at the National Archives in New Delhi 'Selections' from the 'native' newspapers of the period which give a unique insight into contemporary opinion. Right here in Chandigarh itself, the Trustees of the *Tribune* were gracious enough to give me access to the paper's old, 1903-4, files.

My old haunt, Teenmurti House, was useful in locating some relevant books and journals as was the Panjab University Library in Chandigarh. I found their staff, one and all, both helpful and cooperative.

A word on two recent studies which appeared early this year but came, sad to say, a little too late for detailed notice in the introductory chapter. To start with, Charles Allen's *Duel in the Snows: the true story of the Younghusband Mission to Lhasa* (John Murray, London, 2004) which offers a fascinating account resting for most part on the diaries, letters and memoirs of British military officers commanding Indian troops, of non-combatants such as officers from the Medical Corps, and of ordinary British soldiers, BORs (British Other Ranks). Above all, on the private diaries or little known accounts of newspaper correspondents who accompanied the mission. Allen who claims to offer "a more human perspective" of events also had the advantage of retracing on the ground a large part of the invading army's route to and from Lhasa. Briefly, he has set the record straight on the Younghusband-Macdonald stand-off insisting that contrary to received wisdom, the commander of the escort was more sinned against than sinning. For in sharp contrast to Younghusband, a compulsive writer with a whole army of friends, Macdonald was a man of few words and even fewer friends. Trained to do things by the book, he was a complete foil to the charismatic if also a wee bit adventurous leader of the expedition.

Another study, not yet to hand, is by a Bhutanese researcher: Sonam Kinga, *Ugyen Wangchuk and the Younghusband Mission to Lhasa* (Thimpu, 2004). Kinga avers inter alia that the future Bhutanese ruler's grasp of both "imperial realpolitik and the Tibetan outlook" made him an "invaluable" mediator. And insofar as he enjoyed the trust both of Younghusband as well as the Dalai Lama, the Bhutanese leader was, Kinga insists, able to effect "a peaceful" settlement with the Tibetans.

It is most pleasant for me to place on record my appreciation of the efforts of my publishers who decided on a fresh composition in place of a reprint of the old book. They were also receptive to some of my suggestions to help improve the end-product.

As is not unusual, my old friend and colleague Dr S R Bakshi was a great help in many ways. As a matter of fact, much of the credit for the new edition goes to him.

It remains to record my sincere thanks to my wife who as always was a wonderful support. So was Isrun Engelhardt. It is a pleasure and a privilege to dedicate the new edition to them both.

Chandigarh   Parshotam Mehra
April 2004

Acknowledgments

To say that this book grew out of a thesis for a doctoral degree from the Johns Hopkins University more than a decade ago would be factually correct, although in the process the transformation from the original has been beyond recognition. A varied career, in and out of the strictly academic world, kept the author from undertaking a major revision which the availability of new source material in the intervening years had made absolutely imperative. Lately, thanks to the seemingly invisible, yet remorseless, inexorable pressures of University life the idea of publishing the work, without any change whatever, first suggested itself early in 1962. It would be only fair to record my warm appreciation of the fact that the publishers were willing to undertake this without ado. On second thoughts, however, it appeared that while the original may stand in its entirety, an introductory chapter might be added which would survey not only the new research-material available, but comprehend such work as had made its appearance in the interregnum. When the task was finally undertaken, in the latter half of 1962, the inadequacy of this approach became evident. It was clear that the entire script needed a thorough re-examination and in fact, the last three years have been spent in planning, bringing up-to-date and re-writing the whole. What has emerged is the net result of this fascinating, if time-consuming, process.

A work of this character is inevitably a co-operative venture if only in the sense of a very large number of people making it possible. Nor is it always easy to list adequately all those whose help is often-times so generously, indeed unstintingly, given. Distinctions in such cases are bound to be invidious at best and whether a name occurs in the beginning or towards the end is more fortuitous, less deliberate.

The author's deepest debt of gratitude is to Professor Owen Lattimore, under whose guidance the work was first undertaken. Despite the tremendous strains to which he was then exposed—his *Ordeal By Slander* bears a deep impress of the agony of those fateful years—Professor Lattimore took a keen, personal interest in nearly everything connected with my research. He read the script with utmost thoroughness and made most valuable comments in improving it. I am also grateful to Professor Ernest F. Penrose who was my second supervisor. Professor Fritz

Machlup, Chairman of the Committee under whose sponsorship the doctoral work was conducted, was most understanding and helpful too.

The revised volume now presented, was made possible partly through the courtesy of the British Council which was generous with a four-month Bursary award. Through Miss Cranmore, the Council in London enabled me to visit Oxford, where at Christ Church I was able to work on the 'Salisbury Papers'. She also made it possible for me to meet Lieutenant-Colonel Hadow, one of the few surviving members of the 1904 expedition, at Chudleigh, near Exeter. The Colonel was kind enough to loan to me his private diaries for 1903 and 1904 which, though sketchy, proved most useful. I was also able to make a brief visit to Kedleston Hall, outside Derby, the ancestral home of Lord Curzon and his forebears. In London itself, apart from working at the India Office Library and the British Museum, I was able to meet Mr. Leonard Mosley, Lord Curzon's latest, if most controversial, biographer. Sir Harold Nicolson, who knew the Indian Viceroy at first-hand, was most generous with his time and this despite his age and numerous other preoccupations.

The typescript was read and most usefully commented upon by Sir Olaf Caroe. It gained more from him than I could adequately acknowledge here. He was good enough too to write a Foreword. I should also like to acknowledge my debt of gratitude to Mr. Kenneth Rose of the *Daily Telegraph* who has a first-rate understanding and knowledge of Lord Curzon and was so kind as to read through the manuscript and make useful observations. Mr. Hugh Richardson offered many helpful suggestions in the earlier part of the script.

To the Library authorities at the Johns Hopkins University and the staff of the Library of Congress in Washington, D.C., my debt, though old in years, is yet deep and abiding. Mr. S. C. Sutton, Librarian at the India Office Library, was extremely helpful in my work in London; at Delhi, Mr. V. C. Joshi of the National Archives and Mr. Girja Kumar of Sapru House were most accommodating. Mrs. V. M. Yaryemkovaskaya, visiting Lecturer in Russian at the Panjab University (1964-65) was helpful in translating parts of Leonte'yev's book, as was Colonel Geoffery Wheeler of the Central Asian Research Centre in London in locating some Russian material. At Chandigarh my task was eased by Dr. Jagdish Sharma and his very energetic staff in the University Library to all of whom I am deeply indebted.

Through the good offices of the 14th Dalai Lama, I was able to look through parts of the biography (rNam Dhar) of the 13th incarnation. Unfortunately, it is far from enlightening on aspects of Tibet's political history with which this treatise is principally concerned.

Dame Eileen Younghusband, daughter of Colonel Francis Younghusband, was gracious enough to loan to me the private letters of her father which, written at the time of the expedition, offer a most important clue to an understanding of its various facets. Lieutenant Colonel the Lord Kingsale who shares with Colonel Hadow the proud distinction of being a suvivor of the Lhasa Mission was kind enough to loan to me his rich collection of photographs pertaining to it.

In typing the script and getting it ready for the press a team of young men—Keshav Chandra, Madan Sharma, H. S. Raja, R. C. Goel and Ramesh Kumar did a difficult job, sometimes in trying circumstances. I was also able to utilise part of the typing facilities afforded me by the Dictionary of Nationalist Biographies project, through the courtesy of the Institute of Historical Studies and its Director, Dr. S. P. Sen.

A word on the plan of the work may not be out of place here. The attempt in these page, as the title indicates, has largely been to *interpret* the course of events which indeed is otherwise so well known. In doing so the author has leaned heavily on the private papers, diaries and personal, sometimes intimate, correspondence of the chief men directly involved. A major difficulty that this treatment presents—and on which the avid critic will readily pounce—is the repetition of the same source at more than one place. Yet its greatest strength lies in that it lays bare—as State papers, official despatches and Foreign Office memoranda so successfully camouflage—the motives and motivations which the policy-makers had so near at heart.

Again, in the narrative unfolded, an effort has been made to view the entire sequence of events in the light both of an overall picture of India's landward periphery with its rich, yet difficult legacy and the political philosophies, such as these were of the men who conceived, planned and finally executed the project of the Mission. Additionally, the expedition has been viewed not in isolation but as an essential, indeed integral, part of the manifold aspects of Lord Curzon's Viceroyalty.

Two gaps in this work, spring readily to mind. One, underlined by Sir Olaf Caroe, is the lack of definitiveness regarding the nature and extent of Russian intrigue. The intelligence reports from Kathmandu, which I was able to look through at the Public Record Office in London, are unfortunately not very rewarding. Another source one could think of was Russian source material. Here in spite of my best efforts, it was not possible to work at the Archives in Moscow much less unearth any 'papers' or Memoirs of Count Benckendorff, then Russian Ambassador at the Court of St. James or the contemporary records of the Russian Foreign Office. The fact that Russian works, viz. V. P. Leonte'yev's or A. Popov's do not list such material is intriguing and may plausibly argue for its non-existence. Yet a thorough search needs to be undertaken and should prove extremely illuminating.

Another problem relates to Mr. Brodrick's role in doing Younghusband down. The present writer does not, on the evidence to hand, entirely share the views held by other authorities in regard to the then Secretary of State's alleged acts of omission and commission in this context. For a final word here too must await a more thorough research. The Curzon manuscript which I was able to look through at the India Office Library offers to an extent a corrective, as does Balfour's at the British Museum. What however should be most revealing in this case are the *Brodrick Papers* made available in London in the fall of 1963, which unhappily synchronised with my own return to India. Later efforts, supplemented by several friends, to make the Museum authorities relent and permit microfilming or in the alternate manage a brief visit to London, proved singularly unavailing. In both cases, the author is acutely conscious of the lacunae and could only hope that these may be remedied at a later stage.

I should be failing in my duty if I did not acknowledge here my debt to two of my distinguished precursors in this field whose work saw the light of day before mine could. Dr. Alastair Lamb's *Britain and Chinese Central Asia* is an extremely competent study as is Colonel Peter Fleming's *Bayonets to Lhasa*, a work of great merit and worth. I had the privilege of meeting both of them and had the benefit of their counsel.

A Hundred Years On

A little over a hundred years ago, on July 18, 1903 to be exact, Francis Younghusband preceded a few weeks earlier by a small band of officials and an escort of 500 men crossed the forbidding 17,500 feet high Kangra la and quartered at Khamba Jong, some 25 odd miles inside Tibet. His ostensible objective, to negotiate with officials from the Dalai Lama's administration and those of the Chinese Amban in Lhasa. A number of minor irritants on the Sikkim frontier and alleged Tibetan impediments to cross-border trade were the principal issues that needed to be sorted out. A bipartite conference with the Tibetans, with the Chinese acting as facilitators, it was reasoned, would help find a solution.

As a backdrop to Curzon's determined pitch to force entry, was a strong belief that across the deserts to the north, St Petersburg had been up to some mischief. That Tibet's then ruler, the youthful if ambitious 13th Dalai Lama (and his coterie) was privy to a secret understanding with the Great White Tsar. More, behind the back of the British, the Russians had worked out an understanding with Tibet's political masters, the Manchu rulers of China. And the land of the lama was now up for grabs.

As is well known, what started as a peaceful mission to negotiate small frontier and trade disputes ended up as an armed expedition that had, with some occasional brushes with an "army" of untrained, and ill-accoutered, lamas thrown in, eventually wended its way to holy Lhasa. And, in the wake of the Dalai Lama's flight, "negotiated" a settlement of sorts with the deposed ruler's nominee and such Tibetan authorities as were ready to hand.

The September 1904 Lhasa Convention, as it came to be called, had sought to establish a virtual British protectorate over Tibet but was modified in some material respects before it was ratified. And later, at the time of China's "adhesion" to its terms (1906), watered down further. In the event, all that Curzon and his understudy Younghusband had sought to achieve, in the short run at any rate, failed to materialise.

Viewing the century that has elapsed in retrospect, a few facts stand out. For one, the Russian threat, actual or potential, to Tibet's integrity needs serious reexamination. Here the role of Agvan Dorjief, a Buryat Mongol from Russia's

Trans-Baikal region, who became the Dalai Lama's "roving ambassador" to the court of Tsar Nicholas II (r. 1894-1917), has undergone a complete metamorphosis. His autobiography (ca 1922-3) apart, there is impressive evidence to suggest that he was *not*, contrary to what Curzon and his ilk believed, a sinister figure, an *eminence noire,* who had wormed his way into the Tsar's confidence as well as the Dalai Lama's. In actual fact, he was a man of great learning who had *inter alia* set his heart on preaching Buddhist values- and establishing a (Buddhist) temple at St Petersburg.

While drumming up support of Russian 'lamaists' at the Tsar's court, Dorjief also sought to persuade the Tibetan ruler and his people to inch closer to his own. The compact he allegedly concluded on the Lama's behalf and the arms and men the great white Tsar is said to have promised to fight Tibet's battles against British aggrandizement, turned out to be no more than figments of a fevered imagination. For the stark absence of any Cossacks arrayed on the side of the irregular Tibetan levies added to the antiquated weaponry used by them in their "battles" with the expeditionary forces, furnishes "the clearest proof" that Lhasa had not received any "clandestine" assistance (read Russian arms and men) from without.

It may be recalled that the only known outcome of Dorjief's hectic to-ings and fro-ings between Lhasa and St Petersburg, at the turn of the century period, was the establishment of a confidential Russian consulate. This, after a long and contentious debate (1901-2), at the small town of Kandin (also Ganding) in Sichuan, on the main trade route between China and Tibet. It had telegraphic links with Chengdu and there was a waterway from Kandin to Shanghai. From Kandin it took 20-25 days, sometimes even 15, to reach Lhasa. The objective in setting up the consulate was not so much to establish close contacts with Tibet as to maintain vigilance on the activities of the French and the never-idle British in southern China .

The consul Budda Rabdanov, was well versed in spoken and written Russian as well as Mongol languages apart from a good working knowledge of Chinese and Tibetan. His mission was to collect information about Tibet and show an interest in the activities of foreign missionaries as well as the Chinese government in Sichuan. And report to St Petersburg about all that was happening. The establishment of the consulate also showed Tibet's interest in fostering contacts with Russia and its readiness to fully finance the new outfit. Oddly though Robdanov matured at Kandin only in the autumn of 1903 while his Tibetan counterpart, with whom he was to liaise "in the strictest secrecy", never put in an appearance. By December 1904 when his translator died, Rabdanov too called it a day and returned home.

With no mean prescience, Count Nesselrode, the redoubtable foreign minister of Tsar Nicholas I (r. 1825-55), referred to the Great Game as "a tournament of shadows". Aptly called the end-game of the Victorian Cold War, the GG really was, as the late Harry Hodson put it, "a game with scores but no substantive prizes".[1] In the present context, a close scrutiny of Russia's alleged designs on Tibet and China's reported willingness to barter away the land would lead one to the conclusion that the Lhasa expedition, rated the "most pointless" of British India's military adventures, was also "a classic example of perceptions and misperceptions" to dictate intelligence assessment.[2] It should follow that the Buryat apart, another hard look at some facets of the expedition including the role of its principal dramatis personae, briefly touched upon in the following pages, should pay rich dividends. In the long run, the British aggression too turned out to be less predatory, more benevolent, for its major contribution would appear to lie in opening up the forbidden land. A process that has been taken to its logical conclusion with Tibet's new rulers throwing its doors ajar as never before. As a matter of fact, in the past decade or two, with literally thousands of tourists pouring in, year in year out, the land of "mystery and snow" looks no longer that mysterious much less impassable. And the physical barriers that separate it from the rest of the world have largely been overcome to allow reasonably untrammelled access.

II

Curzon and those of his way of thinking, the Russophobes in particular, were strongly persuaded that the dangers to which Russian expansion gave rise were real; in the event, it was imperative for Britain to contain the Tsarist advance. This is not to suggest that, as St Petersburg viewed it, the threat the British posed was less real. The fact was that John Bull opposed the Russians almost everywhere; established alliances against them and in the Crimean War (1853-5), even mounted an invasion of Russian territory! Whereas it is not true that Russian expansion was directed against Britain—for Russia was merely conquering the neighbouring lands she coveted—British expansion was definitely directed against Russia. Britain did not desire for herself territories such as Afghanistan in which she intruded and that she later defended against Russia. Nor did she take any interest in them for their own sake. All that Britain cared was that Russia did not get them.

Nor was it irrational of St Petersburg to fear Great Britain's designs. For one, it had deliberately placed itself between the advancing Russian armies and the warm waters of the sea to the south. Even as the US did much later in regard to its Pacific sea coast, the Russians viewed outposts on the Indian Ocean as their historic destiny. And the British placed every obstacle in their path to realize this objective.

It should thus be obvious that the Great Game in Asia was played for real stakes. It may also be conceded that of the many causes of Anglo-Russian rivalry some were irrational while others lapsed with time, and circumstance. And yet the initial cause that Russian expansion would overthrow the balance of power—and result in Russian domination of Eurasia—was real and admitted of no compromise. That, in the final count, it was a question of Russian or British supremacy as Queen Victoria (r. 1837-1901) put it bluntly, if somewhat crudely, was not far from the truth.

By the close of the nineteenth century, the Manchu empire in China was in "terminal decline"; in the event, the Amban's decrees in Lhasa were ignored both by the Dalai Lama as well as his administration. Russia on the other hand was an expanding imperial power whose armies continued marching across Central Asia acquiring through the latter half of the century on an average, it has been computed, some 55 odd sq miles of territory a day. Meantime the Raj was in the process of consolidating and defining its relationships with states on India's northern border. Its policies however were mapped out in Whitehall, which understandably was more inclined to prosecute its interests direct both in St Petersburg as well as Peking. The background to the Younghusband expedition was therefore "asymmetry" of the diplomatic triangle among Great Britain, Russia and China and the attractions of a reclusive Tibetan entity that beckoned at once adventurers and explorers, missionaries as well as scientists.

Nor when it came to Tibet, were Russian designs a mere figment of the imagination. Or, for that matter, the British line of reasoning insubstantial. For almost a hundred odd years John Bull had striven hard, and successfully, to keep the Russians out of Afghanistan. And it would look very "foolish" if now it meekly let them into Tibet. Which inter alia would involve incurring additional expenditure to mount a defensible frontier for Sikkim, Bhutan—and Assam. It may help to recall what Tsar Nicholas II told the leader of a secret Kalmyk mission to Tibet (1904) namely that he should "incite" the Tibetans against the British. The mission's unambiguous objective was to find out "what was going on there" and in particular what were the English "doing", or up to. Intriguingly the Tsar wanted the whole enterprise to be kept a closely guarded secret for he desired the war minister, General Kuropatkin, to "tell nothing about it" to his colleague, the foreign minister!

The leader of the seven-member Kalmyk mission, Naran Ulanov, was a Don (Buzava) Kalmyk who had earlier, in 1901, served as a Mongolian-Russian interpreter for the official Tibetan mission to St Petersburg led by Agvan Dorjief. Interestingly, Ulanov had also suggested that the shortest route to Tibet lay via Tashkent and the Pamir mountain ridges, *not* across the Outer Mongolian wastes.

Among others, the Tsar had been close to Pyotr Alexandrovich Badmaev (1841–1920), a baptized Buryat doctor of Tibetan medicine who commanded impeccable social linkages and had for long been advisor to the Russian foreign ministry on Mongolian affairs. He had inter alia submitted a secret memorandum proposing the construction of a 1,200 mile railway line, linking his Trans Baikal heartland across Mongolia, from Irkutsk, via Kiakhta, to Lanchow, the geometrical centre of China. And onward to Beijing (then Peking/Peiping). Badmaev, it may be recalled, was close to the finance minister, Count Sergei Witte (1849–1915), who was also a strong advocate of friendly relations with the Dalai Lama as an integral if important component of Russian policy in Mongolia. In the wake of the Tibetan ruler's plea for a Russian protectorate allegedly relayed through Agvan Dorjief, the "highly respected Buryat high lama", the Tsar's interest in Tibet seems to have been aroused further. Thus part of the war minister Kuropatkin's diary entry for March 1, 1903 read:

> I told Witte that our sovereign has grandiose plans in his head: to seize Manchuria for Russia and proceed toward the annexation of Korea... He is dreaming also of bringing Tibet under his rule. He wants to take Persia and to seize not only the Bosporus but the Dardanelles as well...[3]

It may be of interest to note here that it was the liaison between the Kalmyks, the Buryats and the Dalai Lama's Tibet that brought Russia its first awareness of the land of the lama. To start with, both these communities had been Shamanists. Tsarist Russia's real concern, as may be obvious, was the defence of its 2,000 verst long (approximately 1,340 miles) border for which purpose special Buryat-Cossack regiments had been raised as early as 1764. For St Petersburg, this was a matter of vital importance since there was a major Russo-Chinese linkage via Kiakhata, a prominent trading post in southern Trans Baikalia.

The principal attractions for the Buryats as well as the Kalmyks were the monasteries of Ganden and Erdene-Zuu in Outer Mongolia, Labrang and Kumbum in Eastern Tibet (Amdo) and Drepung, Sera and Ganden in Lhasa. Other than the Dalai Lama, there was the partron-chief Jetsen Dhampa Khutuktu (in Mongolian, 'Kutugtu'/ 'Hutukhtu', stands for the Living Buddha) in the Outer Mongolian capital of Urga. With Lhasa and its Dalai Lama as well as Tashilhunpo and its Panchen Lama relatively inaccessible, most Buryats made do with ordainment in Outer Mongolia. Besides, their homeland had earlier been part of Mongol territory.

That the Buryats had a distinct Tibetan presence may be gauged from the fact that around 1900 the Russian Buddhist colony in Lhasa comprised 47 Buryats of whom 42 were enrolled at Drepung for religious studies. Not unoften, the Dalai Lama used some of the colony's inmates for keeping his own lines of communication with Dorjief open. It is important to bear in mind the fact that as with Dorjief so also the Buryats, politics and religion were two sides of the same coin. Which would largely explain why the Tsarist government as well as later the Soviets "used" the Buryat-Kalmyk pilgrims as "convenient pawns" for political purposes. And the latter actively participated in secret reconnaissance and diplomatic missions to Tibet in 1904-5, 1921-2, 1923-5 and 1926-8. In the event, it would be wrong to suggest that Russia had no interest in Tibet. And as to the latter, the visits of hundreds of Russian subjects to Lhasa were a major source of revenue for the Dalai Lama's government. After Younghusband's expedition, traffic in Russian pilgrims declined while in the wake of the Soviet revolution (1917), the colony in Lhasa was almost completely isolated. Difficulties in the Buryats' access however were largely the making of Tibetans, not the British.[4]

While Russia's own interest in Tibet goes way back to the first half of the eighteenth century, its more active involvement relates to the latter half of the nineteenth century. The indefatigable explorer Colonel Nikolai Prejevalski (also Przhelvalsky) whose scientific research easily camouflaged the political goals of his explorations was acutely conscious that the British had an eye on Tibet. No wonder, he had urged his sponsors to preempt them. His first expedition (1870-3) had the Russian general staff's unambiguous objective of scientific exploration apart from intelligence gathering about the political regime in Tibet, its relations with neighbouring countries and the possibility of establishing, and strengthening, ties with the Dalai Lama. This, it was argued, may open the way for Russian influence "over all of Inner Asia, right through to the Himalayas". On return, Prejevalski had inter alia advised a potential military confrontation with Russia's "insolvent" Chinese neighbour, final annexation of the Sungari basin as well as northern Mongolia up to the latitude of Urga. He was also of the firm view that should British pressure on Tibet increase, the Dalai Lama may move his residence to Urga itself.

Among a clutch of Prejevalski's ardent associates, especially P. K. Kozlov, A. N. Kaznakov and B. L. Grombchevski, there was unbounded enthusiasm for the exploration of Tibet after the great explorer's death (1888). While they succeeded in scouring northern Tibet extensively, Lhasa somehow remained elusive. A major Russian preoccupation about this time was thwarting Britain's "sinister" designs, all too evident in the conclusion of the Anglo-Chinese convention on Sikkim in 1890 and the then seemingly impending establishment of a British protectorate over Tibet. The Dalai Lama, it appears, wrote repeatedly to the Bogdo Hutukhtu about his apprehensions and squarely blamed the Manchu Amban at Lhasa whom he charged with being in the pay of the British.

This did not quite tally with the Russian game plan which Badmaev had articulated namely the annexation of the "Mongolo-Tibeto-Chinese East" to the Tsar's dominion. The project had the blessings of Tsar Alexander III (r.1845-94) who had among other things provided Badmaev with a loan of two million rubles. For his part, the highflying Buryat visualized an anti-Manchu, pro-Russian agitation to be mounted throughout Manchuria, Western China and Tibet by a host of Buryat travelling-salesmen. To be sure, Badmaev planned mobilizing some 400,000 horsemen, for most part his lamaist coreligionists, marching on the Chinese capital to overthrow the Manchus. As if in readiness, in 1893, his "P. A. Badmaev & Co" had established its offices in St Petersburg as well as Chita. A precipitate decline in the fortunes of the Manchus registered by their debacle in the war against Japan (1894-5) and the advent of the Trans-Sib railway (construction work had started in 1891) were two great boosts for Badmaev's fortunes. His agents had by 1895, as we would notice presently, got in touch with Agvan Dorjief in Lhasa.

The distinguished Russian diplomat Ivan Korostovetz has suggested that "sometime before" Younghusband's expedition to Tibet, the Tsar had promised to support the Dalai Lama in the event of an invasion of his territory by British armed forces, even though the promise had been made "rather thoughtlessly at one time." The Ulanov mission, briefly alluded to in a preceding paragraph, Korostovetz has further underlined, was both "sponsored and financed" by the Russian war ministry and its general staff.[5]

In more ways than one, Colman Macaulay's abortive mission in 1886 was a precursor to the Younghusband expedition. With a formidable escort of 300 sepoys, its largely unstated goal was to establish a British presence in Lhasa under the guise of regulating trade. In British imagination, the Dalai Lama was an odd Peruvian beast, the Llama, who practiced Buddhism. And it is revealing that the celebrated (London) *Punch* showcased him as such in its cartoons.[6] Understandably, the Lama would avoid the humiliating parade of submission to which the British would no doubt have subjected him. And for obvious reasons. He was the trophy of the hunt, the biggest of the Game. In the event, happily for him, and his people, he successfully eluded both Curzon—and Younghusband. They butchered, but it was he who bolted.

Curzon, it should be evident, did not share the general British helplessness about Russian expansion for he would not admit (April 1899) that "an irresistible destiny" may plant Russia in the Persian Gulf or at Kabul or Constantinople. South of a certain line in Asia, Russia's future, he was strongly persuaded, would be "much more what we choose to make it" rather than what she could "make it herself."[7] Thus, in retrospect, the most important aspect of the Younghusband expedition, as the Indian potentate and not a few of his Russophobe friends viewed it at the time, was that HMG disavowed an otherwise highly successful mission lest the Russians should consider "provocative" British domination of a country bordering India—and far from Russia itself. It was a measure of how far the Great Game had, they bemoaned, "swung" in Russia's favour!

A word here on Agvan Dorjief who looms so large, and portentously, in the crowded events leading to the Younghusband expedition. A brief reference has already been made to the explorations of Nikolai Prejevalski but it may be of interest to note that even before he started, the Russian general staff had not exactly been inactive. For as early as 1869 it was planning secretly to dispatch an agent tagged on to a Mongolian embassy going to Lhasa, with the clear objective of gathering intelligence. St Petersburg, it may be recalled, had in the 1860s launched a major exploration of Khalka and, in 1861, established a diplomatic agency in Urga for what was euphemistically called information gathering. In the second Mongolian embassy to Lhasa (1873), two Russian Buryats joined, one of them being Dorjieff.

Born in a small Buryat village, some fifty odd miles north east of Verkhneudinsk (Ulan-Ude), Agvan Lobsan Dorjief (1853/4-1938) came of humble parentage and as a boy received his education in a Mongol school. Until eighteen he led the life of an average Buryat householder or family man. Presently however he met a Mongolian lama, became a Buddhist scholar-monk, took the vows of a celibate layman (*ubashi*) and left home. About 1872, in the company of a Tibetan lama he set out on a journey to Lhasa in the guise of a Khalka Mongol. He did not stay there for long and returned to Wu-tai-shan where he studied for a while. Dorjief was to come to Lhasa again in 1879, enrol at Drepung and for ten long years study Buddhist philosophy. In 1889 he was appointed one of the seven "tsenshabs" to the Dalai Lama. As spiritual and philosophical assistants to a high lama, "tsenshabs" are highly qualified scholars who serve as spiritual colleagues and assist their master in the study of philosophy, literature, poetry and other related topics. In the case of the Dalai Lama, "tsenshabs" have official rank in the Tibetan government and in some cases, are elevated to the esteemed position of a tutor.

Bell translates "tsenshab" to be a "work-washing abbot". And as one Dorjief's duty it was to sprinkle water, scented with saffron flowers, a little on the person of the Dalai Lama, but more on the walls of his room, on the altar, and on the books, as a symbol of cleansing. Dorjief was thus, the Lama's biographer concludes, in a "close relationship" with the Dalai Lama.[9] More, this proximity impressed the young Tibetan ruler with the equally young Buryat's erudition and personal charm of manner. No wonder, many a Mongol in Lhasa as well as outside it thought no one was "so elevated" as Dorjief.[10]

In his Russian autobiography, Dorjieff affirms that he revealed to the Dalai Lama his Buryat origins and the role his community played in the Tsar's empire where they enjoyed full religious freedom. The benign nature of Russian rule was highlighted by the fact that it did not interfere with the Buryats' faith much less with their ways of living. Meantime in Lhasa itself, a pro-Russian faction of whom Lonchen Shatra was a prominent figure encouraged Tibetans to break away from China as it had been unable to protect Tibet's interests. And as a matter of fact had, in collusion with the British, robbed the country of its legitimate claims on Sikkim. The fact that Russia did not border Tibet seemed not to bother Dorjief, it merely reinforced his argument that St Petersburg would not encroach on Tibetan territory. Understandably, the Chinese lobby was strongly opposed to any new orientation of policy in Lhasa and heavily underlined the massive endowments, which came from Tibet's big and powerful neighbour to the east. Meantime, Dorjief's stories about Tsar Nicholas impressed the Tibetans no end, especially that on his way back home from his odyssey in the far east (1891), the then prospective Russian ruler was accorded a warm reception by the Buryats. Convinced that such a bodhisattva Tsar as him would bestow great favours on Tibet, and its faith.

The Japanese monk-adventurer Kawaguchi has pointed out that Dorjief was the author of a pamphlet that identified Russia with the mythical kingdon of Shambala and its ruler as an incarnation of Tsongkapa, founder of the Dalai Lama's reformed Gelugpa sect. It may be recalled that for their part, the Russians sedously cultivated the belief that the Tsar was the "tsagan" or White Khan, heir to the legendary Mongol empire of Ghenghis Khan. Meantime in 1895, two of Peter Badmaev's "Trade Agents" had met Dorjief in Lhasa who evidently lent them a helping hand; his reward, a gold watch embossed with the imperial monogram. Just about this time, in a memorandum to his master (May 1896), the Russian finance minister, Count Witte, argued inter alia that British attempts to penetrate the country had increased Tibet's political importance and enhanced its economic influence. While Britain was desirous of seizing the land, Nepal had already encroached on Tibetan territory. In the event, Russia should do all it could to counter these moves. It may be of interest to note that in 1896, Badmaev had approached the Tsar afresh for a second loan to promote his cherished project of purloining more territory in central Asia. Tibet, he had pointed out, was important and by annexing it Russia will make England more amenable to its dictates.[11]

Meantime towards the fag-end of the 1890s, with active prompting by Dorjief, the Dalai Lama sought a political relationship with Russia. Later in 1900 and 1901, as we will notice presently, the Buryat was to travel to St Petersburg as the Tibetan ruler's personal representative. In the milieu in which the Great Game was then played, neither Russia nor yet Britain could visualize that a citizen of one or the other country may not share the goals by which the mother country swore; that he may well have an agenda of his own. In the event, since Agvan Dorjief was a Russian subject, the Raj "naturally assumed" that St Petersburg controlled all his acts.

On the face of it, Dorjief did provide a counter-weight to dangers which both of Tibet's neighbours, China as well as the Raj, posed. And his activities during the crucial half a dozen years of Curzon's viceroyalty (1899-1905), and the expedition to Lhasa, would appear to suggest that he was not unaware of the impact he may have on developments. Until then most Tibetans did not know much about Russia but by the 1890s, as we have noticed in a preceding paragraph, Dorjief had equated it to Shambala, a mythical kingdom to the north of Tibet often identified with Central Asia. Whose king, it was widely believed, would eventually subdue the earth's evil empire and save its people, and Buddhism, from tyranny. The Dalai Lama, it should be obvious, sought protection from mounting British pressures for as he later confided in Bell he had genuinely feared that in the wake of their expedition, they would annex Tibet. And, if they succeeded, the survival of Buddhism itself would become problematical. Dorjief's Russian card, the Lama thus hoped, would not only protect him from an impending British stranglehold but may also perhaps help him loosen the Chinese grip on his land.[12]

The British for their part speculated on a possible linkage between a Russian explorer and a Buryat-Tibetan spy. And not unlike many others believed that Dorjief had even been recruited by none other than Prejevalski; as a matter of fact, he was identified as a member of the great explorer's 1884 expedition! A closer scrutiny of the archives however reveals that this was not true, that Dorjief had in fact more dimensions than a stereotype, that he was at once a man of the inner and the outer world. A genuine holder of Tibet's highest religious degrees, he was a scholar, a philosopher and a prelate whose spiritual status among his Asian coreligionists was indeed high. The Buryat's charm and charisma were appreciated among the top social and intellectual circles of European capitals for it may do well to point out that he had the rare distinction of performing Buddhist rituals at the Musee Guimet in Paris as well as the Buddhist temple in St Petersburg. Curzon was to use him as a stalking horse, to mask his own ulterior objectives but failed to see that for the Buryat to pass the highest religious tests could not conceivably have been "a mere ploy" to gain the pontiff's trust on the Tsar's behalf![13]

In 1897, the Dalai Lama dispatched Dorjief on a mission to Paris and St Petersburg to probe as it were the political situation. The trip was to be made incognito and the Buryat pose as an ordinary Buddhist monk. Since British efforts to penetrate Tibet had persisted, it was argued, the Russians may be persuaded to do all they could to stall John Bull. Dorjief arrived in St Petersburg (February 1898) and was granted an audience by the Tsar through the good offices of Prince Esper Ukhtomsky (1861-1921). The Russian ruler with mentors such as the explorer Prejevalski and Prince Otto van Stubendorf possessed a fair knowledge both of Tibet as well as Central Asia. Even as Ukhtomsky urged the dispatch of a Russian representative to Lhasa,

Dorjief underlined the need for some preliminary discussions as well as contacts at appropriate levels. From St Petersburg, the Buryat proceeded to Paris with his attendant, Budda Rabdanov. In the French capital, he is said to have met Clemenceau and possibly called at the Quai d'Orsay. It appears that Dorjief wrote to the Dalai Lama about his experiences in St Petersburg as well as Paris and lavished praises on the Tsar.

It was about this time that the Kozlov expedition (1899-1901) to Tibet, referred to in detail a little later in the narrative, was being planned and Dorjief is said to have lent a hand in selecting gifts for those on whom it was intended to call. Interestingly, another Buryat explorer, Gombojab Tsybikov (1873-1930), disguised as a Mongolian Buddhist pilgrim, had arrived in Lhasa around the turn of the century period. A Russian agent and, not unlike Dorjief, a pan-Mongolist, Tsybikov was to provide his masters with useful information on Tibet's government and its army as well as the size and status of the Chinese garrison.

Meantime Dorjief returned to the Tibetan capital sometime in December (1899) and was appointed chief khenpo, loosely monastic preceptor or abbot, by the Dalai Lama. It would appear that this time round there were three factions in Lhasa, pro-British, pro-Russian and pro-Chinese in their respective political leanings. With the pro-Russian faction taking the lead and suggesting a new, revolutionary change in the age-old Tibetan orientation, Dorjief was sent (March 1900) as the Dalai Lama's "official representative" to request the Tsar become Tibet's patron. He travelled via India and China and on 30 September was received at the Livadia palace, outside Yalta, by the Russian ruler. Realizing the necessity of "establishing liaison" with Tibet and a "mutual exchange" of information, the Tsar is said to have promised "support and protection" to Tibet, though in "rather vague" terms.

In the course of his visit, Dorjief had audiences among others with Lamsdorf, the foreign minister; Witte, the finance minister; and Kuropatkin, the war minister. All three of them are said to have agreed to offer protection to Tibet but on the understanding that a Russian consulate be established at Lhasa. To this Dorjief, as we know, was resolutely opposed for fear it may lead to an influx of other European powers and be ultimately detrimental to Russian interests. Kuropatkin is said to have promised Tibet some (German) Krupp guns acquired by the Chinese and captured by the Russians during the siege of Peking in the aftermath of the Boxer rising (1898-1900). A real hassle though was the problem of logistics and to overcome it, it was suggested that the guns be deployed in East Tibet (Kham). Dorjief's return to Lhasa was an occasion for the Kalons to celebrate for as a result of his efforts, Tibet had, to all appearances, now found another patron— "more powerful and reliable" than China.

In 1901 Dorjief was to go back for the third time his objective, to conclude a formal treaty "on more solid foundations." His visit was billed as the "culmination" of the Buryat's attempts at a Russo-Tibetan rapprochement. And at stalling the "pernicious and foul" activities of the British. Dorjief who reached Odessa (12 June) and later arrived at St Petersburg, was already a focus of public attention. The

Russian press which gave wide coverage to Badmaev's letter furnishing more details hailed his mission as "extraordinary", for Tibet was now seeking a "possible rapprochement and cementing of good relations" with Russia. The possibility of establishing a permanent Tibetan embassy in St Petersburg for "correct intercourse" was also broadly hinted.

On June 23, the Tsar received Dorjief in audience with the customary exchange of letters and gifts. The Emperor's assurance that "given the friendly and fully well-disposed attitude of Russia, no danger will threaten Tibet" may be regarded as the high watermark of the Buryat's mission. For the Tsar's "gramota" (literally, 'charter') inscribed in solid gold letters agreeing to the "protection and defence" of Tibet, was to produce a strong impression in Lhasa where most people came to believe that the Dalai Lama had been given a written assurance that Russia would "stand by" Tibet. Korostovetz however is categorical that "no formal agreement" that made Tibet into a Russian protectorate was ever concluded. The Tsar's ministers, he further avers, were determined "not to become involved" and their ruler had, at best, been non-committal.

Nonetheless the possibility of providing some arms to Tibet is said to have been discussed. Kuropatkin it would appear was not averse to making a provision for "some amount of arms" as well as providing some Russian "military instructors" of Buryat and Kalmyk ethnicity. A final decision on the issue was however held over until the following year. Interestingly Korostovetz makes a mention of some of Dorjief's "fantastic plans" which implied Russian advance across the Himalayas so as to liberate the "oppressed people" to the south. He also portrays the Buryat as a remarkable personality who knew how to gain other people's sympathy and confidence. More, Dorjief who could easily have passed for a Catholic priest but for his Mongolian eyes and broad cheekbones, spoke with an authority and expertise that "mightily pleased" the Tsar. His knowledge of European politics and its workings however was "superficial" and Korostovets refers to the Buryat's "undercover intrigues" and "secret diplomacy" as "Asiatic machinations." While both of his assistants repaired to Tibet, Dorjief was to make another trip to France in the fall of 1902.

Had Dorjief's to-ings and fro-ings been kept under wraps, nobody would seem to have bothered. But the Russian press in general, and Peter Badmeyev in particular, made sure that these receive maximum publicity exposure. With the Buryat's role and importance unduly highlighted, the attention his visit attracted made the (London) *Times* carry frequent reports from its St Petersburg correspondent sometimes with, and at other times without, comment.

The bubble though did not take long to burst. For, in essence, as a knowledgable Russian author suggests, Dorjief's Russo-Tibetan alignment was both "precarious and awkward" and largely a product of the Great Game. It was to collapse as soon as an Anglo-Russian rapprochement (which was to culminate in the Covention of 1907) began to take shape and form. Russian reactions to the Dalai Lama's overtures were from the very beginning, it may be recalled, both "restrained and wary" for all

St Petersburg could offer was "moderate" diplomatic support and "moral encouragement." For the Raj on the other hand Tibet, like Afghanistan and Eastern Persia, was a natural strategic buffer providing access to India's northern frontier and British-controlled Himalayan kingdoms. In sharp contrast, for Russian diplomacy Tibet was no more than a covert instrument of political pressure for its Buryat and Kalmyk subjects alike looked to Lhasa for their spiritual sustenance. While an arrangement for a modest supply of arms was not "something absolutely incredible", it was not a viable proposition. Again, by turning to Russia for help, the Dalai Lama was opening up a new round for competition in Central Asia. It could not have endured.

As to Curzon, some of his "fears and suspicions" may have been "well founded" while others were "imaginary." It may be of interest to note that, in retrospect, both the Russian Consul in Bombay and their ambassador in Peking were to view the British invasion of Tibet as a "counter-thrust" provoked by St Petersburg's occupation of Manchuria. Kuropatkin's view of the six-member mission of Naran Ulanov, referred to earlier, may be gauged from the fact that its leader had been trained as an instructor who was to go to Lhasa by a new route and in the guise of a scientific mission. Later Kozlov was to suggest that Russia send an "expeditionary force" to Tibet to counter British Indian activity and persuade the lamas to open up their country. And secure for the Russians the same privileges as the British were seeking. What undid the St Petersburg plan was the outbreak of the Russo-Japanese war (February 1904). For the record though, even as Ulanov died en route, his mission did succeed in reaching Lhasa.

All the same, by the time it did (May 1905), the Dalai Lama had already fled and Younghusband returned home after his successful venture. The new leader of Ulanov's mission met the Tibetan regent and urged him to align with Russia/China in place of England, as the latter was professedly hostile to Buddhism. Meantime the run-away Dalai Lama who was in Urga pleaded with Russia to take Tibet under its "protection" and proposed inter alia that he return home under a (Russian) Cossack escort. Sadly for him, the Tsar's response was disappointing, in the negative. "This opportunity," not a few in St Petersburg were to bemoan later, was "irreversibly" lost by "timid and vacillating" Russian diplomacy. For those who met him at Urga (early 1905) were struck by the Tibetan ruler's "strongly pro-Russian" leanings and his desire to effect a Russo-Tibetan alliance. The Dalai Lama's "alluring" offers to mediate in the Russo-Japanese war and to take some Russians, including Kozlov, with him to Lhasa were not taken seriously. St Petersburg, it would appear, was now only too keen to wash its hands of Tibet and its Dalai Lama. The latter, to no one's surprise, was "utterly disappointed." In the event, in September 1905, the Tibetan ruler dispatched Dorjief to Russia as his "special envoy" for further discussions![14]

Despite his Russian visits and meetings with the Tsar and his ministers and all the hype in the press, the Buryat's goals may have been modest. For his principal, if overarching, objective would appear to have been a pan-Buddhist, pan-Mongolian confederation—not a political state but a loose religious fraternity embracing Buddhists of all shades and persuasions. And all the way from his own expanse of Trans Baikalia, through Mongolia, to Tibet. This large religious brotherhood, with its enormous physical expanse, and by no means unimpressive numbers, under a vague Russian aegis would, he was convinced, enjoy a respectable measure of autonomy in the Tsar's vast and varied empire.

Was Dorjief then the Tsar's agent or a Buryat nationalist whose aim in life was to preach Buddhist values and defend the interests of the lamaists? Or, had his association with the Dalai Lama, and Tibet, engendered in him a sense of Tibetan nationalism? "In all probability", concludes Tatiana Shaumian, a knowledgable Russian scholar, the Buryat had dedicated his life to preaching Buddhist values. In the event, he tried to safeguard the interests of the Dalai Lama from those encroaching upon his independence and authority as the centre of the Buddhist world.

Patrick French, the well-known British authority on Tibet and its affairs and a biographer of Younghusband, is emphatic that there was "no evidence" that Dorjief was a Tsarist protégé. Rather, he was a "roving ambassador" of the Dalai Lama who attempted to gain support among the higher echelons of Russian society. More, he was, in fact, a Tibetan agent seeking Russian help which, sadly for him as well as the Dalai Lama, did not prove forthcoming.[16]

A word here on the Japanese monk Ekai Kawaguchi whose account of his stay in Tibet (1901-2) was first published in Japan in 1903-4 in 155 daily issues of two Osaka newspapers. And this long before it was to appear in English—*Three Years in Tibet* (1909). Curzon's government, it would appear, had access to all that Kawaguchi saw and heard through a devious channel. This was his Indian tutor, and benefactor, the somewhat controversial Sarat Chandra Das (1849-1917) who, Kawaguchi discovered, had a bad name in Tibet as the "very incarnation of evil." And everyone associated with him, viewed as a spy. Das had, over the years, served the Raj most loyally, and was privy to passing all scraps of information he garnered from the Japanese monk. Including the lurid bits about Dorjief being personally responsible for establishing an arsenal at Lhasa through the import of American guns from Mongolia!

A reputable British author, Scott Berry (*Monks, Spies And a Soldier of Fortune*), has suggested that Kawaguchi's book reveals its author to be "a bungling, likeable but often fearfully bigoted bag of contradictions." That "a madcap adventurer", he was at the same time, a sensitive linguist whose real interest in life was "solitary study". In all, the Japanese monk spent fourteen months in the Sera monastery and in and around the Tibetan capital. Though highly critical of the "greed and hypocrisy" among high lamas, he was comparatively tolerant of the 'soldier monks' who knew little of their religion. Berry has deduced that Kawaguchi "listened to a little too much gossip" and that his reports on Dorjief, then "a trusted advisor" to the Dalai Lama, may therefore be accepted with some caution.

Kawaguchi's work, it may be recalled, has often been cited as evidence that he himself was a British spy who had viewed Dorjief as an "extremely shadowy and sinister" figure. It may be of interest to note in this context that his book was, at best, a loose compilation of the marathon interviews the Japanese monk gave to journalists; its text never seems to have been exposed to any rigorous editing. More, during his two years in Tibet—the third was spent in the tiny village of Tsarang, in the kingdom of Lo—he was all the time in clever disguise. With his very survival depending upon his relating to people from all walks of life, gave Kawaguchi a rich, down-to-earth experience. His tales were a legion. And many of his countrymen simply did not believe them, to start with at any rate.

Nor was that all. Somewhat of a loose cannon, on his way home via Nepal, Kawaguchi told its prime minister, Chandra Shamsher that in the wake of Dorjief's return from Russia (1901), the Dalai Lama had taken "a hard line" in his quarrel with the British. This bit of information was duly relayed to Curzon personally by the Nepalese prime minister.

If not in the pay of the British, was Kawaguchi then a Japanese spy? Oddly though there is no positive evidence to sustain the charge. Possibly, the monk was a self-appointed defender of his country's interests in Tibet. That he had pro-British political leanings goes without saying; in any case, he painted more from hearsay and bazzar gossip than authentic verification a dark, and far from correct, picture of Dorjief's activities before 1902.[17]

A word here on Wilhelm Filchner and Pyotr Kozlov both of him were fascinated by Tibet and its Dalai Lama. Filchner, viewed as some sort of a German Sven Hedin and recipient of his country's National Prize (1938), was a Bavarian explorer who headed three expeditions to Tibet, in 1903-4, 1926-8 and 1935-7. Interestingly, his oft-quoted *Sturm uber Asien* (1924) rests on a half fictional account revolving principally around the exploits of the Buryat Dorjief and his understudy Tserempil (also Zerempil). Inter alia, Filchner has maintained that Dorjief was in close contact with the Russian foreign ministry and the information section of the general staff as far back as 1885. According to Scott Berry, Filchner had, in 1928, a chance encounter with Frank Ludlow, the English Headmaster of the Gyantse school (who later was to have a brief stint in Lhasa), while on a trek in Skardu.

The German admitted, Ludlow recorded, that the name Tserempil (meaning "darling of the Tsar") was fictitious and that he had got hold of some of Dorjieff's papers and "fictionalized" them. "In the main he said", Ludlow noted, that "the acts ascribed to Tserempil were those of Dorjief." Years later in his autobiography, *Ein Forscherleben* (Wiesbaden, 1950), Filchner was to confirm the above and further wrote to suggest that his book treated "in novelistic form political questions of Central Asia, especially the modern history of Tibet based on the experiences of the secret agent Dorjief and my own experiences." More, he was to reveal that the work itself was composed in two weeks during "a very cold winter-time, wrapped in my fur coat." Sadly, while Filchner's Tserempil among other details appears to have been a figment of the author's fertile imagination, Robert Rupen (*Mongols of the Twentieth Century*), and not he alone, take him seriously as an historical figure![18]

It may be noted if only in parenthesis that a Russian journalist too has suggested that Dorjief was the most important agent of his country's general staff and was known under the nickname of Shambala. Sadly, he has adduced no documentary evidence to sustain his case.

Pyotr Kozlov, not unlike his master, the famous Nikolai Prejevalski of whom he was a great favourite, was obsessed with Tibet. Unable to find the lost city of Khora-Khotu in the Gobi desert in the course of his first expedition (1899-1901), Kozlov explored the Tasidam wastes in northern Tibet, found the source of the Yellow River and spent nearly six months in the Mekong River basin. His second expedition (1907-10) on which the Russians were "very keen" and which also attracted support form the Royal Geographical Society in London revolved around defining Tibet's geographical limits. And to ascertain whether Kokonor was part of the country.[19] Although sorely disappointed in not being able to visit Lhasa, Kozlov had two memorable meetings with the Dalai Lama, in Urga (1905) and at Kumbum (1909). On the first occasion, when the Tibetan ruler invited Kozlov to go to Lhasa, he himself was a fugitive from his kingdom; on the second, on his way home after his long "wanderings" in the wake of the Younghusband expedition.

To revert to the opening years of the twentieth century. It should be obvious that it was the Tsar, *not* Dorjief, who was fishing for trouble. The Russian foreign ministry too was sometimes innocent of what the emperor was about. The British diplomat Spring Rice has alluded to Nicholas II's "romantic fascination" for the East and the possibility of a role for himself in another unworldly religion. More, the Tsar was vaguely interested in exotic healing and religions that spawned it. Understandably Drojief, it would appear, used these well known dispositions of the Tsar to foster closer Russo-Tibetan ties.

Both Dorjief as well as the Dalai Lama tried to strike a balance between British/ Chinese/Nepalese threats. And here the Russian card could, the twosome must have calculated, be useful. The game eventually failed albeit not for want of trying; its bane, the intrinsically peripheral interest both Russia as well as Britain had in Tibet. Everything everywhere else was more important.

By late 1903, as we have noticed, Dorjief had become for Curzon and his likes the 'Evil Genius' at the court of the Dalai Lama, a product of Eastern mysticism which by the late 1890s, was so much in vogue in Russian high society. And prominent among the latter apart from Badmaev, was Prince Ukhmtomsky, a gentleman of the bedchamber who was close to the person of the Tsar. Dorjief, it appears, was strongly persuaded to put out feelers and divert the attention of the Russian government towards Tibet. And more especially gain the land of the lama his country's diplomatic support, both against China and Britain. There is no doubt that some elements in the Russian administration supported the Buryat's concept of a pan-Buddhist unity between Tibet and the Tsar's eastern empire. Besides, there are clear indications that the Tsar on his own "encouraged Great Gaming" in Tibet. In the final count then, it was this "random meddling" of the Russian ruler and his army officers which fuelled Curzon's paranoia.[20]

The charge that suspicions about Russian activity in Tibet were made up by the Indian Viceroy and his friends as "an excuse" for mounting the expedition to

Lhasa does not truly hold. The fact is that it was their genuine fear of Russian expansion, which made the Viceroy invent flimsy excuses for sending Younghusband and his men across the border. Curzon apart, many of his persuasion had a firm, if misguided, conviction that Russia and Tibet had signed secret treaties and the devil-incarnate behind this clever game was none other than the Buryat Agvan Dorjief.

Sadly, thanks to Russian pamphleteering and Kawaguchi's reports, Dorjief was painted as an "embodiment of evil and trouble" by the British. In the event, his presence and activities were a cause for concern, if not hysteria. Younghusband conceded that Dorjief's visits to Russia in 1900 and 1901 were the alibi for his own mission. Bell believed Dorjief responsible for the Dalai Lama's actions. The British journalist Chandler called him "an arch intriguer and adventurer". Waddell specifically blamed him for the need of the mission and repeated Kawaguchi's accusation that Dorjief poisoned the young Lama's ears against the British. And created the Shambala -Russian myth. More, ensconced in the Lhasa arsenal, he was supervising Tibet's war preparations!

One and all, they helped firmly establish Dorjief as a source of danger, even a spy, in the eyes of the British public. Curzon reacted sharply to the Buryat's visits to St Petersburg, convinced he was a Russian agent, acting simultaneously as tutor to the Dalai Lama. No wonder the Buryat aroused the Viceroy's worst apprehensions. Rumours about treaties allegedly concluded as a result of his journeys to and fro were the real source of the Indian potentate's discomfort. Since at the turn of the century period Russia posed a threat—its armies had lingered on in Manchuria without any apparent justification in the wake of the Boxer rising—there was a lot of credence to reports of St Petersburg's insatiable appetite for territory and its penchant to continue to expand, unless checked. Younghusband's obvious expectation of Tibetan resistance to his advance rested squarely on his knowledge of Kawaguchi's yet unpublished account.

How much, in the final count, did the Younghusband expedition succeed in its goal of a preemptive strike to warn the Russians away from further expansion in South-Central Asia? Dorjief it appears served as a lightning rod for British panic about alleged Russian plots; beginning in 1901, he provided a "perfect scapegoat" for Curzon to justify his actions. Russia alone, the Viceroy was convinced, must be pulling the strings for no non-European power could possibly have a goal that did not serve a European nation's interests.

In 1905, in the aftermath of Younghusband's expedition, Dorjief settled down in the Russian capital to continue his mediation work towards a Russo-Tibetan 'political' alliance and was still engaged in this exercise until 1914. After the Soviet revolution (1917), the Buryat was to resume his activities as a Tibetan diplomat and helped the new Russian regime re-establish contacts with Lhasa. He was also head of a religious reform movement both in Buryatia and Kalmakiya (1922-9). In the wake of Stalin's notorious purges, in the fall of 1937 Moscow charged Dorjief with being an undercover Japanese spy! Arrested, he was to die under mysterious circumstances in the prison hospital at Ulan-Ude. By then however the Tibetan-Mongolian mission he had set up at the Buddhist temple in St Petersburg (now Leningrad) had closed down and its personnel persecuted.

In the light of recent researches, it would appear that Dorjief was no one's puppet; he certainly was *not* a Russian master-spy. The Buryat may have worked for closer relations between the Russian emperor and Tibet but he was *not* interested in serving the Russian emperor *per se* or later the Soviet state for that matter. It is important to bear in mind the fact that Dorjief viewed religion and politics, even as most Tibetans do, as two sides of the same coin. He was a pan-Mongolist and a pan-Buddhist; his entire career dedicated to serving those interests. Insofar as he was a Mongol dealing with non-Mongols on the periphery of his steppe domain, he dreamed of a pan-Buddhist Mongolian entity central to Eurasia as the palm of a hand joining the "fingers" of Chinese/ Tibetan/ Russian Buddhists. And, in the bargain, relegating the imperial powers of the periphery to a much more modest position than they might "arrogantly claim." It should follow that a man in Dorjief's position may actually be more dedicated to religion than to politics.[21]

However flexible he may have been in the manner in which he achieved the goals he had set himself, Dorjief was certainly innocent of many of the activities of which he was accused by Kawaguchi and Filchner (and later Stalin), activities that were used as a justification for the 1903-1904 expedition. Not long after Younghusband had returned from Lhasa, the American diplomat Rockhill found Dorjief in Beijing (1908) "a quiet, well-mannered man, impressionable like all Mongols" who bore little resemblance to the "sinister *eminence noire* of past propaganda."[22] An image the British had so sedulously fostered. It may be added if only in parenthesis that under the Soviets, Dorjief continued his efforts to pull the Mongols together. For, as earlier under the Tsar, in the wake of the Soviet revolution (1917) too, he had continued to work hard to keep Buddhism alive in Russia until halted in his tracks. Nor, would it be true to say that his vision of a Mongol union, at once religion-centred, and secular, is exactly dead even today.

III

Younghusband was not the butcher charged with the massacre of the Tibetans at Chumi Shengo, or the more familiar Guru, for technically Macdonald, *not* Younghusband, was commanding the military contingent. The Tibetans, much as the Mahatma some decades later, engaged in passive resistance, non-violent protest. For their youthful commander just about sat in front of the wall; neither willing to fight nor yet withdraw. This was new, and indeed a unique encounter for a European power; all it had known was to use its superior physical, and armed might, against anything that came in its way. For their part, neither the Lhasa general, much less his men did realize how powerful and superior, British weaponry was as opposed to their ancient matchlock guns, swords and slings. Which would go a long way to explain the enormity of the slaughter.[23]

The massacre itself was viewed by Tibetans as British treachery; by the British, as Tibetan stupidity. And as Patrick French has put it, turned a "diplomatic excursion" into a " bloody invasion." Weeks later, Colonel Brander's assault on the Karo la 18,000 ft above sea level and rated the highest skirmish in military history, was mounted on the dishonest plea that it threatened the British supply line. The fact was that it did *not*. The pass lay some fifty odd miles to the east of Lhasa!

The term Tibetan "soldiers" was a misnomer. They were, for most part, irregulars armed with age-old, if rusty matchlock guns, swords, spears, slingshots and the like. Their leader, Depon (general) Lhading, had received Younghusband at his camp on 13 January (1904) at Guru. On the battlefield later in March, the British had induced the Tibetans to extinguish the fuses of their guns and, in the aftermath, opened fire with machine guns from the surrounding area. The heroic Tibetan 'soldiers' with their hands disabled, fell on the wasteland and were savagely butchered. Tibetan accounts make it abundantly clear that the British had been "guilty of a massacre" achieved "through treachery"—by first persuading their adversary to put out their gun fuses and then attacking them. British versions, on the other hand, laid stress on the fact that even as the Tibetans disarmed, the Lhasa general jumped on the back of a pony and shouting hysterically, threw himself upon a sepoy. More, he drew his revolver and shot him in the jaw. This was the match that lit the powder keg and made the British response unavoidable.

It has been suggested that, in fact, the attempt to disarm Tibetan soldiers triggered the opening shot, while the scenario of a wild general with the revolver was a myth that grew up later. One of the British officers, Hadow, was to note that "shooting men walking away" was for him a repugnant sight; that Tibetan "stoicism, gallantry and dash" were unmistakable. For the record, a grand total of three Russian rifles were found on the battlefield!

A brief reference to a couple of expressions of contemporary opinion on the "fighting" at Guru may be of interest. While an Indian newspaper noted that British soldiers had "without any temptation" slaughtered those poor wretches "in cold blood without any risk" to themselves, a British contemporary underlined the truism that the firing was "not a military necessity" but had been resorted to "as a punishment." Another sidelight was an over-zealous prelate hailing the shedding of Tibetan blood as "a blessing." Arguing that once Tibet ceased to be a sealed book, it would provide an "excellent" field for carrying on "proselytizing work." Later another Indian paper referring to reports of "our troops" setting fire to and destroying Tibetan villages, asked the bishop "if it were the torches of enlightenment and Christianity" that were used on the occasion for "firing" the doomed villages with?[24]

The massacre at Guru has been viewed, not ineptly, as the "symbolic pivot" of the expedition. For once blood had been spilled on such a scale—nearly seven hundred lay dead on the battlefield—there was no turning back for either side. Curzon and his men were strongly persuaded that in violating a treaty and spurning intercourse, the Tibetans were patently in the wrong; a neighbouring land had no right to refuse treaty relations. On the other hand, the Lhasa general and his people saw no reason why they should not be left to their own devices. The fact of eturning Curzon's letters unopened was a moral refusal to communicate, so also he Lhasa general's behaviour at Guru: he would not fight nor yet would he surrender. As the Raj saw it, Younghusband was "exceptionally patient"; as the Tibetans viewed it, he was "cunningly duplicitous." The British were convinced that only "a hrashing or a wholesome beating" (Younghusband's words) would persuade the Tibetans to any modicum of "good" behaviour. The Commissioner and his men saw the monks as "oppressors" of their people, he had referred to them as "those selfish, filthy, lecherous lamas" who stirred "anti-British feeling" and needed to be aught a lesson.[25]

The Dalai Lama's counsels were sharply divided, for the four-member Kashag ncluding Shatra Paljor Dorje (in 1913-4 he was to be the Tibetan Plenipotentiary to he tri-partite Simla Conference) had inter alia advocated a policy of constructive engagement with the British. It was exposed to considerable embarrassment by the Tsongdu who questioned their loyalty. All the four, as we know, were sent into exile and replaced by a new Kashag.

With Manchu power on the mainland in sharp decline, by the opening decade of the twentieth century Chinese influence in Tibet had grown extremely weak. In the event, the Amban wielded little if any authority. Nor did he have any influence whatever either on the negotiations leading to the expedition or on the conduct of military operations between the opposing sides. The Dalai Lama and his entourage were convinced that should they advance on Lhasa, the British would kidnap the Tibetan ruler and later transport him to India, a contingency they would, understandably, avoid at all costs.

The Tibetan approach to the world was one of "splendid isolation", of NO CONTACT! It was not different from putting one's head in the sand. Not to talk of negotiations, any contact *per se* was taboo. Hence the refusal to receive any communication, be it from the all-powerful Viceroy in Calcutta, or a much lesser fry—Younghusband at Khamba Jong.

In retrospect, the British expedition made the Chinese realize how fragile, and vulnerable, their security was especially from the southwestern corner. This would go far to explain why the Guomindang, and later the Communists, had a major preoccupation in plugging this loophole. In reverse, British India's policy towards Tibet was far from consistent. For much depended upon the personality of the Viceroy and the political complexion of the government in Whitehall. And the larger imperial interests to which British India's concerns were rated somewhat peripheral. In other words, while for Curzon (and Younghusband) India's needs lay at the centre of the diplomatic universe, for the tall, "languid and cynical" Balfour, they were only of marginal interest.

As a perceptive British author has put it, it was "axiomatic" that any subject of the Queen had an "inalienable right" to make money out of whomsoever he wished. The "insolent" Tibetans who were not interested were made to see reason. The telegram of 6 November (1903) authorized the advance to Gyantse "to obtain satisfaction" on matters of diplomacy and trade whatever that may mean. Unstated, to establish the truth about Russian influence in Lhasa.[26]

The physical combat apart, there was a classic if head-on clash of cultures. Clapping Tibetans were not so much mounting a welcome for Younghusband and his men as attempting to drive off evil spirits. Similarly, fancy dress performances put up by the British at Lhasa were viewed by their Tibetan hosts as merely funny. The behaviour of the Lhasa general at Guru would fall into the same slot; to the British, it was incomprehensible.

Among Tibetan delegates at Khamba Jong, there was the Dalai Lama's chief secretary, Lobsang Trinkley and a senior Depon, Tsarong Wangchuk Gyalpo, whose father had earlier (1888) demarcated the Tibet-Sikkim border. For the Chinese, there were Ho Kuang Hsi who represented his country at Shigatse and Captain Randall Parr of the Chinese Customs Service. Pronouncedly pro-British in his leanings, Younghusband found Parr useful, if irritating. Inter alia, he told the Commissioner that the Russians were moving on Lhasa and that the Tibetans counted on their support. Not surprisingly, the Tibetan delegates took no notice of Parr while Younghusband was quick to inform Dane that 20,000 Russians were said to be on their way to help the Tibetans!

The Amban's power and authority were purely ceremonial. The Commissioner was rightly convinced that "not a hundred Ambans" would make the Tibetans talk business. Nor were Parr or even Ho any help. The Tibetan decision not to negotiate at Khamba Jong may have been "based four square on infantile obstinacy,"[27] but surely it was not inconsistent with their steady refusal to have anything to do with unwelcome interlopers. Younghusband and his men did their best to invent lame excuses. For the much talked of two Sikkimese prisoners were none other than O'Connor's untrained spies; Curzon's charge about Tibetan obstruction to trade, "simply disingenuous"; access to Tibet's supposedly lucrative market, a presient theme in Indian despatches, a fake. So also Tibetan troops attacking Nepalese yaks and carrying many of them off, described as "an overt act of hostility", truly laughable. The advance to Lhasa, an inevitable result of the mission's original existence was, in the final count, a result of manipulation by Curzon, indecision by HMG, and chance circumstance of the Amban's indiscretion. In each instance, of reaction rather than action.

A word here on Tibet's "lucrative" trade market! Official statistics belied the claim, pointing out that the total value of both imports as well as exports for the year 1903 was a little less than rupees 14 lakhs [roughly £ 90,000]. The official concerned ascribed the astonishing brevity of his report to the "apparent futility" of expatiating at length on "such a peddling trade"![28]

Younghusband was persuaded that Curzon's manner, however insufferable, was tampered by a "remarkable tenderness of heart" and a gift for warm and loyal friendship. Besides, the governor-general was a strong chief who would see his men through and stand for them if things went wrong. George Hamilton who as Secretary of State was Curzon's political boss once told Godley, for long Under Secretary of State at the India Office, that "strong self-reliant men" recognized in Curzon "a mastermind" but the "mediocrities feared and disliked him."[29]

The Commissioner spent five months at Khamba Jong while the Chinese equivocated and the Tibetan delegates refused to negotiate. What Younghusband longed for was a British protectorate over Tibet and the liberation of a people who were slaves to its "ignorant and selfish monks". Curzon's objective was not very different. He wanted a commercial treaty and the stationing of an Agent at Lhasa so as to spike Russia's alleged designs. Sadly for the two of them, their imperialist ambitions were at variance with the objectives of a punitive expedition Whitehall had so very reluctantly authorized.

The charge that Curzon "chose to virtually abandon" Younghusband on the road to Lhasa does not really wash. Not only was there more than one exchange of communications between the two, the Viceroy is known to have fought his own, and the Commissioner's, battles with his political masters with determination and vigour while away on leave.[30]

Nor did Curzon's absence from India prevent him from influencing the course of events. For the last chapter of the Tibetan drama, played out between March and October (1904), was the outcome of a four-cornered contest. Between Curzon and Brodrick (who enjoyed the full backing of Balfour) disagreeing in England, while nearer home Younghusband in Tibet and the Indian government at Simla failed to see eye to eye with each other.

Before he left for England on home leave, Curzon had counselled Ampthill not to meddle with the Tibetan Mission. And if something had to be done, it must be the reverse of what the foreign department (under Louis Dane) advised. Meanwhile Brodrick, conscious that Younghusband was a little too jumpy and eager to advance, had asked Ampthill to advise him "against precipitancy." Curzon's charge that the acting Viceroy was contemplating the failure of the mission for whose success he was straining every nerve does not truly hold. Ampthill ascribed his churlishness to about of ill-health whileGodleycommentedthatevenasthiswould be "unpardonable" in other persons, it was to be forgiven in Curzon's case.[31]

In Whitehall it was accepted that if the Mission failed in concluding the kind of settlement desired, it should effect a withdrawal after destroying the Lhasa arsenal, walls and other fortifications. And romp home with "as large an indemnity" as it could manage.

Curzon told Ampthill that the latter's dispatch arguing for a British Agent in Lhasa received as much attention in Whitehall as it would "if read out in the streets of Lhasa". It was Younghusband's force of personality added to the Amban's hectoring of the Tibetan negotiators that brought about the conclusion of this "extraordinary" treaty. There was also the signal contribution, midwifery if one may call it, of Captain Jit Bahadur, the Nepalese Agent and the Tongsa Penlop, the future ruler of Bhutan who had virtually shadowed the Mission all the way to the Tibetan capital. For his part, the Commissioner had viewed the occupation of the Chumbi valley as the only strategical point of value in the entire northern frontier, over its entire stretch, from Kashmir to Burma.

Two themes which find a deep resonance later in the narrative are deserving of a brief mention here. Both claimed a lot of newspaper attention in India while officialdom tended to pooh-pooh and sort of sweep them under the carpet. The first related to the price tag for all the expense incurred, the second to the enormous loot that was to accrue from investing a land culturally so rich in all that related to its faith. To start with, the decision that India pick up the tab for the costs of the expedition understandably outraged public sentiment with hardly a newspaper that did not bemoan the sad story of India's "poverty stricken millions" having to pay "for this folly" ! Shamefacedly though, the Raj persisted and a motion adopted in the British Parliament stipulated that the House "consents to the revenues of India being applied for military operations beyond the frontiers of His Majestry's Indian dominion for protecting" the political mission "dispatched" to the Tibetan government!

Another important facet of the expedition which received very little attention and, not unoften, was deliberately sought to be ignored relates to the "looting" of monasteries. Even though there was an occasional mention in the press and official dispatches now and then, the matter was largely hushed. And for obvious reasons. It did not reflect well—or did it ?—on the conduct of the Mission's officers and the large retinue of hangers-on who followed them. And they were a mixed bag : press correspondents apart, there was a veritable army of cartographers, plant and insect hunters, geologists, avid curio seekers. You name it.

An admirable craving for knowledge yoked to an "atavistic desire for plunder" held the key. For, as a recent study has revealed, the "scramble" for books, manuscripts, curios was rated important, "a central plank" indeed of the philosophy of the Mission. Making the British administration a party to the "most blatant looting" of religious objects from the monasteries. Whose custodial monks were a demoralized lot unable, if also perhaps unwilling for fear of reprisals, to put up any resistance.

And no one, just no one, from the top downward, not excluding the Viceroy and his Commander in Chief, and the leader of the expedition (and his nagging wife) was above board. More, the scale of looting and the fact that it was "institutionalized" made it embarrassing, if not indeed shameful. That it was resorted to in the face of official assurances that the monasteries were "not to be pillaged", made it doubly disconcerting, even mortifying.

Michael Carrington's detailed research on the looting of monasteries is revealing with the added advantage that it places the issue in its proper context. Inter alia, the author avers that there was an insatiable demand for *oriental* artifacts and that it was the British state's scramble for knowledge which produced "ideal conditions" for this shameful exercise. Carrington lays open the sad truth that not only was looting rife but that not unoften Tibetans were murdered in the process of acquiring items! More, in the official correspondence between the various departments an attempt was made "to sanitize" the removal of this considerable hoard. And while an "immense proportion" was sold for profit, there was a lot that went to various institutions (viz. the British Museum) to reinforce their notions of "colonial superiority".[32]

Brodrick's so called "vindictiveness" against Younghusband was occasioned largely by his "sudden" conviction that HMG's Tibetan policy had been "deliberately upset" by Curzon. And insofar as the Viceroy was beyond reach, his protégé must answer for his master's sins of omission and commission. And made the scapegoat. Balfour was persuaded that Curzon was culpable and that honour demanded "a public repudiation" of Younghusband. The Commissioner had copied, the British Prime Minister was to note, "the least creditable methods" of Russian diplomacy. Valentine Chirol, the (London) *Times* correspondent, ascribed Brodrick's behaviour to "stupidity" and his "jealousy" of Curzon and viewed the "meanness of the subterfuges" used against Younghusband as "almost past belief". The Commissioner, Chirol charged, had been "censured and snubbed" and awarded "the lowest possible decoration," the KCIE.

At his interview with Younghusband, Brodrick "in a kind of galumphing way" intended to be cordial and told him that he was the "victim of circumstances". At the same time, he sounded a note of warning to the Indian government that they "could not behave as they liked." [33]

In the minds of the Cabinet, Younghusband was closely aligned with Curzon and his policies and was the inevitable target. The "heady tensions" between Curzon and Brodrick introduced what Nicholson has called "a tortuous malignity" into an already complex affair. Besides, Curzon's refusal to submit to HMG on matters of policy had brought both Brodrick as well as Balfour to "a point of exasperation." What went down badly against the Commissioner was that when summoned to explain his indiscretions, he took, ill-advisedly, an "aggressive line." And as if on cue, his supporters began a concerted campaign against the Minister whom, in private, Younghusband had called "one of those pig-headed thunderers who ruin the Empire." While it may be conceded that Brodrick's behaviour was a little less than fair, there is little doubt that the Commissioner's claim of innocence was "disingenuous".

There is no question that he had exceeded his instructions and insofar as there was a complete absence of any political sophistication to beat a tactical retreat, Younghusband's plans did go awry. The Commissioner's oft-repeated plea that while he sacrificed his life for the country, he was thrown overboard by an incompetent boss did not buy him much support. Here it is important to bear in mind the fact that the immediate area of dispute was *not* the treaty but "that favourite British obsession"; the question of Honours. The KCIE conferred on the Commissioner was viewed with a certain disdain as an honour usually "reserved for Indian clerks". What rankled even more was the knowledge that Macdonald too was awarded the same honour! Something Lady Younghusband was to find "intolerable"

An impressive 18,000 strong in numbers, it was a powerful if striking contingent that marched into Tibet: Sikh Pioneers, Grukhas, a Maxim gun detachment, field hospitals, medical staff, military police, telegraph and postal officers, specialist engineers, road builders. The transport menagerie included six camels, 3000 ponies, 5000 yaks and buffaloes, 5000 bullocks and 700 mules.

Theirs was a pyrrhic victory, at best. For, not unlike the much touted if non-existent WMDs in Saddam Hussein's Iraq a hundred odd years later, the British discovered no Cossacks in battle array, much less any Russian munitions in Tibet. In the event, what was to be a triumph of diplomacy ended up as an exercise in military prowess. The objective of fostering Tibetan friendship and cooperation was completely defeated. Instead, in the short run at any rate, there was alienation and contempt. Its "random epic grandeur", to borrow the words of Younghusband's biographer notwithstanding, the expedition was to prove "historically insignificant" if also perhaps one of the most controversial in the annals of British India.

The end-result, in retrospect, was not exactly path-breaking except in one unique respect namely, that the treaty was an inordinate nine feet long! If perhaps distrustful of the Commissioner and his men, the Regent had insisted that he would not affix his seals to disparate sheets of paper. Oddly though, both the British as well as the Tibetans were to ignore the Convention which represented at once total British triumph and, for the Tibetans, abject humiliation. The price paid was heavy by any reckoning: 3,000 dead, unhappily all Tibetan. The British obtained the right to station two Trade Agents, at Gyantse and Yatung and install a telegraph line, all the way from India to Gyantse. The Chinese, however, were to reap the maximum advantage for they climbed back into Lhasa on Younghusband's shoulders!

A word on the principal dramatis personae may not be out of place. By end-1902, with the Durbar behind him Curzon was looking for, to use his own words, "fresh fields to conquer" and Tibet was chosen as one for "a culminating triumph." The Viceroy's decision to send troops into the land of the lama however proved to be "an arrogant gamble" with his career, and his reputation. Yet he seemed to be dead set on winning this last round of the Great Game against Russia; in retrospect though, his determined "pitch" for prestige was to carry an expensive tag.

On the eve of the Commissioner's arrival in Lhasa, an Indian newspaper noted that there was "not the slightest evidence" that Tibet was playing into the hands of Russia or that Russia was seeking to have a hand in its affairs. More the "safety" of the frontier and the security of the Empire have had no more to do with Lord Curzon's "buccaneering" than the "pretence" about a trade treaty. It was, the paper concluded, the Viceroy's "unpardonable" desire to perpetuate his name that one of the "most unjustifiable" expeditions ever was mounted.[36]

Younghusband's was a split, two-dimensional personality. A swashbuckling imperialist and a peaceful, harmonious mystic he was also an autocrat, a racist and a chauvinist. Yet at the same time, more than the sum of these parts. There was a lack of human dimension in his perception which meant that he viewed the world, the empire—and the Tibetans, as stereotypes. His encounter with the Russians in the Pamirs (1891) was a warning of his "sudden, unyielding fits of arrogance" when placed in the position of sole representative of his nation. A contingency that was to repeat itself in the case of the expedition to Lhasa.

The Commissioner had manoeuvred and manipulated successfully against John Claude White. Designated Joint Commissioner, he was kept tied down in

Sikkim to organize mule and coolie traffic into Tibet! This would, Younghusband calculated, keep him out of harm's way. It was said of the Commissioner that he and his wife belonged to the race of wirepullers. The immediate effect of this, as Godley put it, was to create a strong reaction against him in the minds of those not accessible to his influence but well aware of his "tortuous proceedings."

Both Curzon and Younghusband had a shared background as fellow travellers during a formative period of their lives. This had a more "portentous" effect on their Tibetan venture than is commonly appreciated. The twosome had among others been powerfully influenced by Sir Charles MacGregor, a confirmed Russophobe who had for long presided over the Indian intelligence department. His then 'recent' book, the 'Defence of India' had underlined the importance of "military preparations on the frontier" for should these be "neglected" and Russian encroachments not repulsed by "decisive and purposeful" action, the empire of India could be lost.[37] There is no doubt that Curzon's forward policies gained immense support from men of such persuasion. In the Tibetan context, it should be clear that both Curzon as well as Younghusband knew from the very start what their purpose was and pursued it with "perfect clarity and accord" while smokescreening it from the Home government.

His experiences in Tibet were for Younghusband a rich, veritable journey of personal discovery and development. Sadly for him, and the expedition, his relations with Macdonald were "dangerously unsatisfactory." A plodding Royal Engineer, Macdonald's previous military career was anything but distinguished. In sharp contrast to an experienced if impulsive Himalayan veteran, the Engineer in uniform was by nature a cautious man. His detractors viewed him as "rigid and stolid" as a donkey, "a regular stick", an old fashioned leader of men who elicited no great respect.

In sharp contrast, while he may have exasperated his enemies, among his men Younghusband inspired devotion and loyalty. The last great romantic imperialist, he was also the first Westerner to visit Lhasa *without* disguise. His expedition was a formidable military achievement. The odds it faced were forbidding : long supply lines deep in hostile territory, a ferocious and unfamiliar terrain and an abhorrent climate. Above all, a courageous foe. In the event, its survival was a triumph in its own right. As a veritable bonus, it had to its credit some spectacular feats of courage and endurance.

Ampthill had referred to Younghusband as "a very high strung" person who had his "ups and downs". Not to talk of the prolonged strain to which he had been exposed, the Commissioner's bouts of disappointment came from unappreciative political bosses as well as an impossible foe, apart from Tibet's trying climate that claimed a heavy toll. No wonder, as Ampthill put it, Yunghusband was often "going off the rails." His threat to resign which came "within a whisker" of being accepted was symptomatic of his mental state. Macdonald too had his difficulties for apart from insomnia and gastroenteritis, he was a heavy smoker and, in command, "characteristically indecisive." With intensive negotiations in progress in Lhasa, "Retiring Mac" soon faded into insignificance. And earned his new, not ill deserved, sobriquet of the "chowkidar", literally caretaker.

Sadly for the British, the apparent enthusiasm of the Lhasa crowds on the arrival of the mission was not so much a sign of welcome as a display of grave displeasure. The only official willing to talk to the Commissioner was the charming if "incompetent" Chinese Amban. His influence though was minimal; his arrogance towards the Tibetans, no substitute for any genuine power. The harsh if unpleasant truth was that the latter hated the Chinese who in turn felt frustrated for they knew little if anything of what was going on. Happily, Younghusband took a fancy to the Regent, the Ganden Tripa whom he refers to as Ti/Tri Rimpoche, the honorific title by which the holders of the office were known.

The task that the Commissioner faced in Lhasa was difficult if not indeed well-nigh impossible. Curzon was home on leave busy fighting his own endless battles with the Cabinet. The acting Viceroy (Ampthill) had no strong views on the subject; the British government "no coherent" policy on Tibet. As if that were not bad enough, the worse was Macdonald with his unending refrain on a quick withdrawal. It was a major complication.

An apt description of what Younghusband was up against on arrival in the Tibetan capital may be gleaned from a report in an Indian newspaper. Far from sure as to what the Commissioner will do, it quipped: "die of sheer *enui*"? Or, may be ask for advice from Lord Ampthill "who has possibly none to give". And the government at home: "We fancy not." Curzon wants an English Resident, the Prime Minister will not have it. The paper wound up wondering aloud as to how the government will wriggle out of this "apparently intricable position"?[38]

Happily there were a number of factors that helped. For one, the Tibetans had virtually no cards up their sleeves and offered no resistance to the Commissioner's terms. Tucked far away in Mongolia, the Dalai Lama was out of all reckoning. Nearer home, neither Tibet's Manchu rulers, nor yet their Amban in Lhasa mattered, one way or another. They had no proposals to offer. Younghusband's two stipulations about the Gyantse Trade Agent having the right to visit Lhasa, if necessary, and the Chumbi valley remaining in British hands for 75 years until the indemnity had been fully paid, evoked no opposition.

IV

A principal lacuna in the earlier edition relates to an unfortunate omission as to how the expedition was viewed in and by the media. In the event, the following paragraphs should hopefully fill in the gap, if perhaps only partially. An attempt has been made here to mesh what appeared in the "native" (i.e. Indian language) papers with all that was relevant in the "native-owned" English language papers. The latter, not unoften, drew on their British contemporaries, not always in a very comprehensive manner. In the event, their coverage was bound to be coloured by editorial preferences: biases in favour as well as prejudices against individual newspapers as well as men and events. For convenience of reference, the matter has been arranged under appropriate sub-heads.

The Beginnings

If the "peaceful" mission was concerned solely with questions of trade and frontier delimitation, why was there "so persistent" a refusal of adequate information to the public? And why was time for the advance so chosen when Parliament was not sitting and "inconvenient" questions could not be raised? (The *Bengalee*, December 29, 1903). The paper posited the view that Lord Curzon was "hankering after the Earldom of Lhassa (sic)" even as one of his predecessors had been rewarded with that of Burma.[39]

Amazing, said the *Indian Empire* (February 9, 1904), to call a mission escorted by 4,000 soldiers and mountain guns in abundance, "political"![40]

All that the Tibetans wanted was to be "left alone in their isolation." "What right" had Lord Curzon or anyone else "to act as Providence"? "Is the limits of civilisaion reached" by mountain guns, shells and shrapnells?" *(Indian Mirror,* March 3, 1904).[41]

The *Hitavadi* (Calcutta) of March 11 (1904) bemoaned the "despicable" manner in which Lord Curzon had made "baseless rumours" and "false and exaggerated incidents" appear as real truth. Again, was it not "criminal" of "uncivilized Orientals" (viz. Tibetans) to dislike (resist) the "free passage" of "civilized" Englishmen into their country."[42]

In its leader, entitled "The British Invasion of Tibet", the *Tribune* of April 16, (1904) referred to the mission, escorted by over 3,000 troops and accompanied by artillery and large hosts of followers who have settled upon the country as locusts. It cited from the *Indian People* to the effect that an "aggressive" Western power was seeking "to deprive" an "innocent" people of their independence by measures that make one "positively sick."

The *Amrita Bazar Patrika* of July 7 expressed the view that it was one man (viz. Lord Curzon) who "conceived the idea" of invading Tibet and this one man "carried his point without consulting" either the English people, Parliament or the Cabinet.[43]

In its "Notes and Comments" for November 21 (1903), the *Tribune* cited the *Pioneer* for the view that Lord Curzon was fired with the "ambition" of becoming another Lord Dufferin. For in regard to Tibet, as earlier in the case of Burma, the "trading difficulty" was the "first excuse of interference."

The "Action" at Chumi Shengo (Guru), March 1904

The *Bengalee* (May 11) bemoaned the "mowing down" of Tibetans on the "pretence" that they opposed the Mission and insisted that the "voice of humanity" protests "emphatically" against the spilling of more blood. It was clear that the people will "hardly applaud" British bravery and British enterprise in mowing down the primitive and unkempt Tibetans.[44] Later, in its issue of May 21, the same paper referred to one Bishop Weldon who had hailed the shedding of blood in Tibet as a "blessing". Arguing that once Tibet ceased to be a sealed book, it will provide an "excellent" field for carrying on "proselytizing work".[45]

The *Daily Hitavadi* (Calcutta) of June 10, wondered why call a military expedition a "peaceful" mission and wage war upon the people of Tibet with the money of "famished, helpless" Indians? [46]

The *Indian Mirror* of June 24, referring to "reports" of "our" troops setting fire to and destroying Tibetan villages asked Bishop Weldon to "tell us if it were the torches of enlightenment and Christianity" which were used on the occasion for "firing" the doomed villages with?[47]

A correspondent for the *Pioneer* reported that the mountain battery "came into action and tore their (viz. Tibetan) line" with shrapnel. In the event, a terrible "trail of dead and dying marked their line of march." (The *Tribune*, April 5). In its leader, "The Invasion of Tibet", on May 17, the same paper cited from the *Free Press Journal* to the effect that "it is plain" that the soldiers had "without any temptation" slaughtered those poor wretches "in cold blood," without "any risk" to themselves. On May 31, the *Tribune* quoted the (London) *Daily News* to the effect that "it is admitted" that the firing was "not a military necessity" but was resorted to as "a punishment". And referred to Lord Curzon's "utterly unnecessary" interference "undertaken treacherously" in Tibet's affairs under the mask of peace.

The *Tripura Hitaishi* (Comilla) of July 26 referred to King Edward VII's public declaration that he wished to establish peace in the world and enquired, "Is then the massacre in Tuna the outcome of His Majesty's peace proposals?"[48]

Indian Trade

The *Tribune* of December 29 (1903) defined "Indian trade" as the "trade of British merchants" in India and expressed the view that the "forward" party was in favour of Tibet's annexation for it would provide "a pleasant sanatorium" for our Anglo-Indian officers.

Under the heading "Tibetan Expedition and Indian Trade", the *Tribune* on July 16, reported that the value of export and import trade with Tibet which in 1902-3 stood at Rs 33.5 lakhs had decreased to Rs. 21,87,568.

In its issue of September 20, the *Tribune* cited the (London) *Financial Times* of 20 July for the view that the "one remaining pretext" about the "interests of so-called trade" had been exposed by Vincent C. Henderson, the Chinese Commissioner of Customs at Yatung. Statistics revealed that the total value of trade, imports as well as exports, for the year 1903 was only Rs. 1,373,365, roughly (£ 90,000). "The astonishing brevity" of the report was ascribed by the Commissioner to the "apparent futility" of expatiating at length on "such a peddling trade."

The Costs

The *Hitavadi* (Calcutta) of March 11 (1904) deeply bemoaned the fact that "it is the poor people of India" who must pay the cost of the Tibet war as they had earlier in the case of the Afghan and Burmese wars.[49]

To the *Hindoo Patriot* of July 5 it was clear that the decision "to saddle" India with the cost of the Tibet expedition was "a distinct violation" of the statute which laid down that Indian revenues should not be charged with the cost of "any warlike enterprise" beyond the frontier.[50]

The *Indian Empire* of July 19, expressed the view that the expedition was likely to absorb the "greater part" of 1 million pound sterling and it was the "poverty stricken millions" of India who were "having to pay for this folly."[51]

The *Tribune* in the course of its leader, "The Invasion of Tibet" II (June 30, 1904), cited Sir Henry Cotton to the effect that such an expedition at the cost of Indian revenues beyond the limits of British India "cannot constitutionally be undertaken" without the assent of Parliament. Earlier, under the heading "The Cost of the Tibetan Raid", the same paper in its issue of February 16, termed the expenditure of Indian revenues as "both unjust and illegal" except on the principle that India must be bled, even if she should perish. Again, on May 14, taking note of the Tibetan debate in the House of Commons, the paper referred to a motion adopted by the House that it "consents to the revenues of India being applied" for any military operations which may become necessary "beyond the frontiers" of HM's Indian possessions for "protecting" the political mission "dispatched" to the Tibetan government.

The Loot

The *Bengalee* of July 26, referred to the "piles of loot" which it reported were being accumulated at Gyantse by the British and queried, "Is this the way Lord Curzon hopes to bring about the "enlightenment" of the Tibetan nation ?"[52]

In its issue of September 8, the *Tribune* reproduced a report from the *Morning Leader* (London) to the effect that any sack of Lhasa, covert on avowed, would excite universal disgust and indignation. Reporting that Younghusband's authority had evidently failed to prevent looting on the march up, it wondered if it will now "prove sufficient among the far greater temptation of Lhasa?"

A Miscellany

On January 12, the *Tribune* referred to the "very harsh" measures employed for recruiting coolies and alluded to a Kathmandu report that a man being pressed into service had begged to be excused for the poor condition of his wife. He was however compelled to register. In the event, he tore the recruiting havildar apart and was later captured and hanged.

In its leader, "The Invasion of Tibet" I (February 12), the *Tribune* quoted Sir Henry Cotton to the effect that the Mission was "a diplomatic blunder", that if there were indeed good reasons for good action, the government should "publish them without the least possible delay."

Later, under another leader, "The Tibetan Expedition and Parliament" (June 16), the same paper referred to the speech of Lord Hardwicke, the Under Secretary of State for India, in the debate in the House of Lords and expressed the view that "the only conclusion that intelligent men" could draw was that the government was "hopelessly in the mud" and had no policy, "definite or indefinite." More that things will be managed the way Lord Curzon had wanted from "the very outset", something "very much" to be regretted. Two days later the same paper referred to the "present ill-timed, ill-conceived and ill-conducted" business across the Himalayas.

The *Indian Nation* of August 1 expressed the view that there was "not the slightest evidence" that Tibet was playing into the hands of Russia or that Russia was seeking to have a hand in its affairs.[53] A week later (August 8), the same paper expressed the view that the "safety" of the frontier and the "security" of the Empire have had no more to do with Lord Curzon's "buccaneering" than the pretence about a trade treaty. It was, the paper concluded, his "unpardonable" desire to perpetuate his name that one of the "most unjustifiable" expeditions ever was mounted.[54]

The *Bengalee* of August 24, expressed the view that "time" had revealed that the trade treaty was "a myth" and the Mission, the "nucleus" of a large army "threatening" the independence of Tibet.[55]

On August 16, the *Tribune* reproduced a report from the *Amrit Bazar Patrika* about the mission's arrival in the Tibetan capital but was not sure as to what it will do: "die of sheer *enui*?" Or, may be ask for advice from Lord Ampthill, "who has possibly none to give." And the government at home: "We fancy not." Curzon wants an English Resident, the Prime Minister will not have it. And wondered aloud as to how the government will wriggle out of this "apparently intricable position."

In its issue of September 8, the *Tribune* quoted from the (London) *Globe*, about the terms of the treaty and referred to the fact that Mr. Brodrick was "unable as yet" to specify the exact terms. There was not much money at Lhasa but the difficulty "might be surmounted" by the Dalai Lama consenting to "a rectification of the frontier, a lot-needed concession." In other words, what Russia did in Manchuria. "God save England from her advisors," the paper concluded.

On September 10, the *Tribune* under the column "Contemporary Opinion" cited from the *Daily News* (London) to the effect that "the disgrace and infamy of a cowardly and treacherous campaign conducted under false pretences and with a flagrant disregard to the pledged word of British statesmen can never be atoned for." The paper also quoted the (London) *Times* for the view that "if we turn from the political to the military" side of this expedition, "it must be accounted a very brilliant feat of arms."

In its issue of September 8, the *Tribune* reproduced a report in the *Manchester Guardian* to the effect that as the Dalai Lama had fled and refused to return, the lamas left behind were practising "a sort of passive resistance." And referred to a gompa with 6,000 to 8,000 lamas which was approached for food by a detachment that was kept waiting for hours till it was almost reduced to firing. And then kept waiting after it was promised that its demand would be met. In the end, the monks produced "a ridiculous" 100 lbs of meal with which the detachment had to go away content!

The *Charu Mihir* (Mymensingh) of September 13, expressed "no small regret" for so much innocent Tibetan blood that had been spilled and said that it could not "on any ground" justify the Mission. Was it a "peaceful" mission that was responsible for "all the unrest" it had created and "the havoc" it had wrought among the people of Tibet?[56]

In its issue of February 23(1903), the *Tribune* referred to Lord Curzon's *Problems of the Far East* (1894) and said that "for the providential shaping of already rough hewn ends" he was the "divinely appointed" agent. And that in Asia "there was but one British policy" and Lord Curzon was "its Prophet".

On October 22, the *Tribune* under its column "Notes and Comments" referred to a recipe which "somebody" had discovered for the Lhasa Ice Pudding a la Dalai Lama in the Young Husband's Cookery Book. "Make a treaty first and keep it unobserved in a pigeonhole in some cool place like Simla. When you think every body has forgotten all about it, take it out and mix it with the Imperial Coy's Extract of Treaty Obligations. Now you want powder and shot but if you cannot afford them call the whole dish a mission and get the cheaper quality procurable in India free of charge. This gives it a piquant flavour besides making it so cheap. It is superior to the Russian way of preparing it. Kill a few thousand monks and the flavour is improved greatly."

In its leader "Buddhism and the Tibet Mission", the *Tribune* of 6 September referred to a news item, the "Annual Gathering at Urga" by the (London) *Daily News* correspondent, A G Hales which alluded to the desecration of the Lhasa temples that had agitated the large assembly of 24,000 Buddhist priests. The vast concourse, it reported, "stood around with flushed cheeks and blazing eyes with the angry blood swelling in every vein until the name of England stank in the nostrils".[57]

The Finale

The *Indian Empire* of October 11, reported that the mission had to return unless it wanted to be "snowed up." So it "scampered off" with a "useless scroll of paper" which they have been pleased to term a "treaty." This is the "nett (sic) result" of that "luckless mission.[58]

The *Indian Mirror* suggested that unless the Viceroy was "forgetful", the "accommodating" Tongsa Penlop and the "obliging" Amban may find their names in the next New Year's Honours List.[59] The net result was best illustrated in the story of the mountain in labour. The scroll of paper which Colonel Younghusband now holds in his hands is the little mouse of the fable. (The *Tribune*, September 22).

The (London) *Times* referred to the mission's achievement of lifting the veil "from the face of the Central Asian sphinx". And expressed the view that "be the fruits" of this arduous expedition "great or small", "nothing can undo the abiding fact that a British Mission has been seen in Lhasa ." (The *Tribune*, October 8).[60]

No comment is called for. It should be obvious though that the minutiae apart, the broad essentials of all that was contained in state dispatches and exchanges at the highest levels of government between Calcutta and Whitehall was shared by a large segment of the Anglo-Indian as well as the "native" press. Nor, it would appear, was a critical appraisal of men and events inhibited by any visible much less invisible constraints.

Notes

1.   Karl E. Meyer & Shareen Blair Brysac, *Tournament of Shadows: the Great Game and the Race for Empire in Central Asia,* 1999, p. 557.
2.   David H Schimmelpenninck van der Oyer, "Russia's Great Game in Tibet" *Toronto Studies in Central and Inner Asia,* no. 5, 2002, 35-52, p. 52.
3.   Diary of Kurorpatkin cited in Arash Boormanshinov, "A Secret Kalmyk Mission to Tibet in 1904", *Central Asiatic Journal,* 30, 3-4, 1992, 161-87, p. 175.
4.   Alexandre Andreyev, "Russian Buddhists in Tibet, from the end of the nineteenth century-1930", *Journal of the Royal Asiatic Society,* series 3, 11, 3 (2001), pp. 349-62.
5.   "Per-war Diplomacy: the Russo-Japanese Problem; Dairy of J.J. Korostovetz". London, 1920, p. 48 cited in Arash Boormanshinov, *op.cit.,* p. 175.
6.   There of these cartoons, "Forced Favours", "Another Sideshow" and "Business First" are reproduced in the text on pp. 230, 250 and 311 respectively. All the three are drawn by Bernard Partridge.
7.   David Dilks, *Curzon in India,* London, 1970, 2 Vols. I, p. 214.
8.   David Gillard, *The Struggle for Asia 1828-1914 : A Study in the British & Russian Imperialism,* London, 1977, p. 173.
9.   Charles Alfred Bell, *Portrait of the Dalai Lama,* London, 1946, pp. 61-2.
10.   Alexandre Andreyev, *Soviet Russia & Tibet: the debacle of secret diplomacy 1918-1930s,* Leiden, 2003, p. 23.
11.   For more biographical details regarding Dorjief and of Tsarist Russia's interaction with Tibet in the eighteenth and nineteenth centuries, see *Ibid,* pp. 10-26.
12.   Helen Hundley, "Tibet's Part in the Great Game (Agvan Dorjiev)", *History Today,* October 1993, pp. 45-52.
13.   Julia Brown Trott, " 'One Turn of Pitch & Toss' : Curzon, Younghusband and the Gamble for Lhasa, 1903 to 1904", unpublished Ph D thesis, University of Hawaii, December 2000, pp. 335-46.
14.   For a more detailed coverage see "Tsarist Russia & Tibet: An Unwelcome Rapprochement", chapter I (pp. 1-68) in Alexandre Andreyev, Soviet Russia & Tibet, *op.cit.*
15.   Tatiana Shaumian, *Tibet: the Great Game and Tsarist Russia,* Delhi, 2002, p. 31.
16.   Patrick French, *Younghusband: the Last Great Imperial Adventurer,* London, 1994, p. 241.
17.   "On the Road to Nature's Mandala", chapter 2 (pp. 25-57) in Scott Berry, *Monks, Spies & A Soldier of Fortune,* London, 1995.
18.   Dr Isrun Engelhardt's letter to the author, dated February 17, 2002. See also Scott Berry, *op.cit,* p. 74.
19.   Wendy Palace, "The Kozlov Expedition of 1907-10 & the Problem of Kokonor", *Asian Affairs,* February 2002, pp. 20-29.
20.   Patrick French, *op.cit.,* p. 187.
21.   Trott, *op.cit.,* pp. 336-7.
22.   Tournament of Shadows, *op.cit.,* p. 419.
23.   For a detailed and well-informed discussion see Michael Carrington, "Younghusband, the Last Great Imperial Butcher?" in *Tibetan Review,* November, December 1998.

January 1999, pp. 17-20; 19-22; 17-19, 21.

24. Also see "The 'Action' at Guru" (March 1904), *Infra*, section IV.

25. Patrick French, *op.cit.*, pp. 220-6. Also his interview with the editor of *Tibetan Bulletin*, 4.1, January-April 2000, pp. 1-5.

26. Nicholas Fenn, "In the Footsteps of Younghusband: the Centenary Tour of Tibet", *Asian Affairs*, October 2002, pp. 179-89.

27. Peter Fleming, *Bayonets to Lhasa*, London, 1962, p. 76.

28. The *Financial Times* (London), 20 July 1904 reproduced in the *Tribune*, September 20, 1904. For more details, see 'Indian Trade' under section IV.

29. David Gilmour, *Curzon*, pp. 97 and 162.

30. Anthony Verrier, *Francis Younghusband and the Great Game*, 1991, p. 201. For Curzon's letters to Younghusband at Lhasa see text pp. 377-78 and 380.

31. David Gilmour, *Curzon*, p. 288.

32. Michael Carrington, "Officers, Gentlemen and Thieves: the Looting of Monasteries during the 1903/4 Younghusband Mission to Tibet", *Modern Asian Studies*, 37, 1, (2003), pp. 81-109.
    Curzon was to acquire "certain Tibetan curios" from a Calcutta exhibition (January 1905) of "rare and valuable manuscripts, armour, weapons, paintings and porcelain" while "a large collection of porcelain" was "also dispatched" to Kitchener.

33. David Gilmour, *Curzon*, p. 291.

34. Patrick French, *Younghusband*, pp. 256-8.

35. Anthony Verrier, *op.cit.*, pp. 157-8. Also see Trott, *op.cit.*, p. 216.

36. The *Indian Nation*, August 1 & 8, 1904. For more details see section IV under the heading "A Miscellany."

37. Trott, *op.cit.*, p. 162. Curzon was to refer to it as MacGregor's 'famous unpublished memorandum.' Trott suggests that it must have had 'a wide circulation' and its contents 'generally known.'

38. The 'Amrit Bazar Patrika' cited in the *Tribune*, August 16, 1904.

39. *Report on Native Newspapers in Bengal* (abbreviated, et seq, *RNNB*) for the week ending January 2, 1904.

40. RNNB for the week ending February 12, 1904.

41. *Ibid.*, for the week ending March 12, 1903.

42. *Ibid.*, for the week ending March 26, 1903.

43. *Ibid.*, for the week ending July 9, 1904.

44. *Ibid.*, for the week ending May 21, 1904.

45. *Ibid.*, for the week ending May 28, 1904.

46. *Ibid.*, for the week ending June 18, 1904.

47. *Ibid.*, for the week ending July 9, 1904.

48. *Ibid.*, for the week ending August 6,1904.

49. *Ibid.*, for the week ending March 26, 1904.

50. *Ibid.*, for the week ending July 16, 1904.

51. *Ibid.*, for the week ending July 23, 1904.

52. *Ibid.*, for the week ending July 30, 1904.

53. *Ibid.*, for the week ending August 6, 1904.

54. *Ibid.*, for the week ending August 13, 1904.

55. *Ibid.*, for the week ending August 27,1904.

56. *Ibid.*, for the week ending September 19, 1904.

57. *Ibid.*, for the week ending September 10, 1904.

58. *Ibid.*, for the week ending November 5, 1904.
59. Ugyen Wangchuk, the governor ('penlop') of the province of Tongsa in central Bhutan who had from the very outset followed the Mission like a shadow; in 1907 he was to be installed as his country's first hereditary king.

    Yu-t'ai, the Chinese Amban ('viceroy') at Lhasa was later impeached by his government for cowardice, embezzlement of funds and corruption.

    Both the Amban as well as the Bhutan chief had rendered no small help to Younghusband to 'negotiate' with the Tibetans.
60. A brief word on the newspapers and journals cited in the preceding paragraphs may help place them in sharper focus. To start with, there were three *Bengali* language dailies; two of these, the *Hitaishi* (1897) and the *Hatavadi* (1897), published from Calcutta and a third, the *Charu Mihir* (1904) from Mymensingh.

    Among the *English* language dailies from Calcutta mention may be made of the *Bengalee*, the *Indian Empire* (1904) and the *Amrita Bazar Patrika* which was a weekly to start with (1885) but became a daily six years later (1891). The *Indian Mirror* (1904) was another daily in English from Calcutta. The *Indian Nation* was a weekly in English which also appeared from Calcutta.

    The *Pioneer* (1901) was a *daily* in English published from Allahabad with George Allen as its publisher/editor while the *Tribune* (1902) appeared from Lahore and was a *tri-weekly* in English.

    The Bengali language newspapers listed above have all disappeared and so have a number of their English contemporaries. Among the latter, the better-known, *Amrita Bazar Patrika*, the *Pioneer* and the *Tribune* are very much around and, professionally at any rate, doing well.

    Among the English language press, the *Bengalee*, the *A B Patrika* and the *Indian Mirror*, all published from Calcutta, and the *Tribune* from Lahore, were prominent supporters of the nationalist (read Indian National Congress) cause. As to the Anglo-Indian papers, the *Stateman* (*& Friend of India*) broadly supported the Congress and was sympathetic to Indian editors; the *Pioneer*, on the other hand, offered stiff opposition to the nationalist viewpoint and rated the Indian language papers as "disloyal vernacular rags". Sadly for it, they had "penetrated into remote villages". Thus the *Hitawadi*, on account of its audacious and more outspoken criticism of government policies, sold (1900) 35,000 copies, the highest in the country!

    The *Bengalee* was a languishing English daily (1879) when Surendra Nath Banerjee purchased it. And by dint of his industry, devotion and ability made it into an important paper: in 1904 it enjoyed a circulation of an estimated 3,000 copies. The *Tribune* sold (1902) 1,700 copies and the *Pioneer* (1901) 5,054 copies. The *A B Patrika* which sold 2,237 copies in 1885 was, in 1901, converted into a daily from a weekly. The *Statesman* (*& Friend of India*), an English daily published from Calcutta, had a circulation of 4,000 copies (1904).

    The *Report on Native Newspapers* was compiled in the office of the Translator and was treated as a highly confidential document. Such items as had any administrative or political bearing were translated for the persual of officers holding the rank of Divisional Commissioner or above. The selection was exhaustive and covered even the cartoons. The *Report* in respect of Bengal also included such papers as were published in the adjoining French territory of Chandranagar as well as modern day Bihar, Orissa and Assam.

    From 1901 onwards Indian-owned English language newspapers were reported separately in the second part of the *Report* by the Police Department of Bengal and North-Western Provinces (re-christened United Provinces after 1 April 1902 and now, post-1947, Uttar Pradesh). The English language newpaper, the *Tribune*, was included in the *Report* dealing with the vernacular press.

The *Pioneer* Press Library at Lucknow contains the old files of the paper which was then published from Allahabad. The National Library in Calcutta has among its holdings copies of the *Amrita Bazar Patrika* and the *Bengalee* as also the *Indian Nation* and the *Indian Mirror*.

Bibliographic Note

Apart from the present work, two full-length studies on the expedition to Tibet should be of interest. The earliest, Peter Fleming's *Bayonets to Lhasa* (1961) is the "First Full Account" of the British "Invasion", essentially though for the lay reader. The "ultimate motive" of the expedition, the author avers, was the ghost of Russian intrigue operating "from a base in Lhasa", to disaffect Nepal, Bhutan and Sikkim. The fear, though misplaced, was not "unreasonably entertained." "A shot in the dark", the expedition itself was " bedevilled" by "remote control" in Whitehall while its success nearer home was "jeopardized" by Macdonald's "egotism and over-caution." Fleming successfully recaptures the turn of the century period and, in broad strokes, sketches the principal events; nonetheless, he misses out on important details (viz. the Curzon-Brodrick relationship for one). And, in the event, should be accepted with some caution.

Another study, by an American author, is Julia Brown Trott's " 'One Turn of Pitch & Toss': Curzon, Younghusband and the Gamble for Lhasa, 1903 to 1904", a doctoral dissertation presented at the University of Hawaii in December 2000. A well-researched work, Trott's principal thesis is that the expedition was "a gamble and a cultural odyssey", an encounter between people with "extremely divergent perspectives." And, an "exercise of the imagination." Determined that the British reach Lhasa before anybody else did, both Curzon and Younghusband, she insists, had to find "political ploys" to justify their action. Needing a small army to overcome Tibetan resistance, Curzon sent one to escort his representative. The expedition, she is persuaded, was "a chase or hunt" for a chimerical beast, the Tibetan Grand Llama. While both the Viceroy as well as his understudy knew from the beginning what their purpose was, they successfully smokescreened it from others. Especially their political bosses in Whitehall, by creating "a veritable pea souper" of a fog.

Two other interesting pieces on the theme are by Helen Hundley, "Tibet's Part in the 'great game' (Agvan Dorjiev)", *History Today*, and Michael Carrington, "Younghusband, the Last Great Imperial Butcher?" I-III, *Tibetan Review*. The first is a meaningful reassessment of the Buryat lama and the role he played in Tibet's affairs. The American academic makes the point that "recent archival evidence" supports the theory that as far as the land of the lama was concerned, the Russian foreign ministry "initiated nothing" and that "even" important "British observers of the time" (viz. Spring Rice) agreed with this view. Carrington's is a refreshing attempt to apportion blame for the massacre at Guru on the Commissioner/Macdonald and his men/the Lhasa Depon (general) and his Tibetan rabble of an army. The author underlines the fact that the number of Tibetans killed in the first firing in the vicinity of the wall was 340 dead and 150 wounded. Another 288 were killed and 72 wounded in the chase to, and action at Guru. The unasked question is "if Younghusband was so sickened by the slaughter at the wall, why did he allow it to continue?" Carrington also suggests that the contemporary ideology of the 'new' imperialism of the period played a dominant role in reporting and interpreting "the mostly one-sided violence" during the 1904 expedition.

Among recent studies about Russia's designs on Tibet mention may be made of a long introductory chapter, 'Tsarist Russia and Tibet:an Unwelcome Rapprochement' in Alexandre Andreyev's *Soviet Russia and Tibet', the debacle of Secret diplomacy, 1918-1930s,* Leiden. 2003. There is also Nikolai Kuleshov's *Russia's Tibet File,* Dharamsala, 1996 as well as Tatiana Shaumian's *Tibet: the Great Game and Tsarist Russia,* Delhi, 2002. The author's "Tibet and Russian Intrigue" and Alastair Lamb's "Some Notes on Russian Intrigue", both published in the *Royal Central Asian Journal* (London) in the late 1950s, still serve as useful backdrop. While the late John Snelling's *Buddhism in Russia: the story of Agvan Dorzhiev, Lhasa's Emissary to the Tsar,* Shaftesbury, 1993 is almost indispensable.

In his "Russia's Great Game in Tibet", *Toronto Studies in Central and Inner Asia,* no 5, 2002, David H Schimmelpenninck van der Oyer broadly endorses Tom Grunfeld's observation (*The Making of Modern Tibet,* New York 1987, 1996) that while Tsarist Russia did have interests in Tibet, "it was unlikely" to exert much effort to pursue them for the country "simply was not important enough."

In his half-fictional account, *Sturm uber Asien* (1924), Wilhelm Filchner has claimed that Dorjief was in contact with the Russian foreign ministry and the information section of the General Staff as early as 1885. This has been 'confirmed' by a Russian journalist (Oleg Shishkin) who insists that the Buryat, then rated the Kremlin's "most important agent", was known by the nickname of "Shambala". Sadly, neither Filchner nor yet the journalist in question have cited any evidence to buttress their claims.

Michael Carrington's, "Officers, Gentlemen and Thieves: the Looting of Monasteries during the 1903/4 Younghusband Mission to Tibet", *Modern Asian Studies,* 371 (2003), is not only well-researched but also revealing. It has the added advantage of placing the issue in its proper context. Inter alia, the author suggests that there was an insatiable demand for *Oriental* artifacts and that it was the British state's scramble for knowledge which produced "ideal conditions" for this shameful exercise. Carrington reveals that not only was looting rife but that Tibetans were murdered in the process of acquiring items! More, in the official correspondence between various departments, an attempt was made "to sanitize" the removal of this considerable hoard. And while an "immense proportion" was sold for profit, there was a lot that went to various institutions (viz. the British Museum) to reinforce their notions of "colonial superiority."

Patrick French's impressive tome, *Younghusband: the last great Imperial*

Adventurer, 1994 (as well as a number of perceptive studies under the general rubric of the "Great Game") devotes considerable attention to Younghusband's progress to, and performance at, Lhasa. Here a recent study, Karl E. Meyer and Shareen Blair Brysac's voluminous (650-odd paged), if impressive, *Tournament of Shadows : The Great Game and the Race for Empire in Central Asia*, 1999 as well as a number of books by Peter (now Sir Peter) Hopkirk and a bunch of articles in the special centenary issue of *Asian Affairs* (Journal of the Royal Society for Asian Affairs), February 2002, make both for interesting, and instructive, reading.

A number of studies under the rubric of the 'great game', more especially Younghusband's role in it, make for useful inputs. Anthony Verrier's *Francis Younghusband & the Great Game*, 1991 offers a perceptive analysis of the expedition to Lhasa but has to be accepted with some caution especially on the linkages between the Commissioner and his political boss, the Viceroy. The author heavily underlines the fact that Curzon had "a unique gift" for antagonizing his friends and "a habit" of "unwittingly" misleading his subordinates. That may well be true but to suggest that he chose to "virtually abandon" Younghusband even as he was entering the Tibetan capital does not really hold. Nor yet the author's "inescapable" conclusion that around this time Curzon had "washed his hands" off the Tibet business.

Gerald Morgan, "Myth and Reality in the Great Game", *Asian Affairs*, 60, 1, February 1973, is useful in demystifying the Anglo-Russian rivalry. Morgan reveals the interesting fact that from the 1860s there was "only one expert" on Russia in the whole of Whitehall and he was attached to the India Office! Only in 1876 were his studies of Russia and translations made available to the Foreign Office and the War Office. Similarly in India there was *one* expert on China—Ney Elias—and for most of the time he was away from Calcutta on other duties! David Gillard's slim volume, *The Struggle for Asia 1828-1914: A Study in British and Russian Imperialism*, 1977 underlines the fact that the "celebrated" rivalry between British and Russian imperialism in the 19th century would seem to be a "classic case" of "futility, mutual misunderstanding and the arrogance of power." His sum-up makes for interesting reading. Between 1828 and 1833 the British perceived a "major shift of power" in Russia's favour; by 1860, they had "spectacularly" reversed this. After 1860, the balance tipped gradually in favour of Russia. By 1908, in the face of a common threat from Germany, the twosome had called it a day.

David Fromkin, "The Great Game in Asia", *Foreign Affairs* (New York), Spring 1980, offers some refreshing sidelights on the significance of the 'game' in the *Asian* context. He underlines the fact that what was "so especially frightening" about Russian expansion in Asia was its "persistence and seeming inevitability." The stakes were high, real and the ultimate question was of Russian or British supremacy in the world.

Of more than peripheral interest is Michael Edwardes' *Playing the Great Game: A Victorian Cold War*, 1975. The author cites with approval the 19th century Tsarist Russia's celebrated foreign minister Count Nasserode's reference to the GG as "a tournament of shadows", a secret war of illusions. More specifially, he makes the point that both Curzon and Younghusband were defeated "mainly by a rapidly changing world", that the mission was the "last great event" in the tournament but was not "quite the end" of the GG itself. Another study, James Morris, *Farewell the Trumpets: an Imperial Retreat*, 1978 underlines the fact that the expedition "never rang true" and that there was "no heart in it." In the event, it "brought no glory." While Curzon was "a notorious exponent" of the forward policy, Younghusband was much concerned with "face" and image and other peoples' opinion. "An eager puller of strings", he could both be double faced and "aggressively imperialist."

Wendy Palace's "The Kozlov Expedition of 1907-10 and the Problem of Kokonor", *Asian Affairs*, February 2001, does not relate directly to the 1904 expedition to Lhasa but offers useful insights. Arash Boormanshinov's "A Secret Kalmyk Mission to Tibet in 1904", *Central Asiatic Journal*, is a well-researched piece that elaborates at length the Tsarist game plan on the eve of Younghusband's expedition. Nikolai S. Kuleshov's "Russia and Tibetan Crisis: Beginning at the 20th century", *Tibet Journal,* offers an excellent survey of the so called "Russian intrigue'.

Nayana Goradia, *Lord Curzon: the Last of the British Moghuls*, 1993 furnishes some interesting sidelights on the Viceroy's personality. She suggests inter alia that Curzon's "nervous exhaustion" began barely two years after his assumption of office. This made him intolerant of all opposition and, at the same time, persuaded him to drive his officials remorselessly. In the event, none dared differ with him for fear of imperilling his career. Later, in the events leading to the expedition and its aftermath, the Viceroy was to complain bitterly of Brodrick's "animus" against him and thought the Secretary of State "untiring in his malevolence". He it was who later "jockeyed" Curzon out of office and treated him "as worse than a dog".

Two studies by Alexandre Andreyev make for interesting reading: to start with, there is his "Russian Buddhists in Tibet, from the end of the nineteenth century_1930", *Journal of the Royal Asiatic Society* (Cambridge). And the same author's "Indian Pundits & the Russian Exploration of Tibet: an unknown story of the Great Game Era", *Central Asiatic Journal* (Wiesbaden). In the former Andreyev furnishes useful biographical sketches of "a few more outstanding" Buryat and Kalmyk *Iharmpas,* holders of the theological degree that Dorjief too had earned after eight years of very hard work. The second piece dilates on the fact that the Russians had "keenly monitored", and absorbed, the work of the Indian Pundits over a period of time.

Introduction

In the long and chequered history of Tibet, the opening years of the twentieth century occupy an important place. For once the veil was drawn off from the face of the Hermit kingdom and its long-guarded and sedulously-cherished isolation shattered; the British in India had led an armed expedition to the seat of the Tibetan government — to Lhasa, 'the abode of gods'.

The story of the Younghusband Mission, though old in years, has never ceased to evince the interest and excite the curiosity of students of frontier affairs, even in lands far removed from the barren and treeless wastes of Tibet. Today that story has assumed added importance for, the specialist apart, any intelligent student of international relations finds it exceedingly hard to grasp the meaning of much that has lately passed over a country traditionally known only for its mystery and snow, without a reasonable familiarity with the aims and objectives visualised — and the results that flowed from this expedition. Simply told the episode is a brief one and relates to the summer of 1903 when Lord Curzon, then Viceroy and Governor-General of India, chose a Major Younghusband to lead a small number of 'frontier diplomats' to negotiate some trading rights, and settle a few outstanding border disputes, with the representatives of Tibet's 'god-king' and of the Imperial Chinese Resident at Lhasa.

The British commercial mission, escorted by a couple of hundred well-armed troops, penetrated a little over a score of miles into the country to initiate the parleys. Nonetheless it folded up as a full-fledged military expedition that dictated terms to the battle-worsted Tibetans in the audience-chamber of the golden Potala. This chapter in Indo-Tibetan relations which Baron Curzon of Kedleston thus opened has not yet drawn to a close. For verily it would seem that the (Communist) Chinese invasion of Tibet in the fall of 1950, the 'Agreement on Trade and Intercourse between the Tibet Region of China and India' in April 1954, the March (1959) Rebellion in Lhasa with the Dalai Lama a fugitive from the land of his birth and faith, followed by the more recent demotion of the Panchen Lama and Tibet's 'elevation' to the status of an 'Autonomous Region' of the People's Republic are part of the chain reaction that started on its course more than half a century ago.

Nor could it be maintained that the last word has been said on the Younghusband performance at Lhasa. To be sure the treaty which the victorious British Commissioner concluded there marked the beginnings of controversies whose reverberations still fill the pages of learned books and journals. The Curzon-Younghusband team though it had succeeded in persuading a reluctant British government to sanction the advance to the Tibetan capital, failed woefully in carrying conviction after the initial goal had been reached. The two of them—'old friends and fellow-travellers', to borrow Lord Curzon's words—had visualised a political settlement that would have left the British in supreme control, with a territorial and an economic stranglehold over the land which would have been hard to shake. The Conservative government of Arthur Balfour shrank from the prospect at the very moment of its realisation, and repudiated some of the most vital adjuncts of what their Commissioner had committed them to. There are indeed few instances in history where an expanding imperial system thus deliberately set limits to its expansion and denied itself the very means whereby it subsisted and flourished.

Armed encounters, then as now, lead to violent reactions. Younghusband and the men he commanded had borne the brunt of the monks' wild, if futile, fury—at Guru, on the way to and at Gyantse itself. Hot blood too had marked the trail of British progress and yet after the (Gyantse) jong had been taken, albeit the lamas' scowls persisted, there were no battles, few ugly incidents and little if any bloodshed. The return of the expedition was peaceful—for though the Tibetans could not readily believe the fact of withdrawal, they yet saw it with their own eyes!

In planning the expedition to Lhasa the British had to be mindful of Tibet's immediate neighbours to the south. Sikkim's recalcitrant Maharaja, Thutob Namgayal, and his wilful Gyalmo were then living at Kurseong, virtually as state prisoners. No wonder the picturesque Himalayan kingdom's mood was none too pleasing, a fact that entailed resultant dislocations of movement for men and material to the land beyond the Nathu-la. Bhutan too long sat on the fence and an effort was required to bring the Tongsa Penlop on to the British side.

To both the kingdoms of the Thunderbolt, Nepal's Gurkha Prime Minister was a sharp contrast. For Chander Shamsher not only helped the British with all the intelligence (little distinct though from wild bazaar gossip) that his Agent could garner at the Tibetan capital, but rendered all possible assistance, short of men, to make the British effort succeed. What is more, in August-September, 1904 Captain Jit Bahadur, as no doubt Bhutan's Tongsa Penlop, played a most significant role in bringing to a successful fruition the labours of the Younghusband expendition.

One of the Himalayan kingdoms was Britain's protectorate and, small and tiny as they are, could have been in no position to resist Calcutta's imperious dictates. What is amazing about the British venture is not their part, but the role played by the Chinese Amban Yu Ta'i. He was, until the very last, extremely helpful, indeed remarkably co-operative : he nearly appended his signature to the Lhasa Convention. The British were agreeably surprised, the Wai-chai-pou so embarrassed as to order his subsequent recall and eventual humiliation, to save 'face'.

Peking apart, St. Petersburg of Czar Nicholas II was long considered an interested party. Indubitably one of the most crucial factors that decided the Home Government on launching Younghusband was the fear of Russian intrigue, real or imaginary. The name of Aguan Dorjieff, a Buryat Mongol who was a Russian subject and a close confidante of the 13th Dalai Lama, loomed large, and portentously, in Lord Curzon's most intimate correspondence as it did in ponderous Command Papers and Foreign and Political Department Proceedings.

Having humbled the Tibetans, and toppled over the Dalai Lama—who had taken flight to Urga across the frozen Chang Thang—Younghusband and his men did not tarry long in Lhasa. Nor, in retrospect, did the land of the lama become a British protectorate. To be sure, in the wake of the British expedition, the Chinese asserted control and the last few years of the tottering Ch'ing on the mainland witnessed an armed occupation of the Tibetan capital by Chinese forces under the control of the redoubtable Chao Erh-feng.

What has been telescoped in the few paragraphs above is the story unfolded in the many pages that follow. It is a long, and one hopes fascinating, narrative, in which an effort has been made to lend depth and dimension by viewing Tibet as an important factor in the larger whole of India's landward periphery, of her long, and sprawling, northern frontier. So too the expedition to Lhasa has been studied, not indeed in isolation but as an integral part of the manifold aspects of the colourful, if controversial, viceroyalty of Lord Curzon.

INDIA AND TIBET : HISTORICAL GEOGRAPHY

1
India's Land Frontiers

In its strictly geographical connotation a frontier is a 'line of demarcation between territories with independent sovereignties,' or constitutes 'an area of separation' between two regions of 'more or less homogeneous, and usually denser, population.'[1] It is of such 'frontiers' that Lord Curzon spoke when, in his classic essay bearing that name, he described them as 'the razor's edge' on which hang the modern issues of war and peace, and of life or death to nations.[2] From this it may follow that much of human warfare in Europe, no less than in Asia or elsewhere, has raged around and for the defence of frontiers. Indeed, names such as the Alps, the Pyrenees, the Danube and the Rhine, no less than the Tacna-Arica between Bolivia and Peru, conjure up crowded memories. Equally well-known and looming somewhat portentously in the storied past of these countries, are the Great Wall of China or the Khyber pass in India.

Frontiers of more recent and topical interest are the 38th parallel in Korea or the 17th across the two Viet Names, the long and sprawling land frontier extending over two thousand miles between India and China which, hitherto dormant, is now the subject of a bitterly raging conflict between the two countries. Again, there is the potentially much more dangerous Russo-Chinese frontier including, for convenience, the Mongol-Chinese sector, stretching all the way from the Tumen river on the Korean border to the Pamir roof adjoining Wakhan's tongue of land in Afghanistan. Here too the long-simmering Moscow-Peking dispute, now boiling over in public, threatens to make live what had been for long a relatively not-so-active a frontier.[3] Yet again, and despite some thawing of the cold war, there is the still active, if intangible, East-West frontier that has riven Europe—and not Europe alone—in twain for nearly two decades now. For them and around them, wars hot and cold have been waged in the past nor has the threat, as discernible at present, altogether abated for the foreseeable future.[4]

In the making of frontiers, international law has a significant role to play. The recognition of the existence, sanctity and permanence of frontiers is one of the foundations on which the law of nations has been built. Constituting as they do the very warp and woof of international covenants, frontiers once negotiated and demarcated cannot be denounced and torn up unilaterally. They thus remain inviolate and unalterable save through negotiation, for any use of *force majeure* in such cases would be a denial of international law itself.[5] Vital as the element of power politics is, and the preceding lines are a testimony to its import, it does by no means stand alone. As a matter of fact, human geography plays an equally important part.[6] For what makes for frontiers, and frontier problems, are such factors as race, population, language, geography and access to the sea.[7] One need hardly stress that religion in varying degrees plays an important role, e.g., the birth of Pakistan (1947) and Israel (1948), and that the slogan of self-determination has been a powerful weapon in creating new frontiers by disrupting ancient ones.[8]

Students of political geography draw a further distinction between a 'boundary' and a 'frontier'. It is held that the geographical and historical boundaries, shown as lines on a map, represent in fact the edges of zones or 'frontiers', that the boundary does not merely demarcate geographical regions or divide human societies but represents the optimum limits of growth of a particular society.[9] In an address to the Royal Society of Arts, in 1935, Sir Henry McMahon maintained that a frontier meant a wide tract of border land which, because of its ruggedness or other difficulties, served as a buffer between two states. A boundary, on the other hand, was a clearly defined line expressed either as a verbal distinction (delimited) or as a series of physical marks on the ground (demarcated); the former thus roughly signified a region, while the latter was a positive and precise statement of the limits of sovereignty.[10] It would follow that the Great Wall of China connoted the domain that it was thought proper to include in the Chinese *tien h'sia*, marking it from the 'outer darkness' of the barbarians. So too did the Roman Empire's frontiers along the Danube, which separated it from the uncivilised tribes beyond its pale.[11] Much the same would hold true of the Khyber in Indian history. For the problem here, as in the two earlier instances, was not only one of keeping the 'barbarians' out, but also of setting limits to the expansion of an imperial system.

Another factor deserves to be constantly kept in view. Many geographers and other keen students of the social scientces, speak of natural barriers as if these were active forces 'forbidding' or 'prevening' passage. It is easy to slip into this practice but, in fact, in the relationship between man and nature, it is man who is active; nature is passive. It is important to make the distinction, because by so doing one approaches the historical aspect with an unimpeded mind. For instance the Himalayas, or the Pyrenees for that matter, present a different kind of barrier to primitive or less advanced societies than to an industrialized society that is equipped with aeroplanes or the frightening armoury of thermo-nuclear weapons: here it is not nature that has changed, but man,[12] Again, whereas a mountain system—and the extent to which it is a barrier is inversely proportional to the ease with which it can be crossed—tends to mark a separation between economic and strategic regions, a river—and the larger and more navigable it is, the more important this aspect— forms an artery within a region. Trade tends to converge towards the river from both sides. Inevitably thus, when a large river is made to demarcate a frontier between states, two principles come into head-on collision: that of political separation in the midst of a natural economic unit.[13] This conflict characterized the history of such rivers as the Rhine or the Indus and portends, in the not distant future, to become important in connection with such a river as the Amur.

In the light of the recent breath-taking advances in the domain of science and the art of warfare such as polaris submarines and thermonuclear rocketry, not to mention the cosmonauts, one wonders if the age-old division between natural and artificial frontiers has any validity today. Thus, will the sea, the desert, the mountain and the river and what may perhaps be nonexistent today, namely, the barrier of forest and marshes that separated the states of the Heptarchy in Saxon England, or the Pripet marshes which stood as a defensive stockade in the western frontiers of Russia, any longer guarantee natural security as they once did? For the matter of that, even such artificial contrivances as a neutral territory, state or zone, or a buffer state, e.g. Afghanistan and Tibet during the British period, or one secured by international guaranteses, e.g. Laos or Austria or the Mongolian People's Republic, do not inspire in the guarantors, much less among those so guaranteed, any measure of confidence. For frontiers today are fast evolving from being mere geographical barriers into human bulwarks against political ideologies and systems of government, each of them claiming ultimate perfection and allowing at best a modicum of peaceful, if highly competitive, co-existence.[14]

An apt study of a frontier wherein both the geopolitical, as well as the human geography elements have played significant roles in that of India's long and sprawling land frontier which, for most of its length, is conterminous with Tibet. For convenience, and, a clearer understanding of its impact on the land of the lama it may be worthwhile to analyse, however briefly, its historical geography under the two obvious subdivisions into the north-west and the north, north-east segments.

From the very inception of its recorded history, and the fight of Chandragupta Maurya against that post-Alexander satrap Seleucos, India's north-west frontier has been a subject of considerable concern to her rulers.[15] For here a number of passes, including the Khyber, had, like 'narrow sword-cuts in the hills', provided the invaders a royal road to the northern plains.[16] One may go further and say that principally it was to protect these passage-ways against heavy onslaughts from 'barbaric hordes' that every powerful Indian Empire evolved a 'frontier' policy. Thus, examined against the background of their respective times, the policy of Chandragupta Maurya against the post-Alexander Greeks, or of Anandpal vis-a-vis the Ghaznavids, was in no whit different from that of Balban against the Mongols or of Akbar or Aurangzeb when faced with threats from Central Asia.[17] Ranjit Singh's thinking, and perhaps more so his handling of the frontier in the post-Nadir Shah-Ahmad Shah Abdali period, has brought him the well-merited tribute of his British successors. The latter, whose span has been the most recent in Indian history, deservedly demand a somewhat closer examination if only to underline their legacy to the present.

Under British rule, the North-West frontier first attracted notice when, in the opening years of the nineteenth century, the fear of a Tsarist advance through Persia became acute. Actually, ever since the days of Czar Peter's apocryphal will, a Russian advance to India has been regarded almost as axiomatic. Later, the alliance of Napoleon Bonaparte with Czar Alexander I sealed at Tilsit (July 1807) posed a far more serious threat. And while it may be true that the John Company's territorial domain was as yet far distant from the North-West frontier, intense diplomatic activity was in evidence with missions being simultaneously despatched to the courts of Ranjit Singh, the Amirs of Sind, and the Afghan and Persian rulers. Later, in the eighteen-thirties, the Napoleonic bugbear yielded ground to an intense fear of the Russian colossus and the rapid advance of the Tsarist empire, across the steppes of Central Asia,[18] appeared at once sinister and pregnant with dangerous portents. The British Governor-General Lord Auckland's war against Afghanistan (1839-42) was designed to lay low this ghost. In the wake of the war, and not unconnected with it, came the annexations of Sind (1843) and of the Panjab (1849) which together brought India's British rulers face to face with the problem of a long and difficult border stretching all the way from Baluchistan in the south to the Hindu-Kush in the North. In actual fact, this 650-mile frontier tract contiguous with Persia on the Mekran coast and with Afghanistan through the Khyber, Bolan and intervening passes, fell under the two separate provincial administrations of Sind in the south and of Panjab in the north. This largely explains why the 'frontier' policies evolved in the two parts were distinct, and indeed divergent, from each other.

An interesting evolution in frontier thinking and this applied to the north-west no less than to the north-east was the concept of a strong and united, if viable and friendly, buffer. It was this fact that transformed Afghanistan (and later Tibet) in the nineteenth century from the much more familiar role of a thoroughfare in history into that of a buffer, maintaining 'a sort of equilibrium produced by the pressure of two almost equal powers' from the north-west and the south-east.[19] Later, two major settlements in the closing years of the (nineteenth) century helped to delineate boundaries and thereby define Aghanistan's status. The first, the demarcation of the Durand Line in 1893, laid down the southern and eastern limits of the Amir's dominions, the negotiating parties regarding the agreement as a 'full and satisfactory settlement of all the principal differences of opinion' which had arisen between them in regard to the frontier.[20] Its importance notwithstanding—and it did put an end to the existing uncertainty about the boundary—the story of the frontier since 1893 would seem to suggest that the Durand Line accentuated tensions and increased the chances of a collision for 'an international line that divides the allegiance of a tribe is a fertile cause of disturbance'.[21]

A second major achievement in this direction was the Anglo-Russian demarcation of the Pamir boundary which came about in 1895. The British feared lest the Russian annexation of the Amir's Wakhan valley in the north-east corner of his dominions should, by outflanking the frontier agreed upon in 1873, bring their Indian empire into actual physical conterminity with the Tsarist.[22] They had indeed endeavoured hard, albeit unsuccessfully, to interest the Chinese, for it was here that the western limits of their (Chinese) empire met those of the British on the south and of the Russians on the North.[23] By a self-denying ordinance, the two signatories agreed not to exercise any political influence or control across the line from their respective territories. In this way the northern frontier of Afghanistan was now clearly defined, as was its southern and eastern. So indeed was its alignment which, through a consistent (British) policy of gifts, subsidies and a generous supply of arms, leaned heavily towards their Indian empire.

Yet despite definitions—and the Durand Line—the problems of the north-west frontier did not vanish with the end of the old century. Actually they were to persist in the shape of the perpetual tug-of-war between the 'civilising' activities of the British political authorities and the no less active pursuits of the tribes in what was euphemistically called 'no man's land,' being the tract of territory between the administrative boundary and the Durand Line.[24] Nor did independence for the subcontinent usher in a new era for the frontier, as the problem has not fundamentally altered since the British handed over authority to the Pakistan government.[24a] As of today, the North-West Frontier Province no longer exists as a separate entity—a clear enough repudiation of what was done by Curzon—being now a part of the larger, if amorphous, political amalgam of West Pakistan. And yet, the old if somewhat elaborate paraphernalia of allowances, Khassadars, Scouts, Frontier Constabulary and Political Officers has remained practically unchanged.[25] Besides, political rumblings of a disturbing nature have been injected by the Afghan claim for 'Pakhtoonistan' which threatens to undo the very basis of the existence of the Durand Line and hence of Pakistan's western boundary. Two caveats, however, may be entered here. One, with the exit of Daud Khan from the Kabul scene, the Pakhtoonistan threat, for the present at any rate, has taken a back seat. Two, paradoxical as it may seem today, Pakistan itself appears to have been transformed into a buffer as between Russian and Chinese spheres of influence, and power, in Central Asia. Yet in a situation of considerable complexity it is not quite certain whether Afghanistan today plays its now familiar nineteenth century role of a buffer state or the Indian Republic has any direct link with the problem of the north-western frontier 'save possibly as financial backers to any scheme of frontier defence intended to safeguard the whole subcontinent'.[26] Afghanistan apart, the concept of the buffer is closely, almost inextricably, linked up with Tibet and one may therefore, with advantage, turn from a study of the north-west to that of the north-east.

Compared to the north-west which has been somewhat of a perpetual trouble-spot down the ages, the north, north-east has been until very recently, a source of little if any anxiety. Perhaps, in consequence, it came to be taken for granted. So formidable has the physical barrier been that no known invaders appear to have scaled its heights, much less negotiated its difficult snow-laden passes to invest the rich Gangetic plains on the other side. Again, an imperial power in India almost since the days of the Epics would seem, as a matter of course, to extend its bounds to the Himalayan ranges. Thus Arjuna in the *Mahabharata* is said to have defeated the people living around lake Manasarowar, while the Ramayana makes a mention of the founding of the city of Pragjyotish.[27] Much later, on the coins of Samudragupta, appears the figure of Haimavati, while Kamarupa (Assam), Nepal and Kartaripura (Kumaon and Garhwal) are said to have acknowledged that ruler's authority and paid him tribute.[28] In much the same manner, Hiuen Tsang mentions the presence of the tributary King of Kamarupa at Harsha's assembly at Kanauj.[29] Nor did this broad pattern which came to be accepted tacityly all the time register any change under Muslim rule in India.

In contrast to the north-west, British contact with the northeastern frontier was of a much earlier date. Thus trade prospects with Nepal were explored, and the expeditions against Bhutan dispatched, in the period of Warren Hastings whereas the first direct contact with Afghanistan came, as was briefly noticed, with Lord Auckland's war in the early forties of the nineteenth century. Again, the fight against the Gurkhas of Nepal(1814-16) as also the first war against Burma (1824-26), took place in the opening quarter of the nineteenth century, while the British did not enter into full inheritance of the problems of the north-west until the annexation of the Panjab in 1849 or the occupation of Sind a bare half a dozen years earlier.

And yet all this 'primacy' notwithstanding the north-east has long continued to be a 'forgotten' and a 'neglected' frontier. Indeed the young, and otherwise imaginative Lord Dalhousie pronounced the Assam frontier to be 'a bore' while the wife of an officer attached to the Abor expedition of 1911, expressed herself much to the same effect in clear, and no uncertain, terms:

It is such a bore that my husband has to go of on that silly Abor expedition to fight those stupid aborigines with their queer arboreal habits.[30]

Nor had things changed even as late as the early forties for a well-known Indian scholar, writing in 1943, publicly bemoaned the fact that 'serious students of frontier history' continued to confine their attention to the routes taken by Alexander and his followers and had been 'altogether indifferent,' to the eastern part which, from the political no less than the military standpoint, was of the greatest significance'.[31] Again, Sir Charles Bell, a noted authority on this part of the frontier, frankly confessed that 'the north, northast frontier of India does not receive the attention that it deserves. The Indian Government ... devotes a preponderating attention to the north-west.'[32]

What lay at the bottom of this studied 'neglect'? Why was the north-east a 'forgotten' frontier? The explanation is partly to be found in the fact of the 'Himalayas' presenting an almost impassable barrier. Indeed the 'abrupt and absolute' character of this formidable 'abode of snow' has had a profound impact on the Indian mind and, on Indian history. Thus, as was briefly noticed earlier, compared to the disturbed state of the north-west, the north-east has been remarkably quiescent. Through thousands of years of its recorded, and oft-times unrecorded history there is no single mention of an invasion from the north, nor is a large-scale armed expedition from the south known to have crossed the mountains, in search of unconquered lands.[33]

As a necessary qualification to the above, one may mention the British expedition to Lhasa, with which this treatise is principally concerned, in the early part of the century. It is important, however, to bear in mind the fact that the Younghusband venture, which doubtless ended as a military expedition, was initially conceived as a peaceful embassy dispatched to negotiate a commercial agreement.[34] If only to straighten the record, one may also list the Chinese incursions into Nepal (1792) which were clearly in retaliation for the earlier (1788) advance of the Nepalese into Tibet and their sacking of the Tashilhunpo monastery at Shigatse.[35] Later, attempts were made both by the Dogras (1834-41)[36] and the Gurkhas (1855-57) to browbeat the Tibetans in the west, no less than in the east. In either case, however, the period synchronized with the decline of the Manchu authority over the mainland with the result that the Tibetans yielded ground, nor was any retaliation visited on the invaders. On the contrary, Zorawar Singh's attempts to wrest Ngari ended in the Dogras securing their hold over Ladakh,[37] while in the case of Nepal, the rights of extra-territoriality for their nationals as also of trade in Tibet, were obtained. These were, of course, unilateral.

The fact of the invasions, listed in the preceding paragraphs, should not be deemed to alter the general pattern of the inviolability of the snow-clad Haimalyas. For it is important to remind oneself that fundamentally both Nepal and Kashmir, either as aggressors or as victims of aggression, belong to a different physical milieu than do the plains of northern India or for that matter, Tibet vis-à-vis the northern plains.

It has already been suggested that John Company's relations with the states on this part of the frontier were established earlier than with those on the north-west. The first armed encounters with Bhutan (1773), Nepal (1814-16) and Burma (1824-26) have been briefly alluded to. With Sikkim, by contrast, the first contact was of a peaceful character—the British ceding to her some territory which Nepal had earlier (1817) wrested.[38] Later in 1835, however, the Raja of Sikkim was made to surrender 'unconditionally' the Darjeeling tract, under a deed of 'grant'. Except in the case of Nepal, however, this represented not the end, but the beginning of a vigorously pursued British attempt to push India's borders to the outer limits of these mountainous states. Yet relations with the latter were not to be stabilized until the mid-sixties of the nineteenth century, when Sikkim, reduced to the position of a protectorate, became an Indian 'State' in the then idiom, while Bhutan though never part of India agreed to be guided by her in its foreign relations.[39]

Subsequently attempts were made by the Chinese, and the Tibetans, to rake up their old, if somewhat shadowy claims to the lands of the Thunderbolt. The British rejoinder was the Treaty of 1910 negotiated with Bhutan by Sir Charles Bell, the then Political Officer.[40] Nearly forty years later, anticipating aggression by the Chinese in Tibet which actually came within less than twelve months, independent India despatched troops to Sikkim in 1949 and in the same year concluded a fresh treaty with Bhutan which broadly confirmed the earlier relationship established in the British period.[41] Basically, however, the distinction must be clearly drawn: Bhutan is not a part of India, Sikkim, in effect, is. As for Nepal, she remained sovereign and independent but friendly and closely aligned to the (British) *Raj*. The aid it rendered in quelling the (Indian) Rebellion of 1857 was valuable, as no doubt were the sinews of war furnished to the British military machine in the shape of the recruitment of the Gurkhas. Lately, India's independence no less than the emergence of a strong and powerful regime in China, have injected new stresses and strains in the Himalayan power equilibrium. More recently, Peking's aggression against India, and Pakistan's growing intimacy with China despite her close alliances with the Western bloc, have exposed Nepal to contrary pulls, resulting in an even more complex juxtaposition of forces.[42]

Notes

1. Brigadier-General Sir Osbert Mance, *Frontiers, Peace Treaties and International Organisation* (Oxford, 1946), p. 1, and C.B. Fawcett, *Frontiers, A Study in Political Geography* (Oxford, 1921), p. 21 Two other studies may be listed here: Sir T.H. Holdich, *Political Frontiers and Boundary-Making* (London, 1920) and Owen Lattimore, 'The Frontier in Human History' in his *Studies in Frontier History* (Oxford, 1962).

2. George Nathaniel Curzon, *Frontiers : The Romanes Lectures* (Oxford, 1907).

3. In an article, quoted by Tass, the Soviet Communist newspaper *Pravda* maintained that the attitude of the Chinese Communist party leadership on a thermonuclear war 'aims at undermining not only the struggle against imperialism itself' but that Peking's refusal (to sign the test ban treaty) 'placed her in the company of the most bellicose sections of imperialism', *The Statesman*, Calcutta, August 14, 1963. Later (*The Statesman*, April 5,1964) the same paper charged that Peking 'went over to open political warfare,' aimed at dividing the international communist movement and intentionally 'doing everything to exacerbate differences'.

4. The fact that Peking has openly repudiated, and France tacitly torpedoed, the nuclear test ban treaty initially signed by the U.S.A, U.K. and the U.S.S.R. early in 1963 (and later subscribed to by a very large number of countries, including India) bodes ill for the easing of international tensions.

5. W.K. Fraser-Tytler, *Afghanistan: A Study of Political Developments in Central Asia*, 2nd edn. (Oxford, 1953), p. 308.

6. Harold George Nicolson, *Peace-Making* (London, 1919), pp.130-31, charged that geographical, economic and transport considerations were not given enough weight in determining the best frontiers for a stable territorial arrangement at Versailles.

7. Sir Osbert Mance, *op.cit.*, p.1.

8. Sir Alfred Cobban, *Self-Determination*, 2nd edn. (Chicago, 1948), is a valuable contribution to an understanding of the havoc wrought by the workings of this doctrine.

9. 'All objective frontiers have some width. The common conception which is expressed in such terms as 'frontier line' and 'border-line' is a result of the natural human tendency to think of things in sharply defined separate compartments: it is not based on a careful observation of facts'. Fawcett, *op.cit.*, p.17.

10. Sir Henry McMahon, 'International Boundaries', *Journal of Royal Society of Arts*, Vol. 84, 1935-36.
    Professor Lattimore contends that 'the linear frontier', as it is conventionally indicated on a map, 'always proves, when studied on the ground, to be a zone rather than a line.' Owen Lattimore, 'The Frontier in Human History,' *op. cit.*, pp. 469-70.

11. Owen Lattimore, *Inner Asian Frontiers of China*, 2nd edn. (New York, 1951), pp. 238-40.

12. 'The changing significance, for changing societies, of an unchanging physical configuration.. leads to the axiomatic statement that frontiers are of social not geographic origin.' Owen Lattimore, 'The Frontier in Human History,' *op.cit.*, p. 471.

13. And here it is as well to remember that of the two main functions of a frontier – that of securing protection and of facilitating or, at any rate, allowing intercourse—the precise use varies considerably both in time and place.

14. Reference here is to the 'Iron Curtain' or its counterpart in Asia, loosely, and certainly very inaccurately, described as the 'Bamboo Curtain.' These 'curtains' have a connotation apart from mere geography. UNESCO's emblem stressing that defence against war must be built in the hearts of men is another case in point, as also is the Berlin Wall.

15. In R. C. Majumdar (General Editor), *The Age of Imperial Unity* (History and Culture of the Indian People, II), Bombay, 1951, Dr. Radha Kumud Mookerji gives (Chapters 2 and 3, pp.39-70) a connected account of foreign invasions both Persian and Macedonian, and the evolution of a Mauryan Imperial Policy towards them.

16. A.S. Beveridge, 'The Khaiber as the Invaders' road to India', *Journal of the Royal Central Asian Society*, 13 (1926), pp. 250-58 and 308-74, attempts to trace the routes of the seven great invaders of India from Alexander (327-26 B.C.) to Nadir Shah (1738-39). The Journal is henceforth abbreviated as *JRCAS*.

17. Fairly accurate, though inevitably brief, accounts of these policies may be delineated through the appropriate volumes of the Cambridge History of India or the more recent, though as yet incomplete, ten-volume History and Culture of the India People. A one-volume history for ready reference is R. C. Majumdar, H. C. Raychaudhari and Kalikinar Datta, *An Advanced History of India*, 2nd edn. (London, 1950).

18. It is held that the first Russian plan for the invasion of India was hammered out in the heat of the Ochakov affair (1791) resulting from an unsuccessful British effort to make Russia give away to Turkey the Ochakov fortress on the Black Sea which it (Russia) had captured after a costly combat.
    Even before the Treaty of Tilsit, Czar Paul had suggested to Napoleon, in 1800, the plan of sending a joint expedition to overthrow British rule in India. When the French showed lack of warmth, he decided to go it alone and ordered General Orlov, of the Don Cossacks, to mount an invasion and proceed "from the Indus to the Ganges." Later, at Tilsit, an invasion of India was definitely planned as between the Czar and Napoleon. For an excellent study, though with pronounced Russophobia, see Alexis Krausse, *Russia in Asia, 1558-1899* (New York, 1899). Also see H. Sutherland Edwards, *Russian Projects against India: from Czar Peter to General Skobeleff* (London, 1855), Charles Marvin, *The Russian Advance Towards India: Conversations with Russian Generals and Statesmen* (London, 1882) and 'An Indian Officer', *Russia's March Towards India* (London 1894).

19. A. J. Toynbee, 'Journey in Afghanistan and the North-West Frontier', *JRCAS*, 49 (1962), pp. 277-88.

20. After Sir Mortimer Durand who negotiated and signed the agreement with Amir Abdur Rahman. This laid down a boundary, as delimited on a map, which was attached to the treaty.
    For the full text of the Agreement a reference may be made to C.U. Aitchison (Compiler), *A Collection of Treaties, Engagements, and Sanads Relating to India and Neighbouring Countries* (Calcutta, 1929-30-31),14 Vols., XIII.

21. For a critical evaluation, see Sir Olaf Caroe, *The Pathans* (London, 1958), pp. 382-83 and C.C. Davies, *The Problem of the North-West Frontier* (Cambridge, 1932), pp. 161-62.

22. Parliamentary Papers, 1895, CIX, Cd. 7643 and *Report on the Proceedings of the Pamir Boundary Commission* (Calcutta, 1897).

23. For an interesting analysis, see W.K. Fraser-Tytler, *op.cit.*, Appendix IV ("Where Three Empires Meet"). And Owen Lattimore, *Sinkiang, Pivot of Asia* (Boston,1950), Appendix III.

24. In official parlance it was 'tribal territory' which, under the Act of 1935, was part of India, though not of British India. It included the 'Frontier States'.

24. Professor Toynbee has made the point that Pakistan cannot be the same make-weight to Russia on the other side 'as the British Indian Empire' supported by the United Kingdom, used to be. For the greater part of the military strength of the sub-continent is not turned outwards towards the North-West Frontier, 'as it used to be in our time', it is turned inwards. Toynbee, *From the Jamuna to the Oxus* (London, 1962), p.34.

25. Under the constitution, promulgated on February 1, 1962, Pakistan (as earlier since 1956) comprised the two provinces of West Pakistan and East Pakistan, each headed by a (Provincial) Governor. The former NWFP thus became a part of the 'One Unit' (actually 'one unit' was established at the end of 1955, as a prelude to the first Pakistan constitution of 1956) West Pakistan. The frontier States of Swat, Dir and Chitral were designated as semi-autonomous areas. Critics aver that this extreme centralisation would imply a relative neglect of the frontier and its problems.
Sir Olaf Caroe who visited the NWF in 1956, after it had become part of the one-unit, noted that the 'Deputy Commissioners and Political Agents were sitting pretty in just the same places, and apparently doing their work in exactly the same way, that they have still the same 'Scouts Corps' which have been strengthened.' Sir Olaf Caroe, 'Pakistan Revisited', *JRCAS* 44 (1957), pp.175-86.

26. 'But with the departure of the British in 1947 the whole fabric of the defence of India through the buffer state has come to an end, in fact if not in diplomatic theory. Fraser-Tytler, *op.cit.*, p. 297.

27. For brief references, see 'The Historical Background of the Himalayan Frontier' in *Notes, Memoranda and Letters Exchanged Between the Governments of India and China, September-November 1959*, abbreviated as *White Paper No. II* (New Delhi, 1959), pp.125-32.
For details, see R.C. Majumdar (ed.), *The Vedic Age* (London, 1951), pp. 288-93 and 294-304.

28. B. G. Gokhale, *Sumudra Gupta* (Bombay, 1962), p. 52. The writer, however, indentifies Kartaripura as Kartarpur, a town in the Jullundur district of the Panjab.

29. Radha Kumud Mookerji, *Harsha*, 2nd edn. (Delhi, 1959), pp. 43-44.
Verrier Elwin, *India's North-East Frontier* (Oxford, 1959), Introduction, p. xvi.

31. Anil Chander Banerji, *The Eastern Frontier of India*, 1784-1826, 2nd edn. (Calcutta, 1945). The citation is from the preface to the first edition (September, 1943).

32. Sir Charles Bell, "The North-East Frontier of India", *JRCAS* ,17 (1930) pp. 221-26

33. 'No other fact has had a greater significance on the evolution of Indian history. It (the Himalayas) had in the past cut India off from its continental affiliations. To the Hindus the world ended with the Himalayas... It is a matter of significance that there has never been the slightest disturbance of social life by invasion from the side of the Himalayas'. K. M. Panikkar, *Geographical Factors in Indian History* (Bombay, 1959), pp. 66-67.

34. Sir Eric Teichman, *Travels of a Consular Officer in Eastern Tibet* (London, 1922), p.10. Sir Basil Gould, 'Tibet and her Neighbours', *in International Affairs* (London), 26 (1950), pp. 71-76, describes the Younghusband expedition as 'a political mission with a military escort'.

35. For a fuller account, see D. R. Regmi. 'The first Gorkha-Tibet War' in his *Modern Nepal* (Calcutta, 1961), pp. 167-207.

36. Actually Zorawar Singh Dogra was acting for Gopal Singh Dogra who, in turn, was nominally acting for Ranjit Singh, the Sikh ruler and, after 1839, his successors.

37. For Basti Ram's eye-witness account of Zorawar Singh's advance into Tibet, see A. Cunningham, *Ladakh* (London, 1854), also K.M. Panikkar, *The Founding of the Kashmir State* (London 1953), pp. 74-89, the same work having appeared earlier as *Gulab Singh* (London, 1930).

38. John Claude White, *Sikkim and Bhutan* (London, 1909), p.17.

39. White, *op.cit.*, pp. 280-81.
    Also see P. L. Mehra, 'Lacunae in the Study of the History of Bhutan and Sikkim', *Indian History Congress, Proceedings of the 23rd Session* (Calcutta, 1961), 2 Vols., II. pp.190-201.

40. Bell, *Tibet, Past and Present* (Oxford, 1924), Appendix II, pp. 280-81.

41. For the full text of the treaties, see C. H. Alexandrowictz (Editor) : *Indian Year Book of International Affairs* (Madras, 1953), II, pp. 319-22.

42. Girilal Jain, *India Meets China in Nepal* (Bombay, 1959) and Anirudha Gupta, *Politics in Nepal* (Bombay, 1964).

2
Tibet and its Geography

From the general to the specific. A rapid summary survey of India's land frontier in the preceding chapter leads inevitably to the more restricted question of the place occupied therein by Tibet.

Broadly speaking, in any comparative assessment of India's north-west with her north-eastern frontier, some important factors may be kept in view. To start with, the principal geographical feature of the 300–mile odd tract from the tri-junction of Burma, India and Tibet in the east to Bhutan in the west, are high mountain ranges (from 8,000 to 12,000 feet), an almost impenetrable forest and numerous unforded rivers and streams, fed by a rainfall as high as any in the world. Again, while Burma in the south was under British sway, China—later Manchu or Nationalist—did not present any actual expansionist threat for, throughout the nineteenth century, beyond the peaceable Tibetans 'there lay rather than loomed China'. It is true that Chinese claims were never actually forsworn, yet the fact that their authority was non-existent meant that there were no troubled waters for the tribes to fish in. No less significant is the fact that all along this part of the frontier the border is.conterminous with Tibet for there is no intervening state—no Bhutan or Sikkim, not even a Nepal.[1] Again, while some inter-tribal trade must have trickled through, there was no large-scale commerce with any of the northern states—either with China or for that matter with Tibet. Thus for a hundred years or more, with a difficult geographical configuration, with a complete absence of any threat of aggression from without, and with almost no commercial intercourse with the countries across the border, the frontier in the east was at best a *cul-de-sac*.

Today the old picture has well-nigh completely altered. For the first time in history there is an actual confrontation of India and China on the Himalayas whereas during the British period, to go no farther back, from Warren Hastings to Louis Mountbatten, there was always a Tibet in–between. Besides, Burma is now an independent state and Communist China, casting a long and fearful shadow, poses a major threat not only to India but, across the seas, to the whole of south-east Asia.

As one moves westwards from the Assam hills, the northern frontier no longer touches Tibet directly. For, intervening between India and Tibet lie Bhutan, Sikkim and Nepal, in that order. Together sometimes aptly described as the 'inner ring' of states, as compared to the 'outer', they had an important bearing on defence problems in this part of the frontier.[2] Here it was physical geopgraphy, added to Tibet's autonomy—effective until the Communist take-over in 1950—that largely determined the shape of things. Nor were there any big garrisons stationed, nor yet any fortified cantonments or frontier constabularies. No wonder there was a signal absence of any 'romance' of frontier life here, and when a military or 'political' officer talked of the 'frontier', he behaved 'as if the North-western were the whole'.[3]

An interesting way of looking at the frontier, more especially in its nineteenth-century British Indian context, is of being the pivot or hub of a system of security and defence comprising, as it were, three concentric zones or rings. In the outermost lay, on one side, the maritime route from the eastern Mediterranean, through the Middle East, to the Indian Ocean, and on the other Indo-China, then an integral part of the French Empire in the east and the Dutch East Indies controlling the vast Indonesian archipelago. The sea-route was vital and the British mastery thereof ensured an undisputed control over it; so also was a workable understanding with Britain's European neighbours, the French and the Hollanders. The intermediate circle or shell constituted a ring of states such as Afghanistan in the west, Sinkiang in the north and Tibet in the north, north-east. And finally, there was the soft under-belly comprising Baluchistan, the North-West Frontier tribes and states, Gilgit and Leh, Sikkim and Bhutan and the tribal areas sundering Assam from its neighbours in the north and in the south—with Nepal occupying a very 'special' position in this ('inner') ring.[4] Principally thus, apart from a thorough knowledge of major events in Europe and the juxtaposition of the balance of power there, any understanding of India's land frontiers, and the problems connected therewith, would entail a clear grasp of the political geography of these states vis-a-vis India.

In the outer periphery, the first two, namely Afghanistan and Sinkiang, fall outside the scope of this study, and yet one may tarry awhile if only to underline the fact that alongside Tibet they present an identical problem. And this, to borrow Lord Lytton's picturesque phrase, is one of the survival of earthen pipkins between iron pots.[5] A condition precedent to the existence of such states is that Russia and China in the north should hold aloof from India (and Pakistan) in the south, for in proportion as the iron pots approach each other, the earthen pipkins are endangered.

In his 'Political Testament' the Amir Abdur Rahman of Afghanistan, compared his country's plight to that of a swan swimming in a pond, with a bear on one bank and a lion on the other. In another context, he referred to it as 'a goat between these two lions' or 'a grain of wheat between two strong millstones of the grinding mill.' And he counselled his successors, for a long time to come, to keep to deep water. For while he was afraid of a Russian advance very close to the borders of his country, he was at the same time convinced that this would act as a permanent deterrent to England, for thereby she would be warned that 'Russia is close enough to advance upon her'.[6] As for Tibet, Sir Charles Bell thought her to be an 'ideal' buffer and cautioned against the possibility, and danger, of either China or Russia dominating her.[7] Much the same holds true of Sinkiang, as she stands at the backdoor of India and Pakistan which is at the same time the front door of the Soviet Union, and at an angle of the hinterland frontier which, for centuries, has been regarded as the backdoor of China.[8] Besides, the frontiers of Sinkiang which touch the (Inner) Asian Soviet Republics, are 'the geographical centre of gravity' of the non-Chinese territories of China.[9] It would thus seem that a closer, detailed look at Tibet, in the context both of its geography and history, would be an aid to a better understanding of all the three countries in the outer periphery.

To say that Tibet's geography has, and in a profound manner, influenced life on India's northern frontier would be stressing the obvious.[10] here it is necessary to revert to a point, briefly alluded to above, namely that the relative development of societies in India and the mountainous regions beyond has conditioned the respective attitudes of these countries to the problems of terrain on this frontier. For while physical barriers may be static, the working of the minds of men behind them is not. And it is the men and ideas behind the barriers that matter. An historical conspectus thus becomes as relevant as an understanding of the physical geography.

Tibetans call their country 'Bod', the colloquial pronunciation being 'Po', in Western Tibet rendered as 'Böd' . Early Tibetan works refer to the country as 'Tobbat', 'Tubbat' or Tibet, the word Tibet being a corruption of 'Bod stod' ('Po To') .[11] According to the Chinese, 'Tu Fan', or depending upon a variant in the old pronunciation of the second word, 'To Bo' is the country's name : 'To' being a phonetic rendering of the Tibetan word for highland, while 'Bo' is the name the Tibetans give to themselves.[12] Sanskrit chroniclers of the seventh century refer to it as 'Bhot' and its inhabitants as 'Bhot-ias.'[13] To Europeans it came to be called 'Tibet', probably because the great plateau, with its uplands bordering the frontiers of China, Mongolia and Kashmir, through which travellers reach here, is called by the natives 'To Bhot' (high Bhod) or 'Tibet'.

For most part Tibet is a wild, desolate, arid waste in the heart of Asia's steepest mountains. Thus her northern boundary is formed by the Kuenlun and the Tang la ranges while to the west stretch the Karakoram and the south is bounded by the Himalayas. The eastern ranges, however, are pierced through by Asia's mightiest rivers—the Yangtse, the Mekong and the Salween—which make the Tibetan plateau as inaccessible from the east as do the mountain ranges on the other three sides. The lie of the land or its slope, is from west to east—and from north to south. In sum, Tibet may be viewed as an elevated plateau, with an average height of 15,000 feet, ringed around by a great quadrilateral of mountain rages.[14] It is a high upland, for the most part bleak and barren and cut by mountain chains stretching all the way from Kashmir to West China: an inhospitable waste of a frozen desert, windswept and waterless, frightening and almost formidable in its geographical features. Necessarily it is barren of trees or of vegetation, and offers few possibilities for large human habitation.[15]

The Tibetan Plateau ranges in height from 9,000 to 29,000 feet above sea level, nearly three-fourths of it lying above 10,000 feet, while in large areas all elevations exceed 16,000 feet. A wellknown geographer computers that in Tibet, between the Himalayan and the Karakoram ranges alone, there are 50 summits of over 25,000 feet in height.[16] Interspersed with these mountain ranges, however, are broad river valleys such as those of the Indus, the Sutlej and the Tsangpo or the much more familiar Brahmaputra. Mention may also be made of the Kham area where deep river valleys and forests materially alter the look of the country. Except for these, however, most of the rest of the land is sparsely peopled not only by reason of its unusual elevation and the sharp temperature contrasts between day and night but also for its lack of adequate water resources. Nor should that be surprising in a land where precipitation is almost nil and travelling, therefore, hazardous.[17] A caveat, however, may be entered here. Hazards notwithstanding, lateral movement is far easier on the Tibetan plateau than in the Himalayan gorges which lead it on to the Indian side. Hence the enormous tactical advantage enjoyed by China with her troops on the plateau, given time for acclimatization.

Physically, Tibet has two broad divisions : the Chang Tang and the rest of the country.[18] The former is the vast unexplored plateau of the north and central Tibet, occupying nearly 75 per cent of the entire area. Though the country's mean height is about 16,00 feet, many of its peaks range above 20,000. Again, since it is at once barren and desolate, Chang Tang is principally dependent on the southern region even for the barley necessary to feed its domesticated yak, no less than its itinerant nomad. The remaining part of the country, nearly one-fourth in area, may be further sub-divided into three regions. One of these, the valley of the Tsangpo and the broken country along the northern foothills of the Himalayas, is quite a distinct geographical unit. It is an area of Tibet's highest density of population, its plateau affording good pasture; the valleys below, excellent farming land. The climate here is relatively mild; the winter being no colder than Peking, and not nearly so cold as Mongolia. Tibet's main food supply comes from here too; her barley and potatoes, her beans and vegetables. In parts of the valley, where some irrigation has been made possible, wheat and even some soft fruit are grown.[19]

The second physical sub-division comprises the Tsaidam and the Koko Nor basins in the north-east and that 'land of great corrosions', the Kham plains in the east. These are mainly pasture lands, and afford possibilities of un-irrigated agriculture.[20] A noteworthy feature of the Kham area is the plateau ridge between valleys which the Tibetans call 'gang'. The third area embraces the districts of western or upper Tibet, known as Ngari which borders India's Ladakh and is reputedly rich in minerals, more specifically gold.[21]

To define Tibet's physical boundaries and thus her area as well as population, is at best a difficult, tricky business. Knowledgeable writers easily distinguish three Tibets : the geographical, the cultural and the historical, pointing to a hard core common to them all. This last, 'the Tibet of our maps', is what is called political Tibet.[22] It may be worthwhile to underline here the fact that geographical or ethnographical Tibet is a further extension of political Tibet and points to an area which people of Tibetan extraction once inhabited exclusively but wherein increasing Chinese infiltration has gradually submerged them.[23] Thus geographical Tibet embraced, inter alia, what emerged in 1928 as the Chinese provinces of Chinghai and Sikang, which have always been regarded by the people of Tibet as part of their land. So also a sizeable area of what, theoretically at any rate, Tibetans deem as a part of their country lies within Sinkiang. These factors help largely to explain the wide divergences in the estimates made regarding her physical measurements. Thus Dr. Richard gives Tibet's greatest length, east-west wise, as 1,240 miles; its greatest breadth, north-south, as 740 miles and its area as 463,320 square miles.[24] This estimate of nearly half a million square miles, though widely accepted, in some cases just about doubles itself. Resultantly, population figures are also extremely varied. Thus, in 1907 the Chinese government computed the population at 6,430,000 while 15 years later its figures fell to 1,500,000! This leaves a margin of five millions between the lowest and the highest estimates,[25] which obviously vary according to the physical boundaries one keeps in view.

Broadly speaking, two facts emerge from this necessarily brief survey. At the outset one notices the compelling fact that for its large area, the country is, for most part, uninhabited. If a generous figure of 2,000,000 be accepted for its population and the area be reckoned at no more than 500,000 square miles, the density (per square mile) does not exceed four. Actually, in the most thickly peopled areas around Lhasa it has been estimated to be 15. This thinness of population seems to be a matter of concern even to Tibet's new masters.[26] The sparseness, stark as it is, is further accentuated by the large number of monasteries in the country and their armies of idle monks or lamas. The preceding thesis, though widely accepted, is not yet supported, according to Mr. Richardson, 'by any reliable and systematic evidence.' As if this were not enough, the prevalence of polyandry has meant a declining birth-rate, although here too, the same authority contends, the theory is increasingly suspect for unless there is evidence of a large number of unmarried or childless women, it may be hard to sustain.[27] The real working population was nonetheless fairly small, [28] yet it was able—before the Chinese arrived—not only to feed itself but also maintain sizeable reserves of foodstuff. That helps partly to explain why Tibet's resources, until lately, remained completely unexplored and she lived in what Sir Charles Bell calls 'the feudal age.'[29] Until about a decade ago she was, as far as transportation was concerned, a country without a wheel—barring, of course, the well-known Tibetan prayer-wheel. It may be noted, however, that the Communist (Chinese) occupation of Tibet has wrought profound changes in every sphere of Tibetan life, the social no less than the economic and the political. Broadly speaking, therefore, the description of a feudal Tibet may no longer be strictly valid ,[30] as of today. There is the added fact that a fairly large (Tibetan) refugee population in India and Nepal has rapidly adjusted itself to life in the contemporary world without a too-obvious surrender of the spiritual values which are the hall-mark of a Shangri-la civilisation.

The foregoing survey leads to another interesting conclusion namely, that Tibet's scanty population is largely concentrated in the valley around Lhasa, wherein settled agriculture has been possible. Professor Lattimore maintains that nearly five-sixths of the settled area of Tibet is distributed over an arc, running from west of Lhasa in the Tsangpo valley around by the east and the north-east, to the Kansu frontier. The valley—more accurately a system of valleys comprising the Brahmaputra and its tributaries—is easy of access from the other areas of Tibet and marks a dividing line between the settled agricultural area surrounding it and the outlying pasture lands.[31] It extends for more than a 1,000 miles between the Trans-Himalaya and the Himalaya, with the upper Indus river in the west and the upper Brahmaputra in the east. The valley includes the chief towns of Tibet— Lhasa, Shigatse and Gyantse—and provides a sizeable proportion of the country's requirements in agriculture and animal husbandry, albeit the role of the Kham area in this context need not be underestimated.

As for its locale, in regard to Tibet's principal neighbours, the valley is comparatively distant from markets in lands to the east and north, though relatively closer to the south. Thus, though by no means ideally situated, it has become the real nerve-centre of the country, and the focal point for its principal highways.[32] Here, besides the old Kalimpong (India)–Yatung—Lhasa road, through the Chumbi valley and the heart of central Tibet, the Chinese completed, late in 1954, two major highways—the Chinghai-Tibet road linking Sining with Lhasa and the Sikang-Lhasa highway running from Kantse and Chamdo to the Tibetan capital. There is also the West Tibet road running up the valley to Gartok and joining there with Sinkiang by the route, now a major highway, across the Aksai Chin. The trend of criss-crossing the Tibetan uplands with roads, especially those running down to the Indian frontier, has been further accentuated by the conflict with India over the border. Lhasa, the Mecca of all Tibetans and for many another beyond her borders, is situated in the valley and is the seat of the Tibetan government.

Along her southern border, over a distance of nearly 1,500 miles, and stretching all the way from Ladakh in the west to the North-East Frontier Agency in the east Tibet's neighbour is India. The actual physical contact, however, occurs only at two places. In the east, for over 300 miles, Tibet touches NEFA, while in the west Uttar Pradesh (hill-districts of Pithoragarh, Chamoli and Uttarkashi), parts of Himachal Pradesh, Panjab (Spiti) and Kashmir (Ladakh) border on the vast deserts of Western Tibet. For the rest, the inner ring of states—Nepal, Sikkim and Bhutan – intervene between the two. The picturesque Sikkim is India's main gateway to Tibet via Gangtok and the Nathu-la and the Kalimpong-Lhasa route, over the Jelap-la, the principal artery of commerce and intercourse between the two countries.[33]

With her powerful, and populous, neighbour in the east, Tibet's frontier has been a subject of an age-old dispute. It has been pointed out earlier that Chinghai and Sikang, as also parts of Kansu and Szechuan, though provinces of China now, have always been regarded by the Tibetans as their rightful domain.[34] The arguments of the opposing sides, in an effort to delineate the frontier, proved to be the major preoccupation of the tripartite Simla Conference in 1913-14 which, insofar as agreement between the two was concerned, proved abortive.[35]

Apart from the boundary dispute, China's frontier with Tibet has been regarded as a type by itself. Thus whereas her northern 'is an open frontier of indefinite

lepth' and the southern 'artificially closed, but not quite successfully', that with
Fibet has been conditioned by the geography of a land that is 'almost impassable
and almost impenetrable'.[36] And yet all this notwithstanding, the absorptive-
integrative processes of Chinese expansion and growth never came to a halt on
Tibet's borders, for the pressure from her eastern neighbour remained (more
particularly since the early part of the eighteenth century) relentless, inexorable.[37]
This, however, was a reversal of an earlier trend witnessed in the eighth-ninth
centuries of the Christian era when Tibet itself constituted a source of aggression
and her armies occupied and ruled a large area of Western China including Kansu,
the greater part of Szechuan and northern Yunnan. In fact, this phase of Tibetan
military activity, so 'widespread' and persisting 'for so long', has been a subject of
considerable speculation among serious students of Tibetan history.[38]

Russia in the north does not touch Tibet directly, albeit Sinkiang's pivotal
position between that country and China has been a matter of great interest, not to
say anxiety, to the Tibetans.[39] For though not precisely a neighbour, Russia's close
proximity, especially during phases of her history when the energies and dynamism
of the Empire turned east, had not altogether left her uncouncerned with Tibetan
affairs.[40] Thus early in the twentienth century, the conclusion of the Anglo-Russian
Convention, which accepted Tibet as lying outside the sphere of influence of the
two powers, was in itself evidence enough that the Russian interest in the country
was not altogether fortuitous.[41]

From the preceding lines it should be evident that the three great land masses
of Asia—India, China and Russia –are on the periphery of Tibet. They have all
influenced Tibet's past and have, to some extent, been influenced by it.

Notes

1. For descriptive accounts, mostly travelogue, see Colonel F. M. Bailey, *China, Tibet and Assam* (London, 1945), and *No Passport to Tibet* (London,1958), Geoffrey Tyson, *The Forgotten Frontier* (Calcutta, 1945), and W.F. Kingdon-Ward, *Assam Adventure* (London,1941). For frontier delimitation, see J. P. Mills 'Problems of the Assam-Tibet Frontier', *JRCAS*, 37 (1950), pp. 152-61.

2. Three recent studies are K. M. Panikkar, *Problems of Indian Defence* (Bombay, 1960), Satyanarian Sinha, *'The Chinese Aggression* (New Delhi, 1961), and Romesh Sanghvi, *India's Northern Frontier and China* (Bombay, 1962).

3. Sir Charles Bell, 'The North-Eastern Frontier', *op.cit.*

4. This line of reasoning is developed in C. S. Venkatachar, *Geographical Realities of India* (New Delhi, 1955) pp. 50-51, and Sir Olaf Caroe, 'The External Problems of India and Pakistan', *Asiatic Review*, 44 (1948), pp. 303-9.

5. At the interview which Lord Lytton gave in Simla (October, 1876), to the British Muhammadan Agent, Atta Muhammad, stationed at Kabul. For details, see Lady Betty Balfour, *History of Lord Lytton's Indian Administration* (London, 1899).

6. Cited in Sir Evelyn Howell, 'Some Problems of the Indian Frontier', *JRCAS*, 21 (1934), pp. 181-98. For the two citations, see Sultan Mahomed Khan (ed.), *The Life of Abdur Rahman* (London, 1900), 2 Vols., II, p. 281.

7. Bell, 'The North-Eastern Frontier, *op.cit.*

8. Owen Lattimore, "Sinkiang, Pivot of Asia", *op.cit.*, p. vii.

9. *Ibid.*, pp. 220-21.

10. 'In fact, the vast barren uplands behind the Himalayas provide the most magnificen defence in depth imaginable.' K. M. Panikkar, 'Geographical Factors in Indian History' *op.cit.*, p.70.

11. Bell, *The People of Tibet* (London, 1928), p.1.

12. Tsung-lien Shen and Shen-chi Liu, *Tibet and the Tibetans* (Standford,1951), p. 4

13. According to W.W. Rockhill, *Notes on the Ethnology of Tibet*, based on collections in the U.S. National Museum, *Annual Report of the Smithsonian Institution for the year ending June 30, 1893* (Washington, 1895), Tibetans from whatever part of the country they come from speak of themselves as 'Bod pa' or Bod people. The word Tibet represents two Tibetan words meaning 'Upper (high) Bod' by which name the central and westen portions are called to distinguish them from the easten which is sometimes referred to as 'Man Bod,' or 'Lower Bod'. Mongols use the term "Ta-ngut" for the Tibetans of the north and west and 'Tibet' for those of the centre and the south.

14. The French geographers Jean Brunhes and Camille Vallau : *La Geographie de l'Histoire* (Paris, 1921) describe Tibet as a high altitude desert backed by rugged mountains. Cited in Robert Strausz-Hupe, *Geopolitics* (New York, 1942), p. 232.

15. Sven Hedin, *Trans-Himalayas, Discoveries and Adventures in Tibet* (London, 1909), 2 Vols., II, p. 197 gives an instance where during his travels in the northern frozen desert (Chang Tang) he did not, for 79 days of an arduous journey, come across a single human being.

16. George B. Cressey, *Asia's Lands and Peoples*, Second Edition (New York, 1950), p. 160.

17. H.E. Richardson, *Tibet and Its History* (Oxford, 1962), p. 3 cites 'a kind of national hymn of the ninth century or even earlier' which describes Tibet thus: 'The centre of high snow mountains; the source of great rivers, a lofty country, a pure land.'

18. David Macdonald, *Tibet* (Oxford, 1945) gives three geographical divisions : North Tibet, South Tibet, and what he calls Western or Upper Tibet. Professor Lattimore ('Inner Asian Frontiers', *op. cit.*, p. 207) confining himself to Tibet 'as an area of human habitation,' divides the country into two: the centre 'a land of great height' and around the periphery of the central mass' where streams break down from the upper levels.' Cressey, 'Asia's Lands and Peoples', *op.cit.*, lists seven physical divisions : the Himalayan system in the south; the Karakoram routes in the west; The Tsangpo valley; the Chang Tang plateau; the Altyn Tagh and the Kuenlun systems in the north; the Tsaidam and the Kokonor basins; and Kham in the east.

19. An excellent, first-hand description of the Chumbi valley may be found in Tsewang Pemba, *Young Days in Tibet* (London, 1957), pp.13-28 and 62-72.

20. Robert W. Ford, *Captured in Tibet* (London, 1957), Eric Teichman, *op. cit.*, Marion H. Duncan, *The Yangtse and the Yak* (London, 1952), Robert B. Ekvall, *Tibetan Skylines* (New York, 1952) furnish reliable accounts of this region, as also do Andre Migot, *Tibetan Marches* (London, 1959) and G.A. Combe, *A Tibetan on Tibetans* (London, 1926).

21. A Reeve and Kathleen M. Heber: *In Himalayan Tibet* (Philadelphia, 1926), Alexander Cunningham, *Ladakh* (London, 1854), and Captain Hamilton Bower, *Diary of a Journey Across Tibet* (London, 1894).

22. Schuyler Cammann, *Trade Through the Himalayas* (Princeton, 1951), p. 3.

3. H. E. Richardson, *op.cit.*, pp.1-2, following Bell's earlier usage, has graphically presented (p. 2) a three-fold concept : 'Political Tibet', 'Limits of Ethnographic Tibet' and 'Extent of Tibetan Influence in 6th to 10th centuries.'

4. L. Richard, *Comprehensive Geography of the Chinese Empire*, translated by M. Kennelly (Shanghai, 1908). *Tibet*, prepared by the British Foreign Office, Historical Section, Vol. XII, No. 70 (London, 1920) gives the east-west length as 820 miles and the estimate of area as 500,000 square miles. Bell, *The People of Tibet*, p.1, estimates the area at 800,000 square miles; Cressey, *Asia's Lands and Peoples*, p.160, at 1 million square miles. For the 'Tibetan highlands' comprising Chinghai, the Chinghai-Sikang canyon country, the Chang Tang and southern Tibet. Theodore Shabad, *China's Changing Map* (London, 1956), p. 261 gives the area as 900,000 square miles and the population as 3 million.

5. Edward Thomas Williams, 'Tibet and her Neighbnours', *California University publications in International Relations*, Vol. 3, no. 2 (Berkley, 1937). Bell, *Tibet* estimates the population at between 4 and 5 millions; W. F. O'Connor, *Report on Tibet* (Calcutta, 1903), places it between 3.5 and 5 millions. According to Chinese census figures— census operations were conducted in 1953—the Tibetan Autonomous' chu has an area of 580,000 square miles and a population of 1,272,969. Theodore Shabad, *op.cit.*, p. 286.

6. Lately intensive efforts are known to have been made to people Tibet, if possible by large-scale transplantation of the Han, a trend that appears to have been re-doubled since organized Tibetan resistance disappeared with the suppression of the March (1959) Rebellion. Chairman Mao Tse-tung in an interview, as early as November 1952, is reported to have emphasized that Tibet must give more attention to her population problem and suggested that she must have at least 10 million people. *The New York Times*, November 26, 1952.

7. Richardson, *op. cit.*, p. 7.
    Two recent journalist-visitors had this to say: 'The return to lay life of thousands of monks who are now marrying and producing families and the decrease of polygamy and polyandry in a more prosperous society will rapidly increase the population. But the most important immediate factor is that the new medical services are reducing the incidence of sterility by treating venereal diseases and maternal and infant mortality by ante- and post-natal care.' Stuart and Roma Gelder, *The Timely Rain* (London, 1964), p. 49

8. Bell, *Portrait of the Dalai Lama* (London, 1946), p.17.

9. Loc. Cit.
    Professor Pedro Carrasco, *Land and Polity in Tibet* (Seattle, 1959), poses the question of Tibet being a feudal society. For a summary of the discussion, see *Ibid.*, pp. 207-8.

0. The Dalai Lama, *My Land and My People* (London, 1962), pp. 57-60, suggests that some of these changes were already on their way before the Chinese forced the pace by means which left a lot to be desired.

1. Owen Lattimore, 'Inner Asian Frontiers', *op.cit.*, p. 207.

2. *Ibid.*, p. 214. Professor Lattimore considers Lhasa a convenient 'transfer-point' for Tibet's eastern and southern neighbours.

3. There are two major roads to Tibet across the Himalayas : The Hindustan-Tibet road, which was the very first attempt to connect India with the Trans-Himalayan plateau and the Leh-Kashgar route which used to be frequented by caravans from Sinkiang. The latter became inoperative after 1951 when Sinkiang was declared a 'closed area' by the Chinese People's Republic.

34. *Supra,* pp. 60-61
    The Dalai Lama, *op. cit.* (map opposite page 64) shows Tibet's eastern boundary as
    running to the east of Tachienlu and of Sining in the north and this he calls "the ancient
    boundary" between China and Tibet.
35. For detailed proceedings of the Conference, see *The Boundary Question between China
    and Tibet* (Peking, 1940). The ramifications of the Simla Conference, more especially
    in regard to the McMahon Line, have figured prominently in acrimonious diplomatic
    exchanges between New Delhi and Peking over the border dispute. For details, see
    White Papers II and *III* (New Delhi, 1959, 1960).
36. Owen Lattimore, 'Inner Asian Frontiers', *op.cit.,* p. 206.
37. Owen Lattimore, *Situation in Asia* (Boston, 1949), pp. 18-20, calls the Chinese type of
    empire' 'absorptive' as compared to the 'accumulative' (British) and the 'incorporative'
    (Russian). He contends that the adoption of certain western methods by China in the
    nineteenth century, such as the building of railways, increased 'beyond all comparison'
    her ability to penetrate and make Chinese in population her frontier territories, viz.
    Manchura or Inner Mongolia. In other parts, remote from the actual penetration of
    railways, the acceleration of economic and social change also speeded up the rate of
    absorption of non-Chinese minorities.
38. Richardson, *op.cit.,* p. 31.
    Bell, *Tibet,* p. 30 maintains that it was Buddhism which checked 'if it did not sap' the
    martial ardour of a race (Tibetans) 'akin to the devastating hordes of Jenghiz Khan'. It
    may be noted, however, that Buddhism was abolished in 848 and did not recover for
    another 200 years. There was not much of 'martial ardour' in evidence during the
    period of its eclipse though quite a lot of fighting after it revived.
39. Owen Lattimore, 'Sinkiang, Pivot of Asia', *op.cit.,* Introduction.
40. D. J. Dallin, *The Rise of Russia in Asia* (London, 1950), p. 148. It is instructive to
    recall that on the morrow of Russia's military discomfiture at the hands of the Japanese,
    the Russian Foreign Minister Isvolsky wrote to the Tsar that 'no plans concerning
    Tibet should be made.' *Novyi Vostok,* XX-XXI, pp. 39 ff.
41. 'The fear of Russian designs and ignorance of Russian motives which historians find so
    difficult to understand are, unfortunately, the common places of our own times'. Michael
    Edwards, *Asia : The European Age* (London, 1961), pp. 176-77. Talking of Russia's
    place in Asia, K. M. Panikkar, *Asia and Western Dominance* (London, 1953), pp. 16-
    17, makes two interesting points which deserve consideration here : 'Russia is
    permanently in Asia, a geographical fact, which will become increasingly apparent as
    time goes on. The three major states in the east, India, China and Japan, border on
    Soviet territories. Also the Soviet influence is continental and not maritime and in this
    respect it differs fundamentally from the influence that Europe exercised over Asia for
    400 years.'

TIBET, INDIA AND CHINA:
EARLY CONTACTS

3
Tibet Vis-a-Vis (Pre-British) India and China

India's relationship with Tibet goes back to a long, hoary past. Thus the country's first known historical king, Song-tsen Gam-po (more correctly Srong-brtsan-sgam-po) who both unified the land and contributed appreciably to its military greatness is believed to have come from Ladakh, and the latter's proximity to the Indus, and hence Indian influence, is widely accepted.[1] Songtsen Gampo, who lived in the seventh century A.D., looms large in Tibetan annals : with him is said to begin 'the dawn of Tibetan civilisation', he gave the land a strong and powerful impulse, was at once a law-giver and an educational reformer.[2] Again, he and his successors incorporated parts of Bengal and, in the west, Hunza and Swat into a vast Central Asian dominion which included Koko Nor and large areas of what came to be known much later as Chinese Turkestan. Meanwhile, India's cultural impact was both powerful and considerably articulate. Thus the King is reported to have sent a mission of sixteen officials, headed by his Minister Thonmi Sam Bhota, to India where it tarried long and travelled widely. On their return, chroniclers tell us, the Minister and his compatriots created the Tibetan alphabet and translated some Buddhist scriptures into the new language.[3] A famous successor of Songtsen Gampo, Ti-song De-tsen—the two together with a third constitute the trinity of the "Three Religious Kings"[4]—was responsible for cementing the bonds closer. He summoned the Tantrik Buddhist pandit, Padma Sambhava, from Udhayayana to give form and content to what is popularly, though erroneously, called Tibetan Lamaism.[5] Along with his disciple Virochan, the Indian saint dealt a severe blow to Tibet's indigenous (Bon) religion though in the resultant process a great deal of Bon practice became part of (Tibetan) Buddhism. As a visible symbol of his activity the Tibetan ruler, with the help of Padma Sambhava and Bodisattva Khenpo, founded in the last quarter of the eighth century, the famous Samye monastery, located a bare 50 miles south-east of Lhasa.[6] The power and impact of Indian influence was to gather momentum in subsequent reigns: the priesthood was organized and increased,

temples sprang up and Buddhism spread. It may be noted, however, that under th
rule of the Kings, Buddhism was part of court practice living together, quite amicabv
one may suppose, with the concurrent practice of Bon. At the same time traffic wi
India was by no means a one-way affair, it operated as a two-way street for whi
Indian teachers came and translated religious works, their counterparts repaired t
the holy land of the Buddha to study the religion and the language of the sacre
books.[7]

Lamaism, which later was to incorporate sizeable influences both from th
Chinese and the Mongols, was initially a commingling of the corrupt norther
Indian Buddhism of the eighth century and the indigenous (Tibetan) Bon religion
Here apart from Padma Sambhava, and a host of others who followed in his wak
there was the well-known Dripankara Srijanna, popularly known as Atisha, who i
the eleventh century gave considerable impetus to the new faith. Within years c
his arrival in Tibet were founded some of the earliest of a succession of famou
monasteries, which were later to exercise such a powerful impact on the country
history. A cave where the Indian savant is said to have lived, lies a few miles outsic
Lhasa and is still preserved : its construction constituting 'a fitting home' for
religious reformer possessed of the zeal of Atisha. Although he had arrived on a
invitation from the ruler of Western Tibet, his religious activities are said to hav
extended far into the central part of the country and it was under his inspiration tha
ruling nobles all over the land both accepted and lent a great deal of stimulus to th
revival of Buddhism. Among the 'traffic' in reverse was a long line of monks, includir
the well-known Rinchenzanbo who preceded Atisha and a number of monk studen
at Nalanda and Viksramashil universities, who were adepts at rendering India
classics into Tibetan.

Two factors, however, militated against this dual flow being maintained in late
years. One was the impact of Mongol invasions from the north : Tibet's attentio
was, as a consequence, now increasingly diverted towards happenings in Chir
and other parts of Central Asia and was for long, to be riveted there.[9] Again, th
Muslim conquest of India, more particularly of Bengal, rudely interrupted the religior
intercourse. There was the additional fact of a well-nigh complete eclipse c
Buddhism in India, the land of its birth, which came in the wake of this conquest an
dried up as it were, this extraneous source of Tibet's religious and cultural inspiratio

To say all this, however, is not to deny that caravans of traders from India n
longer wended their way across the Himalayas, or that a steady stream of pilgrim
ceased visiting Mount Kailash, the abode of gods, or Lake Mansarowar wherein
bath absolves a Hindu of all his worldly sins, or Gangotri, the source of the sacre
Ganges. Wars and conflicts continued too, not with India as such but with he
peripheral states—with Kashmir and Nepal, with Bhutan and Sikkim. Yet the area c
hostilities was, for fairly obvious considerations of a practical nature, localized an
there was no question ever of occupying Tibet, much less of claiming dominic
there. In a nustshell, the fundamental character of Indo-Tibetan relations, prior t
the British conquest, continued to be non-military and non-political—the chi

emphasis was on cultural ties, though a good deal of commerce was thrown in on the side.

The sundered link with India, consequent on the Muslim invasions and Tibet's own preoccupations with the Chinese and the Mongols, was not to be forged afresh until centuries later and in a very different socio-political milieu. For the East India Company's first encounter with Tibet, towards the last quarter of the eighteenth century, was not motivated by religious, much less cultural, considerations. The aim here, as will be presently noticed, was commerce and the immediate occasion an armed intervention in a neighbouring Tibetan 'dependency'.

Before embarking on a brief conspectus of Britain's first efforts to open up as it were this mystic land of the lamas, [10] it may be well worthwhile to bring the Sino-Tibetan relationship into a sharper focus. The influence of Lama Buddhism and its early associations with India have already been alluded to. Despite these and other binding links it has been maintained, that in the case of India and Tibet there is no real blending of the climates and physical contours of the two countries and that this acts as a serious impediment to intercourse. Thus, it is held, there are sharp lines of demarcation both in the mountain-barrier which is negotiable at comparatively few points as also in the social organization and conditions of life on either side. An apt summary of the view that China's impact was more powerful may be found in Bell,

> We may, in fact, say that the present civilization of Tibet was taken mainly from China, and only in a lesser degree from India... the general appliances of civilization, apart from religion and in a less degree religion also—have come from China. It is noteworthy that in the early days of Tibetan Buddhism, the Indian influence was considerable... (Later, however) the common kinship—partial, though not complete, of Chinese, Mongolians and Tibetans asserted itself against outside influence.'[11]

Whether one accepts this thesis, or rejects it with reservations, it may be readily conceded that Indian Buddhism played an important role by combining what were no better than territorially isolated social groups into a community held together by this identity of a common (religious) outlook. Monasticism, however, and the influence of the church, which kept the social groups bound one to the other, remained supreme throughout the ninth, tenth and eleventh centuries of the Christian era. It may be pointed out, however, if in parenthesis, that it was only when Buddhism became Tibetan, i.e. with the establishment of Samye, and the growth of Sakya, Drikung, Talung and Karma that a 'combining' influence was exerted. The Indian impact was in providing and renewing streams of doctrine and philosophy, not in working on the social side of monasticism. Another fact, briefly alluded to above, needs to be underlined here namely, that in the earlier phase of their history—the period of Songtsen Gampo and his successors—the Tibetans were able to display a remarkable, and widespread, military prowess. Not only did they control the Koko Nor region, and large tracts of what later came to be Chinese Turkestan, but for a week or so even held the then capital of the country Ch'ang An (modern Sian) itself. Over Hunza and Swat too, they held sway. How precisely could a country, whose demographic and other resources were as meagre as those of Tibet, afford this continuing and somewhat heavy strain is a moot point, but that it actually did so is an incontestable fact.

By the beginning of the tenth century, however, when Tibet withdrew from her Central Asian and South Himalayan commitments, relations with China were no better than 'courtesies and skirmishes' with border tribesmen of Szechuan and Yunnan. [12] These were to persist until, early in the thirteenth century, both the countries fell a prey to the Mongols, then sweeping across the whole of Asia. While it is true that Chingiz Khan had obtained the formal submission of the leading lamas and abbots of Tibet early as 1206-7, and to that extent may be said to have conquered the land, the first known, and authentic, Mongol invasion of Tibet took place in 1239 under Ogadai's second son Godan, then Governor of Kansu. [13] Chingiz's grandson, the famous Kublai Khan, had recognized the feudatory status of Tibet even before he assumed his Monglol patrimony in 1260. He did so by accepting the headship of one of the religious sects—the Sakyas, in this case—with the title of Tisri (Ti-shih) and by acting both as the pope of their (Lama) Church, as also the temporal ruler of the land. [14] The Mongols thus became effective overlords of Tibet long before they had, as the Yuan dynasty, completed their conquest of China. Later, their downfall in the middle of the fourteenth century was to be followed by a great deal of chaos in Tibet, with each lamasery claiming independence and forming alliances either with the new rulers of China or with some Mongol tribes.

The weakening of Mongol authority which followed, synchronized with a decline in the power and influence of the Tisri and the birth of a new monarchy under King Chang-Chub Gyal. This emergence of Tibet's second monarchy, known as the 'Sitya' is regarded as the upsurge of a 'national revival'. [15] Its beginnings, however, implied that the old links with China (forged as a result of the two countries' subordination to the same masters) were now broken, with Tibet regaining its independence of Mongol authority entirely in its own way and in its own time. Later when the Ming had got securely in the saddle, the political power of the Chinese receded almost entirely from the Ningsia-Kansu or the north Tibetan border region. Nor need much be read into the 'tribute missions' which are reported to have gone from Tibet, headed by scholar monks, ostensibly to pay fealty to the country's liege lords and masters. The Ming were not a strong dynasty at home, nor could they have been very powerful abroad even if one leaves out of account the fanciful Chenese interpretation of the tributary system. [16] A knowledgeable Tibetan scholar maintains that whereas letters from the Emperors of the Yuan (Mongol) dynasty to the Tibetan lamas sometimes contained detailed instructions on monastic administration, those from the Ming were of a purely complimentary nature. Added to the fact that Ho Lin's inscription in Lhasa mentions that Tibet was a vassal of China only from the beginning of the C'hing period, it may be reasonable to deduce that Tibet was not a tributary in the period of Ming rule. [17]

Under the Manchus, however, it was a different story, the more so as Tibet itself had been undergoing a transformation. It may be recalled that the downfall of the Mongols in the fourteenth century, and the later rise of the Ming in their place, had spelt not only a near-anarchy in Tibet, but also the recession of Chinese authority, almost in its entirety, from the north Tibetan border region. Meantime the Mongols had been split into smaller and smaller tribal factions or 'federations'. Thus there were the western or the Oleot, the northern or the Khalkha, the southern or the Ordor-Tumet-Chahar and the eastern or the Manchurian, to enumerate only the most important. Both these developments threw into special importance these regions of northern Tibet, viz. Amdo, Kansu and Ningsia. And it was in this area that Tsongkapa (1357-1417), the well-known religious reformer of Lamaism, was born.

At a time when the country was sharply split into rival factions, religious no less than temporal,[18] Tsongkapa founded the new, and reformed Ge-lugpa. Forbidden to marry or to drink, its zealous band of monks—called the 'Yellow Hats,' in contradistinction to the older 'Reds'—enjoined a stricter code of morals and were responsible for the two main lines of pontifical succession in the county. For the Panchen Lama of Tashilhunpo, believed to be the incarnation of Amitabha, 'the boundless light', as also the better known Dalai Lama of Lhasa, the embodiment of Avolokistevara, 'the Lord of Mercy', trace their lineage back to Tsongkapa's original sect.[19] Church tradition also associates him with Lhasa's three great monasteries, the Ganden, the Dre-pung and the Sera—together known as 'Den-sa Sum' literally the 'Three Pillars of State.' It has been thought likely that a major result of Tsongkapa's reforms was to subordinate the southern influences of Buddhism, emanating from India, to those coming from the north and derived from Buddhism, Manichaeism and Nestorian Christianity that had flourished in Central Asia from the seventh century onward. Nor, it has been maintained, may his teaching be viewed as simple, unsophisticated process of 'borrowing' from the north, but truly a more urbane reflection in Lhasa, and the part of Tibet dependent on it, of a 'new northern regional ascendancy'.[20] This thesis, however, appears to be a little far-fetched and more than the tenuous array of facts can bear. For basically, besides the new, stricter code he enforced Tsongkapa's chief contribution lay in choosing one distinct line of tantric texts, in preference to another, as the basis of his teaching.

The institution of the Dalai Lama took shape and content at a time when the sway of the western Mongols over Tibet had loosened to an extent that it was non-existent. Under Tsongkapa's successors—his nephew Gedun Truppa, who founded Tashilhunpo and Sonam Gyatso, a keen scholar and zealous exponent of the faith—the loyalty of most of the Mongols to the new sect was, however, assured. It may be noted for instance that the fourth Dalai Lama was a royal Mongol himself. Later, when the western or the Oleot chief Gusri Khan (also spelt Gusi Khan) conquered Tibet, he broke the power of the Tsang rulers and their principal spiritual supporters, the Karamapa. While he handed over authority to the chief pontiff of the Yellow, [21] Gusri remained, as did his successors long alter him, King of Tibet. The relationship between the Prince and the Priest—the lay prince buttressing the authority of the high priest who, in return, extended his spiritual support to the former —was by no means an exclusively eastern concept. The best example in Europe was the relationship of 'Chela' and 'Guru', between the Holy Roman Emperor and the Pope whereby the temporal 'Chela' allowed his spiritual 'Guru' to maintain a papal state in Italy.

To resume the narrative, after Gusri's death in 1655, the Lama gathered more and more power into his hands, encouraged by the fact that the Mongols showed little interest in their new dominion, beyond appointing viceregents to exercise sway on their behalf. Meanwhile Nyawang Lobzang Gyatso, [22] who became the fifth Dalai Lama, and is oftentimes referred to as the Great Fifth, established the Lama hierarchy on a firm footing. Besides building the world-famous Potala, he is also said to have instituted the office of the Panchen Lama by bestowing that title on his old teacher who, with his seat of authority at Tashilhunpo, was to emerge in later years as a powerful, if rival, figure. [23] Thus despite the fact that Gusri's successors right down to 1720 enjoyed the title of 'King', from the time of the fifth Lama the sovereignty of Tibet was to vest squarely in the persons of the Dalai and the Panchen Lamas, their successors being considered merely as their respective reincarnations.

By the first half of the eighteenth century, the power of the Mongols had given way to that of the Manchus. These fifty years, in fact, saw the Manchu ascendancy in China well-established for the new dynasty had, in battle, worsted its chief rivals, the western and northern Mongols, and thereby emerged as the paramount power of Central and Easten Asia. [24] The fact that the Gelupga, which now exercised authority over the whole of Tibet, commanded a near-complete spiritual sway over the otherwise disunited Mongol tribes presented the Manchus with a prospect that was none too pleasing. It was fairly obvious too that the one way out was to secure control over the high priest of this spiritual unity—the Dalai Lama himself. [25]

The painstaking Italian scholar Luciano Petech, whose work has been rated as the *locus classicus* for this period, traces in detail the events leading to what he calls the establishment of a Chinese 'protectorate' over Tibet. [26] The exact form and content of the mainland's institutional control, and the varied political experimentation through which the Manchu-Tibetan relationship passed in its early phases, needs a careful analysis both for its immediate outcome as well as its long-range impact. Thus starting with a complete absence of any direct political authority over the country—with the Emperors possessing no more than a mere 'shadowy form of suzerainty' inherited from their yuan and Ming predecessors—the K'ang H'si ruler tried to establish a vague dominion. [27] There was, however, no military occupation nor yet a regular Resident in Lhasa; the 'protectorate', being dependent entirely upon the personal loyalty towards the Emperor of Lhabzan Khan, the Mongol 'King' of Tibet. [28] This meant the near-elimination both of the spiritual authority as well as the political status of the Dalai Lama who, for Lhabzan Khan, was no more than a convenient instrument to subserve his own ends. [29] His brief

(1706-18) interlude in Tibet's history was followed by the Dzungar holocaust (1718-20) with the latter maintaining the fiction of governing in the name of an absentee Dalai Lama.[30]

Consequentially when the K'ang H'si ruler invested Tibet in 1720, he posed both as a 'liberator' from the Dzungar loot and pillage and a 'pacifier' after the disturbances of Lhabzan Khan's reign. The emperor took the opportunity, however, to station a garrison in Lhasa whose commandant was charged with supervising the country's administration. Since the new Dalai Lama, Kesang Gyatso, was a child, the question of his exercising authority was, at best, academic. In any case, the ruling junta was appointed by the Chinese although, by reason both of distance and bad organization, it was little if at all controlled by them. The Emperor's chief objectives, however, of securing 'a footing in Lhasa' and of acquiring 'the key to religious control', over Mongolia, were amply met. Again, here were the beginnings of what turned out to be nearly two hundred years (1720-1912) of Manchu overlordship of Tibet brought about not indeed by conquest, but by 'skilful opportunism'.[31]

Nonetheless the K'ang H'si ruler's control, was followed in the next few years (1723-27) by the withdrawal of the Chinese. It is true they were unpopular yet their departure once again left the country very much to its own devices.[32] A direct consequence thereof was a violent civil war (1727-28) complicated by the role of the young Dalai Lama's father, a host of his court protégés, and the active intervention of the Dzungars who, not far from Tibet's borders, were still an important factor in the situation. The return of Chinese garrisons thus became, once again, imperative. This meant, however, and not unexpectedly, a complete exile for the youthful Lama whose indirect complicity in the domestic squabbles had attracted widespread notice.[33]

To guard against a repetition of what threatened to be a set pattern, the Tibetan Council was reconstituted. Simultaneously two Ambans, as the (Manchu) Emperor's personal representatives, were to be stationed in Lhasa and assisted by an armed garrison, placed under a military commandant.[34] It is significant that even when the Dalai Lama returned to Lhasa, after a seven–year forced absence in Litang, his functions were strictly limited to religious affairs while his temporal authority was not restored.[35] In fact, it has been suggested that the institution now reverted to the position it had occupied earlier in the sixteenth century when the Lama was no more than a 'much respected spiritual chief without a valid title to temporal rule'. Again, Phola Teji who had emerged victorious in the civil war of 1727-28, carried on the administration and soon won the confidence of the Emperor, as he did of the Tibetans and of the Mongols, while the presence of Chinese armed forces made it clear that Manchu authority could not be disregarded with impunity. Symptomatic of the regard in which the Tibetan ruler was held was the conferment on him, in 1740, of the title of 'Prince' or 'King' by the Emperor.[36]

Phola's death (1747), however, was to precipitate a fresh political crisis. For his successor Gyurme Namgyal, who was very unlike his father, soon came into conflict with the Imperial Ambans while the latter in turn, were plotting to have him murdered.[37] Although Gyurme was no favourite among the Tibetans—he is said to have been 'thoroughly hated by his subjects'—his martyrdom, at the hands of the Ambans, won him wide sympathy and the people of Lhasa, in an excited mob fury, killed both the Manchu representatives as well as their officers and men.[38] The Dalai Lama, however, had now come of age, handled the situation with firmness and skill, he even dissuaded the mob from its overt ambitions, and opened the gates of the Potala to the victims of its insatiable rage. Later, appointing a Pandita as Senior Minister to take over the day-to-day administration, he got in touch with the Emperor in Peking. Thus the Imperial troops on arrival found their task relatively easy, for all they had to do was so to overhaul the administration so as to avoid their previous mistakes.[39]

The Dalai Lama who became 'heir to the sovereignty of Phola' now came into his own, not indeed through any formal pronouncement from Peking but so imperceptibly as to suggest that he had always exercised the powers and performed the functions to which he staked his claims. It has been held that this implied 'not so much the revival of Gusri's domination', as the establishment of a new title of sovereignty, for the fifth Lama had controlled the Government 'without actually undertaking it'.[40] Institutionally, however, the Council, or the *bkalon* as the Ministers were called collectively, was restored and the Dalai Lama could act only through them, while the Ambans retained their earlier powers of supervision and control over the general administration. Yet important as the Ambans' functions were, in the final analysis the reforms of 1751 meant giving the Dalai Lama, who now became the virtual head of (Tibetan) government, a good deal of initiative and authority. What an energetic person could do under this system is evidenced by the life and work of the Thirteenth Dalai Lama.[41]

Another significant landmark in Tibetan affairs was the year 1792 which witnessed a Gurkha invasion from Nepal with the invaders coming as far as Shigatse which they both pillaged and sacked. Four years earlier when the Gurkhas made their first incursions, the Ambans' representatives, and the Dalai Lama's, had acted in collusion to buy them off, while the Emperor at Peking was kept grossly misinformed about the true state of affairs.[42] Later, when he came to know of the facts, Ch'ien Lung was determined to do a thorough job of it. The Chinese army, now braving the difficult and arduous journey from Szechuan, not only threw the Gurkhas back but pursued them within miles of Kathmandu and dictated terms of peace to a war-worsted foe. Nor was that the end. [43] For, in the wake of their resounding military victory, the Manchus introduced two major innovations in the organizational set-up at Lhasa so as to ensure a stricter political control.[44] One of these related to the Dalai Lama who, in future, was to be selected through the use of the golden urn, of which the Emperor made a present to Lhasa. The second related to Tibet's exchanges, or diplomatic communications with foreign countries which, henceforth, were to be routed through the Ambans. On paper, the changes looked formidable for they not only ensured rights of control and supervision but what smacked of an almost direct participation, and imposition of full Chinese sovereignty, in the affairs of the Tibetan administration.[45] The Chinese government, under the Manchus, Professor Petech concludes, "thus wound their way through several experiments to the only possible form of control over Tibet".[46]

For a brief sum-up like the present, it is not necessary to go into the details of the lamaist church organisation, much less the theory underlying the succession of the Dalai and the Panchen Lamas, through the doctrine of Re-incarnation.[47] In much the same manner a fuller discussion of the relationship between the two Lamas in the larger context of the spiritual hierarchy, would fall outside the limited scope and purview of these pages.[48] Yet a few salient points may bear examination in passing. Thus it has been held that the doctrine of re-incarnation was invented as a justification for the fact that 'those who controlled the political power' found it 'inconvenient' to select and appoint the incumbents of church office[49]—a proposition that on the face of it does not carry much conviction. For even an elementary acquaintance with Buddhism reveals that the doctrine of metempsychosis lies at the very heart of it, even as it does of Hinduism : there was thus no need to 'invent' re-incarnation, it already existed. Another viewpoint, however, has greater validity and it is that the office of the Panchen was made use of 'as a counterweight' to undo the immense religious prestige of the Dalai Lama. Thus in the years that followed, the Chinese not only fanned the flames of 'the rivalry' between Lhasa and Tashilhunpo, but built up the position of their favoured Lama by large claims on his behalf to 'temporal authority over parts of Tibet and also to spiritual superiority, over the Dalai Lama.[50]

Again, while native Tibetan control of the internal affairs of the country approximated to a monopoly of Church domination in the hands of powerful families, 'foreign imperial control', especially under the Manchus, 'manipulated' the apparently impersonal apparatus of the Church in a different way. This was by selecting as pontiffs not only minor children but children of insignificant families. For the pontifical succession, it has been held, seemed to subserve two major purposes : it was a sop to Tibetan pride and it accepted the fact of Chinese suzerainty. In this way, Professor Lattimore argues, the Manchus succeeded in Tibet, as they did in Mongolia, in arresting the processes of tribal and regional alteration and variation and maintaining and fostering in its place, 'a dead level of stagnation'. A neat balance was thus sought to be struck between frontier pressure on China and the 'unsettling expansion' of the Chinese into frontier regions.[51]

Two caveats may be entered here . One, that there could be no escape from the selection of children as pontiffs, for once the idea of a *truklu* is accepted, the new authority has to be a child.[52] Two, the preceding lines presuppose that the Manchus exercised a powerful influence in the choice of incarnations. An important fact to underline here is that the use of the urn was prescribed only for the highest among them. Obviously, therefore, the Manchus had no say in the choice of scores, if not hundreds of those incarnations who were lower down in the spiritual hierarchy. Again, the urn was sidestepped by the Tibetans in collusion with the Ambans and thus even its limited applicability was sometimes reduced to nought. In sum, while the Manchus no doubt contributed their share to maintaining and fostering 'a dead level of stagnation' in Tibet, the exact nature and scope of their 'contribution' may be a subject for debate.

Notes

1. For the early history of Tibet in general, and of Songtsen Gampo in particular, see A. H. Francke, "The Kingdm of Nya-khri-btsanpo, the first king of Tibet", *Journal and Proceedings of the Asiatic Society of Bengal* (Calcutta), VI (1910). Reverend Francke contends that the pre-Songtsen gampo Tibet must correspond broadly to Ladakh. Francke's viewpoint, however, should he taken with a goodly pinch of salt. It is interesting that neither Bell (*Tibet*, p. 23) nor Mr. Richardson (*op.cit.*, pp. 28-29) mention Ladakh in this context. The Dalai Lama too (*op.cit.*, pp. 62-63) is silent on the point.

2. One is struck by the fact that later accounts of this king read like those of Peter the Great of Russia or even Alfred of England. Thus he is reported to have retired into seclusion for four years to learn reading and writing; or again, to have evolved a written character for the Tibetan language so that the sacred books, brought from India, could be translated, Bell, *Tibet,* pp. 23-25. Carrasco, *op.cit.*, p. 15 gives the dates c. 600-650 for him, while the Dalai Lama, *op.cit.*, p. 63, gives his birth as the Earth Bull year (A.D. 629). The latter is impossibly late for the Tibetan ruler died in 650 and was succeeded by a grandson.

3. For the best account of this king, based on Tibetan sources, see W. W. Rockhill, *The Life of the Buddha* (London, 1884), pp. 211-15 , also S. W. Bushell, 'The Early History of Tibet from Chinese Sources', *Journal of Royal Asiatic Society* (London), XII (1880) pp. 435-541.

4. The third was Ral-pa-chan (died 838) in whose reign Tibetan armies are said to have over-run westen China. The three are regarded as 'the outstanding figures in war and peace', Bell, *Tibet*, p. 29. The Dalai Lama, *op.cit.*, p. 64 , calls them the 23rd , 37th and 40th Kings: 'The greatest in the history of Tibet, and our people honour them to this day'.

5. Thubton Norbu, *Tibet is My Country* (London, 1961), p. 40 insists that the term 'Lamaism' is rather loosely employed and, that the best description of his country's religion is 'Tibetan Buddhism'.

6. Among the Indian scholars accompanying Padma Sambhava were Santa Rakshita and Kamalashila.

7. In Tibetan the word used for India is 'rGya-gar' which roughly rendered means 'the great land where people wear white'. Another expression commonly employed is 'Phags Yul', which is nearer to 'holy land'.

8. Apart from the Dalai Lama's, *op.cit.*, Appendix I ('An outline of the Buddhism of Tibet'), pp. 212-27, see L. A. Waddell, *The Buddhism of Tibet or Lamaism,* 2nd edition (Cambridge, 1939). Professor Lattimore calls the early religion of Tibet 'syncretic Buddhism'. He maintains that since Padma Sambhava came into Tibet from Kashmir and, therefore, presumably through Ladakh, the supposition that the Lhasa Kingdom was created by a conquest based on Ladakh and resulting in the transfer of the royal capital from Ladakh to Lhasa would be very much strengthened. Owen Lattimore, 'Inner Asian Frontiers', *op.cit.*, p. 223.

9. *Infra* pp. 71-75.

David Macdonald, *Tibet* (Oxford, 1945), calls the country 'the Hidden Land' , 'the Mystic Land' and 'the land of the Lamas'. Sven Hedin, *A Conquest of Tibet* (New York, 1934), refers to the country as the 'Snow Land'.

Bell, *Tibet*, pp. 25-26.

Richardson, *op.cit.*, p. 33.

Ibid., p. 34.

'The Sakya period represents the beginnings of modern Tibet. There we find the first monastic hierarchs as rulers of the whole country, the beginning of a direct supervision of Chinese (actually Mongols) over Tibetan affairs, the first attempt at centralisation'. Carrasco, *op.cit.*, p. 23.
Mr. Richardson holds that Kublai was the patron of the Sakya sect, but was not Tisri. Actually he had appointed a Phagpa, nephew of the old Sakya Pandita, as his (Kublai's) Viceregent with the title of Tisri. Richardson, *op.cit.*, p. 34.

Chang-Chub Gyalsten was a prince of the noble family of Pagmortu, that lived in the valley of the Tsangpo. It was this family which broke the power of the Sakya hierarchs who had increasingly depended on the Mongol emperors. For details, see Bell, *Tibet,* p. 32 and Richardson, *op.cit.*, p. 35.

A typical, though much later instance is the letter addressed by the Manchu ruler to the British sovereign and entrusted to Lord Amhert who had led a trade mission to the Ta Ch'ing emperor in 1816. After admonishing the (British) ruler against 'these embassies' which were troublesome because of the 'indecorous scenes' to which they gave rise and making clear that the presents were of 'no interest' or 'use', the emperor continued: ''In future do not bother to despatch them for they are merely a waste of time. You will be better employed administering your subjects and improving your defences. If you loyally accept our sovereignty, there is really no need for these stated appearances that you are indeed our vassal'. Cited in Maurice Collis, *The Great Within* (London, 1951), p. 324. It may also be recalled that the barge carrying Lord Macartney's mission in 1793, flew a pennant identifying him as a 'Tribute-bearing Embassy from the Red Barbarians'. For details, see J. L. Cranmer-Byng (ed.), *An Embassy to China* (Longmans, 1962).
An excellent, scholarly account of the tributary system under the Manchus is to be found in 'On the Ch'ing Tributary System' in John King Fairbank and Ssu-Yu Teng, *Ch'ing Administration: Three Studies* (Harvard, 1961), pp.107-217.

Richardson, *op.cit.*, p. 38.

Actually, the Middle Ages in Tibet, as for most part elsewhere, are popularly regarded as 'dark'. There were political divisions complicated by growing ramifications of various monastic orders. Thus apart from the Sakya rulers, there were the Drinkhung, the Tshal and Tshurpu hierarchs, each with a powerful, private army. The Sakya ascendancy was followed by those of Pagmortu (1359-1436) and later still came the Rimpung (1436-1565) and the Tsang rulers (1565-1641). The latter two favoured the Karamapa sect, which was an offshoot of the Kargyupa on which the Pagmortu had relied.

For details, see P. L. Mehra, 'The Dalai and the Panchen : Tibet's Supreme Incarnate Lamas', *India Quarterly*, XV , 3 (July-September, 1959), pp. 262-89, and *T'oung Pao Archives*, XLVII (Leiden, 1959).

Owen Lattimore, 'Inner Asian Frontiers', *op.cit.*, p. 229.

'It was then in the Water Horse Year (A.D. 1642) that a Dalai Lama received temporal power over the whole of the country and the present form of Tibetan government, known as Gaden-Phodrung was founded'. Dalai Lama, *op.cit.,* p. 65.

22. The Fifth Dalai Lama was the son, according to what the Thirteenth Dalai Lama told S
    Charles Bell, of a poor man at Chung-gye, two days' journey to south-east of Lhasa.
    is said that he asked the Oleot Mongols to help him against his enemies and that it w
    in response to this appeal that Gusri Khan came to his aid. Bell, *Tibet*, p. 35.

23. It has been held that when, in 1728, the Panchen Lama was offered the sovereignty
    wide areas in north, central and westen Tibet, the Lama accepted the districts near h
    monastery only and in these his authority approximated to that wielded by any oth
    monastery or by the feudal nobility. Richardson, *op.cit.*, p. 53.

24. Thus the Manchu conquest, in spite of the sudden success of 1644, actually occupie
    two generations from 1618-83. It was completed only by Nurhachi's fourth successc
    K'ang H'si and reached 'its height of power' under Chien Lung (1736-95). Edwin
    Reischauer and John King Fairbank, *East Asia : the Great Tradition* (Boston, 196C
    p. 356.

25. The K'ang H'si ruler, it is held, 'naturally regarded' the Dalai Lama as 'one key to tl
    control of Mongolia' where 'Lamaism, was already claiming a large number
    followers. *Ibid.*, p. 362.

26. Luciano Petech, *China and Tibet in the Early 18ᵗʰ Century, monographic du Tour
    Pao*, I (Leiden, 1950). Another definitive authority for this period is a work of tl
    American scholar-diplomat W.W. Rockhill, *The Dalai Lamas of Lhasa and the
    Relations with the Manchu Emperors of China* (Leiden, 1910).

27. Mr. Richardson believes that the Ming held no shadow of suzerainty over Tibet ar
    that quite consciously the Manchus started from scratch. The K'ang H'si ruler's initiati
    in this respect was commendable: 'being himself a Central Asian, he possessed
    sympathetic understanding of the minds of his Central Asian neighbours'. He 'als
    enjoyed some exceptional good luck'. Richardson, *op.cit.*, p. 47.

28. When the Fifth Dalai Lama died in 1682, his temporal successor was his reputed
    natural son Samgye Gyatso who, it seems, was responsible for the discovery ar
    enthronement of the sixth Dalai Lama in 1696. His worst offence, in Chinese eye
    however was his cultivation of the Dzungar Mongols, a major unsettling factor in tl
    then situation in Central Asia. Hence the Manchu Emperor K'ang Hsi's tacit support
    Lhabzan Khan—Gusri's successor to the Kingship of Tibet—in removing Samg:
    Gyatso and later even the sixth Dalai lama who, a lyrical poet ('a gay toper'), wa
    obviously unfit to discharge the responsibilities of a great religious headship.

29. Lhabzan Khan's removal of the Sixth Dalai Lama (Tsangyang Gyatso), whose dea
    later on his way to China was widely suspect in Tibetan eyes, made his position
    Lhasa highly untenable. In return for the Emperor's support, which Lhabzan no
    solicited, the former secured the regular payment of the tribute, 'the first occasic
    when a Mongol King of Tibet had made such a payment to the Manchu rulers.' Lhabza
    Khan's choice as Dalai Lama was a 25 –year old monk, reputed to be his own natur
    son.

30. Actually, the Dzungars had launched their invasion for the ostensible purpose of undoir
    Lhabzan –whom they killed —and of restoring the rightful Dalai Lama, whom the
    were unable to secure, for he had fallen into the hands of the Manchu Emperor.

31. Richardson, *op.cit.*, pp. 49-50. The Lhasa stone pillar inscription in four languages-
    'a magnificent example of Chinese skill in the art of specious propaganda'—howeve
    misrepresented the facts so as to imply that ever since 1640, the Machu Emperors ha
    enjoyed a special position in regard to Tibet and that the Emperor was the overlord
    Lhabzan Khan.

2. Historically, the presence of Chinese troops in Lhasa has always been associated, in Tibetan eyes, not only with overt control but with a shortage of supplies and a consequent rise in prices. This has partly accounted for their unpopularity.

3. The civil war was 'partly' an attempt 'at the restoration of the power of the Dalai Lama' yet seemed to ruin 'for ever' all prospects of his temporal rule, Petech, *op.cit.*, p. 218. There is a certain lack of clarity here and it may be useful to set the record straight. The civil war was brought about by a complicated situation and was precipitated, inter alia, by the powerlessness of the Ambans to intervene effectively. As for the Dalai Lama, within less than 25 years he was the virtual ruler of Tibet—in matters temporal, no less than spiritual.

4. It may be noted that the Residents 'had no powers of intervention'. Their tasks being solely 'to keep the Emperor informed.' Petech, *op.cit.*, p. 240.

5. Actually, although the Seventh Dalai Lama was a minor during the period of the civil war, the Manchu Emperor distrusted him. In 1728, therefore, he was invited to visit Peking but got no further than Litang where he was kept for seven years and later returned to Lhasa 'on the strict condition' that he would refrain from political activity. Richardson, *op.cit.*, p. 52.

6. Petech, *op.cit.*, 219.
    Pooh-poohing the Tibetan tendency to regard him a traitor, 'because he did not openly oppose Chinese overlordship of Tibet', Mr. Richardson considers Phola 'one of the best rulers Tibet has had, for he gave the country 18 years of prosperous and peaceful' government. He also reduced Manchu supremacy to 'a matter of form only'. Richardson, *op. cit.*, p. 53.

7. Earlier, in 1748, the Emperor 'allowed himself to be cajoled into a very foolish step'— the withdrawal of a major part of the Lhasa garrison. 'From every conceivable point of view it was a grievous mistake' actually, it made the Ambans ineffective. Petech, *op.cit.*, p. 187.

8. *Ibid.*, p.199.

9. 'There was no rebellion to put down... A full–sized expedition to Tibet seemed clearly out of place and likely only to produce mistrust and unrest in the country'. *Ibid.*, p. 203.

0. *Ibid.*, p. 220.

1. 'The reforms of 1750 put the temporal supremacy of the religious hierarchy on a lasting basis which was never afterwards challenged'. Richardson, *op.cit.*, p. 58.

2. For details, see D. R. Regmi, *op.cit.*, pp.171-73. It appears that while Nepal was to obtain an yearly tribute of Rs. 13 lakh ingots of silver from Tibet, it had also agreed to send 'a five-yearly tribute mission to China,' a fact which puzzles the scholar and makes him ask 'if the price of victory was vassalage'.

3. 'The situation in Tibet was simply deplorable. But we fail to understand as to how this had opened the way for aggression by the Nepalese neighbour who had cared little to note that this invasion would face a Chinese counter-attack in (sic.) behalf of Tibet.' *Ibid.*, pp. 168-69.

4. For details of the war, of Chinese intransigence, of British interest, the actual extent of Chinese advance and how the latter finally withdrew, see *Ibid.*, pp.176-207.

5. Richardson, *op.cit.*, p. 70, insists that in looking at these far-reaching changes 'the elements of fiction and artificiality in Chinese relations with Tibet and the one-sided character of most versions of Sino-Tibetan history' should be fully borne in mind. For 'the practical effect' of the new system was 'no greater or more lasting a degree of

imperial authority than had been exercised under the previous arrangements'.

46. Petech, *op.cit.*, p. 240.

47. For a detailed examination, see Waddell, 'Tibetan Buddhism or Lamaism', *op.cit.* Marco Pallis, *Peaks and Lamas* (London, 1940) and the Dalai Lama, *op. cit.*, Appendi ('An Outline of the Buddhism of Tibet'), pp. 212-25.

48. For a preliminary assessment, see P. L. Mehra, 'The Dalai and the Panchen', *op cit.*

49. Owen Lattimore, 'Inner Asian Frontiers', *op.cit.*, p. 232.

50. Richardson, *op.cit.*, pp. 53-54.

51. Owen Lattimore, 'Inner Asian Frontiers', *op.cit.*, pp. 231-33.

52. It is necessary to underline the fact that Christ was a child when the three wise men followed the star to Bethelhem—a very close parallel to the vagaries which preced the recognition of a new Mahayana reincarnation.

4
The Missions of George Bogle and Samuel Turner[1]

The earliest efforts to 'open' Tibet belong to the period of Warren Hastings' Governor-Generalship of Fort William in Bengal.[2] Events had conspired as it were, to make this possible even before Hastings assumed the reins of office. Thus Captain Kinlock's expedition to Nepal in 1767, although militarily disastrous, had aroused considerable British curiosity in the lands beyond the Company's immediate territorial domain.[3] Another incentive came through a surgeon named James Logan who had repaired to Nepal in 1769, ostensibly to deliver a letter to the Gorkhali ruler yet in reality to lend support to the claims of Kathmandu's Raja, then pitted in war against the Gorkha invaders. The British surgeon's underlying aim was to secure access to Tibet, through the Raja's territory.[4] It was widely held that the latter's close association with the (Tibetan) Lama would help establish trade relations with his country.[5] The attempt, however, proved still-born, for in that very year Nepal fell a prey to the Gorkhali ruler, Pratap Narayan Sah. And the latter's advent was to mean, for many a year to come, a blighting of normal trade channels which had subsisted hitherto between the rulers of Nepal and their northern nighbours.[6] Meantime, in March 1768, the Court of Directors in London had asked their factors in India to assess the prospects of opening trade relations with west China and Tibet, through Nepal—a directive for undertaking similar explorations in Bhutan and Assam being repeated three years later.[7] It may be recalled that while these developments were taking place Harry Verelst, and not Warren Hastings, was the Governor of Bengal.

In 1772, some Bhutanese freebooters descended, as was their wont, on the small picturesque state of Cooch-Behar. The latter was not part of the territory of Bengal, Bihar and Orissa for which the Company held the rights of Diwani (involving both revenue collection and civil administration) which had been granted them in a formal 'firman' of August 12, 1765 by the Mughal Emperor Shah Alam. Yet Cooch-Behar bordered Bengal in the north and the ruler had appealed to, and sought, the Company's protection. That there was something not quite straight about the

Governor of Bengal lending armed assistance to the ruler is evident from the fac
that, for a long time afterwards, the Company was on the defensive, explainin
away and offering excuses for its actions.[8] It may, however, be pointed out tha
inasmuch as the Maratha threat to Bengal was rated imminent, this new dange
from the north posed a grave menace to the Company's possessions, and henc
the decision to lend armed aid to the ruler of Cooch-Behar.[9]

Critics aver that Hastings' real aim was far from being an altruistic one and tha
in reality, a very advantageous deal was struck before armed assistance was actuall
given. For the Raja had pledged a cash subsidy, half of his state's revenue as a
annual tribute and an acknowledgement of the Company's supremacy.[10] Interestin
as these sidelights are, even more so was the sequence of events that now unfolde
itself. As it turned out, no sooner did the British troops march into the state an
drive the Bhutanese out, the Panchen Lama of Tashi-lhun-po interceded wit
Hastings on behalf of his ward—'I now take upon me to be his mediator'—the De
Raja of Bhutan. The latter, the Panchen pleaded, 'dependent upon the Dalai Lama
who rules in this country' and whose charge during the Lama's minority, ha
devolved upon him (Panchen Lama), should be prevented from further molestatior
Should Hastings defer to this request and 'cease all hostilities against him,' h
(Warren Hastings) 'will confer the greatest favour and friendship upon me'. Th
Governor-General, pleased beyond measure, hastened to ingratiate himself with th
Lama to earn that 'favour and friendship' now so generously proffered.[11]

Nor is his action difficult to understand. Hastings could afford to be liberal t
the Bhutan Raja as long as his own gains, at the expense of Cooch-Behar, had bee
fully secured.[12] Again, the personal intercession of the Panchen seemed to offe
him the possibility—"the present occasion appears too favourable to b
neglected"—of establishing trade contacts with Tibet. This was a prospect doubl
pleasing, and not only as a source of supply for gold and silver, but also in that th
Directors had been laying considerable stress on the opening of trade relation
with the neighbouring lands, and this, as has been noticed, before Hastings too
over as Governor-General. An equally important factor may have been the latter'
own unbounded curiosity about the Orient—what his contemporaries often, an
half-contemptuously as it were, called his 'Pandit-hunting'.[13] It has also bee
suggested that the Governor-General's knowledge of Raja Chait Singh's direc
dealings, religious no less than commercial, with Tashilhunpo must have been a
additional spur to action and to a determination to seize this opportunity for th
Company.[14] It is hardly necessary to emphasise that Warren Hastings was perhap
the greatest, if the first, of the British Governors-General and a man of immens
foresight and imagination. It would thus follow.that his action in this case wa
neithter casual nor up-premeditated. Finally, the halo of mystery that then, as indee
now,[15] has tended to surround Tibet must have played its part too.

The receipt of some presents from the Lama persuaded Hastings to despatch
personal representative, and the choice fell on a young, barely 27–year old, Benga
civilian, George Bogle, then acting as Secretary to the Select Committee.[16] Apar

rom some precious gifts for the Tibetan Lama, Bogle carried a great variety of
rticles, chiefly of British manufacture, which may have been of interest to the
ibetans in establishing the new trade links. Charged with opening 'a mutual and
qual communication of trade' between the two countries, he was diligently to
nform himself of the 'manufacture, productions, goods' introduced into Tibet by
ther countries, 'of the nature of the road between Bengal and Lhasa', and of
ntercourse 'between Lhasa and the neighbouring countries'.[17] In short, his appeared
o be an exercise in 'commercial reconnaissance,' concerned almost entirely with
trade rather than diplomcy'.[18]

Bogle, despite Hastings' encouragement and optimism, was not sanguine about
ne success of his mission which, as it turned out, was a limited one.[19] Hamstrung
ight at its commencement and asked by the Tibetan ruler to abandon his journey
vhile yet in transit through Bhutan, he nevertheless was able to continue, and
omplete it.[20] At Tashilhunpo his meetings with the Panchen were frequent and
narked by extreme cordiality : they met without much ceremony and conversed in
Hindustani with which the Lama, through his mother, was familiar.[21] Again, his
doption of, and adaptation to , Tibetan customs—he ate their food, dressed like
hem and is even said to have married a Tibetan wife—made him a valuable observer.[22]
He met many of their traders including a group from Lhasa which, despite the
Panchen's intercession, he was not able to visit. Yet aided by the active interest
nd sympathetic understanding of the Lama, he made every possible effort to ease
he path towards the fostering of closer commercial ties with Bengal.[23] So also
plans were laid by the Lama, as well as Bogle, for a direct approach to the Manchu
Emperor in order to override, or in any case circumvent, Lhasa's known opposition.
ndeed, it is in this personal contact, which was thus established between Hastings'
envoy and the ruler of Tashilhunpo, that the chief value of Bogle's mission may be
said to lie. The two hit it off, as it were, extremely well and relations between the
British in India and Tibet thus 'got off to an auspicious start'.[24]

Circumstancs were propitious too. For the third Panchen was a learned, able,
powerful and, at the same time, as Bogle bears out, a very cultured personality. The
fact that the eighth Dalai Lama—the seventh had died when the Panchen Lama was
ust twenty—was a minor gave added strength, and influence, to the ruler of
Tashilhunpo. And though the Regent at Lhasa could, and did act as a stumbling-
block, the Lama's own undoubted authority and the prestige of his office went a
long way towards making Bogle's task easy. It is necessary to remind oneself here
that, undeterred by Lhasa's known hostility, the initiative, both in regard to Bhutan's
as also Bogle's visit, was entirely his own. The Lama even undertook to interecede
with the Manchu Emperor Ch'ien Lung on his (Bogle's) behalf.

And yet all said and done, the debit side of the mission was no less important.
Thus Hastings' envoy was debarred from proceeding to Lhasa—the Regent's
opposition was unmistakable and unremitting on that score.[25] Nor was he able to
obtain permission for the Europeans to trade and reside in Tibet. Bhutan too refused
to agree to what it must have viewed as an atrocious demand.[26] Bogle's general

report on Tibet, as also on the trade of that country is, within limits, a comprehensiv survey.[27] And yet despite this, and his own best efforts, the volume of goods i either direction is not known to have increased as a result of his visit. Essentiall the same trickle persisted down to the end of the nineteenth century.

Bogle's failure, however, as may be evident, was not for want of trying. He ha encouraged the Panchen, with whom he had cultivated the most intimate of ties, t plan the sending of Tashilhunpo's envoys to Calcutta from where, besides seein the Governor-General, they may be able to undertake pilgrimages to holy places. He also lent countenance to the Lama's plan of founding a monastery on the bank of the Ganges where Tibetan pilgrims could go and stay.[29] Again, he was able t persuade the Panchen to write to the Grand Lama in Peking suggesting that th latter send some representative people from China to visit India.[30] Later not only di he embark upon a second mission in 1779—abandoned just before death laid it cruel hands on him—but drew up a Memorandum proposing that the Panchen then on a visit to the Emperor in Peking, 'exert himself to procure me', either facilitie for an overland journey, or send 'some person from himself to Canton' with passports so that he (Bogle) might get to Peking while the Lama was still there.[31]

Before going into the deeper, underlying causes of Bogle's failure to achieve his objectives, it may be well to pass briefly in review another commercial mission to Tibet sponsored by Warren Hastings towards the end of his incumbency. This wa: led by a kinsman of the Governor-General, a certain Lieutenant (later Captain) Samue Turner.[32] The need for it arose from the almost simultaneous deaths of Bogle, and the sixth Panchen Lama, with whom he had negotiated.[33] Earlier the Governor-General had been the recipient of some letters from the Regent at Tashil-hunpo which had encouraged him not a little.[34] Again, he also doubtless visualized a sizeable increase in trade owing to the end of the American War of Independence and the near-cessation of Franco-British hostilities. And what if he could open up Tibet and, through Tibet, may be even China.[35] Yet, whatever his real objective, the ostensible purpose of the new mission was to congratulate the Regent and to present regards to the old Lama in his new incarnation.

Turner, though superficially nonchalant, was a much more astute and careful observer than Bogle.[36] a close scrutiny of his 'Account of an Embassy' would bear that out. His interests appear to have been wider too: his love of sport, ice-skating in particular;[37] his meticulous observations of the region, of its flora and fauna; his detailed survey of Tibet's mining and mineral resources;[38] his fairly accurate descriptions of the life and culture of Tibet, no less than that of Bhutan. Yet like Bogle before him, he too was unable to gain admittance to Lhasa,[39] nor did he fare any better in regard to Bhutan.[40] Thus, one fails to notice those 'substantial' concessions from the Regent at Tashilhunpo to which Sir Francis Younghusband vaguely refers in his book.[41] For the Regent's promise to afford all facilities to Indian merchants 'that may be sent to traffic in Tibet on behalf of the Government of Bengal',[42] of which much has been made, was implied, if not explicitly stated, in the old Panchen's conversations with Bogle.

To be sure Bogle pointedly, and persistently, referred in his reports to Hastings that European merchants were by no means essential to carrying on trade with these northern countries—confession at once of failure to achieve his principal objective, as no doubt of an alternative that alone seemed practical. Indeed it would be hard to believe that within so brief an interval as lapsed between Bogle's departure and Turner's arrival, any very marked change in the Tibetan attitude could have taken place. If anything the death of Pal-den Ye-she, the sixth Panchen Lama, acted as a principal inhibiting factor both for the Regent at Tashilhunpo as also for the authorities in Lhasa.[43] And although the real cause of failure to follow up Bogle's mission was Turner's own and the Panchen's death, the element of Chinese influence could not be gainsaid. Nevertheless it has been suggested that what Turner took for Chinese obstruction was, in fact, obstruction by the Regent at Lhasa who was 'a powerful figure completely dominating the Ambans', and not too well-disposed towards Tashilhunpo which had sponsored Turner's, as earlier Bogle's visit.[44]

Basically, as will be noticed presently, the reasons for the failure of Hastings' envoys had very little to do with the personalities of the two men. Hence Sir Francis' over-sanguine remark may be qualified by a recent writer's observation that he (Turner) did not accomplish 'very much' and at best cemented 'already existing' relations.[45]

A neglected figure in the domain of early British commercial intercourse with Tibet is that of Purangir (also rendered as 'Puran Giri'). He was the Gosain who acted as a liaison agent with Raja Chait Singh of Benares, brought the Panchen's letter to Hastings, and not only accompanied his two envoys but also made possible their journeys to Tibet. Later, he was to be the Panchen's close associate who attended on his master during the latter's mission to meet the Emperor in Peking. Whether the Lama actually supported the British case in his parleys with the Chinese ruler is disputed,[46] but there could be no question that the Gosain himself was well-disposed and helped in the general cause.

In placing in its proper perspective the failure of the two envoys, a few observations may be relevant. It may be well to remind oneself that essentially John Company was a trading corporation [47] and that consequentially any openings for a possible expansion of British commerce would be readily seized by its factors in India. Thus, as has been pointed out, it was only when 'opportunities for commerce with the northern countries', meaning perhaps Nepal, were tending towards a low ebb that the Company began to take an active interest in the possibilities of trade with Tibet.[48] An additional factor in the situation was that of contracting trade prospects in Bengal itself, owing largely to the famine of 1770. It will be recalled that Hastings' anticipation of a flow of greater trade, as a result of the end of the American War of Independence, was sufficiently persuasive as to make him despatch Turner. Nor could there be any doubt that the reports of both the envoys were exhaustive studies of Tibet's and Bhutan's potentialities for trade with the Governor's own domain in neighbouring Bengal.

Contrasted with this eager, commercial-minded diplomacy of the Company was the not unnatural mistrust of the *firinghis'* ulterior motives. Generally suspect in the east, the European is doubly so in such relatively remote, unsophisticated, and deeply religious lands as Tibet. [49] One wonders though whether it is his religion, so much at variance with those in the Occident, which makes him the subject of such mistrust. The fact that in earlier times the Capuchins were able to establish, and maintain, a mission in Lhasa and that for centuries Muslims were tolerated and even permitted to engage in business in Tibet, albeit in certain specified occupations, would militate against this thesis. [50] It would seem that in Tibet the formal expression of an attitude is likely to be cast in religious terms, even when real causes are other than religious. Thus the Muslims, the Europeans and other non-Buddhists have been tolerated—and indeed liked[51]—when they were not regarded as forerunners of a political threat but when they were feared for *political* reasons, the attempt to keep them at a distance was expressed in *religious* terms. Besides, had not British dealings with the native states in India, or later with Cooch-Behar or Bhutan on Tibet's periphery, already further fortified this deeply-ingrained distrust? Or, for that matter was it ill-founded either? Bogle's account abounds in passages essaying the armed strength of these lands, their potentialities for resisting a British onslaught, and of his own ingeniously thought-out plans 'for handling' Bhutan, Assam and Nepal. [52] As Dr. Cammann has aptly observed :

Such an aggressive attitude on the part of officials of an expanding Empire could not be easily concealed from the peoples of the surrounding nations. And it would probably have been difficult to convince the Bhutanese or the Tibetans that a policy directed against others might not some day be directed against them. Especially as the former had already enjoyed a somewhat too intimate experience with it. [53]

Should it then be a matter of surprise that both the envoys were allowed admittance after considerable hesitation, that neither was able to conclude any binding commercial agreement, nor permitted to go to Lhasa? Again, that the 'substantial concessions' which Turner is reported to have secured did not, in reality, amount to much nor yet result in anything beyond a mere verbal promise?

Finally, and perhaps of major import, was the fact that the two missions arrived at a time when the Manchu ascendancy was at its acme of influence in these lands. Dr. Petech's work, to which a reference has been made, is explicit on this point, as is any text-book of Chinese history. [54] Even more appropriate is an astute observation of Sir Eric Teichman that the Chinese influence has been the maximum in the wake of their marching armies in Tibet : in 1720, in 1750, in 1792, in 1908-10 and –one may add—in 1950. [55] The Bogle-Turner missions are thus sandwiched between the two earlier invasions. One may recall that Bogle found the Chinese a 'major stumbling block' astride all his paths and that his efforts to work up some feeling in the Panchen that Tibet was an independent entity proved still-born. [56]

Probably his most ingeniously wrought effort in this direction was an attempt to persuade the Lama to conclude a binding treaty with the British in Bengal which was designed to serve as a deterrent to the repeated Gorkhali aggressions in Sikkim. The Panchen avoided and evaded even this bait, how very tempting it may have looked or was made to.[57]

The preceding paragraph apart, it is possible to interpret repeated Manchu incursions as waves of military activity, often reluctantly undertaken beause of the expense, followed by a gradual fall in the temperature until another military expedition proved necessary. It would thus seem that the acme came in 1750 followed by a decline in actual exercise of influence and then another peak (perhaps lower in fact than 1750) in 1792. It was the death of the Panchen followed by the ban on foreigners resulting from 1792 which did the final damage; otherwise it is arguable that the 'foreign devils' might well have continued their relations with Tashilhunpo at least.

Not that the Chinese yoke was not resented. In fact, both of Hastings' envoys clearly underlined, as has been briefly noticed, the too obvious Tibetan resentment of Chinese interference. Yet they also observed that the alien impact was sufficiently powerful and seemed to overawe the Tibetans in all their dealings.[58] Thus the specific failure of the two missions may, in the final analysis, be squarely laid to the general averseness of the celestial kingdom to permit any intercourse with the 'foreign devils'. It follows that as long as the Chinese exercised the least vestige of authority in Tibet, it would remain a forbidden land, and so in fact it did despite the pleasantries exchanged and the gifts that passed between Calcutta and Tashilhunpo.[59]

Notes

1. Apart from George Bogle's 'Diary' edited, and copiously annotated, by Clements R. Markham, *Narratives of the Mission of George Bogle to Tibet and of the Journey of Thomas Manning to Lhasa* (London, 1876), abbreviated et. seq. as *Narratives*, and Samuel Turner, *An Account of an Embassy to the Court of the Teshoo Lama in Tibet, containing a Narrative of a Journey through Bhutan and part of Tibet*, second Edition (London, 1806), a summary of Bogle's impressions on Tibetan trade may be found in *Selections from Indian State papers presented in the Foreign Department*, 1772-85, I, pp. 251-54. For a brief account reference may be made to Younghusband, *India and Tibet* (London, 1910), pp. 7-29, and for a critical appraisal to Schuyler Cammann, *op.cit.* Three papers D.B. Diskalkar 'Bogle's Embassy to Tibet', *Indian Historical Quarterly*, IX (Calcutta, 1938), L. Petech, "Bolge and Tuner according to the Tibetan Texts, *T'oung Pao*, XXXIX (1949) and S.C. Sarcar, "Some Notes on the intercourse of Bengal with the Northern countries in the second half of the Eighteenth Century", *Bengal, Past and Present*, XLI (Calcutta, 1931), give useful and scholarly interpretations. A brief, though excellent sketch is in Sir Olaf Caroe, *Englishmen in Tibet* (Tibet Society, London, 1960).

2. Warren Hastings was Governor of Bengal from 1772-74; under Lord North's Regulating Act of 1773, however, he became from 1774 to 84, 'Governor General of the Presidency of Fort William in Bengal'. His most authoritative biography is Reverend G. R. Gleig, *Memoirs of the Life of the Right Hon'ble Warren Hastings* (London, 1841), 3 Vols. Three others are, A. Mervyn Davies, *Strange Destiny: A Biography of Warren Hastings* (London, 1935), Penderel Moon, *Warren Hastings and British India* (New York, 1949)

and Sophia Weitzman, *Warren Hastings and Philip Francis* (Manchester, 1929).

3.   The Compay's real expert on Nepalese affairs was Rumbolt, Chief of the Patna factory who was the mastermind, it would seem, behind Kinlock's expedition to save the valley from the onslaught of Prithvinarayan Sah.

4.   Ostensibly, Sargeant James Logan was entrusted with the task of delivering a letter from the Governor to the Gorkhali ruler Prithvinarayan Sah promising him support and recognition. In actual fact, he negotiated for permission, from Raja Karan Singh of Saptari, so that the British may go to the Chumbi valley by the Morang-Teesta road and thereby explore the possibility of sending (British) merchandise into Tibet.

5.   The trade was highly lucrative for a large volume of Tibetan gold passed through Nepal the value of which, in Kathmadndu, was 50 per cent less than what it brought in Patna.

6.   On the eve of the Gorkha's rise, Nepal's three principal rulers were located in Kathmandu, Lalita Patan and Bhatgaon respectively. For a detailed discussion of this phase of Nepal's history, see D.R. Regmi, *op.cit.*, Chapter 3 (*Gorkha Becomes Kingdom of Nepal*), pp. 52-103.

7.   An account of these early 'adventures' is found in S.C. Sarcar : 'Some Notes on the Intercourse of Bengal with Northern countries in the second half of the 18th century', *Bengal, Past and Present* (Calcutta), XLI, 1931, pp. 124-25.

8.   During his meeting with the Panchen (Teshu) Lama we find Bogle explaining away, time and over again, how it was that the Company acted as it did in support of the ruler of Cooch-Behar.

9.   The first Anglo-Maratha war started in 1775 and lasted through 1785.

10. Cammann, *op.cit.*, pp. 26 and 155-56, contends that Hastings' motives were far from being unselfish and that he was deliberately fishing in the troubled waters of the state. Gleig: *Memoirs,* I, pp. 255-96, reveals that in his private correspondence Hastings admitted that his real purpose was to gain possession of Cooch-Behar for the Company— apart from whatever he may have hoped to gain at the expense of Bhutan.

11. For the full text of the letter (with annotations), see Markham, *op.cit.*, pp. 1-3. The sequence of events may be carefully kept in view: the Company's troops marched into Cooch-Behar in May 1773; Hastings received the Panchen's letter, interceding on the Deb Raja's behalf, on March 29, 1774; a reply had been dispatched before May 4, when he submitted a Minute on the subject to the Board.

12. Throughout Markham's 'Narratives' one notices the somewhat confusing fact that Hastings always referred to Tibet as 'Bhutan'—evidently a corruption of 'Bhot', the Tibetan word for their country. Cooch-Behar, which now forms part of West Bengal, is not to be confused with Bihar which then, along with Orissa, formed a part of Bengal.

13. Along with Wilkins, 'Asiatic' Jones and Halbed, Hastings was responsible for founding, in 1782, the Asiatic Society of Bengal—a body that has done a great deal of useful work in the field of oriental research. He contributed an introduction to Wilkins' first translation of the *Bhagvad Gita.* What, however, came most to the notice of his contemporaries were his not infrequent disputations with learned Brahmins on Hindu philosophy and religion. Moon, *op.cit.* pp. 351-52.

14. Two Tibetan missions had visited Benaras—in 1771-72 and 1773-74, and their leader had encouraged Chait Singh to send envoys to Tashilhunpo, Bogle found, and conversed with one of them at the Panchen's court. 'The vakils of Cheyt Singh and Kashmiri Mull also came to see me and afterwards frequently repeated their visits', he recorded. Markham, *op.cit.*, p. 102.

15. 'Next morning we wakened in the 12th century, in a world where characters out of Shakespeare did not look at us from a theatre stage, or pictures in books, but walked with us in the streets of the city and stood patiently while we photographed them and talked with them about their lives', Stuart and Roma Gelder, 'Journey to Lhasa', *Eastern Horizon*, II, 8 (August, 1963), pp. 17-25.

16. For Markham's 'Biographical Sketch' of Bogle, see 'Narratives', *op.cit.* pp. xxxi-cliv.

17. *Ibid.*, pp. 6-7, 'private commissions', ten in all, included *inter alia*, 'one or more pair of animals called *tus*' which produce shawl wool and 'some fresh ripe walnuts for seed'.

18. S. C. Sarcar, *op.cit.*, pp. 32-33.

19. Constantly smitten by remorse as he (Bogle) was, Hastings gave him all possible encouragement. 'But as you express an anxiety.... I am perfectly satisfied and pleased with every circumstance of your conduct, and equally so with the issue of your commission'. Letter from Warren Hastings (undated) on his (Bogle's) return. 'Narratives', *op.cit.*, p. 46.

20. It was here that Gosain Purangir's intervention on his (Bogle's) behalf proved decisive. *Loc. cit.*

21. *Ibid.*, pp. 83-84.

22. 'As I always like to do at Rome as they do at Rome', *Ibid.*, p. 88.
    'He married a Tibetan lady, described as a sister of Panchen Lama, by whom he had two daughters. The girls were later educated at Bogle's ancestral home in Aryshire. All references to Bogle's Tibetan wife seem to have been suppressed when his papers were edited for publication'. Richardson, *op.cit.*, p. 65.

23. 'I found in the Lama', Bogle wrote to Warren Hastings, 'the readiest disposition to co-operate with you in removing the obstacles to a free trade, and in adopting such measures as might increase the intercourse between the country and Tibet'. 'Narratives', *op.cit.*, p. 197. Also see *Ibid.*, pp. 133, 160-61 and 163.

24. Richardson, *op.cit.*, p. 66.

25. Actually, the Lhasa Regent Gesub Rimpoche (as Bogle calls him) was opposed to his mission from its very inception. Thus we know that he had written to the Panchen warning him 'that the *fringhies* were fond of war, and after insinuating themselves into a country raised disturbances and made themselves masters of it'. Later, after the Panchen had given him (Bogle) admittance, Gesub 'wrote to Tashi Lama to prevent my coming to Lhasa, and repeated this in several letters after my arrival'. 'Narratives' *op.cit.* pp. 131-32.

26. In a letter to Warren Hastings from Cooch-Behar, Bogle said: 'There was, I beg leave to assure you, no possibility of obtaining his (Deb Raja's) consent to allow Englishmen to travel into his country...' or again, 'I have more than once mentioned the impossibility of procuring leave for Europeans to trade into Bhutan...nor hope to obtain the sanction and concurrence of the administration at Lhasa'. *Ibid.*, pp. 185-86 and 188 respectively.

27. *Ibid.*, pp. 191-206 and 124-29.

28. *Ibid.*, p. 134.

29. *Ibid.*, p. 198.

30. *Ibid.*, pp. 134, 146 and 199. Although not as sanguine as the Lama: 'I do not altogether despair, by your favour of one day or other getting a sight of Peking'.

31. 'If I succeed in procuring passports, I shall then be in a position to urge any points at the court of Peking with the greatest advantage.' *Ibid.*, pp. 207-10.

32. For a biographical sketch, see the *Dictionary of National Biography*, XIX. pp. 1281-82 and 'Narratives', *op.cit.*, p. lxxi, note 2.

33. Bogle died on April 3, 1781, while the Panchen expired on November 12, 1780, in somewhat mysterious circumstances. The Lama was then on a visit to the Emperor in Peking.

34. Turner, *Embassy*, pp. 449-56, gives the text of the two letters.

35. Turner felt that it would probably be by means of their Tibetan contacts that the English would find it possible to reach Peking. *Ibid.*, p. 373.

36. Sir Olaf Caroe rates Bogle much higher: 'He had great charm, and a sweetness of disposition which is rare among Europeans and commends itself to Asians. Surely to care for *man* is more important in an envoy than a love of sport or a study of flora-fauna'. Olaf Caroe, Englishmen in Tibet, *op.cit.*

37. Turner, *Embassy*, pp. 331-32 and 355.

38. *Ibid.*, pp. 369-70.

39. The Regent promised that although he could not permit Turner's going to Lhasa, he would communicate direct to the Governor (Warren Hastings) about what the Dalai Lama thought of relations with the English. *Ibid.*, p. 373.

40. Actually, a civil war in Bhutan had bedevilled an already difficult situation besides delaying Turner's mission. *Ibid.*, p. 148.

41. Younghusband, 'India and Tibet', *op.cit.*, p. 29.

42. Turner, *op.cit.*, p. 374.

43. Turner too seemed to be conscious of this. *Ibid.*, p. 364.
    In his Tibet Society brochure, *op.cit.*, Sir Olaf Caroe dismisses Turner with scant grace: 'But of him there is little to say'.

44. Richardson, *op.cit.*, p. 67.

45. Cammann, *op.cit.*, p. 96.

46. Cammann, *op.cit.*, p. 79, casts serious doubts on the veracity of Purangir and of the two Tashilhunpo officials 'all of whom had much to gain from flattering the English'. Richardson, *op.cit.*, p. 68, however, disputes this.

47. Holden Furber, *John Company at Work* (Harvard, 1948) throws interesting light on this period. Of special interest, in the present context here, will be Chapter VII : "Trade and Politics in Bengal', pp. 225-59.

48. Cammann, *op.cit.*, pp. 25-26. It may be recalled here that in March (1768) the Directors had asked if cloth and other European commodities could find a market in Tibet and West China, by way of Nepal. In 1771 they had asked for similar reports about Bhutan and Assam.

49. To the pages of his 'Diary', Bogle confided: 'The government at Lhasa considered me as sent to explore their country which the ambitions of the English might afterwards prompt them to invade, and their superiority in arms render their attempt successful'. Or again, 'I was at much pains during my stay among the inhabitants of Bhutan and Tibet to remove their prejudices'. 'Narratives', *op.cit.*, p. 203.

50. The Capuchin mission at Lhasa was founded in 1707 by Father Guiseppe d'Ascoli and Francois de Tours and continued until 1745. The Jesuit Missionary, Ippolito Desideri spent five years (1716-21) in the Tibetan capital. It may be recalled that Ladakhi Muslims, who were recently (1963-64) repatriated to India by the Communist regime, always occupied a very important position in Lhasa, and Tibet's commercial life.

51. Sir Olaf Caroe holds that in many ways Tibetans take to Europeans more easily than do Indians. Both Tibetans and Europeans (or at any rate British people) 'are more patient, and in a sense superficial; while Indians are more withdrawn, sensitive and subtle'.

52. Of Bhutan, Bogle wrote 'Two battalions, I think, would reduce their country but two brigades would not keep the communications open....' 'Narratives', *op.cit.*, p. 57.

53. Cammann, *op.cit.*, p. 40.

54. 'Thus after a good deal of trial and error the political power in Tibet was firmly incorporated in that of the Ch'ing Empire where it was to remain until 1912'. The earlier reference is to the armed intervention of 1750. Reischauer and Fairbank, *op.cit.*, p. 363.

55. Sir Eric Teichman, *op.cit.*, p. 2.

56. 'They (Lhasa merchants) answered, that Gesub Rimpoche (the Regent) would do everything in his power, but that he and all the country were subject to the Emperor of China. This is a stumbling block which crossed me in all my paths'. 'Narratives', *op.cit.*, p. 148.

57. *Ibid.*, pp. 150-51.
    Bogle recorded, after he had mentioned to the Panchen Lama the new alignment he had proposed: 'He seemed to be much pleased with what I had said and asked me if he might write this to Gesub'.

58. Turner: *Embassy*, p. 253.

59. Younghusband, *op.cit.*, p. 31, lauds Warren Hastings' efforts as 'not merely statesmanlike', but 'humane'. He used no threats, was not impatient, committed no aggression.

5
India, China and Tibet to 1890

For a hundred years or so after Turner, until the closing decade of the nineteenth century, there is little of major interest in Indo-Tibetan relations, commercial or otherwise. Basically, with Warren Hastings' departure in 1784, the architect of an active and deliberate policy of opening up the country for trade and commerce—his approach had scrupulously eschewed all territorial ambitions at Tibet's expense—was no more. Besides, there were fewer opportunities. As has been noticed earlier, it was clear that after 1792 a conscious effort was made as it were to seal the country from contact with the outside world.[1] Again, fewer still were the envoys despatched who would knock at the gate to seek admittance. Nevertheless there is, in 1811, a certain Thomas Manning, reportedly possessed of a smattering of medical knowledge, who repaired to Lhasa in disguise as a Chinese physician.[2] He was to enjoy, for well-nigh a hundred years, the unique distinction of being the solitary Englishman who ever visited the Potala and had an audience with its lord and master, the youthful ninth Dalai Lama, then aged seven. 'The Lama's beautiful and interesting face and manner engrossed all my attention. He was poetically and affectingly beautiful to look upon',[3] the English visitor recorded.

According to Markham, and Manning's own testimony by implication, the pseudo-physician went entirely on his own without any official help or sponsorship. Indeed, he was highly critical of the Company on this score:

> I cannon help exclaiming what fools the Company are to give me no commission, no authority, no instructions! What use are their embassies when their Ambassadors cannot speak to a soul and can only make ordinary phrases through a stupid interpreter?... Fools, fools, fools to neglect an opportunity they may never have again....[4]

All this notwithstanding, an Indian student of Tibetan affairs would have us believe that Manning had been provided with all facilities by Lord Minto, the then Governor-General of India—a sentiment echoed by a more recent Chinese scholar.[5] And this in the face of his biographer's clear assertion that he (Manning) was undoubtedly 'disgusted' with the official treatment he received.[6]

Sponsored or otherwise, through his thinly-veiled disguise Manning's rea identity could never have been seriously in doubt: 'Sometimes, particularly whe he (Dalai Lama) looked at me, his smile almost approached a gentle laugh.' Coul it be that the Lama saw through the disguise? For 'my grim beard and spectacle somewhat excited his risibility'.[7]

Kindly received on the whole, it would seem to follow that Manning' observations of the Lhasa scene could not have been without their value. Amon other impressions imbibed, the half-baked physician noted that there was n organized or sustained hostility to the British *per se* and that the Tibetans woul fain throw over-board the Chinese yoke 'without many emotions of regret'.[8] An not least for the reason that the great Mandarins at Lhasa—meaning the Ambans— 'were generally rogues and scoundrels'.[9] The value of such observations and th interest of the travelogue apart, it may be broadly agreed that Manning's visit ha a mere episodic significance for there was his conspicuous failure to achieve anythin of great moment.[10]

In the years that followed, British efforts to open up Tibet to trade did nc cease. Essentially, however, the position was somewhat complicated. To th authorities in India it appeared that due pressure in Peking would make the latte relent in its opposition to British intercourse with Tibet—for that alone was viewe as a major stumbling block. On the contrary, seasoned 'China hands' were quit clear in their mind that Peking's reluctance was due not so much to an unwillingnes to oblige, as the conviction that the Tibetans were increasingly recalcitrant an would not easily conform, an assessment which was nearer the truth. Thus in th process pressure from India was often-times resisted by British representatives i Peking and an ill-concealed unwillingness was evident in applying it, if at all— fact which invariably made Calcutta restive and even resentful. Finally, it wa found possible to incorporate in the Chefoo Convention (1876) a separate articl laying down that should a British Mission of exploration proceed, by way of Pekin, 'through Kansuh and Kokonor', or 'by way of Szechuan to Tibet and then to India' or even 'across the Indian frontier to Tibet', the Tsungli Yamen (Chinese Foreig Office) will provide all necessary facilities and passports through its 'High Provincia Authorities', and the 'Resident in Tibet' so that its passage be 'not obstructed'.[11]

For a clearer perspective, it may be necessary to recapitulate here briefly som of the developments that had taken place in British relations with Tibet' neighbouring states in the course of the hundred odd years from Bogle to the Chefo Convention. Much of the ground has been covered earlier. For the present, it may suffice to recall that events culminating in the military expedition of 1861 to Sikkin had reduced that state to the position of a British protectorate. In the case of Bhutan the treaty of 1865 had made her a British stipendiary and seriously compromise her independence.[12] As for Nepal she had, on her own, taken upon herself the rol of a close ally of the *Raj*. To complete the picture it may be as well to recall tha Ladakh had long been a part of Kashmir which, after the accession of Gulab Singh now came into direct relationship with the British; that in 1846 the district of Lahu and Spiti had been incorporated into Kangra, in the Panjab;[13] that Kumaon and parts of Garhwal, wherein Tibet and British India came into direct physical contact with each other, were now integral parts of the North Western Province, later the United Provinces of Agra and Oudh. Again, after the incorporation of Assam, British authority gradually seeped into the tribal belt that sundered Tibet from the foothills in the extreme eastern part of the Indian dominion.[14] Thus all the way from Ladakh in the west, to the trijunction of Burma, Tibet and China in the east, British India had penetrated what Tibet rightly or wrongly regarded as areas within her own peculiar sphere of religious and cultural, and hence by implication political hegemony.[15]

The developments outlined above were bound to disturb Tibetan equanimity, and profoundly. What became even more exasperating, from Lhasa's point of view, was the knowledge that some clandestine missions had been sent into their country and operated there, under the active sponsorship of their southern neighbour. Manning, it is true, was disowned but year after year the Trigonometrical Survey had sent in disguise 'native pundits', as these men were called, to carry out a thorough and systematic study of the Tibetan uplands.[16] Thus Nain Singh, Krishna, the famous 'A. K.', Ugyen Gyasto ('U. G.' for short) and even Sarat Chandra Dass did a remarkable job of work.[17] When the knowledge spread that these Indian Agents of the British had travelled about disguised as monks, hiding their prismatic compasses behind the sanctity of (Tibetan) prayer-wheels, their sextants in their begging bowls, and restricted their rosaries to a hundred beads to check off paces, the land of the lama was visibly disturbed.[18] Besides the Pundits, a host of European adventuresome spirits—Russians and Swedes, Danes and Englishman and Americans—made determined efforts, if sometimes through questionable means, to acquire a detailed and thorough knowledge of the country. Among the names that stand out are the brothers Henry and Richard Strachey, first in point of time (1846-48); the Russian explorer Prjevalsky, who established the conformation of Tibet's north-eastern and eastern mountain systems; the American Rockhill, who made two journeys through the north-eastern and eastern districts of Tibet; the Englishman, Captain Bower who explored the western parts, and a Miss Taylor who came to within 150 miles of Lhasa, not to mention the veteran Swedish doctor, Sven Hedin who made three memorable journeys surveying the northern, southern and western parts of the country.[19]

It is with the background of this persistent, well-sustained, and reasonably successful attempt at penetration by an active and powerful neighbour, along the entire length of its southern border, that Lhasa's reaction to the special article of the Chefoo Convention must be viewed. Such protests may not have been possible, and if made carried far less weight, if Chinese authority itself had remained unimpaired. But the knowledge of the humiliating Opium Wars and the long and bitter Taiping Rebellion, which had shaken the empire to its very foundations, could not be long kept from the Tibetans. Added to this was the fact that the calibre of most of the Manchu officials, posted to these far-flung outposts of the empire, was never, as Manning noticed, of a very high order. Additionally, the loss of the Ch'ing

(Chinese name for the Manchu dynasty) power and prestige could not but b
reflected in the reduced influence of the Imperial Ambans at Lhasa.

While the British were thus preparing to cash in on the letter of the law, th
Tibetans were protesting, ever more loudly, against any British Mission being se
through their country. A showdown seemed imminent and would have led t
interesting results. But, as often in such crises, issues did not come to a head an
an open clash was averted. For the British discovered that their need for Chines
recognition of Burma's incorporation in their Indian empire was far more importa
than the problematical results of the concession wrested at Chefoo.[20] The Chines
too were willing to bargain for in this way they would be putting an end to their ow
serious embarrassment. Consequentially, Art. IV of the Anglo-Chinese Conventio
on Burma, concluded in July 1886, provided an eloquent testimony to many a battl
fought behind the scenes,[21]

> Inasmuch as an inquiry into the circumstances by the Chinese Governme
> has shown the existence, of many obstacles to a mission to Tibet provided fc
> in a separate article of the Chefoo Agreement, England consents to counterman
> the mission. With regard to the desire of the British Government to conside
> arrangements, for frontier trade between India and Tibet, it will be the duty c
> the Chinese Government, after careful inquiry into the circumstances, to ado
> measures to exhort and encourage the people with a view to the promotion an
> development of trade. Should it be practicable, the Chinese Government sha
> then proceed carefully to consider trade regulations, but if insuperable obstacle
> should be found to exist, the British Government will not press the matte
> unduly.[22]

'Face' was saved and unpleasant, inconvenient, facts ignored, but for tha
matter these did not cease to be either unpleasant, or cease to be facts.

Tibet's opposition to the despatch of the ill-fated Colman Macaulay Missio
was not difficult to understand. Preparations for it, and the attendant publicity,
coupled with the spearhead of an armed escort being stationed close to the borde
had caused Lhasa considerable alarm. To hold up the advance, if not to retaliat
against it, the Tibetans too had assembled a small force in the Chumbi Valle
Meantime, the enthusiast in Colman Macaulay had, despite a lukewarm Viceroy, ye
with the active support of the Secretary of State, repaired to Peking and secure
from a reluctant Tsungli Yamen, necessary passports and promises for other facilitie
For a time he even pushed into Sikkim whose Maharaja, drawn powerfully toward
Lhasa, had regarded the British yoke somewhat lightly.[24] That their own troop
were thrown back from Litang did not appear to the Tibetans as important as th
fact that the British Mission was countermanded, abandoned. Lhasa conclude
and rightly, that resistance to Chinese dictates was enough to bring the latte
around and yet obviously wrongly, that the British were a weak power for they ha
to all appearances, retreated when the Tibetans held their ground.[25] It is perhaps n
pure coincidence that about this time there was a strong anti-foreign feeling i
eastern Tibet more particularly in Bantang where Roman Catholic missionaries wer

xpelled, some of their converts massacred and the mission house itself burnt own.[26]

Since Hastings' days, the Tibetans had displayed a consistent, if somewhat ncompromising, hostility to the British, born largely of an inherent suspicion of *eir motives. Nor had this lessened with the passage of time; in fact, as British ominion in India continued to expand, Tibetan susceptibilities were aroused and t a fast pace. For clearly Britain's absorption of the whole sub-continent by 1890 et Tibet face to face with a powerful southern neighbour whose borders, as has een noticed, touched her directly through the Kumaon and Garhwal divisions and *e eastern Assam Hills, and indirectly through the 'inner ring' of mountainous tates and districts. With its expanding dominion, British interest in Tibetan affairs ad grown too and, in the process, been transformed. From the mere commercial econnaissance of a Bogle and a Turner, added to the intellectual curiosity of their ponsor Warren Hastings, or the surreptitious visit of the idiosyncratic Manning, it ad grown into the vital interests of an empire which was determined to defend its rontiers against any alien, not to say unfriendly, or hostile, influences on the other ide of the border. The last few decades of the nineteenth century in India belong to vhat has been termed an Imperial state and this not merely because of the formal ssumption of the Imperial title by the queen of England on January 1, 1877. Logically, hese years saw 'Imperial' India become the centre and pivot of a vast political ystem in Asia. A whole epoch was thus stamped as it were by its founding father's anciful vision of 'bequeathing to India the supremacy of Central Asia and the evenues of a first-class power'.[27]

Not that the incentive for trade had declined by any means. On the contrary, he need for new markets had grown and multiplied. It should always be borne in nind that the body of merchants who had founded the East India Company, though inally voted out of existence in 1857, had left a very deep impact on the nature and character of British rule in India. For the *Raj* remained dominated by what its many critics, not unjustly, called its *bania* mentality—its mercantile ethics, its grabbing, usurious traits.[28] Basically, the economic gains which they made as traders continued or as rulers they kept the same objectives in view. This had, it would appear, a very cogent explantation inasmuch as the desire to discover new markets was, if anything, nuch keener after Britain became the world's greatest industrial power, than in the days of Warren Hastings, when the first faint rumblings of the industrial revolution were barely audible. Perhaps a clearer understanding of British empire-building, and latterly of empire-liquidation, could be gauged if an index of growing trade possibilities, or sometimes of contracting commercial prospects, was constantly kept under review.

Meanwhile as British interests, both territorial and commercial, had grown there had taken place a marked decline in Chinese power. This was evident not only in the traditional eighteen provinces of the mainland but even more starkly in Tibet as in other parts of the Emperor's far-flung dominions. Thus, in the poverty-stricken Szechuan-Hupei-Shensi border region, the 'White Lotus' Rebellion (1795-1814) was an early warning of the declining fortunes of the Ch'ing.[29] Again, the nineties which saw the Imperial State in India at its near-climax, witnessed the rapid carving up of China by the Western powers—an operation often referred to as the 'Cutting up of the Chinese Melon'.[30] The Taiping rebellion (1851-64), briefly alluded to earlier, dealt a severe blow to Manchu rule[31] which continued, less by its own inherent strength than by the fact that foreign nations were interested in bolstering it up, through allowing it 'just enough power to keep on ruling badly, without being able to rule effectively'.[32] For obvious reasons there could be no satisfactory or mutually acceptable division of spoils after the sick man had been buried. The Manchus had thus been reduced to a position where they were too weak to exercise any effective control within their own domain and, as a result of this internal bankruptcy and decrepitude, all the more powerless to resist even the most outrageous demands of the Western Powers.

This loss of Manchu domestic authority was manifest at its starkest in Tibet. Chinese armies had braved, as has been noticed, hardships of a redoubtable character to rush to the aid of the Dalai Lama both in 1726 and again in 1792 when Tibet faced the invasions of the Dzungarian Mongols from the north and of the Gurkhas from the south. In between too the Ch'ing had, to uphld Imperial prestige, sent armed forces to Lhasa. A century later, however, when Tibet once again faced the Dogra threat from the north-west (1840) or that of the Gurkhas from the south (1854-55), no large-scale Manchu armies—countary to a popular, yet mistaken, belief[33]—came to its rescue. Left to fend for itself, Lhasa faced loss of considerable prestige in the one case, and the fact of a galling treaty in the other. It would not be far too wrong to conclude that from all this the Tibetans must have drawn a moral, if not indeed a lesson.

Paradoxical as it may seem, although Manchu authority in Tibet had declined precipitately, the form and fiction of the Emperor's sovereign control had persisted. Thus Chinese Ambans had continued to be stationed in Lhasa and Peking had successfully insisted on all dealings with Tibet, being routed through her, and not directly. Hence it was that the Chefoo agreement with China contained the clause, to which Tibet was not a party, permitting a British Mission to travel to China *via* Tibet or, if need be, in the reverse direction. To complete the picture, one might add that it was the defiant Tibetan resistance—could it be at the behest, or indeed instigation of the Chinese?[34]—to this 'concession' which made Peking wriggle out of its earlier commitment. That the fact of Chinese authority had given place to the fiction of Chinese control, is patent enough and yet significantly the fiction itself was now being hugged. It was convenient and useful to the Chinese: any open confession that their control did not exist would be dangerous to prey-hungry wolves, who stood waiting at the door-step and were only too anxious to seize any such opportunity. To the Tibetans it came handy too for the growth of a strongly-entrenched British power, along the entire length of their southern border, presented the most serious threat to their independence. Protestations of Chinese supremacy would thus put off the evil day of an inconvenient, direct encounter. Besides, to acknowledge what Mr. Richardson has aptly called the "politico-mystical aura of he empire",[35] did not amount to a heavy, unbearable yoke, but a near-complete ndependence in all spheres of activity.

In the light of the above, the often-repeated question whether it were the Chinese who deliberately kept the Tibetans secluded, or whether the Tibetans :hemselves desired seclusion, becomes a purely academic exercise.[36] Left to :hemselves, the Chinese did not encourage intercourse with the outside world, for :he Middle Kingdom was self-sufficient and, therefore, shunned trade or commerce with the Western barbarians. Again, of their own the Tibetans never protested more violently than when the foreigners, including the Chinese themselves, showed the least propensity to interference in their affairs. Years later, Lord Curzon was to call the Sino-Tibetan relationship 'a political affectation' which had only been maintained because of its mutual convenience to both parties.[37]

To take up the thread of the narrative, the Convention on Burma, in 1886, had provided for the countermanding of the Macaulay Mission "inasmuch as an inquiry into the circumstances by the Chinese Government had shown the existence of many obstacles" to its fruition. That this was not only a tribute to the strength of Tibetan feeling on the subject, but also a measure of the bankruptcy of Chinese authority on Lhasa, was clear to any but the most casual of observers. The Tibetans, however, as was briefly noticed earlier, because of their ignorance of the true state of affairs drew the obvious, yet palpably wrong, conclusion that Britain was weak and unable to assert itself.[38] And insofar as they still regarded Sikkim to be a part of their domain, they crossed the Jelap la in force and built a fort at Lingtu (inside Sikkim) to block, or in any case forestall, Macaulay's armed escort of two hundred men.[39] This was in the autumn of 1886, when Macaulay was bemoaning his being 'shipwrecked within sight of the promised land'. On the other hand, Lingtu was strategic and, in the words of Buckland, could 'block the road, and... command the steep downs below' in Jelap, 'where Tibetans pastured their sheep and cattle' during the summer.[40]

Consequent upon the Tibetans fortifying Lingtu, Sikkim was projected into the limelight and undoubtedly her role was destined to be the most pivotal. Much to British embarrassment, however, its young, 28-years old Maharaja, Thotab Namgyal, led by his masterful second wife, the daughter of a Tibetan official in Lhasa, had then been for some years residing in Chumbi—and this despite repeated (British) protests.[41] The injection of Tibetan troops into Lingtu, with what looked like the Maharaja's tacit approval, was viewed by the British as a clear violation of the Anglo-Sikkimese Convention of 1861[42] which, *inter alia,* forbade the ruler from allowing any alien troops passage through his country, much less permit him to cede or lease any part thereof. Lhasa, on the contrary, having always regarded the unilateral establishment of a British protectorate over the small, Himalayan Kingdom as a usurpation,[43] and thus convinced that in marching to Lingtu it was well within its rights, viewed this prospect with obvious satisfaction.

Meanwhile a battle royal was being waged between a Governor-General (Lord Dufferin) who, at best, was not over-enthusiastic about Macaulary's proposed venture and the frontier officials of a subordinate local Government, which was convinced that the Tibetans deserved 'exemplary punishment'. There was also Sir John Walsham, the British Minister in Peking who was sensitive to the Yamen's susceptibilities and Whitehall itself exposed to variegated pressures. Inside Parliament some inconvenient questions had been asked, and outside the Chambers of Commerce had shown a remarkable eagerness to push in. Yet Lord Dufferin was anxious to avoid a mention of Sikkim, for fear of a direct assertion of China's suzerainty over the state, and had hoped that the Maharaja could be persuaded to co-operate.[44] The latter, however, cowed down by events in neighbouring Bhutan, proved severely adamant. Meantime, the Bengal civilians were very vocal. The picture of Sikkim becoming a province of Tibet was painted in lurid colours and it was pointed out that this 'would react most formidably on the security of life and property' in neighbouring Darjeeling. Nor, in retrospect, should this appear to be an exaggeration. Sikkim is wholly south of the Himalayan watershed. Chumbi too is south, but there the watershed at Phari is imperceptible; there is no Kanchenjunga to guard the sub-continent.

That the Maharaja, wholly under the sway of his Tibetan wife, was also amenable to the powerful influence of the Chinese Amban is amply borne out. The former, a forceful character, was well-connected, as was noticed earlier, to a powerful Lhasa family; the latter had recently succeeded in bringing the rival Tongsa and Paro Penlops of Bhutan to their heels. At a meeting convened by the Amban in 1886 in the Chumbi valley, the ruler of Sikkim is reported to have said:

> From the time of..... all our Rajas and subjects have obeyed the orders of China …. In such a crisis (forced by the British crossing into his state territory), if you, as our old friend, can make some arrangements, even then in good and evil we will not leave the shelter of the feet of China and Tibet.... We all, king and subject, priests and laymen, honestly promise to prevent persons from crossing the boundary.[45]

Even after the Macaulay mission was recalled, the Tibetans continued to hold Lingtu—defending their territorial claims thereto which, in any case, were far from clearly defined. Nor did they stop there. For they went further, blocked all trade, levied taxes on the local population and showed no signs of leaving. To cap it all, the Maharaja still tarried on in the Chumbi valley while pressure on Calcutta, from the British tea-planters, continued to mount up. Indeed, the latter feared for their investment in what now seemed to them to become disputed territory.[46] Thus circumstanced, Lord Dufferin appears to have made up his mind to push back the Tibetans, for the situation had become seemingly impossible. The tidings disturbed the Tsungli Yamen which took serious exception to any such course of action by the British.[47] Driven to desperation, it dispatched urgent messages—destined never to reach the addressees—to the commander of the Lingtu garrison as well as the Dalai Lama, underlining the justice of the British case, and asking for compliance with an early withdrawal.

Chinese delaying tactics, as the British viewed them, continued. Truly, Peking's stakes were high. For, not only was Lama hierarchy to be supported, the lucrative

Szechuan-Tibet trade, which enjoyed much popular support, maintained but, what was more, dwindling Chinese prestige in Central Asia needed to be powerfully boosted. There was also great anxiety not to expose publicly China's helplessness in making the recalcitrant, if not defiant, Tibetans conform to Peking's wishes and herein presently the choice of the Thirteenth Dalai Lama (March 1888) was to inject into the situation a disturbing element. The British however, were in no mood to await China's convenience. Besides a year's (1888-87) dilly-dalling, a time-limit had been set Peking to ensure Tibetan withdrawal by March 15, 1888. Nothing happened. A letter had been written to the Tibetan commander at Lingtu too, which was later returned unopened. Another had been sent, in February 1888, to the Dalai Lama, but it brought no reply. On March 20 (1888), 2,000 British troops, commanded by Brigadier Graham, drove the Tibetans out of Lingtu and took up positions at Gnatong. Lhasa's irregular levies, which made two more attempts in the autumn, were repulsed with heavy losses while pursuing British troops advanced 12 miles inside Tibet and entered the Chumbi valley. Their withdrawal, however, was immediate and the occupation lasted barely a day. This prompt and decisive action which took place in September was to serve as a signal for the Tsungli Yamen which, though deeply aroused, was restrained by the thought of an unequal conflict with the British at the farthest end of its dominion. The Chinese embarrassment nevertheless was the greater as they had already 'ordered' their Amban at Lhasa to make the Tibetans pull out and effect a settlement.

Desultory negotiations now ensued. The British were anxious that Peking recognise their protectorate over Sikkim, a proposition for which the Chinese had shown no enthusiasm in the past, nor did they any now. Presently, Mortimer Durand, then Foreign Secretary to the Government of India, conducted some fitful parleys with the Amban, stationed in Lhasa. The latter was obstinate and, 'laughingly but meaningly', hinted that unless negotiations proved fruitful it might be 'a question of war between England and China'. The Foreign Secretary's retort was that such a state of hostilities 'would not be decided in Sikkim' which remark made the Amban 'shut up like a telescope' with profuse apologies for his 'joke'.[48]

The 'joke' apart, the chink in the armour was now sufficiently evident and this despite the Amban's clever ruse of secretly summoning the Deb Raja of Bhutan to be present at the meeting. As Durand put it,

> The Amban evidently dares not give way about the 'rights' of Tibet. 'He was' he said 'only a guest in Lhasa—not a master—and he could not put aside the real masters'. He has no force to speak of, and he knows the Tibetans have turned upon a Chinese Resident before now....[49]

The stalemate thus persisted. Exasperated, the British at one stage threatened to close the episode, so far as China was concerned, without any specific agreement.[50] This spurred Peking to a sudden spurt of activity. Broken once the talks finally led to the conclusion of the Anglo-Chinese Convention of 1890, which *inter alia* defined Sikkim's boundary as the water-parting of the Teesta (*Mochu* to the Tibetans), recognised Britain's protectorate over the state (viz, control over its internal administration and foreign relations) and gave a joint Anglo-Chinese gurantee of the frontier as laid down. Certain other issues, such as grazing rights for Tibetans in Sikkim, the mode of communication between the Indian and Tibetan authorities, and the question of trans-frontier trade were, however, left over to be decided later by a joint Anglo-Chinese commission.[51]

Of the three listed above, the real crux was the question of trade regulations and herein the two positions were diametrically opposed. The British had hoped that Indian tea would have unrestricted entry into Tibet—pressure from the Darjeeling tea planters had mounted with the years—while understandably Chinese opposition to such imports was unrelenting.[52] So indeed was their resistance to the British demand for a complete freedom of travel.[53] Finally, after months of haggling, the British insisted on the establishment of a trade mart at P'hari—although, in actual fact, they preferred Gyantse which, in the heart of the province of Tsang, was ideally located. As it turned out, the claim for Gyantse was not overly stressed, instead pressure was exerted for P'hari which seemed the natural emporium for goods from Lhasa, Shigatse and even Bhutan, the Deb Raja's country. The Chinese, however, aware of Tibetan resistance—and their own inherent suspicion of the British—were, at best, prepared to offer Yatung. Barely inside Tibet, this little town was to prove more an uninhabited narrow hole in a deep valley, which the Tibetans later successfully cut off, than as a centre for commercial intercourse.

With the question of a trade mart finally disposed, and Yatung was to be opened 'to all British subjects from the first day of May, 1894' (Art. I), other issues were quickly resolved. Thus the right of extra-territorial jurisdiction for British subjects in the event of trade disputes with the Chinese or the Tibetans was accepted, it being laid down that these be inquired into, and settled, in 'personal' conference, 'by the Political Officer in Sikkim and the Chinese Frontier Officer' (Art. VI). Trade in Indian tea, which had been the major bone of contention, was to be allowed 'at a rate of duty not exceeding that at which Chinese tea is imported into England', but traffic was not to be permitted during the first five years when other commodities were exempt (Art. IV). Communications with the Amban, and between the Chinese and Indian officials, were regulated (Arts. VII and VIII) though, significantly, not with the Tibetans. Again, pasturage was to be subject to such regulations 'as the British Government may, from time to time, enact for the general conduct of grazing in Sikkim' (Art. IX). Imports of arms, ammunition, military stores, salt and liquor, and intoxicating or narcotic drugs, may either be 'entirely prohibited or permitted on mutually agreeable conditions' (Art. III). Other goods while exempt from duty 'for a period of five years', as an experimental measures, were to be reported at the Customs offices in Yatung with full particulars of their 'description, quantity and value' (Arts. IV and V).[54]

Had the Trade Regulations been carried out Indo-Tibetan relations, more specifically mutual trade and commerce, might have developed fruitfully. Some Chinese writers have tried heroically, though not very successfully, to explain away the Tibetan refusal to accept or abide by the provisions incorporated in the

Convention of 1890, or the Regulations which came three years later. Thus it has been contended that the British demands were, in fact, too far-reaching for the Tibetans to accept, that the Chinese had not given 'proper thought' to the Tibetan opposition and the subsequent difficulties involved in enforcing the treaties, and finally that the Tibetans were completely ignorant both of international law and custom.[55] Another Chinese scholar maintains that, under the 1890-93 arrangements, while British subjects in Tibet were to enjoy various privileges, these were not to be reciprocally claimed by the Tibetans in Sikkim. Again, the Tibetans were being asked to abide by such regulations in regard to cattle-grazing in their former vassal state as the British would unilaterally lay down—an obviously indefensible position. The Tibetan refusal to accept the 1890 boundary was also attributed, among other things, to their belief that what had originally been Tibetan territory was now marked off as Sikkimese.[56]

Most of the points made in these 'explanations' have a grain of truth to sustain them, yet basic to the whole argument is the refusal to accept the fact that the agreements of 1890-93 were the result of long drawn-out negotiations and not a hurried *diktat* imposed by the British over the Chinese. Hence the attempt to wriggle out would seem to hide a real snag namely, that the Chinese did not appear to face up to some harsh realities. And the harshest of these was that while they had lost all control over Tibet, they continued to behave as if they still wielded absolute authority and could conclude the most binding of agreements on its behalf.

The British approach to the problem was complicated by a variety of considerations most of which far transcended the merely local in character. Thus the impending negotiations over delimiting the Pamir boundary involved, besides the British and the Afghans, Russian and Chinese interests as well. And in this case, at any rate, the British were keen that the Chinese, as opposed to the Russians, stake claims to the intervening territory. There was also the question of what has been called 'the preposterous Decennial Mission' which, under the Convention of 1886, was to be despatched by the Government of Burma to the Manchu Emperor. Hence, it has been maintained that 'with a view to gaining political objectives in these two spheres' Lord Lansdowne's Government had 'shown forbearance' on the question of the Trade Regulations.[57] In the Governor-General's view the agreement of 1890 with Sikkim was of value 'not so much on account of the commercial interests involved' but 'as an outward sign of neighbourly goodwill prevailing between the two empires'. It would thus seem that the British Government were, for reasons fairly obvious, fully prepared to endorse and accept the Chinese claims on Tibet implicit in the Convention of 1890 and the Trade Regulations that came three years later.

What exactly were British objectives? A good definition may be found in Riseley's *Gazetteer of Sikkim* written at about that time. The author noted that the British had 'not the slightest ambition to meddle in Tibet' which indeed lay 'on the other side of a great wall'. Nor were they under any illusion that the country was a 'modern Brynhilde, asleep in her mountain top' while the Viceroy was a Siegfried out to 'awaken her from the slumber of ages'. For basically, however valuable Tibet may have been from the point of view of the scientist and the researcher, 'who will deny that it would be a piece of surpassing folly to alienate a possible ally in China by forcing our way into Tibet', either on the plea of scientific curiosity or of dubious mercantile prospects.[58]

However self-denying the British objective may have appeared to be, there is little doubt that the settlement of 1890-93 contained within itself the seeds of a future conflict. For the Tibetans behaved as would anyone in their place: they simply ignored the agreements, maintaining that these lacked their consent. It would seem that for well-nigh a decade now (1886-93), so far as the British were concerned, 'the farce of Chefoo' was being re-enacted on a larger scale. To anticipate Curzon, was not Sino-Tibetan 'control-dependence' a palpable absurdity?

Meanwhile the Government of India hoped, and patiently waited, but even as it hoped and waited, the results it had anticipated did not come about. For two major conflicts developed. In the first place, in 1895, the Tibetans occupied certain areas on the Sikkim side of the border to which they had a very valid claim. As may be evident, the 1890 agreement incorporating the Teesta, and its watershed, within the Sikkimese boundary gave the British a legal right to the area above Giagong although this did severe violence to the historical arrangement which recognised Tibetan claims over it. Thus when it came to implementing the convention, by actual demarcation of the boundary, the Tibetans balked at the suggestion. Here was the crux and the real starting-point, of the Anglo-Tibetan conflict. Later, when the Tibetan authorities stationed their men at Dhankiala and Giagong, Bengal was visibly upset and instructed the Political Officer to point out to the Chinese the true, i.e., the legal, frontier. It was the Government of India which now interceded and directed Mr. White not to get involved in controversial matters but 'confine (himself) to trade affairs'.[59]

Another problem related to Yatung which, with all the limitations inherent in its location, was never really opened as a trade mart. As a matter of fact, the Tibetans built walls on their side to prevent anyone from coming down to meet the British Indian traders.

Luckily for the Tibetans, as also the Chinese, the then Governor-General Lord Elgin was, in regard to this part of the frontier at any rate,[60] the embodiment of a policy of patient-waiting rather than of precipitate action. In a letter to the Secretary of State, the Government of India underlined the need for such patience in dealing with the Tibetans and observed that it was as yet premature to lodge a formal protest against their 'obstructiveness'. Lord Elgin, however, was prepared to bring the fact of Tibetan occupation of the disputed area to the notice of the Amban. When the Lieutenant-Governor of Bengal advocated a 'go-alone' policy, of ignoring both the   Chinese and the Tibetans, the supreme Government took care to point out that 'no inconvenience' was caused as a result of 'non-demarcation'. Letter, when the   Tibetans demolished the Jelap la boundary pillars and the Political Officer advocated reparations, Lord Elgin's

Government over-ruled him and noted that the Amban be given another opportunity to bring the recalcitrant Tibetans round to see reason.[61]

In retrospect, it is clear that the Viceroys's whole approach was in such sharp contrast to the precipitate urgency to which he was exposed. He recognised that the Tibetans had a 'reasonable' claim to the area into which they had moved,[62] that the 1890 treaty did not provide for pillars along the frontier and that no very serious damage had been to British trade from an undemarcated[63] frontier. While his detractors condemned the policy as one of 'conciliation' and 'forbearance',[64] apologists could point to the fact that British trade with Tibet had continued to mount up and that it had actually expanded nearly 500 per cent as between 1890 and 1898.[65]

Notes

1. A belief persisted in Tibet that the British had helped the Gurkhas in their war of aggression in 1792. Besides, there had been a gradual extension of British power in the states bordering Tibet, not to speak of the growing activities of Christian missionaries in these areas. 'And so whether in accordance with Chinese policy or not Tibet, after 1792, deliberately closed its doors to foreigners'. Richardson, *op.cit.*, p. 71.

2. Manning, who was a scholar of Chinese, is reported to have acquired his medical knowledge, in six months, in a London hospital. Graham Sandberg: *The Exploration of Tibet* (London, 1904), p. 116. Markham in his biographical sketch of Manning, 'Narratives', *op.cit.*, pp. clv-clxi, makes no mention of this except in a footnote (p. clvii) wherein he (Manning) is listed as 'one of many doctors' who applied to go to China in 1806.

3. For his audiences, see 'Narratives', *op.cit.*, pp. 265-67 and 288-91. See also Sir Olaf Caroe, 'Englishmen in Tibet', *op.cit.*, pp. 2-3.

4. *Ibid.*, p. 218, Markham's annotation herein is to the effect that Manning might have been given a simple passport by the Government of India, recommending him to the good offices of the authorities without any other official recognition.

5. Taraknath Das, *British Expansion in Tibet* (Calcutta, 1927), p. 6. Dr. Yaoting Sung seems to suggest that Manning's mission was officially sponsored, he (Manning) being Lord Minto's instrument when 'he (Minto) resumed Lord Hastings' (*sic*) unfinished task of opening Tibet for British trade'. The Chinese scholar's obvious reference is to Warren Hastings. Yaoting Sung, *Chinese-Tibetan Relations, 1890-1847* (a thesis submitted to the faculty of the University of Minnesota, 1949), p. 15. Markham, *op.cit.*, p. clvii, quotes from a letter written to Lord Minto by the Select Committee at Canton: 'as we consider Mr. Manning eminently qualified for the task he has undertaken, we anxiously hope Your Lordship will not consider him improper to afford Mr. Manning every practicable assistance in the prosecution of his plans'.

6. 'Narratives', *op.cit.*, p. clix.

7. *Ibid.*, p. 265.
   In talking to the Dalai Lama, then a mere child: 'He addressed himself in the Tibetan language to the interpreter, the Chinese interpreter to my Munshi, my Munshi to me in Latin. I gave answer in Latin which was converted and conveyed back in the same language'. *Ibid.*, p. 266.

8. 'Narratives', *op.cit.*, p. 274.

9. *Ibid.*, p. 273.

10. Younghusband has expressed the view that Manning was a private adventurer who went up in spite of and against the wishes of the then Government of India and puts his failure to this 'disgust' at Government's refusal to support him. Younghusband, *op.cit.*, pp. 33 and 39.

11. The Chefoo (or Yeutai) Convention which was forced by Britain on the occasion of the murder of interpreter Margary on the Burmese border (1875), opened ten additional ports and improved the status of foreigners in China.
    At the time of its ratification by Britain in 1885, additional articles relating to opium traffic were incorporated. For details, see H. B. Morse, *International Relations of the Chinese Empire* (New York, 1918), 3 Vols., II, pp. 303-15, and S. T. Wang. *The Margary Affair and the Chefoo Agreement* (Oxford, 1940).

12. A recent study of these states, for most part geographical, is Pradyumna P. Karan and William M. Jenkins. *The Himalayan Kingdoms* (Princeton, 1963).

13. Actually, these two became tehsils of the Kangra district and functioned as such until early in 1963 when they emerged as full-fledged, independent districts.

14. The Darjeeling district was acquired from the Maharaja of Sikkim in 1835 and, as part of the settlement with Bhutan in 1865, the Kalimpong area was attached to British India. Farther to the east, a series of agreements beginning in 1844 with the chiefs of the little-known hill-tribes living between the plains of Assam and the west of the Himalayas were concluded.

15. 'The Government of the Dalai Lama did not exercise direct authority in Ladakh, Sikkim, Bhutan or any area south of the Himalayas except for the Chumbi valley; but the ties of religious homage, trade, racial affinity and the degree of common interest had given Lhasa a special position and influence'. Richardson, *op.cit.*, pp. 73-74.

16. For details see *General Report on the Operations of the Great Trigonometrical Survey of India during* 1866-67 by Colonel J. T. Walker, pp. i-xxix; *Ibid.* (during 1867-68), pp. i-x; *Ibid.* (during 1871-72) by Major T. G. Montgomerie; *Ibid.* (during 1873-74) by Colonel J. T. Walker, pp. i-x. The first (1866) to go was Pandit 'A' (Nain Singh) who repeated his journey with another (Pandit 'C') in 1867. A later one (1871-72) was No. 9 and then another known as 'D' (famous as A. K. or Krishna) in 1873-74.

17. Markham, writing in 1875, tells us that these men were selected with the greatest care, that they have added 'very materially' to our knowledge not only of the country's geography but of the condition of its people and the state of trade; that they, in fact, deserved the highest praise for their 'painstaking accuracy, perseverance and gallant adventurous spirit'. 'Narratives', *op.cit.*, p. cxviii. Also see Holdich, *Tibet, the Mysterious* (New York, 1906), pp. 231-32 and Waddell, *op.cit.*, pp. 8-9.

18. At the Bhutan Boarding School, established at Darjeeling, with Sarat Chandra Dass as its Headmaster, 'Tibetan and semi-Tibetan lads' were to add to their general knowledge. Besides, 'technical training as Surveyors', which was designed to help the exploration of Tibet through the Survey Department, was also imparted. This apart they received an intensive course of training and were equipped, besides money and clothing, with a strong wooden box, a specially concealed secret drawer for holding observing instruments, a prayer wheel with rolls of blank paper instead of prayers in the barrel, on which observations might be noted and lamaic rosaries by the beads of which each hundred paces might be counted, Sandberg, *op.cit.*, pp. 143-144 and 163. Bell was informed by the Tibetan Prime Minister in 1910 that Sarat Chandra Dass' clandestine entry and surreptitious inquiries led to severe punishment, including loss of life and

property, being meted to a host of people among them officials at the barrier-gates and even incarnate lamas, which was 'a most unusual perhaps unprecedented occurrence in Tibet'. Bell, *Tibet*, p. 59.

19. For details, see Graham Sandberg, *op.cit.* Sandberg should, however, be accepted with a good deal of caution.

20. Colman Macaulay was the 'brilliant' Secretary of the Bengal Government. Chosen to lead the mission to China through Tibet and with all formalities completed for his departure, Macaulay had keyed himself up for this expedition to a remarkable degree. Later, when 'imperial' interests dictated its abandonment, he seems to have taken his disappointment seriously to heart and died a few years later—a broken man.

21. Lord Rosebery, in a speech in the House of Lords: 'I shall never forget the anguish ... with which the Chinese Government pressed on us the abandonment of that expedition, and the abandonment of that expedition was one of the main factors in securing the convention concerning Burma'. *Parliamentary Debates*, Vol. 130, p. 1140.

22. Sir Edward Hertslets, *China Treaties*, 3rd ed., I (London, 1908), p. 89.

23. 'Macaulay was obsessed about opening Tibet. He was always wanting to share his hopes with the whole world'. Actually, he had sought permission to publish a full account and it is believed that he may have been responsible 'even if indirectly' for the publication, in February 1886 and subsequently, of details of the size of the escort. Alastair Lamb: *Britain and Chinese Central Asia* (London, 1960), p. 171.

24. The Tibetans instigated by the Nechung State Oracle occupied Lingtu, some 18 miles within the Sikkim border. Meanwhile, the Maharaja 'a Tibetan at heart, heaving married a pure Tibetan wife' had been residing inside Tibet—and this despite British 'remonstrates and expostulations'. Letter from Lord Dufferin cited in Sir Alfred Lyall, *The Life of the Marquess of Dufferin and Ava* (London, 1905), 2 Vols., II, p. 136.

25. It is evident that the then Governor-General, Lord Dufferin was far from enthusiastic about the mission for, in fact, he thought it 'had been imposed upon' him by Lord Randolph Churchill, then Secretary of State for India. Later, when Tibetan opposition seemed certain, he (Dufferin) was willing to beat a retreat. Sir A. Lyall, Dufferin, *op.cit.*, II, pp. 132-33 and Charles E. Drummond Black. *The Marquess of Dufferin and Ava* (London, 1913), p. 261.

26. Bell, *Tibet*, p. 60.

27. Lady Betty Balfour (ed.), *Personal and Literary Letters of ... Earl of Lytton* (London, 1906), 2 Vols., II, p. 200.

28. '... the fact cannot be ignored that as traders they came to make economic gains and as rulers they had the same aim. The gains they made and their effect on the economic life of the people... is the most important subject in an assessment of British rule'. Ram Gopal, *British Rule in India: on assessment* (Bombay, 1963), p. vii. For a candid survey, see Penderel Moon, *Strangers in India* (London, 1945). *Bania* is a Hindi word for a retailer or petty shop-keeper.

29. Reischauer and Fairbank, *op.cit.*, p. 392. The Rebellion 'was finally suppressed in 1804, but already it had signalized the downward turn in the Ch'ing fortunes'. It may be noted that this was long before the pressure of the Western 'barbarians' was to become formidable.

30. Harold M. Vinacke, *A History of the Far East in Modern Times* (New York, 1950) in dealing with China gives this as his chapter heading (pp. 146-63) for the period 1894-1901.

31. '... it revealed the inability of the Imperial Government to carry out its primary duty of preserving peace and order in the country. Such a rebellion even when unsuccessful, is usually the harbinger of the end of a dynasty... it is not going too far from the facts to say that the successful revolt against the Manchus in 1911 was begun in the middle of the preceding century'. *Ibid.*, p. 68.

32. Owen and Eleanor Lattimore, *The Making of Modern China* (Washington, 1944), p. 123.

33. Actually, the force employed to repel Zorawar Singh's invasion of western Tibet was entirely Tibetan, nor had any troops arrived from China. Yet the fact that the Treaty of 1842 mentions 'the Khagan of China', besides the 'Lama Guru Sahib of Lhasa' has led the unwary to conclude that the Tibetans 'with the aid of the Chinese troops despatched by the Chinese Emperor' had invested Leh. For the text, see Aitchison, *op.cit.* For the quotation, *Report of the Officials of the Government of India and the People's Republic of China on the Boundary Question* (New Delhi, 1961), part II, p. 52. Richardson, *op. cit.*, p. 72, states categorically that the force was 'purely Tibetan, although it has sometimes been wrongly described as 'Chinese'.'

34. Charles E. Drummond Black, *op.cit.*, p. 262, talks of Chinese connivance, while Alfred Lyall, Dufferin, *op.cit.*, pp. 134-36 cites a letter from Count 'Bela Szechenyi ('an experienced informant') to Lord Dufferin alleging that a hundred large boxes filled with European gunpowder were sent from China' to the aid of assembled Tibetan troops in the Chumbi valley to resist Macaulay's much-advertised mission.

35. Richardson, *op.cit.*, p. 72.

36. Cammann, *op.cit.*, p. 144. Younghusband, India and Tibet, *op.cit.*, pp. 415-16 and Teichman, *op.cit.*, p. 19, maintain that China deliberately kept Tibet isolated and secluded; whereas O'Connor, *op.cit.*, p. 48 thinks China was a 'very convenient stalling horse' behind which the Tibetans could shelter invincible distrust of Europeans and their methods.

37. *Infra*, Chapter XI.

38. 'After Macaulay had retired ... the Lamas, soldiers and the population massed on the passes shouted 'Victory', living in the idea that they had frightened the Government of the Empress of India. Their boldness and audacity had no limit ... such affronts done to the mightiest Power demand an exemplary satisfaction'. Letter to Lord Dufferin from *count* Bela Szechenyi, cited in Lyall, Dufferin, *op.cit.*, II, p. 136.

39. Lingtu, at a height of 12,000-13,000 feet, lies astride the trade route from India, through Sikkim, to Tibet over the Jelap-la.

40. For the earlier citation, Younghusband, *op.cit.*, p. 47, for the latter, C. Buckland, *Bengal under the Lieutenant Governors* (Calcutta, 1901). II, p. 847.

41. White, *op.cit.*, p. 22.

42. For the text, see Aitchison, *op.cit.*, XII.

43. Till the end of the 18th century, Sikkim was practically a dependency of Tibet where its ruler was designated Governor of Sikkim', *Encyclopaedia Britannica*, Vol. XX, p. 650, a position that has been seriously challenged, *Supra*, Note 14. Actually the present reigning (Namgayal) dynasty, claiming descent from one of the Gyalpos of Eastern Tibet, goes back to 1641. A vigorous defence of Tibetan advance is developed in Das, *op.cit.*, R. C. Majumdar, *History and Culture of the Indian People, op.cit.*, IX, p. 1070 is unequivocal: 'The leaders and people of Sikkim were mostly pro-Tibetan, and as they did not ask for British help, nor desired it, there was no ostensible ground for interference by the British'.

44. White, *op.cit.*, p. 19, reveals that during his first visit to Sikkim in November 1887, his (and Mr. A. W. Paul's) mission was 'to try and induce the Maharaja to return from

Chumbi ... and to spend more time in his own country'.
45. H. H. Riseley (ed.), *Gazetteer of Sikkim* (Calcutta, 1894), p. 126. The Maharaja, of course, did not oblige and this despite the fact that his annual subsidy was stopped.
46. *Ibid.*, pp. xv-xvi.
47. Charles H. Drummond Black, *op.cit.*, pp. 262-64. It is necessary to recall that influence in Lhasa was of the greatest value to the Manchus for its impact on the Mongols. For 'to tame' them (Mongols) with the Yellow Religion was 'China's best policy'. E. H. Parker, 'Wei Yuan on the Mongols'. *Journal, North China Branch of the Royal Asistic Society,* XXII (1887), p. 101.
48. Sir Percy Sykes, *Sir Mortimer Durand: a Biography* (London, 1926), p. 166.
49. *Ibid.*, p. 167.
50. *East India (Tibet) Papers Relating to Tibet*, Cd. 1920 (London, 1904), No. 1, p. 1; cited et seq., as *Tibet Papers.*
51. Tibet Papers, *op.cit.*. No. 5, pp. 6-7. For the full text, see Appendix.
52. *Ibid.*, No. 8. The Government of India felt that Chinese opposition had placed them 'in a false position towards the planters and the trading community in general'.
53. *Foreign Department, Secret E, Proceedings,* August 1893, No. 44; cited, *et. seq.,* as *Foreign.*
54. Called 'Regulations Regarding Trade, Communication and Pasturage to be appended to the Sikkim-Tibet Convention of 1890', the document was signed at Darjeeling on December 5, 1893, by A. W. Paul for the Indian government and James Hart (brother of the Imperial Commissioner) and Ho Chang-jung for the Chinese. For the full text, see Appendix.
55. Yao-ting Sung, *op.cit.*, pp. 24-25.
56. Tieh-tseng Li, *The Historical Status of Tibet* (New York, 1956), pp. 79-80. A revised edition, *Tibet: Today and Yesterday* was published in 1960. References in the text are to the earlier edition.
57. *Foreign,* August 1893, No. 44.
58. Riseley, *op.cit.*, pp. xii-xiii.
59. *Foreign,* October 1894, No. 129.
60. Thus it may be noted that on the north-west, Elgin got Government involved in the fiercest and most protracted fighting with the Pathan tribes that ever took place, viz., the 1897-98 frontier wars.
61. *Ibid.*, July 1895, Nos. 103-4.
62. Tibet Papers, *op.cit.*, No. 16, p. 52.
63. *Ibid.*, No. 13, p. 25. These boundary pillars had been built by zealous British 'frontier' officers and destroyed by infuriated Tibetans. Their (Tibetan) 'aggression' was regarded as sufficient reason for 'strong action, against the offenders'. Younghusband, *op.cit.*, pp. 59-65.
64. Younghusband could barely conceal his dissatisfaction: '... nothing could have been milder, more patient and more forbearing and also, as it proved, less effectual'.
65. Trade figures, as officially released, were:

1890-91	:	Rs. 3, 80, 081
1884-95	:	Rs. 11,49,150
1897-98	:	Rs. 17,03,060

Tibet Papers, *op.cit.*, pp. 50 and 73.

URZON, TIBET'S DALAI LAMA AND CZARIST RUSSIA

6
Curzon's Early Years and India

remarkable change that took place when Lord Elgin handed over the reins of
ce to his successor Lord Curzon,[1] early in 1899, was nowhere better illustrated
in the new Viceroy's approach towards Tibet. Herein from a policy of 'patient
ting' there was now as it were an abrupt shift to one of 'impatient hurry'. It is this
ent break with the past, and the developments consequent thereupon, that form
subject-matter of the present study. Before examining these, however, it may be
antageous to size up the man who played so pivotal a role in the Tibetan drama.
he lesser *dramatis personae*, the part played by the 13th Dalai Lama was equally
ificant for undoubtedly there was something in the personality of the Tibetan
tiff that invited the wrathful visitation of this powerful potentate of British
ia.

George Nathaniel, the first and as it happened the last Marquess Curzon of
dleston, was no stranger to India, or the East, at the time he assumed the
eroyalty. Indeed, as he later confessed, India had 'haunted him like a passion'
n from his infancy, a passion that was to persist for the rest of his mortal
stence. This 'fascination and ... sacredness of India', of its people, its history, its
vernment, above all 'the absorbing mystery of its civilization and its life' had
n born of his unbounded enthusiasm for Britain's vast Asian Empire 'more
pulous, more beneficent and more amazing' than that of Rome.[2]

Apart from his preoccupation with the Empire and its civilizing mission, which
ne to him early in life and grew with the years, the young Curzon displayed from
very infancy a remarkable power for hard work and a rare maturity of the mind.
contemporary at school, Lord Esher held that Curzon remained to the last an Eton
y: 'brilliant, broadminded, lavish of his endowments ... mature at 18'.[3] The Eton
pact was apparent and in more ways than one for the school also gave him his
e-long affliction: a curvature of the spine [4] which because of the iron corset that
ielded it introduced into his mental make-up a degree of impatience, a marked
itability of temperament.[5]

An epithet that he earned in his early years and that stuck to him until late in life
s that of 'superior'. It was noticed that as a young boy he displayed a degree of

self-confidence that bordered on the boisterous, if not indeed the bumptiou studied intolerance towards all opposition, most of which he viewed as perso and an assumption of airs and graces which, in an undergraduate democracy seer to verge on the ridiculous. No wonder he was the subject of many a doggerel : student and later, in his long public life, of as much misunderstanding and criticis To the average man, Curzon seemed 'above average'—as someone, therefore, be derided and condemned'.[7]

Yet, he had his compensations too. His application and 'superior' knowle of men and affairs, though it taxed his physique, earned him many an honour : even 'some real distinctions'.[8] Thus at Eton he was the President of the Liter Society and Captain of the 'Oppidans', at Balliol he won the much-coveted Loth and Arnold Prize essays. Oxford also gave him the proud Presidentship of its Un reckoned then as now, a nursery for future statesmen. And barely had he reacl twenty-four summers when he was elected a Fellow of All Souls.

Nor, after college, did he rest long on his oars for was not his education, be of foreign travel, somewhat incomplete with the sharp ends of mere academ knowledge still to be rounded off? And characteristically, Curzon took to his r 'instruction' with the singular thoroughness, which he had applied to the old. T between December 1882 and February 1895, hardly did a year pass without r ambitious young man, despite his serious physical disability of a curved spin face up to the most arduous travels in far off lands.[10] Apart from his two around t world trips in 1888 and in 1894, he visited, in the course of his extensive journe most of Central Asia, Persia, Afghanistan, the Pamirs and a great deal of wha common parlance was then the Far East: Japan, China, Korea, Indo-China and Si: From these travels too came his early books: *Russia in Central Asia in 1*: appeared in that very year; next came, in 1892, the formidable ('1300 pages an pound weight of solid print') 2-volume study of *Presia and the Persian Quest* which he always regarded as his *chef d'oeuvre;* followed, another couple of ye later, by his *Problems of the Far East.*[11] And although Curzon had contributec well-known journals before, the vigour of his style, the virility and force of conviction as revealed in[12] what now appear to be ponderous tomes, went a l(way towards establishing his reputation as a keen observer of Asian affairs.

Besides much else, Curzon's books represented what was to become increasin characteristic of the man: concentrated application on the one hand and a disti (Curzonian) approach to Asian problems on tne other. One of his contemporar who was then very close to him, tells us that the young author sat through th consecutive nights to complete one of his works (*viz. Problems of the Far East* time for his projected journey to Afghanistan.[13] Thomas Hardy, the novelist, p Curzon a generous encomium when he (Hardy) commended his (Curzor 'monumental' two volumes on Persia for the 'art of labour and enterprise and value to investigators of the facts acquired', which put 'some of us scribblers shame!'[14] It may be recalled that this book contained a map which Curzon k compiled himself and which is said to have been the standby of eastern Pundits many years and reportedly guided the Defence Committee of the British Cabinet in their Persian difficulties.[15] A none-too-friendly reviewer praised his *Russia in Central Asia* by conceding that for a long time there had not been 'so forcible a description of the life of other peoples and of other lands', while another critic described him as a traveller and observer 'of merit and mettle'.[16] In the bargain—and it was a heavy price to pay by all counts—his back gave him 'more severe and constant pain' and he ruined his health for good.[17]

Both by birth and upbringing Curzon's political philosophy was that of a young Tory who was strongly convinced that both tradition and education marked him out as the aristocrat, born to rule. Indeed an American admirer who was Curzon's contemporary at Oxford summed him up as 'my ideal' of what a specimen of the Conservative, and especially the party of privilege should be. It was 'the aristocratic turn' of Curzon's disposition which 'forcibly struck' him and which hitherto he had never seen exemplified.[18] Again, in a letter in May 1881, Brodrick described Curzon as 'that eloquent-tongued, pertinent-visaged, decrier of maidens ... on whom the Tory hopes are fixed in the county of Derby ... '[19] His place indeed seemed to be well marked out for him and if early in his political career he hitched his wagon from Randolph Churchill to Lord Salisbury, the reasons would appear to be far more personal than ideological.[20]

Since his thinking on Asian, and principally Russian problems acquired shape and content at about this time and was to assume greater importance, if notoriety, in the years ahead, it may be well worthwhile to spell it out here.

Basic to Curzon's approach to Asia was his view of Russia's position in the east. Here he was convinced that the growth of the Czar's Asian dominion had been marked by a continuous, almost inexorable, expansion which followed repeated acts of aggression against neighbouring lands. At the same time he conceded that Russia's advance, especially in Central Asia, was of a 'compulsory' nature, as it took place 'in the absence of any great obstacle', and in the face of an enemy whose rule of life was 'depredation' and who understood no diplomatic logic but defeat.[21] Two other factors had aided, and abetted, the Czarist spillover : one, its frontier officers had persisted in forging ahead, sometimes in open disregard of official instructions and two, the 'gullible'—and to Curzon's way of thinking inexcusable— acceptance by the British of repeated acts of Russian duplicity and *mala fide*.[22] No wonder against his own people he felt a sense of righteous indignation for, alone possessed of the power to stop the Russian advance, they 'deliberately declined to exercise it'.

And what were Russia's objectives? The young Curzon did not indeed suggest that St. Petersburg aimed at the conquest of India, or that Calcutta was the dream of Russian ambitions. Its real goal, he was convinced, was access to the warm waters of the Bosphorus, a goal that could be won 'not on the heights of Plevna, but on the banks of the Helmund'.[23] In his own words, the be-all and end-all of Russian policy was 'to keep England quiet in Europe by keeping her employed in Asia'.[24]

But the 'warm waters' of the Bosphorus apart, Russia was seeking an outlet on the Persian Gulf too. To convince his readers that Russian designs against India were not 'the figment of a biased imagination', nor yet a Russian invasion 'outside the region of endeavour',[25] Curzon cited at length from the writings of the well-known Russian general, Skobeloff.[26] Nor did he stop there. With a thoroughness and attention to meticulous detail that was so characteristic of him, he traced at length the Russian schemes of (India's) invasion from the times of Catherine the Great to those of Alexander III, laying a special emphasis on the (Skobeloff) plan of 1878, and showing how precise it was and how the Russian Government had sought to give effect to it.[27]

It would fall outside the limited scope of this brief survey to emulate the author of these works in his fairly exhaustive analyses. It may, however, suffice to say that Curzon described at length the probable routes which a Russian invasion of India could take, the eventualities that Britain would be up against, and the remedies that lay ready to hand.[28] It may also be relevant to refer, however briefly, to his two volumes on Persia and to point out that here too he saw the Russian Colossus preparing gradually to eat up the whole of that country. Indeed, he viewed Russia's position along the entire 1,000 miles from the Aras to the Tejend as one of 'overwhelming superiority'[29] and Russian 'claims and pretensions' in Persia as 'distinctly, and in parts, avowedly hostile'.[30]

To face up to this mortal threat, what was Curzon's remedy? As one pages through his voluminous writings the answer rings clear, if also with a remarkable degree of repetitiousness, added to a good deal of rigidity in thinking and approach. In sum, it may be spelt out thus: Britain must take up the gauntlet, as she alone could, against further Russian encroachments and then strike, should the warning go unheeded. Curzon was convinced, and noted in a language that admitted of little ambiguity—and what was more 'I say with a full consciousness of my responsibility'—that if Russia were not to be checked 'the position of India will be less secure, the defence of India much more difficult, the financial burdens imposed upon India much greater, the independence of India of European politics much more precarious'. Nor was that all, for 'Russia will not bargain where she thinks that she has only to hold out in order to win'. And thereby he posed what was to him, the pivotal question: 'Is not the point, therefore, in sight at which we should make up our minds as to the line at which the advance of Russian interests and influence would halt?'[31] How unmistakable was Curzon's stand is revealed by Lord Salibury's oft-repeated complaint:

> Curzon always wants me to talk to Russia as if I had 500,000 men at my back, and I have not.[32]

Complementary to his view of Russia, and the threat it posed, was the Curzonian rationale on the role of the British Empire. Pompously phrased, not by late-nineteenth century standards though, and yet unambiguous in its meaning, he summed it up in his inscription to the 'Problems of the Far East',

> ... that the British Empire is, under Providence, the greatest instrument for good that the world has ever seen ... [33]

To Curzon, England was Rome's inheritor—indeed it has been said that the admonition of Anchises echoed eternally in his ears[34]—and the Empire a complete expression of the English system. The creed of empire-building was for him not a partisan but a national faith, a faith that evoked and satisfied his sense of race superiority, of race achievement, even of individual justification.[35] That at an impressionable age his imagination was afire with this peculiar pride few who read him can doubt. Thus at 28:

> No Englishman can land at Hong Kong—without feeling a thrill of pride for his nationality. Here is the furthermost link in the chain of fortresses which from Spain to China, girdles half the globe.[36]

But aside from the mere emotional and the sentimental, Curzon's concept of the Empire called forth the more serious and the professional traits as well. Not only was he convinced that 'the best hope of salvation for the old and moribund in Asia' lay in the 'ascendancy of British character, and under the shelter, where so required, of British dominion', but he was equally clear that 'moral failure alone' could shatter the prospect that thereby awaited England.[37] The Empire thus was a 'romance' no doubt, but it was also a 'responsibility'—and one that demanded a deep sense of sacrifice, of justice, of duty. Thus, as a mandatory of the Divine Will, ennobled by its mission of self-sacrifice and virtue, the Empire in checking Russian advance would but be furthering its own (God-given) mission. For one who had so little of the extraneous trappings of religion, how deeply religious was Curzon's imperialism! How fanatically unbending too!

The budding conservative's views on Asian problems in general, and the role of Russia in particular, underwent little change even when his books grew older. Indeed, it has been maintained that 'most of Curzon's basic convictions, the articles of his faith, were absorbed before he left Eton in 1878'.[38] Lord Ronaldshay has successfully traced these back to his school days when he debated the proposition: 'Are we justified in regarding with equanimity the advance of Russia towards our Indian Frontier?'[39]

That he expressed them forcefully when he became Under-Secretary for Foreign Affairs, after a brief tenure at the India Office, is a matter of record.[40] Lord Salisbury, his political patron, who was then Prime Minister and Foreign Secretary, did not share his apprehensions, nor did for that matter many of his friends who felt that Curzon's 'special obsession' as to the advance of Russia in Central Asia, 'marred' his judgement.[41] This near-complete divergence in the two viewpoints, which was apparent so early, was of a fundamental character and is well summed up by Curzon's biographer in these words:

> He (Curzon) was always more ready than Lord Salibury to adopt a policy which depended upon its success upon a willingness to appeal in the last resort to arms. This difference ... was the outcome to a great extent of temperament. George Curzon's gaze was fixed on the goal which he wished to reach rather than on the ground that intervened. He was impatient of obstacles standing in the way and a little inclined, therefore, unduly to discount them .... Lord

Salisbury brought a cold, critical mind and a dispassionate judgement to bear upon the difficulties to be encountered.[42]

Since the gaze, and the goal, remained constant so did his unsparing criticism of the Foreign Office and its entire approach. Thus on December 29, 1899, Curzon, now Viceroy, wrote to Lord Salisbury :

Does not the point at which our interests are threatened and at which retaliation may become necessary arise when we know for certain that some other power has appropriated some portion of Chinese soil?[43]

Or a year later, and to the same correspondent :

Russia is always willing to leave a rotten power on its legs while we have a disagreeable lust for reform that with a reluctant patient, sometimes ends in absorption.[44]

But with St. John Brodrick, who had taken up Curzon's now earlier incumbency at the Foreign Office he could be more forthright:

We have never had and we have not (now) any policy towards China .... No one knows better than you or I who have successively had to conjure up make-believes. But, or course, the supreme lesson of the Foreign Office is that there is no pre-determined policy about anything.[45]

Nor did his views undergo any modification, much less a change, on Central Asia which he viewed as that 'theatre of Imperial diplomacy possibly—*quod di omen avertant*—as the threshold, of international war'.[46] Thus in 1899 he reminded one of his correspondents :

In 1889 I wrote a chapter in may book on *Russia in Central Asia*, upon Anglo-Russian relations and the future that lay before them in Asia, and although that chapter is eleven years old, I do not think that there is a statement of opinion in it that I would now withdraw or a prediction that has so far been falsified.[47]

Was this adamantine, unbending rigidity the cause of 'his greatest disaster'— namely, the end of his Indian Viceroyalty? Could it also be the reason for much that contributed to that 'sublime failure' in a career otherwise so scintillating?

Before touching on Curzon's tenure as Viceroy and Governor-General, it may be as well to refer to his views on India's place in the larger whole of the British Empire. That India haunted him like a passion and that its fascination, nay even sacredness, grew upon him very early in life has been commented upon.[48] But of what was this fascination born? How did this passionate attachment grow?

As he visualized it, Curzon's India was the political pillar, 'the true fulcrum' (to use his own words) of Britain's Asiatic dominion. In another context, he referred to it as the 'noblest trophy of the British genius and most splendid appanage of the Imperial Crown'.[49] The secret of the mastery of the world (viz., the empire of Hindustan) he wrote in the Preface to one of his books, 'is, if truly they knew it, in the possession of the British people'.[50] Nor was this merely an 'idle dream of fancy' but one 'capable of realization'. For he was convinced that Britain's position in India gave her the certain command of the main land-routes and the rail-roads that will lay open the Far East in the not too distant future.[51] Nor was Curzon the first of the proconsuls to echo these sentiments for, barely a half-century earlier Sir Charles Napier had rated Britain among nations 'what the Kohi-i-Noor is among diamonds', and asserted confidently that were he the King of India he 'would make Muscowa and Pekin shake !'[52]

It may be recalled that the India of Curzon's day was not the physically truncated state of today which passes under that name but an India that comprised Burma in the east and Aden and the Persian Gulf ports in the west. Without doubt the then Indian Empire was a continental order—'a political structure based on India and extending its authority from Aden to Hong Kong'.[53] This continental order, which involved only a subordinate participation of India, was symbolized by the Sikh policeman in the Shanghai Municipal concession and the large, and prosperous, Indian trading communities in Hong Kong, Malaya, Mauritius and Fiji, a sprawling 'overseas India' that pulsated with life. It was this Empire of Hindustan which caught the imagination of the youthful Curzon and never lost its charm and fascination for him. And insofar as he regarded the link that bound this Empire' to England as ordained by 'a higher law and a nobler aim', India to him always remained 'the highest touchstone of national duty'.[54] And thus it was that this 'romance of his youth and the consuming passion of his prime'[55] became an unforgettable memory of his declining years and he seemed ever to cast as it were a longing, lingering look back to his years in India.

Curzon's appointment as Viceroy and Governor-General, announced in the fall of 1898, and generally viewed as a well-deserved reward for his talent, had actually, though in behind the scenes activity, been assiduously sought after and worked for over a period of time. In Lord Salisbury's 'Papers' at Christ Church (Oxford) there are two letters which are revealing on this point. The first, written by Curzon and date-lined Berlin (April 17, 1897) puts forth his candidature and 'my wares ... in the shop-window' in no uncertain terms :

... I have for at least 10 years made a careful and earnest study of Indian problems, have been to the country four times and am acquainted with and have the confidence of most of its leading men ... the views or forecasts I have been bold enough to express have ... turned out to be right .... I have been fortunate too, in making the acquaintance of the rulers of the neighbouring states .... At the India Office .... I learned something of the official working of the great machine ... a very great work can be done by an English Viceroy who is young and active and intensely absorbed in his work ... (and who has) a great love of the country and pride in the Imperial aspect of its possession.

Nor was his 'strongest impulse' a personal one at all : 'it is the desire while one is still in the heyday of life to do some strenuous work in a position of responsibility for which previous study and training' may have rendered him a fit candidate.[56]

Salisbury's response must have been encouraging for even though he (Curzon) may not 'hear anything about the subject' to which his (Salisbury's) letter alludes, he (Curzon) was prepared to regard it 'as one of my most cherished possessions'.[57] A year later, however, he was still reminding his chief :

Perhaps unless you have already made or are about to make other and wiser arrangements you may let me have a word or two with you about it when you return.[58]

But probably the Prime Minister entertained, as did many others, serious doubts as to his physical capacity. For, in a letter on June 20, Curzon enclosed a certificate, which a certain Thomas Smith, F. R. C. S., wrote—'without consulting me in any way'—declaring that he (Thomas Smith) 'can find no sign of disease about him'.[59] And although the Prime Minister may have thrown discreet hints earlier, a definitive recommendation was now made to the Queen.[60] Curzon was fulsome in his praise and 'gratitude', for it 'will lend a distinction to the honour that the wining of no other prize in life could give'.[61]

Opinion, however, was sharply split. The influential (London) *Times* appeared to sum up the general reaction pithily when it expressed the hope—'for Mr. Curzon's sake and that of the Empire'—that Lord Salisbury's 'very interesting experiment' will succeed.[62] While his friends hailed the announcement as 'a great and truly merited advancement' ushering in 'a joyful chapter of history',[63] there were others who felt that the Viceroy-designate was 'inclined to ambition'.[64] A British civil servant in India called him an almost 'boy politician', reminiscing no doubt on the Younger Pitt's first tenure as Prime Minister, and remarked that what India needed most was 'patient level-headedness'.[65] St. Petersburg was, and for obvious reasons, gravely disturbed. For the press there depicted the new Viceroy as belonging to the most extreme Russophobe party and (as his books and articles were quite well known) expressed the fear that he was destined to apply his theories, now that he was vested with the requisite power and authority to do so.[66]

This somewhat rough and ready cross-section of current public thinking may afford a necessary corrective to an objective assessment of the new Viceroy's broad policies. Yet for a better understanding of his approach to Tibet it may be worthwhile to know something of his handling of the problems of the Persian Gulf, Afghanistan and, though to a limited extent, even the North-West Frontier. For not only do these furnish much of the ammunition for his critics but what is more provide keen students of his policies with the necessary background to his thinking about the land that lies athwart the Himalayas.

Notes

1:   George Nathaniel Curzon was the eldest son of Reverend Alfred Curzon, fourth Baron Scarsdale of Kedleston Hall in Derbyshire, and was born in January 1859. He was educated at Eton and later at Oxford, being elected a Fellow of All Souls in 1882. Between the latter year and 1885 he undertook two round-the-world trips, visiting most of the countries in Central Asia and the Far East. In 1891-92, he was Under-Secretary of State for India in Lord Salisbury's administration. Three years later, he became Under-Secretary of State for Foreign Affairs and a Privy Concillor, one of the youngest then to be inducted into the fraternity. Between 1898-1905 intervene the years of his Indian Viceroyalty, though his later return home meant political wilderness for well-nigh a decade.

In 1915, he was to emerge as Privy Seal in Lord Asquith's coalition cabinet and later in Mr. Lloyd George's war-time coalition. In January 1919, after the war had been won, he became acting Foreign Secretary to deputise for Balfour who was to accompany Lloyd George to Paris and succeeded the former in his post in October that year. For some time he retained this office under Mr. Bonar Law but on the latter's retirement missed—reaching within inches though—his life-long ambition of being Prime Minister. Mr. Stanley Baldwin appointed him Foreign Secretary, and in a later Cabinet, Lord President of the Council. But Curzon's day was done and he died in 1925. Apart from Lord Ronaldshay' (later Marquess of Zetland), *Life of Lord Curzon*, 3 vols. (London, 1928), cited hereinafter as *Life*; Sir Harold Nicolson, *Curzon, the Last Phase* (New York, 1939); and Lovat Fraser, *India under Curzon and After* (London, 1911) provide authoritative studies. Some critical sketches are Shane Leslie, *Studies in Sublime Failure* (London, 1932); E. T. Raymond, *Portraits of the New Century* (New York, 1921); and *28 Years in India* (Charles James O'Donnell), *The Failure of Lord Curzon in India* (London, 1903). For panegyrics, see H. Caldwell Lipsett, *Lord Curzon in India* (London, 1903) or Sardar Ali Khan, *Lord Curzon's Administration of India* (Bombay, 1905). The Earl of Midleton, *Records & Reactions* (London, 1939) and Sir Stanely Reed, *The India I Knew*, 1897-1947 (London, 1952) provide interesting sidelights on the man and his times as does that critical, if unsympathetic, study; Leonard Mosley, *Curzon, the End of an Epoch* (London, 1960). Of marginal interest are Austen Chamberlain, *Down the Years* (London, 1935) and *Politics from Inside* (London, 1936); Sir Harold Nocolson, *Some People* (London, 1951); Philip Magnus, *Kitchener* (London, 1958) and Kenneth Young, *Arthur James Balfour* (London, 1963).

2. Sir James Fitzjames Stephen's address to the Eton Society first attracted Curzon's thoughts to the Empire. See Lovat Frazer, *op.cit.*, p. 8, and Ronaldshay, *Life*, I, p. 28.

3. Cited in Shane Leslie, *op.cit.*, p. 186.

4. Strictly speaking it was between his departure from Eton at the beginning of August and his arrival at Oxford in October (1878) that Curzon first suffered a severe attack of the trouble with his back. The best medical advice, however, made it clear that it was due to his weakness of the spine 'resulting from natural weakness and overwork', Ronaldshay, *Life*, I, pp. 38-39. The weak spine had its origins in a fall from his horse in 1874 while riding in the woods near Kedleston, when school was closed for holidays.

5. In two long personal chats (July 1963) Sir Harold Nicolson impressed upon the author the fact that no assessment of Curzon could be complete without a realisation that he was althrough his life, and all the time, in constant physical pain.

6. A Balliol 'composition' ran thus:
   I am a most superior person, Mary,
   My name is George N-th-n-1 C-rz-n, Mary,
   I'll make a speech on any political question of the day, Mary,

Provided you'll not say me nay, Mary.
—Ronaldshy, *Life*, I, pp. 41-42.
Another variant on the same theme ran thus :
My name is George Nathaniel Curzon,
I am the most superior person,
My cheek is pink, my hair is sleek,
I dine at Blenheim once a week.

7. Sir Harold Nicolson, *op.cit.*, p. 9.

8. It would be hard even to list in outline, the trophies which Curzon annexed as he wended his way through school and college. But revenge came too in an early (at 19) curvature of the spine. For details, see Ronaldshay, *Life*, I, pp. 17-71.

9. The Earl of Midleton, who as Henry St. John Brodrick was Curzon's contemporary at Balliol, recalls that the latter's curvature of the spine was more or less a self-invited trouble. 'Short of profligacy and alcoholism I do not think any man could have done more than he did to shatter his health. He broke all known rules and derided all advice', Brodrick recorded. He also mentions the fact that when Curzon arrived at Oxford he (Curzon) complained of him (Brodrick) bitterly for 'I would not abet him in defying nature after 3.00 A. M.' Midleton, *op.cit.*, pp. 189-90.

    Curzon and Brodrick, until they fell out in 1904, were great friends and wrote continuously to each other—on all sorts of subjects. In the Curzon papers at India Office Library—*Mss. Eur. F.* 111, cited, *et seq.*, as Curzon MSS., No. 9, contains letters from Henry St. John Brodrick, during the years 1876-93 which beginning with 'My dear Curzon' in 1876 soon (1878) progress to 'My dear Boy'.

10. How rich his 'travels' made him is evident not only from his numerous books but from his *Tales of Travel* (London, 1923) and its posthumously published companion volume *Leaves from a Viceroy's Note-Book* (London, 1926). The latter, apart from such travelogue as 'Kashmir to Gilgit' contains many a vignette as 'A Duel', 'The Interpreter', 'The Valet', 'Hymns' and 'Cheers'. For a brief conspectus, see Ronaldshay, *Life*, I, pp. 72-89 and 118-75.

11. Apart from titles listed in this paragraph and n. 10, *supra*, Curzon wrote a two-volume study, *British Government in India* which appeared posthumously in 1925.

12. In a letter to Curzon, May 24, 1884, Brodrick wroted ' ... there is a dash about your writing which besides making me feel you are the person to do the thing (not me) savours strongly of a mind emancipated by foreign travel and freshness from the dull restraints of this House of Commons life ....' Curzon MSS., *op.cit.*

13. Midleton, *op.cit.*, p. 186.

14. Ronaldshay, *Life*, I, p. 157.

15. Midleton, *op.cit.*, p. 189.

16. The *Star* (November 3, 1889) and the *Daily News* (December 4, 1889) in Ronaldshay, *Life*, I, p. 145.

17. Mosley, *op.cit.*, p. 41.
18. Cited in *Ibid.*, p. 33.
19. Letter to Curzon, May 18, 1882, Curzon MSS., *op.cit.*
20. Ronaldshay, *Life*, I, pp. 107-14.
    See also Leonard Mosley, *op.cit.*, pp. 36-37. 'In Parliamentary life, he (George Curzon) was never to be one who stayed to get his feet wet before deciding that a ship was sinking'. *Ibid.*, p. 37.
21. Curzon, *Russia in Central Asia in 1889* (London, 1889), pp. 318-20.
22. *Loc. cit.*
23. *Ibid.*, p. 321.
24. *Loc. cit.*
25. *Ibid.*, p. 330.
26. *Ibid.*, pp. 322-23.
27. *Ibid.*, pp. 323-32.
28. *Ibid.*, pp. 342-45.
29. Curzon, *Persia and the Persian Question*, 2 Vols. (London, 1892), II, p. 593.
30. *Ibid.*, p. 589.
31. *Salisbury Papers* (Christ Church, Oxford), letter from Lord Curzon to Lord Salisbury, July 12, 1900, sent on the eve of the (Persian) Shah's visit to England.
32. Cited in Midleton, *op.cit.*, p. 193.
33. The text reads :
    'To those
    Who believe that the British Empire
    Is under Providence, the greatest instrument for good
    That the world has seen.
    And who hold with the writer, that
    Its work in the Far East is not yet accomplished
    This book is inscribed'.
34. Harold Nicolson, *op.cit.*, p. 14.
35. 'It (Imperialism) is becoming', he wrote in 1898 'every day less and less the creed of a party and more and more the faith of a nation'. *Ibid.*, p. 13.
36. *Loc. cit.*
37. Curzon, 'Problems of the Far East', *op.cit.*, p. xii. Later in the text (p. 436) there is a verse :
    'We sailed wherever ship could sail,
    We founded many a mighty state,
    Pray God our greatness may not fail
    Through craven fear of being great'.
38. Harold Nicolson, *op.cit.*, p. 14.
39. The debate took place at Wolley Dod's (House Debating Society) on May 7, 1877, Ronaldshay, *Life*, I, pp. 143-44.
40. In 1885, Curzon had for a time acted as Assistant Private Secretary to Lord Salisbury; in the general elections of 1886 he became, for the first time, a

member of Parliament. In November1891, Lord Salisbury offered him the Under-Secretaryship of India which 'concerns matters in which ... you have shown great interest in a very practical way and it carries ... duties which sometimes involve important questions'. He remained in that office until the fall of 1892.

41. Midleton, *op.cit.*, p. 193. Lord Rosebery also warned Curzon against holding such extreme views.
42. Ronaldshay, *Life*, I, p. 251.
    Later (1895-98) Curzon was Under-Secretary for Foreign Affairs.
43. Cited in Ronaldshay, *Life*, I, p. 277.
44. Salisbury Papers, *op.cit.*, letter, July 12, 1900.
45. Curzon MSS., *op.cit.*, letter, May 3, 1899. Also Ronaldshay. *Life*, I, p. 282.
46. Curzon, Russia in Central Asia, *op.cit.*, p. xi.
47. *Hamilton Papers*, Curzon to Hamilton, letter, May 3, 1899.
48. *Infra,*
49. Curzon; Russia in Central Asia, *op.cit.*, p. 14.
50. Curzon, Problems of the Far East, *op.cit.*, p. xii.
51. *Ibid.*, p. 435.
52. Edward Thompson and G. T. Garratt, *Rise and Fulfilment of British Rule in India* (London, 1934). pp. 393-95.
53. Guy Wint, *The British in Asia* (London, 1947), p. 21.
54. Cited in Harold Nicholson, *op.cit.*, p. 15. In a speech, at Southport, on March 15, 1893, Curzon said :
    'It is only when you get to see and realise what India is—that she is the strength and greatness of England—it is only then that you feel that every nerve a man may strain, every energy he may put forward cannot be devoted to a nobler purpose, than keeping tight—the cords that hold India to ourselves'. Ronaldshay, *Life*, I, p. 193.
55. Ronaldshay, *Life*, II. Preface.
    Accepting his appointment as Under-Secretary for India from Lord Salisbury, Curzon wrote to him on November 12, 1891, 'I gratefully accept it ... and beyond measure pleased at the prospect of learning about a subject and doing some work for a cause which have long appeared to me more almost than any others in the field of politics'. Salisbury Papers, *op.cit.*
56. Salisbury Papers, *op.cit.*, letter, April 18, 1897.
    Curzon—then Under-Secretary for Foreign Affairs—had gone to Berlin along with his wife while Parliament had adjourned. Previously, letter of April 6, he had sought and obtained Lord Salisbury's permission to do so. The letter is marked 'Private' and addressed to 'My dear Lord Salisbury'.
57. *Ibid.*, letter, April 29, 1897.
58. *Ibid.*, The letter bears no date but probably belongs to early in (April?) 1898.
59. *Ibid.*, June 20, 1898.
60. *Loc.cit.*
61. *Ibid.*, letter, June 25, 1898.

62. The *Times* (London), August 11, 1898, in Ronaldshay, *Life*, I, p. 300.
63. Letter from Brodrick, September 19, 1898. In a letter of December 14 (1898) Brodrick wrote to say that 'I cannot doubt you will make your Viceroyalty memorable, if not unique' for Curzon had 'knowledge, energy, talent and resolution in a degree ... never previously combined in the history of India ...' Curzon MSS., *op. cit.*
64. The *Spectator*, in Ronaldshay, *Life*, I, p. 296.
65. Charles James O'Donnell, *op.cit.*, p. 2.
66. *Novoe Vremya*, September 3, 1898, in Ronaldshay, *Life*, I, p. 196.

7
Curzon as Viceroy: His Quarrels with Whitehall

ord Curzon assumed the Viceroyalty early in January 1899, and within a few weeks as up against the problems of the Persian Gulf. Briefly, in 1898, the Sultan of Oman d granted to the French a coaling station at Bunder Jisseh, a small port 5 miles to e south-east of Muscat, and the right to fortify it. This arrangement, which became blic knowledge in 1899, was said to violate a secret agreement of 1891, whereby e Sultan had pledged his word to the British not to alienate any part of his minions to another European power. The Viceroy dispatched a small naval quadron from Bombay and the British Political Agent in the Gulf, supported by the ommander of the naval squadron, demanded from the Sultan a public rescission of e French concession under the threat of a direct bombardment of his palace. The ltan was cowed, the French publicly humiliated and Curzon openly vindicated. [1]

On whose initiative did the Viceroy act? Very much on his own, it would seem. or while it is true that the Home Government had telegraphed authority for livering an ultimatum to the Sultan, this was to have been based on a number of fractions of the agreement of 1891, such as the levy of illegitimate taxes on British erchants. [2] But the inclusion in this ultimatum of a formal demand for the cancellation the French lease, and above all of a public disavowal thereof by the Sultan, were urzon's own ideas. For, in a letter to Lord Salisbury he listed these two as points in hich 'your instructions from home have been either exceeded or departed from'. s to the first, he acted on his own initiative and while taking the blame entirely on himself, made it clear that it did not occur to him that in so doing 'we were suming any fresh responsibility' at all. As to the second 'this was done without r knowledge and before we could prohibit it.'[3] In both cases, the Viceroy pleaded rongly in extenuation. The Prime Minister, however, was angry, stigmatized the oceedings as 'a serious mistake' and pointed out that while 'Meade (the British dmiral) was pluming his own feathers, it should have occurred to him that he was ssibly ruffling ours.'[4]

Nor was Lord Salisbury alone 'a good deal annoyed' for Hamilton, the Secretar of State, had felt unhappy too. The latter branded the entire business 'somewh: unfortunate' as if confirming him in the belief that Indian Politicals in their dealing with native princes adopted an attitude of 'high-handedness and harshness. Without being unpleasant, he reminded the Viceroy that 'in transactions of th kind'—in which the Foreign Office had a right of interfering and a power of control— 'it is necessary to look beyond the local results achieved'.[6] He also confided t Curzon that the Prime Minister had intimated to Cambon (the French envoy) 'th: the instructions had been exceeded and I imagine he (Salisbury) expressed regret'

The Viceroy, however, was unrepentant. He may have 'unconsciously' ove stepped the limits, but was it not providential that he had 'misread' the orde telegraphed from home?[8] Riding by now his familiar hobby horse, he reminde Lord Salisbury that France's action in the Persian Gulf—at Muscat, Koweit an elsewhere—was taken 'in deliberate conjunction with Russia, and is subsidiar not so much to French as to Russian ends.' It was, he maintained, tantamount to ' systematic attempt to contest our position' in the area. Again, and this is significan while he may concede that the matter was 'also' one of 'Imperial concern', he w: bound to regard it 'with an Indian eye' and indeed 'from the point of view of Indi: interest.' His watchword, therefore, was one of 'unremitting vigilance.'[9]

Another interesting facet of the Persian Gulf controversy was Curzon's charg and this despite Brodrick's categoric assurances to the contrary, that the Secretar of State had let him down, that there was 'an element of ingratitude' in his (Georg Hamilton's) disagreeing with the Viceroy's views.[10]

Despite the initial difficulties, and the opposition he provoked, Curzon d eventually have his way. It was in pursuance of his policy that the then Sheikh « Koweit was politically buttressed in his dealings with Turkey which had trie consistently to undermine his independence.[11] So also quietly, though firmly, w: scotched Germany's attempt, in 1900, to acquire a site on the Gulf for the termin of the proposed Berlin-Baghdad railway or Russia's bid for a coaling station on tł northern side of the entrance to this waterway.[12] Meantime, the British had becon unusually active. Surveys of the road-steads, the islands and the islets we undertaken and a flotilla of gunboats, for permanent service in the Gulf, was p into commission. Consular establishments were increased and their personnel ar escorts were strengthened while improved steamer and postal facilities we obtained in return for increased subsidies.[13] Symptomatic of the Indian stake in tł Gulf was the fact that apart from the British commercial mission, accredited by tł Board of Trade, another appointed by the Government of India was als established.[14]

The final victory for the Viceroy's views may be said to have been won by tł British Foreign Secretary Lord Lansdowne's declaration, in May 1903, that tł establishment of a naval base or of a fortified post in the Gulf by another pow would be viewed 'as a very grave menace to British interests'. That Curzon thoug this to be a vindication of his policy—which he knew the Foreign Office had earli ewed as 'lacking in sanity, moderation and decorum and to be rather philistine, if ot forward in its sentiments'[15]—is apparent from the letter he wrote to the Secretary State, a few days after Lansdowne's pronouncement had been made :

You may judge how satisfied I was .... This is what I contended for in language which has since become famous in my book 11 years ago; it is what I have argued and pleaded for in scores of letters to you during the last four years ... and therefore ... I cannot help feeling some personal sense of congratulation.[16]

As if to proclaim his success publicly, Curzon visited the Gulf in all his Imperial galia, in 'almost swashbuckling style' as he himself put it. Besides, the Viceroy elped to establish the Seistan mission of 1903-05 which, under Sir Henry cMahon, was to complete the earlier work of Sir Fredrick Goldsmid's boundary elimitation of 1872. He was also instrumental in the extension of the railroad eyond Quetta to Nushki, both for its strategic import as well as its opening up of trade route to Seistan. A consular representative was also stationed in the latter ace.[17]

Certain conclusions seem to follow from the narrative on the (Persian) Gulf. ainly, Curzon was not averse to defying the Home authorities when he felt too uch was at stake, nor to the use of *force majeure* to maintain Britain's imperial osition. 'If Russia', he confided to one of his correspondents, 'announced a line Seistan, I would myself threaten the Shah with an occupation of Seistan; and I ould undertake to have my men there before Russia could get theirs.'[18] And nally, as Viceroy he regarded himself clothed with a degree of responsibility to feguard what he deemed 'truly Indian' interests. With some slight modifications, d appropriate adjustments, these conclusions repeated themselves over fghanistan too, although Tibet was destined to prove their final testing ground.

n integral part of Central Asia owing its existence wholly to its geographical osition, besides being a sensitive spot between an expanding Russia and the orth-western frontier of the Indian Empire, Afghanistan had always occupied a rategic place in Curzon's thinking. To him it was that 'turbulent Alsatian' which one moment invited and at the next repelled the solicitude of Great Britain, a fatal agnet to the venturesome and a bugbear to the timid. Sooner or later this 'Achilles' el of Great Britain in the East,' as the Viceroy called it, proved to be the despair all those who attempted to solve 'the perennial problem' that it posed.[19] In the rly nineties, while on one of his foreign travels, he had got himself invited to abul and stayed with the Amir Abdur Rahman as his guest. This personal counter, which is held to have done more harm than good,[20] must at least have ven the two men an opportunity to size up each other. And it is not without gnificance that Curzon scrupulously kept his hands off Afghanistan as long as e old Amir was alive. It was only when Habibullah's peaceful accession had been sured that Curzon sought to re-open the entire frontier question on the plea that e treaty with the old Amir lapsed with his death and that the problem must be amined *de novo*.[21]

Habibullah, though wanting in all the prestige and authority that his father had commanded, was not altogether bereft of the wily old man's shrewd judgement. Besides, in contrast to the latter, the new Amir's attitude was viewed as 'the reverse of friendly' for he 'not only received tribal deputations from British territory but had also commenced intriguing with certain frontier fanatics and freebooters.' No wonder Curzon now pressed for a revision of the old treaty arrangement which the Amir had hitherto stoutly resisted. Against the Viceroy's well-marshalled arguments, he put forth the view that the old treaty had been concluded between the two countries and was not personal to their rulers, that it had taken fully into account the complicated nature of all the problems which the Viceroy now put forth and consequently did not call for any fresh examination, much less a renewal. Twice over, Curzon invited the Amir to meet him in Calcutta or even Peshawar: on both occasions the Afghan ruler either cleverly evaded the invitation or quietly ignored it.[23] Since the Cabinet at home would not listen to his talk of sending an ultimatum, the Viceroy felt completely nettled. He questioned, nay challenged, his political superiors' right to interfere in matters of which he deemed himself to be the sole arbiter[24] and, as though in sheer agony, cried:

I think in these questions you may really trust me to know how to handle the Amir as well as anyone else at home.[25]

'Trust me!' That plaintive cry rings through most of his Viceroyalty's eventful years.

On another occasion when the Amir failed for long to acknowledge one of his letters—actually, it was Curzon's invitation, in June 1902, for a meeting in Peshawar—the Viceroy suspected the very worst. Could it not have been an underhand Afghan-Russian deal? He wrote to Lord George Hamilton that if the hobnobbing were to be established, he would propose the occupation of Kandahar and the pushing forward of the frontier to Girishk and the Helmund river. And in deep anguish as it were burst forth:

If you do not like to tackle Russia, then at least punish the Amir. If you allow a man and a state of his calibre to flout the British Empire then we had better put up our shutters and close business.[26]

Whitehall obviously was not impressed by this melodramatic outburst and the Secretary of State confided to him that 'so decided and unanimous was the objection to any forward movement,' that they would rather abandon all the present obligations and 'substitute nothing in their place except an attempt to come to an understanding with Russia.'[27]

Rebuffed decisively, Curzon next turned to Lord Knollys, Secretary to the King, and evidently for the latter's ear told him that the Home Government were being 'unnecessarily timid' about the Amir. 'The least hint of action'—in fact doing anything but sit still and wait to see what turns up—'throws them into agonies of apprehension, and brings down upon me a shower of telegrams.'[28] To Lord George Hamilton, he wrote in much the same strain accusing him, and his colleagues at home, of 'ignorance and timidity' in regard to Asiatic 'foreign affairs'.

Elsewhere he charged that the Cabinet seemed 'prepared to sacrifice all our interests in Afghanistan sooner than run the faintest risk.'[30]

In the years that followed, Curzon found himself often-times over-ruled. Ostensibly, he was not far wrong in insisting that a frank personal discussion with the Amir was vital if Britain was to fulfil its obligations towards defending his country, of whose military strength it knew nothing, and of continuing to pay him a large subsidy. Habibullah's defiance, however, was open and—from the Viceroy's viewpoint—unabashed. He refused to kowtow to Curzon and a meeting between the two never took place. What was worse, Whitehall refused to lend its support to the Viceroy so as to bring pressure to bear upon the Amir to enable him (Curzon) to get what he wanted. In this triangular contest, with the odds heavily weighted against him, the Indian potentate found himself repeatedly frustrated. Thus, early in 1904, in a letter he confided to the King :

> The Amir is as tricky and difficult in correspondence as ever: and the Viceroy is conscious that the Home Government want to adopt a much weaker line than he is disposed to recommend, and to give way. Surrender does not pay with Orientals and we never show weakness without suffering for it afterwards.[31]

Later, towards the end of 1904, when Habibullah came round, albeit on his own terms, and the Home Government decided upon sending Mr. (later Sir) Louis Dane to negotiate with the Amir, much against Curzon's express wishes, the Viceroy was deeply perturbed. He charged that the envoy had not 'stated his points as well as might have been done and in some respects has let the Amir astray'; that he (Dane) did not, in fact, possess 'the requisite expert knowledge or authority.'[32] As has been noticed, Dane's instructions had been dictated verbatim by the Home Government : such was the measure of trust which the Viceroy now inspired in London. Annoyed beyond measure, Curzon continued to hark back to his pet thesis that 'really if he (Amir) could be persuaded to come and sit at the same table with the Viceroy' , it could scarcely be doubted that 'in a day or two some ground of common agreement would be discovered.'[33] Another variant on the same theme was that thanks to the 'persistent timidity displayed in dealing with him by the Government at Home,' he (Curzon) was convinced that the Amir had been so inflated with 'false pride and ignorance,' and had been 'so much thrown off his balance' that he (Amir) felt he could 'now stand alone, and dispense, except on his own terms, with our assistance and support.'[34] And thus it was that despite his fulminations, the final settlement reached at Kabul was on terms which the Amir practically dictated and which the Viceroy had earlier condemned, and without qualification.[35]

'Mr. Dane', Lord Curzon wrote to the King, on March 29, 1905, 'has started back from Kabul with a treaty in his pocket. But what a treaty! The Viceroy trusts that Your Majesty's Ministers are satisfied with it. We in India view the future with sincere alarm, since we conclude that we have abandoned all means of putting pressure upon the Amir; and that he can henceforth treat us just as he pleases.'[36]

How wide was the chasm that yawned between the views of His Majesty's Government and their accredited plenipotentiary in India! Yet Afghanistan was by no means exceptional, it was only typical and symptomatic of a trend that was fairly well spread out.

In each of these fields of foreign policy one notices, *inter alia*, two diametrically opposed strands as between the 'prancing' proconsul in India and his political masters at home. Broadly speaking, Curzon's greatest victory was scored in the birth of a separate administrative entity in the North-West Frontier Province (which had obvious ramifications in the field of foreign affairs) while, if by contrast, his most grievous failure was registered in Afghanistan. Yet it was perhaps, the difficulties that arose in the Persian Gulf area in the opening years of his Viceroyalty, and his handling thereof, which characterized much that marked his footsteps for the remainder of his term of office. The gap that revealed itself in this crisis widened with every passing year. He had, it is true, the initial (and to him very welcome) satisfaction of defying Salisbury's express wishes and of upholding officials whose over-stepping of the prescribed limits embarrassed that Prime Minister not a little in the conduct of his foreign policy. One suspects though that at heart, Curzon despised what to him was the doddering inefficiency, more politely the rather cautious and sometimes deliberate inactivity, of Salisbury's supine premiership and even more so of the government of his cousin (Arthur Balfour)[37] that succeeded him. Yet the nemesis came and not before long.

And herein Afghanistan was to provide a testing ground. In his dealings with the Amir, as was noticed, he found himself face to face with a government that was unanimous in its conviction that the Salisbury experience did not bear a repetition. Hence the very unusual and to Curzon personally annoying, and even humiliating, expedient of the Ministry at home dictating verbatim the instructions with which one of the Viceroy's agents was to be charged. Truly speaking, developments in Tibet may be said to lie somewhere between the Persian and Afghan experiences, as they do chronologically. And yet they may not be viewed as if in islolation; for the three were closely interrelated and a common streak as it were, ran through them all. The latter was equally discernible in the acute differences of opinion, which were not long in revealing themselves, on many facets of domestic policy between India Office in London and the Council Chamber in Calcutta. Besides, the increasing uneasiness, if not acerbity, in the personal relationship between the incumbents of the two offices—a reflection of their extreme divergence in outlook—cast its lengthening, and as time passed almost fatal, shadow across the Viceroy's path. Thus an allusion however brief, to some of the differences on domestic issues may help to place these questions of foreign policy in general, and of Tibet in particular, in a sharper, clearer focus.

One of Lord Curzon's early targets for attack was the institution of the Presidency governors of Bombay and Madras. In his ruthless drive to inculcate efficiency, and uniformity in the administrative organism, the reformer in him felt the special privileges of these two offices, an 'unjustifiable extravagance'; their right to correspond direct with the Secretary of State, 'an anomalous and mischievous pretension'; their choice from among men in British public life, 'an unnecessary luxury'. On what a critic had termed their 'qualified privilege of insubordination,' Curzon heaped all his scorn.[38] So great was his venom, so pointed and sharp his barbs, that it seemed for a while that he had stormed the citadel and taken it by a frontal assault. The Secretary of State and the Cabinet, however, stood four-square for a practice which, apart from the fact that it was time-honoured, had some distinct advantages. This was further borne out by the fact that on the annulment of Bengal's partition, many years later, that province reverted to its earlier status of a Presidency. It would seem in retrospect, however, that the Curzonian zeal was misdirected and the knowledge that, at the end of his first year in office, he had been so decisively over-ruled by Whitehall ever rankled in his breast.[39]

Another incident, relatively minor in itself and yet one that had major repercussions, involved a difference of opinion as to whether His Majesty's Government or the Government of India, should defray the expense of the Indian representatives invited to the King's coronation in London. Curzon held, and rightly too, that the money should come out of British coffers.[40] The Secretary of State who was in sympathy with his viewpoint, was actually negotiating with the Exchequer on these lines when Curzon wrote him a sharply-worded despatch. The latter was tantamount, in effect, to a severe 'censure of the Secretary of State in Council,' if not an open 'indictment' of that body. Even the imperturbable George Hamilton was hurt: 'I own that I am deeply wounded at the language and scheme of this letter' and hinted that until it was 'modified,' or 'another substituted for it,' he would not entertain it.[41] So strong was the feeling aroused by its provocative language that Balfour, now Prime Minister, cabled the Viceroy to withdraw it.[42] Curzon who, in private, had referred to HMG's decision as 'this meanness,' expressed the view that unless the change he had demanded was made, 'lasting harm ... will be done to British credit and reputation in this country'. Later he communicated on the subject with the King himself. Despite the extreme resentment aroused, the Viceroy stubbornly held his ground and refused to oblige until his point was fully conceded. While it be true that he won the final round, it was a pyrrhic victory. For the episode left behind it much bitterness, and closed with an 'absolutely universal chorus of disapprobation' from the Cabinet.[43]

Meantime Curzon had begun to smart under any sort of criticism, tacit or implied, of his policies or actions. And when, early in 1902, the Secretary of State's Council composed of experienced officials with long service careers in India, questioned his action both in regard to the appointment of a Police Commission and his programme of projected educational reforms,[44] the Viceroy burst out in all his fury. He had earlier referred half-contemptuously to the Council's members as 'veterans' whose knowledge of India he rated to be astonishingly out of date. Now he went a step further and accused them of being 'hostile and obstructive,' of worrying him unnecessarily with their 'innuendos and suspicions,' of thwarting and hampering him in his work. He even threatened the Secretary of State with his resignation unless not only his support 'but the backing of your Council too, was forthcoming'.[45]

When Lord George Hamilton tried to palliate and soften his ruffled feelings with the suggestion that 'in public life you must give as well as take,' Curzon returned to the charge with an even greater ferociousness. To Godley he was frank:

You send me out to India as an expert and you treat my advice as though it were of an impertinent school-boy [46]

Or, again:

Your old veterans ... are as dogmatic about the subjects they have ceased to understand as a young curate in a pulpit is about those that he has not yet commenced to know. [47]

Yet the Permanent Under-Secretary's assessment of Curzon's not-infrequent paroxysms of rage was nearer the truth—'I admit that this is an exaggeration, but it really is not a very serious one'—than anyone else's. In a letter to Lord Ampthill, Godley had summed it up tersely:

In any of these disputed matters, the thought that seems to rise in his (Curzon's) mind is not 'I will prove to the Cabinet, or to the Council of India that they are wrong about this or that and I am right,' but 'I have given my opinion, I have even reiterated it in two or more despatches, I am the Viceroy of India and confound you, how do you dare to set your opinion against mine.'[48]

Hardly had the earlier controversies died down when matters again came to a head over what is known as the Durbar episode. Unalterably convinced in his mind that the oriental was attracted by the pomp and pageantry of the Imperial link, Curzon had determined to hold a Durbar at Delhi to celebrate the accession to the throne of King Edward VII. Soon enough he was devoting all his energies to planning it and although the more immediate Indian problems were famine and plague, which together and racked the land like hell-fire, Curzon's chief preoccupation now seemed to be to outdo the spectacle which Lytton had staged at a quarter century earlier.

Scheduled for January 1, 1903, the Viceroy's preparations became hectic as the days neared. In the autumn of 1902, it occurred to him that the Durbar be linked with a Royal proclamation of some tax relief. The idea fascinated and soon took hold of him : would not the glitter and splendour of the Durbar be enhanced a thousand-fold, by its association with such a popular measure of tax remission?[49] The Secretary of State and his Council, however, discouraged him on constitutional grounds, observing that it would be a most awkward precedent. Curzon, not so easily persuaded, was by now possessed as it were of the appropriateness, not to say the political import of such a reduction.[50]

Meantime he wrote to Lord George Hamilton in a tone of open defiance, not unmixed with a deep anguish of the heart. He had received the Secretary of State's telegram formally rejecting the Government of India's despatch with great surprise 'amounting almost to consternation' and looked upon a further dispute with the

India Council 'with utter sickness of heart.' His mind was thus made up 'I say, therefore, with the utmost respect, but with emphasis, that I cannot accept the position which you desire to assign to me.'[51]

A day earlier, no November 12, he had telegraphed to Knollys spelling out how he had been grievously hurt by the Secretary of State and his Council whose attitude, he was convinced, was 'narrow, pedantic and unwise ... short-sighted and wrong.' He had asked Lord George Hamilton to revise his stand and 'if he yields' well and good, 'otherwise I will send you a telegram and will ask you to convey to His Majesty my most respectful assurances of the importance of the issue and my earnest request that the King will insist that his own Coronation Durbar shall be an unequalled success, instead of a dismal failure as His Majesty's ministers threatened to make it.[52]

Two days later came the appeal itself for which ground had already been prepared. Hamilton had telegraphed 'absolutely declining' to let him have his way and hence :

I desire respectfully to report to the King that this decision will check the evergrowing sentiments of loyalty in India and convert them into an attitude of disappointment and almost despair and that I cannot assume the responsibility of allowing His Majesty's name to be connected with such a result.[53]

Whitehall stood aghast. George Hamilton pointed out that it was 'the first time' that an appeal had been made to the King to influence a Cabinet,[54] while it had under consideration a question 'affecting the person who had so appealed'.[55] Brodrick who feared lest Curzon threaten resignation in the belief that HMG might give way, telegraphed privately (on November 19) warning him of the strong feelings aroused, called his move 'a most dangerous precedent,' and explained, in a letter two days later, that 'in this instance there has been unanimity of opinion in the India Office and the Cabinet and that they were all determined that if you elected to go on such an issue we must face it.'[56]

Curzon was annoyed, and beyond measure. In a long letter, written from the Viceroy's camp at Abu, to 'My dear Arthur' he took great pains to justify his action, holding the implied censure on him as 'gratuitous'. He had been 'instructed by the King as his representative to hold a Durbar on his behalf to celebrate his Coronation,' had settled with His Majesty the Proclamation that was to be read at the Durbar, he had even been asked for 'a draft of the message' that the King was to send for a public pronouncement by the Viceroy. Now, with regard to what the Viceroy is to say, 'I submit that that is an issue more directly affecting the Sovereign than anybody else,' since its content was very important, nay almost crucial :

Should I have been right to involve the Sovereign on whose behalf I am acting in what I steadfastly believe will be a humiliating failure without letting him know? .... Inasmuch as all the communications about the Durbar have been with the King, I thought it better to telegraph straight to Knollys.... I hold myself entirely justified, therefore, in my action. Indeed, I think that had I not informed the King and had allowed judgement to go against me by default in the Cabinet, I might subsequently have been open to grave reproof of His Majesty.....

Nor was that all. Curzon maintained that he had not been fairly or justly, not to say generously, treated; hinted that the 'logical corollary' of the Cabinet's decision was his recall; and that, in effect, it amounted to 'setting a similar and equally unmerited crown (of failure) upon my own Indian career.'[57]

Balfour's reply to his proconsul's melodramatic outburst was couched in gracious terms, albeit unmistakable in its meaning and import :

I cannot really assent to your view that because the position of the Sovereign was (in your view) affected by the course to be taken at the Durbar in reference to taxation, you were, therefore, justified in carrying on an independent correspondence with him on a point of high policy without the knowledge and assent of your colleagues .... Nor do I think there is any real justification for your view that the Secretary of State 'tacitly allowed you for more than a year' to assume that a remission of taxation might be properly announced at the Durbar.[58]

To cut a long story short, a compromise on the Durbar speech was finally wrought more or less on the lines George Hamilton had suggested earlier : the Viceroy making a general statement of policy, but not a specific one.[59] From the contents of another communication from Knollys to the Prime Minister's Secretary, it would seem that the Viceroy had meanwhile shifted his ground. 'Judging from this letter' (of which an extract was enclosed), the King's Secretary wrote, Curzon had 'no wish to make an announcement of a remission of taxation in the King's name, as I believe we all have thought was the case, but that he should be allowed to announce the remission at the Durbar.'[60] Blown over, the episode yet left a very deep mark on the relations between London and Calcutta. The extremes to which their representative in India could go to defy or repudiate them were doubtless better appreciated in Whitehall in November 1902, than in the previous four years of this very 'interesting experiment.' At the height of the controversy, Curzon had written to Balfour in an extremely unforgiving tone :

You have never served your country in foreign parts. For your sake, I hope you never may. English Governments have always had the reputation of breaking the hearts of their proconsuls from Warren Hastings to Bartle Frere. Do you wish to repeat the performance?[61]

A by no means unimportant by-product of this episode was the wedge it drove into that nearly quarter-century old, and intimate, relationship between Henry St. John Brodrick and his old colleague of Eton-Balliol days, now in India. Curzon had thought Brodrick's conduct in the whole affair inexcusable, revolting as it was to all the canons of the old school tie; and visited him with his immediate displeasure.[62] Momentarily patched up later the breach was, in effect, never healed.[63]

Notes

1. Ronaldshay, *Life*, II, pp. 45-46.
2. *Ibid.*, II, p. 44.
3. Salisbury Papers, *op.cit.*, letter, March 16, 1899.
4. *Ibid.*, In a letter, February 24, 1899, Lord George Hamilton told Curzon that in the telegram which he (Hamilton) had dispatched on February 19, the words 'this is a serious mistake' were inserted by Lord Salisbury himself. Also see Ronaldshay, *Life*, II, p. 48.
5. *Ibid.*, Hamilton to Curzon, letter.
   Also see Ravinder Kumar, 'The Jissah Lease : An Episode in Anglo-French Diplomacy in the Persian Gulf', *Journal of Indian History*, XLII, 2 (August, 1964) pp. 301-13.
6. *Ibid.*, letter, February 24, 1899.
7. *Ibid.*, letter, April 28, 1899.
8. Ronaldshay, *Life*, II, p. 48.
9. *Supra*, n. 3.
10. *Ibid.*, letter from Lord George Hamilton, June 16, 1899. Earlier (March 20, 1899) Brodrick wrote to Curzon to say that 'George Hamilton sticks to you nobly in Council. ...'
11. P. E. Roberts, *op.cit.*, p. 524.
12. In a letter, March 10, 1900, Brodrick wrote to Curzon, 'I have done all I can to pull you through about Muscat. Lord Salisbury, I think went rather far in telling Cambon that in form, though not in substance, he regretted the way in which things had gone.' Curzon MSS., *op. cit.* In a letter, April 28, 1899, George Hamilton wrote to Curzon that Lord Salisbury clearly intimated to Cambon 'that the instructions had been exceeded and I imagine he expressed regret.' Hamilton Papers, *op.cit.*
13. For Russian and British activity, see Ronaldshay, *Life*, II, pp. 309-10.
14. *Ibid.*, p. 310.
15. Salisbury Papers, *op. cit.*, letter. September 18, 1900.
16. *Ibid.*, earlier (July 12, 1900) Curzon had written to Lord Salisbury that he (Curzon) had 'not studied it (Persian Question) for 12 years without forming opinions'.
17. P. E. Roberts, *op.cit.*, p. 524. Also see Ronaldshay, *Life*, II, pp. 308-9.
18. Letter to Lord Percy, cited in Ronaldshay, *Life*, II, p. 309.
19. In his Russia in Central Asia, *op.cit.*, p. 356, Curzon made a scathing condemnation of 'the amazing political incompetence' in British dealings with Afghanistan : 'For fifty years there has not been an Afghan Amir whom we have not alternately fought against and caressed .... Small wonder that we have never been trusted by Afghan rulers, or liked by the Afghan people.'
20. 'To an oriental the visit of the rising statesman who soon afterwards reappeared as the Viceroy of India using moreover the language of a somewhat peremptory ruler, instead of that of a guest, could only present itself as a prearranged plan.' Midleton, *op.cit.*, p. 195.
21. Relations between the Amir and the Government of India between 1890 and 1895 were often strained to the utmost, almost to a breaking point, for repeatedly the Amir was repulsed in his desire to open direct relations with the British government in London. Fortunately both sides were restrained and an open breach was avoided. 'Outwardly' at any rate, Abdur Rahman maintained a friendly attitude twoards the British till his death in 1901. For details, see R. C. Majumdar, *op.cit.*, IX, p. 1053.

In one of his letters to Lord Salisbury, Curzon referred to the Amir (Abdur Rahman) as 'a cantankerous sort of customer (who) loves his little squabble on paper.' Salisbury Papers, *op. cit.*, letter, June 7, 1900.

22. C. C. Davies, *The North-west Frontier of India, 1890-1908* (Cambridge, 1932), p. 166.

23. Curzon's first invitation was extended in the spring of 1902 which the Amir politely declined. In June of the same year, the Governor-General repeated his earlier invitation and strongly pressed the Amir to meet him (Curzon) in Peshwar in October. To this letter, Habibullah vouchsafed no reply until the middle of December (1902). Ronaldshay, *Life,* II, pp. 266-67.

24. Other things apart, there was evidence of Habibullah hobnobbing with the Russians. He had been the recipient of a letter from M. Ignatieff, Political Agent in Bokhara, while the Russian Government had been pressing for direct communication with the Amir 'upon purely local and commercial matters.' Later, in September 1902, at an open durbar he had read a communication from the Russian Government inviting the Amir 'to throw open to Russian' caravans the trade routes between Khushik and Herat and Khushik and Kabul. For details, see William Habberton, 'Anglo-Russian Relations concerning Afghanistan, 1837-1907,' *Illinois Studies in the Social Sciences,* XXI, No. 4. (Urbana, Illinois, 1937), pp. 70-71.

25. Ronaldshay, *Life*, II, p. 266.

26. Letter to George Hamilton, November 27, 1902. Hamilton Papers, *op.cit.*

27. *Ibid.,* letter, December 19, 1902.

28. Letter to Knollys, December 25, 1902. Curzon MSS., *op.cit.*

29. Letter to George Hamilton, January 8, 1903, Hamilton Papers, *op.cit.*

30. Curzon to Knollys, letter, January 15, 1903, Curzon MSS., *op.cit.*

31. *Ibid.,* Curzon to His Majesty the King Emperor, letter, March 9, 1904.

32. *Ibid.,* Curzon to the King, letter, January 11, 1905.

33. *Loc. cit.*

34. *Ibid.,* Curzon to the King, letter, January 25, 1905.

35. Louis Dane was sent to Kabul, in the fall of 1904, during the incumbency of Lord Ampthill, when Curzon was temporarily away on leave to England. On return he (Curzon) strongly condemned the terms of the Amir's revised treaty which the Cabinet were now prepared to accept. The latter had insisted that the terms in which Dane be instructed should be dictated by the Cabinet verbatim. This was protested by Brodrick who was Secretary of State, 'but the situation was regarded as too serious to permit of any risk being taken.'
'Curzon, I was informed, called him (Sir Louis) gravely to account, although he had carried out his orders unswervingly.' Midleton, *op. cit.*, pp. 197-98.

36. Curzon MSS., *op. cit.*, letter, March 29, 1905. 'The Cabinet insisted on carrying its point of view rather than Curzon's—a decision justified by the conduct of the ruler of Afghanistan during the next twenty years. Curzon submitted, but with an ill-grace and with the usual outpouring of ill-considered complaints.' Kenneth Young, *Arthur James Balfour* (London, 1963). p. 238.

37. Balfour's Cabinet was filled with men who had no better claim to office that that they were his—and by implication—Salisbury's relatives. Curzon in a doggerel gave vent to his feelings :
'In Trade's keen lists, no alien herald
His trumpet blows but brother Gerald;

Foreign affairs have cousin Cranborne
To hint that ne'er was greater man born;
While cousin Selborne rules the Fleet,
Even the sea is 'Arthur's seat.'

38. Despatch to the Secretary of State, September 28, 1899, in Ronaldshay *Life*, II, p. 59.
39. '... the Cabinet were practically unanimous in their opposition' and 'firmly refused' to accept the Viceroy's views. Curzon, on his part, accepted the verdict 'without conviction.' Ronaldshay, *Life*, II, pp. 60 and 98.
40. *Ibid.*, II, p. 239.
41. Letter to Curzon, July 31, 1902, Hamilton Papers, *op.cit.*
42. Balfour in his cable termed Curzon's despatch 'so highly controversial a document' and felt it read like 'an indictment of one colleague by another.' Ronaldshay, *Life*, II, p. 240.
43. Letter to Knollys, July 30, 1902, Curzon MSS. *op.cit.* Also see, *Ibid.*, his letter to the King, August 13, 1902, and Knollys to Curzon, September 23, 1902.
44. It may be mentioned here, if only in parenthesis, that the Indian Universities Act of 1904 as also the Police Commission reforms met with vigorous criticism in India. 'The opposition to the Universities Act proved to be the dress rehearsal for the greatest crisis of the Bengal partition', *Oxford History of India*, 3rd ed. (London, 1958), p. 758. See also Lovat Fraser, *op.cit.*, pp. 246-47.
45. Letter to the Secretary of State, May 28, 1902, Ronaldshay, *Life*, II, pp. 236-37.
46. *Ibid.*, Letter, June 18, 1902, p. 239.
47. *Ibid.*, Letter, June 25, 1902, p. 238.
48. Letter, June 17, 1904, *Ampthill Papers*.
49. Curzon told Godley that the announcement will produce 'an electric effect throughout the country.' Later, he informed the Secretary of State that he (Curzon) should have a free hand 'in respect of this Durbar and what is said and done thereat.' Ronaldshay, *Life*, II, p. 241.
50. In a letter to George Hamilton, October 15, 1902, Curzon wrote : 'The Indians will simply fail to understand a Coronation Durban altogether that is merely to consist of a pageant and a plausible speech, and to be associated with no concrete marks of Royal favour ....' Hamilton Papers, *op.cit.*
51. *Ibid.*, Curzon to Hamilton, letter, November 13, 1902.
52. Curzon to Knollys, letter November 12, 1902, Curzon MSS., *op.cit.*
53. *Ibid.*, Curzon to Knollys, telegram, November 15, 1902.
54. The important point here is that the King had no power in practice to accept Curzon's advice *against that of the Cabinet*. Had the king done so, the Cabinet would have reigned. Thus in reality, Curzon put the King in an impossible position.
55. In the same letter George Hamilton expressed himself rather strongly against Curzon's implied charge 'that I have acted in bad faith,' called it a 'sorry return,' confessed that he wrote in 'real sorrow' and that there was a palpable 'unfairness and injustice' in the allegations preferred. Hamilton Papers, *op. cit.*, letter, November 20, 1902.
56. In his letter, November 21, 1903, Brodrick explained: 'I telegraphed because I feared you might think if you threaten resignation or resigned the Cabinet might give way .... By the time this reaches you I hope a protest will be all you will have thought necessary. If not it will be a tragedy.' Curzor. MSS.(Correspondence with Brodrick, 1894-1903) , *op.cit.*

57. The letter to Balfour, November 20, 1902, is marked 'Private and Confidential' and is part of the *Balfour Papers*, Vol. L, in the British Museum; for convenience abbreviated, *et. seq.*, as *B. P.*, B. M.

58. *Ibid.*, B. M., Vol. L. This letter does not bear any date but was obviously in reply to Curzon's. The British Prime Minister disposed of the latter's long-winded reference to being relieved: 'I have differed from you on this or that point—I may have (who knows?) to differ from you on others. But nothing will for a moment diminish either the warmth of my friendship or the enthusiasm of my admiration.'

59. *Ibid.*, B. M., Vol. I. In a letter, November 27, 1902 from Lord Knollys to Mr. Sandars (Secretary to Mr. Balfour), the former wrote that 'His Majesty approves of what the Cabinet I think has practically approved of ...'

60. *Ibid.*, Vol. I, letter, December 3, 1902, from Lord Knollys to Mr. Sandars.

61. Only the first two sentences in this quotation (not the last two) occur in Curzon's long letter in Balfour Papers, *supra*, note 57. For what his biographer calls 'the full text', see Ronaldshay, *Life*, II, p. 244.

62. For three months, Curzon stopped his weekly letter to Brodrick which he had written to him regularly for two years, and in a cutting reference confided in the Vicerine : 'Observe the amicable way in which he informs me that all the Cabinet including himself (a humble participator) were quite prepared to throw me overboard .... I need not comment on it all but what a light it throws on human nature and friendship.'
    Brodrick in his letters (December 12, 1902 and January 27, 1903) explained his stand at length : 'those of us who had backed you as far as we could and looked upon anything which would remove you at so great a moment as a calamity felt we must take the step of warning you .... I only refer to this because I felt the annoyance in your letter to Arthur.' Curzon MSS. (Correspondence with Brodrick, 1894-1903), *op.cit.*

63. *Ibid.* On August 19, 1903, Brodrick wrote: '... I am very glad to get your letter as there is just as much bitterness growing up on our side as yours, and I will do all I can to stop it ....'
    Years after his return to England, Curzon is said to have patched up his old feud with Brodrick and though never again on such intimate terms, they corresponded in a friendly way during and after the War (1914-18) on *official topics*. Brodrick's letters still began 'My dear George'.

8
Lord Curzon and Tibet, 1899-1902

In the light of Lord Curzon's more active and forceful, if indeed aggressive, personality unfolded in the preceding pages and his overall concept of an expanding, adventurous Russia, the marked divergence in his approach to the Tibetan problem, as compared to Lord Elgin's, should not be a cause for surprise. As may be guessed, basic to the Viceroy's conviction was the belief that anywhere on the Indian glacis, which sloped away from the long perimeter of her frontiers, hostile influences may not be permitted to obtain a lodgement, and that on the contrary Indian authority should be unmistakably, 'and indeed ostentatiously', asserted.[1] He could thus scarce accept such activities on the part of the Tibetans as his predecessor had patiently put up with. The thought that the Sikkim boundary pillars had been destroyed with impunity, that a tract of land near Giaogong—which under the Convention of 1890 was a part of Sikkim—had now fallen into the hands of fanatical monks, was enough to disturb the new Viceroy's equanimity. No wonder that within a couple of months of his taking office, he was condemning the old approach towards Tibet as 'both unproductive and inglorious'.[2] As elsewhere, his 'new look', to borrow a somewhat over-worked yet significant phrase, was designed to achieve 'results'. What these were and what glory attended on their achievement will be the principal concern of the pages that follow. Here it may be well to point out that, both from the point of view of chronological convenience and a decisive shift in policy, the Viceroy's despatch of January 8, 1903, marks as it were a watershed in his dealings with Tibet. In the present chapter it is proposed to treat of the years (1899-1902) preceding that despatch.

The Viceroy's preliminary assessment of the Tibetan question was contained in a communication to the Secretary of State, written not long after he assumed office, [3] wherein he made the following points:

That Yatung, on the Tibet side of the frontier, which had been designated under the Regulations of 1893 as a post for Indian trade with Tibet, 'can never be expected to be a real mart'.

That he would be prepared to leave to the Tibetans land in the neighbourhood of Giaogong, which they are 'so desirous of retaining', on the stipulation that P'hari,[4] further up in the Chumbi valley, be thrown open to native traders from British India. It was emphasized, however, that these traders were not to be hindered from conducting business there directly with the Tibetans. Lord Curzon also suggested, and this is significant, that there be an option of sending a British official to visit P'hari and to reside there, 'if this should prove desirabe'.

That negotiations with the Chinese Resident were not likely to prove fruitful. Elsewhere Lord Curzon had expressed himself strongly to the effect, that the 'preset position' was 'most ignominious' and the use of the Chinese Amban as an intermediary 'an admitted farce'.[5]

'We seem ... to be moving', the Governor-General wrote, 'in a vicious circle. If we apply to Tibet, we either receive no reply, or are referred to the Chinese Resident.' And, if the latter be approached 'he excuses his failure by his inability to put any pressure upon Tibet'.

His analysis apart, Lord Curzon posed a significant question,

I do not feel quite sure, however, whether in your opinion we have so far committed ourselves to this method of procedure in the case of Tibet as to render any experimental departure from it impossible.[6]

Born of his impatience with the Chinese 'farce', Curzon was thus suggesting a direct approach to the Tibetans, with a broad enough hint regarding a British official visiting and residing in Tibet, 'if this should prove desirable'. Lord George Hamilton's reaction was very favourable in regard to the first proposition though he was not sanguine about the result of bringing 'diplomatic pressure' to bear on the Chinese Government. As to the British official, he was extremely guarded for he doubted the 'expediency' of this step since it 'might cause complications, and even delay' the settlement of the essential part of the negotiations.[7]

The outlines had thus been sketched out and the initial exchanges were concerned largely with the implementation of the policies now enunciated. Thus on 24 May (1899) Lord Curzon spoke of having laid his hands 'upon one, if not two agents' through whom it may be possible to enter into 'direct relations with the Dalai Lama of Lhasa'.[8] In retrospect, it proved to be a three-pronged assault: through Kazi U-gyen, the Bhutan Vakil; Taw Sein Ko, a half-caste Chinese who was the Government of Burma's Advisor on Chinese affairs and finally Chirang Palgez, head of the triennial Lapchak mission from Leh to Lhasa. The last two did not achieve much although, for the record, it may be mentioned that the former was never tried—Taw Sein Ko was 'too fat', was bound to be regarded in Lhasa as 'an impostor', besides being 'rather inconvenient to spare'[9]— and that the latter, despite persistent efforts, proved barren of results.

In a despatch, late in October (1899), Curzon spoke of the Lieutenant-Governor of Bengal making a 'guarded' use of the Bhutan Vakil, Kazi U-gyen, for an informal though direct approach. Reference was to the Bhutan official's visit to Lhasa in 1898 on which he later briefed John Claude White, the Political

)fficer in Sikkim, imparting to him the precious information, for what it was vorth, that the Tibetans 'did not like the Chinese yoke'. It would seem that the)alai Lama had, in a very broad and general way, asked the Kazi to act for him in nterceding with the British, an offer which he (Kazi U-gyen) reportedly declined. A year later (in 1899), the Kazi who was on a visit to Tibet was persuaded to write o the Lama from P'hari, entirely on his own yet dilating at length on the now vell-known views of the new Viceroy. The Dalai Lama, however, was in no mood o oblige—at best, he was non-committal. It was this letter which Curzon had in nind when (in December 1899) he wrote to Lord George Hamilton that he had ounded Lhasa 'through a native emissary'—who could be none other than Kazi U-gyen—as to whether it would be prepared to 'discuss the frontier question juietly with us' at the boundary. The Lama, however, refused to oblige (although e made it quite clear that he would like to do so) 'for fear of the Chinese Amban'. Here was 'the first attempt'—to which Curzon alluded in his letter to the Secretary •f State—which had 'not been a success'.[10]

Undeterred, in December, 1899, the Bengal Government again persuaded he Kazi to write to Lhasa. The language used now was more direct, the meaning nore unambiguous. Emphasizing that the reigning Grand Mughal was 'the greatest •fficial under the King', U-gyen exhorted the Lama to 'make haste and settle' nd ended up by warning that 'should the Viceroy in Calcutta lose patience, it vould not end well for you'. The reply from Lhasa (March, 1900) was none too ncouraging for all that the Lama promised was to agree to consult with the new Amban who was 'formerly friendly', although whether he still wielded 'any nfluence' was doubtful.[11]

Between the Kazi's second letter to the Dalai Lama and his visit to Lhasa, in he fall of 1901, intervenes the Kashmir Assistant Resident, Captain Kennion's attempt to make use of the Garpons of Western Tibet, at Gartok. Lord Curzon's etter—his first addressed directly to the Dalai Lama—was entrusted to these Tibetan officials who, however, were later to return it unanswered.[12] It is significant hat at this stage, end of 1900, the Viceroy, despite the first somewhat vague eports of Aguan Dorjieff's visit to Russia—which were to gather considerable nomentum in the years that followed—had not yet despaired of his direct approach. He thought the Tibetan mission to the Tsar 'a fraud', for it was 'most unlikely':

Tibet is, I think, much more likely in reality to look to us for protection than to look to Russia, and I cherish a secret hope that the communication which I am trying to open with the Dalai Lama may inaugurate some sort of relations between us.[13]

The occasion was provided by Ladakh's enclave of Minsar, which lies deep nto Western Tibet. Captain Kennion proposed a visit during which he planned o meet the Garpons and entrust them with the Viceroy's letter to the Lama for onward transmission. In due course, as the plan received imperial sanction (July 900), Captain Kennion set out for Gartok where he formally delivered the sealed

massage. In March (1901), however, it was returned with the observation that i̇
had been sent to Lhasa—whence it had come back unopened, for the Tibetaɴ
Government saw no need for its establishing any communication with thɇ
British. It seemed to Captain Kennion, however, that the seals had beeɴ
tampered with and the contents of the letter read. Later, as if to cover thɇ
earlier version, the Garpons denied that they ever despatched the letter tc
Lhasa for were it known that they had entertained any communication fron┐
the British, their own lives would be in serious jeopardy.

Not unnaturally, the emphasis shifted once again to the Bhutan Vaki
although it is interesting to note that, despite the scorn he heaped upon thɇ
Chinese 'farce', the Viceroy was not unwilling to make use of them. Thuꜱ
Lord Curzon now suggested that the British Charge d'Affaires in Peking may
be asked to address the Tsungli Yamen, the Foreign Affairs Board, 'tc
endeavour to obtain their assistance in regard to having free access to P'hari⸵
This approach was based on the reasoning that 'if it prove⸰, as we anticipated₎
that the Chinese are unable or unwilling to give the assistance' asked foɼ
there need be even less hesitation in going ahead with the new policy oꜰ
dealing directly with the Tibetans.[14]

Meantime Kazi U-gyen was preparing to go to Lhasa to deliver whaꜰ
would seem a veritable menagerie—two elephants, two peacocks and a
leopard—to the master of the Potala. He was now saddled with an additionaⅼ
care, namely the Governor-General's second letter (June, 1902) to the Dalaɪ
Lama. In contrast to the first, Curzon's tone was peremptory, his language
indicative of a growing exasperation.[15] The British Government, he warneↁ
the Lama, had shown extreme forbearance to the Tibetans in their past
dealings but if he (the Lama) refused to behave: 'My government must reservɇ
their right to take such steps as may seem to them necessary and proper',
viz., to ensure the observance of the Convention of 1890 and of the Trade
Regulations of 1893.[16]

As if to add fuel to the fire, U-gyen returned in October and brought
back the Viceroy's letter unopened, and with its seals intact. There were
varied rumours as to whether he actually delivered the epistle, it being widely
believed that he never mentioned to the Lama even the fact of its existence.
By November (1901) Curzon appeared both unhappy and disillusioned.

'I do not believe', he confided to George Hamilton, 'that the man ever
saw the Dalai Lama or handed the letter to him. On the contrary, I believe him
to be a liar and, in all probability, a paid Tibetan spy.'[17] This was contrary to
what the Bengal Government thought, yet in close and clear conformity with
the wildest Darjeeling bazaar gossip on which Curzon was now increasingly
fed. And for what it was worth, dame rumour had it that the Kazi never met
the Lama, that the shapes had dissuaded him from delivering the letter in
question, that he had behaved so indiscreetly that the Lhasa authorities had
forbidden his future visits.

These were indeed grave charges and, if only in parenthesis, a word may *e added to put the record straight.[18] An interesting clue is provided by that *astly rich storehouse of Lord Čurzon's 'Papers' to which this writer had access *nd in which there is a letter from 'Rai Ugyen Kazi Bahadur', written from *alimpong on April 12, 1910. Herein the Kazi repudiated the charge that he did *ot deliver the Viceroy's sealed communication to the Lama : 'It has always been *o me a matter of keen regret that Your Lordship may have believed the story' *vhich, of course, His Lordship had. To vindicate himself the Kazi asked Mr. Bell, *he then Political Officer, 'to enquire of the Dalai Lama in Darjeeling whether or *ot my story was true. He did so and found that it was. On this point you can *atisfy yourself by asking Mr. Bell'.[19] Kazi U-gyen concluded with these words: My profound respect for Your Lordship makes me anxious that this matter *hould be put beyond doubt in your Lordship's mind'.[20] One wonders if it was.

That, however, was long after the passions and prejudices of the early years *f Lord Curzon's Viceroyalty. Truly, the urgency, and the exasperation, in the *Viceroy's tone of that period may be seen at its best in his private correspondence *vith Lord George Hamilton. Thus, writing to the latter in January 1901, before *azi U-gyen's second failure, the Viceroy confessed that he felt completely *utraged by the fact that the Dalai Lama had assumed towards him an attitude of *ontemptuous silence, that in returning his letter unopened he, the all-powerful *Viceroy, had been treated as 'the pettiest of petty potentates'. Curzon added: 'It *s really the most grotesque and indefensible thing that at a distance of little *nore than 200 miles from our frontier, this community of unarmed monks should *set us perpetually at defiance'.[21] One half-suspects that Kazi U-gyen's warning *o the Dalai Lama that 'should the Viceroy in Calcutta lose patience, it will not *end well for you',[22] or his description of the reigning Grand Mughal as 'the *greatest official under the King' were inspired.[23]

It is clear nonetheless that the Viceroy's apparent anger, and impatience, *vith the Lama did not take account of the obvious fact that by opening his *letters, and thereby entering into correspondence with him (Lord Curzon), the *Tibetan ruler would be playing into the hands of his numerous detractors at *nome, in the Lamaist world and in not far away Peking. That he suspected the *ambitious Indian ruler of not altogether friendly designs on his land was well *nown. Now, by corresponding with him, and few secrets could be kept in Lhasa *for long, or even successfully, on mattes which had strong political under-tones, *despite their superficial innocuousness, he was likely to be enmeshed deeper *and deeper into a situation from which it may not have been easy to extricate *himself. Hence the Lama's lack of enthusiasm for epistolary exchanges which the *touchy, hypersensitive Curzon was prone to treat as a gratuitous insult.

If it were not the Viceroy, the British Government at any rate was not altogether *oblivious of this viewpoint. And the response of the Secretary of State to such *a strong plea as was made for an 'altered' policy, or the urgent adoption of some *'practical measures', would seem to demonstrate this beyond cavil. Lord George

Hamilton conceded that relations with Tibet had not been satisfactory and therefore, the Viceroy 'would be justified' in adopting 'strong measures'. But having said that he marshalled argument upon argument against any precipitate move. He reminded the Viceroy that Tibet was politically subordinate to China that the difficult nature of the country would make any military operations hazardous, that the Viceroy's ceaseless pressure for closer relations was likely to increase 'distrust of our intentions' and that any ill thought-out, over-hasty action on India's part 'would be viewed with much disquietude and suspicion. Hamilton ended up on a rather stern note : 'In these circumstances, proceed with due consideration'. And, as though it were not enough, asked the Viceroy to take him into confidence 'before any steps are taken that may involve risk of the complications that I have indicated'.[24] Earlier, in private, he had told Curzon that the latter's proposals 'seem to me somewhat aggressive'[25] and that just then 'our military establishments' were in no position to justify 'any expedition of size beyond the frontiers of India'. Besides, in reality the Tibetan hates foreigners with 'a truly Chinese hatred',[26] and hence the opposition to any precipitate move that may be encountered. Barely a week later, he warned Curzon again : 'the Tibetans are but the smallest of pawns on the political chess-board, but castles, knights and bishops may be all involved in trying to take it.'[27]

Nowhere perhaps, was the gap that lay between the Viceroy's viewpoint and that of the Home Government laid bare more vividly than it was here. Curzon had always regarded it as axiomatic that where diplomacy failed there was no alternative except to resort to *force majeure*. As he put it, and herein he was expressing a viewpoint that was then widely held, 'nothing can be or will be done with the Tibetans until they are frightened. I should at once move a few men up to the frontier'.[28] This indeed would seem to be the basic premise that underlay his plea for an 'altered policy'. For the authorities in London , nurtured in the tradition of the cool and phlegmatic Salisbury, what could not be secured by diplomacy they may be willing to forego, though for a price. This stark divergence in outlook had been patent from the day the Honourable George Nathaniel Curzon assumed office as the old Salisbury's Under Secretary for Foreign Affairs. Besides, it was no secret that Lord George Hamilton had been far from happy about the then Prime Minister's choice for Elgin's successor. And now, one would suppose, the Secretary of State's warnings were designed not so much to carry conviction as to bridle and restrain his over-zealous lieutenant. In any case, Curzon had always refused to believe that anyone not prepared to contemplate the employment of force in the last resort, could possibly have a policy worth the name.[29]

The Tibetans, it would seem, were playing his game too. For the return of his second letter, which Kazi U-gyen brought back unopened, the Viceroy now magnified into a major crisis.[30] Convinced that Tibet was either unwilling, or unable, to enter into any direct relationship, the Viceroy now weighed alternatives for putting future relations on 'a more satisfactory footing'.[31] He rejected a complete trade embargo, for this step, he felt, would defeat its own purpose since all traffic would get diverted to Nepal. In the alternate, occupation of the Chumbi Valley 'was not proposed at present.' It is not without significance that the Viceroy did not reject it out of hand for, as he viewed it, the policy he proposed 'kept this course of action more or less distinctly in the background.'

What did he then advocate? Firstly, that the Political Officer tour along the frontier, that he erect boundary pillars wherever these be necessary or desirable, that grazing grounds which the Tibetans might have occupied at Giaogong or elsewhere be cleared, or fees charged for such violations. Secondly, Mr. White was to be accompanied by an escort of one company of Gurkhas, with another in reserve. The Viceroy was persuaded that his proposed course of action offered some distinct advantages : if the Tibetan did not resist, the convention would be observed; if they did—by impeding the Political Officer's advance, by endeavouring to assert Tibetan claims to Giaogong or by destroying boundary pillars—they would have only themselves to blame for the clash that 'may result'. Maintaining that these were 'the minimum' demands he could recommend, Lord Curzon emphasized that if the Tibetans showed an attitude of permanent hostility, he would strongly advocate the occupation of the Chumbi Valley until they agreed to a diplomatic conference at Lhasa.

It is interesting to note that in their actual execution, as no doubt in private correspondence, the Viceroy materially modified these proposals. Thus White was not to erect boundary pillars, nor was the fact of their being dismantled by the Tibetans to be made a cause of grievance. Instead, Lhasa was to be merely pushed out of territory which reportedly did not belong to it. 'I think', George Hamilton wrote, 'the course you propose in your private latter is more effective and less likely to lead to complications outside Tibet ... than that which you recommended officially'.[32]

A point that bears mention about this despatch is Lord Curzon's allusion, not for the first time though, to certain 'factors in the situation' which were bound to invest this problem with 'a wider and more serious significance.' He had already referred to the existing situation *vis-a-vis* Tibet as 'the most extraordinary anachronism of the twentieth century', which must be brought to an end 'with as little delay and commotion as possible'. That Lord George Hamilton should acquiesce so readily in the Viceroy's proposed course of action may, if only indirectly, seem to confirm the existence of these 'factors'. Indeed, Tibet was fast becoming a hotbed of political intrigue and the sprawling land mass of Tsarist Russia appeared to be casting some dark shadows, across the Potala. It is to this part of the story that attention may be directed for it profoundly influenced all subsequent developments in Lord Curzon's Tibetan policy.

Few can read through the Indian Viceroy's official despatches on Tibet in 1901-02, much less his private correspondence, without being powerfully struck by his growing restlessness in regard to the unsatisfactory nature of the relationship with that country. His insistence that more 'practical' measures [33] were necessary in place of the old policy of watchful waiting has already been referred to as also the fact that seriously opposed as the Home Government were to his methods, they did finally concur in a number of his suggestions. As a matter of fact, a shift was already noticeable in the position which Whitehall had previously taken.[34] And though his dark allusion to 'factors in the situation' which boded ill may have carried weight with the Home Government, the latter was certainly not unaware of a state of affairs which had no doubt become disturbing. In fact, not a little of the Viceroy's exasperation was born of this somewhat paradoxical situation: that while the Dalai Lama sent accredited 'diplomatic' missions, accompanied by autographed letters, to the Tsar of Russia, the Indian potentate, who rated himself no less important a Grand Mughal, was treated with seemingly ill-concealed contempt. His sealed letters, sent with special messengers, and addressed to 'the illustrious Dalai Lama, Supreme Pontiff of the Great Buddhist Church'[35] had been returned unopened, on what appeared to the Viceroy, a lame, hard-to-sustain plea that the Lama was barred communication with the outer world.[36] For not only was there increasing evidence of Russian intrigue but perhaps a growing suspicion that the Lama himself was deeply involved in it. Before essaying the role played by Russia and her agents it may, therefore, be well worthwhile to attempt an understanding of the Tibetan god-king whose pro-Russian leanings were making that country's task relatively so easy.

Notes

1. Ronaldshay, *Life*, II, p. 275.
2. Letter to George Hamilton, March 30, 1899. Hamilton Papers, *op.cit.*
3. *Loc. cit.* Also Tibet Papers, *op.cit.*, Cd. 1920, No. 26, pp. 74-75.
4. Variously rendered as Pari, Phari, and P'hari. Literally 'Pig-hill,' the town, 14,300 feet above sea-level, lies 50 miles to north of Yatung, on the Kalimpong-Lhasa route.
5. Letter, Curzon to Hamilton, March 23, 1899, Hamilton Papers, *op.cit.* Elsewhere (letter of May 24, 1899), Curzon called the Amban 'an obstacle and a fraud'. *Ibid.*
6. *Ibid.*, letter, Curzon to Hamilton, March 23, 1899.
7. Tibet Papers, *op.cit.*, Cd. 1920, November 27, 1899, pp. 99-100.
8. Letter, Curzon to Hamilton, May 24, 1899, Hamilton Papers, *op.cit.*
9. *Foreign*, September, 1900, No. 89 and Encl. to 106.
10. Curzon to Hamilton, letter, December 28, 1899, Hamilton Papers, *op.cit.*
11. *Foreign*, No. 94 (September, 1900), Bengal, April 23, 1900.
12. *Ibid.*, September and November 1900, Encls to 106 and 55-56. Government placed on record its 'appreciation' of the 'tactful manner' in which Captain Kennion carried his mission.
13. Curzon to Hamilton, letter, November 18, 1900, Hamilton Papers, *op.cit.*
14. Tibet Papers, *op.cit.*, Cd. 1920, No. 29, pp. 102-3. The creation of the Tsungli Yamen, or more correctly Tsung-li ko-kuo shib-wu ya-men (Office in General Charge of Affairs Concerning All Foreign Nations) was a direct result of the treaties of Tientsin and Peking dictated by the Western Powers in October, 1860. It continued to handle Chinese Foreign Affairs until replaced by the Wai-wu-pu (Ministry of

Foreign Affairs) in July, 1901. This change too was undertaken at the behest of the foreign powers.

15. This was in sharp contrast to the earlier letter which Captain Kennion had carried. The former contained no threats : the British had only wanted to facilitate trade between India and Tibet, to the mutual advantage of both countries, and to foster that direct and friendly intercourse, which should subsist between neighbouring lands. The Viceroy hoped a Tibetan representative would meet him and help settle all outstanding difficulties. For the text, see *Ibid.,* Annexure to Encl. 3 in No. 37, pp. 120-21. *Ibid.,* Curzon to Dalai Lama, August 11, 1900.

16. *Ibid.,* No. 37, June 8, 1901, pp. 18-19.
    Annexure to Encl. 4 in No. 37, pp. 120-21, Curzon to Dalai Lama.

17. Curzon to Hamilton, letter, November 5, 1901, Hamilton Papers, *op.cit.*

18. For a more detailed account reference may be made to Parshotam Mehra, 'Kazi U-gen: a Paid Tibetan Spy?' *JRCAS,* LI, July-September, 1964, pp. 301-5.

19. Owing to the Chinese armed occupation cf Lhasa, the 13th Dalai Lama sought refuge in India during the years 1910-12. Apart from visiting Calcutta and some centres of Buddhist interest, the Lama spent most of his time in Darjeeling. Here part of Mr. Bell's duty, as Political Officer, was to cater to the needs of the Tibetan ruler.

20. The letter is in No. 340 of the Curzon Collection in the India Office Library. It is in a white cover, bearing 2 half-anna stamps franked in Kalimpong and addressed to 'The Rt. Hon'ble Lord Curzon of Kedleston, Carlton House Terrace, London S. W. 1.' and in Lord Curzon's own handwriting, in blue pencil, are the words 'U-gyen Kazi: Tibetan Letter, 1902'.

21. Curzon to Hamilton, letter, January 11, 1901, Hamilton Papers, *op.cit.*

22. Tibet Papers, *op.cit.,* Cd. 1920. Annexure to Encl. 2 in No. 37, p. 120.

23. The Dalai Lama in his conversations with the Kazi is reported to have referred to the Indian Government as 'the big Government', *Ibid.,* Encl. 3, in No. 44, pp.129-30.

24. *Ibid.,* No. 38, August 16, 1901, p. 122.

25. Hamilton to Curzon, letter, July 4, 1901, Hamilton Papers, *op.cit.*

26. *Ibid.,* letter, July 11, 1901.

27. *Ibid.,* letter, August 22, 1901.

28. *Ibid.,* Curzon to Hamilton, letter, June 11, 1901.

29. In a letter to St. John Brodrick on February 1, 1901, Curzon had written : 'The whole explanation of your troubles at home is that for years no British Minister has consented to look one yard ahead. There has been no prescience and, therefore, no policy. You have none for China, Persia, Morocco, Egypt, or any place in the world. Lord Salisbury is adept at handling the present .... But the future to him is anathema'. Ronalday, *Life,* II, p. 206.

30. He announced this in two telegrams to the Secretary of State (Tibet Papers, *op.cit.,* Cd. 1920, Nos. 41-42, dated October 29 and November 3, 1901, p. 125) who in a private letter enquired, 'What do you propose to do' warning he (Curzon) might 'move more cautiously before assuming the aggressive'. Hamilton to Curzon, letter, November 29, 1901, Hamilton Papers, *op.cit.*

31. The Viceroy's proposals were outlined in Tibet Papers, *op.cit.,* Cd. 1920, No. 44, February 13, 1902, pp. 125-27.

32. Hamilton to Curzon, letter, March 13, 1902. Hamilton Papers, *op.cit.* Actually, in a later despatch—Tibet Papers, *op.cit.,* Cd. 1920, No. 47, July 10, 1902, pp. 133-34—the Viceroy modified some of the points in his earlier communication.

33. In a despatch to the Secretary of State, Curzon had called Elgin's policy as one of 'forbearance and inaction', carried to 'unreasonable limits'. Hamilton, letter, September 5, 1899, had himself referred to the 'present' condition of things with regard to Tibet as being 'grotesque'. Hamilton Papers, *op.cit.*

34. An instance in point was the Home Government's sanction of White's visit to the Tibet-Sikkim frontier and the Secretary of State's admission that the situation was such as indeed 'wants attending to'. *Ibid.,* letter, January 4, 1903.

35. Lord Curzon used this form of address in his letter to the Dalai Lama. Annexure, in Encl. 4, Cd. 1920, Tibet Papers, *op.cit.,* No. 37, pp. 121-22.

36. In his discussions with Kazi U-gyen expressing his inability to accept the Viceroy's letter, the Dalai reminded him (Kazi U-gyen) that he was precluded from writing to any foreign government in terms of an agreement concluded by one of his predecessors, by which he felt bound. *Ibid.,* Encl. 3, in No. 44, pp. 129-30.

9
The 13th Dalai Lama and Dorjief

Some general observations in regard to the institution of the Dalai, and of the Panchen Lama, have been made already.[1] It may suffice here to recapitulate that the former goes as far back as the close of the fourteenth century, that it was the third of the line who converted Mongolia and that the Great Fifth was received by the Chinese Emperor, in Peking, as if he were an independent sovereign. As of today it is the 14th reincarnation of Chen-re-zı who, head of the Tibeto-Mongolian world, finds himself a refugee from the land of his birth and faith.[2] This narrative, however, is concerned with the present Lama's predecessor : Nga-Wang Lobsang Tup-den Gyasto to give him his full name or more simply Tupden or Thupten Gyatso, the 13th Dalai Lama.[3] One of his most intimate friends, and confidants in the Western world,[4] whose later years were spent in writing a biographical account of the Tibetan pontiff rated him a 'unique' world figure. And, in the context of the chequered history of the institution, unique he certainly was. For, other things apart, through all the thirty-seven summers of his adult life—and the Dalai Lama had, 'conveniently' for their Chinese masters and their own power-hungry Regents, developed the practice of dying before attaining adulthood—he had the 'unusual' privilege of exercising the full temporal and spiritual authority vested in his high office. Besides, in the words of his successor, he had not only 'clarified and defined the status of Tibet as an independent nation but also achieved a great deal for the betterment of his people.'[5] In any case, it is pretty certain that none before him exercised such powers and, though political prophecy is at best a hazardous preoccupation, it does not seem likely that any of his successors would achieve that distinction either.[6]

A word here may not be out of place regarding the manner of choosing an infant Dalai Lama who, as was his wont, often died before attaining his majority.[7] The early death of the incarnation kept power in the hands of a Regency Council, which corresponded roughly to a coalition of the highest ecclesiastical figures, representing the corporate interests of the great monasteries, and the most powerful families of the nobility. As if to counter this to some extent, it was 'customary' to choose an infant 'incarnation' from an undistinguished and, for most part, a poor peasant family. Obviously, this prevented the kinds of permutations and combinations that were likely to arise if an incarnation were found in the boson of a family that already had great wealth, or wielded absolute power in a particular territorial region.

   To recount some of his biographical details, Thupten Gyatso was born in June 1876, in a family of ordinary peasants in the province of Tak-po to the south-east of Lhasa, a few days' journey from the capital.[8] Although there had been serious differences of opinion as to where precisely the new incarnation would appear, the claims of a western and an east Tibetan province being staked as clamorously as those of Tak-po for this signal honour, it is significant that the Lama's discovery[9] was a particularly clear one.[10]

   Nor, were there any rival candidates. And since the divine indications in his case were so unmistakable, the Tibetan Government refused to use the golden urn—proof positive of the fact, if one were needed, of a growing paralysis of the Manchu overlordship. That there was only a solitary claimant would not, by itself, preclude the use of the urn although it was generally required that there be more than one claimant, thus giving the Ch'ing rulers of China a hand in the final choice.[11] The date itself (1876), however, would connote a period of declining fortunes for the reigning dynasty, because of the Taiping Rebellion and of the calamitous defeats in the war with Britain and France (1858-61)—to pitchfork only two of a host of other humiliations. However, the young child, then barely two years of age, having been chosen was brought to Lhasa. His enthronement nonetheless had to await the confirmation of the Emperor, which took nearly a year, and was celebrated in 1879.[12]

   A young Dalai's life is certainly not very enviable. Torn away from his parents, denied any playmates except, and only occasionally, his own brothers and sisters, encaged within the forbidding walls of the Potala, as if a prisoner, and surrounded by austere-looking monks, the impressionable youth would seem to grow up in an atmosphere far from the normal or what may be either healthy or wholesome.[13] From an early age reading and writing are stressed, as also long meditations.[14] If an account of the personal experiences of a later incarnation may be said to hold true of his former birth, the facts adduced here may be regarded as relevant. The Lama's education begins when he is about six; the first five years being spent on writing Tibetan-'in addition to daily study of the scriptures, morning and evening.' Religious education in dialectical discussion, however, is added at twelve, while admission to the two famed monasteries of Drepung and Sera takes place at thirteen. The young incumbent, to perfect his knowledge of thousands of Buddhist scriptures, is expected to master some hundreds of them, an induction that may leave one 'unnerved' and with 'a feeling of being dazed'—as though 'hit on the head by a stone.'[15]

   The young 13th must have gone through the mill. Besides being taught some arithmetic and the writing of Tibetan— there are four different forms of the script, the two more familiar being U-chen and U-me—he was trained on the problems of general administration, an apprenticeship that he later admitted to be totally inadequate.[16] The special emphasis of his education had however been, and for obvious reasons, on religious studies; thus, it is said, that eight doctors of divinity debated theological subjects in his presence. No wonder that at thirteen he could take a leading part in religious discussions organized by Lhasa's three great monasteries of Drepung, Sera and Ganden, or deliver a sermon to a large assembly of priests on the previous lives of the Buddha or even retire, over long periods, for religious meditation.[17] Completely secluded must have been his life among the priestmonks who surrounded him and his constant bane—'study, and study, and study in the subtleties of this complicated religion.'[18] Inasmuch as priests constantly hovered around him, instructed him and even took him out for long walks—as if the walks or their company could be a substitute for a young boy's natural ambition for play and sport—mundane affairs received scant attention and all possible stress was laid on matters of the spirit.

This marked slant, from the viewpoint of those who imparted such instruction, may not have been unreasonable. Few Dalai Lamas before him had attempted to take over—much less successfully wielded—the secular authority; those who had, did not survive long to exercise it.[19] Hence the stress on matters spiritual. But well-placed, or otherwise, one wonders whether the 13th Dalai Lama's keen interest in worldly affairs, which was a marked feature of his entire earthly career, was not a natural enough reaction to the training of his boyhood?[20] Perhaps justifiable too—as a rebound against all the earlier emphasis on the metaphysics and mysticism of Lamaistic Buddhism?

As he neared adulthood, many obstacles were strewed across his path. The young Lama's Regent, who was the head of the Ten-gye-ling monastery in Lhasa, had employed his own brother as Chief Minister.[21] The two of them with the help of a third, who was also the abbot of a monastery, are said to have worked out a plan aiming at the young ruler's life. Both the precise nature of the plot as also the mode of its discovery, are shrouded in mystery although some of the details may be pieced together. Actually, as the young Dalai Lama came of age it was noticed that he was frequently taken ill. The subject became a matter of concern and the State Oracle at Ne-chung was pressed into service. The latter revealed that a magical diagram, in the form of a wheel, had been written on a piece of paper and inserted into the soles of a pair of shoes which the Minister had presented to the young Lama. The diagram in question had invoked the assistance of the evil spirits to destroy the wearer of the shoes.[22] Great was the horror and indignation with which the discovery of this plot was received. The conspirators, when unmasked, were visited with exemplary punishments—the legacy of the bitterness thus generated persisting even to our own day.[23] Thus it was well-known that the monks of Tengye-ling, the monastery of the deposed Regent and his brother, recipients as they were of all the insults which the Tibetan Government could heap on them, aided and abetted the Chinese armies whenever the latter threatened, or even appeared to threaten Lhasa.[24] To immediate purpose here it may suffice to recall that these

monks were principally responsible for giving currency to the belief that the 13th
Dalai Lama would be the last of the line: 'Another way,' Bell assures us, 'of saying
that he was a sham incarnation.'[25]

Apart from the half-mystical details of the plot, the plain fact of the matter is
that the 13th escaped the fate of his previous incarnations 'because he had the good
sense to dispose of the Regent before the Regent could dispose of him,'[26] that in a
game where stakes were so high no quarter could be given, nor taken.

His triumph, however, did have serious implications. For it meant that besides
creating a powerful monastic faction that would be bitterly hostile he became, in
addition, an obvious eyesore to the Chinese. It has already been noticed that the
Golden Urn was not used in his selection. Could it be that that partly explained why
the Manchu Emperor took well-nigh a year to accord his approval to the Lama's
enthronement? Perhaps the failure of the Regent's plot also connoted a growing
weakness of Chinese authority, for usually it was a joint Amban-Regent edeavour
to achieve a common objective—a thesis, whose validity has been seriously
questioned.[27] The 13th however had, in scotching the attempt, cleared his path and
though entitled to succeed to the sovereignty of Tibet at eighteen (seventeen by
ordinary reckoning for the Tibetans, like the Mongols, take into account both the
year of birth as also the current year),[28] he actually did not take over until two years
later. And when he finally did, he realized that his limitations were of an extreme
character. As he confessed to Bell,

> I came into power when I was 20 years old, but I did not know at all how to
> govern a country. For the first five or six years it was very difficult ..... However,
> within ten years I had, in some degree, improved the Government.[29]

Ambitious—how ardently had he wished to take over control of worldly
power!—and extremely hard-working, the shades of Kedleston indeed seemed to
fall portentously across the Potala's young occopant. His early problems, however,
were to keep in check the power of those who had, for so long as a hundred years or
more, got used to exercising it. Thus one of his very first acts was to 'crack' down
on the 'toughs' whose rule of Lhasa, during the days of the Great Prayer festival,
was synonymous with considerable lawlessness.[30] Again quietly, albeit successfully,
he defeated an attempt by the Chinese Amban to appoint one of his protégés as a
Minister in the Tibetan Cabinet.[31]

While nearer home the young Lama appeared gradually to be overcoming the
difficulties that he was up against, his handling of Tibet's foreign relations showed
a remarkable degree of naivete, a near-complete lack of maturity. That the Manchu
hold, and in consequence the authority of the Imperial Ambans, had weakened was
clear and the young Lama was shrewd enough to ensure that it did not raise its ugly
head again.[32] His other great neighbour was India in the south—physically
propinquant, culturally very closely aligned.[33] It has been noticed that since the
latter part of the eighteenth century, India had, under the British, made repeated
efforts to open Tibet to trade. These attempts had, however, proved singularly
unavailing. Not unavailing though—on the contrary these were extremely

successful—were similar endeavours in the case of Nepal, Bhutan and Sikkim, a fact that must have frightened the Tibetans out of their wits. The story of the numerous clandestine missions sponsored by the Government of India in the eighties of the nineteenth century may be recalled in this context if only to underline the fact that the initial fright of the Tibetans must have grown further.

As if that were not enough there began in 1890 a squabble which was to prove a long drawn-out affair. It related to, as has been remarked, the delimitation of the Tibet-Sikkim frontier and the observance in practice of the Trade Regulations, to both of which the Chinese had pledged the most solemn of assurances on behalf of their self-proclaimed wards. The ill-concealed British anxiety to open Yatung as a trade mart, coupled with what the Tibetans regarded as aggressive encroachments on their territory in Sikkim, made them suspect the very worst. Nor had stories of Christian missionaries in China, much less India, escaped notice and as most news in Tibet travelled by hearsay, accounts may have been exaggerated at the least.[34] In any case, to the Tibetans it appeared certain that the British were intent on destroying at once their freedom and their faith.[35] Hence the widely accepted picture of the latter as aggressive and disagreeable interlopers who must be kept out at all costs.

In a contrast that was strikingly sharp, was the attitude of the Russians. The land frontiers of the Tsar's dominions then, as those of the Soviet Union's today, did not indeed touch Tibet. Yet neither in Mongolia, nor yet in Sinkiang, has Russian influence, or penetration, been either unknown or non-existent. For most part, the link had been through the Mongol tribes who, converts to Tibetan Lamaism, later came squarely within the Russian territorial orbit. There were also the Torgot Kalmuks who had in the mid-seventeenth century, settled in the Volga region. To the Buriat Mongol no less than to the Kalmuk, therefore, Tibet's monks, and their monasteries remained the natural goal for a life-long ambition. For to the Lama Buddhist, Lhasa has always been the Mecca where his education and training reach their final perfection. Indeed while it may not be easy to catalogue such visits, numerous as these were in the eighteenth century, two of the more important ones may be listed here. In 1720 the Kalmuks are reported to have sent contributions for the repair of the Jokhang, while ten years later another of their missions is said to have visited Lhasa.

In the last quarter of the century when Bogle and Turner repaired to Tashilhunpo they culled evidence enough of a flourishing trade traffic with Mongolia. This clearly was carried by the Kalmuks, as well as the Western and the Buriat Mongols; commerce for most part being in Bulgar hides, yaktails, camels, bastard beads, spices and gold. It would appear that contact here served a dual purpose of trade as well as pilgrimage to holy Lhasa.[36] Turner noticed that the Tibetans were well-informed about Russia—they knew of Czarina Catherine and the territorial extent of her dominions.[37] He learned too that Russia had made many overtures in an effort to extend her trade to the interior of Tibet, through the instrumentality of the 'Tarananat Lama'.[38] Here thus were the first intimations of that rivalry which later was to have such drastic, and well-nigh fatal, consequences for Tibet.

Two factors would thus seem to underline a continuous, and indeed unbroken, link between Russia and Tibet. In the first place, traffic by the Mongols (who later became Russia's Asiatic subjects) had been both regular and long-established,[39] more especially after the destruction of the Tangut Kingdom by Chingiz Khan in 1227.[40] Secondly, the Muscovites' familiarity with the Mongol ways of diplomacy added to the widely-held, if sedulously cultivated belief that the Russian Tsar—the 'tsagan' or the 'White Khan'—was heir to the Mongol Khans. Coupled with the fact that Russia itself was a successor state of the Golden Horde, it created a favourable situation psychologically for the extension of the Tsar's rule over these people.[41] Significantly, and in sharp contrast to the British and other European powers, the Russians had wisely restrained Christian missionaries from proselytising in their Asiatic dominions. Both consciously, but perhaps more so unconsciously, the Russian ruler and his agents made large, capital gains out of this fact.[42]

Another point that bears repetition relates to the fact that since about the middle of the eighteenth century the Buriats and the Kalmuks had been Russian subjects, that among the not inconsiderable coterie of their countrymen in Tibet, the Tsarist regime often discovered convenient tools who could be made use of to subserve its own ulterior purposes. Again, since territorial expansion at Tibet's expense had never been, indeed could scarcely be a Russian goal, these Buriat-Kalmuk monks were not, for most part, suspect in Tibetan eyes.

Towards the closing decades of the nineteenth century one of the Buriat monks in Lhasa or, to use Leonte'yev's words, 'one of the leading (outstanding) lamas of Tibet by nationality Buriat,'[43] was a man called Aguan Dorjieff.[44] Dorjieff—his name has many variants, viz. Dorji, Dorjeev, Dorshieff, Dorshevy, Dogiew, Dorjew-was by birth a Buriat of Chorinskaia, in the province of Verchnyudinsk. His first schooling was in the convent of Amochowski in Buriat Mongolia. Later, roughly around 1880, he drifted to Urga in Outer Mongolia and finally to Lhasa itself. A man of wide learning and ability he studied over a number of years in the Drepung monastery where he is said to have taken a theological degree, hence, to the Tibetans, his title of Tse-nyi Kem-po. His reputation as a scholar seems to have earned him the position of a tutor to the young Dalai Lama, a fact that won him his pupil's complete confidence. Soon, as the Lama came of age, Dorjieff found himself to be his 'work-washing Abbot.' In this capacity, part of his assignment was to sprinkle water, scented with saffron flowers, a little on the person of the Dalai Lama, but more on the walls of the room, on the altar and on the books—a symbol of cleansing. The Buriat was thus very close to the person of Tibet's god-king.

Another version of Dorjieff's early career pictures him as an employee of the Russian foreign office, and of the Intelligence Service, as early as 1885. As a member of the 'Service,' he is said to have visited all the capitals of Europe, to be trained as an accomplished diplomat. Later when the 13th Dalai Lama assumed power, 'it was contrived' that Dorjieff should become his tutor.[45] It is interesting in this context to remember that it has been possible to identify Dorjieff as a member of the Russian explorer Prjevalsky's last expedition to northern Tibet in 1884.[46]

Russian at heart and nearly all Buriat intellectuals were pro-Tsarisit and, later as it turned out, pro-Soviet besides in some degree, being incipient nationalist pan-Mongolists and serious scholars and educators[47] – it appears that Dorjieff told the Lama that because of their close proximity to Mongolia more and more Russians were adopting, or more appropriately taking to, Tibetan Buddhism. Added to the fact that the messianic kingdom of legend, Shambala—literally, 'source of (all) luck'—was oftentimes identified with Russia,[48] Dorjieff's advocacy of the Tsarist cause must have made a powerful impact on the Dalai Lama. Leading the latter along the garden path as it were, the Buriat may have even hinted that the great Tsar was already very close to his faith.[49] One could thus visualize the young Dalai Lama afire with the vision of the all-powerful white Tsar standing by his side, a convert to Tibet's great religion! In the limited context in which alone the terms could be used, one may say that the policy of the Dalai Lama *vis-a-vis* the Russians enjoyed a certain 'popular' approval. Again, how vivid must the contrast have appeared between a ruler who was moving nearer to his faith and another that seemed intent on destroying it. Need one wonder then that while Lord Curzon's letters were returned unopened, the Lama sent missions of goodwill, reportedly of a diplomatic character, to St. Petersburg and Odessa and that he looked to Russia to save him from the intense attentions which his southern neighbour was bestowing on him.[50]

Dorjief, it may be obvious, did not talk of trade, or of 'opening up the country' and though the British protested time and again that their principal interest was commercial intercourse, the Dalai Lama must have viewed this as a clever ruse behind which lay hidden their nefarious design of entering his land in order to destroy his (Buddhist) religion.[51] That this was his view of their endeavours is manifest from a letter he wrote about this time to the ruler of Sikkim:

> Why do the British insist on establishing trade marts? Their goods are coming in from India right up to Lhasa. Whether they have their marts or not, their things come in all the same. The British, under the guise of establishing communications, are merely seeking to over-reach us. They are well practiced in all these political wiles.[52]

While his knowledge of the British, and their tricks, appears to have been complete, the Lama's disenchantment with the Russians yet lay hidden in the limbo of an embryonic future. And meanwhile the Buriat Dorjieff, with the active support of the Tibetan ruler, played his cards extremely well—almost to perfection.

On October 15, 1900, the official column of *Journal de Saint Petersburg* announced that the Emperor had received in audience a certain Aharmba-Aguan Dorjieff who was described as 'the first transit Hamba to the Dalai Lama of Tibet'.[53]

Here was the first official mention of the Buriat's active goings-on, as between Russia and Tibet. Public appearances apart, privately of course, the British both in India and at home, were much better informed.

Notes

1. *Supra*, Chapter 3.
2. The title 'Dalai Lama' is Mongolian in origin and is used mainly by the Chinese and the Mongols and, of course, most of the world outside. The Tibetans know him as Kyam-gon Rimpoche (the Precious Protector); Gye-wa Rimpoche (the Precious Sovereign); Buk (the Inmost Protector); Lama Pon-po (the Priest Officer); sometimes also as Kundun (the all-knowing Presence), Bell, *Tibet*, pp. 54-55 and Heinrich Harrer, *Seven Years in Tibet* (London, 1953), p. 123.
3. Dalai Lama, *op.cit.*, p. 22.
4. A world may be said here of Sir Charles Alfred Bell whose *Portrait of the Dalai Lama* (London, 1946) published posthumously is dedicated to the 13th Dalai's 'long and affectionate friendship'. Apart from this, Bell's *Tibet, Past and Present* (London, 1946), *People of Tibet* (London, 1928) and *Religion of Tibet* (London 1931) make him the best-known authority on the country's history. A member of the Indian Civil Service, Bell served in the Bengal plains prior to his transfer to Darjeeling in 1900. So deeply engrossed was he in the land and people beyond the border that by 1905 he was a complete master of their language. His *English-Tibetan Dictionary*, first published in 1905, remains to this day 'the best practical guide to the spoken language'.

    In 1903-4, he was incharge of a party which made a survey for the projected railway line from the plains of Bengal, *via* Bhutan, to Phari in Tibet. When the Chumbi valley was ceded to the British Government, under the terms of the Lhasa Convention (1904), Bell was placed incharge thereof. After twice acting as Political Officer in Sikkim, during the temporary absence of John Claude White, he succeeded the latter in 1908 and remained in this post until 1918. Bell retired in 1919, but was re-appointed as Political Officer in 1920, finally retiring in 1921. Outstanding periods of Bell's career were 1910-12 when he established intimate relations with the Dalai Lama during the latter's exile in India; 1913-14 when the treaty governing British relations with Tibet was being worked out at Simla and 1920-21 when he visited the Dalai Lama and stayed at Lhasa.

    Bell re-visited Lhasa in 1933-35 when, besides Tibet, he travelled extensively in Mongolia, Siberia, Manchuria and China. In 1937, the Royal Central Asian Society conferred upon him its 'Lawrence of Arabia' medal. The citation read in part: '...He (Sir Charles Bell) has acquired a greater knowledge of the Tibetan language, manners and customs than any other Englishman'. In 1939 he retired from his English home to British Columbia so that he may be able to work on the *Portrait* in relative peace. He had barely completed the manuscript, when death claimed him on March 18, 1945.
5. Dalai Lama, *op.cit.*, p. 22. The Dalai Lama cites from the 'Testament' of his earlier incarnation to this effect : 'After I took up the duties of spiritual and secular administration, there was no leisure for me, no time for pleasure. Day and night I

had to ponder over problems of religion and state .... I had to consider the welfare of the peasantry ... how to open the three doors of promptitude, impartiality and justice'.

Or again : 'From that year, the year of the Water Bull, to this present Water Monkey year, this land of Tibet has been happy and prosperous. It is like a land made new. All the people are at ease and happy'. *Ibid.*, p. 23

5. One wonders if the striking combination of those fortuitous circumstances which permitted the 13th maintain his complete independence of Chinese authority, while keeping the Russians and the British at bay, will recur. For the present with the tight (Communist) Chinese control at Lhasa, the 14th in exile as a hapless refugee and the Panchen Lama in disgrace, with the Indian influence well-nigh completely eliminated, his successor's plight appears none too enviable.

7. in a letter to the King, June 16, 1904, Lord Ampthill, then acting Governor-General wrote :

'Your Majesty is, of course, aware that the present Dalai Lama has outlived the ordinary span of his predecessors who were generally put to an early age, and that the existence of a Dalai Lama who is old enough to act for himself is unusual in the history of Tibet.' Ampthill Papers, *op.cit.*

8. An official biography of the 13th Dalai Lama was completed in February 1940. The Tibetan title, rendered in English, reads: 'The Wonderful Rosary of Jewels'. The Regent of Tibet presented Bell with a copy. The chief limitation of this biography, which else should be a very useful source of infromation, is the fact that herein the Dalai Lama does not appear as a human being but as an incarnation of Tibet's patron-deity, Chen-re-zi. Hence he is above human errors—being all-knowing and all-powerful. Bell, *Portrait*, p. 16.

9. 'In Tibetan religion and political theory the individuals who are the human embodiments of the Dalai-hood die, but the Dalai-hood persists. The emergence of a Dalai Lama is, therefore, in essence the return of one who has been temporarily absent to resume an authority and functions which are already, his own.' Basil Gould, *The Jewel in the Lotus* (London. 1957), p. 215.

10. It was the State Oracle at Nechung who finally came to the rescue of these divergent claimants. He maintained that there were often three re-births of a high lama, of his body, his speech or of his mind. It was the first that was required in this case and this, he held, must be found in the province of Tak-po. Bell, *Portrait*, p. 40.

11. It may be recalled that the drawing of lots is preceded by the selection of a panel of candidates by the Church authorities. This 'subterfuge', it has been maintained, enabled the Imperial authorities to make use of an innocuous choice. Bell, *Portrait*, p. 46, and Owen Lattimore, *Inner Asian Frontiers*, *op.cit.*, p. 232.

12. The enthronement ceremony takes place in the Potala and is called the 'Ser Thri Nag Sol'—literally 'the request to occupy the Golden Throne'. The ceremony, which may be interpreted as a proclamation to the people of Tibet that the young boy has been recognised as the returned Dalai Lama, lasts for many days, as each person has to be blessed separately. Bell, *Portrait*, pp. 44-45.

For a vivid, eye-witness account of the ceremony in the case of the 14th Dalai Lama (February 1940) see Basil Gould, *op.cit.*, pp. 221-29.

It may be recalled here that the 14th Dalai Lama was enthroned immediately after being brought to Lhasa, confirmation from Peking being regarded as unnecessary.

13. The present Dalai Lama denying that his early life was 'all work' or that the incarnations were 'almost prisoners in the Potala', reveals that he saw his family, in whose affairs he was able to take 'some part', at least 'every month or six weeks'. Later, however, he concedes: 'I will agree that most of my time was spent in the company of grown-up men and there must inevitably be something lacking in a childhood without the constant company of one's mother and other children'. Dalai Lama, *op.cit.* 45-46.

14. Heinrich Harrer, *op.cit.*, p. 163, gives a graphic account of the 'lonely life' of the young lama spending hours daily 'praying and studying', in the dark palace rooms of the Potala's 'golden prison', with little free time and few pleasures. When the guests at a merry party felt, Harrer relates, that they were being looked at from the roof of the Potala, they vanished as soon as possible from this field of vision. For 'they did not want to sadden the heart of the young ruler who could never hope to enjoy such distractions'.

15. Dalai Lama, *op.cit.*, pp. 37-41.

16. Bell, *Partrait*, p. 48.

17. *Loc, cit.*

18. *Ibid.*, p. 49.

19. 'It happened that ... during a period of about 120 years from the death of (7th) Dalai Lama Kesang Gyatso (1757) until the accession of the 13th Dalai Lama actual authority was exercised by the Lama himself for only seven years', Richardson, *op.cit.*, p. 59. In a private letter, June 2, 1904, from Lord Ampthill to the Secretary of State, the acting Viceroy underlined the fact that 'the normal state of affairs at Lhasa' was of an incarnation of tender years instead of 'the present abnormal condition of a Lama who is old enough and self-opinionated enough to speak and act for himself'. Ampthill Papers, *op.cit.*

20. Dalai Lama, *op.cit.*, p. 22, cites him (his previous incarnation) as saying: 'After I took up the duties of spiritual and secular administration, there was no leisure for me, no time for pleasure. Day and night I had to ponder over problems of religion and state in order to decide how each might prosper best. I had to consider the welfare of the peasantry .....'

21. The Regent who is the head of the six leading monasteries at Lhasa except for Drepung, Sera and Ganden—is chosen for his post by the National Assembly. During the Dalai's minority a cabinet of four, comprising three laymen and one priest, works directly under him, its chief preoccupation being affairs of state. For religious affairs a separate Ecclesiastical Council also works under the Regent. Bell, *Portrait*, p. 38. For a more recent study, see R. Rahul : 'The Structure of the Government of Tibet, 1644-1911', *International Studies* (New Delhi), III, No. 3 (January 1962) and IV, No. 2 (October 1962), pp. 263-98 and 169-93.

22. *Ibid.*, pp. 53-54.

23. Nor only were the Regent and his brothers punished—although the Regent's connection with the plot was not established apart from the Dalai Lama telling Bell that he believed that he (the Regent) was involved—but their next of kin were not spared either. We are informed that the Minister's wife was brutally flogged and made to sit every day for a

whole week, in one of the main streets of Lhasa, with her wrists manacled and a heavy board around her neck. Later, she was exiled. Bell recalls that the legacy of this bitterness survived until the 1930s. *Ibid.*, pp. 53-54 and 56.

24. Heinrich Harrer, *op.cit.*, pp. 170-71 tells us that 'People still speak of the monks of Ten-gye-ling who 40 years ago sought to come to terms with the Chinese'.

25. It may be recalled that many of his detractors said the same held true of the 14th Dalai Lama, a foreboding that threatens to come true in his case. Bell, *Portrait*, p. 56.

26. Ampthill to Brodrick, letter, June 2, 1904. Ampthill Papers, *op.cit.*

27. Alluding to the failure of the plot, a Chinese officer of that period is reported to have said that 'the affair' had been managed very badly. Bell, *Portrait*, p. 38. Mr. Richardson, *op.cit.*, pp. 59-60 disagrees with this view. He contends that the Imperial Residents 'after the short flush of zeal in 1750' grew 'less and less interested and efficient ... and so far from dominating the Regents, allowed themselves to be dominated'. In reality, thus it was 'the ambition and greed for power of Tibetans that led to these plots.'

28. Actually, the formula—Tibetan, Chinese and Mongol—is that on the first (lunar) New Year day, after his birth. a child is counted as 'in his second year'.

29. Bell, *Portrait*, p. 57.

30. *Ibid.*, pp. 57-58: 'The good people of Tibet were grateful to their youthful head for his prompt reform.'

31. The Tibetan Government wriggled out of an embarrassing situation in an extremely ingenious manner. They informed the Amban that his nominee, one Ramba, had 'died' whereas actually, they had sent him to his country home, a few days' journey from Lhasa. The Amban who knew the inside story, accepted the Tibetan Government's version and reported to the Emperor that the person whom he had appointed had 'died'. In the 'vacancy' caused by Ramba's 'death', the Dalai then appointed his own nominee. *Ibid.*, p. 59.

32. *Supra*, pp. 130-33, and foot-notes 11-12, 27 and 31.

33. The Tibetan word for India is rendered as 'the land of Dharama'.

34. Until recently Lhasa had no newspapers, much less a radio network. The best known Tibetan newspaper, now defunct, was a weekly, *Tibetan Mirror*, published by one Mr. Tharchin from Kalimpong, in India.

35. Since the Tibetan rule is to express everything in a religious guise, when they felt that their independence was threatened, they rendered it by saying that their religion was in danger.

36. Markham, *op.cit.*, pp. 125-26. 'Bulgar', probably a corruption of the Bolghar Kingdom on the Volga, stood for Russian leatherhides.

37. Turner, *op.cit.*, pp. 272-73.

38. 'Taranant' is a variant of Taranatha, the Urga Lama's religious title.

39. Moorcroft reported about a party of 600 such persons which visited Gartok about 1812. Later Hodgson, in 1831, talked of British goods reaching Tibet by way of Russia. Richardson, *op.cit.*, p. 81.

40. 'The road to Tibet had been open to the Mongols since the destruction of the Tangut Kingdom by Chingiz Khan in 1227. In the course of their subsequent wars with China, the Mongols crossed the eastern sections of Tibet and occupied some of its provinces'. George Vernadsky, *The Mongols and Russia* (Yale, 1953), p. 75.

41. *Ibid.*, pp. 388-90. 'Since ... the so-called Golden Horde was actually known as the white horde, the Tsar of Moscow as successor of the Khans of the horde, was now called the 'White Tsar'.

42. 'The Mongol element continued to play an important part at the Moscow court ... the effects of the Tartar domination in Russian history were felt long after the Golden Horde had ceased to exist.' Michael T. Florinsky, *Russia: A History And An Interpretation* 2 vols., (New York, 1953), I, p. 63.

43. V. P. Leonte'yev: *Iostrannaya Ekspansiya v. Tibette,* 1888-1919 (Moscow 1956), p 62.

44. The lack of an authoritative account of Dorjieff who played so important a role in Russo-Tibetan relations, and the events leading to the British military expedition to Lhasa, is indeed pathetic. The well-known Russian Tibetologue, Peter Badmeyeff, wrote some biographical details of him in the Russian press at the time of Dorjieff's visits in 1900 and 1901. To what extent these could be relied upon, however, is doubtful for Count Lamsdorff regarded Badmeyeff as 'an eccentric character.'
Among those who have given first-hand account of him, mention may be made of W. F. O'Connor, *On the Frontier and Beyond* (London, 1931), pp. 125-27 and the same author's *Things Mortal* (London, 1940), pp. 48 and 96-98 as well as David Macdonald. *Twenty Years in Tibet* (London, 1932). Bell's mention of him is intriguingly brief—*Tibet*. p. 62 and *Portrait*, pp. 61-62. Robert Rupen discusses him as an important, and integral part of 'The Buriyat Intelligentsia' in the *Far Eastern Quarterly*, Vol. XV (1955-56), pp. 383-98. There is also a mention of him in A. Popov, 'Russia and Tibet'. *Novyi-Vostok* (Moscow), No. 3 (1923) and L. B-n in 'Khambo Agvan Dorjee (in relation to Tibet's struggle for Independence'), *Ibid.*, No. 18 (1927), pp. 101-19. Reference may also be made to Korostovets, *Von Chinggis Khan zur Sowjet republic* (Berlin, 1926), pp. 207-10 and W. A. Unkrig's not-easily accessible writings. Wilhelm Filchner, *Sturm uber Asien* (Berlin, 1926) is useful but must be accepted with great care.

45. Wilhelm Flichner, *op.cit.* In two articles under the title 'A Story of Struggle and Intrigue in Central Asia', *JRCAS* XIV (1927), pp. 359-68 and XV(1928), pp. 89-103, gave a summary account of Filchner's book. Apart from a friend who translated parts of Filchner's original for the writer, these two articles have been drawn upon.

46. Alastair Lamb, *op.cit.*, p. 314.

47. Robert Rupen, *op.cit.*

48. Kashmir, once Buddhist, had later turned Muhammadan. There is an old Tibetan prophecy to the effect that the Muhammadan power will spread until, in course of time, a Buddhist King rises in a country to the north of Kashmir. The country will be north Shambala and its King, breaking the Muhammadan stranglehold, will restore Buddhism. In Lhasa, the Dalai Lama appears to have lent credence to the belief that north Shambala was Russia and that the Tsar was the king who would restore Buddhism. He is said even to have written a pamphlet to prove this. E. Kawaguchi, *op.cit.*, p. 499.

49. He (Dorjieff) envisioned a Tibetan-Mongolian theocratic empire to be headed by the Dalai Lama 'under the protection of Czarist Russia'. Robert Rupen, *op cit.*

50. Bell wrote years later that the Dalai Lama's chief assistant in his pro-Russian policy was the Prime Minister Shatra whom he rated to be a man 'of great ability and patriotism'. Bell, *Tibet*, p. 64. Also see Alexander Ular, 'The Policy of the Dalai Lama', *Contemporary Review*, January 1905, pp. 44-45.

51. *British Parliamentary Papers*, LXVIII, 'Papers Relating to Tibet', p. 58. One of the Tibetan monks is reported to have said that if the British entered Tibet, his bowl would be broken, viz, the influence of his order would be destroyed.

52. Cited in Bell, *Portrait*, p., 62.

Earlier, Bell noted (*Tibet*, p. 64) that the pro-Russian attitude of the Dalai and his ministers was natural enough for they were genuinely distrustful of British designers and 'in their inexperience thought that this would be a good way to check them'.

53. Tibet Papers, *op.cit.*, Cd. 1920, No. 31, p. 113. This was a despatch from Mr. C. Hardinge and was dated St. Petersburg, October 17, 1900.

It is well-known that a Buryat Mongol, Tsybikoff, who was a Russian subject, had stayed in Lhasa in disguise from 1898-1901, that he too had ingratiated himself with the Dalai Lama's household to which he was attached as a scribe. He had a photographic apparatus with him and 'used it surreptitiously'. Tsybikoff left Lhasa for fear of his discovery and in order to place 'his voluminous notes in safety.' Balfour Papers, *op.cit.*, B. M., XCVI, letter from Sir Ernest Satow to Lord George Hamilton, January 25, 1903. The account was given him (Satow) by one C.W. Campbell who had been for a year Chinese Secretary at the British Embassy in Peking.

10
Curzon vis-a-vis Russian 'Intrigue' in Tibet

Lord Curzon's views on Russia and its potentialities for intrigue in Central Asia have been spelt out at considerable length and need no fresh reiteration, though it would be of interest to know what Lord George Hamilton thought of the problem, for between the two of them major strands of policy had to be woven. To be sure the Secretary of State did view a conflict with Russia (in Asia) 'with great apprehension' being conscious at the same time that the Viceroy appeared 'to think it inevitable.'[1]

His fears were numerous : of her (Russian) unlimited resources' of men— whereas Britain's 'real problem' was manpower;[2] of her Central Asian position which 'will be used to annoy,' whenever there was 'serious friction' between the two powers;[3] of her plea of scientific research, a disguise under which the Russians had been caught spying in India.[4] And finally, what was the assurance that the Russians meant business? For had it not been found 'obviously useless to correspond with'[5] them, while one of their best-known diplomats (Mouravieff) George Hamilton had called 'an incurable intriguer' and 'a terrible trickster.'[6] No wonder the Russian's death did not make him unduly sad : he rated it to be a gentle riddance.[7]

Hamilton was convinced that, should the two empires 'unfortunately come into collision,' the Russians will stand 'immeasurably more hammering and more reverses than our more artificial empire.' The Muscovites had great powers of 'incorporation and assimilation' for the governing race had 'so much Asiatic blood' in them. In another context, he referred to Russia as an Asiatic nation whose rule 'spread and established' through 'a far less efficient government,' than correspondingly did the British.[8] A 'vast, self-contained continental empire,' new communications and railroads were giving her, at the turn of the century, internally 'the same advantages' that Britain once derived from its mastery over the seas. For these, to him very valid reasons, Hamilton wanted to come, 'if possible', to some arrangement with Russia.[9] Clearly, both in their respective analysis of the problem and the solution proferred, a wide gulf in thinking separated the Secretary of State from Lord Curzon. This was all the more clearly discernible as the two of them together grappled with the various facets of their Tibetan policy.

In the initial stages at any rate the Indian Viceroy was in two minds about Dorjieff and his reported activities. Calling the Buriat's first visit to Russia as the 'so-called Tibetan mission from the Grand Lama,' he was not sure whether it was 'bogus or genuine,'[10] and a little later dismissed it almost as a 'fraud.' Furthermore, he thought it 'most unlikely' that the lamas had 'so overcome' their 'incurable suspicion' as to dispatch an open mission to Europe. In any case, Curzon refused to be 'much disturbed' by these 'rumours.'[11]

In February (1901) the Viceroy had encountered in Calcutta 'one of the numerous so-called Grand Lamas of Tibet,' who nonetheless seemed to him to be 'quite a first-class imposter'.[12] Yet, Curzon assured Hamilton, this gentleman was not the person who met the Tsar in Livadia the previous year. The latter, and this was all that the Viceroy knew about Dorjieff at this stage, 'appears to have been a Lecturer in Metaphysics in the Daiping Monastery near Lhasa.'[13]

A few months later his disillusionment was complete as he learnt more and more of Dorjieff and his companion. The tone too now verged on the painful:

I am very much exercised over the question of Tibet. Bengal has charge of Sikkim and as a consequence, of the Political relations with Tibet and the whole Tibetan frontier … and they had let slip two Tibetan missions that visited the Tsar, at Livadia last year, and again in this, left Lhasa crossed the British border, passed in one case through Darjeeling and in the other through Segowlie, travelled India by rail and took ship from Indian ports … who would have believed it possible the negotiations could have been passing between Lhasa and St. Petersburg, not through Siberia or Mongolia or China but through British India itself?[14]

Meantime even as Curzon was writing, Dorjieff had been received by the Tsar a second time and his 'mission' attracted a great deal of notice in the Russian press. It was described as 'extraordinary,' and its 'diplomatic' nature was emphasized. As regards its purpose, it was stressed—repeating that worn-out, if much-abused, cliché—that this was 'further to cement' the already existing relations with Russia, that although Tibet was really quite accessible to them (Russians), the Mission's aim was to make it even more so.[15] The well-known 'Novoe Vremya' commented that Dorjieff's reappearance underlined the fact that his previous conclusions had been favourable and that the Dalai Lama had been confirmed in his intention of contracting the friendliest of relations with Russia. For Tibet must have recognised, the paper further argued, that Russia was the only power able to counteract British intrigue, which had persisted for so long and indeed seemed to be awaiting an opportunity to force an entry into the country.[16]

While in a section of the (Russian) press there was some recognition that Tibet's subordinate status *vis-à-vis* China did not make the mission strictly diplomatic, it was pointed out that since Russia alone had upheld the integrity of that country, the Tibetans, though Chinese subjects, naturally came to Russia to pray and look for assistance. And indeed they would be very welcome.[17]

Dorjieff's second mission, which excited all this comment, comprised eight Tibetans with the Buriat himself as their leader. Apart from the attention which it received in the press the mission, officially described as 'the Envoys Extraordinary of the Dalai Lama of Tibet,' was received by the Emperor, the Empress, the Foreign Minister, Count Lamsdorff and the Finance Minister, Count Sergei Witte.[18]

Curzon was visibly upset. Tibet, he was convinced, was 'not necessary' to Russia; the latter had no relations, 'commercial or otherwise,' with that country nor did its independent existence imply any threat to the Tsarist empire. On the other hand, the Viceroy argued, 'a Russian protectorate there' would constitute 'a distinct menace' and 'a positive source of danger' to the Indian Empire.[19] And if Russia had no thoughts in that direction, as she professed—and herein the Viceroy's logic appeared well-nigh irrefutable—'how comes it that this monastic Lama from Lhasa (Dorjieff) ... was received with almost Royal honours by the Tsar?'[20]

Hamilton did not feel altogether unconcerned, and correspondingly the Home Government's reaction was milder, less flamboyant. Lansdowne did indeed instruct the British Ambassador to seek a very categorical assurance from the Russian Foreign Office, which was readily forthcoming. In fact, Lamsdorff took the opportunity to deny unequivocally that Dorjieff's mission had any significance whatsoever, maintained that the Buriat made his visits for the purpose of collecting money for his religious order from the numerous Buddhist subjects of the Emperor, asserted that his visit had no official character and that although he was accompanied by Tibetans, this had no importance whatever. It may be relevant to mention in this context that while transmitting the text of his interview to the Foreign Office, the British Ambassador's tone verged on the sceptical,[21] yet in communicating it, India Office sounded far more reassuring :

Lamsdrorff had so unequivocally denied the diplomatic or political nature of the Mission in St. Petersburg that I thought it better to pin him down to his words and let the Russian Government clearly understand that any disturbance of the *status quo* would not be acquiesced in by us.[22]

The second Dorjieff mission, the knowledge that Bengal had acted in a most inept, if to him positively discreditable, manner in handling intelligence on the Sikkim-Tibet border,[23] added to the fact that his own efforts to open a direct pipeline to Lhasa had hitherto borne no fruit,[24] made Curzon increasingly restive. Thus Lamsdorff's added assurances to Sir Charles Scott that the Buriat's 'mission' had 'no political or diplomatic character,' that at best it could be compared to the Pope's goodwill missions to the faithful in other countries, and that although the Dalai Lama had sent him an autographed letter, it was really an exchange of innocuous courtesies,[25] did not cut much ice with the Indian Viceroy. Nor was the latter alone in drawing such conclusions.[26]

In the light of the Buriat's second mission and the miasma of intrigue that was (in Lord Curzon's view) being woven around him, the Viceroy now suggested a drastic change in British policy. Convinced that they 'both ought to stop and can stop a Russian protectorate over Tibet,' he let his imagination a free rein :

Nothing can or will done with the Tibetans until they are frightened. I should at once move a few men up to the frontier. I would chase out the Tibetans from the corner of British territory .... I would build up the frontier pillars which they have been permitted with impunity to knock down. If they resisted these proceedings .... I would step across and occupy the Chumbi Valley just beyond. By this time, the Dalai Lama and his men ... would probably offer to negotiate. Yes, I would say, by all means, but only at Lhasa. Then perhaps, the abortive Macaulay Mission might be succeeded by something practical : and we could discuss what should be the character of the new arrangements.

And what was to be the basis for negotiations?

I need hardly say that I would not dream of referring to China in the matter. Her suzerainty is a farce, and is only employed as an obstacle. Our dealings must be with Tibet, and with Tibet alone.

Nor would that be difficult for,

My belief is that without firing a shot, it may be possible to get to close quarters with the Tibetans. Of course, we do not want their country .... But it is important that no one else should seize it, and that it should be turned into a sort of buffer state between the Russian and Indian Empires.[27]

Even outside the domain of private correspondence, it may be recalled that Lord Curzon's government was already pressing the Home authorities hard on 'the adoption of some practical measures' leading to an 'altered' policy which must ensure 'the adequate safeguarding of British interests' upon a frontier where these had 'never hitherto' been impugned.[28]

Hamilton, as was his wont, was trying to soft-pedal. He feared lest the threat 'to invade their country for the purpose of negotiating at Lhasa' might 'accelerate the declaration of a Russian protectorate over Tibet.' No wonder he viewed Curzon's proposal as 'somewhat aggressive.'[29]

Meantime as 1901 drew to a close, two major developments took place. The Viceroy now knew more about the 'head of the mission,' who was 'no doubt very familiar' with the priestly junta that ruled in Lhasa, and viewed the results of his activities as 'unfavourable to ourselves.'[30] Kazi U-gyen too had failed in his endeavours and Curzon felt, as has been noticed, deeply disillusioned.[31] Yet it is significant that the latter had not as yet made up his mind as to 'the next move,' which he still thought to be 'a most difficult' proposition.[32]

Early in 1902, however, the 'altered' approach seems to have been worked out. His chief aim, as the Viceroy never tried of repeating, was to frighten the Lama and his small coterie at Lhasa into negotiating with the Indian potentate.[33] 'The minimum' proposed was 'to enforce' the treaty which had been 'allowed to be evaded' and 'ignored' for years.[34] With that end in view he had fromulated the proposals regarding White's tour of the Sikkim-Tibet frontier, proposals that he subsequently modified materially.[35] 'Of course,' the Governor-General confided in Hamilton, 'I want the

Tibetans to open negotiations with us as the outcome.' [36] The Secretary of State as was remarked earlier liked the modified proposals better: 'I much prefer this plan of driving them out' of territory which belonged to the British.[37]

Besides the India Office, the Cabinet in London had poured cold water on Curzon's oft-repeated anxiety to pursue an adventurist policy. Hamilton, and his advisers, had time and again expressed the view that any abrupt move in the direction of Lhasa may not only help to hasten a Russian protectorate [38] but even antagonize Nepal, when a complete understanding with that country was regarded as a necessary prerequisite to any such move beyond India's frontiers.[39] Besides, there were hostilities in South Africa which not only severely restricted Britain's ability for manoeuvre, [40] diplomatic or otherwise, but entailed, as a direct consequence, plans for a cpomplete reorganisation of British armed forces.[41] Despite this, and warnings to the contrary notwithstanding, Curzon had kept the heat on as it were when, early in the summer of 1902, wild rumours of a Russo-Chinese deal on Tibet gained wide currency.

Actually, it was Kang Yu-wei, the Chinese reformer of the short-lived 'Hundred Days' fame and now a nondescript refugee in Darjeeling,[42] whose infromant in Peking wrote to say that the Dowager Empress had concluded a secret treaty with Russia which provided for the cession of Tibet. The Viceroy believed the news 'coincided with rumours,' nor was as 'wildly improbable.' And once again Curzon rode his by now familiar hobby-horse: 'As you probably know my answer to any such proceeding on the part or Russia ... would be very simple. Without the slightest delay, I would put a British army into Lhasa.' And as to the results, he was quite sanguine, 'I think I could undertake that it (Lhasa) should be in our possession in less than 2 months'. [43]

The authorities in London were intrigued too by what Curzon had relayed but Hamilton regarded Kang Yu-wei's 'very interesting' news as no more than 'vague rumours' at best. And thus, his immediate reaction was not to precipitate a crisis in the manner Curzon would have wished—for, other things apart, negotiations with China for a commercial treaty were just then very near a successful conclusion.[44] The Secretary of State's rejoinder, therefore, was a bare 'Sound the feelings of Nepal who may be very closely watching our acting.'[45] And he kept hammering on this theme all through the autumn months—from 'I wonder whether you have any idea of using the Nepalese treaty rights over Tibet as a weapon'[46] through a renfinder of Lee-Warner's 'note' and of the 'great political advantage of associating ourselves with the Nepalese in repelling Russian influence over Tibet,'[47] to ascertaining from the Nepal Durbar as to 'how far their co-operation could be relied upon, assuming we had to move'.[48] Later, the Secretary of State enjoined upon the Viceroy to 'secure their (Nepalese) hearty co-operation' and retain 'their confidence,' in place of having them 'as sullen and suspicious allies.'[49]

Meantime the diplomatic bag from Peking was getting at once fuller and heavier. Rumours regarding a Sino-Russian deal (on Tibet) were becoming more persistent and texts of the alleged 'agreement' were being openly circulated. The pivotal provision of this 12-clause deal was a renunciation by China of all its interests in Tibet in return for a Russian guarantee of the country's territorial integrity.[50] Hectic diplomatic activity followed these sensational disclosures and although the Chinese Minister 'emphatically repudiated' any idea of a Russian protectorate, the British had a sneaking suspicion that 'unofficially some such proposal has been made to the Yamen.'[51] More telegrams from Peking over the 'rumoured protectorate' by Russia followed and Landsdowne hastened to sound a stern warning that in the event of the conclusion of the agreement HMG would take steps 'for protecting the interests of Great Britain.'[52]

The warning from London synchronized with an increasing anxiety in Peking lest White's proposed tour along the Sikkim-Tibet frontier lead to a head-on collision. Wai-wu-pu, therefore, requested for an assurance that the Political Officer's intentions were of a 'peaceful' character and not designed to precipitate matters.[53] Nonetheless HMG was far from being responsive to such a plea, for all that it vouchsafed was that on the Tibet border 'we propose to make effective our treaty rights.'[54]

Lord Curzon's reaction might as well have been anticipated. Not only had the Imperial Government in Peking but what was to him much more important, the Amban at Lhasa had written to him enquiring 'the object and reason' of these 'proceedings.'[55] What was more, a Captain Parr, the (Chinese) Customs Commissioner at Yatung, was despatched to the border to meet Mr. White.[56] The flutter in the dovecots was evident and in this the Viceroy revelled. Even the junta at Lhasa seemed to show signs of certain movement and some Tibetan officials of the Tashilhunpo monastery did make it a point to call on the Political Officer and volunteered to show him the boundary.[57] Lord Curzon was satisfied that his policy was at long last bearing fruit : for were not the Chinese and the Tibetans, after all, 'frightened?' And before the years was out Peking announced that the old Amban at Lhasa was to be recalled, and the new incumbent Yu T'ai, deemed 'especially suitable' owing to his previous experience in Mongolia, was to proceed post-haste to negotiate with Mr. White 'in an amicable spirit.'[58]

The Political Officer's tour in the summer of 1902, despite its professed 'entire success,'[59] appeared somewhat in the nature of an anti-climax.[60] What did, however, serve as a prop was the fact that it synchronized with wild rumours about a Russo-Chinese deal on Tibet. Despite denials from Peking, and St. Petersburg, about the 'apocryphal' text [61] of the agreement, the Viceroy was cleary convinced of its being there:

> I am myself a firm believer in the existence of a secret understanding, if not a secret treaty.[62]

Curzon went a step further. He thought it 'quite intelligible' that China might part with its rather nominal rights of suzerainty over that country to Russia.[63] And inasmuch as it had been demonstrated that Dorjief was no mere figment of the imagination[64] satisfied that his policy was at long last hearing fruit : for were,[64] he reverted to his by now well-worn theme of an unscrupulous Tsarist regime, which 'squeezes us on nearly everyone of our frontiers,' pressing hard along that of the

Indian Empire as well. Russia which had 'no interest' in Tibet, nor 'any trade,' indeed no object in going there 'except one of hostility to ourselves,'[65] was, Tibet apart, now 'nibbling' in Afghanistan and Presia as well.

And what did the Viceroy propose to do? Initially, to hold the Chinese to account: 'to retaliate' against them and 'seek compensation.' He would refuse to be put off with any evasive reply but insist on 'receiving from Peking a definite repudiation,' of the alleged cession. Unless this were received, 'I think that we are entitled to protect ourselves,'[66] with all that that phrase implied.

As for Russia, Lord Curzon could scarce contemplate 'any tampering' with Tibet on its part. Besides, all the cards (he thought) were in British hands : 'the Russians are powerless to move at a distance of several thousand miles.' Yet, unless the menace were checked 'promptly and effectively,' HMG 'shall rue the day' for long years to come.[67] It is at this stage that Curzon's ideas, 'thrown out at the rough' earlier, began to take a concrete shape and the mission to Lhasa loom somewhat portentously in his imagination.[68] Determined to frustrate 'this little game' while there was time, he now proposed to send 'a pacific mission' intended to 'conclude a treaty of friendship and trade with the Tibetan Government.' But the 'pacific' mission was to be accompanied by 'a sufficient force' to ensure its safety while the Nepalese, reportedly 'itching to have a go at Tibet' themselves, were to join in providing the escort. Nor, and herein the Viceroy was quite emphatic, would this be a departure from the earlier policy and he recalled Lansdowne's advocacy of the Macartney mission from which the then Government of India were, 'as I think wrongly,' induced to depart.[69]

On the eve thus of Curzon's well-known despatch on Tibet (January 8, 1903) the situation had, in certain respects become fairly clear. Not only did an endless spate of bazaar gossip, most of which was of dubious veracity, persist and continue to feed the Viceroy and his subordinates in the Government but Lhasa itself was agog with rumour. The story of Russia's treaty with China was said to be widely believed there and it was argued that if Tibet needed assistance both Russia and China would provide it, for they professed the religion which looked on the Dalai Lama as its head and on Lhasa as its Holy of Holies.[70]

It is true that these rumours in the Chinese press were officially denied[71] yet, read in conjunction with the Dalai Lama's dealings with the Tsar, they did add appreciably to the apprehensions felt by the Government of India. Basically, what worried Calcutta was the threat posed by the reported establishment of Russian influence in Tibet and that too with the connivance of China. It may be recalled that Russia was yet to be worsted in an armed encounter with Japan and that the restraints consequent upon the Anglo-Russian entente of 1907 had yet to draw limits to its unbounded ambitions.[72]

For a correct perspective, it may be necessary to bear in mind the fact that while a Chinese army, reinforced by the Tibetans, might conceivably cross Tibet and invest Nepal, as indeed it had done previously, a Russian army could not have negotiated a vast, notoriously difficult country to violate India's frontiers. British resources, despite depletion, would assuredly have frustrated the move, if it were ever seriously contemplated. But in the process Tibet —the chief bulwark of the northern frontier—would have been crossed and this was a matter of no mean importance. A Russo-Chinese understanding would have meant trouble in Burma too—closer to Tibet in race and religion, although annexed to the British empire by superior force. Thus, all the way from Kashmir to the frontiers of Siam, an element of uncertainty and unrest would have been injected into the situation.

In the final analysis, therefore, the picture as it emerged at the end of 1902 was far more complicated than would be apparent from the pages of the Blue Book where the problem was treated essentially as one of frontier negotiations rather than as 'a chapter in international politics'.[73] The Russo-Chinese deal on Tibet, despite disclaimers, was widely believed in and Lord Curzon was determined to crush this 'little game' while there was yet time. He who had from the very beginning, talked of marching an army to Lhasa was now more convinced than ever before that there was a grave urgency in the situation. Russia had ever been suspect to him, nor did he put much faith in Chinese professions and excuses for procrastination and interminable delay. As for Tibet, the Dalai Lama's behaviour in refusing intercourse was, to the Viceroy's mind, unpardonable, inexcusable[74].

The *raison d'etre* thus for a mission to Lhasa was clear beyond a shadow of doubt. Any move on the part of Russia in the direction of Tibet, 'were it confirmed,' would mean—Curzon had made clear—'without the slightest delay I would put a British army into Lhasa'.[75]

It has been held that in the Tibetan drama at this stage, it was the widely rumoured Russo-Chinese deal that played a more important role than did Dorjieff's reported manoeuvres. Besides, the obvious diplomatic complexity of the crisis[76], two caveats may be entered in, in this context. One, that Brodrick who was most intimately concerned with the compilation of the first Blue Book, placed it on record that 'we have made a great deal of Russian difficulty[77],' while the Viceroy too was quite clear in his mind that he had based his case 'chiefly upon the importance of anticipating a Russian protectorate'.[78] Besides, it may be recalled that Curzon's insistence that 'considerable editing of the papers will probably be required[79],' was countered by the Secretary of State's regret that HMG was unable to meet 'your views on all points' and his considered opinion that he regarded the first one as 'the frankest Blue Book ever published'.[80]

The second point is more important. True, there had been a long and respectable line of explorers, enumerated in an earlier context, to the Tibetan wastes. To dismiss Dorjieff, as part of the general run of them all and to fail to draw a distinction between *bona fide* geographical discovery and political intrigue,[81] however tenuous the line may be at places, would be to run a grave risk both in terms of historical inaccuracy and of the intangibles of public opinion. To Curzon, and to the British Government in London, the Buriat represented in a concrete human physiognomy the worst fears they entertained of Russian designs. Dorjieff's political affiliations, and the reported proximity of his relationship with the Tibetan pontiff, placed him in class apart. And to that extent he was not so much a successor to Prjevalksi, .ozlov and Tsybikoff as a forerunner of a breed that was in many ways so very :ifferent in form and manner. It is significant that eyebrows were not raised, nor the :aditional flutter caused, when the Prjevalski medal of the Imperial Geographical .ociety of St. Petersburg was conferred upon Tsybikoff. Yet every attempt made by .amsdorff to convince the British that Aguan Dorjieff was engaged in geographical :xploration was accepted with a goodly measure of disbelief. Hence the need to :ssess the Buriat at his true worth. Besides, it may be necessary to point out that he lack of agents 'as efficient ... as are employed by Russia' was a matter of serious oncern at the highest level of Government in England and that the Tsarist 'superiority n this respect' was openly acknowledged.[82]

Notes

1. Hamilton Papers, *op.cit.,* Hamilton to Curzon, letter October 8, 1902.
2. *Ibid.,* Hamilton to Curzon, letter, April 8, 1903.
3. *Ibid.,* letter, October 4, 1898.
4. *Ibid.,* Hamilton to Curzon, letter, November 15, 1899.
5. *Ibid.,* letter, February 10, 1899.
6. *Loc. cit.*
7. *Ibid.,* letter June 21, 1900.
   'He (Mouravieff) will be no loss so far as this country is concerned for he was an incurable intriguer, apparently without principle or any definite policy ....'
8. *Ibid.,* Hamilton to Curzon, letter, October 8, 1902.
9. *Ibid.,* letter, April 8, 1903.
10. *Ibid.,* Curzon to Hamilton, letter, October 24, 1900. On the very same day, Hamilton was writing to Curzon to enquire if the latter knew anything. Hamilton emphasized nonetheless that he thought the press reports were 'exaggerated' although 'a good many tongues' had begun to wag and letters had appeared in the press 'as to the intrusion of Russian influence into Tibet.'
11. *Ibid.,* Curzon to Hamilton, letter, November 8, 1900.
12. The obvious reference here was to Norzunoff who, a Buryat himself, was Dorjieff's companion during his visits to Darjeeling in 1900 and again in 1901. Curzon did not learn of this until sometime in February 1901.
13. Hamilton Papers, *op.cit.,* Curzon to Hamilton, letter, February 21, 1901.
14. *Ibid.,* Curzon to Hamilton, letter, July 10, 1901.
15. Tibet Papers, *op.cit.,* Cd. 1920, No. 33, pp. 113-14. Extracts from 'Odessika Novosti', of June 12, 1901, and an interview with Badmeyeff published in the St. Petersburg Gazette, *Ibid.,* Encl., No. 34, pp. 114-15. Dr. Peter Badmeyeff (1851-1919), a Buryat himself and a convert to the Orthodox faith, had served in the Asiatic Department of the Ministry of Foreign Affairs, and was with his practice of Tibetan medicine, the rage of high society in St. Petersburg. He dreamed of a grandiose project of joining China, Mongolia and Tibet to the Russian empire. The fact that he was a friend of Rusputin, opened to him many doors in the Imperial Palace. He 'contributed to Buryat nationalism, his plans for a united Central Asian Empire were pan-Mongolist; he was clearly a Tsarist agent; and he played an important role in Buryat education'. Robert Rupen, *op.cit.*

16. 'Novoe Vremya', June 17, 1901, in Tibet Papers, *op.cit.*, Cd. 1920, Encl in No. 34. p. 115.
17. Bademeyeff's interview published in 'Novoe Vremya' June 18, 1901, as also that paper's comment on June 20, 1901. *Ibid.*, Encl. in No. 34, p. 115 and Encl. in No. 35, p. 116.
18. *Ibid.*, Nos. 36 and 43, pp. 117 and 125. The reception by the Tsarina Empress Alexandera Feodorowha, was the subject of a special official announcement in the 'Messager Official.'

    Oddly, the *Memoirs of Count Witte* (New York, 1921) make no mention either of Dorjief or his visits, or even of Tibet.
19. Hamilton Papers, *op.cit.*, Curzon to Hamilton, letter, July 10, 1901.
20. *Ibid.*, Curzon to Hamilton, letter, July 31, 1901.
21. Tibet Papers, *op.cit.*, Cd. 1920, No. 35, p. 116.
22. Hamilton Papers, *op.cit.*, Hamilton to Curzon, letter, July 25, 1901.
23. In a letter to the Secretary of State, November 5, 1901, Curzon condemned the Bengal authorities lock, stock and barrel, for they had 'no aptitude, no taste, no experience and no men for the job' of maintaining intelligence on the border. *Ibid.*
24. On the eve of his sending the second letter to the Dalai Lama, through Kazi U-gyen, Curzon was far from sanguine about his success : 'my belief is that this effort at conciliation will fail like the first.' *Ibid.*, Curzon to Hamilton, letter, February 21, 1901.
25. Tibet Papers, *op.cit.*, Cd. 1920, No. 36, p. 117.
26. In Edmund Candler's, *The Unveiling of Lhasa* (London, 1905), pp. 112-13, the author expressed a similar view:

    'We were asked to believe that these Lamas travelled many thousand miles to convey a letter that expressed the hope that the Russian Foreign Minister was in good health and prosperous and informed him that the Dalai Lama was happy to be able to say that he himself enjoyed excellent health'.
27. Hamilton Papers, *op.cit.*, Curzon to Hamilton, letter, June 11, 1901.
28. Tibet Papers, *op.cit.*, Cd. 1920, No. 37, July 25, 1901.
29. Hamilton Papers, *op.cit.*, Hamilton to Curzon, letter, July 4, 1901. A week later (letter, July 11, 1901), he warned Curzon that his 'show of force' and more so 'actual exercise' thereof would be tantamount to 'an invasion of Tibetan territory'.
30. *Ibid.*, letter, September 11, 1901.
31. *Supra*, Chapter 8.
32. Hamilton Papers, *op.cit.*, Curzon to Hamilton, letter, November 5, 1901.
33. In his letter to Hamilton of February 18, 1902, *Ibid.*, Curzon again talked of 'frightening the junta at Lhasa.'
34. *Ibid.*, Curzon to Hamilton, letter, January 16, 1902.
35. *Supra* p. 149.
36. Hamilton Papers, *op.cit.*, Curzon to Hamilton, letter, February 18, 1902.
37. *Ibid.*, Hamilton to Curzon, letter, March 13, 1902.
38. *Ibid.* On July 4, 1901, Hamilton wrote to Curzon to say that it was not unlikely that our threats 'to invade their country for the purpose of negotiating at Lhasa might accelerate the declaration of a Russian protectorate over Tibet.'
39. This anxiety underlined thinking not only at the India Office in London but even among the Governor-General's advisers in India. Other things apart, it was reckoned that by making Nepal invade Tibet—on the plea of the latter's disregard of sacred covenants—

ritish troops could be kept out. This was the gist of the memoranda put forth both by r William Lee-Warner and Sir Alfred Lyall in the summer of 1902.

W. Monger, *End of Isolation : British Foreign Policy*, 1900-07 (London, 1963), p. 13.

alfour believed that 'we (the British) were for all practical purposes at the present oment (July 1901) only a third-rate power....'

his was undertaken both by St. John Brodrick and his successor (after October 1902), the War Office, Arnold Foster.

ang Yu-wei (1857-1927), Chinese scholar and writer, was introduced to Emperor uang Hsu by the Imperial tutor, Weng Tung-he and was responsible for the reform licts of 1898. After the Dowager Empress seized power, he barely escaped with his ʾe and for 16 long years travelled and resided abroad during which period he lived in arjeeling for sometime. Upon his return home he supported the abortive attempt to store Emperor Hsuan Tung. Later (1917-27) he lived a retired life in Shanghai.

amilton Papers, *op.cit.*, letter, Curzon to Hamilton, June 16, 1902.

may be recalled that W. F. O'Connor in a hand-written, 13-paged note dated Simla, ine 10, 1901, had put forth two theses : One, that a mission 'would have little or no fficulty in reaching Lhasa' and two, that 'I think ... that they (Tibetans) realise the lly of opposing us by arms.... Thus as the result of a bloodless and inexpensive ampaign we should have obtained possession of the fertile Chumbi Valley'. Lord urzon's marginal comments on these pages are, marks of interrogation—and xclamation: (? !). Curzon MSS., *op.cit.*, Bundle No. 340.

id., 'I daresay, therefore Lansdowne will prefer until that treaty is signed, not to take ɔ any other question which might jeopardize the enormous commercial interests hich that treaty touches and covers.' Hamilton Papers, *op.cit.*, Hamilton to Curzon, tter, August 27, 1902. Later (September 24) 'a telegram entirely upon the lines you ıggest,' was dispatched, but Lansdowne 'I think judiciously postponed addressing it the Yamen until the commercial treaty he was negotiating was safe.'

id., Hamilton to Curzon, letter, March 13, 1902.

id., Hamilton to Curzon, letter, September 3, 1902.

id., letter, Hamilton to Curzon, September 11, 1902. This letter had as an enclosure 'Note on Tibet' by Sir W. Lee-Warner in which the latter sought to invoke an article ʿthe Tibet-Nepal agreement of March 24, 1856. He urged that Britain and Nepal act concert : 'China might be told that we are behind Nepal and Nepal being in direct ɔmmunication with Lhasa might of itself demand information as to any arrangements ɛtween Russia and Tibet. If this infromation was unsatisfactory ... might not Nepal ɛ urged to send a force to Lhasa and demand from Tibet an assurance that it would ɛrmit no Russian troops to enter its country?'

id., Hamilton to Curzon, letter, September 17, 1902.

id., Hamilton to Curzon, letter, September 24, 1902.

hina Times, July 18, 1902 gives the text of the alleged 'arrangement'. Tibet Papers, ɔ.cit., Cd. 1920, Nos. 48-49, pp. 140-41.

amilton Papers, *op.cit.*, Hamilton to Curzon, letter, September 11, 1902.

he (British) Minister was Sir Ernest Satow.

ibet Papers, *op.cit.*, Cd. 1920, No. 52, p. 141. It may be relevant in this context to refer a letter written by one W. M. Upcraft, from Yachow (West China) and published in e *Englishman* referring to the importance of Tibetan highlands: 'and with the experience ʿthe Russians in colonizing bands of Cossacks on the prairies of Siberia it might not

be waste for India to look to the lands that in more than one sense dominate her nort
eastern frontier?' The editorial comment of the paper: 'If the valley of that great riv
Yangtse is to be preserved from encroachment, it is important that neither France n
Russia should be allowed to thrust an arm between it and India. We must be domina
in Tibet both on account of present advantages and future possibilities.' Curzon MSS
op.cit.

53. Tibet Papers, *op.cit.*, Cd. 1920, No. 52, p. 141.

54. *Ibid.*, No. 54, p. 143.

55. The Amban's letter to the Viceroy was dated July 8, 1902, *Ibid.*, Annexure in Encl.
pp. 159-60.

56. *Ibid.*, Annexures 3 and 4 in Encl. 7, p. 161 and Annexure 2 in Encl. 22, pp. 176-77.
'The Chinese reaction to our measure in Sikkim was, in fact, identical in 1902 as in 188
and was motivated by the same considerations: to offer negotiations lest the Britis
take any one-sided measures.' Rinchen Lha-mo *op.cit.*, p. 47. Captain W. R. M'd Pa
was incharge of Yatung in succession to one V. C. Henderson. *Foreign*, Part V, No. 11
June 1902.

57. Tibet Papers, *op.cit.*, Cd. 1920, Annexure Encl. 3, in No. 66, p. 158.

58. For Yu Tai's appointment, see *Ibid.*, No. 59, p. 146; for his instructions *Ibid.*, No. 6
pp. 146-47. Yu Tai, who was the brother of Sheng Tai, the Chinese negotiator of tl
1890 convention regarding Tibet, very much looked forward to completing his brother
unfinished task. For his 'plans', see *Ibid.*, No. 67, p. 177.

59. *Ibid.*, No. 66, pp. 150-56. The words are Curzon's own; at another place the Vicerc
remarked that he (White) had conducted his mission with 'expedition and success' ar
had obtained 'useful information.'

60. White had made (to him) the astounding discovery, which Curzon must have accepte
with his tongue in his check, that the grazing rights (of the Tibetans) on the Sikkim sic
were balanced by similar rights which the Sikkimese enjoyed across the border. F
White's report of his tour, see *Ibid.*, No. 66, Annexure 2, pp. 167-72.

61. The 'apocryphal' text of the published agreement, the Chinese Minister in Pekir
assured Sir C. Scott (the British Ambassador), indeed 'its very form and wording
showed that it could not be of Chinese origin. *Ibid.*, No. 57, p. 145.

62. Hamilton Papers, *op.cit.* In a letter to Hamilton, Ibid., November 13, 1902, Curzo
cautioned the Secretary of state against ignoring these warnings 'either as idle rumour
or as *ballons d'essai*,' and warned that it was better to err on the side of 'over-cautio
than of over-confidence.'

63. *Ibid.*, Curzon to Hamilton, letter, May 28, 1902.

64. By 1902 enough of intelligence had poured in to rebut Lamsdorff's oft-repeate
description of the Buryat being 'a member of the Russian Geographical Society' or tha
the Society 'took an interest in his visit.' *Foreign*, Nos. 56-58 and 109, June 1902 an
Nos. 22-62, September 1902.

65. Hamilton Papers, *op.cit.*, Curzon to Hamilton, letter, August 20, 1902. Later (Septembe
3, 1902) Curzon wrote : 'I desire to impress upon you my conviction that Russia, a
she consolidates her railway connections, will embark... upon a policy of sustaine
pressure along the entire land circumference of the Indian Empire.'

66. *Ibid.*, Curzon to Hamilton, letter, September 10, 1902.

67. *Ibid.*, Curzon to Hamilton, letter, August 27, 1902.

. Throughout 1901 and 1902, Curzon had talked of putting troops in Lhasa or of moving a garrison there to forestall the Russians but no concrete proposal as such had emerged.

. Hamilton Papers, *op.cit.,* Curzon to Hamilton, letter, November 13, 1902.

. Bell : *Tibet,* p. 64.

. *Foreign,* Nos. 17-53, April, 1902.

. A plausible explanation of Russian behaviour may be attempted here. There were a few Russians, who were willing to go far afield in intriguing for the possible expansion of Russia's interest and (eventually, perhaps) territory but there was also a group that believed in conservation and consolidation within Siberia and Central Asia, without pushing further. Invariably the 'conservatives' won over the 'adventurists'. To this it might be added, however, that until more responsible people restrained them, the more adventurous minded often stirred up quite a lot of uneasiness through getting access to the Tsar and the Tsarina, both of whom were weak, credulous and easily-influenced.

. Curzon to Brodrick, letter, December 17, 1903, Curzon MSS., *op.cit.*

. 'It is really the most grotesque and indefensible thing that at a distance of little more than 200 miles from our frontier this community of unarmed monks should set us perpetually at defiance.' Hamilton Papers, *op.cit.,* Curzon to Hamilton, letter, June 11, 1901.

. *Ibid.,* Curzon to Hamilton, letter, May 28, 1902.

. Alastair Lamb, *op.cit.,* pp. 271-72.

. Brodrick to Curzon, letter, February 5, 1904. Curzon MSS., *op.cit.*

. *Ibid.,* Curzon to Brodrick, letter, December 17, 1903.

. *Loc. cit.*

. *Supra,* n. 77.

. Alastair Lamb, *op.cit.,* p. 272. 'The last decade of the 19th century saw a most remarkable intensification of Tibetan exploration and it would be an invidious task to draw a distinction between *bona fide* geographical discovery and political intrigue.'

. BP., BM. Vol. XCVI, letter from George Hamilton to Balfour, January 28, 1903. The Secretary of State wrote to the Prime Minister : 'You asked me why we could not get as efficient agents as are employed by Russia. I enclose two private letters which give concrete illustrations of Russia's superiority in this respect.'

THE YOUNGHUSBAND MISSION
ADVANCES INTO TIBET

11
The Tibet Mission takes shape

By the end of 1902, as has been noticed, Curzon was giving form and content to the despatch of a 'pacific' mission to Lhasa that was to be spearheaded by an armed escort. For a clearer perspective it may be useful to place this development in its proper international setting. As a starting point it may be recalled that early in 1902 a major diplomatic revolution had been brought about by the conclusion of the Anglo-Japanese alliance. With Europe already neatly lined up in its Triple and Dual alliances, the British had, for some time, felt their 'splendid isolation' to be increasingly galling, impractical. One need only recall the episode of the Kruger telegram to show how very alarming the position could, in fact, become.[1] The significance of the new alignment nevertheless, lay not so much in that it was between a Western and an Asian nation but that 'it arose out of the abortive attempts to procure an understanding between England and Germany on the one hand, and Russia and Japan on the other.'[2] Hailed then as an historic event, which marked a milestone in the development of Japan as a world power, it also put England 'in a better position' to watch its Indian frontiers.[3]

Yet 'one of the most remarkable features' of this alliance was 'the dislike shown for it by the British Cabinet.'[4] It is on record that the Prime Minister, as most of his colleagues, entertained serious misgivings: 'None liked it, but all were prepared ... to accept it if Lansdowne insisted.'[5] Of significance in our present context was the viewpoint of George Hamilton, the Secretary of State for India, who feared lest Russia, thwarted in the Far East, now turn her attention increasingly towards Central Asia. He even gloomily predicted that, as result of the alliance, the latter area would witness a Russian coup before the end of 1902.[6] In the final analysis thus, whatever its long-term results, the alliance was both a landmark and a first departure from what had become the time-honoured British policy of keeping aloof from entangling alliances. Basically, it would seem Lansdowne had been coaxed into it to avoid isolation in the Far East and had, in turn, forced it upon a reluctant Cabinet.[7]

Another fact needs scrutiny too. By the end of 1902, at more than one nerve-centre along India's land frontiers, British policy appears to have reached a state of near-deadlock. Thus support for Persia itself meant support of a regime apparently under Russian control; and yet a policy of partition, which seemed the only alternative needed military strength that Britain woefully lacked. So also in regard to Afghanistan the growing suspicions entertained about Habibullah made Curzon press for an active policy which, in turn, was opposed by Lansdowne.[8] Hamilton too, with the unanimous support of his (India) Council, believed that 'we should adhere to passive rather than to forcing tactics.'[9]

Thus in both these cases, and additionally in that of the Straits of Bosphorus where Europe's 'Eastern Question' lay as intractable as ever, a remarkable similarity was observable: 'all had demonstrated British weakness, all had shown the need to modify traditional policies, and all had pointed towards the need for agreement with Russia.'[10] Thus it is on record that in December 1902, Hamilton had told Curzon that barring himself and Lansdowne, the whole Cabinet were opposed to 'any action which is likely to produce war or disturbance in any part of the British Empire.'[11] Besides, as he had warned him (Curzon) earlier, Tibet itself was viewed as 'the smallest of pawns' on the international chess-board and he (Hamilton) was plainly loath to commit more to it than was absolutely necessary.[12] As if this were not enough, the Secretary of State reminded the Viceroy that 'the growing dislike, if not abhorrence, of any forward move, or of any action likely to entail military operations' was so strong that he believed that if the matter was put to vote 'there would be disposition to abandon all our present obligations, and to substitute nothing in their place except an attempt to come to an understanding with Russia.'[13]

A word, by way of comment, may not be out of place here. There was, to all appearances, a well-nigh complete contradiction between the policy underlying the Japanese Alliance (Lansdowne's) and that of coming to an understanding with Russia on any terms (Hamilton's). Would it not be too much to say that it was in this divergence of outlook that the Indian Viceroy hoped to find some fertile ground in Whitehall for driving the wedge deeper, and to his advantage?

The preceding paragraphs furnish an essential background to Lord Curzon's despatch of January 8, 1903, outlining a more active and definitive policy towards Tibet. It may be recalled in this context that Yu T'ai's appointment as the new Chinese Resident in Lhasa, was announced early in December (1902) and that the Secretary of State viewed it as tantamount to China 'implicitly accepting responsibility for the affairs of Tibet.' He had further asked the Governor-General whether 'trade and general relations should be included' among the subjects for negotiations, and whether a Tibetan representative should not be associated with the projected parleys.[14] It was in response to this query from London that the Viceroy penned his despatch spelling out, at some length, his analysis of the Tibetan situation and outlining such measures, as he deemed fit to meet it.[15]

Lord Curzon began by reviewing developments from about the middle of 1901 when he had reported his twice-repeated failure—the third attempt was then being made—to get into personal touch with the Dalai Lama, and had suggested 'more practical measures.' The Secretary of State, however, had overruled him and sounded a warning against 'any precipitate action.' The next move was the Governor-General's proposal that the Political Officer, accompanied by an armed escort, should conduct a tour along the frontier. This 'local action' had been agreed to and Mr. White had carried out his mission in the previous summer with 'expedition and success.'[16] Yet the entire performance had, from the Governor-General's viewpoint, been little better than an anti-climax. For, apart from the dubious nature of the claim on Giaogong, it had been found out that the grazing rights of the Tibetans on the Sikkim side were 'balanced' by similar rights which the Sikkimese enjoyed across the border. Again, Mr. White's tour was said to have caused a flutter in the Tibetan and Chinese dovecots. Peking's officials had indeed been detailed to meet him and even Tibetans from Tashilhunpo had volunteered to show him the boundary.[17] Yet the projected pourparlers never took place for Mr. Ho, the Chinese representative, was first taken ill and later recalled to Lhasa for 'important special business' or, as idle tongues wagged, owing to a difference of opinion between the Amban and his associate.[18] And now had come the news of Peking posting a new Imperial Resident for talks on the frontier problems. What was to be the British attitude?

Before charting his new course of action, the Viceroy wanted to remind the Secretary of State of two aspects of the question which, in his view, needed added emphasis. Firstly, that although White's mission was 'crowned with entire success,' and he had obtained 'useful infromation,' the result had *not been* 'materially' to improve 'our position' on the border or to effect anything more than a timely assertion of British authority. The main advantage, the Viceroy thought, had been in the fear inspired among the Tibetans that his tour was only a prelude to some further movement. It was necessary that this advantage be not sacrificed, and this could be done only if 'we are prepared to assume a minatory tone and to threaten Tibet with a further advance,' unless indeed she revised her policy of 'obstinate inaction.'

Secondly, there was a persistent rumour about a Russo-Chinese deal on Tibet and the Viceroy's own conviction that 'some sort of relations' existed between Russia and Tibet.[19] This, in Lord Curzon's opinion, was bound to invest the forthcoming negotiations with considerable importance, for these would involve not only 'the question of our entire future political relations' with Tibet, but also 'the degree to which we can permit the influence of another great power' to be exercised for the first time in that country's history.[20] For Tibet's relations in the past had always been with China, later to emerge as the 'suzerain power,' Nepal or the British in India and Tibetan exclusiveness had been tolerated because it had carried with it 'no element of political or military danger.'

Taking these various factors into account the Viceroy now proposed that the Chinese invitation to a conference should be accepted subject to two overriding stipulations: that the meeting be held at Lhasa in the spring of 1903 and that a representative of the Tibetan Government should be associated with the discussions. The present appeared to be the most opportune moment to enter into negotiations with Lhasa for there was a Dalai Lama 'who is neither an infant nor a puppet.' This was the only way, Curzon felt, whereby 'the wall of Tibetan impassivity, and obstruction' will be broken. As for their scope, the talks should deal not only with 'the small question' of the Sikkim frontier, but 'the entire question of our future relations, commercial and otherwise with Tibet,' and should further result in the appointment of 'a permanent consular or diplomatic representative in Lhasa.'

The rest of this closely-reasoned despatch is concerned with convincing the Home authorities that there was 'nothing revolutionary' about the new proposals. Lord Curzon indeed sought to show, by digging up a British Minister Wade's correspondence, that a similar proposal had been made as early as 1874.[21] Besides, his new course of action was no more than a 'revival' of the policy underlying the abandoned Colman Macaulay mission of the mid-eighties.[22] Nor should the bogey of Chinese suzerainty deter them.

> We regard the so-called suzerainty of China over Tibet as a constitutional fiction—a political affectation which has only been maintained because of its convenience to both parties. China is always ready to break down the barriers of ignorance and obstruction, to opern Tibet to the civilizing influence of trade, but her pious wishes are defeated by the short-sighted stupidity of the Lamas. In the same way, Tibet is only too anxious to meet our advances, but she is prevented from doing so by the despotic veto of the suzerain. This solemn farce has been re-enacted with a frequency that seems never to deprive it of its attractions or its power to impose.

The Viceroy closed by elaborating parts of his proposal and by holding out threats. He insisted that the British Commercial Mission to Lhasa, that he was now suggesting, must be accompanied by an armed escort: 'to overawe opposition' on the way and to ensure its safety while in Lhasa; that assurances may be held out to the Chinese and the Tibetans that our only objective was to establish 'those amicable and friendly relations and means of commerce' that ought to subsist between adjacent and friendly powers;[23] that a policy of the closest collaboration with Nepal should be followed for the latter also felt endangered in much the same way as the Government of India, and indeed her ruler was very well-disposed to co-operate.[24]

As for the threats, brandished in a tone and language that was unmistakable, Lord Curzon reminded London that any government or country in the Empire had a right to protect its own interests and that if these were imperilled seriously—'as we hold ours to be'—the Government of India, by the fundamental law of survival, 'would have to take steps to avert these dangers.' In questions of this nature, he had no doubt, the opinions of the Government of India 'are entitled to carry weight' with HMG. But, should his warnings go unheeded now, the dangerous situation might 'attain to menacing dimensions.' In plain language, he would not be prepared to answer for the consequences.

Critics have charged Curzon with being both inconsistent and rhetorical.[25] Thus it has been held that his fling at China's inability to exercise its boasted rights of suzerainty was really unnecessary, for Tibet had never been too anxious to meet the British demands for trade rights anyway. Curzon's language was indeed strong, hence perhaps rhetorical, but that he was inconsistent would not hold water. In referring to China his purpose was not to demonstrate, as the Chinese scholar, Dr. Lee would have us believe, that that country was the real foe of British trade, but to point out 'the solemn farce' which, with Tibet as a partner, it had enacted with such annoying frequency. The real foe of British intercourse—and the Viceroy was far less concerned with Tibetan trade in tea than would be apparent at first sight—was neither China nor Tibet singly. It was the vicious circle which to Curzon was so uncomfortable to contemplate—a circle which the Tibetans would not break and which the Chinese were either unwilling, or perhaps unable to. The circle had become more deeply etched and its edges blurred with the webs woven by Dorjieff's flirtations and the persistent rumours of a Russo-Chinese deal. And Curzon seemed to ask himself repeatedly—had Russia, China and Tibet joined hands behind his back?

The real 'accusation' against Curzon is not of rhetoric, nor yet of inconsistency, but the brazen-facedness and ill-concealed contempt with which he seemed to treat both China and Tibet. And as for that, and additionally the cleverness with which he camouflaged his own real intent, why should the then Indian potentate alone be singled out—and condemned? For, however strong one's feelings may be and however loud the protestations about the equal rights of small and great powers, one often wonders, if the half century and more that separates these events from our own day has changed matters to an appreciable degree. Did not Tibet enjoy the privilege of being bordered by a 'great' and 'civilised' power? Had she not proved stupidly obstinate in refusing that power's hand for 'amicable and friendly relations—and means of commerce?' Indeed, the moment one accepts Lord Curzon's premise, his entire case stands thoroughly irrefutable.

It is interesting to recall that one of the powers which later was to register a strong exception to Lord Curzon's description of Chinese sovereignty over Tibet as 'a constitutional fiction and a political affectation,' was the United States. Its Ambassador at the Court of St. James's was to remind HMG that thrice in recent years—in the Chefoo Convention of 1876, in the Peking covenant of 1886 and the Calcutta Regulations of 1890—it had recognized Chinese sovereignty by negotiating with that government on questions relating to Tibet and that since then Peking had waived off none of those rights.[26]

How far did 'means of commerce'—and the desire 'to make (Tibetan) people drink Indian tea' who had no liking for it and consumed the Chinese variety instead[27]—dominate Curzon's thinking? Reading between the lines, the despatch makes clear—what the Blue Books, through specious editing, scrupulously avoided doing, namely that Curzon's entire mental make-up was dominated by considerations which were predominantly, if not exclusively, political.[28] And the missing link, indeed the key to the whole problem, is provided by the Viceroy's private correspondence. Here the talk was about the 'little game' between Russia and China which he wanted to frustrate, of his conviction that Russia was 'nibbling' at Tibet, of 'a small expedition' or 'a British army' which he wanted to march into Lhasa.[29] Paradoxical as it may appear, for the most part there is hardly any mention of selling Indian tea or of importing goods into Tibet,[30] and the boundary, or the grazing rights, are relegated exclusively to the background. This was not only observable at this stage when the Mission was being conceived, but much more glaringly as the expedition neared the end of its labours in Lhasa in September, of the following year.

Another fact that stands out in Lord Curzon's despatch is his studious search for precedents and his great anxiety to prove that in his approach he was no more than following a line that had been laid down, though ill-advisedly abandoned, earlier. The despatch referred specifically to the proposal originating with the British Minister in China as far back as 1874 and to the ill-fated Colman Macaulay venture. Another precedent that he never tired of citing, although not in this particular despatch, was of the Macartney Mission.[31] While it may not be relevant to cover this ground again or even exhaustively, it may be as well to point out that both in the case of Wade's proposal as also of the Macaulay Mission, the primary aim in view was the opening up of Tibet to commerce both in its own right but more so as a back-door to mainland China. The political undertones are either absent entirely or their impact is unimportant—at best, perhaps marginal. Again, as for the Macartney Mission, the allusion was far from being apt.[32] For, as a matter of fact, Sir Halliday Macartney, the then Secretary of the Chinese Legation in London, along with Sir Robert Hart, the (British) Inspector-General of Chinese Customs had dissuaded the Yamen from coming to blows with the British in Tibet and instead had induced it to negotiate. The provocation had been provided by the entry of British troops into the Chumbi Valley, in September, 1888.[33] It is revealing that 'stated that he should exert his utmost' here too the (British) Indian Foreign Secretary's instruction to secure an opening for our commercial enterprise.'[34]

In order to have a more accurate assessment of the response which the Viceroy's despatch evoked in Whitehall, two facts may be kept in view. One, that not only was the Secretary of State traditionally a conservative by nature and, therefore, somewhat of a perpetual drag on his over-ambitious, adventurist proconsul but that throughout 1902 he had, as was noticed earlier, continually warned Curzon against engaging in any action beyond the frontiers of India. Time and again he had reminded the Viceroy that the British were far too weak militarily to engage in any fresh ventures just then and took up a continuous refrain of 'using' Nepal so that the (British) involvement in Tibet should be indirect and of the very minimum.[35] As late as December 19 (1902) he had told Lord Curzon of 'the growing dislike, if not abhorrence' of any forward move and even of 'a disposition to abandon all our present obligations.'[36] Early in 1903 he had talked of 'our surfeit of fighting.'[37] This surely had to be seen against the background of the three wars, viz., on the North-west Frontier in 1897-98, in Sudan (1898) and against the Boers (1899-1902).

Nor, it would seem, should the Governor-General have been under any illusion as to the attitude of the authorities at home. Primarily with Afghanistan in mind, yet equally conscious of Tibet, Lord Curzon on his part did not mince matters when talking of his political superiors in somewhat harsh terms,

If the Cabinet are as seriously impregnated as your recent letters lead me to believe both with ignorance and timidity about Asiatic foreign affairs .... It really seems to me as though the fear of Russia dominated like some great nightmare every phase and aspect of the Asiatic situation and that since the South African war the fear is even greater than it was before .... However we are merely asking leave to do in the case of Tibet what Lord Dufferin attempted to do nearly twenty years ago : and I think that a heavy responsibility will rest on any Home Government that affects to see nothing even when the finger has already begun to trace its fatal handwriting upon the Tibetan wall.[38]

Significantly the letter bore the same date as the famous despatch—January 8 903)—and was written, one would imagine, under the great strain to which the urbar episode had exposed his relations with the authorities at home. Yet, to urzon's biographer it seemed to be the veritable touchstone of his ability to conduct policy in which he was out of agreement with the authorities in London. If the tter did not accept his views 'as to the necessity of asserting ourselves in this arter of the Indian glacis,' it was clear 'they would not do so anywhere else.' [39] at would go far to explain why the Governor-General attached a great deal of portance to reactions at home.

That Curzon was impatient, and extremely agitated, over the likely British sponse is clear enough. His despatch reached London on January 24, and Hamilton stened to acknowledge it in a letter four days later.[40] But early in February, the ceroy sent urgent reminders.[41] Meantime the Russians played into his hands. For th rumours galore, and their ears affixed to the ground as it were, they presented memorandum to the Foreign Office in London that on the basis of 'authoritative formation', a British military expedition had allegedly reached Komba-Ovaleko, its way to the Valley of Chumbi. The Imperial Government, the memorandum aintained, looked upon such an expedition as producing a situation of 'considerable avity' which might oblige it to take measures 'to protect their interests' in those gions.[42]

When, on enquiries from London, Lord Curzon confirmed that the 'authoritative formation' contained in the (Russian) note was 'without the slightest foundation,' : British thought it gave them a powerful handle to pin the Russians down on bet. The Viceroy felt here was a good stick to beat the Cabinet with. Thus he ote home to say that it was possible 'that they (Russians) may either have essed or got wind of the idea' that 'we are contemplating' a mission to Lhasa. Yet ir (Russian) trick was far too obvious: 'all the while the object in the background to deter us from any step that we may have in view by a sort of veiled menace in vance and to secure immunity for themselves in doing the very thing.' And anwhile they lodged their protests on the flimsiest of grounds,

Rarely ever, can we cocker up the Foreign Office to ask any question ever about a general movement or about a general advance by them .... What have they got to do with the Chumbi valley on the south of Tibet? Is Tibet under their protectorate or is China under their protectorate? ... with imperturbable gravity we discuss these insinuations and tacitly accept the right of Russia to act the part of watch-dog upon every section of the Indian border ... and I shall not be surprised if the time comes before long when we have to request their permission for an expedition into Waziristan ... (If you so succumb) critics of a later day will wonder how it was that a responsible government, with full warning given to them, could so obdurately shut their eyes to the signs of the times ... [43].

The first official reaction from London to Lord Curzon's despatch of January 8 was a most guarded one. Hamilton was at any rate quite clear about what Curzon seemed to camouflage in a lot of verbiage namely, that a mission to Lhasa could not be conceived 'without fighting.' For his part, he put it rather bluntly: 'I assume that you would be compelled to send an escort of very considerable dimensions.' Besides, he did not apprehend 'any material interference' on the part of the Russians to aid and succour their (Tibetan) friends. But the real nub of the problem was: 'can we establish a good international case for the course of action you suggest?'[44] A fortnight later, the Secretary of State asked very much the same questions and expressed the fear that unless 'satisfactory explanations' to those were forthcoming, the Cabinet 'will hesitate and delay', until it were too late to send an expedition.[45]

Basically, London's rejoinder to Curzon's repeated pleadings was two-fold. Firstly, even if the Russians reached Lhasa, was it not possible that the defence of the Indian Empire, as then constituted, could take care of this threat? In any case, Balfour would be chary of an armed commitment as far afield as the Tibetan highlands: a mission to Lhasa, as Curzon demanded it, would not be acceptable. Again, the best way to deal with the situation was to do some plain-speaking with the Russians. In fact, the Foreign Secretary felt convinced that here was a good opportunity for him to bind them down and, on the morrow of the Russian note on Komba-Ovaleko, summoned Benckendorff. Nor in his conversations, did Lansdowne mince matters. The language of the Komba-Ovaleko note, he maintained, was unusual and 'indeed minatory in tone;' the Russian complaint was 'gratuitous' and it surprised him that the Imperial Government evinced such interest in a matter which was 'within our undoubted rights.'[46] Driven to the defencive, the Ambassador pleaded that the form of the note was unimportant, that the rumours concerning the expedition appeared exaggerated and that his country had 'no political designs on Tibet.'

As if that were not enough, Lansdowne reverted to the subject a few days later. His tone was now firmer, his points more precisely made: 'any sudden display of Russian interest or activity,' he warned Count Benckendorff, would have 'a disturbing effect', on regions which had hitherto been regarded as altogether outside of the Russian sphere of influence. Such interest would entail, on the part of HMG, a display of activity 'not only equivalent to, but exceeding that made by Russia,' i.e. if the Russians sent an expedition the British would do the same, 'but in greater strength.' The Foreign Secretary next advised the Count that the British Government had infromation that Russia had concluded agreements for establishing a protectorate over Tibet, that it had, or intended to have, agents or consular offices in Lhasa. And driving the Ambassador more or less into a corner, politely queried: now that you have disclaimed any political designs by your country on Tibet, would you state categorically that these rumours are without foundation? Certain in his own mind that these had, in fact, no substance, the Count still undertook to make specific inquiries from his Government.[47] No wonder therefore, that when on the day preceding the meeting of the Cabinet on February 19, Hamilton raised the issue of Lord Curzon's despatch, the four most influential members of the Cabinet— Balfour, the Prime Minister, the Duke of Devonshire, Leader of the House of Lords, and Chairman of the Parliamentary Defence Committee, Lansdowne, the Foreign Secretary and Ritchie, the Chancellor of the Exchequer—'almost spontaneously and unanimously' rejected the conclusions at which he (Hamilton) wanted them to arrive.[48] Hamilton's despatches make it sufficiently clear that his views now approximated to Curzon's or at any rate he was lending these his fullest support, although he never said it in so many words. The wonder is that Lansdowne, who clearly was not afraid of Russia, and had actually driven the Russians into a corner, came out against Curzon.

The discussion in the Cabinet which followed 'took practically the same shape' as it had previously in the Committee. Balfour thought Tibet was a part of China and feared other powers 'might demand compensation', for the advantages which the British may obtain there. Lansdowne would rather wait for the fresh instructions which Benckendorff was expecting from St. Petersburg. All told, Hamilton's 'pleadings against delay', fell on deaf ears and the Cabinet 'were unanimously of the opinion' that they would not be prepared 'to run the risk of international complications, disturbance to trade and all the other hindrances and embarrassments' which flowed from what Curzon, now backed by his political superior, had proposed. Indeed, they went further and directed Lansdowne 'to see whether some *modus vivendi* could not be arrived at which would diminish the perpetual friction' between the British and the Russians in Central Asia.[49]

Hamilton's aim now was to impress upon the Viceroy the great significance of the Cabinet decision as representative of 'the trend of political and official opinion' in the country. But Lord Curzon was far from receptive; his reaction, at first 'strong and almost angry,'[50] was later to take the form of sheer despair. He wrote of this 'inveterate flabbiness, this incurable timidity that vitiates the whole of our Asiatic policy.' The Cabinet's approach, he was convinced, was to condemn us to 'eternal sterility' and he dismissed the objections of Balfour and Lansdowne as 'equally wanting in validity,'

> As I read these successive expositions given by you of the attitude and temper of public men at home, the heart goes out of me, as regards the future of our dominion in Asia and I sometimes say to myself 'is it worthwhile struggling on when our own people and their leaders are themselves engaged in tracing the handwriting on the wall'?[51]

One cannot help wondering about two things—if the Cabinet thought Curzon was completely out of step, why did they not dismiss him? Alternately, if Curzon felt his major policies overruled, why did he not resign? The probable answers are: (*i*) the Balfour Cabinet was a very weak one, rather like Neville Chamberlain's half a century later; and (*ii*) Curzon enjoyed power and prestige too much in Calcutta to contemplate resignation. The end-result, therefore, as the following pages reveal, was a series of compromises of a most unsatisfactory character: Whitehall continuously dilly-dallied, Curzon though he beat tactical retreats kept steadfast in his goal.

Despite Hamilton's continued efforts to pour oil on troubled waters—'ultimately the despatch of such an expedition would be difficult to avoid'[52]—or again, unless the Russian reply was categorical, Lansdowne 'quite admits' that 'an ultimatum will have to be issued' or resort to some course 'similar to that you suggest'[53] Curzon remained disgruntled. Meanwhile, on April 8, the long-awaited reply from St. Petersburg arrived and Benckendorff informed Lansdowne, in the most emphatic manner, that 'Russia had no agreement, alliance or treaty of any kind or sort with Tibet;' nor did it contemplate 'any transaction of the kind.'[54] There were no Russian agents, much less a mission in Lhasa, nor was there 'any intention' of sending them there. Russian policy, the Ambassador explained, could he best summed up in the phrase, '*ne viserait le Thibet en aucun cas.*'

All this notwithstanding, St. Petersburg was not totally unconcerned. For it viewed Tibet as constituting a part of the Chinese Empire 'in the integrity of which' it took a keen interest. If, therefore, there were a wholesale disturbance of the *status quo*—such as an annexation or a protectorate would entail—the Russians would be obliged 'to safeguard their interests in Asia,' and seek some form of compensation elsewhere.[55] Lansdowne, disclaiming any intention to annex the country insisted, however, on Britain's 'local predominance,' a position which Benckendorff did not openly challenge.[56]

It is significant that Lansdowne, and even more so George Hamilton, expressed great satisfaction at Benckendorff's reply. The former writing to Balfour noted that the Ambassador was 'quite straightforward and satisfactory,' and that George Hamilton had 'very properly told the other George that he must not send his little army to conquer Lhasa.'[57] Actually the first George had expressed himself undeservedly : 'This (Benckendorff's explanation) is quite satisfactory ... the main reason for sending a mission with force to Lhasa was fear of being anticipated by Russia. All fear of such movement has now gone.' He saw 'no necessity,' therefore, to associate 'the commencement of negotiations with the despatch of a Mission to Lhasa.'[58]

Bearing in mind the timing of Benckendorff's assurance—after the Boxer Rebellion had been crushed and before the Russo-Japanese War had started—it would appear that the Russians were trying to sketch out a bold policy. The latter envisaged *inter alia*, that should China fall to pieces and be carved out into spheres of interest, or influence—St Petersburg had always been somewhat sceptical about the 'Open Door'—their interest would be staked out in Manchuria (not yet overwhelmingly colonised by the Chinese), Mongolia, Sinkiang, and Tibet. In other words, those parts of the Manchu empire which were overwhelmingly inhabited by non-Chinese or, as in the case of Manchuria, historically definable as not always having been inhabited by a Chinese population homogeneous with the Chinese inside the Great Wall.

Whatever Russian assurances, the Viceroy in Calcutta was far from happy : 'Satisfied !—Emphatically No!' was his reply to George Hamilton. He had no faith in Russian promises—had not Hardinge, the British Ambassador in St. Petersburg, mentioned by name the 'actual (Russian) Agent' appointed in Lhasa? Russia was telling 'a deliberate lie,' nor for the first time either.[59] All that had happened was that 'our activity and threats' had stood in the way of Russian proposals 'reaching a more mature or concrete shape.' He cautioned against dropping 'all suspicions' and urged 'ceaseless vigilance to ward off the peril.' [60]

How wide were the differences that supervened between the Secretary of State and his agent? [61] Hamilton firmly believed that the assurances given by Benckendorff were 'more general and implicit' than would have been forthcoming from St. Petersburg;' that these gave the British 'an absolutely free hand in Tibet,' provided they (British) 'stop short of a protectorate or annexation,' and that, in any case, the urgency of an armed mission 'disappears'. [62]

Curzon had been overruled and could not but be acutely conscious of the fact. Yet the despatch from London was full of bits here and there, if only to console the over-bearing proconsul. Thus he was given the 'go ahead' for his negotiations with the Chinese and the Tibetans and asked for his views on the means to be adopted 'to ensure that conditions that may be arrived at, are observed.' [63] It may be recalled that much the same question had been asked by Lord George Hamilton in December, 1902, when the Chinese readiness to discuss matters had been further underlined by the despatch of a new envoy. Three major developments had intervened between December and the following April: the Viceroy's despatch of January 8, 1903 proposing *inter alia* that Lhasa be the venue for a conference; HMG's refusal to adopt such 'strong measures'; and the Russians' emphatic denial that they either had in the past, much less contemplated in the future, any political action in Tibet. It was in reply to the second query from London that the Viceroy put forth his plans for the Younghusband Mission—a commercial mission that was to end up as an armed expedition.

Notes

1. The Kruger telegram (June 9, 1896) marking the first violent outbreak of popular hostility between Germany and England, was only symptomatic of a widening gulf between the two countries. Later, the Boer War provided France, Germany and Russia with a focal point against the 'perfidious Albion.' The British Cabinet feared lest Lord Curzon's policies in Tibet and in the Persian Gulf, should afford these powers another opportunity of 'coming together'. Ronaldshay, *Life*, II, p. 207. Also see William L. Langer, *Diplomacy of Imperialism*, 2 Vols. (New York, 1935), II.

2. The words are of the Swedish geopolitician Kjellen, cited in A. F. Pribram, *England and the International Policy of the European Great Powers*, 1871-1914 (Oxford, 1931), p. 67.

3. 'By cooperating with Japan to protect her rights in China, (England) was in a better

position to watch her Indian frontier.' Lee, *op.cit.*, p. 28.

4. Monger, *op.cit.*, p. 58.
5. *Ibid.*, p. 59.
6. Hamilton to Curzon, letters February 13 and 20, 1902, Hamilton Papers, *op.cit.*
7. Monger, *op.cit.*, p. 62.
8. As if in an agony of pain, Curzon had cried: 'If you do not like to tackle Russia, then at least punish the Amir. If you allow a man and a state of his calibre to flout the British Empire, then we had better put up our shutters and close business.' Curzon to Hamilton, letter, November 27, 1902, Hamilton Papers, *op.cit.*
9. Cabinet Memo. by Hamilton, December 5, 1902, cited in Monger, *op.cit.*, p. 91.
10. *Ibid.*, p. 92.
    A memorandum by Balfour, dated December 16, 1902 laid down that in regard to Afghanistan, the British 'should withdraw ... from any specific pledge to the present Amir,' and 'we should do all that we can, by direct arrangement with Russia to maintain the *status quo.*'
11. Hamilton to Curzon, letter, December 19, 1902, Hamilton Papers, *op.cit.* Earlier in a telegram, he had warned the Viceroy that 'so decided and unanimous was the objection to any forward movement' that he (Hamilton) thought it best to inform him. Ronaldshay, *Life*, II, p. 268.
12. Hamilton to Curzon, letter, August 22, 1901, Hamilton Papers, *op.cit.*
13. *Ibid.*, Hamilton to Curzon, letter, December 19, 1902.
14. Tibet Papers, *op.cit.*, Cd. 1920, No. 61, p. 148.
15. *Ibid.*, No. 66, pp. 150-56. The 23 enclosures and 19 annexures accompanying this despatch cover pp. 157-77.
16. For White's report, see *Ibid.*, Annexure 2, pp. 167-72.
17. *Supra*, p. 172.
18. For Parr's and Ho's letters, see Tibet Papers, *op.cit.*, Cd. 1920, Annexures 3 and 4 in Encl. 7, p. 161, and Annexure 2, in Encl. 22, pp. 176-77.
19. It may be recalled here that the British attitude towards Tibet was that while that country was subordinate to China and her foreign relations were conducted by the latter, she yet was a recognizable entity in her own right. Lord Curzon's policy of dealing directly with the Dalai Lama had been endorsed by HMG only after the inordinate delay and difficulty of getting anything done through the Chinese became apparent. The distinction between Chinese suzerainty, and *not* sovereignty, in Tibet had not yet crystallised.
20. The despatch refers to what it calls 'circumstantial evidence,' derived from a variety of quarters, and all 'pointing in the same direction.' It was this 'evidence,' referred to in the private letters and based on sources some of which were of dubious veracity, on which the Governor-General principally relied. Printed records, of course, do not substantiate this reference.
21. Mr. (later Sir) Thomas Wade was the then British Minister in China. In a despatch (July 14, 1874) to Earl Granville, then Foreign Secretary, Mr. Wade had said : 'If the trade (i.e., between India and Tibet) be worth the effort, I think it might possibly be opened were a mixed official and commercial mission pushed forward without reference to the court of Peking ... and if that mission were authorised in the first instance to spend money rather freely.'
    Tibet Papers, *op.cit.*, Cd. 1920, No. 66, p. 154.
22. '... we regard it as a grave misfortune' that the Macaulay Mission was abandoned, 'by the exigencies of political considerations that had not the remotest connection with Tibet.' *Ibid.*
23. Colonel Younghusband, India and Tibet, *op.cit.*, p. 3., later maintained that the object of his mission was 'to regularize and humanise' pacific intercourse between India and

Tibet and put their relationship 'upon a businesslike and permanently satisfactory footing.'

24. Tibet Papers, *op.cit.*, Cd. 1920, Encl. 23 in No. 66, p. 177, is the text of a letter from the Nepalese Prime Minister who curiously ends by hoping to 'realise all those expectations which the association with a power like that of England may naturally raise in our minds.' Expectations?—and at whose cost?

25. Lee, *op.cit.*, pp. 35-36.

26. *Department of State Archives*, Great Britain Instructions, Vol. 34, pp. 631-39, No. 1455, Hay to (Joseph H) Choate, June 3, 1904. It is worth noting that at the end of World War II when the Nationalist regime in China again showed some brief spurts of activity in Tibet, the United States reaffirmed its view that Tibet was a part of China. This was to tie Washington's hands when later the Tibetans appealed for support (1950) against the Chinese Reds.

27. Lord Rosebery speaking in the House of Lords on February 26, 1904, concluded from the first Blue Book that 'the whole object of the policy of the Indian Government seemed to be to make Tibetans drink Indian tea.' *Parliamentary Debates*, series IV, Vol. 130, p. 1141.

28. Curzon had used such phrases as 'the question of our entire future political relations with Tibet' and of 'the degree to which we can permit' another Great Power's influence to be exercised in that country's affairs. He had talked of negotiating at Lhasa and of breaking 'the wall of Tibetan impassivity and obstruction.'

29. *Supra*, p. 174.

30. It is not correct to say that there is 'no mention of commerce' in Curzon's letter to Hamilton of November 13, 1902 for, in fact, the Governor-General did talk of 'concluding a treaty of friendship and trade with the Tibetan Government.' Alastair Lamb, *op.cit.*, 281.

31. Curzon to Hamilton, letter, November 13, 1902, Hamilton Papers, *op.cit.* It was this letter which, as Curzon claimed later, foreshadowed the despatch of January 8, 1903.

32. The better-known Macartney Mission was the one led by the Earl of Macartney to Jehol and Peking in 1793. The Chinese response to the British anxiety to open up their country was a polite, though firm, 'No.' How far the later (1887-88) efforts of Sir Halliday Macartney to serve the interests of his (Chinese) employers could be viewed as a 'mission,' as Lord Curzon avers, is at best debatable.

33. It is important to set the record straight for despite Sir Halliday's overtures, British troops pushed into Chumbi in September (1888) in hot pursuit of the Tibetans who, in the face of reverses, had been both stubborn and resilient. For more details, see Alastair Lamb, *op.cit.*, pp. 184-87.

34. *Ibid.*, p. 188.

35. Early in 1903 the Secretary of State felt pleased 'that the Nepalese take so sensible and whole-hearted a view' of a Russian move in Tibet's direction adding 'this seems to me to greatly simplify the situation.' Hamilton to Curzon, letter, January 23, 1903, Hamilton Papers, *op.cit.*

36. Ronaldshay, *Life*, II, p. 268.

37. Hamilton to Curzon, letter, January 14, 1903, Hamilton Papers, *op.cit.*,

38. *Ibid.*, Curzon to Hamilton, letter, January 8, 1903.

39. Ronaldshay : *Life*, II, p. 275.

40. In acknowledging Curzon's despatch, Lord George Hamilton made two important points : 'If the two propositions (i.e., Russia and Tibet have an alliance and when we want to take any action against Tibet, Russia would be on her side) are unanswerable, the question arises : can we establish a good international case for the of course of action you suggest ?' Hamilton to Curzon, letter, January 28, 1903, Hamilton Papers, *op.cit.*

41. Tibet Papers, *op.cit.*, Cd. 1920, Nos. 70-71, p. 179.

42. For the text of the Memorandum, in French, *Ibid.*, Encl., in No. 68, p. 178. 'Tchumbi', is a rendering for the more familiar Chumbi, but 'Komba-Ovealeko', though hard to unravel, could be none other than Khamba Jong. A Russian scholar has suggested that 'Ovaleko' is more Russian than Tibetan, that it may be an adjectival form from 'vol' 'an embankment' (fortification), thus equivalent to Tibetan *Jong*. Perhaps an incorrect (adjectival) form used by someone who did not speak Russian perfectly (Dorjieff?) and hence mistaken by them (Russians) for a Tibetan word.

43. Curzon to Hamilton, letter, February 5, 1903, Hamilton Papers, *op.cit.*

44. *Ibid.*, Hamilton to Curzon, letter, January 28, 1903.

45. *Ibid.*, Hamilton to Curzon, letter, February 13, 1903.

46. Tibet Papers, *op.cit.*, Cd. 1920, No. 72, p. 180.

47. *Ibid.*, No. 73, pp. 181-82.

48. Inside the India Office too there was opposition 'by individual member of the Council' although 'undoubtedly' this would have been steamrollered. Hamilton to Curzon, letter, February 20, 1903, Hamilton Papers, *op.cit.*

49. Balfour to the King, February 19, 1903. The latter's comment, however, was characteristic : 'Russia cannot be trusted, as she had but one desire and that is to increase her power and territories in Asia.'
Cited in G. W. Monger, *op.cit.*, p. 116.

50. Hamilton to Curzon, letter, February 19/20, 1903, Hamilton Papers, *op.cit.* 'In the last letter I received from you, you took up the challenge ... and replied in strong and almost angry language.'

51. *Ibid.*, Curzon to Hamilton, letter, March 12, 1903.

52. *Ibid.*, Hamilton to Curzon, letter, March 17, 1903. Herein the Secretary of State also wrote : 'I wish the Government here had agreed with what was practically the unanimous request of the Indian authorities both in India and here.'

53. *Ibid.*, Hamilton to Curzon, letter, March 27, 1903.

54. How important this reply was may be gauged from the fact that Hamilton's letter to Curzon bears the inscription 'April 8, 5 o'clock.' The text is from his letter to Curzon bearing the above date.

55. Tibet Papers, *op.cit.*, Cd. 1920, No. 83, p. 187, Lansdowne to Sir Charles Scott, April 12, 1903.

56. *Loc. cit.*

57. Lansdowne to Balfour, April 12, 1903. *B.P.* B.M. Add. MSS. No. 49728.

58. Hamilton to Curzon, letter, April 8, 1903, Hamilton Papers, *op.cit.*

59. Here Curzon dug out two recent instances : 'De Giers denied that Yonoff was on the Pamirs when he had himself despatched' him; and again it had been 'officially' denied that 'a Russian Mission had left Taskent for Kabul two days after Stolietoff ... had started.'

60. Curzon to Hamilton, letter, April 13, 1903, Hamilton Papers, *op.cit.*

61. 'As to Tibet' the Under Secretary of State, Lord Percy wrote to the Governor-General: 'the objection to your policy was not ... so much the practical difficulty ... as the reflection that the steps you advocated would be as possible and more defensible after Russia had sent her agent than before.' Letter, April 1903, Curzon MSS.

62. Hamilton to Curzon, April 15, 1903, Hamilton Papers, *op.cit.* A few weeks later—May 7 (1903)—the Secretary of State wrote that 'after the categorical denial by Benckendorff of any such agreement and his ready acknowledgement of the special relations which we can claim .... I do not think that Russia can protest against any course that we may adopt.'

63. Tibet Papers, *op.cit.*, Cd. 1920, No. 85, p. 188.

12
The Mission and its Leader

Knowing Whitehall's reactions to be what they were, Lord Curzon had to choose his steps warily, with the utmost care. He informed the Secretary of State that the Chinese delegates, whom Amban Yu had accredited for the talks, had suggested to him that the conference be held at Yatung, or indeed 'at any place acceptable to us.'[1] For his part he chose Khamba Jong,[2] 'which is the nearest inhabited place to the frontier in dispute,' near Giaogong. 'Our representatives,' the Viceroy further suggested—the Amban was to be invited to associate proper Tibetan deputies with the Chinese delegates—should proceed to Khamba, accompanied by an armed escort of 200 men and if the Chinese or the Tibetans failed to appear, should move forward to Shigatse or Gyantse, 'in order that arrival of deputation from Lhasa might be accelerated.'[3]

In a subsequent communication,[4] the Viceroy defined the scope of the negotiations which were to cover not only frontier and grazing questions, but also 'general and trade relations' as between India and Tibet. Special place was to be given to the duty on tea, and to the ten per cent tax levied at Phari on trade in transit. Again, since Yatung had been found to be unfavourable as a trade mart, Phari 'or indeed any other place' in the Chumbi Valley 'where business could be transacted directly' was to be opened up. The Viceroy also thought it necessary that a British Agent be established at Gyantse which was an important trading centre on the main route to Shigatse and Lhasa. 'The best security,' of course, was to have a British representative at Lhasa, but Gyantse would be 'a suitable alternative.' In any case, a British representative on the northern side of the passes would be able to communicate promptly with the capital. If the Tibetans did not deal freely with him, or offered any obstruction 'it will be necessary to resort to the alternative of moving him forward to Lhasa.'[5]

In his private correspondence, the Viceroy was much more intransigent and, of course, franker. His 'inclination' was to 'take a very strong line in negotiation and to frighten the Chinese and the Tibetans into acceptance of our terms.'

It is significant that this business of 'frightening' the Chinese and Tibetans was central to Lord Curzon's entire approach. More than once he talked of it in the very letter wherein he had spelt out his 'Tibetan proposals.' At heart he must have felt satisfied, that 'they are terribly nervous already.'[6]

Another matter to which the Viceroy referred in his despatch was that the British (Indian) subjects were to have all those rights which the Kashmiris or the Nepalese enjoyed; and that all of them (British subjects) duly authorised by the Government of India, were to require the Tibetan Government's permission only when proceeding beyond Gyantse—the permission, itself, however, being merely a formality.

The head of the Mission was to be a Major Younghusband who 'has a great and well-deserved reputation as a Central Asian traveller, who is also a very thoughtful and reliable man, and who has done conspicuously well in the difficult position of Resident at Indore. He knows the Orientalists generally, and the Chinese in particular, by heart, he will be able to hold his own with combined firmness and good temper against their tortuous tactics.'[7]

The Viceroy thought extremely well of his choice, for he could 'confidently rely' on his (Younghusband's) 'judgement and discretion.' Mr. Claude White was to be the Joint Commissioner and a member of the Chinese Consular Service was to be associated with the two of them.[8]

From the proposals outlined in the preceding paragraphs, certain factors emerge which need careful scrutiny. Thus the site which Lord Curzon chose for the Conference was indisputably inside Tibet, actually between 20-30 miles from the frontier and over 70 miles north of Yatung, a fact to which a reference has been made earlier. That HMG agreed to it was due principally to their ignorance and the Viceroy disarming all opposition by suggesting that the Amban's representatives had themselves given him discretion in such a choice. His description of it as 'the nearest inhabited place to the frontier in dispute,' though not incorrect, was deceptive.

The mission was to be accompanied by an armed escort, while 'reinforcements are held in reserve in Sikkim.' Again, as Lord Curzon visualized it, its advance from Khamba to Gyantse, or Shigatse, and further inland—on the non-appearance of the Chinese or Tibetan representatives—was to be 'automatic.' This was later to be specifically countermanded by the Secretary of State who laid down that without a previous reference to London, the Mission was not to advance beyond Khamba— 'even in the event of the failure of the Chinese and the Tibetan parties' to meet it.[9]

Another suggestion of the Viceroy—and he had not made it for the first time—was in regard to a British Agent being stationed 'preferably' at Lhasa, but 'as a suitable alternative' at Gyantse. He was to have the right to proceed to Lhasa if, and when, deemed necessary. Lord George Hamilton, however, categorically ruled out any such 'political outpost' as the Viceroy had in mind. It would entail, Hamilton had informed him, 'difficulties and responsibilities incommensurate with any benefit which ... could be gained.'

And inasmuch as Russia had denied any political interest in Tibet, the Secretary of State pointed out that 'HMG are unwilling to be committed, by threats accompanying the proposals which may be made, to any definite course of compulsion to be undertaken in the future.' For the matter of that, Whitehall laid down that negotiations 'should be restricted' to questions concerning 'trade relations, the frontier and grazing rights.'[10]

Inside India Office, and even more so in the Cabinet, opinion was dead set against the Viceroy's proposed course of action. The Political Committee of the Secretary of State's Council 'were strongly opposed' to the location of any Agent in Tibet; Lansdowne 'disliked the idea,' while the Cabinet were 'unanimous and immovable in their opposition.' They hated a 'permanent embroilment' in Tibet's affairs. The best hope Hamilton could hold out was, and this despite the fact that 'the Cabinet were disinclined,'

> It is self-evident that if negotiations break down and the Tibetans still decline to give assent to the obligations, we must express our disapproval ... (and that could only) take the shape ... of either a blockade or of the occupation of the Chumbi Valley.[11]

Before proceeding to trace the Mission's 'progress' in the task assigned it by its god-parents, it may be as well to say a few words about its leader, Major Younghusband, whose 'great Asiatic experience, discretion and judgement' had been highly commended by Lord Curzon and to whose choice the Secretary of State had deferred.

Paradoxical as it may appear Francis Younghusband,[12] so much unlike George Curzon in many ways, began life with almost the same self-interests. It is true that he passed through Clifton and Sandhurst, instead of Eton and Balliol, and that he did not write large, ponderous, and 'authoritative,' tomes at any early age. Yet, while Curzon was globe-trotting, and drinking deep at the fount of the 'empire', Younghusband, then in his early twenties, was exploring the Asian continent. Love of adventure apart, his preoccupation with a Russian advance was almost obsessive. Besides, he wanted 'to see how far the Chinese would resist any encroachment by the Russians towards the Indian Empire, from which they were only separated by the outlying province of Sinkiang, then better known as Chinese Turkestan.'[13] Curzon started his first journey around the world in 1888, two years earlier Younghusband had already explored Manchuria. A year later he made his classic Peking to India overland journey across, until then for most part unexplored country. From Peking he had reached the Mongolian frontier at Kalgan and then across the Gobi to Hami. Next, skirting the Tien Shan, he followed the caravan route to Kashgar and thence to Yarkand. Here he determined to take an hitherto unbeaten track across the Mustagh into Skardu. It was a difficult, almost impossible journey, that of crossing the pass and a fromidable glacier at an altitude of 19,000 feet, but Younghusband did the trick : 'a notable feat of exploration had (thereby) been successfully accomplished.'[14]

By 1890, Curzon had completed his *Russia in Central Asia*, and warned his countrymen 'of the gravity of the menace which Russian ambitions constituted to the Imperial position of Great Britain in the East.' [15] A few years previously, Younghusband had concluded that 'the Chinese were quite unable to assume the offensive against the Russians and, in Turkestan, would not even be able to hold their own,' and that the Cossacks would have 'little trouble in conquering the whole of Turkestan.' [16] The resemblance between the two men in this context is striking. Curzon had written of the irresistible march of the Russians towards the frontiers of India, to the heart of Persia, to the warm waters of the Bosphorus, Younghusband had likened her southward drive to that of a glacier which, under the pull of gravitation, moves from the higher to the lower regions.[16] Curzon had been interested in Afghanistan, as a possible buffer to check Russia's onward march; Younghusband had been fascinated at a fairly early age by the idea of Chinese Turkestan serving as a powerful bulwark to any advance from the north to India's borders. He had been less vocal about the Empire, but no less devoted a votary : 'We were on the brink of a war with Russia (in 1885) and it was then that I began to take a part, a very humble one at first, and never a great one—in helping to fend off Russia from India.'[17]

Apart from his early explorations, and he was barely 24 years yet, through the dense forests of Manchuria and the vast plains and deserts of the Chinese Empire from the extreme east bordering on the Ocean, to the extreme west adjoining the Roof of the World, Younghusband had also conducted some semi-military, semi-political, missions to the northern frontier. Thus in June 1889, he had crossed the Shimshal pass and proceeded apace, through the Pamirs, 'to examine what passes there might be into Hunza from there.' It was at this spot that he encountered his Russian counterpart, Captain Grombtchesky 'who ... had started from St. Petersburg to carry out this exploration which I had now completed.' [18] The entirely outspoken manner in which the Cossack talked of a Russian invasion of India—'indeed he boasted of it'—must have left an indelible imprint on his young mind. His mission was crowned with success :

> Such passes as there were into Hunza I had explored, I had forestalled the Russian, and arranged for the safety of the caravan route to Central Asia against raiders...[19]

In the summer of 1890 he was sent to the Pamirs again, this time his mission—originally he had himself suggested it to Government—was to ascertain Chinese and Afghan claims on the Pamirs. The gap that yawned between Chinese and Afghan territory, through which Captain Grombtchesky had penetrated in 1899, seemed to him to demand a clearer definition. Indeed, he had spelt out his purpose as one of trying to find out 'what were the precise territorial limits of each of these countries ... and watch every forward move of the Russians.'[20]

This time his route lay through Yarkand. At Kashghar, however, he was met by the Russian Consul-General, one Petrovsky. As Younghusband proceeded ahead with his journey he was accosted by Colonel Yanoff (also rendered Ianoff), with an escort of a hundred Cossacks while he himself had none, armed or otherwise. A few days later the Colonel appeared again and informed the young lieutentant that he was under arrest for what was allegedly a trespass into Russian territory.[21] His protests that he was on Afghan soil being of no avail, Younghusband submitted without further demur. Meanwhile the British Prime Minister Lord Salisbury's remonstrances with de Giers, his Russian counterpart, over this 'arrest' were so sharp in tone that the latter thought it might spell out war. An immediate result, however, was that Younghusband was soon on his way to India. That his detention by the Russians would be of some concern he had no doubt anticipated, but how surprised he must have been to find from none other than Lord Roberts, then Commander-in-Chief, 'that he (Roberts) had mobilised the Quetta division and was quite prepared to go ahead.'[22]

Between his Pamir adventures and the Mission to Tibet, Younghusband had acted as Political Agent in Chitral. Later, he was to spearhead a gallant relief thither to a worn-out group of beleaguered officers and act as the (London) *Times* correspondent—an assignment that he repeated some years afterwards in South Africa. The last chapters of his fascinating, and still instructive, *The Heart of a Continent*, to which a reference has been made earlier in the narrative, speak of his experiences in this remote Himalayan state; his *Relief of Chitral,* previously alluded to, has been regarded both as 'a model of military history within the limits of a minor campaign,' and 'a fine example of a combined operation which worked out with singular accuracy.'[23] His service on the frontier, the 'tact, judgement and ability' and the 'devotion to duty' of this 'most deserving and distinguished officer'—a citation richly earned both in his 'political and military capacity'—was the subject of considerable official comment.[24] His South African adventure, re-captured in the pages of his now well-nigh completely forgotten *South Africa Today*, brings back to life the tension in that land during the days of the Jameson raid. It need not detain one long here, nor should his somewhat uneventful period as Assistant to the Governor-General's Political Agent in Rajputana (1899-1902) or subsequently as Resident in Indore. It was from this latter post that he was recalled when entrusted with the leadership of the Mission to Tibet.

With their political philosophies so closely akin, and that deep, abiding interest in travel, and exploration, which they shared in common, one may wonder if the Political Agent in Indore had personally been acquainted with Baron Curzon of Kedleston before his own appointment to the Tibet Mission? As will be presently noticed, the two men had indeed met and known each other for more than a decade. Their first encounter, which took place in London, was in 1892 : Curzon had taken over as Under-Secretary for India and Younghusband had reapaired home after his arrest in the Parmirs at the hands of the Muscovites. And the latter was certainly very favourably impressed :

The Under-Secretary was, however, very different.[25] He engaged me in a long and real conversation .... No one else I had met not even in India—was so well-informed, and so enthusiastic as he was. And he was young and fresh and very alert and able. His name was George Curzon and this was his first appointment.[26]

Two years later Curzon, then out of office, was visiting places and while on a tour of Hunza, the Pamirs and Chitral was a guest of Younghusband, then acting as Political Agent with the Mehtar.[27] Curzon recalls their meeting in his posthumously-edited *Leaves from a Viceroy's Note-book;* Younghusband in his *Heart of a Continent.* The former's references to the Agent are factual : he had played host and together they had 'crossed the main range of the Hindu Kush by the Baroghil pass and followed the main course of the Tarkhun river' to Chitral.[28] Younghusband's pen-portrait of his guest, a future Viceroy, is much more revealing and affords an interesting sidelight on the two men:

> Lord Curzon was then both a pleasure and a trial. He was perpetually discussing frontier policy, which[29] was agreeable, but he was continually disagreeing with me, which was irritating .... All the same Curzon had an argumentative turn of mind—I suppose it was the House of Commons debating habit—and it jarred on us up there at the frontier .... We formed and expressed our opinions upon what was life or death for us personally in a quieter away than is usual in Parliament or at elections, where ability to talk or argue is the first consideration. And we resented Curzon's cocksureness. His manner grated on us on the frontier, as all through his life it grated on the British public.[30] It might have been toned down if he could have been for a time with a regiment or served on the frontier... soldiers in general he never understood or liked. But to frontier officers he always opened his heart.[31]

What appears to have been their third meeting—early in 1902 and before the Tibet appointment—took place in Simla when Curzon, now Viceroy, asked Major Younghusband and his wife to be his guests at Government House. Here he enjoined upon his visitor 'not to look upon him as Viceroy, but as an old friend and fellow-traveller',[32]

> ... all Viceregal pomposity vanished as he welcomed us. There was not a trace of it as he laid himself out to make us enjoy ourselves. He was just the warmhearted English host .... And never once afterwards, even in the most official dealings, did he treat me as anything else but a friend. [33]

A reference has already been made to the Viceroy's recommendation to the Secretary of State that Major Younghusband be appointed Commissioner for the team of British negotiators who were to resolve the frontier and trade difficulties with the Tibetans and the Chinese at Khamba Jong. This Lord George Hamilton accepted in approving 'policy'.[34] Younghusband's first inkling about it all was from what he called a 'mysterious letter' that put him into 'a state of agitation', and in which an old acquaintance from Simla solicited 'me to take him with me on my journey.' Nor was his hunch very much wide of the mark : 'Probably a mission to Nepal or Tibet'.[35] The 'mystery,' however, soon solved itself,

> I am to go to Tibet incharge of a very important mission. Very strictly in confidence Lord Curzon had intended to send me to Lhasa with an armed

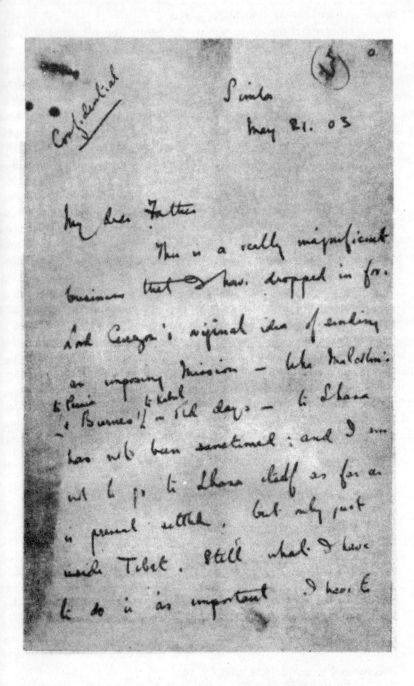

From Simla, to 'My dear Father' dated May 21, 1903

force capable of putting down all resistance .... [36]

It is significant that the above was written before Younghusband reached Simla, or was placed 'on Special Duty', or began drawing up his 'suggestions' regarding the escort which was to accompany the Commissioner and Mr. White, into Tibet.[37] These fromalities, however, were soon gone through and on June 3, Government officially notified him of his new appointment and briefed him on his 'mission'.[38] The letter, in terms of the scope of negotiations as finally determined by the Secretary of State, had been preceded by a long talk in which the Governor-General outlined to him the aims and objectives he (Curzon) had in view and how 'mercilessly' he had been overruled by the Home authorities.[39] Younghusband's own feelings were somewhat mixed :

I was proud indeed to have been selected.[40] .... The whole enterprise was risky. His (Curzon's) own party was very lukewarm over it.... (The Viceroy was) risking much in selecting me. I had never seen a Tibetan, nor served on the North-eastern frontier .... I might make a hideous mess of it with the Tibetans .... I quite saw the risks that Lord Curzon was taking and this made me all the keener to justify his choice.[41]

Whatever Younghusband's initial diffidence, the Viceroy had made his choice after due deliberation—'there was no man in India he would trust better than me' to carry out his plan 'to forestall' the Russians who 'he (Curzon) was convinced', were 'up to some harm'.[42] There is no doubt that Younghusband's previous record of work had inspired confidence and it appears that as early as 1888, after his return from the Central Asian journey, his services had been repeatedly sought for by the Bengal Government for leading punitive expeditions against the Tibetans on the Sikkim frontier.[43] Unknown to him, in each case the Government of India had refused. And now, 15 years later—'it is curious I should have worked to this quarter again'[44]—they were themselves sending him on a not very different undertaking.

Notes

1. Tibet Papers, *op. cit.*, Cd. 1920, Annexure 2, Encl. 1, in No. 99, pp. 195-96.
2. More correctly 'dzong,' literally 'fortress,' and the headquarters of the 'dzong-pon,' the official who heads the district administration. In the narrative both 'jong' and 'dzong' have been interchangeably used.
3. Tibet Papes, *op. cit.*, Cd. 1920, No. 86, p. 189.
4. *Ibid.*, No. 89, p. 190.
5. 'My idea would be to frighten the Chinese and Tibetans into the acceptance of Gyantse by offering them as the only alternative to a representative at Lhasa itself. They will be so ready to bribe us out of the latter proposal that they may concede The former.' Curzon to Hamilton, letter, May 7, 1903, Hamilton Papers, *op. cit.*
6. *Loc. cit.*
7. *Loc. cit.*
8. Tibet Papers, *op. cit.*, Cd. 1920, No. 89, p. 190.
9. *Ibid.*, No. 88, from the Secretary of State to the Governor-General, April 29, 1903, pp. 189-90.

10. *Ibid.*, No. 95, p. 193, from the Secretary of State to the Viceroy, May 28, 1903.

11. Letter from Hamilton to Curzon, May 28, 1903, Hamilton Papers, *op. cit.*
It is not without significance that it was written on the same day as the telegraphic despatch to the Governor-General drawn upon in the previous paragraph.

12. Born in 1863 at Murree, in the Panjab (now part of West Pakistan), Younghusband's upbringing had been Victorian in the best sense of the term, viz., regular daily prayers, inculcation of filial piety, and the veritable Sunday School. At 13, he went to Clifton College which had a traditional role of preparing boys for a career in the Army, and later at 17 to Sandhurst where Allenby and Sir Herbert Lawrence (later Haig's Chief of Staff) were his contemporaries. At 19, he joined the 1st Royal Dragoon Guards, then stationed at Meerut, in India, as a subaltern. His *Relief of Chitral* (in collaboration with his brother 'G. J.') was published in 1895, *The Heart of a Continent*, in 1896 and *South Africa today*, in 1897, all in London. His Tibet expedition is described in *India and Tibet* (London, 1910), and in a brochure *Our Position in Tibet* which gives the text of a talk to the Central (later Royal Central) Asian Society on November 2, 1910. Apart from his interest in Himalayan exploration, which seemed abiding, in later life Younghusband was to turn increasingly towards mysticism—his works in this field are indeed numerous—and the fag-end of his life was spent in founding a World Fellowship of Faiths. Of a score and more of his better-known works in this field, the following may be listed : *The Coming Country, a Pre-vision* (London, 1928), *The Epic of Mount Everest* (London, 1926), *Everest : the Challenge* (London, 1936 and 1941), *The Heart of Nature* (London, 1931), *Life in the Stars, an exposition of the view that on some planets of some stars exist human beings higher than ourselves* (London, 1927), *The Living Universe* (London, 1938), *Modern Mystics* (London, 1935), *The Gleam: the religious experience of an Indian, here called Nija Svabhava* (London, 1923), *Mother World in Travail for the Christ that is to be* (London, 1924), *The Reign of God : a drama* (London 1930), *The Sum of Things* (London, 1939) *Wedding* (London, 1942), *A venture of faith : being a description of the World Congress of Faiths held in London*, 1936 (London, 1937). Apart from stray sketches—one of the best is Herbert Samuel (Viscount Samuel) *Man of Action, Man of the Spirit: Sir Francis Younghusband* (London, 1952)—no full-scale 'Life' of Younghusband, has been written. His own, *The Light of Experience* (London, 1927) is mainly autobiographical. A recent study is George Seaver, *Francis Younghusband* (London, 1952). The writer drew heavily on Dame Eileen Younghusband, M.B.E., J.P., D.B.E., who was generous with her time, Sir Francis' letters loaned to him through her courtesy and Mr. George Harrison, a close friend and associate. The latter's *The Great Adventure: a Younghusband Anthology of divine Fellowship*, in manuscript, was also made available to him through the kindness of Mr. Harrison.

13. Younghusband, *The Heart of a Continent*, 2nd edn. (London, 1937), Introduction.

14. Percy Sykes, *A History of Exploration*, Torch Book Edition (New York, 1961, pp. 248-49.

15. Ronaldshay, *Life*, I, pp. 142-43.

16. Younghusband, *The Light of Experience* (London 1927), p. 40.

17. *Ibid.*, p. 3

18. *Ibid.*, p. 45. Younghusband's account of his adventures, in the realm of a deep communion with nature, during these journeys is found in his *Wonders of the Himalayas* (London, 1924).

19. Younghusband, The Light of Experience, *op.cit.*, p. 48.

20. *Ibid.*, p. 53.

21. The exact place from where Younghusband was turned back by the Russians wa
    Bozai Gombaz.

22. Younghusband, The Light of Experience, *op. cit.*, pp. 56-62. It is interesting to recal
    in this context that Curzon referred to this episode as indicative of Russian bad fait
    and of their penchant of reeling out 'deliberate lies.' He reminded his corresponden
    that 'de Giers denied that Yanoff was on the Pamirs when he (de Giers) had himsel
    despatched him (Yanoff).' Curzon to Hamilton, letter, April 13, 1903, Hamilton
    Papers, *op. cit.*

23. George Seaver, *op. cit.*, p. 167 and George J. Younghusband, *Indian Frontier Warfare*
    (London 1898). Younghusband's Relief of Chitral, *op. cit.*, was written in collaboration
    with his brother Captain George (later Major General Sir George) Younghusband
    though, in the latter's words, 'mostly by Frank'. For brief description, see Major
    General Sir George Younghusband, *Forty Years A Soldier* (London, 1923), pp. 126-52
    and his earlier Indian Frontier Warfare, *op. cit.*, pp. 17-20 and 47-48.

24. The words occur in a memorandum submitted by Colonel R. Parry Nisbet, then
    Resident in Kashmir, while summarising the results of the Chitral expedition. Cited
    in Seaver, *op. cit.*, p. 168.

25. Younghusband was comparing him (Curzon) to Lord Cross, then Secretary of State
    for India, who took 'only a perfunctory interest.' Younghusband, The Light of
    Experience, *op. cit.*, p. 62.

26. *Ibid.*, pp. 62-63.

27. 'Mehtar' (literally 'greater' or 'bigger') is the Persian title of the ruler of Chitral who
    belongs to the Kutur family.

28. Curzon's description in Chapter III (*The Mehatar of Chitral*) of his book is a detailed
    account of his visit. He was very conscious of the importance of Chitral 'owing to its
    geographical position, in the scheme of frontier defence of the Indian Empire' (and
    was convinced of the necessity of closing) 'this small chink in the mountain palisade
    which at that time Russia showed such a persistent desire to penetrate ....' Curzon,
    Leaves from a Viceroy's Note-book, *op. cit.*, pp. 93-146.

29. It is interesting to recall in this context that Curzon's viewpoint on the importance of
    Chitral was directly refuted by another well-known authority on the problems of the
    frontier who held : 'Chitral was never on the high road to India from High Asia and
    never will be... (at best it) must remain as one outlying channel in the mountain
    district northwards. As a military outpost it had little to recommend it.' Colonel Sir T.
    H. Holdich, *The Indian Borderland: 1880-1900* (London, 1901), p. 312.

30. A knowledgeable critic who knew him at first-hand wrote to the author to this effect
    : 'Curzon never understood real men—he lived on paper or in a debating society. But
    he could charm if he thought it worth-while. In many ways he was arrogant and a bit
    of a cad'.

31. Younghusband, The Light of Experience, *op. cit.*, pp. 69-70.
    Sir George Younghusband, Forty Years a Soldier, *op. cit.*, p. 128, recalls Curzon's visit
    when 'with Frank as his guide, philosopher and friend (he) saw a good deal more of
    Chitral and its ruler, than he would have otherwise succeeded in doing. The Mehtar
    was most civil, probably thinking that an M.P. generally sat on the right hand of the
    Queen of England, and was her Chief Adviser. Anyway Frank records that the Mehtar
    asked them to dinner and in return dined with them and that they all played game of
    polo together. It must have been an inspiring sight, that game of polo with Lord
    Curzon in the midst of it.'

32. 'The first part of his injunction was difficult to obey. It would have taken a man with a larger imagination than I have not to look upon Curzon as Viceroy.' Cited in Seaver, *op. cit.*, 198. The source, not indicated, appears to be some Note-Book, or private correspondence.

33. *Loc. cit*

34. Tibet Papers, *op. cit.*, Cd. 1920, No. 92, p. 192.

35. Numbered (erroneously) '2' in the collection of 53 letters which Younghusband wrote to his father—a few are addressed to his sister—and which have an important bearing on the expedition to Lhasa. Here, more than anywhere else, he laid himself bare-open, and one delineates his innermost feelings. The letters, in manuscript, were loaned to the writer through the courtesy of Dame Eileen Younghusband and are hereinafter referred to as *Younghusband Manuscript.* No. 2 is dated Indore Residency, May 7, 1903. His correspondent from Simla was one Gabriel who, at one time his assistant, now worked in the (Government of India's) Foreign Department.

36. Younghusband MSS., No. 1. The letter bears no date ('May 1903') but was written 'on the way to Simla.'

37. Tibet Papers, *op. cit.*, Cd. 1920, Encl. 5, in No. 99, pp. 197-98, June 1, 1903.

38. *Ibid.*, Encl. 6, in No. 99, June 3, 1903.

39. This was over lunch. Curzon praised his (Younghusband's) work at Indore, confided 'there was no man in India he could trust better than me to carry out his plans, and told him (Younghusband) he (Curzon) hoped 'you will be glad to get back to your old work.'

40. There were other men who wanted the job, 'Dane (later Sir Louis Dane) himself would like to have had it and so would Major General Sir Edmund Barrow, who was in China and with Lockhart in Chitral in 1885. *Loc. cit.*

41. Younghusband, The Light of Experience, *op. cit.*, pp. 81-82.

42. Younghusband MSS., No. 3, May 21, 1903.

43. Seaver, *op. cit.*, p. 201.
    In one of his letters to his father, Younghusband MSS., No. 6, there is an allusion to this earlier selection when he was asked 'whether I could check interpretation in Chinese,' to which, of course, his reply was a firm negative.

44. *Loc. cit.*

13
'Negotiations' at Khamba Jong

preceding chapter spells out at length what may be summarily recalled here
ely that the talks which were to commence on Tibet had been originally
gested by the Chinese. White's tour along the border, in July 1902, had aroused
n to the ugly possibilities inherent in such a situation and, apart from the
erial Government in Peking exhibiting increasing anxiety to the British Minister,
Manchu Amban in Lhasa had also been in communication with the Viceroy.
ier it was noted that owing to his 'illness,' and later 'important special business'
hasa, the Amban's representative had not been able to meet Mr. White. This
not seem to bother Curzon, then engaged in one of his major policy wrangles
n the Home authorities. The Viceroy's silence, however, appeared to be
tentous—and disturbing—and late in November 'His Excellency Yu' had written
is opposite number in India, to say that negotiations be resumed and 'matters
hus amicably arranged'[1]. A little later, on January 21, 1903, Mr. Ho. had himself
ressed Mr. White asking him 'to come to Yatung for a few days... and discuss
tier and other matters in a friendly manner'.[2] White, however was in no mood
blige—he lacked instructions[3] and Curzon was certainly not interested until a
Amban had arrived[4]. The Chinese delegates (Mr. Ho. and Captain Parr) tiring
response, addressed another letter to the Political Officer in which, in an
uarded moment it would seem, they expressed themselves thus:
      ... and fearing that the suggestion contained in Mr. Ho's letter of the 21
   January, 1903, to you that you might find it convenient to discuss matters at
   Yatung has not proved acceptable we, therefore, hasten to assure you... quite
   prepared to proceed to such place as may seem to ... the Viceroy more desirable
   ....[5]
Lord Curzon seized upon the words. If only he could have named Lhasa to be
venue! Meantime the Chinese Commissioners' words were echoed by the
ban who reminded the Viceroy that his men had been cooling their heels at
ung for three months 'to begin the discussion of affairs'. *Inter alia*, he averred,
Deputy appointed by Your Excellency can either come to Yatung or the

Chinese Deputies will proceed to Sikkim or such other place as may be deci
upon by Your Excellency'.[6]

From the context it should be obvious to the most casual of observers that
phrases 'such other place' or 'such place as may seem ... more desirable'
relevance only to a place in India—and quite probably Darjeeling was in view.
Curzon grasped the opportunity with both hands and the tone and content of
letter to the Amban would suggest that he was determined to hold him to v
was, at best, an inadvertent slip. He now placed the blame securely for his l
delay on the condition of the passes and the fact that 'the whole tract was ur
snow'. 'Now', however, he (Curzon) informed the Chinese Resident, '... on
understanding that on this occasion the Lhasa authorities will be duly and l
represented', he was prepared for an early meeting of the Commissioners.

As to the venue, he left the Amban no choice, for Khamba Jong is 'the nea
inhabited place to the frontier in question, where such a meeting can take plac
The escort, that was to accompany the British Commissioner, would be 'sm
considering both the rank of the officer[8]—and, in Younghusband's own wc
'he piled it on a good deal about my high position'[9]—the wild nature of
country and not least (owing to) 'Your Excellency's reiterated wishes'.

And what were the subjects to be discussed? Herein the Viceroy enumer
not only the natural rights of grazing 'but also the method in which our t
relations can be improved' and placed upon a basis 'more consonant with
usage of civilised nations, our direct and predominant interests in Tibet, and
friendship with Chinese Government'. The meeting was to take place on July 7
Viceroy's letter was written on June 3) that is before 'His Excellency Yu' c
either gauge the true import of the Viceroy's words, much less have time to prote

Meantime, and even as the Viceroy was informing the Amban, Younghust
had left Simla for Darjeeling, on his way to Khamba Jong. The appointme
White as Joint Commissioner had been made as also of Captain (later Lieuter
Colonel Sir) William Fredrick O'Connor as Secretary. His original brief tha
(Younghusband) 'should go at once' to Khamba Jong and 'if proper (i.e., offi
Chinese and Tibetans did not appear' was to move on farther into the country
they did appear',[11] was later countermanded. Putting a specious interpretatio
his instructions,[12] however, Younghusband despatched White—whom he init
rated as an excellent 'local' man, who 'does everything most comfortably'
could make 'all the arrangements in the easiest way'[13]—with almost the e
escort to precede him, while he himself held back at the head of the Sikkim va
White and his advance-guard crossed into Tibet on July 6, in the face of repe
protests from the Chinese Commissioners who had insisted that Khamba 'b
on Tibetan side of the frontier is an unsuitable rendezvous', but had been infor
that by itself could not 'for a moment be recognised ... as a legitimate objectio
Earlier, on July 5, two high Lhasa officials had met the Joint Commission
Giaogong. They had asked Mr. White to discuss matters there but were told
such talks were 'not feasible', and that 'any discussion must be deferred

val at Khamba Jong'. How earnest the Tibetans were in dissuading the British in crossing into their country may be gauged from the following entry in Captain Connor's 'diary' of that day,

They... pressed forward on foot, and catching hold of Mr. White's bridle, importuned him to dismount and to repair to their tents. At the same time their servants pressed round our horses, and seizing our reins endeavored to lead us away .... The Khamba Jongpen (one of the Tibetan officials) afterwards followed us, and made repeated efforts to induce me to halt .... He was in a very excited and agitated state .... He said 'You may flick a dog once or twice without his biting, but if you tread on his tail, even if he has no teeth he will turn and try to bite you'....[15]

Tibetan officials apart, even Mr. Ho who had arrived on the frontier requested British to remain at Giaogong. Unsuccessful at first, he met them again and ed them to remain there 'in preference to proceeding to Khamba Jong'. His uest however, was 'politely declined'.[16]

Thus it was that Khamba was reached and 'negotiations' started there. How ch of the seemingly uncooperative attitude, even anger, of the Chinese and the etans was a result of British demeanour, of their haughty, proud disdain may be ged, if only partially, from one of Younghusband's private letters, written a few s after he had himself crossed into Tibet and arrived at Khamba Jong,

Politically things are bad. Old White had made a terrible hash of it. He will treat these Chinese and Tibetans as he would the Sikkimese and will not remember that when he crossed the boundary, he crossed out of his own district... and though we may pull through without a row here because the Tibetans are a mild people it will not be any thanks to White. He has never been out of Sikkim : he is a little God there but he is absolutely useless and worse than useless in dealing with high officials of an independent nation ... and bitterly I regret I ever let him come on ahead alone. I have a deal to make up and you know how difficult it is to make up a bad start .... I had no idea he was so appallingly unfit as he had proved himself to be.[17]

There had been a fear that the Tibetan representatives would not arrive for the partite negotiations that had been initially envisaged. To forestall this the British reign Office, early in May, had urged its Minister in Peking 'to lay stress on the cessity of associating a properly accredited Tibetan representative' with the inese Commissioners.[18] Peking did indeed seem to recognise the importance of ch representation, for its Amban in Lhasa was lecturing the Tibetan 'barbarians' discussing matters with the British 'on the basis of reason', and imploring them t even if the latter entered Tibet 'on no account to repel them with arms'.[19] It uld appear that, for some time at least, his admonitions were not without avail the Dalai Lama was persuaded to appoint two officials: Le Po Tsang, described a civilian of the sixth rank and Secretary of the Council in the Treasury partment, and Wang Chu Chieb Pu, a Military Officer of the fourth rank decorated th the Peacock Feather and described as a Commandant in 'Interior' Tibet.[20]

And since Ho Kuang-hsi and Captain Parr had previously been designated Chin Commissioners, with the arrival of the British negotiations could indeed set of a good start. Difficulties, however, were not slow in cropping up. One of these already been hinted at, namely that both the Chinese and the Tibetan officials implored and entreated with the British advance-guard to desist from crossing frontier, but their protests had been brushed aside and summarily rejected. I was that all.

Even as early as July 7, before he crossed into Tibet, Younghusband entertained serious doubts about the respective positions of the Chinese Tibetan delegates. Officially he had informed Government that 'neither of them in the opinion of either White or myself, of sufficiently high rank'.[21] In private. called it 'such impudence' as was bound to 'make the Viceroy's hair stand on er although this was no surprise to him, for he had 'exactly expected ... and, in f predicted' this earlier.[22] This 'discovery' as he called it, was later to be confirm by the expert advice of Mr. Wilton, of the British Consular Service, who had b attached to the Commission. Wilton too thought the officials to be of 'too low rank' and felt the Chinese should have been represented by the Assistant Am and the Tibetan Government by a member of their Council.[23]

With an air of ill-disguised contempt Colonel Younghusband, who had arri at Khamba Jong on July 19, condescended nevertheless to meet the 'low ra delegates in the tripartite negotiations for which the stage was now set. Th days after his arrival, on July 22 to be precise, he addressed them all. But e before he delivered his well-prepared, long, and somewhat laboured perorat which was intended, as he confided to Authority, 'not for the benefit of these pe representatives here ... but to reach the ears of the Tibetan Government at Lhas the Tibetans raised two, what may best be termed, 'preliminary' objectio Firstly, they protested against negotiations being held at Khamba Jong at all as proper place, they pointed out, was Giaogong. Younghusband's explanations t the site was for the Amban, or the Viceroy, to choose evidently did not ca conviction for much 'futile' discussion ensued. Secondly, 'the two Tibeta severely criticized 'the size of my escort.' Since the parleys had been proclaimec be peaceful, they queried, why these armed guards? Younghusband—'with hands tied behind our backs by HMG', to use Lord Curzon's words[24]—tried shut them up by saying that he needed these men to protect himself against 'l characters'. This too did not cut much ice, for 'the fruitless disputations' wh followed could only be put an end to by his motioning to the interpreter commence reading my speech'.[25]

When it was over, the Tibetans refused to discuss it. Younghusband retor by saying that he would enter into such discussions only with (Tibet: representatives 'of sufficient rank and authority'. Meantime, however, they co report on what he had said to their Government. On their (Tibetans) refusing oblige, Mr. Ho put in a plea for their ignorance and pointed to the difficulty dealing with them. As though with tongue in check, he asked if Younghusba ould not meet with them by going to the frontier? The Commissioner somehow managed to parry this inconvenient question and next presented to the Tibetan Grand Secretary a copy of his speech, but 'he (Grand Secretary) could not have got rid of a viper with greater haste than he got rid of that paper'. The Tibetan protested he could, on no account, receive it.

Whatever 'progress' he made with the 'negotiations' Younghusband was convinced that 'the refusal of these two officials to receive, even with Mr. Ho's approval merely the copy of a speech is ... conclusive evidence that they are quite unfit to eventually conduct negotiations' with him. Mr. White and even Mr. Ho, lent their full weight of authority to this unhappy conclusion. Indeed, Younghusband was certain in his mind that 'they (Tibetans) have no authority from their Government'. Nor was Mr. Ho any the better for, apart from lacking any position or authority' on his own, he certainly had 'not the slightest influence' over 'these Tibetans'.[26] Truly, the very first meeting was enough to drive the British Commissioner to the end of his tether. For at its conclusion he wrote to his Government of 'the possible necessity for coercion' before the negotiations could be 'satisfactorily terminated'.[27]

The first 'meeting' of the 'delegates' of the three 'powers' was also to prove to be the last. For the next three months that the British remained at Khamba there were hardly any talks in the strict sense of the term. The Tibetans had underlined what seemed the root cause that filled them with suspicion of British motives and soon enough other sources confirmed it. Thus in mid-August the British Minister in Peking confided to the Foreign Secretary that the presence of the troops could make the Tibetans 'uneasy' and that their withdrawal would be necessary before the negotiations could be carried 'with deliberation'. Khamba's smallness and inability to feed a large force was also being discreetly hinted at.[28]

That the Tibetans, despite their differences, were united on the desirability of a British withdrawal was confirmed by a deputy from Tashilhunpo who arrived at Khamba on July 29, and wanted 'to demand the reason for our armed presence within the country ... and to request our immediate withdrawal'[29]. In his talks with the deputy—'a trifle less bigoted than his Lhasa brethren'—Younghusband was reminded of the same basic problems: Khamba was outside the disputed region, whereas Giaogong was inside it;[30] the Tibetans thought the British had not come with a friendly intent, as they had forced their way into the country;[31] a reduction of the armed escort would appease them[32]. Perhaps the deputy, whom undoubtedly the Commissioner had tried to keep in good humour,[33] threw a clever, yet no whit unmistakable, hint when he told Younghusband that the latter's horoscope indicated that Yatung would be 'a most favourable place for negotiations'.[34]

One wonders how, in the face of such unambiguous evidence of a united demand both by the Lhasa delegates and of the deputy from Tashilhunpo,[35] added to the unwearied Chinese protests that the British armed escort should be withdrawn, Younghusband could conclude, as he did, that the ranks of the party 'with whom we shall soon commence negotiations' are 'considerably divided'.[36]

Again, when every attempt to open negotiations was met by the stock rejoinder 'withdraw to the frontier,' the commercial mission, eager to enforce 'treaty obligations,' found itself at the end of two months not indeed on the way out bu 'entrenched in the open, with maxims trained and ready'.[37] What is more, there were further reinforcements of the escorts, a larger complement of British officers while more were held in reserve in not far off Sikkim.[38] That there was no mistaking the Tibetan attitude is clear from Captain O'Connor's entry (for August 31) in his 'Political Diary of the Commission':

> Their (Tibetan) present policy is one of passive obstruction. They have made up their minds to have no negotiations with us inside Tibet, and they wil simply leave us here....[39]

In more informal correspondence, the Commissioner was making no secret o his determination to force Government's hands.[40] Thus to Curzon he wrote, early in August,

> We shall have to move on to Gyantse before the negotiations are concluded ... we shall have to bring continuous pressure upon the Tibetans to effec anything, and to force ourselves into contact with them, since they so persistently hold aloof. I even think that the new settlement may have to be signed in Lhasa itself.[41]

As a matter of fact the reply to 'passive obstruction' was to be active aggression and the 'peaceful' mission was preparing the ground for a further advance into Tibet. Had not the Colonel, in his very first encounter, talked of 'the necessity for coercion'—a tune on which he continued to harp in the weeks, and months, ahead

Notes

1. Tibet Papers, *op. cit.*, Cd. 1920, Annexure I, Encl. 22, in No. 66, p. 176.
2. *Ibid.*, Annexure 2, in No. 66, pp. 176-77.
3. *Ibid.*, Annexure 2, in No. 99, pp. 195-96.
4. *Supra*, n. 2.
5. *Supra*, n. 3.
6. *Ibid.*, p. 196.
    Dr. Lamb, *op. cit.*, p. 287 contends that it were these words of the Amban which gave Curzon 'the opportunity for which he was looking and out of which the whole structure of the Younghusband mission to Lhasa of 1904 was to emerge.' Actually, as has been shown above, the first to use the expression were the Chinese Commissioners—not the Amban.
7. It may be recalled that under the Anglo-Chinese Convention of 1890 and the Trade Regulations of 1893, Yatung was the only place 'open' to the British in Tibet. By insisting on Khamba Jong, were not the British guilty of a 'deliberate violation' o those very 'treaty obligations' which ostensibly they had set out to enforce? Indeed a British author contends: 'There is not the shadow of a doubt that the violation of the Convention of 1890 carried out with a high-handed disregard for the elementary principles of international law. ... The Home Government was hood-winked and the Tibetan authorities were rushed'. A. Maccalum Scott, *The Truth About Tibet* (London 1905), p. 30.

8. Major Younghusband was, temporarily, promoted Colonel.
9. Younghusband MSS., No. 8, July 7, 1903. Throughout these letters, one notices the striking emphasis, indeed pre-occupation, with 'face'. There is Younghusband's repeated reference to the Foreign Office having 'a good wholesome respect of me' (No. 3), of the fear lest he 'lose dignity' if proper Chinese and Tibetan representatives did not arrive (No. 8). When it was suggested that Ho and Parr were equal in rank to him and White—he asked in pained surprise: 'Did you ever hear such impudence?' and 'it will make the Viceroy's hair stand on end?' (No. 8).
10. Tibet Papers, *op. cit.*, Cd. 1920, Encl. 6, in No. 129, p. 223.
    Also see *Ibid.*, Encl. 7, in No. 99, pp. 200-1.
11. Younghusband MSS., No. 7, June 28, 1903.
12. 'However I am taking these orders as personal to myself—that is to say I am going to read the 'you' in the telegram as meaning FEY only: and I am going to send on the escort and O'Connor and probably White too... I shall give out that my camp equipage has been detained by the rains (which it has) and that I cannot proceed beyond the last inhabited place till it arrives: that in the meanwhile a portion of my escort (really the whole) has been sent to prepare the camp and make all preliminary arrangements ...'
    Loc. cit.
13. *Supra*, n. 11. Younghusband's assessment of White was to undergo a complete change in the weeks and months ahead until he came to distrust and later almost ignore him.
14. For Ho's and Parr's letters see Tibet Papers, *op. cit.*, Cd. 1920, Annexure 1, for White's Annexure 2, both in Encl. 5, in No. 129.
15. *Ibid.*, Encl. 15, in No. 129, p. 226.
16. *Ibid.*, see entries for July 5-6, pp. 226-27.
17. Younghusband MSS., No. 9. The letter is inscribed 'Camp Khamba Jong, July 19, 1903'.
18. Tibet Papers, *op. cit.*, No. 90, p. 191.
19. These words occur in an extract form the *Peking Gazette* of May 23, 1903, entitled 'Supplementary Memorial from Yu Kang' (Chinese Resident in Tibet) and purports to be an address made by the Amban to the Tibetan bka'-blons. For the text, see *Ibid.*, Encl. in No. 97, p. 194. It may be noted here that the Chinese officials' repeated emphasis that they considered the Tibetans 'barbarians' and thus not fully manageable, underlined their (Chinese) legal contention of full sovereignty over Tibet, although 'barbarians' in the sense of being outside the Chinese pale may have been their real meaning.
20. *Ibid.*, Encl. in No. 106, pp. 204-5.
21. *Ibid.*, Encl. 11, in No. 129, p. 225.
22. Younghusband MSS., No. 8, July 7, 1903.
23. Tibet Papers, *op. cit.*, Cd. 1920, Encl. 28 in No. 129, p. 243.
24. Curzon to Godley, letter, July 8, 1903, Curzon MSS. The meaning would be much clearer from the context:
    'We hear that both the Chinese and Tibetans are on their way to Khampa Dzong. But do not be surprised if many months elapse before any real advance is made. We enter the arena with our hands tied behind our backs by HMG....'
    Curzon did regard himself as unduly handicapped—thwarted. In a letter to the Prime Minister on the same day (July 8), *Ibid.*, he told him in no uncertain terms that

'Ambassadors, proconsuls, Governors etc.' were duty-bound, as it were to show the way to their Governments, 'even if they decide, perhaps quite rightly, not to take it', that some of the things 'that I have put forward, and that you have rejected, e.g., Tibet—will of a surety come: and my only discredit will have been to be a little previous.'

25. For the text of the speech, see Tibet Papers, *op. cit.*, Cd. 1920, Annexure, Encl. 21, in No. 129, pp. 232-34.

26. A bare ten days after this, Younghusband was confiding in his father about 'the wretched Chinese Commissioner' who was 'trying to bolt' but 'the Tibetans will not give him carriage', Younghusband MSS. No. 10, August 2, 1903. In a letter to Hamilton, August 12, 1903, Curzon talked of Ho as 'a very timid little man' whose 'one desire' was 'to clear out of the place as soon as he can, and return to more hospitable quarters.' Hamilton Papers, *op. cit.*

27. For Younghusband's remarks, see Tibet Papers, *op. cit.*, Cd. 1920, Encl. 21, in No. 129, pp. 230-32.

28. *Ibid.*, Nos. 107-109, p. 205.

29. *Ibid.*, Encl. 24, in No. 129, pp. 241-42.

30. *Ibid.*, Encl. 45, in No. 129, pp. 257-59.

31. *Ibid.*, Encl. 47, in No. 129, pp. 260-62.

32. *Loc. cit.*

33. Referring to the deputy's visit, Younghusband wrote to his father: 'I had told him to thank his august Master for the kindness he had shown to two Englishmen who had visited him. The man looked surprised; so I added that perhaps His Holiness did not remember as he received these Englishmen 130 years ago in one of his former existences ....' Younghusband MSS., No. 10, August 2, 1903.

34. Tibet Papers, *op. cit.*, Encl. 56, in No. 129, entry in the Political Diary for September 5, 1903, p. 273.

35. The rivalry between the Dalai Lamas of Lhasa and the Panchen Lamas of Shigatse has been as old as the institution of the two offices themselves. A reference has already been made to the popular belief that the Panchen is the Dalai's spiritual superior. The tug-of-war between the two was to culminate in our own day, in the 9th Panchen's flight to China in December, 1923, and his unsuccessful attempt to return at the head of a large Chinese escort in 1936-37. Sixteen years later his successor was to stage a come-back as the spear-head of a Communist Chinese conquest of Tibet; after the March (1959) Rebellion in Lhasa, he stayed back to cooperate with Lhasa's new masters. Later (in 1965) he was removed ostensibly for his failure to cooperate fully with the Chinese.

Despite the early and even at the time of the Younghusband mission to Lhasa, pronounced pro-Panchen Lama learnings of the British, Sir Charles Bell, Sir B. J. Gould and Mr. Hugh Richardson and even Mr. Heinrich Harrer—who remained in Tibet for long and knew the country and its people intimately—turned out eventually to be anti-Panchen Lama.

For a pro-account which should, however, be accepted with considerable caution, see Gordon Bandy Enders, *Nowhere Else in the World* (New York, 1935).

36. Tibet Papers, *op. cit.*, Encl. 24, in No. 129, pp. 241-42.

37. *Ibid.*, Encl. 54, in No. 129, p. 267.

38. Younghusband MSS., Nos. 12-13, August 24 and September 25, 1903. Actually, Government had offered him 'another Pioneer Regiment directly but I put them off till after the rains and have now asked for them on October 1 to be in reserve in Sikkim'.
A little later (No. 14, October 2), he was 'strengthening my escort to 300 men with 4 British officers'.

39. Tibet Papers, *op. cit.*, Encl. 54, in No. 129, p. 267.

40. Actually, Curzon denied this and assured Hamilton that 'he (Younghusband) is incapable of any such tricks'. Curzon to Hamilton, letter, August 12, 1903. Hamilton Papers, *op. cit.*

41. Cited in Curzon's letter to Hamilton, *loc. cit.*

14
The Advance to Gyantse

It has already been pointed out that the ranks of the Tibetan and the Chinese 'Commissioners' had been considered 'too low' and that Younghusband had seriously called into question the authority of either to negotiate with him. The Tibetans' 'far from civilised' behaviour at the first meeting, and subsequently, was an additional reason for insisting that 'proper' representatives should be appointed. Mr. Ho's (whom Curzon called 'a very timid little man') lack of rank—and polish— was enough to condemn him by itself, and what was more he had not even 'the slightest influence' over 'these Tibetans'. Finally, when the Commissioners' own conclusions were confirmed by the arrival of Mr. E. C. Wilton, whose knowledge of Chinese (and Tibetan?) official hierarchy could scarely be bettered, time was thought to be ripe for rectifying this serious lapse. Actually, Younghusband was convinced that the Amban 'was trying it on with us by sending off inferior delegates' and held it against him that he (Amban) refused 'to correspond direct with me, as if I was something' far below him in rank.[1]

Soon enough, Lord Curzon took up cudgels on his deputy's behalf. On August 25, clear in his mind that the old Amban who was to continue for a few more months, 'does not want to do anything at all',[2] he wrote to 'His Excellency Yu' to suggest that the latter himself or the Associate Amban, along with a Councilor of the Dalai Lama and a high member of the (Tibetan) National Assembly, should proceed post-haste to Khamba. The Viceroy also took the opportunity to remove any doubts as to his choice of the venue for these meetings. He argued, somewhat speciously, that since the former convention (which the Tibetans had now repudiated) was concluded on Indian soil and since HMG were not prepared to allow a similar repudiation 'of any agreement at which we may now arrive', the present negotiations must be conducted inside Tibet.

As if to tighten the screw, Curzon warned his correspondent that 'unless very early steps' were taken to complete the negotiations, 'my Commissioners' would select 'some other place' in Tibet to pass the winter, for Khamba Jong's climate during this period was considered 'unsuitable'.[3]

That Younghusband had been consulted with regard to the Viceroy's letter to the Amban is evident and was, in the circumstances, to be expected.[4] What is not clear is the authority for the threat now held out to select 'some other place' in Tibet for passing the winter; for as yet Calcutta lacked a clear, formal sanction from London to talk anything of the kind. It would be apparent, however, that if Gyantse was not mentioned, it was not that it was not in Lord Curzon's mind but that he was being somewhat discreet. For, in a letter to Lord George Hamilton a fortnight earlier he had cited Captain Parr (whom the Viceroy called 'friendly') in support of 'what I have said to you all along' namely, 'that all our efforts would be wasted and that we should do nothing until we insisted upon maintaining an Agent at Lhasa'.[5] Younghusband too had concluded much to the same effect: 'we shall have to move on to Gyantse .... I even think that the new settlement may have to be signed in Lhasa itself'.[6]

As may be apparent, irrespective of clear authority, for Curzon the advance to Khamba, sanctioned by HMG in a most halting, reluctant manner was the thin end of the wedge. And although he continuously talked of Younghusband possessing 'the patience and the immobility of a pyramid', and of being able to spend 'a year or two years, if required in Tibet',[7] he was on his own intolerant of delay. For other things apart, he was anxious to prove 'the essential impracticability' of HMG's[8] plans and in this respect Khamba was a convenient demonstration post that would bear out his own oft-reiterated conclusions. Hamilton, his position in the Cabinet increasingly shaky—thanks to the row over Chamberlain and 'free trade'— sympathised to some extent with his over-bearing proconsul, if only to keep on the right side of him.

For the public eye, at any rate, the Viceroy was building up a strong case based on the alleged 'hostile actions' of the Tibetans, the by-now-well-demonstrated inability of the Chinese to exert any pressure whatever and the often-repeated bogey of Russian activity stiffening the Lama's back. In a despatch, dated September 16, he infromed his political superiors *inter alia*.

(a) That war 'has been definitely decided upon' by the National Council and that the Lhasa Government were 'determined not to negotiate';

(b) That they were collecting troops from all quarters and that 'action' was planned by the middle or end of next month, 'after getting in harvest'. Anticipating this attack, the British Commissioner had already increased his escort by one hundred additional troops;

(c) Two British subjects had been arrested by the Tibetans at Shigatse, and they (Tibetans) had declined to restore them.

As to the prospects for 'negotiations', the Viceroy painted a somewhat gloomy picture. The Chinese Amban, whose appointment had been announced in December 1902, was not supposed to arrive until the end of November—and Curzon thought the delay 'intentional'. Nor could there be any progress until he did, for the old incumbent 'does not wish to impair his popularity' in the few months left to him.[9]

Again, although the Dalai Lama had agreed to Khamba Jong as a meeting place (?)[10] the Tibetans were refusing to negotiate there. Indeed Younghusband, the Viceroy confessed, despaired of a peaceful solution for he (Younghusband) was convinced that until the Tibetans realised the seriousness of our intent—'which they now deride'—nothing could be done.

What were His Excellency's suggestions in the face of these 'grave' developments?

Occupation of the Chumbi Valley, and the advance of the Mission to Gyantse. The Viceroy went further and warned Lord George Hamilton that the occupation of the valley was, by itself, 'insufficient'; that any sort of action will be difficult after November; that a delay would be most injurious to 'our prestige' and would be tantamount merely to postponing the problem without solving it.[11]

Lord George Hamilton on his part had now conceded, though still in private, that 'it was a pity' that the Cabinet 'did not allow you a free hand' in Tibet;[12] that 'the news' from that quarter 'tends to confirm your predictions' and that he feared that 'we shall under less favourable circumstances ... be forced to send a Mission to Tibet'.[13] Yet, as Secretary of State, he refused to relent within the confines of an official despatch. Herein he barely undertook to bring to the notice of the Chinese authorities the hostile actions of the Tibetans, albeit he was 'doubtful' about any satisfactory solution. As for a further advance beyond Khamba HMG, he informed the Viceroy, viewed such a move 'with grave misgiving', although they were disposed to think that the fact that 'we are in earnest', may be sufficiently brought home to the Tibetans by the occupation of the Chumbi Valley 'in the first instance'.[14] Yet this official face-saving notwithstanding, Hamilton was still fighting the Viceroy's battles:

> but I did throw out to him (Lansdowne) a hint that matters were progressing so unsatisfactorily that it seemed inevitable that we should be compelled to take some form of action as you had throughout suggested ... the contest with an army of armed monks would be a novelty, and I should imagine that their defeat, and the slaughter of a few hundred of them, would have a salutary effect right throughout Tibet.[15]

At his end too, Curzon was leaving no stone unturned. He had written to Lansdowne that Tibet 'is going badly, or rather not going at all' and that while Younghusband had a large stockpile of patience and would not move on his own, nothing whatever was going to be done 'until we move or threaten'. For his part 'I will postpone it as long as you like; but sooner or later it is inevitable'.[16]

Apart from the allegedly 'hostile' actions of the Tibetans, Lord Curzon pressed home another vital point : evidence of an increasing disability of the Chinese either to hasten the advance of their new envoy Yu Tai, or to coax or cajole the recalcitrant Tibetans into a more reasonable frame of mind. As a matter of fact, the Foreign Office in London, thanks to the Viceroy's persistent proddings, had been exerting every possible pressure at Peking.[17] In turn, the Wai-wu-pu which had in the

Amban at Lhasa a major link in its chain of command, repeatedly asked him to make the Dalai Lama toe the line. Unfortunately it never worked out for the Amban's prestige and authority had sagged to a point where his 'admonitions' to the 'obstinate and stupid' Tibetan 'barbarians', administrered with increasing frequency, availed little if at all. It is true that the Imperial Resident had, apart from admonishing the Councillors, sometimes 'instructed' them, nay even 'ordered' and 'ordained' and 'enjoined' upon them—the results, nonetheless, were the same in all cases. The Tibetan Government stubbornly evaded submission to his authority.

The India Office too had expressed its own strong misgivings.[18] Thus the conclusion, increasingly irresistible, was that even the new Amban, now nearly a year on the road, when he did eventually arrive would be able to do precious little. A despatch of September 25 (1903) from Sir Ernest Satow, the British Minister in Peking, summed up the situation admirably and may bear citation:

... I am disposed to think that the Chinese Government are really desirous of seeing the matter brought to a satisfactory conclusion between India and Tibet, but from Prince Ch'ing's (Chinese Foreign Minister) repeated allusions to the obstinate temper of the Tibetans and the difficulty the Imperial resident (i.e., Amban at Lhasa) experiences in dealing with them, they are not sanguine as to the likelihood of Yu Tai's being able to expedite the negotiations.[19]

There was yet another string to the Viceroy's bow : the fear, for most part imaginary as it proved, of Russian intrigue. Younghusband spoke of it constantly and Curzon rubbed the point home unremittingly. 'Every letter of his (Younghusband's)' the Viceroy wrote to the Secretary of State on August 26, 'bore eloquent testimony to the fact that the Tibetans are relying upon Russian support. I feel no doubt in saying that any failure on our part in the present negotiations will leave things worse off than they were before, and will precipitate the very ascendancy of Russia which our proceedings are intended to prevent or postpone'.[20] A week earlier, Curzon had written to Lansdowne even more categorically,

I have not a doubt that the Russians, through their Buriat Lamas, are behind the Tibetans and the latter openly proclaim it. We cannot, of course, end with another fiasco like Colman Macaulay's Mission.[21]

In an earlier letter, when Younghusband had been at Khamba Jong for less than a few weeks, the Viceroy had drawn heavily upon the Commissioner and his informers :

Captian Parr, the Chinese Customs Officer ... has told Younghusband in confidence upon his arrival at Khamba Jong that he had good reason to believe that Russians are now actually on their way to Lhasa. Younghusband further telegraphs ... that they (Tibetans) rely absolutely upon Russian support. The same report reaches us from Nepal and ... confirmed a recent *Reuter* despatch ... I am firmly convinced of Russian *mala fides* in the matter ....[22]

Meantime Younghusband was writing what proved to be a veritable disquisition on British policy in Tibet and herein Russia loomed somewhat portentously :

> When we have obtained this access to Tibet and acquired as much influence
> there as is required for keeping Russian influence at bay, we shall have averted
> an insidious political danger to India; we shall have put ourselves in a position
> which will have as a barrier between our frontier and the probable future
> frontier of Russia the whole breadth of the inhospitable Chang Tang plateau;
> we shall have prevented the junction of any possible future spheres of French
> and Russian influence north and south across Asia : and we shall, on the
> other hand, be in a position of support to our own efforts in Szechuan and for
> combining our strength from east to west.[23]

What with valuable aid from Satow and Younghusband, the Viceroy's own
pressure continued, and mercilessly. In July, he had warned Balfour that he was
clear that his (Balfour's) government had been 'slow, sometimes unnecessarily
slow', and that an advance in Tibet 'will of a surety come';[24] early in September,
forwarding Younghusband's long report on Tibet, alluded to above, he wanted 'to
bring fairly home' to the minds of HMG 'three' major considerations. These included
the establishment of a trade mart at Shigatse 'which is now regarded such a daring
and wicked thing to ask', but had actually operated there for nine long years (1783-
92).[25] A near-climax may be said to have been reached when, on the day he wrote
his despatch regarding the hostile actions of the Tibetans, he scored another long
dig at HMG and their 'timidity',

> The Government will be compelled to authorise in the long run what we all of
> us advise, but what was rejected as ill-considered and impracticable. How
> often it happens that a Government in its collective capacity, which is always
> one of timidity, makes a mistake in rejecting the warnings of those who know...
> by postponing strong action now about Tibet, and the Government will not
> postpone or escape it altogether, but that sooner or later we shall be driven to
> the necessity ... of teaching these wretched little people that they cannot at
> our door treat us as if we were a power even more contemptible than
> themselves.[26]

The combined assault—and there was no letting up of heat—had its impact.
On October 1, the Secretary of State informed the Governor-General that HMG
'having again considered the position' were now prepared, 'if complete rupture of
negotiations proves inevitable', to authorise not only occupation of the Chumbi
Valley but also the advance of the Mission to Gyantse, 'if it can be made with
safety'.[27] It may be recalled that only ten days prior to this, Whitehall had viewed
any such action with 'grave misgivings', while a bare four weeks earlier Curzon
had advised Younghusband that 'whatever the Tibetans or Chinese did ... I felt
sure that HMG would not authorise an advance from Khamba Jong in the
forthcoming autumn' and that he (Younghusband) should shape his plans
accordingly.[28]

HMG's telegram of October 1 represented, as may be obvious, a very guarded,
hedged-in approach. Godley had referred to it as authorizing only a 'conditional

advance.' It may be recalled that Lord George Hamilton was on the way out—he
quit office on October 9, 1903—and that the British Cabinet were in the throes of a
grave political crisis. In the light of the controversy that was to rage around it later,
it may be as well to point out that the advance it authorised was, at best, a
compromise solution to a rather complex problem.[29] It was apparent that the Prime
Minister, and his colleagues, had been far from impressed by the 'gravity' of the
situation and were keen to keep away from all entanglements, binding or
otherwise.[30] What was more, Whitehall placed little 'confidence' in the Indian
Government's assessment of the problem in its varied facets. To the Viceroy,
however, here was a major triumph. Himself a powerful advocate of a 'strong'
approach, his chief preoccupation now was to prove beyond cavil that a 'complete
rupture of negotiations' at Khamba Jong was, in fact, 'inevitable' and that the
advance to Gyantse could be made 'with safety'. Meantime, Younghusband was
asked for his opinion and later—on October 11—summoned to Simla 'to consult
with me about the Tibetan advance'.[31] Detailed plans too were drawn up and
discussed at the Council table and with the military authorities, and everything,
from the Viceroy's viewpoint, seemed to augur well for the long-awaited advance.

On October 26, Lord Curzon had penned a fairly detailed despatch to London[32]
outlining 'reasons' why the advance into Tibet had become 'indispensable' and
why the Mission's goal should now be Gyantse, and 'not only' the Chumbi Valley.
As for the inevitability of the forward move, he reminded India Office that there
had been no Tibetan delegates for three months (the two earlier ones having never
been replaced); that a Colonel Chao, who had come in place of Mr. Ho, was
discovered to be 'inferior' in position to his predecessor; that Yu Tai had not yet
arrived and that the present Amban had 'failed to acknowledge the Viceroy's
letter' in which his attention had been drawn to the inadequacy both of Chinese
and Tibetan representation. Meantime, Lhasa had been 'preparing for war' for
months—so defiant, had it become that it had 'tortured and killed' two British
subjects who had earlier been captured. They 'mistake our patience for weakness,
reject our overtures with scorn and despise our strength'. 'In these circumstances',
the Viceroy queried, was there really 'any alternative', except the obvious one to
advance?

And additionally the move forward must be to Gyantse. For the Chumbi Valley,
the Viceroy informed the Secretary of State nor for the first time either, was not
regarded a part of Tibet and the latter country may be disposed to view its
occupation as a 'retrograde step'. Again, in case the valley alone were to be
occupied, 'our present situation will be repeated' at Phari, instead of at Khamba
Jong, and it would require 'stronger measures' to convince the Tibetans that we
were 'in earnest'. Two more arguments were pressed into service. Younghusband
thought that it was 'extremely important' that the British should come into contact
with the Tibetan people—'who are friendly and prepared to enter into relations
with us'—in contrast to the hierarchy of Lhasa monks who were the real

opposition.[33] (What a faithful echo of the line of reasoning Communist Peking was to adopt a bare half century later!) And insofar as the British were pressing for a trade mart at Gyantse, this objective could best be attained by getting there quickly. As for the physical difficulties, the Viceroy was confident that none whatever really existed. 'No serious resistance' was anticipated and though cold, the season 'is entirely favourable'.[34] Basically, Lord Curzon hardly anticipated any problems in 'carrying through operations' and maintaining 'communications and supplies'.[35]

A word may be added here, if only in parenthesis, about the alleged 'torture', and killing, of the 'two British subjects' by the Tibetans, to which the Viceroy had alluded. In an earlier despatch Lord Curzon had mentioned their capture,[36] and since then they had occupied a most important place in all diplomatic correspondence and for a time appeared even to be at the very centre of the stage. Lord Lansdowne had repeatedly asked the British Minister in Peking to secure their release;[37] the Chinese Foreign Office in turn had pressed its Amban at Lhasa with 'orders' to get them set free forthwith;[38] and the latter had done his best to persuade the Tibetans of the errors of their ways,[39] although to no effect. Who were these all-important 'British subjects'?

Initially, in July when the Mission had occupied a fortified camp at Khamba Jong, two men from the Lachung valley in Sikkim, had been sent to the Gyantse-Shigatse area to spy out the land.[40] The former returned with a report that the people of the country were 'in an excited state', that orders had been given to Tak-po and Kang-bo, and other provinces, 'for the assembly of soldiers' and that the monks of the three great Lhasa monasteries[41] had professed themselves as 'ready to march out'. In a land where a major source of news was the idle gossip of the bazaar, the Lachung men did a redoubtable job in bringing in the most fantastic of fibs on which O'Connor, and his master, now fed the Government.

Anyway, 'the two Lachung men', who paradoxically remained anonymous to the very end, 'sent to Shigatse on the 18th of July have not returned', Captain O'Connor noted in his 'Dairy' on August 2. Efforts to track them failed but gradually, over the next few weeks, these two spies were transfromed as it were into peaceful traders.[42] Meanwhile every unsubstantiated rumour that they had been captured, beaten up and put to death was seized upon and bloated out of all proportion. Here at last seemed to be a real 'incident', a deliberate outrage, demonstrating the studied hostility of the Tibetans. How vital they seemed may be gauged from Lord Curzon's despatch of November 5 :

> Perhaps, however, the most conspicuous proof of the hostility of the Tibetan Government and of their contemptuous disregard for the usages of civilization has been the arrest of two British subjects from Lachung at Shigatse, whence they have been deported to Lhasa, and it is credibly asserted, have been tortured and killed.[43]

To anticipate events slightly, a year later the two men were found, perfectly hale and hearty, on the Mission's arrival at Lhasa. Meantime for a whole twelve

upon saying that the whole matter will
have to go before the cabinet on Nov. 6th & he
is very doubtful of its passing. He says too that
the telegram of Oct 1st wd. probably never have been
passed by the cabinet.   This has played the
dickens, for on the strength of the telegram of
Oct. 1st considerable military preparations had been
commenced in anticipation for winter is coming on
and the best season for operations is passing away.
    The Viceroy asked me for my opinion on
Broderick's telegram and this I have given and I
believe he is telegraphing furiously. It really
must be heart-breaking work to a Viceroy
working with a vacillant Cabinet like this
There is no feel of certainty or reliance &

From Simla, to 'Dearest Emmie' dated November 3, 1903

months their imaginary 'torture', and 'death', had served a most useful purpose.[44]

While the Viceroy was preparing for the advance into Tibet and re-assuring the new Secretary of State, Henry St. John Brodrick (who had taken over from George Hamilton) that he (Curzon) will 'proceed with as much caution as possible', take action only 'when absolutely provoked to it' and ensure that our 'preliminary advance' was 'easy and effective', London dropped, what appeared to Curzon, a veritable bomb-shell.[45] Nowhere is the resultant atmosphere better captured than in Younghusband's 'very private' letter to his sister 'Dearest Emmie' written from Simla on November 3:[46]

> There has been, I am sorry to say a serious hitch over these Tibetan affairs. The Home Government are hedging badly. On October 1 the Secretary of State (Lord George Hamilton) telegraphed out that in the event of a rupture of negotiations proving inevitable His Majesty's Government were prepared to sanction an advance of the Mission to Gyantse and the occupation of the Chumbi valley.[47] But a few days ago comes a private telegram from Brodrick (to) Lord Curzon saying that the whole matter will have to go before the Cabinet on November 6 and he is very doubtful of its passing. He says too that the telegram of October 1 would probably never have been passed by the Cabinet.[48] This has played the dickens : for on the strength of the telegram of October 1 considerable military preparations had been commenced in anticipation, for winter is coming on and the best season for operations is passing away.
>
> The Viceroy asked me for my opinion on Brodrick's telegram and this I have given and I believe he is telegraphing furiously.[49] It really must be heart-breaking work to a Viceroy working with a moribund Cabinet like this.[50]
>
> There is no feel of certainty or reliance and so no decided action can be taken....

To set the record straight, both Brodrick and (his permanent Under Secretary) Godley had expressed themselves sufficiently clearly although, to obviate causing any offence, in a guarded language. The former had underlined the fact that the Cabinet was 'most unfriendly to any advance... and they will unquestionably want to know where we are going to stop'. The whole India Council too were 'hostile to advance' and hitherto 'only one member of the Cabinet ready to back it'.[51] Godley affirmed that the feeling in the Cabinet, 'pretty well-known', 'coincides' with that 'of our Council' who were 'very decidedly' opposed to an advance. He ended on a note which was to prove prophetic :

> ... but if, as I expect, you adhere to your opinion and induce the Government to agree, I am afraid that you will find that the obstacles to an advance to Lhasa which exist in this country are much more fromidable than in Tibet.[52]

Curzon, profoundly hurt, and in deep chagrin, protested vehemently against what he called 'throwing over' of the earlier policy of October 1, and wondered if 'an authority of this kind', once given, 'can be withdrawn'. He was convinced not only of the 'reasonableness' of 'our case', but even more so of the 'fact' that 'there is no other alternative'.[53]

This noticeable acerbity in Curzon's language, and the obvious pressure which he now brought to bear on the Home authorities may be difficult to understand without a word on Henry St. John Brodrick—later Earl of Midleton—the new Secretary of State who on October 9, 1903, succeeded to the office.[54] The latter's intimate ties with his old Eton-Balliol friend in India were no secret and, to the superficial observer, Lord Curzon was now placed in a good, strong position. Public postures apart, as a matter of fact however the two friends had very nearly broken with each other towards the end of 1902 : Curzon had visited Brodrick with his dire displeasure over what he (Curzon) believed to be his (Brodrick's) disingenuous role on the 'Darbar' episode[55]—and what contribution the Indian exchequer should make thereto.[56] A few weeks before St. John became the Viceroy's political head we find him writing, in a half-apologetic tone :

> I am exceedingly sorry you feel us to be so much in fault ... there is just as much bitterness growing up on our side as yours, and I will do all I can to stop it .... This issue with your despatch on Pay has made me suffer very heavily at the hands of the Indians press, and has made the difficulty of harmonious working greater than ever .... Honestly we thought, I especially, that while teaching us the benefit of a vigorous policy, you would endeavour to teach India the necessity of adequately supporting it.[57]

On his own, Curzon had been far from happy with the prospect of Brodrick taking over the India Office. George Hamilton who preceded him had, with a rare combination of deftness, patience and a remarkable power of resilience carried on with Curzon a rather difficult role,[58] had sensed the approaching storm and sounded timely warnings. For his part, the viceroy had an inherent distrust of Brodrick's 'never-failing gaucherie' which he thought would prevent his becoming 'either popular or a really capable minister'.[59] On September 24, George Hamilton wrote   to Curzon :

> I have warned Balfour what a howl his (Brodrick's) selection will provoke in India and I doubt whether you will find him easy to get on with, or if he will handle the (India) Council well ....[60]

A couple of weeks later he (George Hamilton) again 'warned' Balfour that Brodrick's appointment to the (India) Office 'would be most unpopular in India', but evidently the Prime Minister 'ignored the hint'.[61] Would it be too much to conjecture that some of these 'warnings' were inspired?

Not that Curzon took it kindly. Actually he too, disturbed by the impending changes had expressed himself, and in no uncertain terms, to Godley :

> It (Brodrick's induction into office) is a new and from some points of view, a rather painful experiment, starting almost at the end of one's time in India with a new Chief ... I cannot regard the situation without some anxiety ... But I must honestly confess there will have to be some change of clothes before

he (St. John Brodrick) can be generally recognised as the whole-harted champion of Indian interests .... [62]

Brodrick, who could probably sense George Curzon's feelings, took the earliest opportunity to allay the latter's fears :

I have never felt that on the subjects which I understood, such as those concerned with the Army, you felt the same regard for my views as I had for yours in matters which you have studied so much longer than myself... I shall never differ form you if I can possibly help it, and I have perhaps an exaggerated view of the necessity of trusting the man on the spot...[63]

It would thus be apparent that the relationship between the two men, as it subsisted in October, 1903, was far from being of an intimate, confidential nature. On Brodrick's part there was a stark awareness that the Viceroy did not quite trust him; on Curzon's a shade of 'anxiety' at what he viewed as a 'painful' experiment.[64] It is against this backgorund that one may examine the Secretary of State's telegram of October 29 expressing his doubts if the advance to Gyantse could be supported, a viewpoint for which he had the fullest backing of the Prime Minsiter and of a preponderant majority, if not indeed his entire Council. And yet Curzon took it to be an insult, a deliberate effort to reverse the earlier policy and throw it overboard. Nor, it should be sufficiently stressed, was either Brodrick or the Prime Minister unaware of what the Governor-General was up to. Thus in his letter of October 27 to 'My dear Arthur', the new Secretary of State wrote :

I do not know that we can actually say negotiations have reached a 'complete rupture' but if the move is to be made at all, I see no means now of deferring it. I believe you are at one with me in wishing the advance could be foregone— from his letters I know that George intends ultimately to go to Lhasa and if I were beginnig the negotiations afresh, I should be disposed .... to avoid making this move...[65]

Balfour's reply has been cited elsewhere. He deprecated 'permanent entanglements' in Tibet for he feared that if 'we 'manchurianise' what is technically a part of the Chinese empire', British diplomacy in the Far East may be gravely compromised. He it was—and not Brodrick—who wanted the decision to await Cabinet sanction unless 'military conditions render this inexpedient.'[66]

Yet in Lansdowne, the Foreign Secretary, the Cabinet had an advocte of 'going forward now', and on Novermber 6, the advance to Gyantse was 'sanctioned'.[67] The riders, however, were important—though not strictly from the Governor-General's point of view. HMG were 'clearly' of the opinion, Brodrick informed Lord Curzon, 'that this step should not be allowed to lead to occupation or to permanent intervention' in Tibetan affairs in any form. In fact, it was made 'for the sole purpose of obtaining satisfaction and as soon as reparation is obtained, a withdrawal should be effected'. Again, the British Government were 'not prepared to establish a permanent mission in Tibet' and the Viceroy was informed not indeed for the first time, nor yet the last, that 'the question of enforcing trade facilities in that country

FORCED FAVOURS.

The Grand Lama of Thibet. "NOW THEN, WHAT'S YOUR BUSINESS?"
British Lion. "I'VE COME TO BRING YOU THE BLESSINGS OF FREE TRADE."
The Grand L. "I'M A PROTECTIONIST. DON'T WANT 'EM."
British Lion. "WELL, YOU'VE *GOT TO HAVE* 'EM!"

["The advisers of the Dalai Lama, having ignored their obligations to us under the Convention of 1890, have now ignored the British Mission;" . . . "an advance is to be made into the Chumbi Valley on the frontier of Thibet."—*Daily Paper.*]

From PUNCH 1903, *Reproduced by permission*

must be considered in the light' of this decision, viz., the decision not to establish a permanent mission.[68]

Curzon had indeed scored a victory, at what cost, he did not quite seem to bother[69] yet, and wished Younghusband godspeed in the express confidence that 'I would make a success of this'.[70] The decision to advance with all its 'ifs' and 'buts'—and, in private, the Viceroy, as will be presently noticed, plunged headlong into a battle royal questioning all the Cabinet's major premises—considerably upset the Chinese. For some time now they had been genuinely afraid that a move of this nature was in the offing : the Governor-General, it may be recalled, had already talked of 'winter quarters' for his Commissioners. Anticipating this in full measure, the Amban at Lhasa had written to the Viceroy on Octover 17 that he himself, along with a Tibetan Councillor, would 'proceed to the frontier', and in the meantime begged him (Viceroy) to restrain his officials form selecting any new (winter) 'quarters'. He had also endeavoured to placate the British by holding out the hope that their two arrested subjects would soon be let off.[71] Almost simultaneously the Wai-wu-pu was making repeated requests that Younghusband be dissuaded from proceeding further. It intimated that the new Amban had been asked to reach Lhasa 'by forced marches';[72] that the present Imperial Resident had been instructed 'to proceed at once' to meet Younghusband and 'arrange matters';[73] that it was ready to 'exact obedience' from the Government of Tibet to Imperial commands to 'forthwith' resume negotiations.[74]

Their abject pleas, and express pleadings, were to be all in vain. Curzon hoisted Peking with its own petard. The Chinese were sternly reminded that their Tibetan wards had 'systematically disregarded the injunctions of the Emperor and the Chinese Government', that they (Chinese) had 'no real influence' in restraining the Tibetans. As for the new Amban, who was supposed to transform the scene, he had 'unnecessarily' protracted his journey.[75] The rejoinder to Chinese representations to stop Younghusband, took very much the same line : HMG could not 'remain inactive'[76] nor could they condescend 'to postpone' the measures which 'the conduct of the Tibetans' had 'constrained' them to adopt.[77] Above all, it was impossible to desist from what had already been sanctioned.[78] The Viceroy's formal reply to the Amban's letters was a variant on the same theme. He told 'His Excellency Yu' that since the Dalai Lama had already taken four months to select his Councillors, he (Curzon) saw no prospect of the Amban ever reaching Khamba. 'In these circumstances', the Viceroy informed him, the place for the negottiations had to be 'some more suitable spot'. And inasmuch as the Amban had warned him that all the passes in Tibet were guarded, the Viceroy intimated that he would be 'compelled' to take measures 'to ensure the safety of my Commissioners'.[79]

The Chinese apart, the Russians had also to be taken account of. As a matter of fact, Lord Lansdowne anticipating difficulties from their end had, almost immediately after the decision to advance was taken, informed Cout Benckendorff that the 'outrageous' conduct of the Tibetans had compelled HMG to take this step. He, however, hastened to assure the Ambassador that there was no intention either of 'annexing', or even of 'permanently occupying' any (Tibetan) territory.[80] For some time the Russians seemed to take it stoically, at any rate there was no immediate reaction. Later, however, the Count made what Brodrick called 'very serious representations',[81] intimating that this present invasion of Tibet by a British force was calculated to involve a great disturbance of the Central Asian situation. He thought it likely to create mistrust in the relations between the two countries, all the more unfortunate at a time when they were about to enter into an amicable discussion regarding their various global frictions.[82]

Lansdowne's rejoinder was couched in 'stout language'.[83] He expressed considerable 'surprise' at the Russian 'excitement'. Need he remind the Count that British interests in Tibet's affairs were 'wholly different' from any which Russia could claim. Was it meet then that these protests emanate from a Government which had 'all over the world' never hesitated 'to encroach upon its neighbours?' Lansdowne reminded the Ambassador of Russian 'encroachments' in Manchuria, Turkestan and Persia and wondered if they (Russians) would have shown the same forbearance (as the British had) in the face of Tibetan provocations? In the final analysis, the Ambassador was persuaded to accept the British pleas to 'the necessity of the advance' and its limited objective of merely obtaining satisfaction.[84]

Notes

1. Younghusband laid the blame squarely on previous practice, for 'unfortunately the Viceroy of India from Lord Lansdowne's time had been in the habit of corresponding direct with the Chinese Resident instead of corresponding through the Foreign Secretary. This has made the Chinese Resident think that he is equal to the Viceroy and that as I am merely a deputy.... I am a very small being and quite beneath his notice.' Younghusband MSS., No. 11, August 16, 1903.
2. Curzon to Hamilton, letter, August 12, 1903, Hamilton Papers, *op. cit.*
3. Tibet Papers, *op. cit.*, Cd. 1920, Encl. 36, in No. 129, pp. 250-51.
4. 'I had a telegram from Government asking for my opinion as to what reply Viceroy should give the Chinese Resident at Lhasa.' Younghusband MSS. No. 11, August 16, 1903. It is also evident that the Commissioner in his reply had sufficiently twisted the Amban's tail for, 'If I mistake not though Lord Curzon will pretty soon send him (Amban) to the right about'. *Loc. cit.*
5. Curzon to Hamilton, letter, August 12, 1903. Hamilton Papers, *op. cit.* It is clear that the words are allegedly those of one of the Chinese Commissioners. Younghusband's letters to his father do not make a mention of this particular conversation though evidently Parr was *persona grata* within the Mission's camp at Khamba Jong.
6. *Loc. cit.*
7. Curzon to Lansdowne, letter, August 19, 1903, Curzon MSS. *op. cit.*
8. Curzon to Hamilton, letter, August 12, 1903, Hamilton Papers, *op. cit.*
9. *Loc. cit.*
10. It is hard to find any evidence whatever in support of the contention that the Dalai Lama ever agreed to Khamba Jong being a meeting-place for the negotiators, unless

his nomination of the two Tibetan officials was taken for such. As a matter of fact, even the Amban had protested against the choice and in his letter to the Viceroy on June 24, 1903, had written :

'But I understand that Khamba Jong is in Tibetan territory; therefore, the British Commissioners and the Chinese and Tibetan Commissioner deputed by me are only able to rendezvous at the boundary near the grazing ground fixed by the Convention of 1890'. Tibet Papers, *op. cit.*, Cd. 1920, Annexure Encl. 23, in No 129, p. 241. It would thus appear that neither the Chinese nor the Tibetans had agreed to Khamba Jong, and that the Viceroy, despite their protests, had faced them with a *fait accompli*.

11. *Ibid.,* No. 112, p. 209.

12. Hamilton to Curzon, letter, July 9, 1903, Hamilton Papers, *op. cit.*

13. *Ibid.,* Hamilton to Curzon, letter, August 26, 1903.

14. Tibet Papers, *op. cit.*, Cd. 1920, in No. 113, p. 210. The occupation of the Chumbi valley, it would seem, had been acquiesced in at the persistent proddings of Younghusband reinforced by the Governor-General. In a letter to Hamilton on August 26 (*Supra,* note 13) Curzon informed him that Younghusband had pleaded 'if not to advance toward Gyantse, at any rate to put some pressure in the opposite direction by a military occupation of a part or the whole of the Chumbi valley.' 'This was the condition', the Governor-General continued, 'foreseen by Lansdowne, and accepted by him as not unlikely'.

15. Hamilton to Curzon, letter, September 15, 1903, Hamilton Papers, *op. cit.*

16. Curzon to Lansdowne, August 19, 1903, Curzon MSS.

17. See for instance Tibet Papers, *op. cit.*, Cd. 1920, Nos. 100-103, pp. 201-2, No. 105-11, pp. 204-8, and nos. 114-15, pp. 210-11.

18. *Supra,* note 14.

19. Tibet Papers, *op. cit.*, Cd. 1920, No. 116, pp. 211-12.

20. Curzon to Hamilton, letter, August 12, 1903, Hamilton Papers, *op. cit.*

21. Curzon to Lansdowne, letter, August 19 (1903), Curzon MSS.

22. Curzon to Hamilton, letter, August 5, 1903, Hamilton Papers, *op. cit.*

23. Younghusband's 'Memorandum on Tibet', p. 41. The 'Memorandum' was written sometime in the third week of August and Younghusband refers to it as 'the long memorandum' in letters to his father. Younghusband MSS., No. 12, August 24, 1903.

24. *Supra,* note 24, in chapter 13, Curzon to Balfour, letter, July 8, 1903.

25. Curzon to Hamilton, letter, September 2, 1903, Hamilton Papers, *op. cit.*

26. *Ibid.,* Curzon to Hamilton, letter, September 16, 1903.

27. Tibet Papers, *op. cit.*, Cd. 1920, No 120, p. 213.
   On October 6, Hamilton wrote to Curzon about a Steuart Bayley, 'who knows a great deal about Tibet' advocating 'as a coercive act', the advance of the Mission to Gyantse further to be 'associated' with the occupation of the Chumbi valley.
   'I am not directing any of the Indian telegrams or despatches', the Secretary of State wrote, 'but Bayley's note made such an effect upon the Foreign Office that they telegraphed to you accepting Bayley's advice' Hamilton Papers *op. cit.*

28. *Ibid.,* Curzon to Hamilton, letter, August 26, 1903. Younghusband wrote to his father that Government may not sanction 'any advance before the winter but something might be done in the spring'. Younghusband MSS., No. 12, August 24, 1903.

29. Godley told Curzon that the telegram of October 1, authorised 'conditional advance' and that the Viceroy's 'new telegram asking for final sanction' was the precursor to

'the cold fit... colder than ever' that had seized the British Cabinet. Godley to Curzon letter, October 28, 1903, Curzon MSS. Curzon in his letter to Brodrick, November 4, took him to task for throwing over the earlier policy: 'When the former (Lord George Hamilton) in his telegram of October 1, quoted the authority of HMG, it naturally never occurred to anyone of us that this did not mean HMG, but only two members of it', *Ibid.,* Curzon to Brodrick, letter, November 4, 1903.

30. In his letter to 'My dear St. John' dated October 28, Balfour noted: 'I am not very happy about this movement into Tibet... I strongly deprecate permanent entanglement in Tibet, particularly because we have as much on our hands as we can look after'. *B.P.,* B.M. Vol. XXXVIII, No. 49720.

31. Curzon to Brodrick, letter, October 14, 1903; Curzon MSS. To his father on October 22, 1903, Younghusband wrote that he had been 'summoned here (Simla) to advise the Viceroy on the situation', that he received a telegram on the 10th, 'left Khamba Jong on the 11th and was here on the 20th'. Younghusband MSS., No. 16.

32. On the same day, Curzon had sent Brodrick a long anxious telegram, seeking authorisation 'for an immediate advance to Gyantse'. Referred to in Brodrick's private telegram to Viceroy on October 29, 1903. *B.P.,* B.M., Vol. XXXVIII.

33. The argument about fanatical monks misleading a relatively peaceful friendly people occurs time and again in Younghusband's own letters and repeats itself in most of Lord Curzon's despatches to the India Office. Typical, and by no means exceptional, is the letter of September 2, wherein Curzon drew a clear 'distinction between the people of Tibet who are good-humoured, sociable set of men, quite prepared to enter into communications with ourselves' and the dominant clique of Lamas who are 'a narrow, intolerant and superstitious ecclesiastical hierarchy, whose continued ascendancy depends entirely upon the exclusion of the foreigner'. Curzon to Hamilton, letter, September 2, 1903, Hamilton Papers, *op. cit.*

34. In his letter to his father from Khamba Jong on October 9, Younghusband confided: 'I hope we shall move early in November. I do not anticipate much fighting but a good deal of cold'. Younghusband MSS., No. 15.

35. Tibet Papers, *op. cit.,* Cd. 1920, No. 123 (October 26, 1903), pp. 214-15.

36. *Ibid.,* No. 112, p. 209.

37. *Ibid.,* No. 114, p. 210; No. 115, p. 211; Encl. in No. 116, p. 212.

38. Thus Sir Ernest Satow wrote to the Foreign Secretary 'The Board (Chinese Foreign Office) has already telegraphed to the Imperial Resident in Tibet instructing him *to order* the Tibetan authorities to release the two British subjects *at once* ....' *Ibid.,* Encl. in No. 118, p. 213.

39. *Ibid.,* Encl. in No. 149, p. 303.

40. The euphemism 'information-gatherers' has been employed for these men by Alastair Lamb, *op. cit.,* p. 291.

41. In his 'Diary' entry for July 31, Captain O'Connor lists in detail the 'information' brought by these men. *Ibid.,* Encl. 30, in No. 129, pp. 244-45.

42. Colonel Younghusband's letter of August 19 to the Foreign Secretary, describes them as 'two Sikkim (Lachung) men who had proceeded to Shigatse to trade', and urged Government 'to take more special notice of the case'. *Ibid.,* Encl. 41, in No. 129, p. 254.

43. *Ibid.,* No. 129, pp. 219-21.

It is not without significance that Younghusband's letters to his father, which are otherwise most revealing and informative, are conspicuously silent about 'these two Lachung men'.

44. When 'the dubious and anonymous British subjects'—to borrow Lord Rosebery's words—were restored, Younghusband held a full durbar and made a great deal of fuss saying these two men formed one of the main reasons why the mission had been moved from Khamba to Gyantse and that he was satisfied that 'the ill-treatment had not been severe'.
    The men were released at the suggestion of the Amban Yu Tai and a medical examination had revealed that they had been 'well fed showing no sign of ill-treatment beyond imprisonment'. Tibet Papers, *op. cit.*, Cd. 2370, Part I, No. 130, p. 52, Part II, No. 265, pp. 224-25 and No. 293, pp. 236-37.

45. Curzon to Brodrick, letter, October 14, 1903, Curzon MSS.

46. Younghusband MSS., No. 18.

47. Later, after consultations with Younghusband at Simla, the Governor-General had pressed the Secretary of State's authorisation for 'an immediate advance to Gyantse.' *Supra*, note 32.

48. *Ibid.*, Brodrick to Curzon, 'private' telegram of October 29. It is obvious, that Brodrick was proceeding in the matter after the closest consultations with the Prime Minister who, in any case, completely distrusted Curzon's judgement and was chary of any 'entanglements'.

49. Hit at what he regarded a soft spot, Curzon deluged Brodrick with his despatches : Nos. 126 and 129, pp. 216-18 and 219-21 and his cable No. 127, p. 218, Tibet Papers, *op. cit.*, Cd. 1920. Privately too (viz. on November 4) he wrote him strong letters.

50. 'He (Kitchener) had just seen the Viceroy and said he was fearfully down (?) about Brodrick's telegram'. *Supra*, note 46.

51. Brodrick to Curzon, letter, October 29, 1903. Curzon MSS. To allay Curzon's anxiety and for fear he (Brodrick) be misunderstood, 'Do not think that I am adopting their comparison when I am explaining it'. And again 'I nonetheless cite these opinions so that you may not ascribe any failure to give effect to your views to my indifferent advocacy'.

52. *Ibid.*, Godley to Curzon, letter, October 29 (1903).

53. *Ibid.*, Curzon to Brodrick, letter, November 4, 1903; also Monger, *op. cit.*, p. 141. In actual fact, the sanction accorded by Balfour, on a Memorandum drawn up by Lansdowne on September 29, was transmitted by Hamilton to Curzon on October 1. This authorisation had not, therefore, received the full sanction of the Cabinet.

54. 'In the reconstruction, Austen Chamberlain became Chancellor of the Exchequer and Brodrick moved to the I.O. (India Office). These changes ... did have a subtle long-terms effect. The departure of the anti-German Joseph Chamberlain, left foreign affairs almost exclusively to Balfour and Lansdowne, who took a much calmer view of relations with Germany and tended to be preoccupied with Russia. (Austen Chamberlain was anti-German as also Arnold-Foster, the new War Secretary). They were balanced by Salisbury (the title inherited by Cranborne in August) and by Brodrick, who was moved to a department directly connected with foreign affairs', George Monger, *op. cit.*, pp. 135-36.

55. *Supra*, Chapter 7.

56. Hamilton told Curzon on February 27 (1903), Hamilton Papers, *op. cit.*, that the Committee on Imperial Defence and more especially Brodrick, Selborne, Lansdowne

and Ritchie 'had come to a fuller sense of Britain's liability in the event of war with Russia and the magnitude of the military assistance which India would undoubtedly require'.

57. Brodrick to Curzon, letter, August 19, 1903. Curzon MSS.

58. Curzon referred to Hamilton as one 'who whether he always concurred with us or not, had both a great familiarity with the working of the machine and also much tact, sympathy and discrimination in the discharge of his important duties', *Ibid.,* Curzon to Godley, September 23, 1903.

59. Hamilton to Curzon, letter August 14, 1903, Hamilton Papers, *op. cit.*

60. *Ibid.,* Hamilton to Curzon, letter, September 24, 1903.

61. *Ibid.,* Hamilton to Curzon, letter, October 6, 1903.

62. Curzon to Godley, September 23, 1903, Curzon MSS. On October 16, one of Lord Curzon's very good friends and confidants, Sir Clinton Dawkins, wrote to him : 'By a curious irony St. John with whom I think your relations in recent times have not been most cordial has gone to the India Office'. In an earlier letter (February 20, 1903) he had described St. John as 'very industrious and vey high-minded but..... more obstinate than any other animal in the world, is not without vanity, and has not really the mind, or imagination necessary for War Office, let alone India'. *Ibid.,* letters, October 16 and February 20, 1903.

63. *Ibid.,* Brodrick to Curzon, letter, October 15, 1903, which he (Brodrick) had called his 'first semi-official letter'.

64. To maintain—Peter Fleming, *Bayonets to Lhasa* (Laondon, 1961), p.92—that the relationship between the two men, as of October 1903, was of a cordial, intimate or friendly nature is, therefore, not correct; 'their life-long friendship' has already been exposed, as had been noticed, to serious strains.

65. *B.P., BM.,* Vol. XXXVIII Add. No. 49720.

66. *Ibid.,* Balfour's letter is dated October 28 (1903).

67. Actually, two days preceding this, Brodrick had circulated a Memorandum among his cabinet colleagues. Herein he listed four points for serious scrutiny : the risks of the expedition itself; the difficulty and expense of maintaining a mission at Lhasa; the effects of violation of Chinese territory; and the wisdom of undertaking a small war when affairs in the Far East were so critical. Monger, *op. cit.,* p. 142

68. Tibet Papers, *op. cit.,* Cd 1920, No. 132, p. 294.

69. How strongly Balfour felt about it, is revealed by the fact that immediately after the meeting sanctioning the advance he wrote to the King : 'The Cabinet are apprehensive that the Viceroy entertains schemes of territorial expansion, or at least of extending responsibilities which would be equally detrimental to Indian interests and to the international relations—of the Empire....' *B.P.* BM. Vol. I
Monger, op. cit., p. 142, maintains that ' the episode had, however, shown a growing divergence between him (Curzon) and the Home Government, and relations between Calcutta and London, embittered by personal antagonism between Brodrick and Curzon and by Curzon's headstrong character, began now to decline rapidly'.

70. Younghusband MSS., No. 19 November 11, 1903 : 'Nothing could be nicer than the Viceroy when I left. He got up from his lying-down chair though his leg was still bad and wished me Goodluck.....'

71. Tibet Papers, *op. cit.,* Cd. 1920, Annexure in Encl. 84, in No. 129, p. 291.

72. *Ibid.,* No. 143, pp. 299-300.

73. *Ibid.,* No. 142, p. 299.
74. *Supra,* note 72
75. Tibet Papers, *op. cit.,* Cd. 1920, No. 139, pp. 297-98.
76. *Loc. Cit.*
77. *Ibid.,* No. 145, p. 301.
78. *Ibid.,* No. 148, p. 302.
79. *Ibid.,* No. 134, p. 295.
80. *Ibid.,* No. 133, p. 294.
81. Brodrick to Curzon, letter, November 20, 1903, Curzon MSS.
82. Throughout November 1903, as earlier in the year, talks were in progress in London between Lansdowne and Count Benckendorff to remove the causes of friction between the two powers. For details, see Monger, *op. cit.,* pp. 104-46. On November 7, Benckendorff told Lansdowne of the Russian Foreign Minsiter Lamsdorff's desire 'to remove all sources of misunderstanding between the two Governments' and urged that there should be 'a change for the better' in 'our relations'. *Ibid.,* p. 142.
83. The words are in Brodrick's letter to Curzon of November 20. Curzon MSS.
84. Tibet Papers, *op. cit.* Cd. 1920. No. 141, pp. 298-99. It is interesting that Monger's work, already cited, which is otherwise so detailed, makes no mention either of Lansdowne's talk with Benckendorff regarding the advance into Tibet or of the Russian Ambassador's later protest.

15
Guru and its Aftermath

AFTER THE REPEATED Chinese requests to stay the advance had been brusquely turned down and the Russian protests squared up, Tibetan resistance was all that was left to be encountered. And here it was not so much the physical prowess of the ill-equipped —armed with spears and matchlocks, not even breechloaders— yet fanatical monks that was dreaded so much, as the difficult Tibetan country and the bitter Tibetan winter. Another fear, magnified out of all proportion to its intrinsic worth, was of Russian intrigue: dread of Russian-trained and equipped soldiers and officers, if not indeed the Cossacks themselves.

The winter that year had been unusally severe and claimed a large number of victims, particularly among the rank and file—and difficulties on that account were not inconsiderable. As a matter of fact, from Gnatong in Sikkim on December 11 (1903) the newly-designated 'British Commissioner for Tibetan Frontier Matters' had written:

> Transport difficulties are very great and it is almost impossible to get beyond Chumbi for sometime yet ... the weather is getting cold. 22° of frost been last night but no snow yet....'[1]

A little over a week later, he crossed the Jelap-la 'On a bright clear, sunny day....'[2] Subsequently, early in January, the Mission had reached Camp Tuna which lay across the Tang-la (15,200 ft). 'Between you and me', the Colonel wrote to his father, 'it was an extremely easy affair'; although 'by Jove', the terperature was minus 20° (with) the coldest and bitter winds nearly all day'.[3] From Tuna, on January 30, he also wrote of:

> a howling blizzard, a tearing wind and finest snow driving along. The thermometer last night was only just at zero, but it has not risen above 20° during the day.[4]

Casualties, at first, were few. 'In going up Sikkim in June', the Commissioner boasted, 'out of 500 men, 3 died: 63 went to hospital. In crossing the Tang-la pass in January, out of the same number none died and only 15 are now in hospital'.[5] To set the record straight, it was Younghusband above all who had been a powerful

advocate af crossing into Tibet in mid-winter because these (Tibetan) passes he
rated to be extremely easy. Yet presently the figures continued to mount and 'even
a Sahib', a young European in the Postal Department, 'had to have both his feet cu
off from frost-bite'.[6] Later, he got it (frost-bite) 'on the stumps' and died.[7]

The winter cold apart, a major fear was of 'armed' Tibetan opposition now tha
a numerous, well-equipped force, was penetrating deep into their land
Younghusband had reported, early in his sojourn at Khamba Jong, that the hills an
passes around 'bristled' with armed (Tibetan) hostiles. Their attack was feared a
the time and, primarily with a view to meet it, his escort had been increased whil
additional reserves were held back in Sikkim. It is indeed a curious commentary o
the observations of the Frontier Commissioner, and of O'Connor who principall
pieced together stray bits of information for him, that none of these much talked o
attacks ever came to pass. Yet the new advance over the Jelap-la posed an entirel
different problem, for here was a frontal march, right into the heart of Tibet. As ma
be imagined, there was a lot of talk of opposition being offered, althoug
Younghusband was optimistic— 'at first, at any rate'.[8]

To start with, of course, there was a gentlemanly refusal. For Captain Parr a
well as the local Chinese official, and the Tibetan general, 'asked me to go back t
Gnatong', where the Amban and the Tibetan Councillors 'would come and discus
matters with me'. Later, they all implored him 'to remain where I was'. Th
Commissioner, however, was not to be so easily dissuaded. Next, the Tibetans trie
'a Chinese Wall stretching across the Valley'. Later still, the same officials 'begge
us once more not to advance'. They made yet another effort:

Exactly, as I passed under the gateway the local official seized my bridle an
made one last ineffectual protest. Then I rode through and the door to Tibe
was at last opened.[9]

Tibetan resistance, however, took no ugly turn yet and the whole thing ende
up as most things do in Tibet— in great good humour'. 'We adjourned to Parr'
house', the Commissioner recorded, 'where first Parr gave us an enormous lunch
then the Chinese and Tibetan officials sent in a meal and themselves came and sa
down with us to eat it. It was altogether a great day of which I am proud.....'[10]

The Commissioner sojourned at Chumbi for nearly a month, while Macdonal
went ahead with plans for a further advance. On January 6, the entire force reache
Phari with no opposition as yet from man though much from nature, for the cold wa
now terrible: 'piercing winds swept down the valley, and discomfort was extreme'.[1]
A day later they encamped at the foot of the Tang-la (15,200 ft.) for the march t
Tuna, which was to serve as a base for the further advance to Gyantse. On Januar
12 three monks from the Lhasa monasteries and the General, who had met th
Mission at Phari asked O'Connor again that the British withdraw to Yatung. Later
the Tibetans are reported to have agreed to discuss matter at Tuna itself.[12] Nex
day, however, they built themselves a wall at the very place where the open plai
was narrowed by a large frozen lake and an outlying spur of one of the mountai
ranges. They indeed 'ran it up in a night. It was their equivalent for a 'full stop' '.[1]

above General and his Staff together
with some British Officers telling him
he must disarm. Behind them off the
picture are the reserve, and behind the
point where the photo was taken from are
the maxims, guns, & mounted infantry.

You will see that they
were in a regular trap. and of course the
Lhasa Gen'. absolutely lost his head
in commencing a fight under these
conditions. Instead of shrugging his
shoulders and saying "All right, odds

From Gyantse, to 'My dear Father' dated May 1, 1904

On the day the Commissioner arrived at Tuna with his 'snug little escort o⁣ battalion 23ʳᵈ Pioneers, 2 Maxims with British detachments, I gun and so⁣ sappers',[14] a camp of some 2,000 Tibetans 'who were six miles off on our flank' ⁣ noticed.[15] If Macdonald had had his way—and one of the first violent squabb⁣ had already taken place between the two men—the Mission would have withdra⁣ and retired to Chumbi. But the Commissioner 'absolutely refused to move' ⁣ stayed put.[16] Meantime the presence of the Lhasa monks, nay their wh⁣ demeanour, was increasingly suspect, for they had behaved at Phari 'in a m⁣ unfriendly way'. Could it be that they had not only not come forth to greet⁣ British, but had prevented the people—'who are friendly'—from selling th⁣ wares?[17] In the light of his early conclusion, which was fully shared by the Vice⁣ and the Home Government, that the power and influence of these 'ill-conditio⁣ monks' must be completely broken before there could be a settlement, and of⁣ persistent talk of what Curzon chose to call 'Dorjieff, or the Mission to Livadia⁣ the Russian rifles in Lhasa', Younghusband made a daring bid both to gauge⁣ full measure of the Lama fury as well as to ascertain 'what their military organizat⁣ was worth'.[18] His visit, unarmed, to the Tibetans in their Camp at Guru was ind⁣ full of risk—though personally he rated the percentage to be extremely low. It ⁣ been called 'a trifle overbold' and 'a single-handed heroic madness',[19] albeit with⁣ doubt, it was an astonishing act of bravery, so astonishing that it hardly deser⁣ to succeed!

Curzon was angry. He conceded that odds were 'I daresay 100: 1, in y⁣ favour'. But supposing he had been seized, even as a British party just about t⁣ time was by the Maharaja of Manipur: 'where should I have been and where wo⁣ the Government of India have been? I suppose that my reputation would have g⁣ irretrievably and that we should have to march straight into Lhasa'.[20]

Far form adopting an apologetic tone, Younghusband justified his action ⁣ in words which were significant. He viewed his visit as 'a great effort in the direct⁣ of peace' and thought his seizure 'would have been the most single proof' ⁣ Curzon's policy of coming to a settlement 'was justified'. Above all,

I thought this visit to the Tibetan camp was worth such little risk as there ⁣ for never before ... had a British officer met a really representative body⁣ Tibetans in their surroundings. I have to advise Government as to how to d⁣ with the Tibetans ... Here was an opportunity though of seeing them face⁣ face, so I determined to push through their barriers of reserve to come to cl⁣ quarters with them, to gauge for myself what they were really worth, to tes⁣ they were in any way amenable to reason, to ascertain without doubt who w⁣ the moving spirits and to see what their military organization was worth...

Whatever Younghusband's justification, and he entirely pooh-poohed⁣ element of danger involved, it is difficult to escape the conclusion that he stak⁣ much more than he seemed fully to realise. It had been very near 'a close shave'⁣ he called it in his letter to his father or wrote of half a dozen years later in his bo⁣ In the words of one of his semi-fictional heroes it may be termed 'not ... foolha⁣

but running pretty near in that direction'.[22] Be that as it may it did, however,
've two useful purposes. Firstly, it convinced the Commissioner that no
npromise was possible with the 'low-bred, insolent, rude and intensely hostile'
nas—hence the inevitability, form Younghusband's point of view, of the
osequent Guru fighting. Secondly, much of the criticism arising out of this fighting,
there will be occasion to notice, was later assuaged on the plea of this meeting.

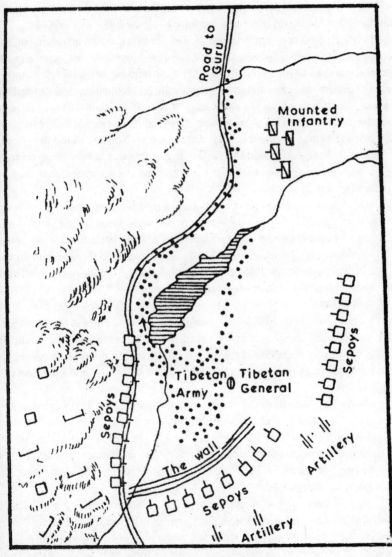

The battle at Guru, March 31, 1904.

The action fought at Guru, on March 31, in the Tibetan attempt to resist
advance of the Mission beyond Tuna, was the first armed encounter which
peaceful commercial Mission was engaged in. The details of how it all started
perhaps unimportant except insofar as they underline two relevant facts. One, t
twice over Macdonald had sought Younghusband's assent, though in vain,
commence the shooting, for he (Macdonald) was convinced that on either occas
it was an impossible position for the troops to be in. Two, that the Commissio
acted with the greatest deliberation and restraint and but for the fact that the Lh
'General' lost his nerve, there may not have been any bloodshed at Guru.

Briefly, almost completely surrounded by the armed escort, advancing in 'atta
formation', Macdonald's men ordered the raw Tibetan levies, with almost
accoutrement, to lay down their arms. On their refusing to do so, an attempt v
made to disarm them forcibly. It was a difficult, tense situation, and beyond do
a mere 'touch and go', when the Lhasa 'General', evidently unable to restr
himself, fired a shot. This proved to be the signal for the *melee* that ensued, fo
was nothing better. Even the official despatch from Younghusband described
Tibetans as 'being surrounded to such a degree that our men were pointing th
rifles into the camp over the wall.'[23] In private, the Commissioner was m
outspoken :

> I did what I could to prevent it and the troops behaved splendidly ... But it v
> a wretched affair—and pure massacre[24]— brought on by the crass stupid
> and childishness of the Tibetan General. They will not believe in our power
> I am fearfully disappointed for I had and wanted to go through without this
> as I have known all along how worthless these Tibetans were both in th
> generalship and military organization all round...[25]

And again :

> I was so absolutely sick at that so-called fight I was quite out of sorts. It was
> the Tibetans' own fault and I am glad I twice restrained Macdonald fro
> commencing firing but of course it was nothing but pure butchery—the po
> things were penned up in a hollow within a few yards and even feet of c
> rifles.[26]

One of the British officers in the armed escort, Lieutenant (later Lieutena
Colonel) A. L. Hadow made this significant entry in his Diary under the headi
'Fight at Guru',

> Started 8 a.m. Accompanied 23 P (Pioneers) in advance in line. Got rou
> ememy's left flank. Did fearful execution. Got back 7 p.m. Awfully done, had
> ride from the Spring.[27]

'Fearful execution' it doubtless was. The Tibetans lost 700 men, dead a
wounded; the British 2 wounded, one of them being Edmund Candler, the (Londo
Daily Mail's correspondent.[28] It is not without significance that more than
months after the fight, the gruesome corpses of that 'fearful' massacre still
strewn around on the Tuna plain.[29]

Younghusband had described the fighting as 'a disaster', 'a terrible and ghastly business', and writing years later wondered if it could possibly have been avoided.[30] Contemporary observers of the scene thought, including Younghusband, that the Tibetans doubted the seriousness of British intent to advance. Actually, the Commissioner had repeatedly referred to the fact that his was regarded 'a doomed mission.'[31] Again, both Curzon and Younghusband had oft-times protested against dark forebodings, openly voiced in Parliament and outside, that the Commissioner was bound to meet the same end as the ill-fated Cavagnari,[32] that he would be trapped in Lhasa. Did the Guru killing, therefore, result from a Tibetan miscalculation?

Another facet of this problem may also be examined. And this related to a British obsession with restoring their 'prestige' on the frontier. Before he quit office, Lord George Hamilton had talked somewhat nonchalantly of killing a few hundred Tibetans prior to the latter doing any business[33] with them and the *Daily Mail*'s correspondent had expressed the view that 'there was no hope of their (Tibetans) regarding the British as a formidable power and a force to be reckoned with, until we killed several thousand of their men'.[34] Again, Younghusband noted at Khamba Jong, as he did later at Tuna, that while a diplomatist must have 'prestige' behind him, he (Younghusband) had 'none' and in an official despatch to Government on January 11 (1904), remarked :

We have, in fact ... not one ounce of prestige on this frontier. I have... nothing to work with in making a settlement ... Rather than being afraid of us, the Tibetans here in Tibet think we ought to be afraid of them.[35]

'What are we, they say'—he wrote to the Governor-General—'against the omniscient and omnipotent Dalai Lama?'

Could it be then that the 'massacre' at Guru was a cruel, if necessary, blood-bath to which the Tibetans must be subjected so as to be fully impressed with the power and pelf of a Great Imperial Power?

This, of course, was only the beginning. And the blame was made to rest squarely, as it certainly did for most part, on 'the ignorance' of the Tibetans and 'the stubborn hostility' of the leaders from Lhasa. To be sure, Younghusband had talked of 'the silly Lhasa General', of his 'crass stupidity', of the Tibetans' 'childishness' and of it being 'all their own fault'. However, with an ugly and ill-concealed satisfaction, one suspects, the British Commissioner noted that one of the Tibetans killed at Guru was the Lama representing the Ganden Monastery : 'the most insolent of the three lamas I saw at Guru in January and a thoroughgoing obstructionist'.[37]

What was the effect of the Guru massacre on the Mission's future role? Younghusband had expessed the hope that the tremendous punishment which the Tibetans had received will be an object lesson, prevent further fighting and induce the Tibetans at last to negotiate.[38] His hope was shared among others by the Viceroy who expressed the view that 'in all probability' the Mission will now reach Gyantse 'without further fighting'[39] and Mr. Brodrick, the Secretary of State, who felt sure that the goal (Gyantse) will be reached 'without much further trouble'.[40] In both respects these calculations were, however, to be completely belied. Tibetan

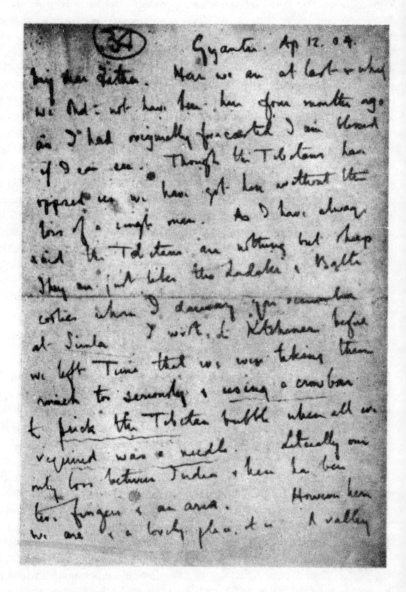

From Gyantse, to 'My dear Father' dated April 12, 1904.

resistance to the further progress of the Mission, however futile it may have seemed, never ceased. For less than two weeks later, Macdonald faced some 2,000 of their men resisting him and another '190 Tibetan corpses' were to mark the trail of the British advance from Guru to Gynastse.[41] How many more hundreds—or may be thousands—countless, and uncounted, of the wounded and the maimed crawled away to hide their agonies 'in mountain dens or peasant hovels', could be anybody's guess.

The 'fighting' at Guru, and subsequently at Tsamdang gorge, had for once put an end to the embarrassments of the Indian Government. In London too, the British Cabinet now felt impelled to seek the formal assent of Parliament, as required under the statute, for 'military operations' beyond the frontiers of India.[42] Indeed had not a hard-pressed, harassed Tibetan general 'lost his nerve',[43] and committed an act of aggression by making an unprovoked attack on a peaceful, commercial Mission? Had not a pistol shot been fired—and an officer lost two fingers and a press correspondent an arm?[44] Henceforth the word 'Tibetan' was replaced by the term 'the enemy' in all the despatches that passed between the Commission and the Government of India and between that Government and London. Diplomacy was to be at a discount and 'military operations' were henceforth to dominate the (Tibetan) scene.[45]

And yet an outer façade of negotiations was kept up—more, it would seem, to assuage uneasy consciences in London than to satisfy the deeply-hurt feelings of the Commissioner. The latter, called a 'rampant adventurer' by an over-exacting Secretary of State, would have, in his then tone and temper, no truck with the Tibetans until in sack-cloth and ashes, they kissed the ground in front of him. But—and on this he stuck out his neck long and with a remarkable power of resilience—no talks, much less negotiations, this side of Lhasa.[46] It is necessary to bear this in mind for when the Commissioner did ultimately go through the stipulated motions at Gyantse these were, at best, of a half-hearted and unwilling player performing what was an humiliating or embarrassing act that he had to, perforce.

Not directly relevant though to the actual progress of the Mission, some of the major developments may be briefly recounted here. The Amban had written to Younghusband, very early in April, that he intended to come and meet the Commissioner but that the 'obstinate' Tibetan 'barbarians' were making it difficult.[47] On his own too, Lord Curzon had imagined the new Amban putting in an appearance: 'deprecatory, conciliatory, and anxious to keep you (Younghusband) back at all hazards, and willing to give every sort of encouragement in order to persuade you to retreat, and to retain for China (distinction?) of having settled the matter and revindicated her suzerainty'.[48] Instead, however, at Guru had arrived not the Imperial Resident at Lhasa but a certain General Ma as his delegate in place of 'Ho, Chao and Li'. He too had asked the Mission to—what many another had valiantly, if vainly, tried before—retire to Yatung.[49] On April 11 Ma informed the Commissioner that the Amban would arrive 'as soon as he could arrange' with the Dalai Lama and additionally that four Tibetan delegates, of unknown position, were on their way to negotiate.[50]

Ma's tidings were not very old when some of the ancient doubts began to revive. For on April 18, Younghusband made the (old—or was it new?) discovery that the delegates designated were of low rank, that they had been halted on their way to receive fresh orders—could it be in view of the fighting which had meantime taken place both at Guru and Tsamdang gorge?[51] On April 22, an official arrived from the Amban bringing the precious information that that dignitary was coming within two weeks. The picture painted by the new envoy about conditions in Lhasa was nonetheless not an encouraging one. For, as Younghusband reported to the Viceroy, although the Dalai Lama[52] had been aroused to 'a sense of our power' yet since the former Councillors were imprisoned, there were 'few' capable Tibetan officials left to negotiate with.[53]

In Calcutta, in the meantime, a profound change had come over the scene. Lord Curzon, the Commissioner's unfailing friend and supporter,[54] had towards the end of April proceeded home on leave, his place there being taken by his *locum tenens*—Lord Ampthill. The Viceroy had placed on record his strong conviction that during his absence 'whatever is done will be done by the Cabinet, in consultation with myself in England', rather than by the 'left behind' Government of India.[55] In actual fact, it turned out to be just the other way round for, among other things, relations between Curzon and St. John Brodrick continued to deteriorate precipitously. Inevitably, the Secretary State developed a greater measure of confidence in the 'left behind' Ampthill and a growing distrust of the Commissioner and his 'rampant' adventurism. Curzon's advice too, as there will be occasion to notice, was at a discount. It is with this essential background that the second phase of the 'negotiations' at Gyantse, and the final advance of the Mission to Lhasa, must be viewed.

In hastening the pace of advance—and the Secretary of State as earlier Curzon himself, though much more mildly, had rapped the Commissioner for what appeared to be his unseemly hurry to proceed to Lhasa[56]—the sound and smell of gun-power and shell played an important role. There was fighting, and of a much more fierce sort than hitherto, both in and around Gyantse.[57] Reluctantly, for Ampthill took a much more balanced view of things than the 'committed-to-the neck' Curzon, the acting Viceroy suggested to the Secretary of State the fixation of a timelimit by which 'proper' representatives, 'invested with full powers', were required to arrive.[58] Within a few days, a tentative date, viz., June 25, for the advance to Lhasa was being discussed.[59] Finally, on May 14, the Secretary of State agreed to 'ultimatums' being dispatched both to the Dalai Lama and the Amban,[60] a move further reinforced by a direct communication from London to the Chinese Government[61].

The 'ultimatums' were not without their effect. On June 23 (later June 25) being the last day named for the negotiations to commence, Younghusband reported that Tibetan delegates were on their way and requested that the deadline be advanced by five days.[62] On the afternoon of July 1, the Ta Lama arrived at Gyantse and accompanied by six representatives of the three Lhasa monasteries, met the Commissioner.[63] Serious parleys, however, were ruled out for Younghusband now insisted that, as a pre-condition, the Gyantse Jong must be evacuated so that 'there may be no risk of further attack on the Commissioner'. And as the Tibetans did not comply, the Jong was assaulted, and taken. Therefore, for a few days, efforts to get in touch with the Ta Lama and his men proved futile.[64]

On July 14, the Mission began its march to Lhasa. Two days later, the Commissioner received a letter (through the Tongsa Penlop, the Bhutanese envoy) and emanating from the Dalai Lama and the Ta Lama, protesting readiness to negotiate.[65] On July 20 , the Tibetan envoys comprising the Ta Lama, the Yutkok Shape and the Grand Secretary met the British Commissioner at Camp Nagartse and implored him to return to Gyanste for negotiations. Younghusband repeated— 'for the fiftieth time' –that he had waited long and patiently; and as for any further parleys reminded them that he had 'the Viceroy's orders to go to Lhasa and, go there I must'.[66] Public postures apart, in private, the Commissioner was much more communicative :

The cussed part is that they are such absolute children in the business of this world. When I told them that we considered it a great insult that the representative of a great power should be kept waiting for a year they said 'Oh, do not let us think of the past. Let us be practical and think only of the present. Here are we now, anyhow, so let us negotiate'. I told them this was all very fine now they had got the worst of it but though I was ready to negotiate, I had to go to Lhasa.

......of course it is very hard to keep my temper with them when they go on for hour after hour with silly argument but I managed to do it through two interviews one of 3¼ and the other of 3½ hours.... I quietly answer their arguments and smile to them and give them tea and cigarettes and leave the solid fact of our advance to produce its effect....'[67]

The 'solid fact' of the Commissioner's 'advance' continued, chiming in with the continuous refrain that the Mission must proceed to Lhasa and that there was to be no half-way house in-between. For both at Chaksam ferry, where the National Assembly promised negotiations and asked the Commissioner not to proceed to Lhasa and at Camp Tolunng where, apart from the Ta Lama and Tasrong Shape, a Chinese official deputed by the Amban and an Abbot, in private attendance upon the Dalai Lama, along with the representatives of the three Lhasa monasteries, met him and implored him against advancing, his reply was the same: 'We must go there'.[68]

Meantime Younghusband had broken the back of what he called the correspondence difficulty; for the National Assembly had sent him 'the very

PUNCH, OR THE LONDON CHARIVARI.—MAY 25, 1904.

ANOTHER SIDE-SHOW.

Master Johnny Bull. " NEED WE GO IN HERE, SIR ? "
Mr. Br-dr-ck. " YES, MASTER JOHNNY. YOU MUSTN'T MISS *THIS* ON ANY ACCOUNT."
Master J. B. " OH, ALL RIGHT. I SAY, IT ISN'T ANYTHING LIKE THE SOMALI ONE, **IS IT ?** "

first letter that has been received by a British official from a Tibetan official'. It bore the seal of the three great monasteries and of the Dalai Lama's great Chamberlain.[69] Later he was to receive a communication from the Lama himself, 'the first, of course, that he has ever written to an Englishman'. In reply, the Commissioner was courteous to a degree but stuck to his point :

> I trust His Holiness will appreciate inconvenience it would be to me to halt anywhere short of Lhasa now that I have left Gyantse. I ended up—'I hope, I may be able to subscribe myself with the highest respect and consideration, Your Holiness' sincere friend, FEY.'[70]

The diplomatic record was thus to prove barren; in the military sphere, however there was a far greater spate of activity and it is to this that the narrative must now revert.

The 'fighting' at Guru on March 31, offered a preliminary, if poor, foretaste of what lay in store. Everyone, not least the Commissioner himself, viewed it as an exemplary 'punishment' that 'will live in the memories of the people for ages'.[71] Nor had there been much of firing for seemingly apologetically Younghusband pointed out that 'the Maxims fired 700 rounds which is 1½ minutes' firing and the average of the infantry was only 12 to 13 rounds per man which is nothing at all with magazine rifles'.[72] Again, this killing of 'poor, harmless peasants' sickened the killers for the real enemy, as they viewed it, were the all-too-ubiquitous, scowling monks in the monasteries who had evaded them[73] hitherto. Clearly, as was noticed previously, both the personnel on the spot, as well as the policy-making, directing authorities in Calcutta or London, did not anticipate any further resistance: the road to Gyantse, and beyond, was now presumed clear.[74]

Contrary to expectations, and the best of surmises, Guru served only as a curtain-raiser. Henceforth, the Tibetans—ill-equipped, ill-led and with a complete lack of planning, much less any awareness of the arts of warfare—offered resistance at every step, how very foolhardy at times it may have seemed. Without getting enmeshed into details, a few of these 'battles' may be examined not so much with a view to their meticulous dissection as it were, but as typical of most of the rest.[75]

The Mission arrived at Gyantse on April 11. A day previously, at Tsamdang gorge, a sizeable Tibetan force with 'numbers of modern rifles in addition to probably 1,000 matchlocks' lay in ambush, in a well-chosen, strong, natural position. They were finally driven out but for long 'stuck to their position pluckily'. The action, not important in itself, showed at once the virility of Tibetan opposition, and their acute awareness of the danger posed by the British Mission.[76]

Macdonald, who had escorted Younghusband to Gyantse, left him there with a part of the force while, with the large bulk of it, he returned to Chumbi. The Commissioner was strongly opposed to Macdonald's withdrawal, as indeed he was to all 'withdrawals'. He expressed his strong conviction that the Mission's halt at

Gyantse 'has made them (Tibetans) revive their resistance' and that the decision to negotiate there coupled with the actual departure of Macdonald's men made a profound difference to Tibetan reaction:

> On our first arrival here the Tibetans were laid out flat. They gave up the fort without a murmur. The Head Lama signed before me.... But then when they saw we were going to negotiate (and Macdonald withdrew)... I saw it (change in their attitude) coming in. There was .... strong proof that they were collecting a great gathering to envelop in here and strike our line of communications...[77]

The ostensible reason for Macdonald's pulling out was the fear that both food as well as fodder for the animals, would be scarce at Gyantse while there was the additional difficulty of maintaining a long, and somewhat arduous, line of communication all the way from the Jelap-la into the very heart of the country. It was, therefore, necessary to send the main force to Chumbi where ample supplies were ensured.[78] Left with a bare 500 men, two guns, and two maxims and a squadron of mounted infantry to boot, Younghusband took the bold decision not only to guard his own position but what was more to disperse a Tibetan concentration athwart the road to Lhasa. The Commissioner's intelligence had revealed a sizeable Tibetan pocket at the strategic Karo-la—16,500 ft, above the level of the sea and 45 miles from Gyantse[79] —which could, theoretically at any rate, endanger the Mission's communications at Kang-ma in its rear.[80] Entirely on his own responsibility Younghusband persuaded Colonel Brander, the Commander at Gyantse and a man very much after the Commissioner's own heart, to do the job:

> I said I have not the slightest objections on political grounds and so far as my military opinion was worth I was entirely in accordance with him. The way to prevent mischief is to knock such a gathering on the head at the start. I thought, and in our strongly fortified post we could well look after ourselves here.[81]

On May 6, battle was joined on the Karo-la. The Tibetans, numbering about 2,500 men, armed with 'Lhasa-made and foreign rifles', were led by many 'influential lamas' and 'officials' from the capital,[82] and with their jingals, matchlocks and breech-loaders kept Colonel Brander's men under heavy fire. After four hours' stubborn fighting, however, 'the enemy' was completely dislodged, the Colonel reported, yielding in the bargain 'two camps, and a quantity of powder, ammunition and stores'.[83]

The decision to send out Brander was the Commissioner's own but much more important was the responsibility to permit him engage in battle. Younghusband's subsequent apologia that 'the only way to prevent (a) gathering of that kind' and arrest fanaticism from developing was 'to hit hard from the start', and before 'they had time to hit you',[84] wears somewhat thin and does not carry conviction. Karo-la as has been noticed, was 45 miles on the road to Lhasa and he had yet no business, nor any authority, to go in that direction. Besides, to engage in that kind of fighting, while ostensibly awaiting the Amban's arrival and that of the Tibetan delegates for the commencement of fresh negotiations, was not to brighten the notoriously dim,

(a)   (b)

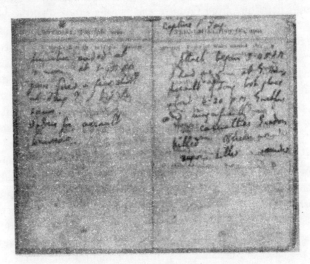

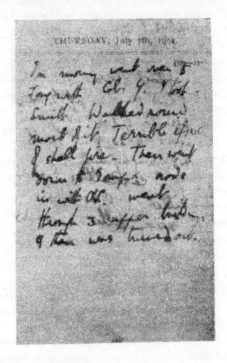

Extracts from Lt. (later Lt. Col.)
A. L. Hadow's diary
[For text see Appendix 10]

dubious prospect of their success. Younghusband later maintained that, with Macdonald's departure from Gyantse and 'strong proof' that the 'enemy' were collecting 'a great gathering to envelop us here', any dereliction of duty on his part may have resulted in Kang-ma being invested and resultantly the Tibetans, all over the country, gathering 'exultingly around us'.[85] While it is difficult to be categorical in hypothetical cases like this, and the Commissioner's picture is no doubt heavily overdrawn, it may be conceded that shorn of its political overtones, the Karo-la fight was perhaps a tactical necessity for without it the Mission, left with only a handful of its escort, could have been beleaguered, starved out and slaughtered to a man.

The decision itself, it would seem, was taken in deliberate, though covert, defiance of express instructions to the contrary which the over-cautious Macdonald had despatched.[86] To the Commissioner, the Commander of the Escort was rather a poor fish, if ever there was one. Up against the Karo-la concentration he (Younghusband) thus acted with a great deal of courage, convinced in his mind that it was the rightful (righteous?) course. A smaller man may have stood hidebound by the letter of Macdonald's written communication, with results that may have been well-nigh disastrous. Younghusband's admission in his letter to his father, is one of disarming frankness. Brander had left on the morning of the 3rd :

On the afternoon of the 4th Murray who commands here in his absence hands me a telegram from Macdonald to Brander ordering him back here unless he is actually committed. If I had sent the message on at once Brander would have got it a march before he reached the Karo-la; and before he was actually committed. But I knew the effect of his returning without fighting when all the Tibetans knew that he had gone out to fight would have been absolutely disastrous. So as it had been left with me to procure a messenger ... and I hoped he (messenger) would reach Brander after his fight. But in case ....I wrote him (Brander) a note saying I had the strongest possible objections on the political grounds to his returning without fighting unless the enemy were so considerably strengthened...

Unfortunately the messenger ....did arrive....before the fight and he (Brander) was greatly unnerved.... But he wrote me a line from the field of battle thanking me for my 'strong and cheering letter' which he had acted on.... I have just had had another note from Brander thanking me for the strong support I have rendered him throughout'.[87]

Meantime while engaged in rendering 'strong support' to Brander, the Commissioner himself faced a major threat. For in the small hours of the morning of May 5, with only about 150 men by his side, Younghusband was taken completely by surprise with a large Tibetan force creeping right up to and investing his camp. The Gurkha troops fought gallantly, as did Younghusband himself, 'with a borrowed rifle and a bayonet.' And ere it was daylight, the attack had been repulsed.[88] Later, the Commissioner calculated that there were about 800 men who had marched 12 miles during the night and managed to reach 'right up under our wall',[89]

It is a little rough to be woken up in the morning by the enemy firing through your own loop-holes only ten yards off! Heaven know what the sentries were doing... Of course once the Tibetans had discovered themselve they were shot down in a moment, and after ¾ of an hour's fighting cleared off. But if they had not fired or begun booing but singly climbed silently over the wall we should have had a precious nasty trim....[90]

Tibetan losses were sizeable, nearly 139 dead-bodies dotted the plain in front,[91] while countless more—rigorously pursued for miles around—sustained injuries, sickened and died.

Both at Karo-la and the siege of the Commissioner's camp at Gyantse, the Tibetans fought stubbornly and tenaciously, yielding ground only when they had to. In fact, these actions stand out in marked contrast to the one at Guru. At both places while Tibetan casualties were heavy, no 'massacres' followed. This could, if partly, be explained by the fact that the men of 'U' and 'Tsang', with a good sprinkling of the Khampas—were better led and displayed considerable valour, in contrast to the raw levles of Guru that permitted themselves to be herded together.[92] A point that deserves scrutiny is the fact that at Guru, the British troops were right up against an armed Tibetan mob—not unlike a crowd in a city; later actions were tactical, real battles with movement in a mountain terrain. Another factor could be discerned in the strongly-fortified positions, particularly at Karo-la and later in the (Gyantse) dzong, taken by the Tibetans in all subsequent actions, while the fact of their numerical superiority was common in all cases. The Commissioner noted that while, 'they are not much good' at offence, they were developing 'a fine capacity for sitting tight'.[93] He was also struck by the fact that despite 'some pretty hard knocks.... they are solid and obstinate as ever'.[94] Yet while conceding their strong points, he was not oblivious of their overall weakness,

The Tibetans certainly did pitch it out very well, they are a solid lot who will stand an astonishing amount of pounding. I adhere, however, to the opinion I held from the first that they cannot be considered a power to be easily reckoned with.... With a loss of less than 40 killed on our side we have killed 2,500 Tibetans. We have repulsed every attack on us. We have turned them out of an almost impregnable fort. And we kept open our communications....[95]

In the military actions that follow Karo-la, the assault on the dzong at Gyantse, on July 5-7, stands out as the most significant if only because it involved the maximum number of fighting men, on both sides. Having received sizeable reinforcements, and poised in readiness for the impending advance to Lhasa, the Mission was no longer, as hitherto, on the defensive. The number of Tibetans involved was 5,000 to 6,000; their losses, 'severer than estimated', were also heavy.[96] The Commissioner called it 'a great fight', waged by 'modern' guns freshly supplied by shells 'of use against walls'. The climb of the assaulting column on the walls of the dzong he regarded an 'almost dramatic' scene.[97]

A word may be added here if only in parenthesis. Whatever the strong point of the Tibetans, it should not be forgotten that the British Indian troops were well-

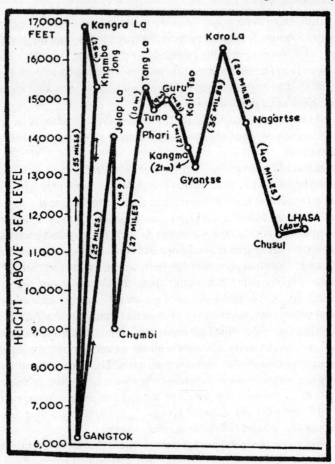

A graphic representation of altitudes enroute indicating important sages.
Horizontal distances (not to scale) are in brackets.

armed with magazine rifles, a few machine-guns and magnificent discipline. Nor did the Tibetans prove to be truly such good fighters on their own ground as say Pathan tribesmen. The Khampas, in their own physical milieu may have proved much better.

There was an old, traditional belief among the Tribetans that Gyantse dzong held the key to Tibet and that if it ever fell into the hands of a conqueror, further resistance would be useless.[98] The capture of the dzong, therefore, was somewhat synonymous with a virtual full-stop to any future fighting, and for all practical purposes—barring a few brief, though decisive, encounters on the way to Lhasa—this turned out to be correct.

For its military action, however, 'one of the most brilliant episodes of the campaign' was the Gurkhas' engagement with the Tibetans at Karo-la, on July 18.

ts way to Lhasa, the main body of the troops forced the pass at 16,400 ft. while
Gu as and the Pathans on the right flank climbed a glacier and fought 'a crisp
e battle' at 19,000 ft.[99] The Karo-la was thought to be impregnable, if strongly
l, Younghusband, never a great admirer of the fighting qualities of the Tibetans,
te to his father of a Pathan Jamadar of the Guides, then serving with the
unted Infantry, who said with a grasp " 'what a chance these Tibetans have
? If we Pathans had held a position like that, there would not have been many
ibs left'". And on his own added, 'If they (Tibetans) have chucked a position
that, I take it we shall not have much more trouble with the Tibetans in the
ting way...'[100]

And that proved to be only too true. For barring some minor skirmishes here
there, in the way of any significant fighting there was none after Karo-la,
er on the Mission's advance to Lhasa or on its way back.

Notes

Younghusband MSS., No. 21, December 11, 1903.

Ibid., No. 22, December 20, 1903.

Ibid., No. 25 January 11, 1904 (actually, through an obvious error, the letter is dated
'January 11, 03').

Ibid., No. 26, January 30, 1904.

Ibid., No. 25, January 11,1904.

Ibid., No. 28, February 25, 1904.

Ibid., No. 28, March 11, 1904. Encamped at Tuna just then, Younghusband talked of
'real winter again. 37° of frost, snow and blizzard.'

Supra, n. 1.

Supra, n. 2.

Loc. cit.

Younghusband, India and Tibet, *op.cit.*, 159.

Tibet Papers, *op.cit.*, Cd. 1920, No. 173, p. 312.

Lieutent-Colonel L.A. Bethel ('Pousse-Cailloux'), 'A Foot-note', *Blackwoods
Magazine* (London), MCCCLX, February 1929, pp. 147-76.
'Pousse-Cailloux' is a 'pebble-pusher', French equivalent of the English 'footslogger'.
The writer, Lt.-Col. Bethel, was then a Lieutenant in the 8th Gurkhas.

Supra, n. 2.

Supra, n. 3.

This took place at Tuna on January 8 and Younghusband gives a graphic account of
how he resisted— for two consecutive days—Macdonald's mounting pressure. The
latter had emphasized that there was 'no fuel and grass and the men would not be able
to stand the cold'. Younghusband justified his action on the ground, *inter alia*, that the
2,000 Tibetans on 'our flank, retired on the very day that Macdonald wanted us to'.
Younghusband MSS., No. 26, January 30, 1904.

Tibet Papers, *op.cit.*, Cd. 1920, No. 169, p. 310.

For details, *Ibid.*, Cd. 2054, Part II, Nos. 36-37, pp. 17-19 and Cd.1920, Nos. 158,
160 and 166, pp. 306-7 and 309. Curzon's words are in his private letter of January
23 to Younghusband, the latter's in his reply from Tuna of February 3 (1904). Curzon
MSS.

19. Seaver, *op.cit.*, p. 218 and 'Pousse-Cailloux', *op.cit.*, p. 163. For further accounts of meeting, see Tibet Papers, *op.cit.*, 1920, No. 174, p. 312 and Cd. 2054, Pt. II, No. p. 19.

    Younghusband, India and Tibet, *op.cit.*, pp. 162-67, gives a graphic account as d 'Pousse Cailloux', *op.cit.*, pp. 160-63.

    In his broadcast talk over the BBC entitled 'With Younghusband to Lhasa', *op.cit.*, Fredrick (then Captain) O' Connor recalled the incident vividly.

20. Curzon to Younghusband, letter, January 23, 1904, Curzon MSS.

21. *Ibid.*, Younghusband to Curzon, February 3, 1904. To his father, the Commissio wrote somewhat nonchalantly about his riding 'without escort into their new camp, miles beyond this'. Younghusband MSS., No. 26, January 30, 1904.

22. This is in Younghusband's partly autobiographical novel, But In Our Lives, *op.cit.*, T remarks are of the hero of the story, Evan Lee. A later writer, while admitting ' severity with which Younghusband made his intuitive decision' to go to the Tibe camp, has commented: 'it is equally impossible to maintain that the escapade reflec a sound judgement'. Peter Fleming, *op.cit.*, p. 135.

23. Tibet Papers, *op.cit.*, Cd. 2054, Nos. 9-12, pp. 5-6.

24. Edmund Candler, the (London) *Daily Mail's* correspondent who was himself seriou injured in the fighting described it as 'not a battle but a shambles, not a stand-up fig but a massacre'. In a subsequent passage in his book he called it 'an inglorious victor and expressed the view that the officers who did their duty 'so thoroughly, had no he in the business at all'. Edmund Candler, *op.cit.*, pp. 109 and 111.

25. Younghusband MSS., No. 32, April 1, 1904. This letter was written within 24 hours the actual fighting.

26. *Ibid.*, No. 33, April 4, 1904. In his private letter to Lord Curzon, the Commissioner f convinced that 'it (Guru fighting) was practically inevitable' and that politically it w important 'to prove to the very hilt that we did not resort to force till we we absolutely compelled to ....' Younghusband to Curzon, letter, April 14, 1904. Curz MSS.

27. *Diary for 1904*, entry for March 31, 1904. For April 1, Hadow noted that he was 'Ve tired after yesterday. Stayed in camp'

28. In the final tally the number of Tibetans, killed and wounded, left on the field was 62 prisoners taken, 222; while 'doubtless a number, slightly wounded, escaped.' As f the Mission, 'Major Wallace Dunlop, wounded severerly, lost two fingers; Candl dangerously wounded, left hand amputated, besides other serious sword wound Native ranks two wounded severely, eight wounded slightly', Tibet Papers, *op.cit.*, C 2054, Part II, Nos. 11 and 37, pp. 6 and 18.

29. Thus Powell Millington. *To Lhasa At Last*, Second Edn. (London, 1905), p. 54, note 'what was left of the corpses of many Tibetans who had fallen in the fight ... som months before'. Lt. Hadow, *Diary*, made this entry for Friday, October 14 (1904) : ' lot of remains lying about at Guru' Millington was on his way to Gyantse (some tim in June) and Hadow on the way out of Tibet.

30. Candler's comment that 'to send two dozen sepoys into that sullen mob was to invit disaster' is undoubtedly very near the truth. A recent writer's observation thereo deserves citation : 'Given the Tibetan Commander's refusal to do it (clear the road fo the British advance), a clash was inevitable; given the British superiority in weapons, was bound to be one-sided'. Peter Fleming, *op.cit.*, p. 152.

Younghusband to Curzon, private letter, February 3, 1904. Curzon MSS.

Ibid., In his letter to Curzon, of April 14 (1904) the Commissioner wrote: 'Lord Rosebery's gloomy foreboding that mine is a second Cavagnari Mission will prove as foundationless as most others of his dismal prognostications.'

'And I should imagine that their (Tibetan Lamas') defeat and the slaughter of a few hundred of them, should have a salutary effect right throughout Tibet'. Hamilton to Curzon, letter, September 15, 1903, Hamilton Papers, *op.cit.*

Edmund Candler, *op.cit.,* p. 112.

Brodrick in his letter to Curzon on April 7, 1904, noted 'I am not sorry personally that the Tibetans should have sustained a smashing defeat, as nothing but *peine forte et dure* would have really influenced them....' Curzon MSS.

Tibet Papers, *op.cit.,* Cd. 2054, Part II, No. 37, p. 18.

Younghusband MSS., Nos. 32 and 33, April 1 and 4, 1904.

Tibet Papers, *op, cit.,* Cd. 2054, Part I, No. 12, p. 6.

Younghusband's 'full report', *Ibid.,* No. 23, p. 9, placed the blame squarely on the Ti betans and praised the (British) troops for their 'exemplary patience and fortitude' in circumstances of 'unequalled vigour and difficulty'.

Loc. cit.

Curzon to Younghusband, letter, April 4, 1904, Curzon MSS.

Ibid., Brodrick to Curzon, letter, April 7, 1904.

Tibet Papers, *op.cit.,* Cd. 2054, No. 25, p. 10.

Supra, note 39.

To Curzon, Younghusband wrote in private that the Tibetan 'General' 'had no nerve or character—much less any martial ardour.... He had orders from Lhasa not to fight. He was also told that if we were not prevented from moving forward, he would have his throat cut'. When the Commissioner ordered the disarming of the Tibetan sepoys 'he (Tibetan 'General') lost his head like a school girl and began personally struggling with a sepoy'. Younghusband to Curzon, letter, April 30, 1904. Curzon MSS.

In a letter to his father—Younghusband MSS., No. 34, April 13, 1904—the Commissioner wrote : 'Literally, our only loss between India and here has been two fingers and an arm'.

A Maccalum Scott, *op.cit.,* p. 44.

Five days after reaching Gyantse, Younghusband wrote to Lord Curzon of 'his firm belief' that 'if we marched straight on to Lhasa we would see the whole Tibetan bubble burst', and that this was 'the easiest and safest way to settle this business once for all'. He was indeed dead set against 'stopping at Khamba Jong, stopping at Tuna and stopping here' which was all 'so lame and halting'. 'It leads to no result' declared the Commissioner and added 'I might negotiate here till I am blue in the face but it would all end in talk'. Younghusband to Curzon, letter, April 25, 1904, Curzon MSS. From now on Younghusband's advocacy of a straight dash to Lhasa was to bring him into increasing conflict with the authorities, both in India and England.

Tibet Papers, *op.cit.,* Cd. 2054, Part I, No. 14, p.7. It may be mentioned here that the new Chinese Amban Yu Tai had arrived at Lhasa, early in December (1903).

Curzon to Younghusband, letter, April 4, 1904, Curzon MSS.

Tibet Papers, *op.cit.,* Cd. 2054, Part I, No. 16, p. 7.

Ibid., No 22, p. 9.

Ibid., No. 30, p.12.

52. Younghusband's references to the Dalai Lama are of the most deprecatory. He c
    him 'this bumptious young Dalai Lama' who was no better than 'a youth caught
    a baby from the bazaar' (Letter to Dane, March 28); 'a young whipper-snapper..
    on a pinnacle of spiritual power' and 'an obstinate, self-willed youngman...
    difficult to manage'. (Letters to Curzon, April, 16 and 25, 1904). Curzon MSS.

53. Tibet Papers. *op.cit.*, Cd. 2054, No 34, p.13.

54. Younghusband confided in Curzon. 'freely ... as between two workers for the go
    the Empire who look not merely to its purely selfish interests, but also believe
    England has a high name to make in the history of the world...', while Curzon wr
    him as 'an old friend', their common goal being 'the good of the Tibetans no less
    the safeguard of Imperial interests'. Younghusband to Curzon, letter, January 1,
    and Curzon to Younghusband, letter, January 23, 1904. Curzon MSS.

55. *Ibid.*, Curzon to Younghusband, letter, April 4, 1904.

56. The Secretary of State, through the Viceroy, had sounded a 'warning' th
    (Younghusband) was showing undue eagerness to go to Lhasa and too great precipita
    Ibid., Younghusband to Curzon, May 15, 1904.

57. *Infra.*, pp. 249-257.

58. Tibet Papers, *op.cit.*, Cd. 2370, Part I, No.7, pp. 3-4. In his private letter to Curzo
    May 15 the Commissioner wrote, 'I had always been buoying myself up with the
    that when the worst came to the worst, Government would always brace thems
    up... Now the worst has come to the worst... instead of severely punishin
    Tibetans for their many insults and for their final iniquity of attacking the Mission,
    still while they are daily firing upon me—to meekly write and ask them to nego
    And having negotiated we are to humbly retire from the scene'. Younghusban
    Curzon, letter, May 15, 1904. Curzon MSS.

59. Tibet Papers, *op.cit.*, Cd. 2370, Nos. 13 and 18, pp. 6 and 8.

60. *Ibid.*, Part I, No. 32, p. 12. To his father on May 27 (1904) Younghusband wrote :
    advancing the Mission to Lhasa to negotiate is no use. I am advocating a regular can
    against the Lamas...' On June 3: 'I have been busy sending off ultimatums today—
    to Dalai Lama and one to Amban, Lhasa general returned both which pleased me gr
    as I highly disapprove of giving them any further chance of negotiating. But the c
    chap has just sent asking to have them...' Younghusband MSS.

61. Tibet Papers, *op.cit.*, Cd. 2370, Part I, No. 56, p. 19.

62. *Ibid.*, No. 63, p. 21. On June 23, Younghusband wrote to his father 'News just ca
    that Tibet negotiators are coming to see me, I only hope it is true'. Younghusband N

63. Tibet Papers, *op.cit.*, Cd. 2370, Part I, No. 72, p. 24.

64. *Ibid.*, Nos. 75 and 83, pp. 25 and 28.

65. *Ibid.*, No. 95, p. 32.

66. *Ibid.*, Part II, Encl. No. 252, p. 211.

67. Younghusband MSS., No. 45, July 22, 1904.

68. Tibet Papers, *op.cit.*, Cd. 2370, Part I, No. 118, pp. 48-49 and Part II, Encl. No.
    p. 217.

69. Younghusband to Curzon, letter, July 25, 1904, Curzon MSS.

70. Younghusband MSS., No.46, August 1, 1904.

71. Younghusband to Curzon, letter, April 14, 1904, Curzon MSS.

72. *Ibid.*, Younghusband to Curzon, letter, April 16, 1904.

73. *Ibid.*, Younghusband to Miller, letter, March 30, 1904.

74. *Supra*, pp. 245-247.

75. For an excellent, first-hand account of the fighting, see Brevet-Major W. J. Ottley, *With Mounted Infantry in Tibet* (London, 1906).
76. Ottley, *op.cit.,* pp. 68-73.
77. Younghusband to Curzon, letter, May 15, 1904, Curzon MSS.
78. Younghusband, India and Tibet, *op.cit.,* p. 187. Tibet Papers, *op.cit.,* Cd. 2370, Part II, Encl. No. 61, p. 125.
79. Both Younghusband as well as Brander believed that a Tibetan position at Karo-la could endanger the Mission's communications at Kang-ma in the rear. For a well-informed analysis, see Peter Fleming, *op.cit.,* pp. 165-70.
80. 'Younghusband must have known that in letting the column go he was placing his own career in jeopardy, he risked with open eyes recall and disgrace'. Besides, he was seriously compromising his own safety as evidenced by the Tibetan attack on the Mission's camp. *Ibid.,* pp. 166-67.
81. Younghusband MSS., No. 37, May 9, 1904.
82. Tibet Papers, *op.cit.,* Cd. 2370, Part I, No. 11, pp. 5-6 and Part II, Encl. No, 72, p. 131, and Nos. 75-76, p. 132.
83. Younghusband to Curzon, letter, May 7, 1904, Curzon MSS.
84. *Loc. cit.*
85. *Ibid.,* Younghusband to Curzon, letter, May 15, 1904.
86. 'The moveable column should not have gone as far as the Karo-la without reference to me. If you are not committed return at once to Gyantse. Fear your action will be considered as attempt to force hand of Government. Younghusband's concurrence does not relieve you of responsibility. You may clear out any Tibetans threatening communications between Ralung and Kang-ma and this piece of road should be reconnoitred. Please acknowledge'. Cited in Peter Fleming, *op.cit.,* p. 168.
87. Younghusband MSS., No. 37, May 9, 1904.
88. Tibet Papers, *op.cit.,* Cd. 2370, Part I, No. 6, p. 3 and Part II, Encl. No. 71, p. 130.
89. It is possible to argue that if Brander had not been engaging at Karo-la, the Gyantse camp would probably have been beleaguered by 3,000 men. Even if they had been successfully beaten off, their losses would have been much higher.
90. *Supra,* n. 87.
91. *Loc. cit.*
   In his letter to Lord Curzon, on May 7, 1904, Younghsband wrote : '140 is, I think, the exact number'. Curzon MSS.
92 Godley wrote to Ampthill that 'the Tibetans have quite suddenly assumed a character of which we never thought them capable; they are no longer stupid, defenceless sheep but ferocious determined fanatics with a steadily increasing perception of the military advantage at their command'. Cited in Peter Fleming, *op.cit.,* p. 183.
93. Younghusband to Curzon, letter, May, 31, 1904, Curzon MSS.
94. *Loc. cit.*
95. *Ibid.,* Younghusband to Curzon, letter, July 12, 1904.
96. Tibet Papers, *op.cit.,* Cd. 2370, Part I, Nos. 77, 80, and 82, pp. 26-28 and Part II, Encl. Nos. 193, 196 and 202, pp. 179, 180 and 184. For a detailed, and graphic account of the assault, see Ottley, *op.cit.,* pp. 180-195.
97. *Supra,* n. 93.
98. Ottley, *op.cit.,* p. 191.
99. Tibet Papers, *op.cit.,* Cd. 2370, Part I, No. 99, p. 40, and Part II, Encl. No. 221, pp.

192-193. See also 'Pousse- Cailloux', *op.cit.*, p. 163. It will be recalled that the author, then Lt. L. A. Bethel, took a part in the fighting. It were 'his' men, of the 8th Gurkhas, who had climbed the glacier.

'The most remarkable feature' of the Karo-la engagement, Ottley wrote, was that the fight took place at 19,000 ft. 'a record which has not been reached by any army of any nation throughout history, and is now open to the armies of the world to beat'. Ottley, *op.cit.*, p. 200.

100. Younghusband MSS., No. 44, July 19,1904. The letter was written from Camp Zara, 16,000 ft. above sea-level, where the Mission, and the force, had camped after dispersing the Tibetans from the Karo-la.

16
Problems: Man-Made and God-Made

The preceding pages furnish, albeit inadequately, an inkling of some of the difficulties which the Mission faced in its campaigning in the land of the Lamas. Though smoothed over and to some extent alleviated by the time of the final advance from Gyantse to Lhasa these had, in actual fact, persisted throughout the year and a quarter of the Mission's sojourn in Tibet. Some were physical, peculiar to the land and its rigorous clime; others were human and almost exclusively personal: the running battle between the Commissioner and his chief military aide, General Macdonald; or the growing distrust between HMG on the one hand and the chief executant of their policy in Tibet on the other, resulting often times in a strain that was perceptible at both ends. It would be difficult to understand, much less appreciate the truth about the Mission or grasp the picture in all its fullness of detail without having a closer look at some of these problems; at once man-made and God-made.

Perhaps one of the chief difficulties which the force was up against was transport, a difficulty made all the more acute by the lie of the land, and its peculiar terrain. For most part the country is, as was noticed earlier, a high-altitude, empty, barren, cold and windswept desert. And until the Communist take-over, the only wheel known in Tibet was the traditional prayer-wheel. The transport problem, therefore, reduced itself to one of advancing into a desert on one's own carrying-power. And herein not only had the load itself to be carried, what was more the carrier had to be supplied the energy with which to carry it. As one of the Mission's officers noted,

The solution lay, *imprimis*, in finding some animal which would work but not eat, or in multiplying its carrying-power that the consumption would be negligible.[1]

Another bottle-neck was 'the wasp-waist of that truly infernal Himalayan crossing', the 14,390 ft. high Jelap-la or for that matter the Nathu-la above Gangtok. The former, narrow and difficult at the best of times and yet one of the principal routes through Sikkim, into the Chumbi Valley, had to be kept open in all weathers ranging from 'calm', through 'frozen sun-shine', to the bitterest of the blizzards. For, the moment it would be cut off the Mission's life-line of supply from its Indian base would dry up. The ultimate solution was found in the twin discovery of the mule and the yak : the mule because it worked, and over-worked in the worst of snow-drifts; the yak because it did not eat away its load.

A problem which knew no remedy, and found no mention in official despatches, was the intensity of the cold. Captain O'Connor's faithful diary records of thermometer readings bear a silent testimony to the sleet and frost and snow through which the men—and their animals—lived and worked, marched and rested. 'Pousse-Cailloux' is, however, more eloquent as indeed are the pages of Lieutenant Hadow's 'Diary' and of Younghusband's book.[2] Thus Lt. Bethel speaks of 'the bitter penetrating cold, still and sterile by night, rising to the incessant grit-laden gales of icy wind which blew with devastating venom', all day long, 'relentlessly, without intermission'. [3]

Some of the entries, picked up at random, from Lt. Hadow's diary are equally expressive:

Thus on *Wednesday, January 6, 1904:*

Marched to Phari, V. cold last night. 6° below zero and a wind, could not sleep much. V. cold when we got up.

And for *Saturday, January 9:*

Yesterday was one of the hardest days we had ... about 14° below zero.

Again, *Wednesday, January 13:*

V. windy with dust, rather trying.

Sunday, January 17 was no better:

A very bad day. Strong wind and dust and did not go down at night. Tent full of dust.

Monday, January 25:

Strong wind all day, and dust blowing.

Wednesday, January 27:

Dust-storm blew, most unpleasant.

Sunday, January 31:

Snow and blizzard all day.

Tuesday, February 9:

Lovely day, V. little wind.

Wednesday, February 17:

..... Some snow on hill in night. Cold wind blowing all day. A sepoy died yesterday and another today.

Friday, February 19:

Another cold, windy day. Very unpleasant.

Wednesday, February 24:

Another sepoy died last night, making 12 deaths up-to-date.

Saturday, February 27 :

Stayed in camp. Very windy and dust blowing.
Friday, March 4:
Windy and V. cloudy. Snow fell at night.
Saturday, March 5:
Snow fell last night.... One sepoy died in night and one sepoy committed suicide in morning, making 15 deaths up-to-date.
Thursday, March 10:
Snow last night. Very cold day. Ass: Post Master died last night making 16 deaths.
Monday, March 14 :
... Heavy wind all day, and cloudy later.
Friday, March 25 :
A fall of snow last night. Stayed in camp.
Saturday, April 2 :
.... V. windy and dust blowing, most unpleasant.

Younghusband's own description of the area around Phari Jong which General Macdonald occupied on January 20, makes interesting reading too:

He (Macdonald) stayed there a couple of nights during which the cold was intense, the thermometer registering about 40° of frost at night. The ground was frozen so hard that a working party of 12 men only succeeded after two hours' hard work, in excavating some 33 cubic feet of earth, and as neither turf nor stones were available, it was impossible to construct any entrenchments.[5]
Later, the Commissioner arrived at Tuna ('the filthiest place I have ever seen'):
We tried to live in the houses, but after a few days preferred our tents, in spite of the cold, which was intense and against which we could not have the comfort and cheer of a fire, for only sufficient fuel for cooking could be obtained, most of it being yak-dung, and much having to be brought from Chumbi....[6]
A month or two later things were no better.
Communications had to be kept up across two high passes right through the winter; a flying-column had to be ready to proceed at any moment to our assistance at Tuna; and supplies and transport had to be collected for our advance as soon as possible to Gyantse. On the Tang-la there was never any great depth of snow and what snow fell, soon cleared away; but there were terrible winds, and the convoys sometimes crossed in blinding, icy blizzards...... On the passes into Sikkim there was much more snow, and they were occasionally closed after an unusually heavy storm. Still, fairly continuously the transport corps plied across them, and supplies accumulated in Chumbi....[7]

The cold created its own problems, with varied ramifications. Thus rifle-oil froze, footwear froze to the very feet, breath froze to the face, 'to make it like a visage'. An entry in Lt. Hadow's diary for January 8 makes interesting reading and is not so much exceptional, as typical:

....The cold last night rendered one lock of maxim and some rifles useless owing to oil clogging. Tried both maxims on the march, only one fired....

Four days later, matters had not improved:

Tried Maxims in the morning, many failures, found fuses (?) spring to (sic) heavy and worked at 2½ to 3 lbs.....

Cases of pneumonia, and frost-bite, were not unusual. The real problem was that every pound of fuel had to be transported—and with the bottle-neck that transport was—and conserved specifically for cooking purposes. Lt. Hadow's diary is full of expeditions for 'collecting yak-dang' but even these did not seem to avail much, for 'from first to last we were dependent for warmth on the natural heat of our bodies'.

The bleak barrenness of the land, its lack of transport added to the acute bitterness of the cold, icy blizzards which blew uninterruptedly across hill and dale created well-nigh insuperable problems, for the Mission. And yet they represented, in reverse, the lamas' major allies—'strong and unfailing'—on whom they did count with a goodly measure of confidence. Could it be that their obstinacy, when face to face with the threat which the Mission posed, was due, if partly, to a child-like curiosity in seeing how long the invaders could stick out their necks against such formidable odds. Younghusband often talked of the stubbornness, of the mulish stolidness of the Tibetans. One wonders how much of this was born of an inherent, ingrained faith in the invincibility of their elements ?

Another aspect of the problem needs scrutiny too. As we shall presently notice, the military authorities were weighed down by the threat posed by the Mission's ever-stretching lines of communication. Younghusband told Macdonald that as for him he was not interested in maintaining the link across Chumbi (when in due course the Mission had advanced beyond Tuna to Gyantse)[8] a proposition to which the ever-wary Scotsman refused to give countenance. But having planted the Mission at Gyantse, the military authorities were averse to any advance on Lhasa. And when they finally did acquiesce in it, Macdonald's view was of a quick dash to and fro: a prospect to which Younghusband was resolutely opposed.[9] The military viewpoint was that both Karo-la and Chaksam ferry, the stage for the fording of the Tasang-po (Brahmaputra) and beyond which lay holy Lhasa, represented two of the most vulnerable spots where any successful hostile action could mean the Mission's severance from its base. Hence Macdonald's advocacy of an advance to, and a halt at, Nagartse and the holding out of a threat to march on Lhasa, but no more. Younghusband was convinced in his own mind that nothing could be achieved, short of Lhasa, followed by a prolonged stop-over at the capital. In the final analysis a compromise was wrought : to proceed from Gyantse without dependence on the base, either for support or even supplies.[10] As the terrain from Gyantse onwards was quite unfamiliar and 'the enemy' at once actively hostile and elusive, besides being ubiquitous, the risks involved, and the consequent difficulties encountered, were considerable.

Again, a by no means unimportant problem was the regular upkeep of supplies. Actually, for most part, the men had to live off the land. The hoarded grain and the mummified carcases of sheep in the monasteries—and in Tibet the latter have been, from times immemorial, havens of refuge for a sizeable part of the population—were to provide the staple, later nick-named 'tummy-twisting', diet. This enforced self-sufficiency, save for food, made the 1,500 men and 3,000 mules who emerged from Gyantse and took the high road to Lhasa—'with every man and mule laden to its ultimate carrying power'—look like 'a veritable marching Army and Navy Stores'.[11]

The physical apart, there were personal, temperamental problems too. On the face of it, there was something slightly odd about Colonel Younghusband, leader of the 'Tibet Frontier Commission' having as his principal military aide a Brigadier-General J.R.L. Macdonald, of the Royal Engineers.[12] The former was inferior in military rank to the latter and yet superior in status. Nor was that exceptional for it may be added, if only as a foot-note, that Younghusband's military rank as a 'Political' officer was only nominal for half the Political Department officers were seconded from the Indian Army. Initially, Macdonald's appointment as 'Commandant Royal Engineers on the road from Siliguri onwards...' was gazetted towards the end of September (1903) and specifically excluded charge of the Mission's escort, then stationed at Khamba Jong. Apparently Curzon, who must have had a nodding acquaintance with his (Macdonald's) previous record in Uganda, in East Africa, was somewhat sceptical about his choice but then 'we were looking to roads and communications' and did not appear very concerned about his being 'a soldier, strategist or commander....' Besides, as the Viceroy confessed later, he was 'over-ruled'.[13] There could be little doubt that this upkeep of roads and communications represented one of the chief problems in regard to Tibet and would largely account for Macdonald's choice. The role of the brilliant commander, of the military genius planning operations in a difficult land was not the one for which the man from the Royal Engineers was cast and, therefore, it was perhaps not quite fair to expect from him something of the stuff he was not made of.

Younghusband who first met Macdonald at Darjeeling in October (1903), reacted to the man, and the post he was earmarked for, with a measure of enthusiasm:

Macdonald is an excellent, sound, solid fellow and we shall get on capitally. Of course, in actual military operations, I have nothing to say. But otherwise I am to be the senior officer to him and the whole expedition is to be a kind of big support to the Mission and I am not to be merely the Chief Political Officer accompanying a military force.[14]

Again, Kitchener was very friendly and cooperative having agreed to the deployment of a 'section of a British mountain battery and two maxim gun detachments all of British soldiers and I will give orders that not a single man to be under six feet'—all that the Commissioner had asked for in October (1903).[15] The Commander-in-Chief went a step further and 'told me to write him privately from up there to tell him how things were going and to ask him anything I wanted'.[16]

It seemed to be an excellent start, for nothing could have been better: 'It is much to be in private correspondence with Lord Curzon and Lord Kitchener'. And of the latter, Younghusband had formed a most favourable impression:

> He is very easy to talk to. No sort of formality or pompousness. You feel you can say exactly what you think... He accepted everything I said both at his dinner and in Council without questioning me as to the grounds for my opinion like Lord Curzon always does—and he did not inquire into the details like Lord Roberts always used to.[17]

Soon, however, the gloss began to wear off the wicket and the first impression proved to be somewhat overdrawn. In November, from Calcutta—and this was weeks before the Jelap-la crossing—the Commissioner was still confiding in Macdonald to 'regard me simply as a precious parcel of goods to be carted from one place to another and taken the greatest possible care of' on the way.[18] Yet in the process of 'carting' the 'precious parcel' serious difference of opinion began to develop. In his initial enthusiasm, the Commissioner had planned to be in Gyanste by Christmas, a prospect of which the Viceroy was extremely sceptical. Soon he was to discover that it was not only the weather and the almost insuperable problems of transport which stood in the way but what was more Brigadier-General Macdonald had begun to drag his weary feet. 'If I am at Gyantse by the end of January, I shall be surprised', the Commissioner wrote from Gnatong (Sikkim) on December 11.[19] To be sure, Gyantse was not to be reached until exactly four months later.

Macdonald, among 'the most cautious and methodical of people', was averse to any advance farther from Chumbi until he could be certain of ensuring a hundred per cent fool-proof safety. The decision, therefore, to station the Mission—'with half a battalion, two maxim guns, a 7-pounder and some sappers and any amount of ammunition and two months' supplies'—at Tuna, in the middle of January, was acquiesced in after a raucous, noisy battle of words. For while Younghusband was convinced that 'caution is all very well to a certain point', and that they were losing 'many advantages through advancing so slowly', the commander of the escort felt certain that 'nothing so desperate was ever done before'.[20] In actual fact, shortly after they crossed the Tanga-la on January 8, Younghusband and Macdonald had their first serious row. The latter, clear in his mind that 'as there was no fuel and grass and the men would not be able to stand the cold', demanded an immediate withdrawal to which the Commissioner's retort was a stern 'No!' Macdonald threatened, stamped his feet hard and asked Younghusband to 'assume all responsibility' and give him (all this) 'in writing'. As the Commissioner held his ground and refused to budge— a proceeding in which the Viceroy later thought he (Younghusband) was 'entirely right'—Macdonald relented and the Mission, encamped in 'three large houses which have been fortified', remained at Tuna.[21]

Meanwhile as Younghusband and his men settled down, they discovered to their dismay that the halt at Tuna was far more protracted than was originally intended. For other things apart, there was 'a most pessimistic head of the staff' at Chumbi who was spreading some fantastic rumours about the strength of the Tibetan camp, not far from the Commissioner's own.[22] To Younghusband the risks involved were well-night negligible :

> If we had any amount of transport, if we were at war with Tibet, if the inhabitants were against us, and if the Tibetans had at any time shown themselves to be warlike and with military aptitude, there might be reason for it.

As matters stood there was 'no war', the people were 'friendly', the Tibetans most 'unmilitary'-like, and the very slight 'military risk' involved clearly overborne by the 'political disadvantages' of delay and 'the great cost' of keeping troops up there. No wonder, Macdonald's caution was not exactly appreciated by the Commissioner.[23]

Later, when probably as a result of Younghusband's own repeated requests, Government asked the Commissioner what was holding up his advance, Macdonald pleaded—'without any expression of his opinion'—that 'if we did not require to keep up communication' beyond Kala Tso to Gyantse, a distance not exceeding 40 miles, he (Macdonald) would be prepared to move immediately. The Commissioner, however, was getting increasingly impatient. There was 'nothing so risky as being cautious' he declared and charged that the 'military have had time enough in all conscience' to make their preparations.[24] Of Macdonald, and his ways, he used strong language:

> I think I told you he (Macdonald) has asked me to give him 'an absolutely free hand' as it (advance to Gyantse) is a 'purely military move'.[25] He has got a head like a donkey's and I cannot drill into it that I cannot give him a free hand and that it is not a military move. Of course he thinks he is fettered by these d-d politicals and if anything goes wrong I shall be blamed for not allowing him to do as he wished....[26]

In the fighting at Guru on March 31, as in the later advance to Gyantse, Younghusband ensured that Macdonald did not have the 'full control' he had demanded.[27] This not only meant that at Guru 'the onus of commencing hostilities' rested with the Tibetans but also prevented the Mission from becoming 'a military expedition pure and simple' which Macdonald would be able 'to order... about as he pleased'. Besides, the military might have taken such disastrous steps 'as the retirement from Tuna' and behaved in a manner 'I highly disapproved of'.[28] Government's reversal of its earlier decision, Younghusband confided in his father, 'gives me more power than I had before—or at any rate assured I had for nothing had up till now been laid down'.[29]

It is clear that both at Guru, and subsequently on the way to Gyantse, Macdonald powerfully influenced by his staff officers and their unrelenting pressure—easily understandable in such cases—for a medal, was exaggerating his role and 'his exploits'. This was something through which his military bosses could easily see.[30] It is also evident that at Guru, the continued firing into an unarmed Tibetan mob—it was far from being a regular army—and what Lord Curzon called 'the unnecessary pursuit' of the runaways by the Mounted Infantry, was over-done and added its own fearful quota to that shameless slaughter.[31] Nor had matters improved weeks later when Ampthill confided to the Secretary of State:

> We are sending you home by this mail two despatches from General Macdonald ... You will see that the whole tone of these despatches is that of a general who is commanding real military operations rather than of a Commander of the escort of a peaceful Mission, but in this respect... a warning has already gone to General Macdonald.[32]

Nor did troubles with Macdonald end with the advance to Gyantse; for many a battle had yet to be waged. As was noticed, the General on the morrow of his arrival there returned to Chumbi where, he maintained, supplies were more plentiful. Yet of this move too Younghusband strongly disapproved. Meantime, serious differences were developing between the Commissioner and the Home Government over the question of the advance to Lhasa. Younghusband was convinced that if his political objectives were to be fully realized, Government would have to be prepared to keep the Mission and a considerable force in Tibet for another year. The military were firmly opposed to this viewpoint, for they not only wanted the whole thing rushed through 'but to get back before the winter'.[33]

It is at this stage, one notices, that the differences between Younghusband and the authorities in London added their own fearful complication to the running battle with Macdonald. Nor was the latter alone, for both Kitchener and (Major-General Sir Edmund) Elles, the Military Member, now became his powerful protagonists—both in and outside the Council Chamber. In fact, they seemed to demand the Commissioner's very head, and on a platter. Two letters from Ampthill to Curzon and the Secretary of State are eloquent of the change in the situation. Thus on June 2 :

> The Commander-in-Chief and Elles are both indignant with Younghusband and want to make him essentially subordinate to Macdonald as merely the Political Officer of the latter's staff. I have to defend Younghusband against the Military authorities....[34]

In August , with the Mission in Lhasa, things were no better:

> Younghusband has very poor opinion of Macdonald who did his utmost to get out of going to Lhasa and has exaggerated the difficulties at every stage, but the slightest hint or suggestion of this in the Council Chamber is enough to make Lord Kitchener and Sir Edmund Elles rise up in arms and deliver a violent counter-attack on Younghusband. I have had to protect Younghusband from their fury on at least a score of occasions and to resist their scheme of 'breaking' him.[35]

The battle was thus joined and raged at white heat, during May-July. In the midst of it, the Commissioner was engaged in what he called 'another furious contest with Government' and sent in 'for the second time', his 'formal resignation'.

A sore point was Macdonald's painting the risks 'in the darkest colours' and demanding a formidably large force both as an escort for the Mission at Lhasa, as also for the post at Gyantse. Later he (Macdonald) was sharply to revise the figures upon which both he and Younghusband had agreed during the latter's brief visit to Chumbi early in June.[36] The Commissioner considered Macdonald's estimates 'excessive', but the military authorities did finally have their way and he was informed that as their objections to the Mission 'wintering' at Lhasa 'were overwhelming' he (Younghusband) should shape his course of action with a view to returning to Gyantse.[37] A compromise was finally wrought : Younghusband stayed at his post and the Commander of the escort did not, on the whole, do as badly as was feared. But this was not without the Commissioner having some truly anxious moments. It is important to bear in mind the fact that as Ampthill's support for Younghusband became increasingly pronounced, the military ranged itself full-square behind Macdonald. Thus at a time when the 'Commander of the escort' was under considerable fire, Kitchener wrote to Ampthill for the information of the Secretary of State that he (Kitchener) was 'quite satisfied' that Macdonald was

> fully qualified to control the Military operations. His estimates and forecast have turned out extremely correct and the experience he has gained makes him the most suitable commander for the Military operations in Tibet....[38]

Nor was that all. For the Commander-in-Chief went further and told Ampthill a few days later that his 'only fear' in Tibet was 'the very pronounced views of aggrandizement' held by Dane (later Sir Louis), the Secretary to Government, and Younghusband and that he could not 'help feeling rather nervous' when the Commissioner got on to Lhasa.[39] But long before the Tibetan capital was reached, Younghusband on his part had begun to be anxious too. Thus barely had the Mission left Gyantse, when Macdonald confided that 'he cannot undertake to attack Lhasa if I have to put pressure'. This made Younghusband exclaim, as though in sheer desperation, 'so what the dickens he has come here for at all. I am blessed if I can discover'.[40]

Later at Peti Jong, half-way through Lhasa, when the Tibetan delegates came to meet him and the Commissioner rebutted their 'silly arguments', Macdonald proffered what was evidently unsolicited advice to the effect—'I should settle with them here' for 'we might not be able to reach Lhasa'. In any case, he urged 'a bird in hand being worth two in the bush'.

Younghusband, conscious that this was simply due to his (Macdonald) having 'a pain in the lining of his waistcoat', took 'no notice' of it. Besides, the Commissioner was in full agreement 'with the leading officers of the force' that there was 'no special risk' in going on to Lhasa,[41] Yet a chief aide like that, on a political mission of such import as the one on which he was now engaged, was sure to drive Younghusband mad.[42]

In Lhasa itself, there was another row between the two, even a 'battle royal' as Younghusband called it. Two of the members of the Mission, White and Wilton, had evidently strayed into the town without previous reference to the General or his staff, which made him (Macdonald) later exhort the Commissioner 'to impress on members of the Mission that they must obey Force Orders'. Younghusband was furious for all that the rebuke implied,

> I wrote back asking him to come and see me. I then told him my officers obeyed my orders not his and that he himself had to conform to my wishes I told him plainly that there could be only one head up here and that I intended there should be no mistake that that head was myself.

Macdonald 'blustered a good deal' about referring matters to Government but finally came round and said 'he would not if I would not'. Younghusband was satisfied : 'He (Macdonald) now understand (sic)', he wrote to his father with an air of confidence, 'his position in the universe'.[43]

The strain and the unpleasant nature of this running sore between Younghusband and Macdonald—and to one of its more important aspects namely, the latter's behaviour at Lhasa more especially in regard to the threat of withdrawal of the entire force from the Tibetan capital, a reference will be made in the following chapter—must have cast its long and deep shadow all the way from the crossing of the Jelap-la to the return from Lhasa. On nearly every occasion, which Younghusband deemed to be of importance, the commander of the escort not only failed to play the game but for most part, proved what may be termed a thorough-going 'obstructionist'. A summing-up of Macdonald by Perceval Landon, the *Times* correspondent—and Ampthill called him 'a hero-worshipper' of Younghusband[44]—appears to be pretty near the truth:

> Macdonald is a slow–moving and cautious man, intensely painstaking and foresightful—if there is such a word—a most pleasant man personally. He is not a strong man and his indecision over serious and trifling matters is notorious.
>
> Also he is strangely touchy about criticism of any kind .... The least dissent from his opinion, or demur at his tardiness ... maddens him and he betrays his mortification at once....[45]

Nor was this exceptional for it is well-known that the General's own staff officers were not entirely happy with him.[46] In any case, the unending row between the Head of the Mission and the Commander of his escort must have had a profound impact on the expedition as a whole.

Notes

1. Pousse-Cailloux, *op.cit.* p. 150.
2. Younghusband, India and Tibet, *op.cit.*
3. Pousse-Cailloux, *op.cit.*, p. 156.
4. This was a youngman, frail of body, a Mr. Lewis. Both his legs were amputated because of frost-bite and he died of the stumps being snow-bitten again.
5. Younghusband, India and Tibet, *op.cit.*, p. 158.
6. *Ibid.*, p. 161.

7. *Ibid.*, p. 169.

8. Younghusband to Curzon, letter, June 18, 1904. The Commissioner was convinced that his position had been fully vindicated and that nothing adverse had come out as a result of planting the Mission at Gyantse 'to hold its own if the worst came to worst'. This 'it had easily done and our communications have never been cut so that I was able to get out when wanted by Government. I do not call that being unduly optimistic'. Curzon MSS.

9. A detailed discussion on these points is in subsequent pages. Younghusband's reference to these was for obvious reasons, scanty in public. Thus his India and Tibet, *op.cit.*, p. 203, is brief. Also Seaver, *op.cit.*, pp. 233-35.

10. Ottley, *op.cit.*, pp. 194-95.

11. Pousse-Cailloux, *op.cit.*, p. 166.

12. For an account of Macdonald's earlier service in East Africa, and the controversy in which he was engaged there with a Captain Lugard, see Peter Fleming, *op. cit.*, pp. 106-9.

    Macdonald's first appointment was made on September 29, 1903, when he was placed under the orders of the Director-General Miscellaneous Works. Later, he was to come under the direct control of the Commander-in-Chief. Younghusband was quite clear in his analysis of Macdonald's appointment—his own information being, very obviously, based on Curzon's. This was to the effect that when the Foreign Office asked for an 'Engineer Officer for Sikkim last autumn—before the advance to Gyantse was anticipated—to do both road work and command the troops in Sikkim', which were stationed there to support the Mission at Khamba Jong, Macdonald's name was recommended. Younghusband MSS., No. 32, April 1, 1904.

13. Ampthill to Curzon, letter, June 23, 1904, Ampthill Papers, *op.cit.* Colonel Peter Fleming's reasoning, *op.cit.*, pp. 108-9, that Curzon did not quite identify him (Macdonald) at the time of his selection is not very convincing particularly in view of the Viceroy's categorical assertion that 'doubts as to his (Macdonald's) selection' emanated from him (Curzon) 'but were over-ruled'. Curzon to Ampthill, letter, September 30, 1904, Ampthill Papers, *op.cit.*

14. Younghusband MSS., No. 16, October 22, 1903. The Colonel had stayed at Darjeeling on his way to Simla from Khamba Jong 'to confabulate' with Macdonald who was to command 'in the event of an advance'.

15. *Ibid.*, No. 17, October 28, 1903.

16. *Loc. cit.*

17. *Ibid.*, No. 18, November 3, 1903.

18. *Ibid.*, No. 19, November 11, 1903.

19. *Ibid.*, No. 21, December 11, 1903.

20. *Ibid.*, No. 24, January 2, 1904.

21. Writing to his father about his encounter with Macdonald in a letter date-lined Tuna, January 30 (1904), Younghusband said as if in a whisper : 'But I will now tell you a thing which neither you nor Emmie must mention to anyone ....'and then narrated the entire episode. *Ibid.*, No. 26, January 30, 1904.

    The Commissioner had also written 'privately' to the Viceroy and Dane.

22. Younghusband was deeply exercised over 'this individual' (none other than Macdonald) who 'sucks in every yarn the Tibetans tell him'; was responsible for the story that the Tibetan camp, '6 miles below here', had been re-inforced by some 4,000 men who

were 'armed with rifles' and who intended to attack the Mission. His own estimat based on a personal visit, was of there being not more than 600 men. *Ibid.,* No. 2 February 25, 1904.

23. *Ibid.,* No 29, March 11, 1904.

24. *Ibid.,* No 30, March 18, 1904.

25. In a letter to Dane, the Foreign Secretary, on March 26, Younghusband told him th when earlier in January Government over-ruled him on the question of Phari he ha 'on account of the difficulty' of running this business with 'a dual control', express the view that the move into Tibet onwards 'be a purely military move'. Now, course, the context was different. Younghusband to Dane, letter, March 26, 1904. Curzon MSS.

26. Younghusband MSS. No. 31, March 25, 1904.

27. Initially Government had ordered 'full control' being given to Macdonald. Again this, Younghusband protested strongly and threatened 'to be relieved of th responsibility'. At this Government climbed down and a compromise was effecte Thus while Macdonald was to have 'military control', Younghusband was to ha over-all charge. The Brigadier was 'to carry out my wishes, unless they involv serious danger to the troops. Curzon MSS., Younghusband to Curzon, letter, Ap 14, 1904.

28. *Loc. cit.*

29. Younghusband MSS. No. 33, April 4, 1904. Arguing out the Commissioner's line reasoning Curzon wrote to Brodrick: '... the mission is a political mission ar Younghusband, not without reason, claims superior control. On the other hand, th advance is a military operation... Younghusband is a little sensitive about his person prerogative, and thinks that Macdonald imperfectly recognizes the diplomatic charact and object of the entire proceedings ...' The situation, however, was one that 'presen itself in almost every frontier war in India'. Curzon to Brodrick, letter, March 3 1904. Curzon MSS.

30. *Ibid.,* Kitchener to Curzon, letter, April 26, 1904. The Commander-in-Chief who ha written to Macdonald assured the Viceroy that he hoped there will be 'no more these incidents'.

31. Ampthill to Brodrick, letter, May 5, 1904. Ampthill Papers, *op.cit.*

32. *Loc. cit.*

33. Younghusband MSS., No. 38, May 24, 1904.

34. Ampthill to Curzon, letter, June 2, 1904, Ampthill Papers, *op.cit.*

35. *Ibid.,* Ampthill to Brodrick, letter, August 17, 1904.

36. Younghusband MSS., Nos. 38 and 42, May 24 and June 17, 1904.

37. For details, see Memorandum of Information, June 6-12 (1904) and Dane to Curzo letter, June 23, 1904. Curzon MSS.

38. Kitchener to Ampthill, letter, June 26, 1904. Ampthill Papers, *op.cit.* Also see Miller to Curzon, letter July 21, 1904. Curzon MSS. Miller refers Kitchener's giving a 'very honourable opinion of Macdonald's capacity'.

39. Kitchener to Ampthill, letter, June 30, 1904, Ampthill Papers, *op.cit.*

40. This was at Camp Zara, below the Karo-la, when the Mission had just about le Gyantse on its way to Lhasa. Younghusband MSS., No. 44, July 1904 (the origin does not bear any date).

41. *Ibid.,* No. 45, July 22, 1904. This was at Peti Jong. Younghusband had hardly conclude his interview with the Tibetan representatives when Macdonald came in. Also s Younghusband to Dane, letter, July 21 (1904), Ampthill Papers, *op.cit.*

2. Despite his rage, Younghusband was deeply affected : 'The poor man', he wrote to his father, referring to Macdonald, 'is on invalid's diet and ought really be on the sick-list'. Younghusband MSS., No. 45.

3. Younghusband MSS., No. 47, August 19, 1904.

4. Ampthill to Brodrick, letter, August 31, 1904, Ampthill Papers, *op.cit.*

5. *Ibid.* This was written from Gyantse on May 11 (1904) and was addressed to Ampthill as 'My dear Dick'.

5. Most of Macdonald's staff officers were on terms of excellent personal relationship with Younghusband—of these Colonels Brander and Hogge may be cited as being typical. Macdonald was not happy with the former for he had technically flouted his (Macdonald's) instructions and as for the latter, 'threatened' him 'with court-martial'. Basically, Younghusband wrote, 'on a business like this he wants to treat everybody like a drill-sargeant would'. Younghusband MSS., No. 33, April 4, 1904.

17

Clash of Wills: Younghusband, Curzon and the Cabinet

Nor did the clash with Macdonald stand by itself. Younghusband who had started under the best of auspices and oftentimes, in his early letters, acknowledged this without qualification, soon found himself under a cloud. That from the first, thanks to Lord Curzon's own tireless advocacy, Lhasa was an obsession is easily understandable.[1] So indeed was its corollary, a pre-occupation with Russian activities in Tibet. This meant accepting for most part as authentic evidence that proved, in nearly all cases, to be little better than the most unreliable of bazaar gossip.[2] Yet the real difficulty was that not only did the Commissioner's private letters breathe these sentiments, but that his official and public despatches were thoroughly impregnated with them. Two entries may be cited here as being typical, and indeed representative, of the much larger number on which the Government of India, and the authorities in London, were increasingly fed:

> Information that the Tibetans are relying on Russian support and that Russian arms have entered Tibet has now been received from several independent sources. It may be assumed... that Dorjieff is at Lhasa; that a promise of Russian support has been given to the Tibetans; and that the Tibetans believe that this promised support will be given to them.[3]

And again,

> Colonel Chao stated that Dorjieff is at present in Lhasa. He said that the arrogance of the Tibetans was due to their reliance on the support of the Russians .... that of late the Tibetans have been taunting the Chinese openly and saying that they now have a stronger and greater power than China upon which to rely for assistance.[4]

From his private letters too, the following may be culled :

> and secondly came the information that Dorjieff ....was actually in Lhasa, and not only there, but in the closet possible touch with this young Dalai Lama, who had just assumed this unprecedented amount of authority in Tibet, and so

influencing him in favour of Russia that it became a foregone conclusion that by diplomacy alone....(it would be impossible) making these obstinate Tibetans observe their treaty rights.[5]

Later, there was to be a shift of emphasis:

What has been proved...is that the Russian support the Tibetans have received is even greater than we have believed. It may not have been given by the Russian Government but it has come from Russian territory and unless we have to see Russian influence grow....[6]

And there was much more to it,

One thing is certain...we have many Lhasa-made rifles (which are really quite useful weapons) and Russian arms arrayed against us now than if we had advanced to Lhasa last year...[7]

Nor were any doubts entertained about Dorjieff's machinations:

For I have always assumed that we have quite enough to go on without inferring that Russian Government had anything to do with it. We have the evidence of the Nepalese representative in Lhasa, and of many traders, that Dorjieff has made the Dalai Lama promises of Russian support, and that the Dalai Lama has trusted in them so much that, on the strength of them, he has defied us and ignored the Chinese.[8]

Left to himself, Curzon fully, and without qualification, shared his lieutenant's enthusiasm—but times were somewhat out of joint. For with Brodrick at the helm of affairs in the India Office, Curzon had to be doubly cautious in drawing up a clear line of distinction between what he himself would have liked to do in Tibet and what the authorities at home would want or had authorized him to. It is thus not without significance that one of the first serious warnings to Younghusband, not to overdraw the picture, and instead be a little more restrained and discreet, was administered by Curzon himself and this was months before he left for home :

But I want to warn you—with a view to publication of papers in the House of Commons, and also to the attitude of the Home Government, whom we have to draw along with us, not to alarm or repel—to be very careful now, in any communication with the Tibetans, or in any dispatch to us, you either (do not?), speak just for the present about Lhasa, or rub in the Russians. In one telegram where you reported that you would negotiate at Lhasa, or words to that effect, I cut out the reference, since it would have involved a certain rebuke from HMG. Neither of us has any authority to speak about Lhasa now, or even to bluff about Lhasa. We may ultimately have to go there....

Events will probably be on the side of you and your policy. But you will greatly jeopardize the latter if you frighten the authorities at home either by showing your hand too plainly or by dragging in Lhasa before Lhasa is required....[9]

Younghusband fully appreciated the Viceroy's line of reasoning; was even convinced that he (Curzon) was 'quite right'. He realized too that the Home Government had to be treated like a 'pack of children' and that his 'diplomacy' had to be executed 'much more in the direction' of the authorities in London than of the

Tibetans.[10] He further confessed that he sought to use Lord Curzon as 'a safety-valve', for it was 'not always easy to contain myself' and there was a possibility he (Younghusband) 'might otherwise break out in the wrong direction'. And then he reasoned out. Had he not shown the 'utmost patience' in treating with the 'ill-conditioned' Tibetan monks who had demanded of him—'the representative of the greatest empire in the world'—a retirement to the frontier? Since there was no 'prestige' to back him, was he not justified in employing a measure of 'mind bluff?'[11] Besides, the Tibetans were 'not a people fit enough to be left to themselves between two great Empires'.[12] His rationalization apart, basically however the Commissioner promised to conform, regretting his 'ill-advised references to Lhasa, and the Russians' and pledging he would 'continue; to carry out 'Your Excellency's policy'.[13]

Neither the Viceroy's 'warnings', much less the Colonel's own solemn promise to toe the line, proved effective over a period. Soon enough Younghusband was back to the old tune, with notes that were far shriller and a manner that was unmistakable in its accent. The Commissioner rebelled at the thought of 'negotiation' for this took little account of 'the humiliations' to which the Tibetans had subjected the British representative, of the fact that the Mission had been continuously 'bombarded', that the lamas had been hostile and far from deferential. Truly he felt outraged,

> I had always been buoying myself up with the hope that when the worst came to the worst Government would brave themselves up and support their representative. Now the worst has come to the worst.... Instead of severely punishing them (Tibetans) for their many insults and for their final iniquity of attacking the Mission, I am still—while they are daily firing upon me—to meekly write and ask them to negotiate! And having negotiated we are to humbly retire from the scene.[14]

Again, he ridiculed what he called the 'farce' of negotiations—and harked back to the inevitability of a march on Lhasa,

> It seems from motives of Imperial policy (though I fancy that that term includes a good deal of supineness and weak-kneedness) that it was necessary to go through this farce of trying to negotiate at Khamba Jong and here but it was evident from the first that Lhasa was the only place to negotiate at and I think HMG might have paid a little more regard to the dignity of the British representative and a little less to the feelings of the Russians and the outcries of the Radicals.....These half-measures never pay with ignorant Orientals...[15]

Younghusband's strident advocacy of a march on Lhasa was not lost on the authorities in India or England. Thus on the morrow of the attack on the Mission at Gyantse, the Commissioner wrote to the acting Governor-General that he was sure 'HMG must see the necessity for going to Lhasa has now been proved beyond doubt'. Besides, there was 'never' going to be a settlement 'till we have got at the Lhasa people themselves' for they were 'the root of all mischief'.[16]

With HMG still publicly committed to the policy of an advance to Gyantse and no more, in terms of the telegram of November 6, the Secretary of State now felt impelled to warn the Commissioner against what he called his 'undue precipitancy', for his 'distinct eagerness' for a further advance—noticeable 'throughout' his despatches—had caused the Cabinet 'some apprehension'.[17] This was early in May, and barely had Lord Curzon temporarily laid down the charge of his office.

Younghusband was cut to the quick; he vigorously pleaded 'Not Guilty'. Was he not already a victim of 'the extraordinary dilatoriness' of the Home Government? Had he not made his proposal (to advance to Lhasa) after 'three despatches to the present Amban' had brought forth no response in terms of the arrival of the Tibetan delegates? Had he not been kept waiting in Tibet 'for nine months?'[18] Was it not 'his duty', as 'officer on the spot', to represent 'the local as against the Imperial view?' His remonstrances were indeed loud and categorical,

....it is (not) fair to charge me with undue eagerness... I should have thought I was more deserving of credit for the patience I had shown than of a charge of precipitancy....[19]

Whatever his justification, there could be little doubt that his long stay in Tibet, with its varied experiences and myriad frustrations, had resulted in overstrung nerves. Nor should one minimize the strain of living, and working with his sort of difficulties—at 15,000 ft. above sea-level. And as Landon, the *Times* correspondent, argued in 'such circumstances' how 'narrow-minded, sensitive, imaginative and altogether ridiculous' could men become?[20] Besides, one 'immediately in contact' with the difficulties of his situation 'tends to push forward'.[21] Actually, Younghusband's 'eagerness and undue precipitancy' grew, despite warnings, and he found himself an unrelenting advocate of extreme courses. It is significant that the impression that such was, in fact, the case was held not only by Brodrick, but shared in varying degrees by Kitchener, Ampthill—and even Curzon, whom everyone rated to be among his (Younghusband's) staunchest supporters.[22]

It has been noticed that the Commander-in-Chief, with whom the Commissioner had started off extremely well, later thought he held 'very pronounced views of aggrandizement' and feared for the worst when he (Younghusband) got to Lhasa.[23] Ampthill too regarded him as 'a man of highly-strung temperament' who had 'his ups and downs'.[24] Significantly enough, Curzon for his part, put him as 'the extremist' in the matter of effecting a deal with Tibet.[25] Would it be too much to deduce that what ended as Younghusband's near-complete defiance of authority at Lhasa, in September 1904, had its early beginnings in his continuous smarting under superior direction? More than once he was rapped for disregard of what was known to be official governmental policy. Each time he emerged, superficial conformity apart, as increasingly impatient of control, as distinctly disdainful of those who sought to direct him. Could it be, therefore, that the end-result proved to be what it was because he (Younghusband) had not been sufficiently 'broken'—to borrow Lord Kitchener's phrase—in time?

It may be recalled that in sanctioning the advance from Khamba Jong to Gyantse, HMG had laid down that the step was 'for the sole purpose of obtaining satisfaction' and that 'as soon as reparation is obtained' a withdrawal should be effected. To start with, as was noticed, it was the lack of prestige on the frontier that needed badly to be boosted; later that the prestige was 'at its height', emphasis shifted to a decisive 'move now' and of utilizing the psychological moment for action'.[26]

In private, the Commissioner had expressed himself in no uncertain terms. The move to Lhasa was 'the easiest and safest way' to settle this business; 'stopping at Khamba-Jong, stopping at Tuna and stopping here' (Gyantse) was a policy that was 'so lame and halting'. At Gyantse he might negotiate 'till I am blue in the face' for 'the only way to settle with the bumptious lamas' really was an advance to Lhasa and 'the dictation of terms'.[27] Officially, within three weeks of his arrival at Gyantse, the Commissioner stoutly confirmed his first impression that the Lhasa Government were 'irreconcilable'.

It is interesting that even the Secretary of State was privately asking the Governor-General for 'some sort of definite communication as a prelude to a further advance',[28] while the Permanent Under Secretary was equally clear that they 'shall have to go to Lhasa after all'.[29] It was with this aim in view that the Government of India wrote to the Secretary of State on May 6 to urge that 'some definite limit of time should now be imposed and that a further advance should at once be made', unless the 'proper' Tibetan and Chinese representatives put in an appearance.[30]

The much-sought for authority was granted on May 12, but in the then mood of the Government and the country, it was hedged in by all kinds of ifs and buts. The telegram of November 6 was referred to specifically and every care taken to ensure that there was no departure from its declared objectives,[31]

We have authorized it (advance to Lhasa) because there is nothing else to do, but naturally not having been anxious for the expedition from the first, we wish to give every loop-hole we can before actually going on to Lhasa...[32]

What a government, the unwary may exclaim! Besides, the position was extremely unsatisfactory from the point of view both of Lord Curzon, and even more so of Younghusband. The latter confessed to a feeling of 'depression'. It was 'butcher and bolt' at its worst, or of being 'thrown to the winds', the Commissioner confided.[33] At home Lord Curzon, then on leave, was waging what was progressively a losing battle with a Government that was 'quite impenitent' and against what Godley termed, not inappropriately, its 'stone-wall attitude'.[34]

To pick up the thread, on May 12 even as the go-ahead for the advance to Lhasa was given, the Viceroy while furnishing details of reinforcements needed was once again impressing upon London the need for 'decisive and early assertion of British power'.[35] As has been noticed, the Dalai Lama and the Amban were informed (on May 25) by the British Commissioner about the time-limit set for awaiting the negotiators' arrival—[36] something of which the Commissioner 'highly disapprove (ed) of,' and out of which he tried valiantly, though vainly, to wriggle out.[37] On June 9, the Secretary of State accorded his formal approval for the Mission to proceed to Lhasa if, by June 25, 'competent' negotiators did not arrive at Gyantse.[38]

There is a noticeable divergence in HMG's attitude at Gyantse as contrasted with their earlier stand at Khamba Jong. There the final move was to be sanctioned in London—and hence the Commissioner's discretion somewhat limited and circumscribed.[39] Here at Gyantse he had a much wider latitude and did avail of it to the fullest. For even when accredited Tibetan representatives put in an appearance, he laid down a somewhat impossible condition as a preliminary to any talks with them: the insistence that the Jong be handed over within forty-eight hours so that, as he put it, 'there may be no risk of further attack on the Commissioner'.[40] Actually, as the Tibetans did not comply, the Jong was assaulted and taken. Thereafter, for a few days, Younghusband's efforts to get in touch with the Ta Lama proved futile.[41]

Whether the negotiations with the Ta Lama, the Grand Secretary and the Shapes would have succeeded if the Tibetans had not been required to evacuate the Jong is a moot point. For, other things apart there was always the Amban, profuse with his promises, yet refusing to stir out of Lhasa on one pretext or another. Could the Commissioner, in his then tone and temper, have condescended to talk to the Tibetans, to the exclusion of the Chinese? Even if he did, would the Tibetans, have come to brass tacks—or to use a crude expression, 'talked business?' Necessarily some of these queries belong to the realm of speculation. And however one may answer, the fact remains that HMG had shifted their ground considerably—despite the critics' oft-repeated charge of their seeming immobility—since the Mission first assembled in Khamba, just about a year earlier. In fact, as the following chapters reveal, their main interest was now focused on the terms of the final settlement with Tibet. And thus quite obviously they had reconciled themselves to the inevitability of an advance to Lhasa.

Notes

1. Immediately after the crossing of the Jelap-la, early in January, Lt. Hadow recorded in his *Diary* (entry of Tuesday, January 5) 'Colonel Younghusband arrived early, had a talk with him. No chance at present of going to Lhasa'.

2. Herein the records of the Mission's Diary at Khamba Jong, as later at Tuna and Gyantse, are instructive.

3. Tibet Papers, *op.cit.*, Cd. 1920, No. 158, p. 306.

4. *Ibid.*, No. 166, p. 309.

5. Younghusband to Curzon, letter, February 3, 1904. Curzon MSS.

6. *Ibid.*, Younghusband to Curzon, letter, June 18, 1904.

7. *Ibid.*, Younghusband to Curzon, letter, May 31, 1904

8. *Ibid.*, Younghusband to Curzon, letter, February 3, 1904.

    In a letter to Sir Hugh Barnes, Lt. Governor of Burma, on February 27 (1904) *Ibid.*, Lord Curzon wrote: 'I have the best authority for saying that, had we delayed much longer (in going to Tibet), the Russians would have been securely installed....' One would imagine that the Viceroy's 'best authority' was none other than Younghusband himself.

9. *Ibid.* Curzon to Younghusband, letter, January 23,1904. Curzon explained himself at length. 'In the eyes of HMG', he told Younghusband, 'we had gone to Tibet not because of Dorjieff or the Mission to Livadia, or the Russian rifles to Lhasa', but because of Tibetan violation of our frontiers and of the earlier Convention. Besides, the Russians had officially denied any intrigues or diplomatic intentions with regard to

Tibet. Uncharitable critics, he warned the Commissioner, were bound to say that it was because the British, were 'obsessed' with the 'Russian nightmare' and wanted to get to Lhasa before they (Russians) did that lay at the bottom of their policy and that 'the infringement of the Treaty etc.' is 'so much humbug'.

10. Younghusband MSS., No. 27, February 5. 1904. To his father, Younghusband referring to Curzon's letter called it 'rather admonitory' in tone, yet expressed the view that he would like a 'philosophical dissertation' from him (Curzon) as an old friend 'rather than official from the Foreign Office'. In an earlier letter, even before he had started for Khamba Jong, Younghusband had expressed his clear conviction 'and my own idea is that I shall have much more delicate work in managing them (Home Government) than with the Chinese and Tibetans. I shall have to carry them with me step by step'. *Ibid.*, No. 5, June 16, 1903.

11. *Ibid.*, letter, February 3, 1904

12. *Ibid.*, letter, January 1, 1904. Herein Younghusband sought to write 'freely to Your Excellency as between two workers for the good of the Empire who look not merely to its purely selfish interests, but who believe England has a high name to make in the history of the world and hard duties to perform in fulfilling its destiny of advancing the welfare of the human race'.

13. *Supra*, n. 11.

14. Younghusband to Curzon, letter, May 15, 1904. Curzon MSS.

15. *Ibid.*, Younghusband to Curzon, letter, May 7, 1904. It may be recalled here that the Tibetan attack on the Commissioner's camp at Chang Lo (near Gyantse) had taken place on May 5 and that Colonel Brander was engaged with the Tibetans at Karo-la on May 6.

16. Younghusband to Ampthill, letter, May 5, 1904, Ampthill Papers, *op.cit.*

17. *Ibid.*, Ampthill to Younghusband, letter, May 2, 1904.

18. Younghusband to Curzon, letter, May 15, 1904, Curzon MSS. In this letter Younghusband told Lord Curzon that he felt 'depressed' over a number of things that had happened— 'above all because of the warning from Ampthill which the Secretary of State had asked him to give me'.

19. Younghusband to Ampthill, letter, May 11, 1904. Ampthill Papers, *op.cit.*

20. Ampthill to Brodrick, letter, August 31, 1904. Perceval Landon, of the *Times*, on his way back home had met Ampthill and told him that 'trials and isolation had a strange effect on the Mission' and that it was 'quite a revelation to me' to find how men behave. Ampthill Papers, *op.cit.*

21. *Ibid.*, Brodrick to Ampthill, letter, May 6, 1904.

22. *Loc. cit*, With Curzon in London, Brodrick wrote. 'Younghusband will not then want for a friend'. On his own, Ampthill told Younghusband that though the latter would miss 'Lord Curzon's powerful support and personal influence' these would soon be exercised 'in personal consultation with Ministers' in England. *Ibid.*, Ampthill to Younghusband, letter, May 2, 1904.

23. *Supra*, Chapter 16.

24. Ampthill to Brodrick, letter, May 25, 1904. Ampthill Papers, *op.cit.*
    The acting Viceroy did not regard Younghusband as being 'impatient under restraint', but one who had 'displayed considerable patience and endurance'.

25. In a letter to Ampthill on July 1, after attending a meeting of the Cabinet in which Tibet was discussed, Curzon wrote that (in regard to Tibet) 'there are practically' three schools of thought, 'the extreme' being represented by Younghusband. He himself,

however subscribed to what Curzon called 'the less extreme' school.

26. Tibet Papers, *op.cit.*, Cd. 2370, Part I, No. 2, pp. 1-2.
   Gyantse was reached on April 11, the despatch telegraphed on April 22. Younghusband to Curzon, letter, April 16, 1904, Curzon MSS.

27. *Ibid.*, Younghusband to Curzon, letter, April 25, 1904.
   On April 30, the Commissioner wrote to Curzon much in the same strain: 'It is getting more certain every day' that we shall never make a settlement 'till we go to Lhasa'. *Ibid.* See also Younghusband to Ampthill, letter, May 5, 1904, wherein he railed against 'those selfish, filthy, lecherous' Lamas whom he was 'determined to smash'. Ampthill Papers, *op.cit.*

28. *Ibid.*, Brodrick to Ampthill, letter, April 22, 1904.

29. *Ibid.*, Godley qualified his statement by saying 'You may be quite sure that the Cabinet won't agree if they can possibly help it'. Godley to Ampthill, letter, May 6, 1904.

30. Tibet Papers, *op.cit.*, Cd. 2370, Part I, No. 7, pp. 3-4.

31. In private, Godley wrote to Ampthill: 'You will do well to bear in mind the fact that the Government are most unwilling to go a step beyond what is absolutely necessary.... The telegram of the 12th authorizing the advance, was drafted not in this office but in the Cabinet, and the reference to the telegram of November 6 was exactly what I expected....' Godley to Ampthill, letter, May 13, 1904, Ampthill Papers, *op.cit.*

32. *Ibid.*, Brodrick to Ampthill, letter, May 13, 1904.

33. Younghusband to Curzon, letter, May 15, 1904. Curzon MSS.

34. Godley to Ampthill, letter, June 9, 1904. Warning the acting Viceroy against reading too much in Lord Hardwick's (then Under Secretary of State for India) answer to questions in the House of Lords, Godley told him that in the Cabinet discussion a few days previously, 'the dominant note was a strong determination to adhere to the telegram of November 6'.

35. Tibet Papers, *op.cit.*, Cd. 2370, Part I, No. 14, p. 7.

36. *Ibid.*, No. 32, p. 12.

37. Younghusband told his father that he was 'greatly' pleased when the Lhasa General refused to accept his ultimatums—but a little later, 'the cussed chap has just sent asking to have them'. The Commissioner 'declined to send them again'. in fact, kept them 'as a curiosity' though he feared 'this will probably make Government hedge in again'. Nearly a week later, he reported: Government got rather stuffy because I was in no hurry to send in that beastly ultimatum'. He was ordered 'virtually recalling me to Chumbi'. Later learning 'I had delivered' the ultimatums Government informed him he might stay at Gyantse, 'if I liked'. Younghusband, however, refused to retract. Younghusband MSS., Nos. 40 and 41, June 3 and 11, 1904.

38. Tibet Papers. *op.cit.*, Cd. 2370, Part I, No. 52, p. 17. On June 23 Younghusband writing to his father from Kangma, on his way back to Gyantse told him 'news just came in that Tibet negotiators are coming to see me. I only hope it is true'. Younghusband MSS., No. 43.

39. In fact, Younghusband had been smarting for the lack of latitude given him 'in managing the Tibetan business'. Younghusband to Curzon, letter, May 15, 1904, Curzon MSS.

40. Tibet Papers. *op.cit.*, Cd. 2370, No. 75, p. 25.

41. *Ibid.*, No. 83, p.28

YOUNGHUSBAND IN LHASA, THE CONVENTION AND AFTER

18
Negotiations and their Scope: Preliminary Exchanges between Calcutta and Whitehall

From its very inception there had been little doubt in Lord Curzon's mind, or for the matter of that in the Home Government's, as to the exact nature and scope of his Tibetan policy. That the Viceroy wanted to plant a British army in Lhasa, that he would have a permanent (British) Agent stationed in the (Tibetan) capital was fairly well known, even to the most uninitiated. His real difficulty was to goad an unwilling, panic-stricken, Cabinet at home into accepting what Godley aptly called the popular facet of a 'strong' forward policy, 'without facing fairly the unpopular and disagreeable' side thereof.[1] How, in the process of its actual implementation, and despite the Viceroy pulling at his hardest, the transformation took place to something considerably short of the ideal, provides a fascinating study albeit one that demands careful analysis.

Long before Curzon became Viceroy, or even entered his political stewardship under Lord Salisbury, he had written about 'the semi-scientific, semi-political' expeditions of the Russian explorer Prjevalski to the Tibetan interior, of politics being 'cloaked and disguised under the garb of Science'. He had also expressed a clear conviction that should the Russian ever enter Lhasa 'he (Prjevalsky) would not leave it without some sort of treaty in his pocket'.[2] Should not Curzon, now Viceroy of Her Britannic Majesty's Indian Empire, go one better?

It is on record that as early as March 30 (1899) Curzon had suggested 'the option' of sending a British official to visit, and to reside at Phari, which he was keen should be opened as a trade mart in place of Yatung.[3] Again, while attempting direct negotiations with the Tibetans, in July that year, he had hinted at paying them 'direct' and 'liberally' for any rights which they (Tibetans) might grant or concede in the Chumbi Valley.[4] Later still, and long before the Younghusband Mission was conceived, the Viceroy had spelt out his views—'very much in advance', as he later told the Secretary of State[5]—regarding a Tibetan settlement, and in no vague or uncertain terms either. Thus in a letter to Lord George Hamilton on June 1 (1901),

> Nothing can or will be done with the Tibetans until they are frightened. I should at once move a few men up to the frontier, I would chase out the Tibetans from the corner of British territory. I would build up the frontier pillars... if they resisted these proceedings... I would step across and occupy the Chumbi valley just beyond... By this time the Dalai Lama, and his men...would probably offer to negotiate. Yes, I would say, by all means but only at Lhasa. Then perhaps...we could discuss what should be the character of the new arrangements.[6]

And as for the 'new arrangement', he talked, in a subsequent communication of securing 'commercial-political facilities' for the adequate safeguarding of 'British interests'.[7]

Here, it may be noticed, the outlines were fairly broadly sketched out. Curzon 'would not dream' of referring to China, whose suzerainty he regarded, nor without reason, as 'a farce and an obstacle'. As for Tibet itself, he wanted it to be 'a sort of buffer state between the Russian and Indian empires' for he would hate to have 'a second Afghanistan' on the north, a viewpoint that was apparently inconsistent for Afghanistan already was a buffer state.

Hamilton must have been shaken and most rudely too. He termed Curzon's proposals 'somewhat aggressive' and wondered if the Viceroy's impending 'threats (for the purpose of negotiating at Lhasa) might not accelerate 'the declaration of a Russian protectorate over Tibet'.[8] A week later, he summed up his proconsul's terms as tantamount 'practically' to an invasion of Tibetan territory, with the object of 'concluding at Lhasa' a treaty to put 'our relations for the future on a better foundation'.[9]

One thing is obvious. Without putting any 'sinister connotation' on his words as the Viceroy later unfairly charged Hamilton with doing, Curzon's chief objective was neither 'grazing rights' nor 'boundary pillars', much leas 'trade in tea'. These it may be recalled, were put forth as the ostensible objectives of the Mission in the Secretary of State's despatch which finally launched Younghusband.[10] Thus it is not without significance that in February (1902) the Viceroy had openly aired in an official despatch, the Sikkim Political Officer's suggestion about occupying the Chumbi Valley 'until the Tibetans agree to a conference at Lhasa'.[11] A few days later he was frank enough to admit that in Tibet it was 'not the frontier itself' that was 'at issue';[12] in August, he held forth the assurance of taking Lhasa 'within 2-3 months';[13] in November, he showed a strong determination not to withdraw his proposed Mission (for 'go it would') which was to be accompanied by 'a sufficient force to ensure its safety'.[14] Again, in his well-known despatch of January 8, of the year following, to which a detailed reference has been made elsewhere, Lord Curzon had clearly indicated that however useful White's trip along the Sikkim-Tibet border may have been, this 'annual re-assertion of authority' as he called it, would not put

Government in a position 'to exercise much pressure upon the Tibetans'. Any negotiations about the fixation of the border, he had dismissed as 'a minor point'. For clearly to him the problem was not 'the mere settlement of a border dispute' nor even the 'amelioration of our future trading relations', but what he called 'the question of our entire future political relationship'. The negotiations at Lhasa, which he envisaged in these proposals were to culminate in the appointment of a permanent British representative, consular or diplomatic, to reside at the Tibetan capital.[15]

Curzon's proposals were, as was noticed in another context, rejected by the Cabinet. Red with rage, the Viceroy termed the latter 'foolish',[16] its logic 'extraordinary', its policy imbued with this 'inveterate flabbiness, this incurable timidity',[17] nor did he as a result deviate from pressing his own course of action with all his might. In brief, a decision was taken—which His Excellency accepted with ill-grace—not to associate 'the commencement of negotiations with the despatch of a Mission to Lhasa'. 'That could be done later', the Secretary of State explained, should the Tibetans prove recalcitrant.[18]

However limited in scope its start, the Younghusband Mission was born. Yet from the first, the Viceroy did not camouflage his immediate goals, much less his long-range objectives. Indeed there had been little, if any, change in his thinking. In his more formal despatch, the Governor-General again suggested that the stationing of a British representative at Lhasa would be 'the best security' for any trade concessions; though grudgingly he may agree to Gyantse as 'a suitable alternative'. He, however, stuck tenaciously to the view that a British representative on the farther side of the northern passes, could 'communicate' promptly with the Tibetan capital, but if there be any obstruction, 'it will be necessary to resort to the alternative of moving him (Agent) forward to Lhasa'.[19]

In private, Curzon could afford to be more outspoken:

My inclination is to take a very strong line in negotiations and to frighten the Chinese and the Tibetans into the acceptance of Gyantse by offering this as the only alternative to a representative at Lhasa itself. They will be so ready to bribe us out of the latter proposal that they may concede the former.[20]

Once again, the Cabinet shot down, and ruthlessly, his proposals—the bases he had mapped out for negotiations with Tibet's lamas. Here Hamilton's words were clear and left little room for doubt:

I had some trouble in this Office...as the majority of the Political Committee were strongly opposed to the location of any Agent in Tibet...Lansdowne disliked the idea of an agent at Gyantse...But the Cabinet were unanimous and immovable in their opposition to the proposal to establish an Agent... I tried to come to a compromise but that modified suggestion met with equal opposition....the Cabinet were disinclined to contemplate coercion...[21]

Not for the first time, Lord Curzon lambasted his political masters at home with 'the bogeys' that allegedly 'dominated their imagination'. He was sure the Home Government had got 'its tail down' and that to its over-wrought nerves 'mole-hills assume the dimensions of mountains, and spectral apparitions fill the air'[22]. In any case, in its despatch of May 23, Whitehall spelt out as well as it could its terms as to the exact scope and content of the negotiations at Khamba Jong—and what a wide chasm yawned between it and its accredited representative in India.

Refusing to broadbase the talks beyond 'questions concerning trade relations, the frontier and grazing rights', the Secretary of State warned the Viceroy,

....they (Home Government) desire that no proposal should be made for the establishment of a Political Agent, either at Gyantse or at Lhasa. Such a political outpost might entail difficulties and responsibilities incommensurate, in the judgement of His Majesty's Government, with any benefits which, in the circumstances now known to exist, could be gained by it...HMG are unwilling to be committed, by threats accompanying the proposals which may be made, to any definite course of compulsion to be undertaken in future. They authorise you then, subject to the conditions above stated, to communicate with the Chinese Resident and Tibetan representative...[23]

As if to underline the gravity of the situation, and there could be little doubt about the seriousness with which the Home Government viewed it, Godley confided in Curzon that the matter was settled 'entirely over the heads of us permanent officials' and that he 'didn't even see' the last telegram until 'it had been marked for despatch'.[24]

Beaten, Curzon manfully refused to cry 'defeat'. Thus a close scrutiny of the 'instructions' for Colonel Younghusband, prior to his departure for Khamba Jong, reveal vividly the working of the Viceroy's mind. To highlight a few points, how important to his Government was the demarcation of the 'frontier'? Art. 4 of Younghusband's 'instructions' read in part:

....a strict insistence on the line of frontier stipulated for in the Convention of 1890 is, perhaps, not essential to the interests of the Indian Government or of the Sikkim Durbar....

As for 'grazing rights',

The question...is not one of great importance. It appears that at present certain mutual grazing rights exist on either side of the border...

Or, was it the establishment of trade marts? HMG, Art. 6 continues,

have decided that we should not press for the appointment of a Political Agent at Lhasa or Gyantse, but if the new trade mart at the latter place is not to be reduced to a nullity from the start, and if any real advance is to be made in our commercial relations with Tibet, it should be possible to secure the application to Gyantse of the provision in Clauses I and II of the Regulations of 1893 under which it was agreed that the Government of India should be free to send officers to reside at Yatung to watch the conditions of the British trade at that mart....[25]

Two comments may be in order. One, the 'Instructions' were drawn on June 3, i.e. after Lord George Hamilton's telegram of May 28 had been received. Two, Younghusband's testimony as to the Viceroy's early views—and his own approximated closely to the Governor-General's—should make clear how far apart

Lord Curzon stood from his political superiors at home. The Viceroy had indeed wanted 'from the first', Younghusband wrote twenty-five years later, 'to send the Mission to Lhasa and to establish a representative permanently there. But this was too much for the Home Government. All they would sanction was the despatch of a Mission to the nearest place inside Tibet.[26] And 'with this half, or rather quarter measure Lord Curzon had for the time to be content'.[27]

As for himself, on the eve of his departure for Khamba Jong. the Commissioner conceived the task to be no mean one:

> I am not to go to Lhasa itself as far as is present settled,...but what I have to do is as important. I have to try and induce the Tibetans and Chinese to allow a permanent British Agent in Lhasa if possible or at any rate in some town in Tibet. I have to put our trade relations with Tibet upon a proper footing and I have to settle the boundary between us.[28]

Notes

1. Godely to Ampthill, letter, May 19, 1904 Ampthill Papers, *op.cit.*
   The unpopular side was 'the necessary expenditure, with its possible result of increased taxation'.
2. Curzon, Russia in Asia, *op.cit.*, p. 252. The young author had also talked of the Dalai Lama who 'with a little war between England and Tibet dragging its tedious length along', would find it 'politic to make a breach in the Chinese wall of exclusion...in favour of the one nation whose rivalry with England might enable them to give him a *quid pro quo*'. The obvious allusion was to Czarist Russia. The 'little war' between England and Tibet, referred to hostilities between the two countries in 1888-89.
3. Tibet Papers, *op.cit.* Cd. 1920, No. 26, pp. 74-75.
4. In a communication addressed to the Chief Secretary, Bengal, July 26, 1899. *Ibid.*, Encl. 4, in No. 29, pp. 108-9. It will be recalled that initially the Political Officer in Sikkim was an official of the Bengal Government.
5. Curzon complained that he had 'suffered somewhat from my readiness to let you always know in advance—often very much in advance—exactly what is passing in my mind'. Curzon to Hamilton, letter, July 31, 1901, Hamiltons Papers, *op.cit.*
6. *Ibid.*, Curzon to Hamilton, letter, June 11, 1901.
7. Government of India's despatch of July 25, 1901, Tibet Papers, *op.cit.*, Cd. 1920, No. 37, pp. 118-19.
8. Hamilton to Curzon, letter, July 4, 1901, Hamilton Papers. *op.cit.*
9. *Ibid.*, letter, July 11, 1901.
10. *Supra,* Chapter 11.
11. Despatch of February 13, 1902, Tibet Papers, *op.cit.* Cd. 1920, No. 44, pp. 125-27. The Governor-General added, however, that he was not 'at present' thinking of occupying the valley, but this might become necessary if 'the attitude of permanent hostility', displayed by the Tibetans persisted.
12. Curzon to Hamilton, letter, February 18, 1902, Hamilton Papers, *op.cit.*
13. *Ibid.*, Curzon to Hamilton, letter, May 28, 1902.
14. *Ibid.*, Curzon to Hamilton, letter, August 20, 1902.
15. For a detailed discussion, *Supra*, Chapter 11.
16. Curzon to Hamilton. letter, February 12, 1903, Hamilton Papers. *op.cit.*

17. *Ibid.*, Curzon to Hamilton, letter, March 12, 1903. In a letter to Godley, April 1 (1903), Curzon wrote that Balfour's approach to problems was 'utterly academic', which fact 'takes the breath away' from the 'startled' official. Curzon MSS.

18. *Ibid.*, Hamilton to Curzon, letter, April 8, 1903.

19. Tibet Papers, *op.cit.;* Cd. 1920 No 89, pp. 190-91. The despatch is dated May 7, 1903.

20. Curzon to Hamilton, letter, May 7, 1903. Hamilton Papers, *op.cit.*
    Earlier (letter of April 13), Curzon told the Secretary of State that to the question whether he was satisfied with the Home Government's decision, he would return the answer 'Emphatically, No!' He warned the Secretary of State against dropping 'all suspicions' and, in fact, advised him to persist with an attitude of 'ceaseless vigilance'. Reference was to Russian designs on Tibet.

21. *Ibid.*, Hamilton to Curzon, letter, May 28, 1903.

22. *Ibid.*, Curzon to Hamilton, letter, June 4, 1903.

23. Tibet Papers, *op.cit.,* Cd. 1920, No. 92, p. 192.

24. The Permanent Under-Secretary also told Curzon that the Cabinet spoke 'with no uncertain voice', that they were 'nervous' and 'evidently will not agree to any effective coercion', Godley to Curzon, May 29, 1903, Curzon MSS.

25. Tibet Papers, *op.cit.,* Cd. 1920, Encl. 6 in No. 99, pp. 198-200.
    The 'instructions' are in the form of a letter addressed officially to 'Major F. E. Younghusband, C.I.E., on Special duty', dated Simla, June 3rd 1903. Younghusband's promotion to the temporary rank of Colonel was gazetted in London on June 26, his first letter, as 'British Commissioner, Tibet Frontier Commission' is addressed from Gangtok (Sikkim) on June 22. On the eve of the Commission's departure for Gyantse (December 10, 1903) Colonel Younghusband's title was changed to 'British Commissioner for Tibet Frontier Matters'. *Ibid.*, Encls. 5 and 6 in No. 129, p. 223 and No. 155, p. 305.

26. It is interesting that before the official instructions, and his own appointment, Younghusband had written to his father that he was 'to go up from Darjeeling through Sikkim to a place called Khamba Jong and afterwards perhaps to Gyantse'. Younghusband MSS., No. 3, May 21, 1903.

27. Younghusband, The Light of Experience, *op.cit.*, p. 81. Curzon's own views, of course, on the telegram of May 28 (1903) were best expressed in his frank avowal to Godley that 'we enter the arena with our hands tied behind our backs by HMG'. Curzon to Godley, letter, July 8, 1903, Curzon MSS.
    Younghusband's 'personal view' was to have 'resumed the proceedings where we had left them when we drove the Tibetans across our border, and had again advanced into the Chumbi Valley, and stopped there till we had effected a properly recognized and lasting settlement'. This course would have better settled the local question, and would have avoided 'much subsequent international complications'. Younghusband, India and Tibet, *op.cit.*, pp. 93-94.

28. Younghusband MSS., No. 3, May 21, 1903.

19
Negotiations and their Scope : HMG's Final 'Diktat'

Not content with the 'half or quarter measure' which the Home Government had conceded, the Viceroy continued to press for more. The four-month halt, and stalemate, at Khamba Jong was followed by mounting pressure to move forward to Gyantse. It has been noticed, in an earlier chapter, how the telegram of October 1 (1903) by Lord George Hamilton sanctioning the advance was later qualified by HMG in its more stringent, if somewhat illogical and contradictory, pronouncement of November 6.[1] Since the latter was to play an important role in the final settlement, it may be worthwhile to reproduce its exact text:

> They (HMG) are, however, clearly of opinion that this step (advance to Gyantse) should not be allowed to lead to occupation or to permanent intervention in any from. The advance should be made for the sole purpose of obtaining satisfaction, and as soon as reparation is obtained, a withdrawal should be effected. While HMG consider the proposed action to be necessary they are not prepared to establish a permanent Mission in Tibet, and the question of enforcing trade facilities in that country must be considered in the light of the decision contained in this telegram.

Curzon tore the logic of this communication to pieces.[2] The object of the Mission, he insisted, was to negotiate a new convention, not to obtain reparation. And 'what reparation'? He reminded the Secretary of State that HMG were ignorant of the fact that the Government of India already possessed, and could exercise 'without protest', the right to establish 'a permanent Mission in Tibet'. Of his own *bona fide*—and obviously this was now increasingly suspect at home—he offered the most categorical assurances. He was 'not in the least anxious', he thundered, for any *coup de theatre* in Tibet, nor in any 'frontier fighting', much less in an 'extension of the frontiers of the empire'.[3]

In any case, for the present Lord Curzon was content to bide his time, and wait for a further opportunity. He was certain in his own mind that events will be on his side—and therefore, he would not 'jeopardize' his policy and frighten the authorities at home either by showing his hand 'too plainly' or by 'dragging in Lhasa before Lhasa is required'.[4] The fighting at Guru, as later at Gyantse, however removed many of the obvious embarrassments which he and his Government had often felt in the past.

Soon, however, an element of considerable urgency was injected into the situation. After a long and fateful struggle with the Prime Minister and the Cabinet, and initially the King had entered strong objections, Lord Curzon had been able to obtain a few months' leave to rest and recuperate at home.[5] Originally due back in September, the Viceroy was actually away from April 30 to December 13, 1904, a period that synchronized with the end of his first term in office and before the resumption of his second. He was determined, while away, to keep firmly in his hand all the major threads of policy and leave Lord Ampthill, his temporary replacement little, if any, initiative.[6] He had hoped, as everyone else did, that by his presence in England he would be able to exercise much greater influence on the framing of policy, being then at its very fount and pivot.[7] On the eve of his departure, therefore, in a private letter to Younghusband, he dilated considerably on the eventual shape which a Tibetan settlement may take,

That we should permanently occupy the Chumbi Valley. What garrison will this require? Where should it be placed?

That we should have a British Agent somewhere in Tibet. You would probably prefer Lhasa... Is it possible to conceive of a native representative, possibly taken from a neighbouring Tribe or country?

That we should possess power of constant access to the Dalai Lama. Would it be a good idea that he (British Agent) should visit Lhasa once a year? Or should he keep a native vakil to transmit his correspondence at Lhasa?

That the new treaty should be signed by the Dalai Lama himself. If this be required, do you think that the Mission should go to Lhasa to do it? Or shall we bring down the Dalai Lama to meet me in the Autumn when I come back?[8]

It is interesting, and no doubt revealing, that at this stage Curzon was emphatic that the Government of India were 'still uncommitted' to the nature and scope of a Tibetan settlement, felt sure it (Government) 'must obtain absolute securities' that British 'retirement' is not followed by Russian 'advance', nor British 'ascendancy' replaced by Muscovite 'intrigue'.[9]

Younghusband who, through his long and somewhat enforced inactivity, if not hibernation after crossing the Jelap-la, must have turned these things over in his mind a thousand times now set forth his side of the case.

For the Agent, he met all the objections his detractors could raise and did not visualize 'any overwhelming disadvantage' in having him 'posted at Lhasa'. He even fixed the escort: '150 would be a suitable number...(These were to be) British soldiers and to include a cavalry escort and I would have 2 guns and 2 maxims'. The Agent, of course, 'should be British'.[10]

Determined to make out 'fuller demands', he promised to think out how the Russians could best be prevented 'from negotiating or intriguing with Tibet'.

The Convention must be signed either at Lhasa or by the Dalai Lama in India. 'Since show and personality' were of 'extreme importance' with orientals, 'Either Your Excellency must go to Lhasa or the Dalai Lama must go to India.'[11]

In his later communications Younghusband's tone, if anything, became increasingly strident—the scope of his demands too multiplied, and appreciably. He took it for granted that the Mission had to go to Lhasa and 'have an Agent there'. The terms too had to be dictated for that was the only way 'to settle' with 'these bumptious lamas' and face 'the unalterable fact' of Russian aid. As he conceived it, his attitude was to rest on the maxim of an open defiance. For, to the Tibetans he would say, 'J'y suis. J'y reste'.[12]

More formally, in May (1904), in a memorandum, the Commissioner had summed up his views on a Tibetan settlement, which were not materially different from those he had expressed earlier.[13] It may be of interest to mention here that Lord Ampthill's Government applied its seal of approval and incorporated these, without much change, in its despatch to the Secretary of State in June.[14] Meantime Lord Curzon, now in England, was pulling his full weight and canvassing all the support he could muster among the Cabinet to have his views accepted. These he later summed up in a (Cabinet) Memorandum.[15] As most of the points in Lord Ampthill's despatch were indentical with the views held by Lord Curzon, it may be relevant to underline only the most important.

A Resident at Lhasa, was to be demanded but failing this, an Agent was to be posted at Gyantse with the right of proceeding to the Tibetan capital to discuss matters with their officials, or the Amban. Younghusband was directed to apprise the authorities of his view 'after you have arrived at Lhasa', and until then Government were to reserve 'our final opinion'.

Formal recognition by the Tibetans of the exclusive political influence of the British was required. The Lamas were not to enter into relationship with any foreign power, or cede any portion of their country's territory to any such power, or to admit to Tibet any representative of this power, without previous British consent.

An indemnity was to be demanded, calculated at the rate of £ 100,000 a month, from the date (i.e., May 4) the Mission was attacked until one month after the signature of the Convention.

Until such time as the indemnity was paid, the occupation to the Chumbi Valley was required both 'as a security for fulfillment of treaty and for payment of indemnity'.

Without British permission, no arms were to be manufactured nor imported while all fortifications between the frontier and Lhasa were to be razed.

Trade marts were to be established at Gyantse, Shigatse, Lhasa and Gartok and, in the east, 'at such other places as may hereafter be found suitable'.

Details regarding the settlement of the Sikkim and Garhwal boundaries, customs duties and trade regulations were to be left over to later negotiations.[16]

Even as these terms were being debated, a good deal of private correspondence was exchanged between Lord Ampthill in India and the Secretary of State and once again the gulf that yawned between thinking at both ends came out in the open. Brodrick complained that,

> Curzon neither sees the disappointment caused by the development of the expedition nor the comparative flimsiness, as we think it, of the case which he would build up against Russia. It hardly seems sufficient to us to say that Dorjieff is a Russian representative, or that Russian rifles are found... the difference between us and Curzon is that we think battle can be better fought out in London than at Lhasa.[17]

Later, Godley confided to Ampthill as was noticed earlier, that the 'dominant note' in the Cabinet was 'a strong determination to adhere to the telegram of November 6'.[18] Besides, the expedition had proved to be 'ten times' more 'troublesome and prolonged' than what the Indian authorities had originally predicted, with the result that the Cabinet would be 'the reverse of anxious' to keep a Resident at Lhasa who 'might require constant support'.[19] On July 1, after Curzon had presented his viewpoint to the Cabinet, Brodrick wrote back at length about his (Curzon's) 'unchanged' views which were 'practically different on all points'[20] from those held by HMG who

> look upon the whole matter as a question between us and Russia (and) would not make a large annual sacrifice in keeping an Agent with a proper support in Tibet in order to force the Tibetans to a trade which they do not desire.... they (Cabinet) are determined to go to Lhasa .... on the ground laid down in our telegram on the 6th November 1903—to obtain satisfaction and reparation. ... our main point is to re-establish our prestige and to make it clear to Russia that we will not surrender our freedom in Tibet to them. In our judgment the mere fact of a British force marching to Lhasa and slaughtering a great number of Tibetans on the way ought even without a treaty to establish our claims and show our power. The occupation of the Chumbi Valley which however little it may annoy Tibet, will be some guarantee...that we mean business...

Reverting again to Curzon and underlining the fact that his viewpoint illustrated 'more clearly' than any other 'the divergence of opinion' between HMG and the late Viceroy, Brodrick pointed out: 'It was freely urged against him...that we would sooner have punishment with no ulterior liability than a Convention with all the liability attaching to it....'[21]

Godley on his part underscored the fact that Curzon's encounter with HMG must have made him 'realise for the first time' what he (Godley) had tried to impress upon him 'during the winter and spring' namely 'the very strong feelling in the breasts of HMG against anything like a forward policy in Tibet.'[22]

Curzon, however, refused to budge. Apart from the stationing of the resident, he had demanded 'much more stringent terms' all along the line. Not surprisingly, HMG was torn between the 'conflicting desire' to get as much as we can for the expedition' on the one hand, and not to lay down proposals that will mean 'an immediate renewal' of it on the other.[23] Taking into account these varied claims, and counter-claims, the Cabinet fromulated its polity at its meeting of July 6 which the Secretary of State later spelt out in a long telegram to India.

On the non-controversial side, while broadly agreeing with the Government of Lord Ampthill on Britain's exclusive political influence in Tibet, Mr. Brodrick suggested that regulations regarding trade and the levying of customs duties should be on the general lines of those attached to the Convention of 1890.

Furthermore, fortifications between the frontier and the point which the Mission may have reached in its advance. were to be demolished. On three points which were undoubtedly the linchpin of the Viceroy's scheme, his replies were sharply categroical and countary to the suggestions made by Simla. Thus,

(a) Neither at Lhasa, nor elsewhere, was a Resident to be asked for;

(b) In regard to the indemnity, the sum to be demanded should not exceed an amount 'which, it is believed it will be within the power of the Tibetans to pay', by instalments if neccessary, spread over three years. 'Colonel Younghusband', the Secretary of State however emphasized, ' will be guided by circumstances in this matter';

(c) The occupation of the Chumbi Valley, which was to be the security for the payment of the indemnity and for the fulfillment of conditions in regard to the opening of the trade marts, was to continue 'till the payment of the indemnity shall have been completed', or the marts opened effectively for three years, 'whichever is the latest'.

In regard to the trade marts, Mr. Brodrick limited the number to two : Gyantse, in addition to Yatung. At each place Tibetans were required to maintain an Agent who was to receive such letters as were sent to him by his British counterpart and was to be 'responsible for the delivery of these (letters) to the Tibetan authorities as well as to the Chinese and for transmission of their replies'.[24]

In a long letter to the Secretary of State, Curzon, then in England, subjected these provisions to an exhaustive and critical examination, suggested detailed amendments, and pin-pointed 'three omissions'. He had no doubt that a treaty that did not provide for the stationing of a British Officer will be 'ineffective'. He feared that if trade with Tibet was to be restricted only to a particular route 'you will find this one strangled and all others closed, and that if the Chumbi Valley ('if you have once occupied it') were to be evacuated 'your treaty will be doomed'. As for the omissions, he reminded Mr. Brodrick that the Giaogong boundary rectifications were necessary, so were 'reciprocal' facilities for 'trade, travel and settlement' of British Indian subjects in Tibet as also safeguards against Russian infiltration 'industrial, mining and commercial concessions'.

Curzon regretted that the terms, as laid down, will neither 'repay' the Government of India, 'for the sacrifices' it had made, much less be of 'lasting value'. Nor was he sure whether his views will carry 'conviction', for he bemoaned the fact that he had never been 'so fortunate' as to carry HMG with him 'at any stage of the Tibetan proceedings'.[25]

Apart from Curzon, Lord Ampthill too suggested some modifications. He desired, in particular, to expand the meaning and scope of the exclusive political influence which the British were to demand suggesting that the conditions against the cession of Tibetan territory should be amplified 'in the usual manner', while some others be secured by 'express stipulations'. He also pressed for the opening of a 'subordinate mart' at Gartok.[26] Two days later, he reverted to the subject and wondered whether the provision regarding the British Trade Agent's proceeding to Lhasa may not be made 'one of the more stringent terms to be exacted should the Mission be opposed'—and added that Younghusband had desired that this 'be included' in the Convention.[27]

As a result of 'your communication and Curzon's', Brodrick wrote to Lord Ampthill, HMG were 'getting into shape' a modified set of instructions.[28] These 'improved terms' were spelt out in the Secretary of State's telegram of July 26, and later elaborated in his despatch of August 5. Both marked a decisive change in the earlier instruction of July 6; more specifically on the question of the new trade marts to be opened as also the precise scope of Great Britain's exclusive political influence. In both cases, it would appear, HMG now veered round to the position taken by Lord Ampthill, and even that of Lord Curzon—a fact of which the latter was not unaware.[29]

On the fundamentals, however, there was no change, tacit or implied. Thus the Resident was declared to be neither necessary, nor even desirable, and Lord George Hamilton's authority was adduced in support of the view that such a political outpost 'might entail difficulties and responsibilities incommensurate with any benefits which may accrue from it'. As for the right of the Agent at Gyantse to proceed to Lhasa this, the Secretary of State thought, 'would be to alter the character of the duties of the Agent...(and) to assimilate them to those of a Political Resident'.

In regard to the indemnity, his 'ignorance' of the resources of the country would make it hard to fix a specific sum. The amount, however, while constituting an 'adequate pecuniary guarantee' should not be such as to be 'beyond the power of the Tibetans', by making sufficient efforts, 'to discharge within the period named (i.e., three years)'.[30]

Another effort to secure a modification of these terms was made on August 1. Lord Ampthill asked the Secretary of State whether, 'having regard to the further opposition' offered by the Tibetans (during the advance of the Mission from Gyantse to Lhasa), he would not consent to the right of the Agent at Gyantse proceeding to the Tibetan capital being incorporated in the revised terms?[31] India Office, however, refused to relent and merely contented itself with a re-affirmation of its earlier position.[32]

Here then matters finally stood. Younghusband was unhappy and distraught beyond words. One can almost picture him up there at 14,000 feet, attacked at close quarters, under the strain of altitude, and with a pusillanimous military commander. The wonder is that he remained sane, and carried through an almost impossible task. On July 12, he confided to Curzon:

We are just starting for Lhasa but under rather depressing circumstances. The Home Government will not hear of our having a Resident there. The military say they cannot keep the Mission there for more than ¾ of an hour.... and as Government are asking such exceedingly moderate terms...what I am afraid in this business is doing only just enough to thoroughly arouse the hostility of the Tibetans...and not doing enough either to completely subdue them...or to attach them to us.[33]

From 'the tone of your recent telegram', Lord Ampthill wrote to the Commissioner on July 11, it would appear that,

You are dissatisfied and disappointed at the terms of settlement laid down by the Home Government. You do not think that you are being allowed to ask enough and you consider that all this trouble, toil, anxiety and expenditure ought to result in more substantial gains. You probably think that the Government of India share your views but they are also being checked and repressed by the Home Government.[34]

Curzon had fought his battles and, what with his own ill-health and Lady Curzon's, was in a highly agitated frame of mind. On July 8, he charged Ampthill with breach of faith, alleging that he (Ampthill) was only 'in partial sympathy' with the late Viceroy's views,

You contemplate with equanimity the retirement or failure of the expedition before it has accomplished the object for which it was sent...I now anticipate that our efforts and sacrifices will have been thrown away and if this be the consequence I shall have no other consolation than that I was completely devoid of responsibility...[35]

A week or so later, however, he felt much better. This, as may be surmised, was a result of Brodrick's 'improved terms'. 'We do not get all that I had pressed for',[36] Lord Curzon wrote, 'but we get a good deal and I hope to have made clear that we retain the power to post a British Officer or Officers at Gyantse ...I would have preferred a man at Lhasa...'[37]

But the scowl soon returned and on August 4 he severely lambasted the Secretary of State:

These telegrams are sent off without any reference to or consultation with me. HMG's policy about Tibet is not my policy. Indeed I regard it as entirely mistaken... The decision about the Chumbi Valley is, in my opinion, particularly inept. It is all due to that fatal telegram of November 6 to which Brodrick in particular had pinned his faith... Some future Government of India will pay a penalty for these blunders... The responsibility for which will doubtless be laid at my door.[38]

Lord Ampthill was far from happy with Curzon's diatribes though officially at any rate, he endorsed the policy of his predecessor.[39] It was no secret that he did at the same time, though in private, appear to be fairly well-satisfied with the terms laid down by the British Cabinet. In fact, he told Brodrick that he was 'really glad' that HMG had decided 'against having any British agent at Lhasa' and added that the terms of settlement which had been laid down were 'entirely in accordance with my personal views'. His Council too, though they would like 'to go a little further', were 'on the whole fairly contented with your terms'.[40]

Thus on the eve of the Mission's arrival in Lhasa, and its conduct of negotiations there, the picture as to the various actors in the drama over the terms on which a settlement was to be effected was pretty clear. Younghusband was a disgruntled man, under great strain, doing his best under constant physical dangers in a climate devastating to the nerves. Yet here was an unwilling instrument of a policy he completely repudiated and heartily disapproved for above all he felt certain it did not fit the local needs. Lord Curzon, his chief sponsor, principal informant and political mentor had made no secret of his complete disgust with HMG and its policy—and what is more let Younghusband know about it.[41] Ampthill in India, was playing a rather difficult game. He 'only a half-Viceroy' or a bare *locum tenens,* as Curzon would have him, had completely forfeited his (Curzon's) trust and confidence while the Commissioner, in direct and regular communication with the Viceroy on leave, scarcely confided in his (Ampthill's) political judgement.

The truly remarkable thing about the Lhasa convention, and the negotiations with the Tibetans, thus is not so much the terms incorporated therein—important though these be in their own right—as the circumstances and the background in which it came to be concluded and in which the parleys were conducted.

Notes

1. Referring to HMG's 'almost mystical faith in the lapidary status of the telegram of November 6', Colonel Peter Fleming makes the point that '…this directive was both vague and inconsequent in its more positive aspects. Taken literally (it implied) that a diplomatic mission with a specific purpose was now regarded in London as a punitive expedition with undefined objectives'. Peter Fleming , *op.cit.,* p. 95.

2. Writing years later, Younghusband referred to this 'curious' telegram which 'I never quite understood'. His indictment was severe: 'It is remarkable that a document which was so often quoted to the Russian Government, to the Indian Government, to the Chinese Government… should have described with so little precision the real purpose of the advance—and this at the culminating point of thirty years' effort on the part of the Government of India', Younghusband, India and Tibet, *op.cit.,* p. 141.

3. Curzon had confessed that he did not 'quite understand' the telegram of November 6, that 'the entire object of our Mission' was to enter upon a new Convention and

that 'we cannot retreat until that object has been attained'. Curzon to Brodrick, letter, November 7, 1903, Curzon MSS.

4. *Ibid.,* Curzon to Younghusband, letter, January 23, 1904.

5. For details, see Knollys to Sandars, May 26, 1903, and Balfour to Knollys, May 29, 1903. On the King's behalf his Secretary had written that 'His Majesty is still of opinion that the Viceroy should only be allowed to remain six weeks, or at the most two months', to which the Prime Minister had replied by recommending that 'his (Curzon's) plans should in substance be accepted'—and this 'in spite of Curzon's extraordinary behaviour and still more extraordinary' letter, at whose 'tone and temper' he (Balfour) confessed to 'being much disappointed'. *B.P., B.M.,* Vol. I.

6. See for instance Lord Ampthill's persistent complaints about serving 'two masters', about being only 'half a Viceroy'; of operating under a 'three-tier system'; of the common belief that 'nothing serious will be done until Lord Curzon's return from leave'. Ampthill to Brodrick, letters, July 27, July 13, and June 2, 1904. A reference should also be made to his (Ampthill's) letter to Godley, June 9, 1904. Ampthill Papers, *op.cit.*

7. On April 4 (1904) Curzon had written to Younghusband in a manner so characteristic of him, that after he goes on leave 'whatever is done will be done by the Cabinet in consultation with myself in England rather than by the Government of India who will be left behind'. Curzon to Younghusband, letter, April 4, 1904, Curzon MSS.

8. *Loc. cit.* In the same letter Curzon had invited Younghusband to apprise him of 'your own view of the state of affairs' and told him that, if he (Younghusband) did not 'catch me in India', he could 'continue to write to me while I am in England'.

9. *Loc. cit.*

10. Younghusband even discussed the names of Agents who would fill the bill. For himself he was not too keen, but as for Sir Hugh Barnes 'nothing could be better': albeit Irwin and O'Dwyer too 'would do capitally'. A man of the China Consular Service or someone 'associated with him for the purpose of tackling this Chinese Amban' was another basic desideratum.
Younghusband to Curzon, letter, April 16, 1904. Curzon MSS.

11. *Loc. cit.* Younghusband advocated the personal factor : 'If Your Excellency could personally meet' the Dalai Lama, nothing perhaps could produce 'better results'.

12. See for instance Younghusband's letters to Lord Curzon, of April 25, May 7 and May 15, and those to Lord Ampthill of June 4, 13 and 24. Also revealing are his letters to Dane, the Foreign Secretary, of June 16 and 18. The year, in all cases, is 1904.

13. Not in Cd. Papers. The Memorandum, however, formed an enclosure in the Commissioner's letter to Lord Curzon of May 27, Curzon MSS.

14. The telegram of June 26, is in Tibet Papers, *op.cit.,* Cd. 2370, No. 66, p. 22.

15. The 'Memorandum' was circulated among members of the Cabinet at their meeting on June 30 which Lord Curzon attended by invitation.

16. *Supra,* note 14.

17. Brodrick to Ampthill, letter, May 20, 1904, Ampthill Papers, *op.cit.*
Curzon who in the meanwhile had had 'long talks' with the Prime Minister and Landowne imploring them 'not to go on repeating these stupid and gratuitous pledges about Tibet', was trying in an herculean effort, to square the circle. Letter

to Ampthill, May 26, 1904, *Ibid.*

18. *Ibid.* Godley to Ampthill, letter, June 9, 1904. Curzon was to have attended this meeting but was 'too unwell', as he told Ampthill, to do so. He wanted 'to prepare' Government for 'a possibly somewhat prolonged occupation of Lhasa', for 'a British Agent somewhere' and against 'any more embarrassing pledges'. Curzon to Ampthill, letter, June 10, 1904.

19. *Ibid.,* Brodrick to Ampthill, letter, June 10, 1904.

20. Curzon too was getting increasingly disillusioned. He charged that the Cabinet were 'anxious to get out of the whole thing' and that they were mostly ignorant of anything 'but large and frequently incorrect generaliszations, and the discussion wanders about under imperfect control'. Curzon to Ampthill, letter, July 1, 1904. Curzon MSS.

21. Brodrick to Ampthill, letter, July 1, 1904, Ampthill, Papers, *op.cit.*
    This last point, Brodrick underlined, 'illustrates more clearly than any other the divergence of opinion between HMG and the late Viceroy'. The Secretary of State further told Ampthill that he was keen to convey the Cabinet view 'frankly' for 'the more you know of our feelings, the easier it will be for you to deal with your own Council'.

22. *Ibid.,* Godley to Ampthill, letter, July 1, 1904.

23. *Ibid.,* Brodrick to Ampthill, letter, July 15, 1904.

24. Tibet Papers, *op.cit.,* Cd. 2370, No. 77, pp. 26-27.

25. Curzon to Brodrick, letter, July 8, 1904, Curzon MSS. Curzon also reminded the Secretary of State that the latter's 'instructions' contained no provision consistent with HMG's despatch of February 27, 1903, wherein it was laid down that 'it is indispensable that British influence should be recognized at Lhasa in such a manner as to render it impossible for another power to exercise a pressure on the Tibetan Government inconsistent with the interests of British India'. A copy of the above formed an enclosure to Curzon's letter to Ampthill of the same date.

26. Tibet Papers, *op.cit.,* Cd. 2370, No. 88, p. 30. The telegram was dated July 11 (1904).

27. *Ibid.,* No. 91, July 13, 1904. p. 31. It is interesting to note that both here and in the earlier telegram of July 11—as also the despatch of June 30—Ampthill was hiding his personal opinion in favour of official policy as laid down by Curzon and his Council. Thus in his letter to Brodrick on June 30 he confessed that in the matter of the Agent 'my personal opinion entirely accords with yours and I repeated your instructions to Colonel Younghusband without a qualm'. Later, on July 13, he told the Secretary of State that in regard to 'the terms of settlement' he had laid down, 'my personal views' were 'entirely in accord' with his (Brodrick's). Ampthill Papers, *op.cit.*

28. *Ibid.,* Brodrick to Ampthill, letter, July 15, 1904; Godley to Ampthill, letter, July 15, 1904.

29. A comparison of Art. 2 in Mr. Brodrick's telegrams of July 26 and of July 6, shows how far he had travelled in accepting the Viceroy's views. A comparison of Art. 5 in the two telegrams is also instructive : on July 6, the marts to be opened were only Yatung and Gyantse; on July 26 Gartok was added. Again, clause 5 (a) makes its first appearance in the latter telegram. By virtue of this clause, in

addition to Gyantse and Gartok, the Tibetan Government was required to undertake to consider 'the question of establishing fresh marts, if required by the development of trade'. In a letter to Ampthill on July 19, Curzon told him that his (Curzon's) own arguments added to 'the excellent and sometimes identical' suggestions made from India had not been 'without effect' as the 'revised instructions' from Whitehall will bear out. Curzon MSS.

30. Tibet Papers, *op.cit.*, Cd. 2370, Nos. 106 and 115, pp. 42-43.

31. *Ibid.*, No. 112, pp. 44-45. Knowing as one does Lord Ampthill's own views on the subject, it is interesting to reflect that the Acting Viceroy was merely echoing a policy he did not really believe in. Little wonder, it carried so little conviction in Whitehall.

32. *Ibid.*, No. 114, p. 45. The Secretary of State's telegram was dated August 3, 1904. The Secretary of State's views in his telegram of August 3 had been repeated to Younghusband and a draft Convention, 'as finally settled', was forwarded to him embodying those views on August 5. Tibet Papers, *op.cit.*, Cd. 2370, Encl. No. 233, p. 198, and annexure, pp. 198-200.

33. Younghusband to Curzon, letter, July 12, 1904, Curzon MSS. Herein the Commissioner revealed that he would feign act as a sort of 'protector' to the Tibetans, 'this would, of course, land us with fresh responsibilities... (but) by giving this assurance we may be able to bind the Tibetans to us'.

34. Ampthill to Younghusband, letter, July 11, 1904, Ampthill Papers, *op.cit.*
To Brodrick, the Acting Viceroy opened out more fully. He revealed that Younghusband had shown 'his dissatisfaction and disappointment' by telegraphing that he 'saw no point' in going to Lhasa:
'As he had to demand so little of the Tibetans and gave further indications of a desire to throw up the sponge... Younghusband is a great anxiety to me as he is so extremely touchy and self-opinionated and he has got into his head an idea that the Home Government are putting the drag on the Government of India...' *Ibid.* Ampthill to Brodrick, letter, July 13, 1904. Earlier to the same correspondent, Ampthill had talked of the Commissioner's 'occasional outbursts of self-opinionated ill-temper' (letter June 22, 1904) and Brodrick, in turn, of his (Younghusband's) being 'rather jumpy' (letter, June 17, 1904).

35. Curzon to Ampthill, letter, July 8, 1904, Curzon MSS. Actually, the starting point here was a letter, June 16, 1904, which Lord Ampthill had addressed to the King and in which he had, *inter alia*, expressed the view that 'personally' he held 'it would be better that the Mission should fail than that Your Majesty's Government should be exposed to a charge of breach of faith or that the resentment and hostility of Russia should be incurred'. Ampthill Papers, *op.cit.* Curzon had some inkling of this communication through Lord Knollys.

36. The obvious reference was to the 'instructions' then about to be issued by HMG.

37. Curzon to Ampthill, letter, July 19, 1904, Curzon MSS.

38. *Ibid.*, Curzon to Ampthill, letter, August 4, 1904. 'These telegrams', of course, refer to those of July 26 and August 3 sent by the Secretary of State to the Governor-General. It is interesting that in a letter to Younghusband at Lhasa, Curzon expressed the very same view. Younghusband wrote to his father that

Curzon had complained that 'quite unnecessarily', Government had committed itself to Russia and that 'just the other day' it sent the telegram regarding the terms 'without even showing it to him'. 'Poor man', the Commissioner concluded 'he has scarcely been out of bed for a month'. Younghusband MSS., letter, August 19, 1904.

39. Ampthill's dilemma can best be realized in his letter to Godley :
    'Another difficulty...I cannot express the views which Lord Curzon left on record because they are at variance with the directions of HMG and partly because they do not exactly coincide with my own; while at the same time I do not feel quite justified, as a mere *locum tenens*, to express my own views...'
    Ampthill to Godley, letter, May 31, 1904. Ampthill Papers, *op.cit.*

40. *Ibid.,* Ampthill to Brodrick, letter, July 13, 1904. Exactly a week later, Ampthill confided in the Secretary of State that 'your views and mine on this Tibet question, seem to be as nearly as possible in accord'.
    Ibid., Ampthill to Brodrick, letter, July 20, 1904.

41. *Loc. cit.* Ampthill told Brodrick (letter, July 20, 1904),
    'I am inclined to think that in writing his memorandum for the Cabinet...Lord Curzon was greatly influenced by private letters which he had received from Colonel Younghusband ... It is also the case, I think that Colonel Younghusband is enthusiastic over the policy which he (Younghusband) advocates because he believes it to be Lord Curzon's...'

20
Younghusband at Lhasa: 'Negotiations' and the 'Negotiators'

tween July 1903 when Younghusband arrived in Khamba Jong and August
)4, when his expedition was knocking at the gates of the Potala, its nature and
nplexion had altered well-nigh completely. As originally planned, the
mmissioner had set out to negotiate with the representatives of the Chinese
ıban and of the Dalai Lama : the proposed talks being confined to the question
the Tibet-Sikkim frontier, of grazing rights in and around Giaogong and the
ning of some new trade marts in Tibet. By the time of its arrival in Lhasa, the
ssion had been transformed into a military expedition in all but name.[1] By
son of its superior armed might, it had forced its way into the country until
v it had reached its political nerve-centre, the hub of the capital itself. The
port and the scope of the talks it still proposed to hold had changed too, and
ısiderably. These were now to be conducted between a victorious British
nmissioner and his war-worsted Tibetan adversaries. China's Amban was
re, but primarily to aid and render assistance in bringing the parties together.[2]
r did grazing rights, and frontier boundaries, occupy any but the least
ıortant place in the final drafts of the convention. The emphasis had shifted
pening more trade marts, to occupying the Chumbi Valley which was to serve
a guarantee for the indemnity that the Tibetans were to pay, and on ensuring
exclusive political influence which the British Government would now exercise
ie land of the Lama. In this now much-altered equation between the negotiating
ties, how were the 'talks' actually conducted?

   The first Tibetan reply to the main demands of the British was thought to be
preposterous' and impertinent that Younghusband intimated to the Amban
: he 'could not even receive it' (i.e., officially).[3] A few days later, the
nmissioner made it clear to the Tibetan official who called on him that the
ıs he (Younghusband) had put forth represented 'the minimum' that would
ccepted.[4] When the two Tibetan Shapes complained to him that the Mounted

Infantry, by now notorious for its depredations, had captured some men fro
Kham he clearly indicated that such 'military operations' would continue un
they (Tibetans) showed signs of agreeing to his terms. Again, when the Tibeta
confided that 'by asking a great deal they intended to obtain a little
Younghusband reminded them that 'our terms' did not admit of bargaining, th
he could not accept the Amban's mediation—the Tibetans had proposed that
'decide between us'—unless it was that his (Younghusband's) terms should
accepted.[5]

And not only were these (terms) not capable of modification, but the thre
of brute force, of military operations—which had always lurked in t
background—was aired openly, and indeed quite frequently. Thus after t
second reply of the Tibetans had been received and found to be 'not qu
satisfactory', Younghusband gave out that he 'would act', if necessary. (
another occasion he told the Amban that either the Tibetans accepted what
was demanding, or he was 'fully prepared to act'.[6] On September 1, when he m
the Amban, the Shapes, and the members of the Tsongdu and handed over t
final draft of the treaty, he warned that he would negotiate for a week longer b
if, at the end of it, the treaty was not signed, he would resume 'military operatior
against them.[7] To all talk for concessions, or alternative suggestions, I
continuous refrain was that the terms embodied the commands of the Briti
Government and 'would have to be accepted', that either the Tibetans must si
the Treaty or 'take the consequences of refusal'. It was this air of 'adamanti
firmness', as he called it, coupled with the not infrequent appeal to the fir
arbitrament of the sword he wielded, that forms the essential background to t
conduct of the 'talks' which led to the conclusion of the Lhasa Conventic
Nearly a quarter century later, the Commissioner recorded :

I was now brutally talking of war when I had so far been talking of peace.
I meant to fight they would fight too. But when I told them that I knew th
could do no such thing, they suddenly collapsed... and forthwith agreed
the whole treaty, lock, stock, and barrel.[8]

With whom was the Commissioner to negotiate a settlement? The head
the Tibetan Government, the master of the Potala, was the obvious choice. Y
for months everyone in the official hierarchy, from the India Office downwar
had been speculating whether, with the Mission arriving in Lhasa, the Da
Lama would not indeed bolt.[9] To allay the Secretary of State's fears, Ampthill p
forth the view that the fact of the Lama's running away need not cause 'a
undue apprehension'; as a matter of fact, the contingency may not even ari
For inasmuch as there was a powerful 'faction' against him, 'a strong possibil
existed' of his (Dalai Lama) being assassinated. Nor was this unusual for it w
'the ordinary fate' of the Dalai Lamas to 'meet with a premature end'. The prosp
did not disturb the acting Viceroy at all,

If events turn out in this way we shall, in fact, find the normal state of affa
at Lhasa instead of the present abnormal condition of a Lama who is o

enough and self-opinionated enough to speak and act for himself... I think that the Chinese will help us in this matter for they have shown that they regard the movement of our troops with indifference.[10]

Ampthill's views about the Dalai Lama being put out of the way, or the help at the Chinese may render in this context approximated closely to the general ~nsensus of opinion among the members of the Mission. Thus on April 29, the ommissioner telegraphing to the departing Viceroy his 'latest views' on the tuation thought the Lama would 'flee',

Suitable Regent may then be found, and normal system of Government be re-established without him (Dalai Lama). Amban may be willing to meet me, but evidently has no power over Dalai Lama.[11]

In any case, the Commissioner rated the Dalai Lama, and his reputed spiritual ~thority, pretty low. Dismissing him as 'a young whipper-snapper' caught up ~ut of the bazaar', Younghusband felt outraged that the Lama had the temerity ~ set 'three great empires by the ears' and had been taken too seriously 'at his ~wn valuation'.[12] In any case, for 'any proper settlement', it was imperative that ~, who was 'at the bottom of all the mischief', be brought 'down on his keens'. is bolting would not, Younghusband argued, do 'any harm' for, being at once ~bstinate and self-willed', he would, should he decide to stay, 'probably be ~ry difficult to manage'. A Regent more amenable would 'suit in fact' and is ~ally 'the normal ruler in Tibet'.[13]

As weeks elapsed, Younghusband's belief in the Dalai Lama bolting 'with ~y luck', and having a Regent of 'our own choice' in his place, persisted. In ~ct, any indications to the contrary angered and even rattled the Commissioner,

It would only have made the Dalai Lama still more conceited and still more stubborn and sulky... luckily the Chinese Government said they had no influence with the Dalai Lama and rather hoped he would run away—in which I entirely agree. I think it would be the best thing that could happen...[14]

There was, however, a decisive shift in Younghusband's attitude as the ~Mission got ready to proceed to Lhasa. For, early in July, to a Dalai Lama ~portedly disillusioned with his Russian friends he was prepared to proffer the ~ost categorical assurances of British 'protection'.[15] Later, on the door-steps of ~hasa, he seems to have undergone a complete metamorphosis. For he confided ~ his father,

We are within 16 miles of our goal... and what I am chiefly afraid of now is the Dalai Lama bolting, so I am angling delicately for him...[16]

Finally, in Lhasa itself when the Commissioner discovered that the Lama ~ad, in fact, left the capital, there was for a time a serious proposal to engage a ~orce 'in pursuit to seize' him. This however, was turned down by HMG both as delaying or compromising' the withdrawal of the main force and as being ~undesirable'—a decision which the Governor-General appeared to regret. Mr. ~Brodrick, however, showed a willingness for an ultimatum being served

threatening dire penalties in case the Dalai Lama 'will not return and treat' or gi
the necessary authority to 'sign treaty'.[17]

Whatever his earlier views, and there is little doubt that his first impressio
had been entirely mistaken, Younghusband found on arrival in the Tibetan capi
that without the Dalai Lama, the situation was well-nigh chaotic,

The worst difficulty, I have at present is finding anyone to negotiate wit
The Dalai Lama has washed his hands of the whole business, handed ov
his seal to an old gentleman who has no other qualifications than amiabilit
The four real Councilors have been imprisoned. The four new ones a
nincompoops and the slightest thing is referred to the Nation
Assembly...responsible to no one, without any President or any method
voting.[18]

More specifically, on the day after his arrival in Lhasa and while returning
his camp through the heart of the city, Younghusband noticed that large crow
looked on 'apathetically'.[19] A few days later he found the confusion even wor
: 'Yutok Shape is ill, Ta Lama is in disgrace, while of the remaining Shapes one
hostile and the other uneless. The Tsong-du is sitting in permanent session'.
Apathy apart, the general attitude of the Tibetans he had found to be not s
much 'hostile' as 'futile'. Indeed without the Lama,[21] the Commissioner foun
the going rather rough; and in the initial stages at any rate, felt complete
befuddled, at his wits' end.

Soon, however, out of this stark confusion, features and figures, began
emerge. Actually, the Commissioner's role was not unlike the catalyst, whic
both helps to precipitate and crystallize : 'without fiddling or interfering b
simply standing up firm and straight', he would have these numerous discorda
elements take form and content around him.[22] Among those who thus revolve
the Amban Yu T'ai apart, of the greatest interest was a Lob-sang Gyaltsen, th
Gaden Ti Rimpoche. He had first visited the Commissioner on August 14 an
was 'most moderate and reasonable in his talk and acknowledged Tibetans wer
beaten'.[23]

The Rimpoche had evidently kept in the background because he was afrai
of the Shapes and, as Younghusband confided to Curzon, of the Dalai Lama
should the latter return and the British retire. Actually, in private, the Commissione
had referred to him as 'the sort of' Regent whom the Dalai Lama left and who ha
approached him (Younghusband) 'to secure my support in case the Dalai Lam
should be deposed'.[24] But, and here was the chief snag from the Commissioner
viewpoint, 'he has not much influence'[25] which fact, did not prove for long to b
an insuperable obstacle. Thus it is noticed a few days later that a telegraphi
report from the Viceroy to the Secretary of State informed the latter that the 'T
Rimpoche is making marked overtures to Younghusband who, in return, i
showing him special attention as the principal in negotiations'.[26]

As matter of fact, the Commissioner, rattled by 'this intangible, illusive, un
get-at-able set of human beings' as he now found,[27] was considerably heartene

by his new 'discovery'. He regarded it as 'a decided advance', although it had taken 'a fortnight of my precious six weeks' to make. His close advisers too sustained him in this assessment,

> The Nepalese Representative said the Regent was a moderate man, more inclined to make a peaceful settlement than the generality of the National Assembly.[28]

The Amban in turn, endorsed the Commissioner's choice assuring (or was it echoing ?) him that the Rimpoche was 'the best man among the leading Tibetans' and what was more, 'came next after Dalai Lama in the Lhasa province'.[29] The die was thus cast and in subsequent dispatches one finds the Commissioner referring to the Rimpoche as the 'acting' Regent.[30]

Matters were finally clinched when, on September 4, three days after Younghusband had given the Tibetans a week's advance notice to make up their minds, before he would resort to military operations, the National Assembly definitely recognized the Ti Rimpoche as the Regent and, with the Amban's consent, permitted him to use the seal of the Dalai Lama.[31] No sooner was the Rimpoche thus 'elected', than he confirmed that the Tibetans 'were prepared to accept our terms'[32]—a bare 72 hours later he was to affix the Lama's seal to this compact.

During the first few weeks of his arrival in Lhasa, the Commissioner appears to have played with the idea of pursuing the Dalai Lama, forcing him to return to the capital and there seal and deliver the Convention which he (Younghusband) had been charged with concluding. It has already been noticed that HMG put its foot down, and firmly—despite 'the very cautious wording' which Ampthill had used—on such a wild goose chase.[33] Simultaneously, Younghusband was persuading the Ti Rimpoche, with sweet reasonableness, to use his good offices to make the Lama return,

> As to the Dalai Lama, I said I was quite prepared to give him the most positive assurance that he would be safe from us if he returned here. I did not wish to discuss personally with him the details of the settlement, but wished him to affix his seal in my presence; and it would certainly be more convenient if he were nearer Lhasa for reference during the negotiations. The Regent said he would send two messengers to him tomorrow, advising him to return.[34]

But evidently, there was another string to the bow. Three days later, the Commissioner confided to Lord Curzon:

> I have made a point of his returning to receive me and if he does return he will have to bow to our will—while, if he does not, everyone here will be only too delighted to seize the opportunity of having him deposed by the Chinese Amban which the Chinese will be glad enough to do under the pressure of our force.[35]

The game was thus clear—and, as Younghusband confessed, it was 'an exceedingly easy one' to play.[36] No sooner thus was it evident, both that the

Lama was beyond easy reach and that Whitehall would not countenance the idea of pursuing him across Tibet's frozen deserts in the north, than the Commissioner shot the second string, as it were, of his bow : to secure the deposition of the Dalai Lama. As will be presently noticed the Amban, and for very good reasons, was prepared to oblige—and both the Viceroy and the Secretary of State thought here was a clever way out of the impasse. It is interesting that the Commissioner attributed the move as originating with, and in fact emanating from, the Amban who probably, it would seem, was already in touch with the Wai-wu-pu on the subject,

> Roundabout way of denunciation of Dalai Lama and exaltation of Panchen Lama would be more satisfactory solution of present difficulties and I would recommend that Minister at Peking be asked to urge Chinese Government to denounce Dalai Lama and to telegraph reply to Amban by India to save time. Amban informs me that he has been receiving no reply to telegrams sent from Lhasa 5th August by Gyantse to Wai-wu-pu. He does not care to mention this to his own Government but is very anxious for reply.[37]

The acting Viceroy in transmitting Younghusband's message expressed his own doubts if there were precedents of the Tashi Lama taking over from the Dalai Lama. Nor was he sure whether the Chinese were not indeed so manipulating as to saddle the British with the 'entire blame', should things go awry.[38] But Mr. Brodirick did not apparently show any great concern. 'At first sight', he telegraphed the Viceroy, 'it smiles on me. To depose the Dalai Lama if it can be done in orthodox fashion, would be a signal stroke'![39]

A major difficulty, however, cropped up and it was the unwillingness of Sir Ernest Satow to press the Chinese authorities—a course of action endorsed by Lord Lansdowne who feared lest the attempt prove 'abortive'.[40] Meantime the Government of India, as no doubt the Commissioner himself, were busy cataloguing precedents and gauging the respective superiority, spiritual or otherwise, of the two incarnations.[41]

Events, however, sped fast and soon enough outpaced discussions in London or even Simla. On August 16—and the Ti Rimpoche had been making 'marked overtures' in the meantime—the Amban informed the Commissioner that he had asked the Rimpoche to send a massage to the Dalai Lama to come back or else he (Amban) would donounce him to the Emperor. It is not without significance that the Amban said this at a meeting where the Commissioner,

> I said the Dalai Lama should certainly either come back, or abdicate; and if he remained away at this important juncture, assumption would be that he had renounced functions of Government.[42]

Reporting to the Secretary of State 'the news from Lhasa upto August 17' the Viceroy informed him that Younghusband, considered it would be possible, even if the Dalai Lama should not return, to negotiate a satisfactory convention in the manner proposed by the Amban, i.e., denunciation of the Dalai Lama, thereby reducing him to a private person and asking the Tashi Lama to resume government in accordance with precedent.[43]

BUSINESS FIRST!

British Lion (*to* Grand Llama). "YES, THAT'S ALL RIGHT, MY FRIEND. YOU MAY GO AWAY FOR THREE *HUNDRED* YEARS, IF YOU LIKE. *BUT THIS HAS GOT TO BE SIGNED FIRST!*"

Four days later, on August 21,[44] the telegram purporting to contain the denunciation of the Dalai Lama—on which the Amban had now definitely decided—had been sent to Younghusband by the Chinese Resident with the request that it be forwarded to Peking via Gyantse, the Commissioner undertaking to do 'this service for him'. Younghusband's own sympathies were hard to disguise :

> I said...I considered he (Amban) was acting with great wisdom in denouncing the Dalai Lama, for it was he who had brought all this trouble upon his country, and he deserved to suffer for it. I was not surprised, however, at so young a ruler coming to grief... For a young Dalai Lama, who had not only temporal, but also supreme spiritual power, the tendency to go wrong must have been almost irresistible.[45]

These sentiments were dutifully echoed by the Amban who affirmed that the Lama had been 'headstrong and obstinate, and had never followed good advice'.[46] What was more to the point, he informed the Commissioner that while the Tashi Lama was to be the spiritual head of the Church, a Regent would be appointed 'for transaction of secular business'.[47] A few days later, replying to a query from Government as to precedents about the Lama's denunciation, Younghusband gave out what was at best a half-truth :

> The fact that he endeavoured to induce the Dalai Lama to come in is well known to Buddhists here, and they are also aware that, after he has definitely fled from the country, it was on the initiative of the Amban[48] that he was deposed. I personally consider the denunciation a very politic act...[49]

And so indeed he did for to his own recommendation he now adduced the authority of the Bhutanese chief as also of the Nepalese Representative both of whom, he reported, 'approve of denunciation'.[50]

Meanwhile rapid developments ensued. The Amban's telegram was received in Peking on August 24, two days later, an Imperial decree was issued reducing the Dalai Lama to the position of a private individual, by 'temporarily' depriving him of his dignity. A threat was held out that should the Lama remain contumacious, he would be permanently degraded.[51] As hectic messages were still being exchanged between the Commissioner and the government of Lord Ampthill and between the latter and the Secretary of State,[52] it would seem that the Chinese action in Peking could not have been on Sir Ernest Satow's initiative. In any case, it would be obvious that the Wai-wu-pu did not only not seem to need pushing or pressurizing in this particular direction—but may actually have welcomed the move as conducive to partly restoring its own, now sharply-dilapidated, prestige in Lhasa.[53]

It is also significant that as for the future, the Amban was charged with the responsibility to 'conduct all Tibetan affairs'. To be sure, the notice of the Lama's deposition as posted in Lhasa, threw an interesting, and revealing, light on the factors leading to his downfall and unwittingly gave away a great deal,

...he did not remain to guard his kingdom...he gave no orders to his subjects to settle the question of the Indian Tibetan boundary, which had been outstanding for more than ten years...he paid no regard to the Emperor, nor to law and justice. These various crimes show that he is not a man who would not be punished... In future...the Amban will conduct all Tibetan affairs with Tibetan officials and important matters will be refered to the Emperor...[54]

What score did the Tibetans set by these pronouncements ex cathedra? How far did they believe in the alleged acts of omission and commission of which their ruler had been found guilty? It is not necessary to go into these questions here, even though it may be noted in passing that no sooner was the proclamation posted than it was torn down and that the people of Lhasa were said to view it with 'complete apathy'.[55] It may be relevant in this context to mention that this was a bare three days after the signing of the Convention and that British forces, with their maxims trained on the Potala, still held sway in the Tibetan capital. One wonders though if this helped to correct Younghusband's oft-repeated viewpoint that the people of Lhasa were 'heartily glad' that the Lama had gone, that they believed he had brought ruination to his land or that his departure was 'not regretted' by them.[56] Maybe towards the latte part of his stay, he began to have second thoughts.[57]

Notes

1. Actually, the military made a strong bid to call the Mission the 'Tibet Field Force', which move Ampthill strongly opposed, for he read into this 'a deliberate attempt to subordinate Younghusband to the military authorities'. Both Kitchener and the Military Member Elles finally gave way on the 'understanding' that Field Service concessions should be allowed without the change of nomenclature. Ampthill to Brodrick, letter, June 30, 1904. Ampthill Papers, *op.cit.*

2. It may be necessary to recall here that despite Lord Curzon's view that China's so-called suzerainty over Tibet was 'a constitutional fiction and a political affectation', such negotiations as took place at Khamba were held among the British, the Chinese and the Tibetan representatives. At Gyantse too there was repeated talk of the Amban arriving but after disappearance of General Ma, who had replaced Ho, Chao and Li, the Chinese took a back seat. At Lhasa, they refused to be a party to the 'talks'. The Amban's role of active co-operation with the British, alluded to at length in subsequent pages, which may be regarded as personal to Yu T'ai, was later severely censured by the Chinese Government and he was summarily dismissed from office. It may also be remembered that Chinese 'adhesion' to the Lhasa Convention was later secured by the 1906 Peking Convention between Britain and China. Lord Curzon's 'fiction' thus proved stronger—and stranger—than the facts.

3. India and Tibet, *op.cit.*, Cd.2370, No. 127, p. 51.

4. *Ibid.*, No. 129, p. 52.

5. *Ibid.*, Encl. No. 261, pp. 219-20.

6. *Ibid.*, No. 134, p. 54, Encl. No. 276, p. 228 and Encl. No. 318, p. 247.

7. *Ibid.*, Encl. No. 305, pp. 240-41 and Encl. No. 341, pp. 261-62. Younghusband. India and Tibet, *op.cit.* pp. 291-92,

8.   Younghusband, The Light of Experience, *op.cit.*, pp. 99-100.
9.   As early as May 27 (1904) the Permanent Under-Secretary had asked Ampthill, 'What are we to do when we get to Lhasa and find the Government gone elsewhere?' Godley to Ampthill, letter, May 27, 1904, Ampthill Papers, *op.cit.*
10. Ampthill to Brodrick, letter, June 2, 1904. Ampthill Papers, *op.cit.*
     Four days later, the Viceroy telegraphed the Secretary of State that at Gyantse, the Bhutanese chief, the Tongsa Penlop, had told Mr. Walsh that 'the Dalai Lama and his Government would desert Lhasa before the arrival of the Mission'. *Ibid.,* Ampthill to Brodrick, June 6, 1904.
     Ten days later, the Viceroy wrote to the King much to the same effect declaring the existence of a Dalai Lama old enough to act as one was 'unusual in the history of Tibet'. *Ibid.,* Ampthill to King, June 16, 1904.
11. Younghusband to Curzon, telegram, April 29, 1904, Curzon MSS.
12. *Ibid.,* Younghusband to Curzon, letter, April 18, 1904. Later in this communication, the Commissioner suggested that to demonstrate clearly to the Tibetans that we are 'not going to be fooled', and to impress the 'orientals' with pomp and pageantry which are 'of extreme importance', the Dalai Lama must go to India to sign the Convention and meet the Viceroy or 'Your Excellency must go to Lhasa'.
13. *Ibid.,* Younghusband to Curzon, letter, April 25, 1904.
14. *Ibid.,* Younghusband to Curzon, letter, May 7, 1904. The Commissioner was convinced that in this way the Dalai Lama's personal prestige, as indeed that of his office, would be completely 'gone' and he would 'remain a derelict'.
15. In a letter to the Secretary of State, the acting Viceroy told him that Younghusband had proposed an amendment of the proposed instructions, suggesting end of clause 2 should read:
     'The British Government will, if a Foreign Power attempts to intervene, take such steps as they may consider necessary to assist the Tibetan Government to exclude such intervention'. Ampthill to Brodrick, July, 11, 1904, Ampthill Papers, *op.cit,* Also see Younghusband to Curzon, letter, July 12, 1904, Curzon MSS.
16. Younghusband MSS., No. 46, August 1, 1904. The letter was written from 'Camp on Lhasa river'.
17. The Secretary of State to Viceroy, telegram, August 16, 1904. Ampthill Papers, *op.cit.* Also see *Ibid.,* Ampthill to Brodrick, August 17, 1904, 'I had hoped that the very cautious wording (of the proposal to pursue the lama) ... would have made it acceptable to you'.
18. Elsewhere, Younghusband told Lord Curzon that although he had met 'the highest Lamas' in Lhasa and they were all 'extraordinarily quaint and interesting' and 'good fellows' yet they were 'utterly hopeless as negotiators'. Younghusband to Curzon, letter, August 8, 1904. Curzon MSS.
19. Tibet Papers, *op.cit.,* Cd. 2370, No. 121, pp. 49-50.
20. *Ibid.,* Nos. 105 and 123, pp. 41 and 50. The Yutok-Shape and the Ta Lama, (later Tsarong Shape), besides the Chief Secretary, were the Tibetan officials who had met Younghusband at Nagartse on July 19 and vainly dissuaded him from proceeding to Lhasa. Of them, the Commissioner wrote : 'The Yu-tok Sha-pe... was calm and polite and ... cordial in his manner ; the Ta Lama, though more excited, was not ill-mannered...the Chief Secretary ...excited throughout, and argumentative and querulous'. Younghusband, India and Tibet, *op.cit.,* pp. 225-32.

21. On reaching Lhasa on August 2, Younghusband had wired that the Dalai Lama was believed to be in a private monastery, a few miles away; on August 5, that he was at Reting; on August 8, that he was three days' distant; on August 11, at Nagchuka 'eight marches to the North'; On August 17, that he was believed to have 'almost certainly' fled beyond Nagchuka; on August 20 that he had left Nagchuka for the North 'twelve days ago'. *Ibid., Encl.* Nos. 239, 243, 249, 259, 267, and 280 respectively.

22. Younghusband to Curzon, letter, August 17, 1904, Curzon MSS.

23. Tibet Papers, *op.cit.,* Cd. 2370, No. 129, p. 52.

24. Younghusband, India and Tibet, *op.cit.,* pp. 273-75, gives a fuller account of the Commissioner's first interview with the Rimpoche. Also see Younghusband to Curzon, letter, August 17, 1904, Curzon MSS.

25. Younghusband, India-Tibet, *op.cit.,* Cd. 2370, Encl. 261, pp. 219-20.

26. *Ibid.,* No. 130, p. 52. The telegram from the Viceroy to the Secretary of State is dated August 23 and gives 'news from Lhasa to 17 August'. Actually, as Younghusband wrote later, during his visit to the Amban on August 16, the latter reportedly said that he 'recognised the Ti Rimpoche ...as the principal in the nigotiations'. Younghusband, India and Tibet, *op.cit.,* p. 277.

27. Younghusband, India and Tibet, *op.cit.,* p. 268.

28. *Ibid.,* p. 269.

29. India and Tibet, *op.cit.,* Cd. 2370, Encl. No. 318, p. 247.

30. *Ibid.,* Nos. 131, 146 and 148, pp. 53, and 59-60.

31. *Ibid.,* Encl. No. 316, p. 245.

32. After he had made this declaration, 'Regent then affixed his private seal to a Tibetan translation of draft Convention... and I have informed Regent that convention itself will be signed in the Potala'. *Loc. cit.*

33. *Supra,* n.17.

34. Younghusband, India and Tibet, *op.cit.,* p. 275.

35. Younghusband to Curzon, letter, August 17, 1904, Curzon MSS.

36. *Loc. cit.*

37. The text of Younghusband's proposal as 'emanating from Amban'—and actually in the Commissioner's own words—was telegraphed to the Secretary of State by the Viceroy on August 25, 1904. Ampthill Papers, *op.cit.*

38. *Loc. cit.*

39. Secretary of State to Viceroy, telegram, August 26, 1904, Ampthill Papers, *op.cit.*

40. *Ibid.,* Secretary of State to Viceroy, telegram, August 28, 1904.

41. *Ibid.,* Viceroy to Secretary of State, telegrams, August 26 and September 8, 1904. The Viceroy, relying principally on Sandberg's book, *op.cit.* contended—and this was contrary to what Curzon had written in his Memorandum of June 23—that the Tashi Lama had 'much older spiritual authority', than the Dalai Lama; that the Lhasa people were 'heartily glad' that the Dalai Lama had gone and doubted whether the Lama would return 'as a rival Russian Pope' if the Tashi Lama were set up in his place.

42. Younghusband, India and Tibet, *op.cit.* p. 226.

43. Tibet Papers, *op.cit.,* Cd. 2370, No. 130, p. 52; Viceroy to Secretary of State, telegram, August 23, 1904.

44. It was probably around August 19, that the Commissioner received 'certain information' that the Lama had 'finally fled' and in so doing had written to the

National Assembly that the English were 'very craftly people' and warned its members to be 'careful' in making an agreement with them. His departure, Younghusband recorded, 'was not regretted' by Tibetans. Younghusband, India and Tibet, *op.cit.*, p. 279.

45. *Ibid.*, pp. 281-82.

46. *Loc. cit.*

47. Tibet Papers, *op.cit.*, Cd. 2370, No. 132, p. 52 and Encl. Nos. 273 and 319, pp. 227 and 249.

48. From the above, it should be evident as to whose was the 'initiative' in deposing the Lama. Younghusband had been keen on it long before he reached Lhasa and the Amban found in the move new crutches to elevate his well-nigh lost power. Who 'collaborated' with whom would, therefore, at best be a debatable proposition. Dr. Li's suggestion about giving Younghusband 'every benefit of the doubt' is enigmatic at best. The fact of the matter is that Younghusband wanted the Lama to be deposed—he thought it would ease his path and in this the Amban came handy. See Li, *op.cit.*, pp. 105-7.

49. Tibet Papers, *op.cit.*, Cd. 2370, No. 149, pp. 60-61. See also Viceroy to Secretary of State, telegram, September 8, 1904. Ampthill Papers, *op.cit.* Younghusband put forth the view that the contemplated action would show 'impracticability of Tibetans restraining us and Chinese (from) working together'.

50. Viceroy to Secretary of State, telegram, September 8, 1904, Ampthill Papers, *op.cit.*

51. Tibet Papers, *op.cit.*, Cd. 2370, No. 135, p. 54.

52. Thus writing to Younghusband on August 26, Ampthill told him that he had 'just sent' him (Younghusband) a telegram about precedents for deposing Dalai Lamas and 'the irregular appointment of the present fugitive pontiff' which he hoped may be useful. He also confessed that both he and Dane had been studying 'Sandberg's book and other records'. The writer discovered this letter in Miss Eileen Younghusband's collection, wherein it is marked '4'.

53. When the British Minister in Peking informed the Chinese Vice-Minister about the Mission's proposed advance to Lhasa on June 25, 'no surprise was manifested by the Vice-Minister...nor was any objection raised by him... He remarked that the Dalai Lama, who was ignorant and pig-headed, was entirely in the hands of the three great monasteries'. *Memorandum of Information* (concerning Tibet) for June, 1904.

54. Tibet Papers, *op.cit.*, Cd. 2370, Annexure, Encl. No. 362, pp. 274-75.

55. *Ibid.*, Encls. 331 and 332, p. 257.

56. Younghusband's letters and despatches are full of remarks to this effect. References are Viceroy to Secretary of State, telegram, August 26, 1904. Ampthill Papers, *op.cit.*, and Younghusband, India and Tibet, *op.cit.*, pp. 279 and 281.

57. Ampthill to Brodrick, telegram, September 24, 1904 in which Younghusband reported from Lhasa that the Dalai Lama was 'a few marches beyond Nagchuka' and that he may return when the Mission leaves Lhasa in which case the position of the Amban may be rendered difficult 'as the feelings of the people are against the Chinese'. Ampthill Papers, *op.cit.*, also see Younghusband's reverie on the hill outside Lhasa, on his way back. For the text from his 'Vital Religion', see eaver, *op.cit.*, pp. 248-50. Also George Harrison, 'The Great Adventure : a Younghusband Anthology of Divine Fellowship' (in manuscript).

21
The Commissioner Versus the Amban

Apart from the Ti Rimpoche, whose star shone all the more resplendent after the Dalai Lama had been denounced, and was thus out of the way, the Chinese Amban played a most significant role in nearly all that led to the success of the Mission, culminating in the conclusion of the Lhasa Convention. The Manchu Yu T'ai was a brother of Sheng T'ai who had earlier negotiated the Sino-British Convention of 1890. Not unlike most other Manchu officials, spread thinly over the vast Chinese domain all the way from Manchuria to Tibet, he kept up an outer façade of dignity, excellent good manners, an air of 'something very much akin to superiority', and solid intellectual capacity. Younghusband did not rate him to be 'indeed strikingly clever'[1]—but then the Commissioner was perhaps a poor judge of character. Indeed, it has been held that he 'never, at any rate, saw through the Amban'.[2]

It has already been noticed that Yu T'ai's appointment had been announced early in December, 1902; that as 'the throne' attached 'much importance' to the Tibet frontier question he had been 'ordered to proceed at once' to the frontier and negotiate with Mr. White 'in an amicable spirit'.[3] It was clear that the previous incumbent, Yu Kang, had failed dismally in much the same Mission. Unfortunately for the new Resident too many delays supervened before he could make a start. His original intent of voyaging through the ocean and reaching Tibet, via India, had been given up for fear it might engender suspicion among those 'grossly stupid and ignorant people' whom he had set out 'to enlighten as far as lay in his power'.[4] For the next twelve months, however, his slow peace—and a progress that was slower still—on the long overland journey became a subject of considerable comment in nearly all diplomatic correspondence relating to the Tibet question and, in the bargain, Yu T'ai acquired a not ill-deserved notoriety.

To be sure, almost immediately after he had been ordered to proceed 'at once' to his new post, Peking gave out that he could not be expected in Lhasa until July next year.[5] This served as a convenient handle for the Viceroy to press his peremptory proposal on the Secretary of State, charging that the Chinese were not serious.[6] Later when, towards the close of September, 1903, Yu T'ai was still discovered tarrying around Chengtu, capital of Szechuan, the British Government were to put to good account his by now frequent, and somewhat inordinate postponements.[7] And though the embarrassed Prince Ch'ing, then head of the Wai-wu-pu, explained that the delay had been due to the difficulty of collecting troops, the British insinuated that the Amban-designate was unnecessarily protracting his journey and figured out his arrival in Lhasa at 'an uncertain, but in any case remote date'.[8]

Nor did Chinese appeals to stay Younghusband's advance, pending the arrival of Yu T'ai, fall on any but deaf ears. In fact, HMG, as Lord Lansdowne pointed out, refused to countermand the measures it had already sanctioned (viz. the Mission's despatch). For not only had the Tibetans shown increased hostility, and systematically disregarded the injunctions of the Manchu Emperor, but what was still worse, the Chinese had demonstrated no real power, much less influence, in restraining them.[9] And herein the British Government had concurred entirely in the conclusion to which their Minister in Peking had been driven namely, that though the Chinese were desirous of bringing about a satisfactory solution of the Indo-Tibetan dispute, Prince Ch'ing's repeated allusion to the obstinate temper of the Tibetans made him (Satow) feel that 'they (the Chinese) are not sanguine as to the likelihood of Yu T'ai being able to expedite the negotiations'.[10]

In the last stages of his journey, ordered again to 'proceed at once' and hasten by 'forced marches', the new Amban was still at Ta-chien-lu twoards the third week of November.[11] Although the precise date of his arrival in Lhasa is disputed, he is said to have been there when the British crossed the Jelap-la into Tibet on December 3. Later, reportedly he sent 'strict orders' to the Tibetan commander, for what these were worth, that while he might reason with the British, he should not resort to force.[12] From then onward Yu T'ai emerges fully into the limelight, more so in his now frequent epistolary exchanges with Younghusband. Thus one is told that on March 19, and again on March 27, he was endeavouring to collect carriage and start out to meet the British Commissioner but that the Tibetans would not allow him 'to carry out the orders of the Emperor'.[13] Again, on April 3 'he now intends to come and meet me as soon as possible', Younghusband informed the Viceroy from Tuna.[14] Meantime, and what was more to the purpose, the Amban had blessed the Mission's project of going to Gyantse, in view of 'Tibetan obstinacy', though the Dalai Lama had written to him that 'we (British troops) should go back to Yatung'.[15] A day later, however, Younghusband is accosted not by the Amban but by his delegate, a General Ma.[16] On the Commissioner's arrival at Gyantse on April 11, and Yu T'ai had promised to greet him there in person, the Commissioner had only to be content with Ma's assurance that the Amban will come 'as soon as he can arrange with the Dalai'.[17] A fortnight later arrived another despatch bringing the precious news that the Amban 'is coming within a few weeks'. Yu T'ai had, however, hastened to assure Younghusband, having probably read all the accounts of the Guru affair (the Commissioner later confessed the Tibetans had laid the blame for the disaster squarely on British treachery), that the

Lhasa General was 'the aggressor' and that 'my (Younghusband's) compassion in releasing the prisoners and in caring for the wounded, and my humane motives, have conferred incalculable blessings on Tibet'.[18]

What measure of a man? Curzon had visualized Yu T'ai's putting in an appearance at Gyantse where, in a letter to Younghusband, he pictured him arrive,

> puffing in, deprecatory, conciliatory, anxious to keep you back at all hazards and willing to give every sort of encouragement in order to persuade you to retreat, and to retain for China the credit for having settled the matter and revindicated her suzerainty.[19]

By the end of April (1904) Younghusband's own assessment of the Amban was no whit different from Lord Curzon's. He 'may be willing to meet me', the Commissioner confided, 'but evidently has no power over Dalai Lama'.[20]

With May, the Amban's letters become somewhat less frequent. Now, it seemed, was the Commissioner's turn. On April 23, the latter wrote to Yu T'ai, expressing disappointment at his 'continued dilatoriness' which, he warned, will not 'naturally predispose Government to be lenient'.[21] On June 1, he addressed him as he did the Dalai Lama, in terms of those 'beastly' ultimatums—which took him a few days in actual delivery[22]—announcing, inter alia, the Commissioner's intended advance to Lhasa.[23] On July 13, on the eve of the Mission's departure for the Tibetan capital, Younghusband wrote to him again.[24] At Chaksam ferry—just a few days' march this side of Lhasa—Younghusband heard from the Amban but merely to the effect that he (Amban) had communicated the contents of the Commissioner's letter to the Lama.[25]

No sooner did the Mission arrive at Lhasa than Yu T'ai's former intimacy seemed to return. He visited Younghusband within a few hours of his arrival and not only promised all help in impressing upon the Tibetans the urgent necessity of making a speedy settlement, but 'had already collected two days' supplies and was ready to arrange more'. He had also made, Younghusband noted with no small satisfaction, a special present of food to the troops.[26] These food 'gifts' must be viewed against the background of the fact that the Mission was now entirely dependent upon local supplies, which were not always readily forthcoming. Apart from such a welcome attention right at the commencement of Younghusband's admittedly difficult assignment, Yu T'ai's role in rendering all possible assistance was by no means, a small favour. A few questions naturally spring to mind. What motives guided him? What purpose was the Amban working up to?

Properly to appreciate Yu T'ai's behaviour, it would be necessary to recall that the Amban's office had suffered a considerable eclipse, both in authority and prestige, during the latter half of the nineteenth century. That eclipse was due principally, if not indeed entirely, to the sore straits to which China's own power had been reduced, and a reference to which has been made earlier in the narrative. Besides, the Ambans were—and Yu T'ai was no exception—invariably not happy choices and in their character, and deportment, left a great deal to be desired,[27] Yu T'ai's own appointment coincided with the aftermath of the famous-infamous

(d)

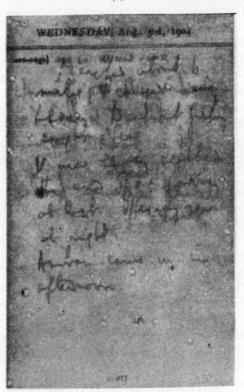

Extracts from Lt. (later Lt. Col.)
A. L. Hadow's diary
[For text see Appendix 10]

Boxer Rebellion. Never before had the Emperor, much less his Court, been subjected to such a great humiliation. Meantime the young, and reportedly headstrong, Dalai Lama had come into his own and the Chinese Imperial Resident, never popular in Tibet, began to be treated with extreme indifference, bordering on ill-concealed contempt.[28] No wonder that the Amban's 'decrees' and 'orders' to the Tibetan authorities were obeyed more in the breach than in their observance. Essentially, therefore, where Yu Kang had found the situation 'so untenable' as to have 'begged' the Emperor 'to relieve' him,[29] Yu T'ai was not likely to fare any better.

From the above it should be clear that, while it is difficult to affirm the validity of the oft-repeated complaint of the new Amban that the Tibetan Government would not afford him the necessary facilities for travel so that he could go out to meet the British Commissioner, two facts may be borne in mind. Firstly, the old Amban Yu Kang, or for that matter his predecessor, had made a similar complaint, and more than once.[30] Secondly, the complaint, even if true, has been held by itself to offer no valid justification for his inability to stir out of Lhasa. In fact, a recent Chinese scholar has put forth the hypothesis that Yu T'ai could have gone out to meet the British Commissioner; that lack of transport was, at best, a 'pretext'; that as a matter of fact it was his 'cowardice' which prevented him from shouldering his proper responsibility on behalf of the Imperial Government, or for doing something for the Tibetans when he was most required to.[31] This line of reasoning leaves one rather cold. If the position of two of his immediate predecessors was indeed so 'helpless' that they could not stir out of Lhasa and, in fact, finally 'begged the Emperor' to relieve them, how could Yu T'ai's be supposed to have improved ? Or, is it implied that they were cowards too and lack of transport, in their case also, was no more than 'a pretext'?[32]

Yu T'ai's relative lack of communicativeness, not to say coolness, towards the Commissioner during the latter's sojourn at Gyantse may not be difficult to explain. Two small incidents help serve as a clue. Thus on May 10 (1904) Younghusband telegraphed to the Foreign Secretary that Captain Parr's guard of Chinese attendants was beaten up by the Tibetans, that his two Bhutia servants were killed and that all his property had been looted. Nor was that all. For 'General Ma and all Chinese officials', are practically besieged, and dare not leave their quarters, the Commissioner reported.[33] It may be recalled that Captain Parr was the Chinese Customs Officer at Yatung, that he was one of the two delegates chosen by the previous Amban to negotiate with Younghusband at Khamba, and that General Ma had been sent by Yu T'ai himself on a similar assignment. Could it be that Lhasa, or the Amban himself, was immune from the repercussions of these 'incidents'?

Another occurrence is equally revealing :

Wilton hears from a Chinese source that Amban recently received letter from representatives of the great Lhasa monasteries. They denied that Dalai Lama had power to ratify a treaty, and said it was compulsory on Dalai Lama to work conjointly with the great monasteries. Amban was notified he might negotiate as much as he pleased with British, but Tibetans had nothing to do with them and Amban was warned against making any treaty allowing British to proceed beyond Yatung.[34]

Would it not be legitimate to argue that sensing the climate of opinion around him, the Amban heeded the warning and restrained his epistolary zeal as far as the 'all-wise Sahib' was concerned?[35]

Turning finally to his behaviour at Lhasa, it would appear that the arrival of Younghusband, synchronising as it did with the flight of the Dalai Lama, afforded him (Amban) an opportunity that he had been long waiting for. The British Commissioner noted that he did not see him (Yu T'ai) 'at his best', that the Tibetans had put him 'in a most humiliating position' and yet 'he kept up appearances and made a brave show with all the aplomb of his race'.[36] Actually, to the Amban, Younghusband came handy. On the coat-tails of the British—and General Macdonald and his men ruled the roost as long as they were in Lhasa[37]—he strove, and hard, to regain his lost authority. Significantly eloquent of his line of thinking, and an early expression thereof, were the ill-chosen 'congratulations' which he showered on Younghusband on his 'victory' at Guru. He even proffered the unsolicited comment that it was the Tibetans who were the aggressors. It may be recalled that he blessed the advance to Gyantse. And there could be little doubt that he heartily welcomed the Mission's arrival in Lhasa. Again, Younghusband's own despatches noted that it was the Chinese who appeared to gain the most from British victories over the Tibetans.[38] It may be recalled that the Amban expressed to the Wai-wu-pu, his firm conviction that the (Tibetan) situation would take a favourable turn if the Tibetans should meet with 'another great defeat'—of course, at the hands of the British.[39]

Not unnaturally, therefore, at Lhasa Yu T'ai went out of his way to toe the line which Younghusband was pursuing; if for no other reason than that it answered in its entirety to his own, and his country's, long-term and even immediate, interests. He welcomed, it would seem with ill-concealed grace, the Commissioner's slightest hint about the deposition and denunciation of the Dalai Lama, and went the whole hog with it in what appeared to be indecent hurry. He hastened to recognize the Ti Rimpoche as Regent, after Younghusband had found him to be 'a sensible man', a move for which Peking later denied him any authority.

Yu T'ai went a step further. He told the Commissioner repeatedly, what each one of the Tibetan negotiators persistently, and almost to the very end, repudiated namely that there was no objection on their part to any of the terms of his Convention. He dismissed Tibetan protests as spurious, over-rode their objections with imperious fiats, put on an air of 'superiority' and treated them altogether with 'disdainful contempt'?[40] It was on the cards that he would have affixed his seal to the 'Adhesion Agreement', thereby ratifying the treaty on behalf of his Government, were it not for the fact that the Chinese Foreign Office specifically barred him from so doing.[41] A measure of the 'confidence' he inspired in the authorities at Peking is afforded by the fact that no sooner was the Wai-w-pu able to re-assert its control, after the departure of the British, than Yu T'ai was summarily dismissed from office, humiliated and charged with crimes whose enormity was indeed reckoned grave.[42]

What modicum of popularity did he enjoy among the Tibetans may be gauged from the jeers and ridicule with which they received his exhortations that they 'must not transgress' his orders lest any punishment befall them—even as it had their ruler.[43] It is also significant that more than once, the Tibetan negotiators threw broad enough hints to Younghusband to deal directly with them, rather than the obviously unwelcome intermediacy of the Amban.[44]

It is somewhat paradoxical, and no doubt intriguing, that while Chinese historians have charged that Yu T'ai 'played into' Younghusband's hands,[45] knowledgeable British authorities contend, as has been noted earlier, that the Commissioner never, in fact, 'saw through the Amban'.[46] Actually, apart from what has been said above, two observations may be relevant in this context. One, that the Amban's role was that of a shrewd man of affairs, who played up to the British on the spot, while at the same time advising his Government that the British, by humbling the Tibetans, were in reality giving China a chance to re-assert and buttress its own authority. This pandering to the British, which was one of the charges levelled against him at his impeachment, however humiliating a confession it may have been to the pride and self-esteem of the Manchu court,[47] would certainly appear to be a clever and shrewd assessment of the existing situation. Nor was there anything 'queer' about it. Besides, it would also fit in with the fact that in order to win Younghusband's confidence, it would suit the Amban to assure him (Younghusband) that only higher orders prevented him (Amban) from affixing his seal in immediate approval of the Commissioner's covenant.

One could go even further and say that merely because he was later summarily dismissed from service 'within a few years' need not necessarily imply that Yu T'ai did not inspire confidence at that time in his superiors at Peking. Court favour is traditionally arbitary and fickle. In fact, in the last decades of the dynasty—and this was the very last decade—the court knowing its own weakness, was most suspicious of the best servants of the state, simply because their capacity won them prestige and this was something to frighten a dying dynasty. Besides, it is evident that Yu T'ai was not unlike the sacrificial lamb who must serve as a scapegoat for Britain's success at Lhasa which, to Peking, was synonymous with China's own defeat and discomfiture.[48] As for Younghusband not seeing through the Amban, the Commissioner's peculiar limitations must be constantly borne in mind. His apparent 'relief' in talking to a man of the world, after 'so many long, dreary and ineffectual interviews with the obtuse and ignorant Tibetans',[49] ned not blind us to the fact that the Commissioner was severely hedged in both in terms of time and space. Besides, he had the most specific instructions neither to ignore nor yet by-pass Chinese suzerainty. In the administrative and governmental chaos that Lhasa presented on the morrow of his arrival, the Amban seemed to be the only ray of hope. And Yu T'ai played the Commissioner's game to near-perfection. Besides, to by-pass him, as the Tibetan negotiators suggested, was perhaps another invitation to land himself in that hopeless morass of interminable talk from which he had, with the greatest difficulty, extricated himself. For Younghusband was shrewd enough to see that

> Chinese suzerainty was definitely recorded in the Treaty and all the way through the negotiations I had tried to carry the Resident with me. It was no part of our policy to supplant the Chinese... as I always tried to treat the Resident with respect, I expected, and did, in fact, receive, his hearty co-operation. We each of us could and did help the other to the advantage of both.[50]

Nor is it possible to deduce that the Commissioner was so supine or unintelligent as to be unable to strike back when occasion demanded. Thus, even as he wrote to his father on September 16:

> Of course, the wily Heathen has weighed in at the last moment with an objection to the whole proceeding because China's suzerainty is not sufficiently recognized. I told the Amban that if he talked too much about the rights of suzerainty I would begin to talk about the responsibilities. These operations had cost us a million sterling and for that we had a perfect right to bill the Chinese. He coiled up at once but can do nothing without orders from Peking and Peking is probably influenced by France and Russia.[51]

Two expressions may be underlined : 'the wily Heathen' and 'can do nothing without orders from Peking'. It should be evident that Younghusband was not the innocent lamb who never, in fact, 'saw through the Amban' nor yet was the latter, so overawed by the former, as to have 'played into his hands'.

Notes

1. Younghusband, India and Tibet, *op.cit.*, p. 263.
2. *Infra* 323-324.
3. Mr. Townley's telegram from Peking announcing Yu T'ai's appointment is dated December 6, 1902, Tibet Papers, *op.cit.*, Cd. 1920, No. 59, p. 146.
4. *Ibid.*, No. 67, p. 177.
    Yu T'ai had called upon Mr. Townley in Peking on January 5, 1903.
5. *Loc. cit.*
6. Thus as early as February 11, 1903, the Viceroy telegraphed to the Secretary of State that Yu T'ai's reported arrival in July 'supports our view that there is intentional delay'. Lord Curzon further underlined the fact that the situation was 'extermely serious and early action necessary'. *Ibid.*, No. 71, p. 179.
7. Telegraphing information from the British Consul-General at Chengtu, Sir Ernest Satow, the Minister in Peking, told Lord Lansdowne (on September 28, 1903) that Yu T'ai was holding consultations with the new Viceroy of Sezechuan on Tibetan affairs, that there were differences of opinion between the Resident and the Assistant Resident and that the former was scheduled to leave Chengtu on October 11 (1903) 'with an escort of some 40 soldiers'. *Ibid.*, No. 117, p. 212.

8. *Ibid.,* Nos. 116, 139, and 145, pp. 211-12, 297-98 and 301.

9. *Ibid.,* Nos. 139 and 148. pp. 197-98 and 302.

10. *Ibid.,* No. 116, pp. 211-12; the despatch from Sir Ernest Satow in Peking was sent on September 25, 1903.

11. *Ibid.,* Nos. 142-43 and 146, pp. 199-201.

12. Yao-ting Sung, *op.cit.*, p. 139. Li, *op.cit.*, note 218, p. 248, makes this laconic comment: 'Yu K'ang was finally replaced by Yu T'ai and left Tibet in the spring of 1903'. Younghusband, India and Tibet, *op.cit.*, p. 88, notes that Yu T'ai reached Lhasa after 'thirteen critical months of his appointment; actually on February 11, 1904'. *Ibid.,* p. 172. According to Younghusband, the old Amban had memorialised the throne, sometime in July (1903), that he had told the Tibetan Councillors of the British intent to bring troops into Tibet, that 'they must on no account repel them (British-troops) with arms, but instead discuss matters 'on the basis of reason'. *Ibid.,* pp. 89-90.

13. Tibet Papers, *op.cit.* Cd. 2054, Nos. 5 and 7, pp. 3-4. Dr. Sung, basing his account on the Memoirs of Chang Ying-tang, informs us that 'upon learning of this critical situation (Younghusband's crossing of the Jelap La) the Chinese Government instructed Yu T'ai to proceed to the frontier at once in order to stop the British advance...Unfortunately, Yu T'ai lost his chance by not going to the frontier in person on no other ground than that of the Tibetan authorities refused *(sic.)* to furnish the means of transport. Instead, he sent an ordinary officer to make the call'. Yao-ting Sung, *op.cit.*, p. 39.

14. Tibet Papers, *op.cit.,* Cd. 2054, No. 14, p. 7.

15. *Loc. cit.*

16. *Ibid.,* No. 16, p. 7. 'Ma' is almost always a Muslim name. It is not unlikely that General Ma hailed from Kansu province which would indicate a Peking policy of using one kind of frontier minority, the North-Western Muslims in this case, against another. the Tibetans.

17. *Ibid.,* No. 22, p. 9.

18. *Ibid.,* No. 34, p. 13.

19. Curzon to Younghusband, letter, April, 4 1904, Curzon MSS.
A little later, the Viceroy confessed to the Commissioner that a settlement was a difficult affair 'complicated by the fact that the fiction of Chinese suzerainty is to be retained'.

20. *Ibid.,* Younghusband to Curzon, telegram, dated April 29. 1904.

21. Tibet Papers, *op.cit.,* Cd. 2370, Encl. No 63. In his letter to Lord Curzon, on May 7 (1904), Younghusband noted that the Chinese Government had informed the British that it 'had no influence with the Dalai Lama and rather hoped he would run away', a view 'in which I entirely agree'. Curzon MSS. Earlier, on May 2, the Acting Viceroy telegraphed the Secretary of State that Younghusband had heard from the Amban to the effect that 'he (Amban) cannot get a reply to his representation from the Dalai Lama', five days later that Younghusband's 'fourth despatch to present Amban has produced no more result than previous three'. Ampthill Papers, *op.cit.*

22. Originally Younghusband despatched the ultimatums on June 3. These, however, were returned by the Lhasa general—'which pleased me greatly'. The general, however, soon retracted but Younghusband was rather chary of sending the ultimatums again. Later, Government 'got rather stuffy' and 'sent me a telegram virtually recalling me to Chumbi'. In between, he actually 'had delivered' these documents. For details, see Younghusband MSS, Nos. 40 and 41, dated June 3 and 12, 1904.

23. Tibet Papers, *op.cit.*, Cd. 2370, Encl. No. 212, p. 186.
24. *Loc. cit.*
25. *Ibid.*, Encl. No. 236, p. 201.
26. *Ibid.*, No. 119, p. 49, and Encls. Nos. 239 and 264, pp. 205 and 223-24.
27. *Supra*, p. 60. Manning had suggested that the great Mandarins at Lhasa, meaning the Imperial Ambans, 'were generally rogues and scoundrels'. Colonel Peter Fleming quotes, with approval, a remark of his, 'It is a very bad policy thus perpetually to send men of bad character to govern Tibet'. Peter Fleming, *op.cit.*, p. 232. So does Younghusband, 'the haughty Mandarins were somewhat deficient in respect, and I noted the same thing'. India and Tibet, *op.cit.*, p. 321.
28. *Supra*, Chapter 9.
    Li, *op.cit.*, p. 65, notes that in 1900, the Dalai Lama killed his own tutor Demo Hutukhtu who had been in power upto 1895 and had 'always enjoyed the confidence of the Imperial Court'. Besides, after the Boxer Rebellion, 'he (Dalai Lama) and the Tibetan officials listened to the Resident's advice only when it was acceptable to them, and orders, regulations and treaties, which were distasteful to them were utterly disregarded'.
29. *Loc. cit.*
30. Tibet Papers, *op.cit.*, Cd. 1920, Annexure in No. 129, p. 291, and Encl. in No. 149, p. 303. Evidently Yu Kang's predecessor, Resident Kuei Huan, could not in 1896 'get transport...nor Tibetan officials to accompany the trip' in order to demarcate the frontier with the British. Li, *op.cit.*, p. 96.
31. Li, *op.cit.*, pp. 92-93.
32. Dr. Li concedes that Yu Kang and his deputy faced 'more difficulties', detailed in their memorials to the Emperor, and that Yu T'ai found himself in a 'helpless situation'. Li, *op.cit.*, note 218, p. 248.
33. Tibet Papers, *op.cit.*, Cd. 2370, Encl. No. 86, p. 135. Also see Ibid, Encl. No. 81, p. 134.
34. *Ibid.*, Encl. No. 91, p. 139. The Commissioner's telegram from Gyantse is dated May 11, 1904.
35. The title ('all-wise Sahib') was used by the Tsongdu (Tibetan National Assembly) in addressing Younghusband ; the Dalai Lama had been more literal and called him 'the Sahib sent by the English Government to settle affairs'. *Ibid.*, Nos. 111 and 118 pp. 44 and 48. See also Younghusband, India and Tibet, *op.cit.*, pp. 235 and 242.
36. Younghusband, India and Tibet, *op.cit.*, p. 263.
37. 'But with this splendid force at my back', Younghusband wrote to his father on September 9, 'the Tibetans had to give in and the only difficulty was in applying the pressure so as to secure acceptance without resentment'. Younghusband MSS., No. 50, September 9, 1904.
38. Tibet Papers, *op.cit.*, Cd. 2054, no. 26, p. 10.
39. Li, *op.cit.*, p. 93.
40. Younghusband, India and Tibet, *op.cit.*, pp. 301 and 322.
41. Tibet Papers, *op.cit.*, Cd. 2054, No. 162, p. 65. Li, *op.cit.*, p. 96, maintains that the Wai-wu-pu not only refused to give sanction but 'admonished him (Yu T'ai) for having let the Tibetans enter into such a questionable agreement with the British'.
42. Colonel Peter Fleming has cited from a translation of the indictment found among the 'papers' of Mr. (later Sir) Ernest Wilton who, a member of the (Birtish) Chinese

Consular Service, had joined the Mission at Khamba Jong early in August 1903. Fleming, *op.cit.*, pp. 230-32. See also Younghusband, India and Tibet, *op.cit.*, p. 3

43. Tibet Papers, *op.cit.*, Cd. 2370, Annexure in Encl. No. 362, pp. 274-75.
44. Younghusband, India and Tibet, *op.cit.*, pp. 283 and 285. The Commissioner noted : 'I now came to the conclusion that the Tibetans were trying to make dissension between the Resident and myself'. To Lord Ampthill 'he wrote that the Regent had put out feelers to him and that 'if I had lifted my little finger', the Tibetans would have come over 'to our side' and that 'the only sentiment in my speech' the Tibetans resented was wherein the Commissioner had talked about recognizing the suzerainty of China. Younghusband to Ampthill, letter, September 26, 1904, Ampthill Papers, *op.cit.*
45. Li, *op.cit.*, p. 93.
46. Peter Fleming, *op.cit.*, p. 235.
47. Symptomatic of Chinese thinking may be Dr. Li's assertion that for Yu T'ai 'it did not require any effrontery' to inform Younghusband that he (Yu T'ai) had been unable to see him for lack of transport from the Tibetan authorities. Li, *op.cit.*, p. 93.
48. Years later, Younghusband noted that Yu T'ai's dismissal, and later imprisonment 'in fetters', as also his Secretary's humiliation, were no doubt 'inspired by a desire to sweep away all Chinese officials' who had helped conclude the Convention at Lhasa. 'A similar resentment' against Tibetan officials was also shown —'two Councillors and a General being degraded'. Younghusband, India and Tibet, *op.cit.*, p. 345.
49. *Ibid.*, p. 263.
50. *Ibid.*, p. 175.
51. Younghusband MSS. No. 51, September 16, 1904. It is only fair to note that this was in a private, family letter.

22
The Tongsa Penlop and Captain Jit Bahadur

U-Gyen Wangchuk who as Tongsa Penlop was the de facto ruler of Bhutan and had emerged victorious from the last civil war in that country in 1885, had shown a measure of friendliness to the British during the period of their short-lived hostilities with Tibet in 1888.[1] And yet, as the Mission advanced from Chumbi to the Tuna plains, the Commissioner had been 'in considerable anxiety'[2] about what Curzon called 'the incomprehensible hirerarchy who preside over the hills that literally overhang the camp'.[3] To be sure, Bhutan lay on the right of the advancing columns and with close affinity to Tibet could be a source of considerable embarrassment, if not positive anxiety. Feelers were first thrown through the Commissioner of Darjeeling and later 'an official of some standing', the Trimpuk Jongpen, met Younghusband at Tuna and pledged his whole-hearted support. He even promised 'and gave permision, on payment', to make a road up the Amo-chu. His intercession, on the Mission's behalf, with the Lhasa monks at Guru proved a positive gain to Younghusband revealing as it did Tibetan obduracy and, in the bargain, helped to draw Bhutan closer.[4]

This was, by itself, no small a gain. The Commissioner felt 'perfectly certain' that, barring the Paro Penlop, the other chiefs of Bhutan 'are most thoroughly amicable towards us'. And this meant, with Nepal thrown in, that the whole frontier 'right up to the Himalayan watershed' was ranged 'on our side'.[5] Lord Curzon was 'delighted' at the 'success' of 'your negotiations'[6]—a gain, which the Commissioner attributed chiefly to his refusal to retire form Tuna when the military had asked him to do so in January.[7]

Early in June, the Tongsa Penlop himself appeared on the scene accompanied by his somewhat heterogeneous band of retainers. 'In theory', Landon, the *Times* correspondent noted, he had come to act as a 'mediator' in the lamas' quarrel with the British, for he was 'most anxious to effect a settlement'. In practice, he leaned far too heavily even for British comfort, on the Commissioner's side.[8] His usefulness, as a pipeline for communicating with the Tibetans, and more particularly the Dalai Lama, was a great boon. For he acted, most of the time as the Commissioner's mouth-piece—expounding the British terms of settlement, dressing down the Tibetan delegates in behind-the-scenes encounters and before their meetings with Younghusband, in stately 'durbars'.

More specifically, at Gyantse he lent a helping hand in such 'negotiations' as were conducted there with the delegates form Lhasa.[9] Indeed, he exchanged many a mesage with the Dalai Lama and other dignitaries before the former deigned to address the 'all-wise Sahib'.[10] The Lama had, in fact, pleaded with the Penlop to intercede on his behalf with the British and 'assist in peaceful settlement, fighting being bad for both animals and men'.[11] Through him, the Commissioner too let the Lama know 'an outline of the terms we should demand'.[12]

After reaching Lhasa, the Penlop reverted to the not unfamiliar type who invarialby apes his master and chimes in with every nod of his head. But when he does not, it is on the tacit understanding that the master had already consented to the change. Thus on September 4 (1904), during the discussions on the payment of the indemnity the Penlop suggested, and Colonel Younghusband 'assented', that the amount be reduced from Rs. 76,00,000 to Rs. 75,00,000!![13] On an earlier occasion he asked Younghusband not to occupy the Norbulingka, the Dalai Lama's summer palace, owing to its religious associations. The Colonel who had merely 'made a pretence' of going there, 'consented to occupy the next best residence in Lhasa'.[14]

What influence did he wield over the Lama may be gauged from the fact that no meeting-ground could be found that would prevent the Mission's advance to Lhasa. As for the 'weight' he carried—the Commissioner had noted that the Penlop's representation 'carried weight'[15]—after the Lama had left, it need must be emphasised that everybody who had anything to do with the Mission, or the Commissioner for that matter, reflected something of the power and authority that flows naturally from well-accoutred troops and trained Maxims.

Younghusband found him to be most useful and, in consequence, continued all through to underwrite his great 'importance'. Despite the many embarrassments to which the predatory raids of his men exposed the Mission,[16] the Commissioner wrote him an excellent testimonial: 'The Tongsa Penlop I found to be a straight, honest-looking, dignified man[17] of about forty-seven years of age. He bore himself well, dresed well, gave me costly presents (to condone, one would suspect, his followers' notorious depredations in the countryside)[18] and altogether showed himself a man of importance'.[19]

For 'services (he had) rendered', the Penlop was to receive the signal honour of a Knight Commander of (the most Distinguished Order of) the Indian Empire.[20] Later, in 1906, when Sir U-gyen Wangchuk became the hereditary Maharaja of Bhutan, with the Lopons and the whole body of Lamas and the State Councillors swearing 'allegiance to him and his heirs with unchanging mind', the British Government were duly represented at his installation.[21]

Captain Jit Bahadur, the Nepalese representative in Lhasa—courtly, courteous and clever—had spent many a summer in the county and had, therefore, first-hand knowledge of its affairs. His Prime Minister in Katmandu, Maharaja Chandra Shamsher, had decided upon giving the 'Raj' his 'whole-souled' support and offered to co-operate 'in whatever way might be thought most desirable' either 'within or beyond the frontier'. For he too, not unlike the British, regarded Russian designs on Tibet as 'utterly inconsistent with the interests of his own country.'[22] His plighted word, like a true Rajput, he 'amply fulfilled', and to the last day of the Mission. Thus he wrote long, well-reasoned, even threatening, letters to the Dalai Lama, and his Councillors, which could not have stated the British case better, nor indeed more forcefully.[23] Besides, he placed nearly all his intelligence resources, and these were of no mean a magnitude, at the disposal of the British Resident[24] at Katmandu. At Khamba Jong, his 'present' of the sorely-needed, and what the Commissioner viewed not only as 'of great practical use, but of still greater political significance', 500 yaks to the Mission[25] was an act of extreme friendliness. It may be recalled that it was the Nepalese government that directed Captain Jit Bahadur to render the Mission 'every assistance' and as the Commissioner later recorded 'no one could have been more helpful'.[26] He had the local knowledge and the quickness of wit, which the Penlop lacked, and employed these to the Mission's maximum advantage.

Long before Younghusband arrived in Lhasa, Captain Jit Bahadur had reported regularly, and at great length, to his government about the goings-on in the Tibetan capital. In a cloud of what, for most part, was bazaar gossip and unsubstantiated rumour-mongering, his intelligence because of his peculiar advantages had provided a certain substratum of solid worth. His usefulness was widely acknowledged and, in July (1904) before the Mision left Gyantse, even the Secretary of State had suggested to the Acting Viceroy to 'employ' him in such negotiations as may be entered into with the Dalai Lama.[27] It may be recalled that earlier in January (1903) Whitehall had given serious thought to a proposal by Sir William Lee-Warner that instead of the British sending an armed expedition, 'might not Nepal be urged to send a force to Lhasa' and demand assurances of (Tibetan) good behaviour?[28] Later there was even a suggestion, evidently seriusly meant, that the British might subsidise the Nepalese for such intelligence as the latter may garner— in place of having their (British) own agent at Lhasa who may be merely 'shut up' and 'put under guard'.

Inasmuch as his government had lent active aid and succour to the Mission, Captain Jit Bahadur's role had to be cast in a lower, subordinate key. Yet he it was who 'discovered' the Ti Rimpoche,[29] impressed upon the Commissioner that here was 'a moderate man' more inclined to make a peaceful settlement than most of the others. Henceforth there was no move which the Commissioner made in his negotiations with which the Nepalese representative was not closely associated, hardly a meeting to which he was not invited, scarcely a detail which either escaped his notice or attention.

Notes

1. On the outbreak of hostilities, in 1888, the Bhutanese had not only warned the Tibetans of the consequences of refusing to come to terms with the British but what was more 'refused' them any 'assistance'. White, *op.cit.,* p. 281.
2. Younghusband, India and Tibet, *op.cit.,* p. 169.
3. Curzon to Younghusband, letter, April 4, 1904, Curzon MSS.
4. Younghusband, India and Tibet, *op.cit.,* pp. 169-72. To the Jongpen's advantage Younghusband recorded that he (Jongpen) was 'the first sensible man' he (Younghusband) had met on the frontier'.
5. Younghusband to Miller, letter, March 30, 1904. Curzon MSS.
6. *Ibid.,* Curzon to Younghusband, letter, April 4, 1904.
7. *Ibid.,* Younghusband to Dane, letter, March 26, 1904. If the Mission had retired, as Macdonald wanted, 'Bhutan which was then sitting on the fence would have come on the Tibetan instead of our side', the Commissioner wrote to the Foreign Secretary.
8. Landon noted that his (Tongsa Penlop's) 'unblushing and openly-admitted preference for the English was not entirely satisfactory even to us. It suggested a biased mind....' Landon, *op.cit.,* II, pp. 62-63. See also Younghusband, India and Tibet, *op.cit.,* p. 204.
9. Younghusband, India and Tibet, *op.cit.,* pp. 208-22. Landon, *op.cit.* II, pp. 64-65.
10. At Gyantse, Younghusband noted that 'at my request' the Penlop wrote to the Ta Lama about the Commissioner's readiness to carry on negotiations 'en route to Lhasa'. Younghusband, India and Tibet, *op.cit.,* p. 222.
11. Tibet Papers, *op.cit.,* Cd., 2370, Nos. 63, 72, 78 and 83, pp. 21, 24, 26 and 28 respectively.
12. *Supra,* n. 10.
13. Tibet Papers, *op.cit.,* Cd. 2370, No. 317, pp. 245-46. Younghusband, India and Tibet , *op.cit.,* p. 298.
14. Younghusband, India and Tibet, *op.cit.,* p. 298. Years later Younghusband noted: 'With the object of getting into the next best house in Lhasa, I made a pretence of wishing to go into the Dalai Lama's Summer Place... and eventually arranged that the house of the first Duke in Tibet should be at my disposal'. *Ibid.,* p. 267
15. *Loc., cit.*
16. Landon, *op.cit.,* II, p. 63, noted that the Penlop's men 'with his full sanction, took advantage of the presence of our troops to harry the land far and wide, and do what looting they could on their own account'.
17. *Loc. cit.* Evidently the *Times* correspondent regarded him (Tongsa Penlop) 'not a particularly dignified adjunct to the Mission'.
18. *Loc. cit.* In a footnote (p. 63) Landon noted that 'looting by his (Tongsa Penlop's) attendants in the Nagartse district caused such widespread distress that the inhabitants came in to us for food', and further that the Bhutanese 'deprived the wretched peasants of grain and money alike'.

19. Younghusband, India and Tibet, *op.cit.,* p. 204.
20. White, *op.cit.,* pp. 105-83, gives a detailed account of his 'First Mission to Bhutan' undertaken for this purpose.
21. *Ibid.,* pp. 211-36.
22. The matter had been first broached with him by Lord Curzon at the Delhi durbar (January, 1903). Younghusband, India and Tibet, *op.cit.,* pp. 134 and 170.
23. Younghusband gives a resume of one of these which the Maharaja sent to the (Lama's) four councilors sometime in September (1903). See *ibid.,* pp. 135-37. Another was addressed to the Lama himself, early in June (1904). *Ibid.,* pp. 206-7.
24. Col. Pears and later Lt.-Col. Ravenshaw, British Residents at Katmandu, had regularly sent in to Calcutta extracts of reports received by the Government of Nepal from their representative at Lhasa..
25. Younghusband, India and Tibet, *op.cit.,* p. 133. 'This welcome offer' was accompanied by another of 800 yaks within a month. *Ibid.,* p. 134.
26. *Ibid.,* p. 267.
27. Brodrick to Ampthill, letter, July 22, 1904, Ampthill Papers, *op.cit.* Five days later the Secretary of State wrote to say that he thought the letters of the Nepalese Representative at Lhasa 'have been encouraging'. *Ibid.,* letter, July 27, 1904.
28. *Supra,* Chapter 11.
29. Younghusband, India and Tibet, *op.cit.,* p. 268.

23

The Lhasa Convention: The Indemnity and the Agent

On the afternoon of September 7, in the audience-hall of the golden Potala—and the Tibetans had made a last, desperate, though vain, bid against the sacrilege involved[1]—the British Commissioner, resplendent in his full-dress diplomatic uniform, arrived to have the convention signed and sealed. The atmosphere was that of a Durbar and every possible care had been taken to ensure that no detail was missed that may impress the Asiatic with the power and majesty, the glory and the grandeur, of the British Empire and this, one of its unique, notable feats of armed might. The ceremonial indeed 'deeply impressed' the Tibetans.[2] As for the Colonel, the effect of signing the treaty in the Potala's audience-hall, was as important as the contents of the treaty itself.[3]

General Macdonald had taken all necessary precautions against any last-minute mishap: 'a battery to fire a salute or to bombard the palace' had been stationed in a suitable position and the entire route leading up to the Potala, as also its side passages, were lined with troops.[4] Nor had the Colonel forgotten his camp-table 'and on it was laid the flag' which had flown over the Mission headquarters throughout. The Ti Rimpoche, and 'the mass of Tibetans', were present too. So were the Tongsa Penlop and his motley crowd of retainers, the portly Nepalese representative and, of course, Yu T'ai who appeared to preside over this solemn, if quaint, assembly.

At the appropriate moment, the signatures were appended on the dotted lines and the seals affixed[5] on a convention 'negotiated' for the past five weeks at Lhasa, though drawn up indeed at Simla. The Commissioner took care that no available seal was omitted: the Dalai Lama's, the Council's, those of the three great monasteries or of the National Assembly. The great ceremony tailed off with a speech by Younghusband in which he very appropriately reminded the Tibetans that most of their misfortunes had been due to disrespect which they had shown to the British representative. Indeed, he exhorted them 'You will find us equally good friends, if you keep the present treaty and show civility'[6]—a promise that was, for many a

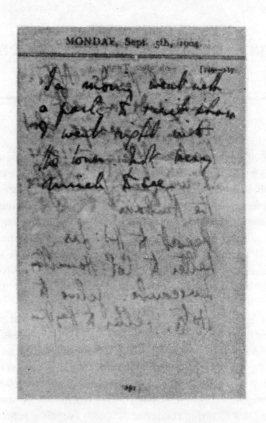

Extracts from Lt. (later Lt. Col.)
A. L. Hadow's diary
[For text see Appendix 10]

ear, made good and honoured by both sides.

It has been noticed that the Secretary of State had laid down a very definite
olicy both in regard to the indemnity that was to be demanded and the Agent, who
as not to be appointed. The preceding pages also reveal, and vividly, that the
ommissioner's own views on the subject ran completely counter to those of his
olitical superiors in Simla, though much more so in London. And although Lord
urzon had placed the Commissioner at the extreme end of the political spectrum,
far as policy towards Tibet was concerned, Younghusband's thinking came the
osest to him. Nor is it without interest that in concluding the convention at Lhasa,
ne Commissioner's gaze was focussed not so much on the instructions, for most
art clear and unambiguous, that he had received from the Secretary of State, with
heir near-complete endorsement from the acting Viceroy, but on his own views,
owerfully endorsed by Lord Curzon. It is necessary to underline this aspect of the
uestion in order to understand both the Commissioner's initial action at Lhasa and
is later apologia in explaining it away.

On the issue of the indemnity to be demanded, the Secretary of State's telegrams
f July 6, 13 and 26 and of August 3 and 31 addressed to the Government of India
nd repeated by the latter verbatim to Younghusband in Lhasa as well as elaborated
n his later despatches, made the position clear beyond a doubt.[7] And although the
xact sum to be stipulated was not clearly mentioned, it was to be such as may not
e 'beyond the power of the Tibetans to pay'. An additional rider was that the
Chumbi Valley, which was to be occupied as a security for this payment, was to be
vacuated at the end of three years—it being implied that the indemnity would
ave been paid by that time, albeit in instalments. 'Some degree of discretion',[8]
owever, was left to the Commissioner who 'will be guided by circumstances in
his matter'.[9] In actual fact, Younghusband stretched the period of payment, and
vith it the resultant occupation of the Chumbi Valley, to 75 years. Would 'some
legree of discretion', vouchsafed him by Authority, comprehend this departure?

The Commissioner later maintained in his defence—or as Brodrick termed it
vindication'—that the suggestion for the longer period actually came to him from
he Tibetans and that in accepting it he was doing no more than acceding to their
vishes to 'suit', as it happened, 'their convenience'.[10] It is necessary to straighten
he record here, and be more specific as to how the provision came to be incorporated.

In the first reply which the Tibetans gave to the British terms of settlement—
nd the Commissioner had demanded 'more than Government have sanctioned my
sking... what Government of India *proposed* not what Secretary of State
anctioned'[11]—they had taken exception to each one of them. On the specific
question of the indemnity, the Colonel reported, 'they decline to pay any, saying we
ught to pay them an indemnity instead (of) their paying one to us'.[12] A few days
ater when the 'impertinence' of their 'unsatisfactory' reply had been brought home
o them, and they ware asked to be 'more amenable', the question still rankled.
Even the soft-spoken Ti Rimpoche, who had been 'discovered' in the meantime,
conceded that the problem presented difficulties.[13]

The Tibetans handed over their second reply on August 19 and therein indicated, for the first time, a willingness to pay 'a small amount' on the specific condition that the boundary be fixed at Giaogong. The Commissioner, however, was adamant and told the Amban that while the period in which the indemnity was to be paid could be a subject for discussion, the payment itself was not.[14]

The sum suggested by the Government of India—the Secretary of State had pleaded his inability to fix any, owing to his self-confessed ignorance of Tibet's resources—it may be recalled, was to be computed at the rate of £ 100,000 a month, or Rs. 50,000 a day, and was to be reckoned from the date (i.e., May 4) the Mission had been attacked at Gyantse. On August 23, Younghusband informed Government that he considered their stipulated sum 'excessive', and would not press for it 'seriously'. He further thought that the demand, as it stood, would make the British very unpopular and suggested instead the 'securing of additional facilities for trade', and perhaps 'mining rights' as well.[15] As it transpired, the Secretary of State rejected the latter, for he thought it will 'at intervals necessitate support and pressure from us', while making it clear that the figure for the indemnity was 'altogether excessive'.[16]

Before Government could reply to his communication he reported again on August 30, that the Tibetans had accepted all his terms except the one relating to the indemnity, but that he (Younghusband) had indicated that 'it would have to be paid' one way or another.

Meantime the Commissioner's views were undergoing a sharp change. Thus on September 1, we find him informing Government that the sum, which he had found 'excessive' only a week earlier, could be paid 'without undue hardship'—a fact which did not go unnoticed in Simla[17]—and that 'in spite of their protests of poverty', the Tibetans cold really 'pay the indemnity'.[18]

With this sudden metamorphosis we find the Commissioner's mind working on another track. Ostensibly to lessen the Tibetans' hostility to the payment, he was hard at work devising some way out. Thus on August 21,

The Ti Rimpoche had said that the Tibetans had little cash. If that was so, I was prepared to consider the question of extending the period in which the payment of the indemnity could be made... The Ti Rimpoche said he wished the settlement with us to be fully completed now so that we could have it over and be friends, but if the Tibetans had to go on paying us an indemnity for some years after, the row would be kept up and friendship would be difficult.[19]

The Tibetan position was clear and unexceptionable; they were opposed to any extension of the period over which the payment was to be made.[20] But Younghusband had his own ends in view for with the payment was linked up, inextricably as it were, the occupation of the Chumbi Valley. A week later he returned to the subject:

I quite recognised the difficulty they had in paying the indemnity in cash within three years. I would, therefore, be prepared to receive proposals from them as to modifications in manner of payment. If, for instance, they thought it

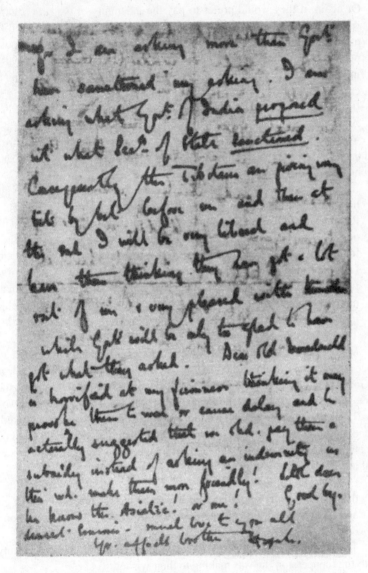

From Lhasa, to 'My dearest Emmie' dated August 22, 1904

impossible to pay the whole indemnity in three years, and would like the term extended to five, I would submit such a proposal for the orders of the Vicero Or again, if they would prefer to pay the indemnity *at the rate of a lakh o rupees a year for a long term of years*, I would ask Government if the difficult might be met in that way...[21] I would be also prepared to submit proposals fo privileges or concessions in Tibet which might be taken in lieu of part of th indemnity.... They (the Ti Rimpoche, the Yutok Shape and the Tsarong Shape expressed their disappointment at this answer.... The Tsarong Depon said.. It was hard.... That we should demand so much from Tibet, and the Nationa Assembly would be very much disheartened at the result of this interview..."

Younghusband's hints were broad enough, but the Tibetans were shrewd to and they seemed to grasp the implications of his demand. On August 31, he agai touched on the question,

.....The Ti Rimpoche then again dwelt upon the impossibility of paying wha he considered so heavy an indemnity. I repeated my old arguments. ... The Rimpoche said that we were putting on the donkey a greater load than it woul possibly carry. I replied that I was not asking the donkey to carry the who load in one journey. It could go backwards and forwards many times.. Dropping metaphor I told the Acting Regent .... if... they could not pay th full amount in three years, I would receive proposals as to paying in a larg number of years.... The Ti Rimpoche replied that the Tibetans disliked th idea of prolonging the time during which they would be under obligation to u They wanted to settle the business up at once and have done with it...[23]

Matters, however, now moved fast. The interview, detailed above, had take place on August 31. A day earlier, i.e., on August 30, Younghusband had telegraphe to Government for permission to arrange payment of the indemnity by instalmen of one lakh of rupees a year: the total amount, May through September, would ru into 75 lakhs. On September 4, without receiving the approval he had asked for, h found an obliging Ti Rimpoche (who had been that day 'definitely recognised b the National Assembly as Regent' and with the Amban's consent 'commenced usir seal left by the Dalai Lama') again darken his door,

He said Tibetan Government were prepared to accept our terms, but begge that the indemnity might be paid in annual instalments of one lakh each... agreed in anticipation of sanction from Government. I trust my action will l upheld...'[24]

The Commissioner, however, took care not to leave the Tibetans in any dou as to the 'concession' he was making to their wishes,

I pointed out to them such a concession was very great deal more than it appear to them. Seventy-five lakhs in 75 years was only equal to a very much small sum within three years.... They must, however, clearly understand that und the terms of the treaty we should retain the right to continue to occupy th Chumbi Valley till the full payment of the indemnity was paid. .... The Rimpoche eventually affixed his private seal to the daft Convention.[25]

In private he was franker,

This (payment spread over 75 annual instalments) of course is a great reduction but as one of the conditions in the treaty is that we retain the Chumbi Valley till the indemnity is paid such a concession is of the greatest use to us. ... Lord Curzon will, I know, be delighted but how the Home Government will view it, I don't know. If they like to be idiotic they of course need not exercise the right to occupy the Chumbi for 75 years ...[26]

In view of the controversy that was to rage, and fiercely, around this question, the sequence may be laid threadbare. It was Younghusband who, on August 23, told Government that he regarded the amount proposed for the indemnity 'excessive'; two days earlier, he it was who had suggested to the Tibetans 'extending (of) the period' over which the payment was to be made. Again, it was from him that the specific proposal for payment being made at the rate of a lakh of rupees a year 'for a long term of years' first emanated: the donkey could go backwards and forwards many times. Throughout, that is until the fateful day of his being recognised Regent, the Ti Rimpoche maintained a consistent stand on the settlement 'to be fully completed now'. The Tibetans, he had told Younghusband repeatedly, 'disliked' the idea of 'prolonging the time' during which they would be 'under obligation to us'—and 'the row' would be kept up.

No sooner had the Ti Rimpoche capitulated, than the Commissioner hastened 'to sign, seal and deliver' the Convention. The settlement relating to the indemnity was incorporated in Clause VI which stated inter alia,

The indemnity shall be payable... in 75 instalments of one lakh each on the 1st January in each year, beginning from the 1st January, 1906.

The subsequent clause (VII), however, still paid lip strive to the Secretary of State's mention of three years as the period for payment,

As security for the payment of the indemnity, the British Government shall continue to occupy the Chumbi Valley until the indemnity has been paid and until the trade marts have been effectively opened for three years whichever date may be the latter.[27]

On September 12, the Viceroy telegraphed to Mr. Brodrick that the Convention had been signed, as finally approved by the Home Government, 'with modifications', and the main one was in regard to the indemnity—another was not to be known in Simla much less in London, for some time. Explaining the Commissioner's action, Lord Ampthill pleaded that Younghusband 'with considerable demur' was 'obliged to give way', owing to the 'special request' of the Ti Rimpoche. Having regard both to the necessity of obtaining early signatures, and to the Tibetan anxiety to conclude a settlement, the Viceroy felt that the agreement 'should.... be accepted as it stands'.[28]

To say that Mr. Brodrick was surprised, would be an understatement. His initial reaction—'I heartily congratulate Colonel Younghusband... his action will be supported...'—was qualified, less than 72 hours later, by inserting 'generally' before 'supported' and the all important rider: 'further communication will be made to you as to indemnity'.[29]

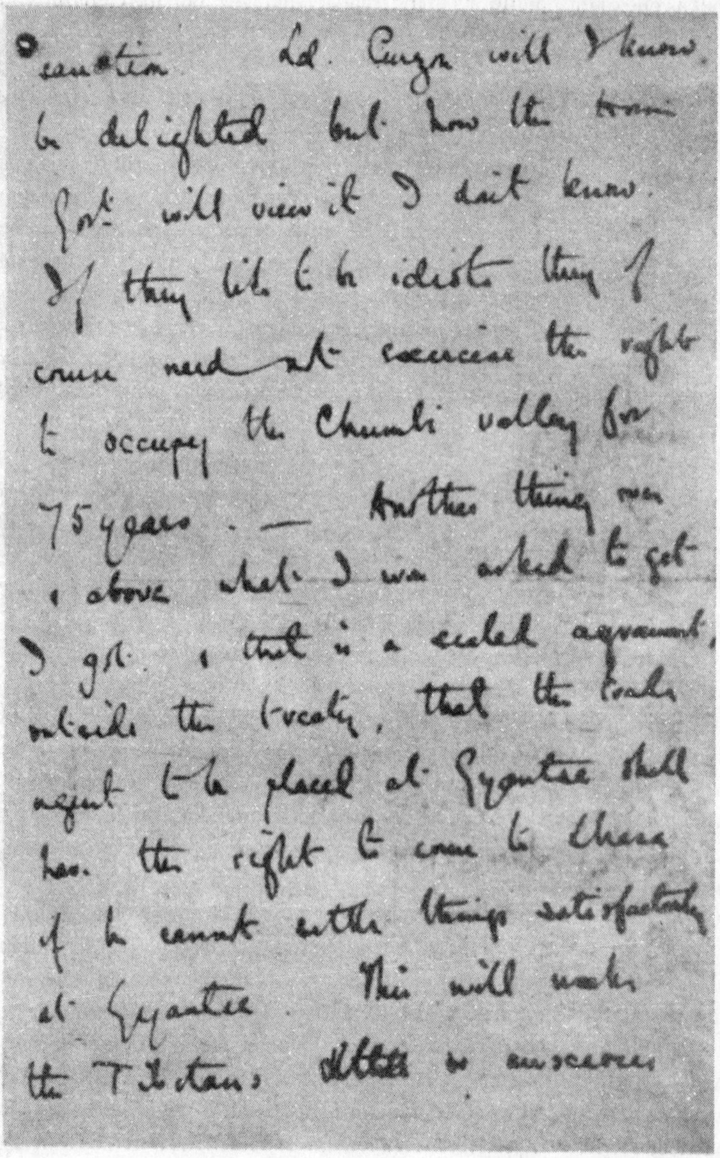

From Lhasa, to 'My dearest Emmie' dated September 9, 1904.

Actually, a day earlier he had already pointed out to Lord Ampthill the very obvious—that the mode of payment of the indemnity, read in conjunction with Clause VII, would mean that 'our' occupation of the Chumbi Valley 'may have to continue for 75 years'. And he underlined,

This is inconsistent with the instructions conveyed in my telegram of the 26th July last and with the declaration of HMG as to withdrawal.[30]

On September 16, Mr. Brodrick was more specific. Calling the indemnity –'as at present fixed'—a 'permanent tribute', he 'authorised' the Viceroy to reduce the amount to 25 lakhs. The sum was to be paid within three years at the end of which period 'the occupation of the Chumbi Valley' was to cease. His 'orders' were to be carried out by Younghusband and the 'necessary changes' incorporated in the Convention.[31]

Here, however, came the rub. For even though Mr. Brodrick had made up his mind, so had Colonel Younghusband. On September 18, anticipating criticism, he had wired to Government,

.... In reality, an indemnity of Rs. 75,00,000 payable in instalments spread over 75 years, is equivalent to about half the amount required to be paid in three years. Rs. 36,00,000 is only half the annual revenue of the State of Indore, and Tibet is a country far richer than Indore... But had I insisted on this amount being paid in three years they would have been left with a sense of oppression. A nasty racial feeling would have sprung up....

And with what correspondence to facts did he report, may best be left to the reader's judgment,

The arrangement which I adopted was put forward by Tibetans themselves, who preferred it to the various suggestions... all of which were put before them by the Nepalese and Bhutanese.[32] The feeling now prevailing here is altogether better, the Tibetans to all appearances being well-contented with the settlement which I have concluded...

Why had he preferred this particular mode of payment and herein, perhaps unwittingly, Younghusband gave himself away,

My view is that our responsibility is greatly diminished by terms of the Convention. With Chumbi Valley in our occupation and the Tibetans well disposed our merchants and trade agents at Gyantse and Gartok marts will be secure; whereas their position might have been precarious after our withdrawal from Chumbi, had Tibetans' resentment been aroused by their having to pay indemnity in a short time.

Arguing his position thus, the Commissioner informed the Viceroy that he 'deprecated any alteration of terms at present', for he felt that his proposal had incurred the 'minimum of responsibility, with the maximum of reparation'—a phrase which he apparently stole from one of Mr. Brodrick's despatches.[33]

More fully aroused than their Agent, the Government of India reminded Younghusband, in a telegram on September 19, that HMG had 'authorised' the reduction of the indemnity and an early termination of the occupation of the Chumbi

Valley. He was further advised that they considered it 'most desirable' that before leaving Lhasa he would secure the consent of the Tibetans to this change and that they trusted he would endeavourer to meet their (Government of India's) wishes 'on this point'. He was also informed that he could stay in Lhasa until October 15.[34]

The Commissioner, however, was in no mood to oblige. Though he had received Government's telegram (along with which Mr. Brodrick's had been repeated) before he left Lhasa, he wired back to say that it had been communicated to him too late; that the present arrangement was 'distinctly preferred' by the Tibetans; that if he had attempted to alter—'at this stage'—a settlement made with 'such solemnity', the main objects in view might not have been attained. As for meeting the express directives of HMG,

I hope to give opinion on arriving in India. Present was not the most suitable moment for arranging the matter...[35]

The mode of payment of the indemnity alone was not fund 'to be inconsistent'—to repeat Mr. Brodrick's words—either with his specific instructions or the previous declaration of HMG. Soon, in another particular, the revelation of what had transpired at Lhasa came to him as a still ruder shock.

Elsewhere in these pages it has been noticed that Mr. Brodrick, even as his predecessor, had taken a resolute stand in regard to the appointment of a Political Agent at Lhasa. Or for that matter, of permitting the Trade Agent at Gyantse to proceed thither, if and when he had matters to discuss that could not be settled locally. His telegram of August 3 to Lord Ampthill had closed the scope for any further discussion, as far as he was concerned.[36] Throughout Younghusband's stay at Lhasa, neither the Government of India, nor yet the Secretary of State for whom the former were the principal channel of official intercourse, had heard anything from their Commissioner on this subject. Nor indeed did the convention, signed in the Potala, make any mention of an Agent.

On September 9, however, Younghusband had penned a communication, which was not to reach Simla until about the end of the month, to the Government of India informing them that he had made a formal arrangement with the Tibetan Government whereby the British Trade Agent at Gyantse could visit Lhasa—'when it is necessary to consult with high Chinese and Tibetan officials on such commercial matters of importance' as he (Trade Agent) had found impossible to settle at Gyantse.

Being of a less formal character than the rest of the convention, he had drawn it up separately. Recommending its acceptance he now pleaded that it would prove 'a useful spur' to the Tibetans to transact business with the British Agents 'with despatch'.[37]

Appended to the agreement was the Commissioner's 'explanation' as to what led him to conclude it even in the face of the Secretary of State's instructions to the contrary. The apologia was indeed simple. On the authority of a telegraphic communication from the Viceroy—reference was to the draft initially proposed by the Government of India in June[38]—he had inserted this clause among the term which he had communicated to the Tibetans, through the intermediacy of the Tongsa Penlop. Later perhaps, he may find it more difficult to incorporate it. It is true, he argued, that subsequently instructions had been received not to press this point but he had let the clause stand, for he felt it may be useful in later negotiations as a bargaining counter.[39]

When I found the Tibetans raised no specific objection to the clause, provided only the Trade Agent came here on commercial, and not political, business, and only after he had found it impossible to get this commercial business disposed of by correspondence, or by personal conference with the Tibetan Agent at Gyantse, I thought there would be no objection to taking an agreement from the Tibetans to this effect, for under such limitations and provisions there could be no ground for assuming that, in coming here... (he) would be taking upon himself any political functions or adopting the character of a Political Resident.[40]

Readily convinced that their Commissioner had done no violence to the explicit directions he had received, the Government of India, in forwarding the 'agreement' to the Secretary of State, expressed the view that 'in the light of the circumstances explained by him, as further fortified by the fact that the Tibetans had raised no objection to it', they thought HMG would approve of the Colonel's action. Lord Ampthill's Government had no doubt that the right would be of 'great' value to us 'hereafter' and hedged in as it was by many 'ifs' and 'buts', it 'did not commit' Government to any political control over Tibet.[41]

In private, however, Lord Ampthill was much more outspoken. He confided to Mr. Brodrick that the Commissioner had acted 'in distinct contravention', even in 'violation', of 'your orders'. But for the rest he was a strong and powerful advocate of his action :

Now what I have to say.... If you do not like this agreement, which does not form part of convention and will not be publicly known, all that you have to do is to say nothing about it.... The main objection to it had disappeared seeing that the Tibetans accepted it without the slightest demur and considered it thoroughly reasonable.... In any case, I hope that you will not blame Colonel Younghusband.... I need not dwell on the inexpediency of disavowing the acts of our agents

And more so when reference to headquarters was 'impossible' and 'discretion' was allowed 'man on the spot'.[42]

To Godley, a day later, the Acting Viceroy not only expressed his 'hope' that the Colonel will be 'fully upheld' by the Home Government but that it will be a 'great political mistake', both 'from the Imperial and party points of view', to throw him over. Besides, Lord Ampthill thought it 'quite possible' to adjust the final settlement to 'the pledges of HMG...'[43]

Notes

1. 'The Tibetans objected strongly... suggested that the treaty should be signed in the Resident's Yamen, but I said I would be content with no other place (except the Potala)... they began murmuring other objections, but the Resident told them the matter was settled' and admitted of 'no further discussion'. Younghusband, India and Tibet, *op.cit.*, pp. 300-1.
2. *Ibid.*, p. 306.
3. 'But those who have lived among Asiatics', the Colonel wrote, 'know that the fact of signing the Treaty in the Potala was of as much value as the treaty itself.... It was to give an unmistakable sign which all other countries could understand that our prestige was re-established in Tibet...' *Ibid.*, p. 302.   One wonders whether the European, or the Western, mental make-up is different. How about the repeat performances in the Hall of Mirrors at Versailles?
4. *Ibid.*, p. 303.
5. Younghusband recorded that the Tibetans at the ceremony, who 'throughout' showed prefect 'good temper', often 'laughed over the operations of sealing'. Was it at the worthlessness of the seals and the Colonel's apparent fondness for them?
6. For the full text, see Tibet Papers, *op.cit.*, Cd. 2370, No. 360, p. 271.
7. These were repeated to Colonel Younghusband on July 7, 14 and 28, August 5, and September 6 respectively. The first telegram was acknowledged by the Commissioner on July 9. Mr. Brodrick's efforts to get the dates of acknowledgement of the later telegrams by the Commissioner did not bear fruit. Secretary of State to Viceroy, telegram No. 94/175, February 7 (1905) and Viceroy to Secretary of State, Nos. 120 and 124/175, February 16 and 20, 1905. Curzon MSS.
8. Younghusband, India and Tibet, *op.cit.*, p. 295.
9. *Supra*, Chapter 19.
10. 'Memorandum by the British Commissioner', Tibet Papers, *op.cit.*, Cd. 2370, Encl. in No. 189, pp. 80-83. See also Younghusband, India and Tibet, *op.cit.*, p. 294.
    In a private letter to Lord Ampthill from Pete Jong on September 26, Younghusband wrote: 'But I had not thought till the Regent made the proposal to me that any extension of the time of payment would be acceptable to the Council.... At the last moment, however, the Regent made the 75-year proposal....' Ampthill Papers, *op.cit.*
11. Younghusband MSS., No. 48, August 22, 1904. Younghusband's 'strategy', it seems, was to make the Tibetans agree 'bit by bit' and then 'at the end I will be very liberal'. This will make the Tibetans 'very pleased with themselves while Government will be only too glad to have got what they asked'.
12. It is interesting to recall that Macdonald too thought along much the same lines, for as Younghusband confided to his sister: 'Dear old Macdonald... suggested that we should pay them a subsidy instead of asking an indemnity as this would make them more friendly! Little does he know the Asiatic ! or me!' *Loc. cit.*
13. Tibet Papers, *op.cit.*, Cd. 2370, No. 127, p. 51, Encl. Nos. 260 and 261, pp. 219-20 and Encl. Nos. 289-91, pp. 233-36.
14. *Ibid.*, No. 134, p. 54, and Encl. No. 318, p. 247. For the full text of the Tibetan reply, see Annexure in Encl. No. 318, pp. 247-49.
15. *Ibid.*, No. 139, p. 57 and Encl. No. 286, p. 232.
16. Secretary of State to Viceroy, Telegram, August 31, 1904, Ampthill Papers, *op.cit.* Initially marked 'Private' it was later (*vide* telegram of September 5) made 'Official'.

17. *Ibid.,* Secretary of State to Viceroy, telegram, September 13 and Viceroy to Secretary of State, telegram 'September 16. Lord Ampthill had reported that the Colonel had 'altered' his earlier opinion and now believed that the Tibetans 'could pay the amount fixed'.

18. Tibet Papers, *op.cit.,* Cd. 2370, No. 148, p. 60, and Encl. No. 303, p. 240.

19. The meeting took place at the British headquarters in Lhasa on August 21. Among those present were, besides the Commissioner, the Ti Rimpoche, the Tongsa Penlop, and the Nepalese representative. For details, *Ibid.,* Encl. No. 317, pp. 245-46.

20. In his letter to Lord Ampthill on September 26, *Supra,* note 10, from Pete Jong. Younghusband underlined this again : 'But the Tibetans seemed reluctant to have the time extended or give another trade mart'.

21. To Lord Ampthill, Younghusband wrote that initially he had decided 'to make them agree to pay Rs. 75 lakhs in eight years, and then recommend to Your Excellency to reduce the amount on ratification. At the last moment, however, the Regent made the 75-year proposal....' Younghusband to Ampthill, letter, September 26, 1904, Ampthill Papers, *op.cit.* Also *supra,* n.10.

22. Tibet Papers, *op.cit.,* Cd. 2370, Encl. No. 328, pp. 254-56.
    This meeting was held at British headquarters on August 28. Among those present were the three Tibetans (named in the text) and the inevitable Tongsa Penlop. It is interesting to note that the Penlop too now urged the Commissioner to 'take into consideration the sufferings the Tibetans had already gone through', and asked that a reference be made to the Viceroy. See also Younghusband, India and Tibet, *op.cit.,* pp. 284-85.

23. At this meeting, on August 31, the Ti Rimpoche, the Tongsa Penlop and the Nepalese representative were present. Tibet Papers, *op.cit.,* Cd. 2370, Encl. No. 340, p. 260. It is clear that the resistance of the Ti Rimpoche was being gradually worn out for, at this particular interview, he is reported to have said, *inter alia,* that 'while he personally saw the wisdom of agreeing to our terms, he could not persuade the National Assembly to be reasonable'. Younghusband, India and Tibet, *op.cit.,* p. 288.

24. *Ibid.,* Encl. Nos. 316 and 343, pp. 245 and 263. Significantly, the Rimpoche was accompanied by the Tongsa Penlop—who, for some time now 'on his own initiative had been selling the idea that they (Tibetans) should let us (British) collect customs duty at the marts, and get the amount of the indemnity' adjusted against that source— and the Nepalese Representative, besides a Secretary of the (Tibetan) Council. Younghusband, India and Tibet, *op.cit.,* p. 294.

25. Tibet Papers, *op.cit.,* Cd. 2370. Encl. 316 and 343, pp. 245 and 263.

26. Younghusband MSS., No. 50, September 9, 1904.

27. For the full test of the Convention, as originally signed at Lhasa, see C.U. Aitchison, *op.cit.,* XIV, Part 2, pp. 22-25. The treaty also appears, as an appendix, in Younghusband, India and Tibet, *op.cit.,* pp. 441-43.

28. Tibet Papers, *op.cit.,* Cd. 2370, Encl. No. 151, pp. 61-62.

29. Secretary of State to Viceroy, telegrams 292 and 295 of September 12 and 15, 1904, Ampthill Papers, *op.cit.*

30. Tibet papers, *op.cit.,* Cd. 2370, No. 153, p. 62.

31. *Ibid.,* No. 156, pp. 63-64.

32. *Supra,* Ns. 10 and 21.

33. Tibet Papers, *op.cit.,* Cd. 2370, No. 164, pp. 67-68. Years later, long after the heat and dust of controversy had settled down, Younghusband revealed that he wanted 'if I could to leave them better disposed to us'. And in this 'I could now feel that we had

succeded' for they were now 'firm friends' and 'did indeed actually ask me to take them formally under British protection'. Younghusband, Light of Experience, *op.cit.*, p. 102.

34. Tibet Papers, *op.cit.*, Cd. 2370, No. 169, p. 68.
35. *Loc. cit.*
36. *Supra*, Chapter 19.
37. The 'agreement', along with Younghusband's forwarding letter, is in Tibet Papers, *op.cit.*, Cd. 2370, Encl. No. 349, pp. 265-66.
38. *Ibid.*, No. 66, p. 22.
39. Younghusband MSS., No. 50 of September 9, 1904. See also Younghusband, India and Tibet, *op.cit.*, pp. 299-300.
40. *Supra*, n. 37.
41. Tibet Papers, *op.cit.*, Cd. 2370, No. 182, pp. 72-75.
42. Ampthill to Brodrick, letter, September 28, 1904. Ampthill Papers, *op.cit.* Earlier, the Viceroy had assured the Secretary of State that 'it really does not matter much' if Younghusband had left Lhasa without incorporating the changes suggested. For the Trade Regulations could be negotiated from Gyantse 'by the Commercial Agent'; the reduction of the indemnity 'can be made by myself' while ratifying the convention; and the Chinese adhesion 'is not a matter of immediate urgency'.
43. *Ibid.*, Ampthill to Godley, letter, September 29, 1904.

24
The Lhasa Convention: HMG's Disavowal

The Secretary of State had been furious from the outset. Even before Younghusband left Lhasa he told the Viceroy, and in no uncertain terms, that the Colonel's indemnity clause would be 'most unacceptable' and that he thought there was hardly any precedent for 'an official disregard of instructions to such a degree'.[1] As a clearer picture of what transpired at the Tibetan capital emerged, the Secretary of State's 'annoyance' mounted 'in intensity'.[2] He officially informed the Viceroy that there had been 'defiance of express instructions', that the British Government were 'not prepared' to modify the cardinal principles of their policy 'by accepting a situation created for us by our representative's disobedience to orders'. Mr. Brodrick went further and accused the Commissioner of contravening 'our instructions in a most important particular'.[3]

In private, the Secretary of State was more explicit for both the Prime Minister and the Foreign Secretary had been extremely unhappy over the whole bussiness,[4]

... we must make it clear that Younghusband had 'sold' us. It had become too much like the usual Russian device as it was. Things got really bad at the Foreign Office as Lansdowne felt his honour involved...

Despite this, Mr. Brodrick still hoped 'to get an accommodation' without 'too open an esclandre'.[5] This feeling, however, did not last long for soon enough it was evident that things had got to be mended—and drastically. The realisation grew that Younghusband's 'mistake' had landed the Home authorities into 'very deep waters'.[6] A week later Mr. Brodrick warned the Viceroy (referring especially to the Indian foreign secretary, Louis Dane's impending mission to Kabul),

That Dane should understand clearly that... Curzon's views are not the views of the Government here, they have been deliberately put aside and that we do not intend to have a repetition of Younghusband's conduct at Lhasa. Our instructions must be followed...[7]

On October 28, the Secretary of State repeated that Younghusband's action had given them a powerful jolt, 'a considerable shock'. He still hoped, however, that the supplementary Convention 'will be allowed to stand' for difficulties may arise with the Tibetans 'by disavowing our agent'.[8]

This hope, however, was unusually short-lived. On November 3, the Cabinet, hitherto preoccupied with the Russian problem, met and 'very fully' discussed the Tibetan situation. And, with 'practical unanimity', decided not to accept the supplementary agreement. And 'although', Mr. Brodrick told the Viceroy, 'you will think this a mistake',

> But the Foreign Office feeling is so strong that it would be impossible to refuse Russia the right of sending a commercial agent, if she desires to, that I am afraid it is part of the old story—either we must make Kabul of Lhasa, or we must refrain from doing at Kabul... On the other hand we are most desirous that the reversal of Younghusband's policy should be made as quietly as possible, and that as little public attention may be attracted.... I am afraid that the feeling excited by his want of respect for the injunctions laid on him will not easily subside....[9]

In conformity with the above, the India Office now formally directed the Viceroy that the separate 'Agreement' was to be disallowed and that the provisions regarding the indemnity were to be amended in accordance with its earlier directives. On November 11 (1904) Lord Ampthill, while ratifying the Convention, incorporated both these changes.[10]

The strong terms used by the Secretary of State in regard to the action of Younghusband—and such words and phrases as 'disobedience', 'disregard to orders', 'defiance of express instructions' had been employed—had cut him to the quick. Even before he arrived at Simla, some of HMG's severe censure had been passed on to him. The Viceroy too, though defending him (Younghusband) 'magnificently' in public, was 'scolding' him 'in private'.[11] No wonder the Commissioner was in a dark mood,

> My return to India is now marked by a sense of deep regret that I consented to be an Agent in carrying out... in a time too limited to admit of proper reference to London, a policy decided in detail by HMG before they were aware what the political situation in Lhasa was or in what circumstances the Agent would find himself placed...[12]

Elsewhere he had expressed the view that 'all the way through this business', he had tried his best 'to approximate my action', as closely as was possible, to the views of MHG 'even where these were sadly against my own inclinations and opinions, as to what was wise'.[13]

With his whole being 'strung to its full', and sad at heart at this 'wholly underserved' reprimand—how striking must have been the contrast with his feeling exactly a year earlier when he talked of 'a most genial and communicative letter (from Lord Curzon) which encouraged me much'[14]—Younghusband was clear that he would be able to vindicate himself. He even hinted at representing the position both to the King and to the Prime Minister, evidently over the head of the Viceroy and the Secretary of State.[15] Seething with indignation when he reached Simla, he soon set himself the task of justifying his conduct. In a long Memorandum, which he drew up on October 18, he spelt out in detail his main defence as he felt it conditioned both by 'the political situation in Lhasa' and 'the circumstances' in which he found himself. Some of its main points may be summed up here:[16]

(a) That the despatch of the Secretary of State, dated August 5, in which it was specifically laid down that the amount of the indemnity was not to be more than what the Tibetans could pay within three years, did not reach him 'till after I had accepted the Tibetan proposal'. The terms of the draft convention had of course, reached him earlier, but 'a certain amount of latitude was left to me in the matter';

(b) That since the military authorities had fixed September 15 as the date of departure from Lhasa, he had perforce to limit himself to this period for 'negotiations';

(c) That in the draft terms which he presented to the Tibetans on September 1, he had put the figures for the indemnity at 75 lakhs, and the period of payment at three years. Later, on September 4, he made the change when the Ti Rimpoche 'begged' of him;

(d) That Tibet could well afford to pay 75 lakhs, but the major difficulty was that there was no cash. If he had insisted on 25 lakhs within three years, 'I should have left behind me a raw in Lhasa';

(e) That since the indemnity was fixed both for the expense incurred in military operations and 'for insults to, and attacks upon the British Commissioner', he thought 25 lakhs—only £ 10,000!'*— was 'a small amount' to enter into a treaty 'as satisfaction for insults and attacks upon the British Representative';

(f) That, in the final analysis, he had to act upon his own responsibility for extending the period for payment of the indemnity, and thought he should so act as to 'suit the convenience of the Tibetans';

(g) That if he had remained behind in Lhasa his stay would have aroused suspicion and he would have forfeited 'all the confidence I had so hardly won'. Besides, 'though I certainly had the power to insist upon the alteration, I hardly had the right to'.

What doubtless started as an explanation ended, however, as a warning, and in sounding this note the Commissioner gave away a great deal. To quote his own words:

But while reducing the amount of the indemnity, HMG wish also to limit the period of occupation of the Chumbi Valley. This is a very serious sacrifice of the interests of the Government of India. Chumbi is the key to Tibet. It is also the most difficult part of the road to Lhasa. With Chumbi in our possession we

---

* An obvious error; rupees 25 lakhs in 1904, was equivalent to £ 166,650.

have a clear run into Tibet.... With Chumbi in possession of Tibetans, the difficulties of an advance into Tibet are trebled... Nor do the Tibetans show any resentment at the idea of our prolonged occupation of Chumbi, for the valley is not looked upon as a part of Tibet proper...[17]

On the day he penned these lines, the Colonel confided to his father that he felt 'very depressed', that it was not a pleasant thing to have to write his defence after achieving what one of his correspondents had called 'just the hardest bit of business that has ever been done beyond the frontier'.[18] No wonder, he felt convinced, that 'we have the most despicable system of Government for dealing with Imperial affairs'.[19]

A week later, Colonel Younghusband wrote to Lord Curzon whose 'warmly appreciative' message, had given him such a feeling of 'comfort and encouragement' in the enveloping gloom and 'depression'. Apart from his personal regard for his old friend, he rated Curzon as 'the only true man' in his 'hour of trial', when 'neither the Home Government nor Government of India supported me'.[20] Younghusband confided in him (Curzon) his fervent hope that 'with the principle' of securing Chumbi for 75 years and of getting permission for our Agent at Gyantse to proceed to Lhasa, 'I know you will agree'. He further assured him that he 'acted for what I considered the best in a rather complicated position'. As for his conduct,

I am held to have acted contrary to instructions but as a matter of fact I had none. On August 30 I did telegraph asking whether the instalments might not be paid at the rate of one lakh each. But on August 31, Macdonald said he would have to leave on September 15.... I was in a tight place and having to get the job finished as best I could and without leaving behind any feeling of resentment...

Did he not feel rather bad and upset now?

...like a criminal impeached for high treason and I feel I shall always now be regarded by the Cabinet Ministers as a dangerous man who, cannot be trusted... that it was not particularly fair on me to send me into space tied down to return by a certain time and yet expect me to get a treaty through letter for letter the same as had been laid down in London before anything of the conditions at Lhasa had been known.[21]

Writing years later, Younghusband had nothing much to add to what has been noted above. He had to act in circumstances that were 'very exceptional' and he was 'not' taking 'more latitude' than such circumstances 'naturally confer on an Agent'. As for the Home Government's pledges these,

were given with a qualification, but the main pledge that we would not annex Tibet or establish a protectorate over it, or interfere in its internal administration, had not, in my view, been infringed by the Treaty I signed.

The maximum he was prepared to concede and, at best, grudgingly:

We may assume that Government had some pressing international considerations of the moment which necessitated their taking no account of the qualification to their pledges....[22]

'Separate Agreement', regarding the British Trade Agent's visits to Lhasa; duly signed and sealed. Erroneously referred to by Younghusband as 'Seals Affixed to Treaty'

Nearly every aspect of the Colonel's apologia has been examined, and answered, in the preceding pages and nothing appears to betray him more than his own letters and despatches. Thus was the proposal for the extension of the period of payment first made by the Tibetans? Did not the Ti Rimpoche insist, time and again, for a settlement 'once and for all'. Again, would the scope of discretion allowed to the Commissioner cover the gap between three years— and 75? As for the 'right' to insist upon an alteration, did he have the 'right', in the first instance, to impose a treaty? Rights, it appears, for the weak and the defeated never existed then, nor for that matter even today: Younghusband's demand was for signature on the dotted line, a more recent variant thereof has been 'unconditional surrender'.

Nor need it be forgotten that if the Tibetan winter, severe as it is, did not hinder the Mission's initial advance through the Jelap-la, across the Chumbi and over the Tang-la into the very heart of the country, why was it so frightening, or forbidding, on the return journey ? Throughout his letters and despatches, Younghusband had underlined the fact that the military were unnecessarily exaggerating the hazards involved in the Mission's return. In the final analysis, he had fought hard—though unsuccessfully—for staying on in Lhasa for the winter, and without any British troops ? Or again, was there any ambiguity about the Government's final instructions to him,[23] despite the alleged refrain on 'no binding entanglements' coupled with 'the maximum of satisfaction or reparations'?

Upon other aspects of Younghusband's defence, comment is superfluous. Thus, how could one compute 'the satisfaction' to be demanded for 'insults to and attacks upon' the British Representative? Or, assess Tibet's ability, or lack thereof, to pay the sum demanded? In the one case, honour is a many-faceted thing and the price of its vindication has varied both in time and place. Nor has it been possible then, or even now, to assess very fully Tibet's economic potential in terms of ready cash.[24] Here again, unfortunately, it is the Commissioner's own words which weaken his case considerably. How was it that the very amount which he had found 'excessive' on August 23, could be paid 'without undue hardship' a week later ?

But above all, it is his words of warning—and unabashed confessions to his personal friends and correspondents—which compromise his position and with almost no qualification. Thus the letter to his father, on the morrow of the conclusion of the Convention, is clear and admits of little ambiguity. On the 75-year occupation of Chumbi he thought Curzon,

> will I know be delighted, but how the Home Government will view it.... I
> they like to be idiotic....

For whose sake was the Convention being concluded—his own and Curzon's or the Home Government's ? This is an aspect of the question to which it is proposed to revert later.

Again, he explicitly forbade his father to breathe about the 'agreement' regarding the Gyantse Trade Agent proceeding to Lhasa:

However do not mention a word about this for the Secretary of State absolutely forbade my asking for this.[25]

In his 'Memorandum' of October 18, Younghusband had underlined, rather heavily, 'the interests' of the Government of India which were so dear to him. And inasmuch as the Chumbi Valley constituted 'the key to Tibet', he set his heart on a long lease of years for which the stranglehold could be secured. All that now came, therefore, between him and his cherished goal had to be sacrificed. In this case it happened to be the Secretary of State and his none-too-convenient directives.

Another angle from which the question needs to be examined may also be considered. There may be a very good case for the Commissioner's inability to stay on in Lhasa after the date set by General Macdonald—and 'retiring' Mac's behaviour at Lhasa, as elsewhere, had left a lot to be desired. It may also be said, in all fairness to Colonel Younghusband, that Mr. Brodrick's instructions on this point—to Lord Ampthill—were somewhat vague.[26] There is also some validity in the Commissioner's contention that he hated to make any drastic alternations in the terms of the Convention on the morrow of concluding it with such solemnity ? Yet, all said and done, the gravamen of the charge would still stand out. Did his instructions, and the terms of the draft Convention, provide him room enough for manoeuvre ? Again, was 'a certain amount of latitude', which he pleaded in extenuation, enough to alter the period of payment—and hence the very scope and complexion of the consequent agreement ?

At Gyantse, we have noticed, he put in the stipulation regarding the Trade Agent's visit to Lhasa without clear sanction from London. At the Tibetan capital he confessed to asking 'what Government of India *proposed,* not what Secretary of state *sanctioned'* ? And did he not plead guilty, however roundly he put it :

And although I admit that my action was not covered by my instructions, I regret that Home Government should consider that it was defiance of them.

Years later—and long after the din and dust of controversy had died down—the Commissioner again sought to answer those who thought that the 75-year occupation would have involved a repudiation of the solemn pledges which the British Government had held out repeatedly to Russia since the Tibetan trouble started, and as late as June 2 (1904). The Colonel argued—not very convincingly though—that the promise of Lord Lansdowne 'not to annex Tibet, to establish a protectorate over it, or in any way control its internal administration' was conditioned by the saving clause that the action of Government must, to some extent, depend upon the conduct of the Tibetans themselves. He maintained that the latter continued the fighting after June 2—they had indeed attacked the Mission's base-camp at Kang-ma, and 'fired on us', at Nagartse Jong. Nor had they sent in any negotiators on the appointed day, i.e., June 25, at Gyantse. Was not all that, he queried, justification enough for HMG to depart in 'some slight degree' from the earlier policy which had commended itself to them before the exact nature and extent of Tibetan opposition was fully known. Again, did the right to occupy the Chumbi Valley constitute in any way a breach of the pledge to the Russians,

> Would the occupation of Chumbi, a valley lying altogether outside Tibet proper on the Indian, and not on the Tibetan, side of the watershed, a valley which had not always belonged to Tibet, mean annexing Tibet, establishing a protectorate over it, or controlling its internal administration ?

Besides, by signing the Convention he was,

> Simply acquiring for Government the right to occupy the Chumbi Valley for seventy-five years if they wanted to, and if they did not want to, they could go out whenever they liked. I was not 'compelling' the Government to occupy the Chumbi Valley; I was simply acquiring the right, which they could abrogate if they did not want it.[27]

Notes

1. Brodrick to Ampthill, letter, September 15, 1904, Ampthill Papers, *op.cit.*
2. *Ibid.,* Ampthill to Godley, letter, October 6, 1904. Ampthill at the same time hastened to assure the Permanent Under-Secretary that he could 'fully understand the feelings of HM's Ministers' and was 'most anxious and eager' to meet 'their wishes'.
3. Tibet Papers, *op.cit.,* Cd. 2370, No. 170, p. 69. Mr. Brodrick's telegram was dated October 8, 1904. It is interesting that Godley writing to Ampthill, a day later, thought the question was not 'a very important one', felt there was no 'harm to ourselves, or our prestige' by first insisting upon 'something more'. He hoped 'Satow (Sir Ernest) will manage it skillfully' for 'all' seemed to depend upon him 'now'.
4. *Infra,* Chapter XXV.
5. Brodrick to Ampthill, letter, October 6, 1904, Ampthill Papers, *op.cit*
6. *Ibid.,* Brodrick to Ampthill, letter, October 13, 1904.
7. *Ibid.,* Brodrick to Ampthill, letter, October 20, 1904.
8. *Ibid.,* Brodrick to Ampthill, letter, October 28, 1904.
9. *Ibid.,* Brodrick to Ampthill, letter, November 4, 1904.
    In his letter of date, Godley wrote to the Viceroy 'of the strength of the feeling' in the Cabinet against 'a strong policy in Tibet'. He also revealed that the Cabinet 'entirely refused to adopt the additional clause' of the Convention 'in spite of the Secretary of State's entreaties'.
10. Tibet Papers, *op.cit.,* Cd. 2370, No. 185, p. 77. See also Aitchison, *op.cit.,* XIV, Part 2, pp. 22-25. In his 'Declaration', appended to the convention, the Viceroy was 'pleased to direct' as an 'act of grace' that the indemnity be reduced to 25 lakhs and the amount be paid in three instalments. A further letter from the Secretary to the Government of India informed the Ti Rimpoche that 'the Viceroy while fully appreciating the good feeling shown by the Tibetan Government in giving such an undertaking (regarding the right of the Trade Agent at Gyantse to proceed to Lhasa) considers it unnecessary to embody its provisions in a formal instrument'.
11. Mr. Brodrick praised the policy as 'very magnanimous' but doubted whether it 'would have had the effect... you anticipate'. Brodrick to Ampthill, letter, October 28, 1904, Ampthill Papers, *op.cit*

12. Telegram from Younghusband to Government of India, October 11, 1904, omitted from Tibet Papers, *op.cit.*, Cd. 2370.
    Younghusband, India and Tibet, *op.cit.*, p. 332: '... and I bitterly regretted ever having undertaken so delicate a task with my hands so tied'.

13. Younghusband to Ampthill, letter, September 26, 1904, Ampthill Papers, *op.cit*

14. This was at Khamba Jong, Younghusband MSS., No. 15, October 9, 1903.

15. Apparently, on receipt of the Commissioner's telegram, Lord Ampthill wrote to Mr. Brodrick, 'He is suffering from swelled head and the malady is aggravated by his wife who has it in an even greater degree. You will see that I am not exaggerating when I tell you that Colonel Younghusband's latest is a demand to go home and lay his case before His Majesty and the Cabinet and that Mrs. Younghusband fully expects that a peerage will be conferred on her Lord and master'. Ampthill to Brodrick, letter, October 12, 1904, Ampthill Papers, *op.cit*

16. The 'Memorandum' by the British Commissioner comprises 16 paragraphs. Tibet Papers, *op.cit.*, Cd. 2370, Encl. in No. 189, pp. 80-83.

17. Ampthill told Brodrick that he (Ampthill) thought that Colonel Younghusband 'makes a very good defence' except in the matter of the indemnity. Ampthill to Brodrick, letter, October 20, 1904, Ampthill Papers, *op.cit*

18. These words were used in a letter addressed to Younghusband by the *Times* correspondent (Hensmann) and the co-editor of the *Pioneer.*

19. Younghusband MSS., No. 52, October 18, 1904.

20. *Loc. cit.* Younghusband's praise for Curzon was fulsome, and unqualified: 'he was warmly appreciative of every difficulty, and he was able to put into me all his own keen enthusiasm.... He supported me in all my requests. He was patient with me in my many irritabilities.... And he kept a steady flow of encouragement and good counsel running unceasingly to me'. Younghusband, Light of Experience, *op.cit.*, pp. 102-3.

21. Younghusband to Curzon, letter, October 26, 1904, Curzon MSS.
    In what may best be termed his prefatory remarks, Younghusband told Lord Curzon that what he had 'most looked forward to was the warm welcome I know you would have given me' and that he had hastened back from Lhasa 'on purpose to be here on your first arrival'.

22. Younghusband, India and Tibet, *op.cit.*, p. 341. Also see *Ibid,* pp. 293-300.

23. One of the very last telegrams which Younghusband received from the Viceroy before leaving the Tibetan capital read: 'You now have authority to remain until the 15th October at Lhasa...' Tibet Papers, *op.cit.*, Cd. 2370, No. 169, p. 68.

24. This observation may be regarded as true today, 15 years after the Communist Chinese occupation of the country, as it was in Younghusband's time. See for instance the *Statesman,* June 2, 1964.

25. Younghusband MSS., No. 50, September 9, 1904.

26. Thus putting Mr. Brodrick's second telegram of September 13 alongside his telegrams of September 16 and 18, it is clear that the Secretary of State wanted to reduce the indemnity, but whether he wanted Younghusband definitely to stay back at Lhasa in order to negotiate this satisfactorily is not quite evident. Thus on September 16,

    in no circumstances is the force to stay at Lhasa for the purpose of obtaining more favourable terms than those already agreed to.
    On September 18 however,

there is no objection to Younghusband remaining behind at Lhasa provided he can do so in safety....

The commonsense view would seem to be that the latter telegram superseded the former. But who was to ensure the Commissioner's 'safety' ? 'Retiring Mac' or the broken reed of an intensely-hated, and unpopular, Amban ? Tibet Papers, *op.cit.,* Cd. 2370, Nos. 153, 158, and 161, pp. 62-63 and 65.

27. Younghusband, India and Tibet, *op.cit.,* pp. 296-97. It is not without significance that Younghusband then, or later, did not offer any defence for his 'agreement' in regard to the Gyantse Trade Agent proceeding to Lhasa. The maximum he conceded was that he acted upon 'my own responsibility'. *Ibid.,* p. 299. In his later work, The Light of Experience, *op.cit.,* pp. 96-105, he scrupulously avoided any mention of this controversy.

25
The Scapegoat ?

In a covering letter to the Secretary of State, stoutly upholding the main points of Colonel Younghusband's 'Memorandum', the Government of India had commended his 'great perspicacity and fearlessness of responsibility' which they thought, 'would be a great mistake to discourage in any of our agents'. And though they conceded, however grudgingly, that his 'error of judgement' was a serious one, they maintained that the circumstances in which it was made 'afford sufficient reason for generous condonation'.[1]

In private too, Lord Ampthill 'stuck up' for the Commissioner. Knowing him to be 'sick and sore'—and egged on to resentment by a wife "who is inordinately proud of him and despises the whole race of 'officials'"[2]—the acting Governor-General refused to under-rate his very considerable achievements. Thus in a letter to Brodrick on October 26,

I am afraid from the tone of your recent communications that you are inclined to make a scapegoat of Colonel Younghusband and publicly repudiate his action. If this is really your intention, I earnestly hope that you will think better of it. I venture to think that it would be more generous and politic to treat Colonel Younghusband with honour and distinction, give him the rewards which the public consider his due and which in many ways he has fully deserved and treat his disregard of instructions as a mere error of judgement forced upon him by the unusual circumstances of his position. It would savour strongly of Russian methods to publicly disavow the action of our Agent and everybody would think that we had only done so under pressure from Russia. After all, Colonel Younghusband's achievement has been very considerable, for in spite of the impossible attitude of the Tibetans throughout all the stages of the Mission except the final one, he has got the Convention signed with thoroughly and generally friendly feeling. He has turned the suspicion and dislike of the Tibetans into....real confidence and esteem... A generous attitude on the part of the Government... for there can be no doubt that in due course of time the fact will become known.[3]

A day later, Ampthill told Curzon that HMG were getting 'more and more irritated' over Tibet and that he was doing 'my utmost' to defend him 'against the wrath of His Majesty's ministers'.[4]

On the very day he wrote to Lord Curzon, the acting Viceroy mailed to the Secretary of State an advance copy of his forwarding letter to Younghusband's Memorandum, to which a reference has been made already. Lord Ampthill had altered the original Foreign Office despatch—'which seemed to give him away on points on which he had excellent defence'—to emphasise that the Colonel had 'ample justification' in the India Office telegram for 'not holding in at Lhasa' after the Convention had been signed.[5]

Meantime, alive to the climate of opinion in Whitehall, Lord Ampthill was growing increasingly anxious for fear the Colonel was being thrown to the wolves. Thus on November 3, he wrote to Godley,

> Please stick up for Younghusband as much as you can. It would be a terrible mistake to make a scapegoat of him.[6]

Luckily for Ampthill, and the former Commissioner, Godley too endorsed this line of reasoning. Younghusband's performance, the Permanent Under Secretary thought, was creditable,

> Four or five months ago, as I reminded Mr. Brodrick, HMG were very much inclined to believe that they, in the person of their envoy, would have to come back from Lhasa with their tails between their legs, without a treaty, and with the whole thing to do over again next year. The actual situation is a very different one from this, and I think they ought to show some gratitude to the man to whom their escape from a very awkward position is largely due....[7]

It is not without significance that Mr. Brodrick, who in recent studies has been painted as the devil of the piece in the game of doing Younghusband down, stuck up vigorously for the additional clause empowering the Gyantse Trade Agent's visit to Lhasa and that it was the Cabinet which stood in the way. In reality it was 'they' who 'entirely refused to adopt (this clause) in spite of the Secretary of State's entreaties'.[8] In fact, the feeling among his colleagues was 'so strong' that Mr. Brodrick's 'appeal' had little, if any, effect and a 'reversal of Younghusband's policy' became inevitable.[9] Only a week earlier the Secretary of State had thought it probable that the supplementary convention 'will be allowed to stand' for he would hate 'to disavow our agent'.[10]

Thus it would appear that by the time Younghusband's 'explanation' was received in London, the decision of the Cabinet on a 'reversal' of the former Commissioner's policy—and this in despite Mr. Brodrick—had been taken. No wonder that the India Office now reacted in a much sharper tone,

> It is almost trifling with us to say that he had not received the despatch of the 3rd August when he had in his possession the very clear telegrams of the 6th and 26th July. He makes a great deal of not remaining on after he got the instructions to change the treaty; and he has here a better case. But it is very weak of him at the end of his apology—if apology it can he called—to press so

strongly the retention of the Chumbi Valley, on which, as a matter of principle, HMG have a right to decide, and had already decided. Moreover, he makes no reference whatever to the second convention, and his whole tone is impenitent. I am sorry for it....[11]

On November 18, Mr. Brodrick still talked of the 'very strong... feeling' that 'the I.C.S. ought to have a lesson as to behaving as Y. has done',[12] while Godley confessed he was not sure whether the 'comparatively mild draft' he (Godley) had prepared would go through 'the ordeal' of the Cabinet without serious mishap. The Permanent Under Secretary further revealed that 'various members of Government are, to my knowledge, inclined to insist upon a serve censure of Younghusband' although he for one was not 'prejudiced' against the former Commissioner.[13]

It was against this background that the India Office mailed to Lord Ampthill its considered views regarding Younghusband's performance at Lhasa. The language was harsh and the Secretary of State repeated his earlier charge against the former Tibet Commissioner both in regard to the indemnity and the separate 'agreement'. He viewed Younghusband's disregard of instructions as 'serious' in nature and reminded his (Younghusband's) principals that in matters of Indian frontier policy the course to be pursued must be laid down by HMG alone nor should its agents— in this case the Government of India—'under the pressure of the problems which confront them on the spot'—fail to conform. For, in the final analysis, it was the Supreme Government which had more immediately before them the interest of the British Empire as a whole.[14]

There the matter ended for the present. Brodrick later confided to Ampthill, what was pretty apparent, that if he (Ampthill) were to have been a permanent, in place of being a temporary, replacement of Curzon, the despatch would not have been 'as vigorous' as the one he (Brodrick) was 'forced to' send.[15] At the same time he made it clear that while he (Brodrick) did not 'complain' of 'a frank statement of views',

> I wish... that the despatches with regard to Younghusband had been a little less pronounced, as when they come out, it will look as if there had been a sharp divergence of opinion.[16]

In his private letter to the Secretary of State on October 26, as was noticed, Lord Ampthill had expressed his fear that 'you are inclined to make a scapegoat of Colonel Younghusband and publicly repudiate his action'. He had cautioned Brodrick against this course and 'earnestly' hoped 'you will think better of it'. A week later Curzon's *locum tenens* was exhorting the Permanent Under Secretary at the India Office to 'stick up for Younghusband as much as you can; it would be a terrible mistake to make a scapegoat of him'.[17] In later years, Sir Francis himself put forth the view that Mr. Brodrick's opposition to Lord Curzon's policy—which 'centred on the question of having a permanent political agent at Lhasa'—was somewhat personal and maintained that 'the mutual indignation of these two great men split over my poor head'.[18]

More recent students of Lord Curzon's Tibetan policy have repeated the charge with added force, accused Mr. Brodrick of a dark 'conspiracy', of 'an arbitrary but (as it proved) implacable malevolence', and as not only thirsting for the Commissioner's 'blood' but of wishing to forestall 'any possibility of reprieve for the scapegoat'.[19] It has been further maintained that 'for not easily fathomable motives', the Secretary of State had embarked on 'a vendetta' against Younghusband and that he pursued 'by dubious methods' his 'strange campaign' against the Colonel.[20]

Reiterating further Younghusband's own analysis, the writer cited in the preceding paragraph has expressed his firm conviction that 'the hounding of Younghusband could only be explained as a by-product of Mr. Brodrick's breach with Curzon' and that on this breach 'some indirect' light is thrown by what he calls 'the secret pamphlet' of 1926. The latter could not have been based, contrary to Mr. Brodrick's assertion, on 'a careful review of correspondence' but makes only 'a shallow pretence of impartiality'.[21]

Another competent authority on the subject has explained away Younghusband's disobedience of his instructions to the 'conflicting concepts of his superiors' as to what the Tibetan problem was all about and in such circumstances the Commissioner must be 'entitled to use his own discretion than he would have been on a more conventional diplomatic mission.'[22]

A biographer of Younghusband, Dr. George Seaver, has also made a bold bid for his subject. In this context he has revealed the existence of a 'private note' which the Commissioner left 'for his own future justification'. There are also the two letters which Younghusband wrote on his way back from Lhasa—one to Lord Ampthill, to which a reference has already been make in the text, and another to Lord Lansdowne. Dr. Seaver has also sought to condemn Mr. Brodrick, for his ignorance of some essential facts and his suppression of some others which were 'inconvenient'. His editorship of the Blue Book, for instance, was 'partisan in its nature and scope'.[23]

A great deal of familiar ground has already been covered in regard to Colonel Younghusband. It is interesting, and revealing, that Brodrick's detractors have condemned the Colonel's 'apologia' as 'ill-judged', his failure to express even 'a semblance of contrition' over his actions as 'a cardinal error' which he (Younghusband) should have had 'the gumption to avoid'. It has been further maintained that 'he spoilt his case by his refusal to eat the humble pie, his inability to conceal his conviction that he had been right all along'.[24] This apart, two aspects of the controversy deserve careful scrutiny. Thus at the outset it is necessary to underline the strong conviction, shared by the acting Viceroy and most members of the Cabinet, from the Prime Minister downwards, that in behaving the way he did, Younghusband was profoundly influenced by Curzon's views; that he deliberately chose to flout the instructions of his political superiors to pursue 'an adventure of his own'. Thus on September 29, Lord Ampthill told Godley that he (Ampthill) was sure Younghusband had 'deliberately' exceeded his instructions. Indeed,

He went to Tibet as Lord Curzon's man and thoroughly imbued with Lord Curzon's ideas which he was enthusiastically determined to carry out. I have not had him entirely to myself for I know that he has been in regular correspondence with Lord Curzon to whom he has been looking for support and final approval...[25]

A week later, the acting Viceroy was writing to the Secretary of State on much the same lines,

I should not like to say that Colonel Younghusband's action was deliberate but I may remind you between ourselves that he is before everything else Lord Curzon's man. He started on his mission thoroughly imbued with Lord Curzon's ideas and convinced of the ignorance and pusillanimity of the Home Government. He has, I know, been in regular correspondence with Lord Curzon since the latter went home and it is therefore more than likely that the all-powerful influence of Lord Curzon's views has actuated him though perhaps quite unconsciously...[26]

It is revealing that the author of these lines in either case was pleading that the Commissioner be not thrown over, and that he was prepared to make 'great allowance' for him.

On October 6, Ampthill laid bare his mind once again—and in no uncertain terms. Writing to Godley that he for one was 'most anxious and eager' to meet the wishes of His Majesty's ministers whose feelings he 'fully' understood,

You must know... Younghusband gave me the slip and I think you will recognise that it was not in my power to have prevented him from doing what he did....[27]

In subsequent communications too, as has been noticed in another context, Ampthill went out of his way—as he told Curzon—'to defend him (Younghusband)' against the 'wrath' of His Majesty's ministers. And it is to this aspect of the question that it is necessary to turn now for to single out Brodrick alone as the culprit is being both unfair to the man and even more so to the facts.

It is true that on September 22, Brodrick wrote to Balfour that,

If, as the papers allege, you are going to Balmoral, please support me with the King against decorating Younghusband till we get the other names. George Curzon strongly objects to his getting an honour till his work is done, and the provision as to '75 years' is a direct violation from orders of July 26 and has made things difficult....[28]

It is important to bear in mind the fact, that Brodrick was not the only one to feel disturbed by the news of the Lhasa Convention for the Russians, the Germans and even the Americans had expressed grave concern over its conclusion. Nor was that all, for on September 27 the British envoy in St. Petersburg, Sir Charles Hardinge, underlined the 'transcendental importance of adhering to the very strictest interpretation of our assurances to the Russian Government'. The Foreign Secretary too was of the same opinion. He told Hardinge that Younghusband's action had placed Government 'in a very embarrassing position' and declared that although

British interests in Tibet must be protected, the seventy-five year occupation of the Chumbi Valley was 'quite inadmissible' and 'none of us here would listen to it'.[29]

Nor was the strength and vehemence of this feeling against Younghusband's action by any means confined to Lansdowne. It was shared, and without qualification, by Balfour himself. In fact, the latter confided that by his disobedience to orders Younghusband had 'touched the honour of his country' and that by owning up his conduct Government will inevitably share in the resultant 'discredit'— a course which he would refuse to adopt.[30] To the King, Balfour was even more explicit. Explaining at length how Younghusband's action had landed government in a quandry,

> But I do not see how we are to avoid the imputation—grossly unjust though it is—that in thus disavowing one portion of the Treaty which Colonel Younghusband has negotiated, we are acting not in obedience to the principles of international good faith, but to pressure from Russia. The only chance of any permanent arrangement with that power in Central Asia depends upon the mutual confidence that engagements will be adhered to, and if, as I fear, Colonel Younghusband, in acting as he has done, wished to force the hands of the Government (whose policy, doubtless, he disagrees with) he has inflicted upon us an injury compared with which any loss to the material interests affected by our Tibetan policy is absolutely insignificant.[31]

Earlier, Balfour had used such expressions as by 'disobeying our explicit orders', Younghusband had 'placed us' in a 'very false position'; that in regard to Tibet both 'in policy and in honour' Government were committed 'to a non-intervention policy'; that 'in defiance of orders' he made arrangements to occupy the Chumbi Valley for 75 years, 'a period difficult to distinguish from permanent occupation'; that the Colonel's 'indiscretion' made it impossible fully 'to clear ourselves from the very unjust imputation of copying the least creditable methods of Russian diplomacy'.[32]

To such strong expressions, Edward VII too could not have been immune. He 'greatly' regretted that Colonel Younghusband should have acted 'in such an extraordinary way'—'in direct and deliberate defiance of instructions'—and now formally withdrew 'the wish which he had originally expressed'.[33] This probably refers to the King's initial idea of announcing a decoration for the former British Commissioner, immediately the Lhasa Convention was signed. It would follow that the decision to defer the Honours was that of the King's, taken at the powerful intercession of the Prime Minister, although it may be conceded that Brodrick was actively concerned.[34]

A second aspect of the question concerning Colonel Younghusband relates to what his superiors regarded his underhand methods. Not only in Tibet had he behaved as though he were carrying out 'a private adventure' of his own, or at Curzon's behest: it appeared that even after his return he proposed to carry the fight to the King's court. Two distinct references to this may be gleaned in Lord Ampthill's and Sir Arthur Godley's communications, besides a host of others. There is also to hand a sizeable piece of evidence to show that the Colonel had through his friends, and relatives, a direct pipeline to the King. And that he used these means not only to vindicate himself—which may, in the final analysis, be regarded as legitimate enough—but to bring into disrepute the instruments through whom alone a constitutional monarch could function. It is significant that a person of the sobriety of Sir Arthur Godley should have called Younghusband 'a wire-puller'.

The case against Colonel Younghusband may thus seem formidable even if Brodrick were completely unprejudiced against the Commissioner. Not only did the latter fail to show any contrition for conduct for which anyone would have him censured—but what was worse was to hold, as he did, that no error had, in fact, been committed. Thus his 'apologia' was 'a vindication'. The Colonel went further and used all the means at his disposal through private correspondence, through friends near the King, to bring the India Office and the British Government into open contempt. It may be argued that in so doing he strongly offended Mr. Brodrick—and offended him deeply. That in Tibet and outside it, the Commissioner behaved and acted as Curzon's man could have been no solace to the Secretary of State whose relations with the Viceroy had now reached almost their nadir. What the record bares out is the Secretary of State's extreme displeasure with the Commissioner —whom he certainly tried to do down in the award of Honours—but neither evidence nor yet motives of his 'implacable malevolence' or 'vendetta' against Younghusband are easy to fathom.

Notes

1. Tibet Papers, *op.cit.*, Cd. 2370, No. 189, pp. 77-80 and No. 182, pp. 72-75. The two despatches make interesting reading and show the extent to which the Government of India could go in defending every act of omission and commission with which their agent had been charged.
2. Ampthill to Godley, letter, October 20, 1904, Ampthill Papers, *op.cit.*
3. *Ibid.,* Ampthill to Brodrick, letter, October 26, 1904.
4. *Ibid.,* Ampthill to Curzon, letter, October 27, 1904.
5. Curzon MSS., Miller to Curzon, letter, October 27, 1904.
6. Ampthill Papers, *op. cit.,* Ampthill to Godley, letter, November 3, 1904.
7. *Ibid.,* Godley to Ampthill, letter, November 4, 1904.
8. *Loc. cit.*
9. *Ibid.,* Brodrick to Ampthill, letter, November 4, 1904.
10. *Ibid.,* Brodrick to Ampthill, letter, October 28, 1904.
11. *Ibid.,* Brodrick to Ampthill, letter, November 11, 1904.
12. *Ibid.,* Brodrick to Ampthill, letter, November 18, 1904.
13. *Ibid.,* Godley to Ampthill, letter, November 18, 1904.
14. For the text, see Tibet Papers, *op.cit.,* Cd. 2370, No. 193, pp. 84-86.
15. Brodrick to Ampthill, letter, February 10, 1905, Ampthill Papers, *op.cit.*
16. *Ibid.,* Brodrick to Ampthill, letter, January 18, 1905.
17. *Supra* pp. 359-360.
18. Letter to the *Times* (London), April 19, 1939.
19. Peter Fleming, *op.cit.,* pp. 273-74.

20. *Ibid.,* p. 279.
21. *Ibid.,* p. 291.
22. Alastair Lamb, *op.cit.,* pp. 305-6.
23. George Seaver, *op.cit.,* pp. 268-70.
24. Peter Fleming, *op.cit.,* p. 277.
25. Ampthill to Godley, letter, September 29, 1904, Ampthill Papers, *op.cit.*
26. *Ibid.,* Ampthill to Brodrick, letter, October 5, 1904.
27. *Ibid.,* Ampthill to Godley, letter, October 6, 1904.
28. Brodrick to Balfour, letter, September 22, 1904, *Balfour Papers,* B.M., Vol. XXXIX.
29. Monger, *op.cit.,* p. 170.
30. Balfour to Lansdowne, October 4, 1904. *Balfour Papers,* B.M., Add. MSS. 49729.
31. *Ibid.,* B. M., Add. MSS. 49684, Balfour to Knollys, October 6, 1904.
32. *Loc. cit.*
33. *Ibid.,* letter, Knollys to Balfour, October 15, 1904.
34. *Supra,* note 33, Knollys told Balfour that he had two letters from Brodrick 'on the same subject', which he had shown to the King.

26
Retrospect — and Prospect

An attempt has been made in the preceding pages to examine the circumstances that led to the despatch of the Younghusband expedition and to review at some length, the sequence of events at Lhasa and the Commissioner's alleged acts of omission and commission. At this stage in the narrative it may be possible to gather together the main threads and put the principal conclusions in focus.

Any proper understanding of the Tibetan expedition would presuppose a good working knowledge of the historical as well as the political geography of India's land frontiers. The sharp, yet revealing contrast between the ever-active and virile north-west and the until very recent dead and forgotten north-east, presents in itself a fascinating subject for serious study which could be highly rewarding. The opening chapters barely essay to telescope the long-storied past of these regions into a summary statement, perhaps necessarily unsatisfying, and then proceed to an examination of what by far is the most important factor that has conditioned developments on India's landward periphery. And this unquestionably is the vast physical expanse of Tibet lying athwart the mighty Himalayas, all the way from Kashmir to the North East Frontier Agency. On the face of it, it seems hardly credible that the barren and treeless wastes of this high plateau with a small, and by no means growing population, living under a mediaeval if not a primitive social system, should have excited the cupidity and invited the wrath of an alien army. The oddity, such as it is, becomes the more striking when one recalls that long and intensive explorations, in the latter half of the nineteenth century, in and around Tibet, the Karakorams and the Pamirs had led to the highly satisfying discovery—how satisfying for the then intensely rival British and Russian imperialisms contending for supremacy in these regions—that no viable passage-ways existed across high Asia which could be used for artillery and wheeled traffic. All this notwithstanding, what made the land of the lama important then was her geographical location vis-à-vis her huge, populous and powerful neighbours in the south and the east and the sprawling, yet by no means distant land mass of Asiatic Russia that loomed, and portentously, to her north and west. Today the old physical configuration remains, though the political has well-nigh completely altered. For China, not Russia, by occupying Tibet has, for the first time in history, set up a confrontation between the two greatest masses of population in the world.

The brief historical conspectus attempted in the second part highlights the principal features of Tibet's relationship, over the centuries, with both India and China. In tracing these one is powerfully struck by the closeness of early Indo-Tibetan ties. To knowledgeable students (although lately it has been fairly contentious ground) the origins of the Lhasa kingdom which brought about the final political consummation of the three distinct and disparate regions that comprise Tibet, from that of Ladakh in the seventh and eighth centuries of the Christian era, is highly suggestive of early Indian influences.[1] Even more important was the borrowing of the then prevalent syncretic Buddhism of northern India which was later accepted, and adapted, to suit Tibet's own peculiar needs, and the traffic in religious books and teachers between the two countries that has persisted down to our own day.

There is also the fact of the striking military prowess of the Tibetans in the heroic age of the Cho-gye when their arms held sway over nearly the whole of Kansu, the greater part of Szechuan and northern Yunnan and even spilled over into Hunza and Swat. Later, when the Lhasa Kingdom receded into its own and the Tang and the Yuan spread out over Asia's vast heartland, came the Chinese impact –powerful and no doubt lasting albeit, for most part, in material things. Thus the habit of drinking tea, the mode of dress of the people, of furnishings in a Tibetan home were in the nature of unobtrusive gifts from the Chinese. Still later came the Mongols who, with their varied tribal ramifications, long held sway far and wide and controlled Tibet too, for a time as part of their vast Chinese dominions. The successors of Chinghiz were also to act as catalysts for the institutions of the Dalai and the Panchen, the emergence of a reformed Tibetan church and the broad outlines of the patron-chaplain relationship between their chiefs and the Lamas of the Gelugpa sect.[2] Like much else, this too was a bequest to the Manchu rulers of China who, in fostering new ties with the pontiffs of the Yellow hat in Tibet, were not unmindful of their value and import in the context of Mongolia itself, now turned largely (Lama) Buddhist. The Manchu relationship with the Dalai Lamas in Lhasa was to undergo some major institutional changes during the eighteenth century principally in the wake of their armies marching across the land, ostensibly to repel the attack of the Mongols from the north, and of the Gurkhas from the south, yet in reality to tighten the reins of their control over the Lama's dominions.

Sandwiched somewhere between the eighteenth century Chinese incursions may be placed early British efforts to open up the land of mystery and snow. Primarily the aim of Warren Hastings, as of the Hon'ble East India Company whom he served, was to find new markets for British goods. It is not unlikely that a somewhat vague feeling was also entertained that through this little known backyard of hers, China itself might be made more accessible. Essentially, therefore, the missions of Greoge Bogle and of Samuel Turner were essays in commercial diplomacy. That both the envoys of so enthusiastic a sponsor as Hastings failed in their attempt to establish trade marts or even to obtain, for their English factors, access to the famed lands of the Thunderbolt was a great surprise. Nonetheless it was due not so much to their want to trying, as to the fears and doubts which assailed Tibet's lamas in terms of the dark, perhaps not easily fathomable, motives and motivations of the firingies.

In the chequered story of Britain's repeated efforts to open up Tibet, the next hundred years were far from eventful. True, the half-eccentric Manning succeeded in reaching Lhasa, or the 'brilliant' Colman Macaulay prepared himself, with evident relish, to lead an official mission across its high wastes. But for a corrective it may be recalled that Manning, who went in disguise, achieved practically nothing while the 'exigencies of political considerations' led to the countermanding of Macaulay's projected venture. All this notwithstanding, these hundred years had wrought a major transformation in the overall picture. The wars of 1861 and 1865 with Bhutan and Sikkim had brought British dominion in India right up to Tibet's doorsteps and thereby helped to confirm the lamas' earlier suspicions of British intentions. Nor were the clandestine Indian explorers, sponsored by their British masters, who roamed the Tibetan countryside with their sextants and prisms and measured beads designed to allay the doubts and suspicions already aroused. Meantime another important development had taken place, for in the second half of the nineteenth century the power and prestige of the Manchu Ambans in Lhasa began to suffer increasingly and shrink grievously.[3] This gradual erosion of their authority which reflected the defeats and humiliations of the Middle Kingdom at the hands of the foreign devils happened to synchronise with the emergence, towards the close of the century, of the powerful figure of the 13th Dalai Lama.

The true import of these varied, yet interrelated, developments came out in sharp relief when the Chinese, for and on behalf of their wards, concluded with the British Government in India the Sikkim Convention of 1890, and the Trade Regulations of 1893. The former sought to define the Tibet-Sikkim boundary, the latter spelt out in detail the trading facilities which British subjects were to enjoy in the land across the Nathu-la. It is significant that the country most vitally concerned in these arrangements was not a party to either. That would go a long way towards explaining the subsequent drama: Tibet's blunt refusal to be bound down by any of the stipulations entered into on her behalf, China's now fairly obvious inability to make her do so and growing British discontent, if not exasperation, with the resultant situation. Yet despite manifold frustrations, Lord Elgin's government in India displayed a remarkable forbearance with the doings of some fanatical hotheads across the Sikkim border and a sympathetic, even generous, understanding of the veritable delays and circuitous diplomacy of the Chinese.

The policy of patient waiting, however, was not destined to last for the new incumbent to the Viceregal throne, who was to play so decisive a role in the Tibetan drama, was signally lacking in this admirable quality. The third part is devoted largely to an understanding of Lord Curzon's 'new look' against the background of his early career and his Viceroyalty's manifold problems. Of Elgin's successor it has been held, and with a measure of truth, that almost always he did the right thing in the wrong way. Equally truly it may be said that nowhere is he better revealed than in his early books and travels. Thus the prancing proconsul with a megalomania for territory, and one may add imperial influence, emerges clearly from the otherwise well-reasoned pages of a *Persia and the Persian Question* or of a *Russia in Central Asia,* or the globe-girdlings which increasingly, yet forcefully, brought home to him the unique fascination and the mission of 'the Empire'. Nor could it be sufficiently emphasized that he had been Under Secretary for India, and for Foreign Affairs, before he took over as Governor-General. Both facts are of great import. For strange as it may seem, one gets the unmistakable impression from the career of this otherwise remarkable man that his mental horizon did not much widen after his late teens and that the obsessions of his early school days, confirmed by his travels, were expanded and elaborated in his books even as he continued to wrestle late in life with some of his initial experiences in administration. Thus the proposition, 'Are we justified in regarding with equanimity the advance of Russia towards our Indian frontier?', which he debated at Eton while not yet twenty—and of which his books breathe a strong under-current— did not cease to be the subject of his serious preoccupations for almost the entire span of a long and distinguished public career. Another 'flame' which has been traced in the narrative to his youthful years at Oxford, was the 'Empire' and it is remarkable that the sanctity and sense of dedication with which he viewed the duties and responsibilities it entailed did in no whit diminish even after many an early, and zealous, votary had been disillusioned by the jolts administered by World War I.

Not yet forty, the brilliant, ambitious, and to use an epithet which stuck to him all through life—the 'superior'—Baron, later Marquess, Curzon of Kedleston Hall in Derbyshire, stepped into the shoes of the patient, and somewhat taciturn Elgin. Few men could have been better qualified for the (Indian) Viceroyalty; fewer still could have had his richness and variety of experience and the deep knowledge and understanding of Asian problems that he alone commanded. India had been the fever and passion of his youth, central—nay perhaps pivotal, to his concept of the 'empire'; he had visited the country four times before he landed hither to be its lord and master. Of Asian rulers, as of Asian lands, there were hardly any that he did not know at first hand. Thus he had met the Shah of Persia, the Amir of Afghanistan, the King of Korea, the ruler of Siam (with whom he frequently corresponded), the Emperor of Annam and the King of Cambodia; with Li Hung-chang, the Chinese statesman whom he had met in London while at the Foreign Office, he was known to be on terms of considerable intimacy.

It is against this essential background of the man, and his ideas, that his handling of the Tibetan problem must be examined. Nor should that question be viewed, as though in isolation. For, as the narrative reveals, there is a considerable bearing of both the Persian and the Afghan problems on his dealings with Tibet.

Lord Curzon's policies in regard to all the three were closely akin for the basic question, as he viewed it, was the same in each case. Shorn of all extraneous trappings and hyperbole it could be simply worded thus: how to check, and indeed forestall, the Russian advance as far away from the Indian glacis, and as effectively, as possible? Another powerful factor that cast a grim, fearful, and as time went on, a lengthening shadow across the entire gamut of his Tibetan policy was the growing tension that progressively developed in his relations with his political superiors at home. The 'battles' which he waged with them, both on matters of domestic and foreign policy, and the 'victories' which he reportedly scored in consequence, left a deep wound that grew deeper as the years rolled by.

In analyzing Lord Curzon's policy towards Tibet two distinct phases are readily discernible, the watershed as it were being provided by the despatch of January 8, 1903. Early in his Viceroyalty, beginning of 1899, he bade farewell to the policy of forbearance and conciliation associated with his predecessor's name, and tried one of a direct approach to the master of the Potala. China was to be completely ignored and the Tibetan Pontiff reminded of the seriousness of British intent. Unfortunately for the Governor-General's sealed letters and special agents, and generous promises of 'liberal' payments for concessions obtained, the Lama proved singularly unresponsive. It is revealing, and perhaps characteristic of the then Viceroy that far from having a sympathetic understanding of the Tibetan ruler's peculiar difficulties, he grossly misjudged the conduct of the men employed and suspected them for the worst. That the Dalai Lama had the temerity, one had almost say the cheek, to return the Indian Grand Mughal's letters unopened was sufficient cause, in Lord Curzon's eyes, for a march on Lhasa, if only to show the Tibetan barbarians some elementary rules of civilised behaviour, of a code of (international) conduct! But the Lama's offence, grave and inexcusable as it was, became seriously compounded when he began, almost simultaneously, to despatch his extraordinary missions and special 'diplomatic' envoys to the Tsar of Russia.

Was the Buryat, in fact, a secret agent of the Russian Intelligence Service who had wormed his way into the confidence of the Tibetan Pontiff, or was he merely a religious zealot whose role as a faithful Russian subject, and an intelligent Buryat nationalist, need not have been a trumped-up affair, is hard to establish with any categoric assurance. What is plain is that Dorjief had convinced himself, and succeeded in convincing his youthful Tibetan master, that the Great White Tsar of the legendary kingdom of north Shambala, and hosts of his innumerable subjects were only too anxious to lend all the aid they could to the Lama's faith. It may also be conceded that the weight of all the evidence that can be mustered would seem, and this despite the flamboyant and sensational stories to the contrary, to point to the second conclusion. Basically however, thanks to the remarkable paucity of authentic source-material, Dorjief's figure remains shadowy, as ghost-like he flits across the Tibetan stage. A qualification, however, may be added. The Buryat's visits to Russia and the publicity attendant thereupon, reinforced by the attention which the Tsar bestowed upon the Lama's representatives, seem to have confirmed the Pontiff in his cherished, wishful belief that the lay supporter, whom he had sought elsewhere in vain, had at last been discovered. And the contrast appeared to be so sharp and to such grave disadvantage for the activities of his southern neighbour. Had not indeed the latter occupied Darjeeling and Sikkim, allegedly parts of Tibet, and repeatedly demanded new trading concessions and rights to open additional marts? And now, through these clever, insidious epistolary exchanges, on his own and through his agents, was not the Indian ruler, coveting Tibet itself?

The second phase of Lord Curzon's relations with his neighbouring domain covered by Chapters 11-17 opens with his strong, unqualified advocacy of an armed mission, though commercial to all outward appearance, forcing its way to Lhasa and demanding there a conference with the Chinese and the Tibetans. Its ostensible objective was to settle all outstanding problems at this tripartite meeting. The urgency which the Viceroy injected into his proposals, formally made early in 1903, derived largely from the persistent rumours, then widely current, of a Sino-Russian deal on Tibet and later even a direct Russo-Tibetan compact or understanding. It would have been only natural to expect that when both the one and the other were denied, and in the most categoric of terms, by the power concerned—denials which were accepted as satisfactory by the British Government—much of the wind would be taken out of Lord Curzon's sails. Yet paradoxical as it may seem, it was typical of the then Viceroy's mental make-up that Russian assurances served but to confirm his own innate suspicions of the Muscovites' dark intent. To make it more palatable to Whitehall, however, he did shift his emphasis from an armed mission with commercial overtones to a commercial mission with an armed escort! Yet a mission negotiating at Lhasa continued to remain his principal objective even though he may have temporarily relented and made some tactical retreats on minor points.

The choice of Colonel Younghusband as the leader of the Mission was not due, as may be obvious from the text, to a fortuitous circumstance but was the result of cold logic and well-calculated risk. One may suspect though that in the case of the 'Commander of the Escort' the same deliberation was not evident, yet the difficulty here lay in the Viceroy being, as he later maintained, 'over-ruled'. Macdonald he had perhaps never met, but Curzon knew backwards as it were the mountaineer, the Pamir-explorer and the 'fellow-traveller' whom he had virtually hand-picked, other things apart, for the implicit trust and faith he could place in his (Younghusband's) political judgement. It is significant that from the very outset the Colonel, deeply impregnated with the Viceroy's political ideology, was convinced that the Tibetans must be taught their proper place in the scheme of things, that the Amban's role was farcical, that the Dalai Lama was no better than a whipper-snapper caught out of the bazaar. Was he not, as head of these 'bumptious' lamas at the fount of all the Commissioner's troubles? And one, therefore, that deserved to he summarily put out of the way. Yet before many months elapsed Younghusband whose 'views and wishes' had always been notoriously so far apart from those of

Whitehall, had outpaced his own political mentor as well. It is indeed revealing that long before the expedition reached Lhasa Lord Curzon, then on leave in England, had begun to categorise the Commissioner as situated at the very extreme of the political spectrum that had emerged in terms of the settlement that was to be effected. Nor was he alone in his thinking, for the Secretary of State, as no doubt the acting Viceroy, were admittedly uncomfortable about Younghusband being rather 'jumpy' and somewhat 'precipitous'.

A reasonable defence of the Commissioner's behaviour may be that the progress of the Mission had been far from smooth; in fact, its path lay strewn with all sorts of pitfalls not the least important of which were the altitude and that continuous sniping, guerilla-fashion, by the Tibetans which persisted for most part. To make sure that it did not prove abortive, one of Lord Curzon's early compromises, and an admitted tactical retreat, was his acceptance of the four-months long halt at Khamba Jong where the initial tripartite 'negotiations' had commenced in the later part of July, 1903. Though it posed a major problem to Younghusband's endurance, as it did no doubt to the Viceroy's, the halt proved to be a temporary one. For the advance from Khamba to Gyantse—actually the Commissioner and part of the force had initially retreated and later again advanced via the Jelap-la and the Nathu-la[4]—with a brief stop-over at Tuna, at the head of the Chumbi Valley, and from then on to Lhasa may have been slow and devious but was, in retrospect, steady and sure. While the narrative reveals the momentary checks and restraints which HMG imposed from time to time, the more abiding impression remains that in every case the Viceroy eventually succeeded and got away with nearly all that he wanted. He coaxed and cajoled, threatened and pleaded, seemed to yield ground now and yet remained unbending, singly and by turns, until Lord George Hamilton, Mr. Brodrick or Mr. Balfour gave way. It is imperative to note, however, that in attaining his desired objective in each case some of the means to which His Excellency was willing to resort were decidedly questionable. The choice of Khamba itself, as the venue for the talks, demonstrates how cleverly he had rushed both the Amban and the Tibetans and succeeded in hoodwinking his own masters at home. His later representations to Whitehall to obtain its sanction for the advance to Gyantse did severe violence, as the voluminous correspondence reveals, to those twin ideals of truth and forthrightness which Lord Curzon had publicly proclaimed to be peculiarly Western in their 'conception' and as occupying 'a high place' in its moral codes.[5]

Again, with a brazen-facedness bordering almost on the semi-comic, he catalogued the 'war-like preparations' of the Tibetan lamas and tried to convince the newly-inducted successor of Lord George Hamilton at the India Office that not only had a breach of negotiations taken place at Khamba but that one was inevitable. What finally removed many of Lord Curzon's obvious embarrassments was the 'fighting' at Guru which, shorn of all the trappings of diplomatic despatches, could scarce be distinguished from a cold-blooded massacre of raw, ill-trained and ill-equipped Tibetan levies. Yet the Viceroy's conscience was now at rest, for the

lamas' hostile intent, nay the charge of aggression itself, had been proved, and to
the hilt. Later, in its wake began those 'military operations' which were to transform
a peaceful commercial mission into an armed expedition. The final goal could now
no longer be in doubt, for the advance to Lhasa had been secured.

With the last part of the book, the victorious military expedition reaps its by
now well-earned fruit: the Lhasa Convention is signed in the audience-hall of the
golden Potala. This final consummation also serves to underscore that yawning
chasm between the Commissioner, now located in the Tibetan capital, and his
political masters, in Calcutta and Whitehall. The gap, apparent from the beginning,
had been repeatedly coverd up, with its deep fissures thickly papered over as it
were by the all-too-frequent 'surrenders' of the Secretary of State in London to the
ever-aggressive and pushful advocacy of Lord Curzon who consistently, and
stoutly, championed the cause of Younghusband. The appearance of the *locum
tenens,* as Ampthill called himself, slightly complicated the situation but did not
materially alter it. For Younghusband remained, and functioned to the last as
'Curzon's man' and this despite every effort of the acting Viceroy to win him over
and furnish him with a more accurate and faithful interpretation of the mind of
HMG, as indeed of his own. To that extent is may be conceded, and without
qualification, that despite the extreme difficulty of his role as only 'a half-Viceroy',
its varied embarrassments and sometimes lack of forthrightness —not to mention
what he later termed Younghusband's 'betrayal'—Ampthill emerges out of a
somewhat sorry, shoddy business remarkably well.

As for HMG its repeated cries of a halt, of going thus far and no farther, after
grudgingly, and sometimes with ill-grace, yielding to one demand after another,
sounded at best like a refrain, if not a punctuation. And it is evident that by the time
Mr. Brodrick made up his mind to yield no more ground, it was already a little too
late in the day. Both he and his predecessor had fought, and lost, many a battle and
the determination not to lose the last round in the final encounter was demonstrative
less of strength than the drowning man's vain bid to catch at the traditional straw.
No wonder Younghusband gravely miscalculated Whitehall's mood. It must also
be said that in the last few and crucial weeks in Lhasa when he needed sound
advice most the one man who alone could tender it—for Younghusband would
take it from no one else—failed miserably in so doing. On the contrary one has the
rather uncomfortable feeling that Lord Curzon's omission—a steadier and more
sure-footed man would have behaved differently—grossly misled Younghusband
when obviously he alone could have saved him (Younghusband) from falling
down the precipice.

II

A clearer understanding of Younghusband's stay at Lhasa, and his negotiations
with the Tibetans there, also throws an interesting, and revealing, light on some
dubious aspects of the Commissioner's dealings. Reading between the lines of
official despatches, not to mention his private letters, two conclusions seem to be
fairly obvious. Firstly, the deposition of the Dalai Lama, ostensibly carried out by

the Manchu Emperor on the recommendation of the Imperial Amban at Lhasa, had the tacit approval of Colonel Younghusband, if not his active support. It is not unlikely that the Commissioner's acute eye saw at once that without the deposition being effected, the legality of much that he did at Lhasa would be in serious jeopardy. And herein the slightest hint from the Colonel was doubly welcome to the Amban whose honour, and the numerous humiliations to which he had been subjected at the Lama's hands, could in no manner have been better vindicated.

Another interesting fact, and it is closely related to the one outlined in the preceding paragraph, was the meteoric rise of the Ti Rimpoche for whom the path lay open once the Dalai Lama had been put securely out of the way. It is significant that from a person who 'commanded no influence', to borrow the Commissioner's own words, the Rimpoche emerges, in a matter of a week or so, not only as the principal Tibetan negotiator but also as the recognized Regent. And the whole comic opera culminates as it were in the affixing of his private seal to an agreement to one of whose major clauses the Rimpoche's oft-reiterated opposition had been unwearied. Would it be too much to say that Younghusband not only conquered Lhasa but, in order to negotiate 'properly', set up a government of his own choosing one of whose principal functionaries was no better than a British protégé?

It is also possible to view the sequence of events at the Tibetan capital from another angle, which puts a slightly different construction on them. Having reached Lhasa, and with the Lama's flight preceding his arrival, Younghusband had to negotiate with someone or else return empty-handed. Nor did he want the convention undermined by having the Chinese say that he had set up his own puppets to sign it. Therefore, at first he may have been doubtful as to whether the Rimpoche was a big enough man to be his opposite number, but gradually Younghusband and the Chinese felt each other out. When it became plain that the Chinese wanted to take the Dalai Lama down a peg or two, a sentiment in which Younghusband found himself to be in cordial agreement with them, it was equally clear that they would not raise the accusation of puppet against the Rimpoche, and this meant that the British could hold any future Tibetan Government to the validity of the Convention. Thus strictly speaking Younghusband did not have to set up a government; all he had to do was to act as though the Tibetans with whom he dealt were, in fact, the duly-constituted authorities. Two facts, however, may to an extent militate against this hypothesis. One, that the actual state of affairs Younghusband found in Lhasa on arrival bordered on the chaotic, with no one prepared to accept responsibility for anything. Who, therefore, suggested what to whom and took the initiative in so doing, would perhaps not be of much relevance. Secondly, the Amban, from the very outset, showed himself more than ever anxious to do the Commissioner's bidding, the more so when their admittedly rival interests appeared to be so closely concerted at points.

Lhasa also proved to be the focal point for much of the controversy that later raged around some of the principal terms of the convention. Here, in the face of instructions which left little room for ambiguity, the British Commissioner displayed an open disregard for authority which later earned him a not unmerited censure.[6] It may be noted, however, if only in parenthesis, that 'face' would have been saved all round by just dropping these offending clauses. In fact, it has been suggested that HMG acted like the weak, conservative Government of Arthur Balfour would be expected to act, getting the whole picture out of focus, and actuated by a fatuous sense of *amour-propre* such as only a weak man will show. The record however, as the narrative spells out, is revealing in two specific instances: the suggestion for an extended period of payment for the indemnity to be imposed, and the right of the British Trade Agent at Gyantse to proceed to Lhasa to negotiate on matters which had not yielded satisfaction locally. The Commissioner later maintained that it was the Tibetans who had made the initial suggestion regarding the extended period and thereby willingly consented to a long-term occupation of a part of their land. His despatches, not to mention his private correspondence do not, however, bear the Colonel out. The plain, unvarnished truth appears to be that on more than one occasion he had spelt out his ideas in this respect with a broad enough hint that these be accepted. The Tibetans however, and to the very end, kept up a stiff, stubborn opposition until they succumbed to the gleaming British bayonets, and the inevitability of a surrender. The second revelation is even more damaging. On whose authority, one may ask, did the Commissioner conclude that separate 'agreement' which permitted the Trade Agent at Gyantse to proceed to Lhasa? For if there was one point on which the position taken up by Lord George Hamilton, and later consistently upheld by Mr. Brodrick, had been clear-cut and reiterated with an almost nauseating frequency, it was the question of the Agent. That there was something fishy about the deal in Younghusband's own mind is evident, apart from a host of other evidence, from the following: the 'agreement' was not made a part of the terms of the Convention; the Commissioner did not mention it in any of his frequent telegraphic despatches from Lhasa; and above all, its existence was not known at the India Office, and even in Simla, until weeks after it had been signed and sealed in the Tibetan capital.

An interesting sidelight on Younghusband's 'negotiations' at Lhasa relates to Lord Curzon's role. An omission has been noticed earlier, one wonders about his acts of commission? There were 'dark hints' in Parliament, the Indian Viceroy later wrote to Younghusband, 'that I was the real culprit'.[7] It may perhaps be useful to enquire as to what extent he shared the blame.

In Younghusband's correspondence there is a mention of 'a private and very confidential letter' which the Commissioner received in Lhasa from the Viceroy on leave. He told his father that it had been written 'in the strictest confidence and you will not of course repeat it'.[8] The epistle written from London in the middle of July (1904), made three interesting points. *One,* that 'the policy which you advocate is, in my opinion theoretically the 'right one' and that 'we may be forced to adopt more of it than the Cabinet at present contemplate or desire'. *Two,* that 'all that HMG as a whole know or care about Tibet is that it is a nuisance and an expense and all that they want to do is to get out of it in any way that does not involve positive humiliation'. *Three,* that there was no use 'in yielding to depondency or in resigning', and that 'what we have got to do is to make as good an agreement as we can in the circumstances and to point out clearly to those in authority the responsibility that they incur in over-ruling us but as far as possible to keep them straight'.[9] Whatever his own assessment of the situation and this did, in a marked degree, go much farther to the extreme than did Lord Curzon's, the Commissioner must have felt fortified in the thought that not only did he enjoy the utmost confidence of the Viceroy but that the latter would be back in India to sustain and buttress him by the time he himself returned from Lhasa. Thus circumstanced, Younghusband may have felt sufficiently strong to run counter to the express wishes of HMG, and of the acting Governor-General. Curzon may not have directly encouraged him, yet did nothing to dissuade, much less discourage him from taking a course which he could have, in Younghusband's case, reasonably well anticipated and foreseen. It is significant that he had not even a word of criticism for the Commissioner's conduct at Lhasa although the latter had his own moments of doubt.[10] And as for Younghusband, Curzon was the one man to whom 'the real credit' was due for his (Younghusband's) success, 'the only true man who in my hour of trial', when both the Home Government and the Government of India clearly deserted him, 'stood by my side'.[11] Again, on the morrow of the conclusion of the convention, and in the context of its controversial clauses:

> Lord Curzon will I know be delighted but how the Home Government will view it, I do not know. If they like to be idiotic...[12]

There is a mention in Dr. Seaver's biography of a private note of Younghusband, alluded to earlier, which he left for 'his own future justification'. Here the Commissioner refers to another 'private and very confidential letter' from Lord Curzon which he wrote after an interview with Lord Lansdowne and wherein the latter is credited with the view that 'the pledge we had given Russia not to occupy Tibet did not prevent us from occupying the Chumbi Valley'.[13] The present writer has not been able to locate this letter, nor is there a mention of it in Younghusband's correspondence with his father. There is nonetheless a reference to it in a private letter of February 22, 1905, which the Viceroy wrote to the former Commissioner,

> It is perfectly true that Lord Lansdowne told me on my return to England that there was nothing in his assurances to Russia to debar us from a permanent occupation of Chumbi: I wrote this to Lord Ampthill as well as to yourself. I was, therefore, as much surprised as you were when I found the proposal subsequently treated as an offence.[14]

Would it be too much to deduce that the 75-year clause, which could be scarce distinguished from 'a permanent occupation', owed its direct genealogical origin to the above-cited unequivocal declaration of Lord Curzon, allegedly based on the then British Foreign Secretary's assurances?

Another interesting fact emerges too. Clearly Curzon wrote to Younghusband as he did to Ampthill and much to the same effect. The letter to the acting Viceroy is datelined Walmer Castle and was written on May 26, 1904,

I have, however, had long talks with the Prime Minister, Lansdowne and Balfour. I have implored them not to go on repeating these stupid and gratuitous pledges about Tibet in the House of Commons—pledges which must in some cases be broken. Lansdowne has to some extent committed himself to the Russians whose assent he wishes to procure to the Egyptian agreement. But I gather his assurances do not go beyond a promise—

(i)   Not to annex Tibet—which need not apparently preclude a permanent occupation of the Chumbi Valley. The latter, indeed, is hardly a part of Tibet;

(ii) Not to establish a protectorate, which I imagine that none of us desires;

(iii) Not to interfere permanently in the internal administration of the country, which is not inconsistent with a somewhat prolonged occupation of Lhasa should this be found to be necessary....

The Government are very much against a permanent agent at Lhasa or any- where. But I have said that I do not see how they can avoid it in some form or other although steps may be required to qualify the appearance...[15]

Somewhere in June, it is obvious, while the Commissioner was still at Gyantse poised for the final march to Lhasa, he had been fully, and in the most categoric of terms, posted with Lord Curzon's thinking on the vital points of a projected treaty. It is thus likely that while handing over a preliminary draft of the terms to the Tongsa Penlop—that the Lama and his men may have time to digest them—the Commissioner put in the clause concerning the Gyantse Trade Agent visiting Lhasa which in its innocuous wording was tantamount to 'steps... required to qualify the appearance'. Later, unmindful of Mr. Brodrick's telegrams and Lord Ampthill's resolute underpinning thereof, the Commissioner stuck to it to the last convinced, one would imagine even more fervently than Curzon—'I do not see how they can avoid it in some form or other'.

The indemnity and the Agent apart, a fundamental question arises. Was Younghusband at Lhasa carrying out the directives of his superiors—of the Secretary of State, transmitted to him through the Governor-General—or of the man who originally despatched him on his mission? From all available evidence one is driven to the reluctant, yet remorseless, conclusion that the Commissioner owed a greater sense of loyalty to Lord Curzon and a lesser to the Indian Government of Lord Ampthill or Mr. Brodrick in Whitehall. Yet while conceding Younghusband's 'loyalty', there is not a shred of evidence to sustain the charge, which an uncharitable critic then made in Parliament, that Younghusband's 'defiance' had been made with Lord Curzon's 'knowledge and acquiescence'.[16] Curzon, in London, may have made a reasonably good guess of how Younghusband would act, but had no foreknowledge of it; there is at any rate no trace of a dark conspiracy between the two men.

A point that is closely interelated remains yet to be answered. In disobeying 'instructions' what precisely were the Commissioner's motives—apart from the obvious one that as 'Curzon's man' he was determined to do what would have most pleased his master. Two clues may be of interest in this contest. One, the march from Gyantse to Lhasa was an eye-opener to everyone, not least to Younghusband. The land that now came into view was in such marked contrast to the barren, desolate wastes around Tuna or Kang-ma. Nor had the Gyantse plain been an improvement. Now on his way to the Tibetan capital, it is clear, he was deeply struck and at more than one place expressed his sense of unabashed amazement,

> The country is very fertile and this Lhasa river on which we are encamped is as big as the Thames at London bridge. The Valley is two or three miles broad and covered with cultivation. Tibet, in fact, is a much richer country than Kashmir.[17]

Or again,

> ...it is becoming more evident with each day's march that Tibet is by no means the desert, worthless country it has been believed to be.... The Brahmaputra Valley is not what we had expected to find it—a deep, narrow gorge like the Valley of Jaleum between the Wular Lake and Kohala. It is a valley three or four miles wide with lots of cultivation. And the hill-sides are not bare but covered with rich pasturage.... The villages are all remarkably well built and flourishing looking and I don't know where in the whole length of the Himalayas you would find a more prosperous country...[18]

What was more, Younghusband was clear that the Tibetans bore him, or the British for that matter, no ill-will. There were 'no scowls' as he moved through Lhasa's crowded streets and he was certain in his own mind that the people did not care 'a two penny dam whether we went there or not'. The monks too had 'no sort of fanatical feeling' and actually 'for the most are good fellows'.[19]

Could it be that his cupidity was excited—and whose would not?—by 'the fertility of these valleys, the affluence of the people, the wealth of the temples and what is more extraordinary still the good disposition shown to us everywhere by all' except the few out and out anti-foreign Lamas?[20] No wonder even as he 'rammed down their throats' the whole treaty, he was sure not only that the Russians will be 'kept out for ever' but also that their (Tibetan) payment of the annual tribute will be 'the means of gradually tying them (Tibetans) to us'.[21] What if, in the bargain, he exceeded some (inconvenient) instructions?

Younghusband was a man of honour, of integrity and both his earlier career, as indeed his later years, bear an eloquent testimony to this. The maximum that can be held against him was that perhaps he was politically a little amateurish—viz. Godley's charge of his being a 'wire-puller' and Ampthill's that he was 'Curzon's man'. In extenuation, however, it may be urged that in Tibet he was carrying out an incredibly difficult responsibility in a strange and distant country, 14,000 feet above the sea. Again, for a corrective it is as well to remember that he was essentially an explorer and a mystic and not an adept at the jigsaw puzzle of politics. There could be no doubt that the dread hold of Lord Curzon on his mind was deep and abiding and that like the great Viceroy he too wanted to make his own small contribution—'a very humble one at first, and never a great one'—to the common cause of 'helping to fend off Russia from India'.[22] A later writer has explained away Younghusband's lapse at Lhasa in apt phrases,

> in the exhilarating atmosphere of a successful expedition, in a remote and unknown country, he saw the opportunity of securing without difficulty greater advantages for his country than were contained in his instructions.[23]

But that would be a paraphrase, and at second-hand, of the former Tibetan Commissioner's own inimitable words,

> My humble little effort to improve the shining hour and get a trifle little more for my country than I was specifically ordered to obtain.[24]

III

In concluding this survey a few words may be in order regarding the precise place that the Younghusband expedition occupies in the chequered story of British India's relations with Tibet—a saga that was later to be part of the British bequest to the Government of free India. Broad generalizations apart, it is obvious that a more accurate, detailed and documented answer would demand a greater familiarity with subsequent developments than is known to exist as of now. There are, in fact, a host of problems in this period which though they could be readily stated, cannot as yet be fully or adequately answered. For other things apart, access to relevant material is not yet forthcoming and in its absence research lags woefully behind.

In assessing what actual purpose the expedition served in the years that followed, it is necessary to draw a clear line between the objective of the Viceroy and his agents in India and those of the British Government in London. That cleavage apart, and the physical besides the mental isolation was often-times complete, Younghusband's Convention had demonstrated both the positive fact of Tibet's ability to conclude its own international compacts as also, and very markedly, China's calamitous lack of authority or control in Lhasa. It is true that the Commissioner had been advised to secure the Amban's 'adhesion' to his convention, but it is equally a fact that throughout the progress of the Mission and even more so during its sojourn in the Tibetan capital, the powerlessness and ineffectiveness of that functionary was clearly, and unmistakably, exposed. The Lhasa Convention which was to form the chief basis of all subsequent political dealings between the Government of India and Tibet had marked a clear, healthy departure from an old practice—namely, that all matters concerning Tibet should be routed through China.

Unfortunately, political compulsions of international relations supervened on the morrow of Younghusband's return. Legal pundits pointed but that without China's 'adhesion' the compact lacked 'validity' and conscious of the value attached to its signature, Peking raised its price and insisted as it were on 'complete satisfaction'. The tortuous negotiations spanning a period of nearly two years, which were twice broken and conducted inconclusively in Calcutta before they reached fruition in Peking are at once a testimony to the latter's growing intransigence and of the British fighting a rear-guard action all along the line. In the result, some of the major gains made at Lhasa had to be compromised, if only temporarily.[25] Thus though the Peking Convention was free from such clichés as the powers of the sovereign or the suzerain *vis-à-vis* the feudatory, the fact that China was not to be recognized as a foreign power, in terms of clause IX of the Lhasa deal, restored to her a position which Britain had overtly assumed in 1904. The Chinese gain was thus clear, and tangible and the British retreat obvious enough for all to see.[26]

A year later came the entente with Russia. What had been implicit in 1906 was now made explicit. For by the Anglo-Russian Convention of 1907, the British not only tacitly 'recognised' Chinese right in Tibet, but further bound themselves down to a position of conducting no independent negotiations with that country except through their (Chinese) intermediacy. They further undertook, as did the Russians, not to send a representative to Lhasa nor obtain 'any concession for railways, roads, telegraphs, and mines, or other rights in Thibet'.[27]

Lord Curzon, now free from the trammels of office,[28] and Sir Francis Younghusband, whose career as a frontier officer had come to a virtual close with the Tibet expedition,[29] attacked both the deals, and violently. The former Viceroy held that the so-called self-denying clause in the convention with Russia was tantamount to an absolute surrender, that the efforts of a century had been sacrificed with 'a wholesale abandon' and that John Bull had suffered his greatest humiliation.[30] Sir Francis' lament was couched much in the same key. He deplored the fact that the British had no 'settled, pushful and aggressive policy', that Whitehall had not accepted what appeared to him a 'permanent solution' of the problem—namely, the appointment of a British Agent at Lhasa.[31]

Nor were the two alone, much less without reason. The plain truth is that the two conventions took the position back to where it belonged before the expedition to Lhasa. Not only were the old barriers to direct relations with Tibet up again but what was more the Chinese, in the wake of British retreat, were in a position to erect bigger and better ones. Yet to Sir Edward Grey, and the Liberal Government to which he belonged, 'an effective buffer had been built to a Russian advance, there was freedom from an anxiety that had often preoccupied earlier administrations, an end had been put to a frequent source of friction and a possible cause of war'.[32]

Besides much that had been yielded across the table, events in Tibet conspired too, and disastrously. The British expedition by its sudden withdrawal on the morrow of a resounding military 'victory', had helped in creating a power vacuum which the Chinese, despite their varied preoccupations at home, did not neglect to fill.[33] Thus by 1910 Peking's troops were in complete control of Lhasa and the Dalai Lama once again a fugitive from the land of his birth and faith. The contrast between the two occupations, however, was striking and exercised a most powerful impact on what transpired subsequently. The British had demonstrated that, however formidable the physical barriers, and however forbidding the rigours of Tibet's climate—not to mention the innumerable difficulties of transport in a country that until lately knew of no wheel except the prayer-wheel—they could still reach Lhasa. Since they had dared to cross the Jelap-la in the frozen cold of a January, it was patent that they could cross it whenever they chose to. Indeed many a Tibetan who had convinced himself that Lhasa was not accessible to a large force and that the gods would whisk the British away before they dared the sacrilege of reaching the gates of the golden Potala, found himself sadly disillusioned. Before their dazed eyes, the spectacle was not of the foreign devils fleeing from the scourge of angry heavens but the chief of their gods who, at their approach, found himself a helpless fugitive.

Another equally revealing experience for these people was the behaviour of the British and Indian troops. Stray cases of looting may have occurred and the fact of continuous exhortations to the contrary, in official despatches and private papers, could indeed help to confirm these.[34] Yet on the whole the troops appear to have created a very favourable impression. The monasteries were respected nor were their supplies ruthlessly seized. True, hoarded grain and carcasses of sheep were requisitioned—adequate food supplies in the Lhasa valley for a large force has been an endemic problem—but the owners in every known case were handsomely recompensed. Above all the wounded in battle were properly cared for, and the prisoners taken treated well.

The Chinese levies who followed not long after, presented a study in contrast for, besides much else, the 'shame' of the British expedition had to be avenged, right and proper.[35] Again, the invasion of 1910 is said to mark a clear break with previous policy. For now, in sharp contradistinction to earlier occasions, a Chinese army had reached Lhasa 'against the will of the Tibetans'—an exception that indeed was to become a rule, a precedent.[36] In any case, spoliation of monasteries and the seizure of men and property of the 'barbarians' must have been resorted to without any scruples. The British had come in at their own sweet will, but did not tarry long beyond the signing of the Convention; the Chinese sneaked in when they could, and threatened to stay put. The Tibetans, at the receiving end in each case, noticed the marked difference between the two. It is said that they compared the British to a frog and the Chinese to a scorpion. The frog, though frisky and classed a fierce animal—in Tibet, at any rate—is not rated as deadly as the scorpion. And as the Tibetans put it: 'When one has seen a scorpion, one looks on the frog as divine".[37]

Not unconnected with their behaviour, and the relatively easy terms of the Lhasa Convention—early in 1908 the Chumbi Valley had, despite clear breaches on the other side, been evacuated[38]—was the marked change towards the British in the attitude of the Dalai Lama. This began to manifest itself in the closing years of the Lama's first exile,[39] and became the more apparent when, in 1910, he again found himself a fugitive from his native land. It is significant that he now sought shelter from his relentless foes not in the vast expanse of Mongolia, which lay in such close proximity to the domains of the White Tsar, but in the holy land of the Buddha. What was more, he now appealed to the British who until yesterday had been his sworn enemies. How did this sudden transformation, so complete as to take on the character of a metamorphosis, come about?

On his flight from Lhasa, hot on the heels of the British expedition, the Dalai Lama must have found that although the Manchu court could 'depose' him, its authority was actually in such decay that it did not consider it discreet to interfere with his passage, which lay entirely through territory over which China, i.e., the Manchu Emperor, claimed sovereignty. When he got to Outer Mongolia, his keen eye must have noticed that Russia was actively conducting a sphere of influence policy there and that the prestige the Russians enjoyed at Urga cast a fearful shadow over that of the Manchu-Chinese. Shrewd as he was, he must have realized too that the actual policy of the Russians in Mongolia was in marked contrast to their mere verbal expressions of friendly interest in Tibet.[40] This was further underlined by the cordial, yet formally couched, message which he received from the Tsar and which did not go beyond an exchange of commonplace pleasantries. Hence the Lama's ill-concealed overtures to the British, alluded to earlier, during his brief and none-too-happy a stop-over in Peking. Hence too the appeal which he had addressed to 'Great Britain and all the Ministers of Europe' to intercede with the Chinese to stay the despatch of their troops to Lhasa. This was in 1909 while he was still on his way back home via Peking, from his long wanderings. His return to the Potala was followed, with scarcely a breathing spell, by the arrival of a Chinese army of invasion, and occupation, and he barely managed to escape— even as a later incarnation did in our own day—with a price on his head. Now, during his two-year sojourn in India, the Tibetan ruler made the astounding discovery that the British summarily dismissed his repeated requests to proclaim his country a protectorate 'on the same terms as Bhutan enjoyed....'[41]

Thus when the Lama eventually returned to Lhasa after his two exiles and varied, yet enriching, experiences and after the Russians had been defeated by Japan and the Manchus overthrown and replaced by a Republic that staked far sweeping claims on his domains, he appears to have reached certain broad conclusions. The most important perhaps was the one relating to the British. The latter had shown in their actual behaviour that they did not covet his land, nor did they seemingly wish to impose a control which assuredly it was in their power to impose. The Russians were friendly but distant and regarded Tibet merely as an outer and remote fringe of Mongolia, which was the zone of their interest and activity. In clear contradistinction to these two powers were the Chinese who, whenever they penetrated into Tibet, would not withdraw if indeed it was in their power to stay. Thus he must look to the British interest in maintaining him as the ruler of a buffer state, and to their power to sustain a policy of that kind. Besides, one would suspect that memories of Younghusband and his troops' generally decent and honourable behaviour, reinforced by the Lama's own personal friendship with Bell, inclined him to take this course. With minor modifications, necessitated by the exigencies of changing circumstances from time to time, these broad conclusions continued to be the guiding principles of the 13th Dalai Lama for the score or more years that now remained to him. One could go even further and say that Tibet's basic approach did not register any major departure even under his successor, and that it was the Chinese aggression of October 1950 which again violently shook and completely undermined the old pattern.

One final word. The Younghusband expedition sounded a clear note of dissonance in an otherwise long tale of amity that had marked the relationship on both sides of the border over the centuries before the British arrived, and even under them. It is perhaps of the greatest import that this departure was realised to be such by the successors of Lord Curzon. For under the gravest of provocations in 1910-11, and again in 1950-51, not a single British solider, nor yet an Indian, did again dare cross Sikkim for a march across the Valley of Chumbi to the city of gods. Nor perhaps would a future Younghusband ever again lead a mighty host, in combat formation, to hold in fealty this neighbouring land of mystery and snow—now a hallowed memory. Actually, and it is a grim, sobering thought, with the vast armies now poised in Chumbi, may not the Nathu-la be a witness to a movement in reverse?

Notes

1. N. B. Roy, 'India and Tibet, Cultural Contacts', *Modern Review* (Calcutta), LXXXIII, March 1953, pp. 205-6, suggests that in making what he calls their 'fabric of civilization', the Tibetans borrowed impulses primarily from India. Roy reveals that a Tibetan Minister, Thou-mi-Sambhotta, was deputed to India, in the middle of the seventh century, to study and transcribe Buddhist texts and that before Padma Sambhava went to Tibet another Indian saint, Santa Rakshita had been invited by Tibet's chief, Ti-Song-De-Tsen.

   A Chinese scholar, however, enters a caveat: 'There was indeed very early religious contacts between India and Tibet.... But the Tibetans, as shown by a study of the loan-words in their language, appear to have received names and objects from the Chinese prior to their contact with India'. Li, *op.cit.*, p. 12.

2. Lest this summary statement give a false impression, it may be emphasized that the most powerful Mongol impact on political institutions in Tibet was not under the Yuan (i.e., Mongol) dynasty in China (1260-1368) but in the sixteenth and seventeenth centuries by which time Mongol ascendancy had been gradually eroded and superseded by the Manchus. Thus the most important Mongol influence was during the period of 're-arrangement' in Inner Asia characterized by the decline of the Ming (late sixteenth century) followed by a piecemeal Manchu conquest of China, Mongolia, Tibet and Sinkiang.

3. A news-item in the *Statesman,* of March 1890, makes interesting reading: 'The Chinese in Calcutta have apparently been deluded into considering the Amban as a heavenly-sent messenger in close relations with 'the Lord of the Universe' as they style their Emperor, and in some respects connected by family ties with the moon and the greater constellations whereas he is nothing of the sort. A minor representative of the invisible emperor of China, he has been received with exaggerated honours'. The *Statesman* (Calcutta), March 13, 1890.

   A day previously, the same paper had reported the arrival in Calcutta of 'His Excellency Sheng-tai' deputed to settle the 'Tibet dispute' with the British, *Ibid.,* March 12, 1890.

4. From east to west, three passes—the Jelap-la, the Nathu-la and the Sebu-la—afford good routes into Tibet. Initially the British had used the Jelap-la which lies exclusively through Sikkimese territory. Later, after the Trimbuk Jongpen had met Younghusband at Tuna, the Bhutanese allowed the British to by-pass the Jelap-la and use a route over a less intractable pass, the Nathu-la.

5. In an address to the Calcutta University Convocation on February 11, 1905, Lord

Curzon said: '... the highest ideal of truth is to a large extent a Western conception... undoubtedly truth took a high place in the moral codes of the West before it had been similarly honoured in the East, where craftiness and diplomatic wiles have always been held in much repute... oriental diplomacy by which is meant something rather tortuous and hyper-subtle'. *Speeches by Lord Curzon of Kedleston,* Viceroy and Governor-General of India, 4 volumes (Calcutta, 1906), IV, p. 75. Also see Shane Leslie, *op.cit.,* p. 211.

6. Later attempts to whitewash Younghusband's conduct take the form either of putting the blame on Brodrick's stupidity—he was 'deaf to persuasion and would consult no one' and 'was totally without experience of conditions' in India as well as in those areas (Seaver, *op.cit.,* p. 254), or his 'implacable malevolence' against the Commissioner (Peter Fleming, *op.cit.,* pp. 273-74); or again 'to conflicting concepts of his (Younghusband's) superiors as to what the Tibetan problem was about' whereby 'he was better entitled' to use his own discretion (Lamb, *op.cit.,* p. 305), and not least Whitehall's 'obsession with Russian susceptibilities' and its 'sense of injured dignity in that a subordinate should venture to exceed his *(sic.)* orders' (Richardson, *op.cit.,* p. 92). One fails to see how Brodrick's alleged sins of omission or commission, much less differences of opinion between the Viceroy and the Secretary of State or a vindication of Whitehall's 'sense of injured dignity' be held to justify Younghusband's defiance of instructions.

7. Curzon to Younghusband, letter, February 15, 1905, Curzon MSS.

8. Younghusband MSS., No. 47, August 19, 1904.

9. Curzon to Younghusband, letter, July 13, 1904, Curzon MSS. It is obvious that this letter was received in Lhasa on August 19. *Supra,* note 6.

10. 'With the principle of securing Chumbi for 75 year and of getting permission for our Agent at Gyantse to proceed to Lhasa, I know you will agree. But whether I was wise under the circumstances to make such arrangements I daresay you doubt'. *Ibid.,* Younghusband to Curzon, letter, October 16, 1904.

11. Younghusband MSS., No. 52, October 18, 1904.

12. *Ibid.,* No. 50, September 9, 1904.

13. Seaver, *op.cit.,* pp. 251-52.

14. Curzon to Younghusband, letter, February 22, 1905, Curzon MSS.
    The Curzon letter is also alluded to in Younghusband's later correspondence with the Viceroy wherein while referring to the 75-year clause,
    'I agreed, knowing how satisfactory that agreement would be to us and having in my possession that private letter from you (which as it was marked 'very confidential', I cannot quote either to Lord Lansdowne or to Mr. Brodrick) stating that in Lord Lansdowne's opinion the pledges to Russia not to annex Tibet did not necessarily stand in the way of our occupying Chumbi'.
    Ibid., Younghusband to Curzon, letter, February 23, 1905.

15. Curzon to Ampthill, letter, May 26, 1904. Ampthill Papers, *op.cit.*

16. *Parliamentary Debates,* Vol. 140, p. 464, Mr. Gibon Bowles, the critic in question, had also insinuated that Lord Curzon, 'a military and strategically-minded man' wanted to take into India an 'unconquered border' for political purposes.

17. Younghusband MSS., No. 46, August 1, 1904.

18. Younghusband to Curzon, letter, August 25, 1904, Curzon MSS.

19. *Ibid.*, Younghusband to Curzon, letter, August 6, 1904.

20. Younghusband MSS., No. 50, September 9, 1904.

21. *Loc. cit.*

22. Younghusband, The Light of Experience, *op.cit.*, p. 3.

23. Richardson, *op.cit.*, p. 92.

24. Francis Younghusband, letter to the *Times* (London), April 19, 1939. This was an aftermath of Henry St. John Brodrick's (later Earl of Midleton), Records and Reactions, *op.cit.*, which the same paper had, a fortnight earlier, hailed as a work 'in the great tradition'. *Ibid.*, April 4, 1939.

25. The Convention 'was a clear acknowledgement of Tibet's direct powers to make treaties and contained nothing whatsoever to suggest the suzerainty of or even any special connection with China'. Richardson, *op.cit.*, p. 93.

26. 'Chinese rights in Tibet were thus recognized to an extent to which the Chinese had recently been wholly unable to exercise them'. *Ibid.*, p. 94.
    Grover Clark, *Tibet, China and Great Britain* (Peking, 1924), p. 14, maintains however that the Convention of 1906 'does not seem to have abridged' either Britain's special interest in Tibet or her right to deal with her (Tibet) direct.

27. The citation is from the text of the (Anglo-Russian) Convention.

28. It may be recalled that Lord Curzon resigned from his Indian Viceroyalty in August 1905, although he did not return to England at once, and that it was not until 1915, that he became a member of Mr. Asquith and later Lloyd George's war-time coalition Cabinet.

29. Between 1905-9, Sir Francis was Resident in Kashmir. He retired in the latter year being convinced that his peculiar talents were not being properly employed. Seaver, *op.cit.* p. 273.

30. 'The Russian Convention', Lord Curzon wrote on September 25, 1907, 'is in ,my view deplorable. It gives up all that we have been fighting for years and gives it up, with wholesale abandon that is truly cynical in its recklessness. Ah me! It makes one despair of public life and the efforts of a century sacrificed and nothing or next to nothing in return'. Ronaldshay, *Life*, III. p. 38. Also *Parliamentary Debates*, Vol. 184, p. 537.

31. Sir Francis Younghusband, *Our Position in Tibet* (Central Asian Society, London, 1910. Little known this small brochure gives the text of the talk by Sir Francis and the very interesting discussion that followed. The proceedings were held under the auspices of the then Central Asian (later the Royal Central Asian) Society.

32. Grey of Fallodon, *Twenty Five Years* (London, 1925), p. 154.

33. The Chinese had started by attempting to absorb Eastern Tibet, the in-between area stretching east of the Salween to the borders of Szechuan, wherein Lhasa's control was principally 'spiritual' and to that extent perhaps shadowy and vague. Later, in 1905 came the appointment of Chao Erh-feng who was to prove most effective in establishing authority over this vast region.

34. Secretary of State to Viceroy, telegram, August 16,1904, Ampthill Papers, *op.cit.* specially enjoined: 'In no case must there be looting by the troops'. On August 1 1904 Ampthill wrote to Brodrick that, 'It was, however, a comfort to hear that I should be supported in any directions I might have to give for the destruction of buildings. the confiscation of property and the seizure of hostages.....' *Ibid.*
    Taraknath Das, *op.cit.*, p. 64, quotes from a despatch of the *Daily Mail* correspondent

alleging looting of the Lhasa monasteries. Mohammed Barkatullah, *The Forum* (New York), 1905, pp. 128-40, refers to the systematic spoliation carried out by the British in Lhasa and concluded: 'The English have such a special knack of looting, and they do it in such an adroit manner that no one can venture to call it by its true name'. Tibet Papers, *op.cit.*, Cd. 2370, No. 122, p. 50, contains a telegraphic directive from the Viceroy to Younghusband forbidding any looting of monasteries.

35. 'Chao (Erh-feng) would appear to have construed our mission of 1904 as the shadow of an ultimate annexation. To meet this imaginary danger, he designed to convert Tibet into a Chinese province by establishing throughout the country, under Chinese officials, the form of political and administrative organization that obtains in China'. Rhin-chen Lhamo (Mrs. Louis King), *We Tibetans* (London, 1926), p. 54.

36. Richardson, History, *op.cit.*, p. 99.

37. Bell, *Tibet*, p. 70.

38. In its dispatch of July 18, 1907, the Government of India gave a formidable list of such breaches, Tibet Papers, *op.cit.*, Cd. 2370, No. 196, but the Secretary of State over-ruled them and ordered evacuation for reasons 'of policy and expediency'. *Ibid.*, No. 199.

39. During his sojourn in Peking, the Lama received Sir John Jordan, the British Minister, in audience and 'expressed a desire for friendly relations with the Indian Government'. Later he was to address an open appeal to 'Great Britain and all the Ministers of Europe'.

40. The Tsar's telegram to the Lama read: 'A large number of my subjects who profess the Buddhist faith had the happiness of being able to pay homage to their great High Priest during his visit to northern Mongolia, which borders on the Russian Empire. As I rejoice that my subjects have had the opportunity of deriving benefit from your salutary spiritual influence, I beg you to accept the expression of my sincere thanks and my regards'. Bell, *Portrait*, p. 68.

41. Tibet Papers, *op.cit.*, Cd. 5240, Nos. 347 and 349.

Appendices

Appendix 1

Convention between Great Britain and China relating to Sikkim and Tibet, signed at Calcutta, March 17, 1890.

Whereas Her Majesty the Queen of the United Kingdom of Great Britain and Ireland, and Empress of India, and His Majesty the Emperor of China, are sincerely desirous to maintain and perpetuate the relations of friendship and good understanding which now exist between their respective Empires; and whereas recent occurrences have tended towards a disturbance of the said relations, and it is desirable to clearly define and permanently settle certain matters connected with the boundary between Sikkim and Tibet, Her Britannic Majesty and His Majesty the Emperor of China have resolved to conclude a Convention on this subject and have, for this purpose named Plenipotentiaries, that is to say:

Her Majesty the Queen of Great Britain and Ireland, His Excellency the Most Honb'le Henry Charles Keith Pethy Fitzmaurice, G.S.M.I., G.C.M.G., G.M.I.E., Marquess of Lansdowne, Viceroy and Governor-General of India;

And His Majesty the Emperor of China, His Excellency Sheng Tai, Imperial Associate Resident in Tibet, Military Deputy Lieutenat Governor;

Who having met and communicated to each other their full·powers, and finding these to be in proper form, have agreed upon the following Convention in eight Articles:

ARTICLE I

The boundary of Sikkim and Tibet shall be the crest of the mountain range separating the waters which flow into the Sikkim Teesta and its affluents from the waters flowing into the Tibetan Mochu and northwards into other rivers of Tibet. The line commences at Mount Gipmochi on the Bhutan frontier and follows the above mentioned water-parting to the point where it meets Nipal territory.

ARTICLE II

It is admitted that the British Government, whose protectorate over the Sikkim State is hereby recognised, has direct and exclusive control over the internal administration and foreign relations of that State, and except through and with the permission of the British Government, neither the ruler of the State nor any of its officers shall have official relations of any kind, formal or informal, with any other country.

ARTICLE III

The Government of Great Britain and Ireland and the Government of China engage reciprocally to respect the boundary as defined in Article I, and to prevent acts of aggression from their respective sides of the frontier.

ARTICLE IV

The question of providing increased facilities of trade across the Sikkim-Tibet frontier will hereafter be discussed with a view to a mutually satisfactory arrangement by the High Contracting Parties.

ARTICLE V

The question of pasturage on the Sikkim side of the frontier is reserved for further examination and future adjustment.

ARTICLE VI

The High Contracting Parties reserve for discussion and arrangement the method in which official communications between the British authorities in India and the authorities in Tibet shall be conducted.

ARTICLE VII

Two joint Commissioners shall, within six months from the ratification of this Convention, be appointed, one by the British Government in India, the other by the Chinese Resident in Tibet. The said commissioners shall meet and discuss the question which by the last three preceding Articles have been reserved.

ARTICLE VIII

The present Convention shall be ratified, and the ratifications shall be exchanged in London s soon as possible after the date of the signature thereof.

In witness whereof the respective negotiators have signed the same and affixed thereunto the seals of their arms.

Done in quadruplicate at Calcutta this seventeenth day of March in the year of our Lord one thousand eight hundred and ninety, corresponding with the Chinese date the twenty-seventh day of the second moon of the sixteenth years of Kuang Hsu.

> Lansdowne
> Sheng Tai
> Chinese seal and signature

Note: *The Convention was signed at Calcutta with no Tibetan representative being either present or taking part in the negotiations.*

Instruments of ratification were exchanged in London on August 27, 1890.

Appendix 2

Regulations regarding Trade, Communication, and Pasturage to be appended to the Convention between Great British and China of March 17, 1890, relative to Sikkim and Tibet. Signed at Darjeeling, December 5, 1893.

1. A trade mart shall be established at Yatung on the Tibetan side of the frontier, and shall be opened to all British subjects for purposes of trade from the 1st day of May 1894. The Government of India shall be free to send officers to reside at Yatung to watch the conditions of British trade at the mart.

2. British subjects trading at Yatung shall be at liberty to travel freely to and fro between the frontier and Yatung, and to rent houses and godowns for their own accommodation, and the storage of their goods. The Chinese Government shall undertake that suitable buildings for the above purpose shall be provided for the officer or officers appointed by the Government of India under Regulation I to reside at Yatung. British subjects shall be at liberty to sell their goods to whomsoever they please, to purchase native commodities in kind or in money, to hire transport of any kind, and in general to conduct their business transactions in conformity with local usage, and without any vexatious restrictions. Such British subjects shall receive efficient protection for their persons and property. At Lang-jo and Ta-chun, between the frontier and Yatung, where rest-houses have been built by the Tibetan authorities, British subjects can break their journey in consideration of a daily rent.

3. Import and export trade in the following articles: arms, ammunition, military stores, salt, liquors, and intoxicating or narcotic drugs, may, at the option of either Government, be entirely prohibited, or permitted only on such conditions as either Government, on their own side, may think fit to impose.

4. Goods, other than goods of the description enumerated in Regulation 3, entering Tibet from British India, across the Sikkim-Tibet frontier, or vice versa, whatever their origin, shall be exempt from duty for a period of five years, commencing from the date of the opening of Yatung to trade; but after the expiration of this term, if found desirable, a tariff may be mutually agreed upon and enforced. Indian tea may be imported into Tibet at a rate of duty not exceeding that at which Chinese tea is imported into England, but trade in Indian tea shall not be engaged in during the five years for which other commodities are exempt.

5. All goods on arrival at Yatung, whether from British India or from Tibet, must be reported at the Customs Station there for examination, and the report must give full particulars of the description, quality and value of the goods.

6. In the event of trade disputes arising between the British and Chinese or Tibetan subjects in Tibet, they shall be inquired into and settled in personal conference by the Political Officer for Sikkim and the Chinese Frontier Officer. The object of personal conference being to ascertain facts and do justice, where there is a divergence of views, the law of the country to which the defendant belongs shall guide.

7. Despatches from the Government of India to the Chinese Imperial Resident in Tibet shall be handed over by the Political Officer for Sikkim to the Chinese Frontier Officer, who will forward them by special courier.

    Despatches from the Chinese Imperial Resident in Tibet to the Government of India will be handed over by the Chinese Frontier Officer to the Political Officer for Sikkim, who will forward them as quickly as possible.

8. Despatches between the Chinese and Indian officials must be treated with due respect, and couriers will be assisted in passing to and fro by the officers of each Government.

9. After the expiration of one year from the date of opening of Yatung, such Tibetans as continue to graze their cattle in Sikkim will be subject to such Regulations as the British Government may from time to time enact for the general conduct of such grazing in Sikkim. Due notice will be given of such Regulations.

GENERAL ARTICLES

1. In the event of disagreement between the Political Officer for Sikkim and the Chinese Frontier Officer, each official shall report the matter to his immediate superior, who in turn, if a settlement is not arrived at between them, shall refer such matter to their respective Governments for disposal.

2. After the lapse of five years from the date on which these Regulations shall come into force, and on six months notice given by either party, these Regulations shall be subject to revision by Commissioners appointed on both sides for this purpose, who shall be empowered to decide on and adopt such amendments and extensions as experience shall prove desirable.

3. It having been stipulated that Joint Commissioners should be appointed by the British and Chinese Governments under Article VII of the Sikkim-Tibet Convention to meet and discuss, with a view to the final settlement of the questions reserved under Articles IV, V, and VI of the said Convention; and the Commissioners thus appointed having met and discussed the questions referred to, namely trade, communication, and pasturage, have been further appointed to sign the Agreement in nine Regulations and three General Articles now arrived at, and to declare that the said nine Regulations and three General Articles form part of the convention itself.

    In witness whereof the respective Commissioners have hereto subcribed their names.

    Done in quadruplicate at Darjeeling, this 5th day of December, in the year 1893, corresponding with the Chinese date, the 28th day of the 10th moon of the 19th years of Kuang Hsu.

    A. W. Paul, *British Commissioner*

    Ho Chang-Jung ⎫
    James H. Hart   ⎬ *Chinese Commissioners*

Note: *A Tibetan Minister was present at the negotiations in Darjeeling but took no active part nor did he sign the Regulations.*

Appendix 3

Convention between Great Britain and Tibet, signed at Lhasa on the 7th September, 1904.

Whereas doubts and difficulties have arisen as to the meaning and viabilities of the Anglo-Chinese Convention of 1890, and the Trade Regulations of 1893 and as to the liabilities of the Tibetan Government under these agreements; and whereas recent occurrences have tended towards a disturbance of the relations of friendship and good understanding which have existed between the British Government and the Government of Tibet; and whereas it is desirable to restore peace and amicable relations and to resolve and determine the doubts and difficulties as aforesaid, the said Governments have resolved to conclude a convention with these objects and the following articles have been agreed upon by Colonel F. E. Younghusband, C.I.E., in virtue of full power vested in him by His Britannic Majesty's Government and on behalf of that said Government and Lo Sang Gyal-Tsen, the Ga-den Ti-Rimpoche, and the representatives of the Council, of the three monasteries Se-ra, Dre-pung and Ga-den and of the ecclesiastical and lay officials of the National Assembly on behalf of the Government of Tibet.

I.   The Government of Tibet engages to respect the Anglo-Chinese Convention of 1890 and to recognise the frontier between Sikkim and Tibet, as defined in Article I of the said Convention, and to erect boundary pillars accordingly.

II. The Tibetan Government undertakes to open forthwith trade marts, to which all British and Tibetan subjects shall have free right of access at Gyantse and Gartok, as well as at Yatung.

The Regulations applicable to the trade-mart at Yatung under the Anglo-Chinese Arrangement of 1893, shall, subject to such amendments as may hereafter be agreed upon by common consent between the British and Tibetan Governments, apply to the marts above mentioned.

In addition to establishing trade-marts at the places mentioned, the Tibetan Government undertakes to place no restrictions on the trade by existing routes, and to consider the question of establishing fresh trade-marts under similar conditions, if necessary development of trade requires it.

III. The question of the amendment of the Regulations of 1893 is reserved for separate consideration and the Tibetan Government undertakes to appoint fully authorised delegates to negotiate with representatives of the British Government as to the details of the amendments required.

IV. The Tibetan Government undertakes to keep the roads to Gyantse and levy no dues of any kind other than those provided for in the tariff to be mutually agreed upon.

V.   The Tibetan Government undertakes to keep the roads to Gyantse and Gartok from the frontier clear of all obstruction and in a state of repair suited to the needs of the trade and to establish at Yatung, Gyantse and Gartok and at each of the other trade-marts that may hereafter be established a Tibetan agent who shall receive from the British Agent appointed to watch over British trade at the marts in question any letter which the latter may desire to send to the Tibetan or to the Chinese authorities. The Tibetan Agent shall also be responsible for the due delivery of such communications and for the transmission of replies.

VI. As an indemnity to the British Government for the expense incurred in the dispatch of armed troops to Lhasa, to exact reparation for breaches of treaty obligations, and for the insults offered to and attack upon the British Commissioner and his following and escort, the Tibetan Government engages to pay a sum of pounds five hundred thousand—equivalent to rupees seventy-five lakhs—to the British Government.

The indemnity shall be payable at such place as the British Government may from time to time after due notice, indicate whether in Tibet or in the British districts of Darjeeling or Jalpaiguri in seventy-five annual instalments of rupees one lakh each on the 1st January in each year, beginning from the 1st January, 1906.

VII. As security for the payment of the above mentioned indemnity and for the fulfillment of the provisions relative to trade-marts specified in Articles II, III, IV and V the British Government shall continue to occupy the Chumbi Valley until the indemnity has been paid, and until the trade-marts have been effectively opened for three years, whichever date may be the later.

VIII. The Tibetan Government agrees to raze all forts and fortifications and remove all armaments which might impede the course of free communication between the British frontier and the Towns of Gyantse and Lhasa.

IX. The Government of Tibet engages that without the previous consent of the British Government—

a. No portion of Tibetan territory shall be ceded, mortgaged or otherwise given for occupation to any foreign power;

b. No such power shall be permitted to intervene in Tibetan affairs;

c. No Representatives or Agents of any Foreign Power shall be admitted to Tibet;

d. No concessions for railways, roads and telegraphs, mining or other rights shall be granted to any Foreign Power or to the subject of any Foreign Power. In the event of consent to such concessions being granted similar or equivalent concessions shall be granted to the British Government;

e. No Tibetan revenues, whether in kind or in cash, shall be pledged or assigned to any Foreign Power, or to the subject of any Foreign Power.

X. In witness whereof the negotiators have signed the same, and affixed thereunto the seals of their arms.

Done in quintuplicate at Lhasa this 7th day of September in the year of our Lord one thousand nine hundred and four, corresponding with the Tibetan date, the 27th day of the seventh month of the Wood Dragon year.

Thibet Frontier Commission *Seal of British Commissioner*		*F. E. Younghusband, Colonel,* *British Commissioner*		*Seal of the* *Dalai Lama* *affixed by the* *Ga-den Ti-* *Rimpoche*
Seal of Council	Seal of Dre-pung Monastery	Seal of Sera Monastery	Seal of Ga-den Monastery	Seal of National Assembly

In proceeding to the signature of the Convention, dated this day, the representatives of Great Britain and Thibet declare that the English text shall be binding.

Thibet Frontier *Commission*		*F. E. Younghusband, Colonel* *British Commissioner*		*Seal of the* *Dalai Lama* *affixed by the* *Ga-den Ti-* *Rimpoche*
Seal of Council	Seal of Dre-pung Monastery	Seal of Sera Monastery	Seal of Ga-den Monastery Ampthill, *Viceroy and Governor-* *General of India*	Seal of National Assembly

This Convention was ratified by the Viceroy and Governor-General of India in Council on the eleventh day of November, A. D. one thousand nine hundred and four.

S. M. Fraser,
Secretary to the Government of India,
Foreign Department

Note: Here was the first direct treaty between Great Britain (acting for the Government of India) and Tibet. As has been noticed in the text, although the Chinese Amban at Lhasa was present at the negotiations—his role was indeed pivotal—he did not sign the Convention.

Declaration signed by His Excellency the Viceroy and Governor-General of India and appended to the ratified Convention of September 7, 1904.

His Excellency the Viceroy and Governor-General of India having ratified the Convention which was concluded at Lhasa on 7th November 1904 by Colonel Younghusband, C.I.E., British Commissioner, Tibet Frontier Matters, on behalf of His Britannic Majesty's Government; and by Lo-sang Gyal-Tsen, the Ga-den Ti-Rimpoche, and the representatives of the Council, of the three monasteries, Sera, Dre-pung and Ga-den, and of the ecclesiastical and lay officials of the National

Assembly on behalf of Tibet, is pleased to direct as an act of grace that the sum of money which the Tibetan Government have bound themselves under the terms of Article VI of the said Convention to pay to His Majesty's Government as an indemnity for the expenses incurred by the latter in connection with the dispatch of armed forces to Lhasa, be reduced from Rs. 75,00,000 to Rs. 25,00,000; and to declare that the British occupation of the Chumbi Valley shall cease after the due payment of three annual instalments of the said indemnity as fixed by the said Article, provided, however, that the trade-marts as stipulated in Article VI of the Convention; and that, in the meantime, the Tibetans shall have faithfully complied with the terms of the said Convention in all other respects.

Ampthill,
Viceroy and Governor-General of India

This declaration was signed by the Viceroy and Governor-General of India in Council at Simla on the eleventh day of November, A.D. one thousand nine hundred and four.

S. M. Fraser,
Secretary to the Government of India,
Foreign Department

Appendix 4

'Separate Agreement' regarding the Gyantse Trade Agent.

The Government of Tibet agrees to permit the British Agent, who will reside at Gyantse to watch the conditions of British trade, to visit Lhasa, when it is necessary to consult with the high Chinese and Tibetan officials on such commercial matters of importance as he has found impossible to settle at Gyantse by correspondence or by personal conference with the Tibetan Agent.

Sealed and signed at Lhasa the 7th September 1904, corresponding with the Tibetan date, the 27th day of the 7th month of the Wood Dragon year.

F. Younghusband, Colonel,
British Commissioner.

Seal of Dalai Lama affixed by the Ti-Rimpoche
Seal of the Council
Seal of the Dre-pung Monastery
Seal of the Sera Monastery
Seal of the Ga-den Monastery
Seal of the Tsong du (National Assembly)

Note : HMG disallowed the 'Separate Agreement' as being 'unnecessary and inconsistent' with the principle on which their policy had been based. Lord Ampthill, thereupon, declared it to be invalid and ignored it while ratifying the Convention.

Appendix 5

Dear Lord Ampthill,

I am most grateful to Y. E. for your kind and encouraging telegram which reached me yesterday evening. I think after the attack on us this morning HM's Government must see that the necessity for going to Lhasa has now been proved beyond all doubt. I had hoped on our arrival here that there was still a chance of effecting a settlement. But evidently when the Lhasa Govt. saw that we were not going on to Lhasa and that Macdonald with the guns and part of the force had returned to Chumbi they perked up again; and for the last week I have seen signs that they meant more mischief. Orders had been sent from Lhasa to collect together all the soldiers about here and a representative from the Ga-den Monastery at Lhasa had come round to incite the people. We shall never make a settlement therefore till we have got at the Lhasa people themselves. They are at the root of all the mischief and it is them we must bring to book.

Nor do I think we ought to let off the Chinese. If they pose as the suzerains of Tibet they should have kept these Tibetans in order and the very least we might have expected of them is that they should have given us warning this morning of the attack. There is a General Ma here who is by way of being a representative of the Amban and he should have sent word over to me.

The Tibetans this morning certainly showed a kind of stolid courage, founded mainly I think on the belief that the magic the Lamas exercise will save them from our bullets: and fortified also by a dread of what will happen to them and their families if they do not obey their leaders' orders. One man stood by a tree not twenty yards from our wall with his arms folded quietly looking on and was of course shot down. Many others were almost as stolid. But they have no real leaders and no fighting instinct and no military aptitude. In fact they are always showing themselves most inept and instead of attacking us while it was dark waited till day had broken. We were then woken by a wild boo-ing and firing. But most of the shots missed even the house.

I expect they will make another attack tonight but our position is quite impregnable, and the poor beggars have not a chance. Of course now that they have deliberately attacked us our blood is up and we are not so sorry for them as we were. Still there is something very pitiful in seeing these poor peasants who have really no other wish than to be allowed to plough their fields in peace being mown down by our merciless magazine rifles. It makes me all the more determined to smash those selfish, filthy, lecherous Lamas who are bringing all this trouble upon their country for their own ends. Two things strike me up here, one the impassiveness of the people generally and their keenness to trade with us: and the other the intense hostility of the Lhasa monks and especially of the Dalai Lama. If then we smash the Lama's power our way will I think be clear.

While I am writing I have received the telegram dt. May 2nd from Foreign (office) saying the London F.O. had asked the Chinese Govt. to tell the Dalai Lama through the Amban that we had no desire to remain in Tibet and were prepared to withdraw the Mission as soon as our settlement was made. I wish it were possible to consult me before such messages are sent for it is that class of message which makes the work of local officers so very difficult. The more we talk about withdrawing to such ignorant people as the Dalai Lama and his advisers and the more obstinate they remain. I should have thought Ld. Lansdowne with his experience out here wd. have appreciated that fact. I think it is the withdrawal of Macdonald (unavoidable of course) which has made the Lhasa Govt. revive their resistance as they have lately done and however much H. M. Govt. intend to withdraw I think they would be wise not to mention the fact more than necessary. I tried with all my resources by reason and persuasion and speaking mildly to the Tibetans to make a settlement: but once they have definitely entered into a quarrel I think it is wiser to shove soft words aside and stiffen ourselves a bit.

With many thanks to Your Excellency for your encouraging words, Believe me

Yours truly,

F.E.Y. (Francis Edward Younghusband)

Appendix 6

Viceregal Lodge
Simla

Lt. Colonel F. E. Younghusband, C.I.E.

Dear Colonel Younghusband,

I hope that you are glad that I did not allow you to resign when for the second time you expressed your desire to do so. However things may seem to you, to us they seem more hopeful just at present and I for one am convinced that you will bring this business to a satisfactory conclusion. I should like to remind you by way of a friendly hint that on-lookers see most of the game and this maxim is no less applicable to the large game of politics than to the more limited fields of athletic contests. At present both the Government and the general public regard you with a favourable eye; you are getting full credit for all that you have hitherto done and if you achieve only that which we ask of you there will be general satisfaction even though the result may fall far short of your own personal desires. The relief of mind to the Government and to the general public to see this Tibetan business at an end will be so great that there will be but little criticism of the actual results, and the man who achieves this much-desired object will be hailed with ample gratitude and satisfaction. It would be a thousand pities if you were to throw away this chance of personal distinction for want of a little more patience and a little less impatience of the views of those who have to regard the Tibet Mission as only one of the thousand anxious concerns of the Empire.

It is evident from the tone of your recent telegram that you are dissatisfied and disappointed at the terms of settlement laid down by the Home Government. You do not think that you are being allowed to ask enough and you consider that all this trouble, toil, anxiety and expenditure ought to result in more substantial gains. I may be wrong in my impression but it seems to me that a great part of your dissatisfaction is due to your belief that the Govt. of India share your views but are being checked and repressed by the Home Government. Now if this is your belief it may be of use to you to know that you are mistaken. My Colleagues and I are quite well satisfied with the terms of settlement laid down by the Home Government; we have come to the conclusion that the establishment of a political Resident at Lhasa is unnecessary for our purposes, that it would be a most undesirable addition to your responsibilities and that we can attain our objects just as well by the posting of a commercial Agent at Gyantse and at any other marts which may be established.

Annexation or a Protectorate as I have explained to you are out of the question in view of the pledges of His Majesty's Government but we should not in any circumstances desire them; our burdens and responsibilities on our frontier are already sufficiently great. Now if you read the terms with due appreciation of the latitude with which they can be interpreted you will see that we have got practically everything which we wanted and that within the main principles which have been so emphatically laid down from the beginning there is little else that we could ask for. My opinion is that Gyantse is geographically better suited to be the commercial centre of Tibet than Lhasa' and that once a flourishing trade is established there other influences will be focussed in the place. When that is done Lhasa would become a purely religious centre and could be left to the sensual monks whom you so much detest. This is of course only an idea of distant future possibilities, but the Brahamputra seems to me to form a natural boundary between the part of Tibet with which we wish to deal and the more negligible northern part of the country. I should be glad to know what you think of this view of the case. I have told you officially why I think it essential that the Mission should go to Lhasa without delay and I may inform you that not only do my Colleagues unhesitatingly agree with me in this opinion but the whole Consensus of responsible public opinion takes the same view.

I have also told you why it is impossible to make arrangements for you to stay at Lhasa throughout the winter and I hope you will come around to our opinion that this is unnecessary. Once we have demonstrated our power of going to Lhasa if and when we choose and thus prevented any future misconception, the threat of returning ought to be sufficient, and if we are eventually to treat Gyantse as the centre of our influence the sooner we begin to do so the better.

Now a few words in reply to your letter of the 24th June for which many thanks. I can assure you that His Majesty's Government have not thought lightly of the attacks on the Mission and the person of their representative; but would you after mature reflection desire to inflict heavier punishment on these unhappy and misguided people than they have already suffered? You have told us yourself that they are between the devil and the deep sea and that they only took to fighting us because they feared worse things at the hands of their own leaders. All that you have said from time to time justifies us in the belief that when a settlement has been made the Tibetans will become our very good friends. Would you desire anything to be done which would destroy that possibility and leave an enduring bitterness? And after all there is such a thing as magnanimity on the part of a great Empire towards a small and half-civilized nation. Do think of the matter from this point of view.

You refer very naturally to your prolonged absence from Mrs. Younghusband and your little daughter and this is a matter in which I can sympathize with you most strongly and sincerely. I hope that the separation will not be for much longer and that the circumstances of your return will in some measure make up for all the hardships of the long absence.

I hear that Mrs. Younghusband is coming to Simla and Lady Ampthill and I much look forward to the pleasure of making her acquaintance.
Believe me

Yours sincerely

Ampthill

Appendix 7

Walmer Castle
Kent
July 13, 1904

My Dear Younghusband,

I sent you a brief telegram of congratulation on the brilliant capture of the Gyantse Jong. You are now on your way to Lhasa and will, I devoutly hope, be permitted to arrive there.

The policy which you advocate is in my opinion theoretically the right one and it is quite likely that we may be forced to adopt more of it than the Cabinet at present contemplate or desire.

But before I came back to England—indeed while I was on the sea—Lord Lansdowne had gone and committed himself to a series of pledges to Russia (in my judgement unwise and uncalled for)—pledges against to get Russia's consent to the new financial arrangements in Egypt. I have accordingly been very much handicapped in the struggle that I have been waging. All that H.M.G. as a whole know or care about Tibet is that is a nuisance and an expense: and all that they want to do is to get out of it in any way that does not involve positive humiliation. This is the not unnatural attitude of an administration never strong and now tottering to its fall.

I have fought hard to get them to consider
(a) the possibility of a longer stay at Lhasa;
(b) the necessity of an agent in Tibet;
(c) the necessity of retaining the Chumbi Valley.

The Indian military authorities have pretty well killed the first. I have only so far succeeded in the second as to get the Govt. to agree to our right to put agents wherever we have marts, on the lines of the Trade Regulations of 1893. I have also got them to agree tentatively to the 3rd. I am now working to secure a modification or rather expansion of the orders of the telegram of July 6, which was sent off without ever being shown to me. I have been somewhat handicapped by my illness: since I have scarcely been out of bed for a month: and have had to do everything except one interview with the Cabinet, by correspondence.

There is no use in yielding to despondency or in resigning. If you have cause to feel it much more have I. What we have got to do is to make as good an agreement as we can in the circs, to point out clearly to those in authority the responsibility that they incur in overruling us, but as far as possible to keep them straight.

When you get to Lhasa or while you are there please be very careful to stop any pillaging of the temples or monasteries. Any other country would strip them bare. But let us set an example as at Peking. Of course enormously important discoveries may be made in respect of manuscripts. But let there be no burning or wanton destruction.

I need hardly tell you that this letter is written in the strictest confidence. I hope to be back in India in October.

Your sincerely,

Curzon

Appendix 8

St. James's Lodge
Delahay Street
Westminster

Dearest Francisco,

I send you a few words. Today I have had a long talk with Brodrick urging your (and George's) views, but they cling to Kitchener who says that the 'whole transport of India' couldn't store and keep you for the winter, which seems to me nonsense. They funk two things, the electorate, and a war with Russia, which, as a matter of immediate fact, might come at any moment: chiefly as a save-face for Russia. I argue that to have taken so much time and money and then to bolt in a month would to the Asiatic (and perhaps to the European also) imply defeat. Nothing is settled yet. God bless you. I wish I were with you. If you want to wire to me wire "Esteeming" London and I shall get it, and use Christian names for Ministers and authorities.

Yours ever

Harry Cust

Note: Addendum to the above letter in Younghusband's own handwriting:
This must have been written before the treaty was signed at Lhasa—probably while I was on the way up and while I was depressed by the idea that I would be allowed only a few weeks at Lhasa within which to negotiate the Treaty as the Military authorities did not want all the Transport mules—about 5,000— kept locked up in the line of communications.

Appendix 9

Private and Confidential   *The Standard Editorial Offices*
103, 104 and 105, Shoe Lane,
Fleet Street, London E.C.
27th January 1905

Colonel Sir F. E. Younghusband, K.C.I.E.

My dear Sir,

Our mutual friend, Colonel Frank Rhodes, took you a message some time ago from me to the effect that there was a possibility of your conduct of the Tibet Treaty being called into question. Being convinced that your work in Tibet has been for the good of the Empire I feel that an opportunity should be given you of knowing what is being done by those in authority in regard to the question of the Treaty which you concluded. I should be obliged if you would treat this letter as purely confidential. I write to you as a friend of Frank Rhodes and I feel sure that you will respect the confidence.

Tonight I had received the following letter from Mr. Brodrick. It is in circular form and most likely has been sent to every Editor with whom Mr. Brodrick is personally acquainted. He says: 'I am sending you early tomorrow the Blue Book on Tibet. It is, as the notice accompanying it shows, not to be published till Monday, and will not be sent to any of the Sunday papers or news associations until Sunday afternoon.

'It may be useful to you to know that the important and governing despatches are those of the 5th August, 3rd October, 7th November, and the final dispatch of the 2nd December. From these you will see that the policy of the Government has been the same throughout. Their desire has been to 'sterilise' Tibet in order to keep out foreign powers, but not to attempt an occupation of the country, or the maintenance of a Resident, which might prove at any inconvenient moment a heavy strain on our resources. This view, although repeatedly pressed upon the Indian Government from the beginning of 1903, and laid down formally in the telegram of the 6th November, 1903, did not prevent our representative pursuing a somewhat more adventurous policy, and it was therefore impossible for us to ratify the convention he had obtained in its entirety. Trustworthy evidence has since reached us that the points in the Convention, which were modified by the Government, were those which were the most strongly resented by the Tibetans, and which would have certainly led to trouble.

'These remarks, of course, are only for your confidential guidance in dealing with the Blue Book.'

If you will remember I asked Colonel Rhodes to warn you that such a step as this was likely to be taken by those in authority and I need scarcely tell you that if you care to take any action I am at your disposal.

Yours very truly,

H. A. Gwynne

Appendix 10

Text of Extracts from Lt. (later Lt. Col.) A. L. Hadow's Diary

a. **Tuesday, July 5th, 1904**

Arimistice ended at 12 noon. At 1-45 p.m. guns fired a few shots at Jong and I did the same. Orders for assault tomorrow.

b. **Wednesday, July 6th, 1904** Capture of Jong

Attack began at 3-45 a.m. I had one gun at G (Gurkha?) House. Assault of Jong took place about 4-30 p.m. Gurkhas did magnificently. Our casualties Gordon killed Officers wounded (?) sepoys kiled (?) woulded (?) .

c. **Thursday, July 7th, 1904**

In morning went over to Jong with Col. Y (Younghusband) and took Smith. Walked round most of it. Terrible effect of shell-fire. Then went down to Gompa. Rode in with O'Connor. Went through 3 upper buildings and then was turned out.

d. **Wednesday, August 3rd, 1904**

Marched about 6 miles and camped near Lhasa. Went out fishing and caught a few. V. nice having reached the end of our journey at last. Heavy rains at night, Amban came in afternoon.

e. **Monday, September 5th, 1904**

In morning went with a party to visit Lhasa and went right into the town. Not very much to see.

Bibliography

A. **Primary Sources**
   1. **Unpublished Manuscripts**
   Younghusband Manuscript, being (53) letters written by Colonel Francis Younghusband to his father, some are addressed to his sister, while in Tibet, in 1903-4
   Curzon Manuscript, in the India Office Library, London.
   Hamilton Papers, in the India Office Library, London.
   Ampthill Papers more specifically those relating to the period March-December 1904, in the India Office Library, London.
   Balfour Papers in the British Museum.
   Nam dhar of the 13th Dalai Lama made available through the courtesy of the 14th Dalai Lama, Swarag Ashram, Dharamsala, Panjab.
   Salisbury Papers, at Chirst Church, Oxford.
   Dairy for 1903, 1904 of Lt. (later Lt. Col.) A. L. Hadow.
   2. **Government Documents**
   Foreign Department, Secret E, Proceedings.
   Bengal, Political and General Consultations.
   Forest, Sir George W., Selections from the Letters, Despatches and other State Papers Preserved in the Foreign Department of the Government of India, 1772-1785 (Calcutta, 1890), 3 Vols.
   East India (Tibet) Papers Relating to Tibet, presented to both House of Parliament by command of His Majesty (London).

1904	Cd. 1920
1905	Cd. 2054 and Cd. 2370
1908	Cd. 3750
1910	Cd. 5240
1912-13	Cd. 6604

General Report of the Operations of the Great Trigonometrical Survey of India during 1866-67, 1867-68, 1871-72 and 1873-74.

Notes, Memoranda and Letters Exchanged Between the Governments of India and China, September-November, 1959, and November 1959-March 1960, abbreviated as While Papers II and III (New Delhi 1959-60).

Report of the Officials of the Governments of India and the People's Republic of China on the Boundary Question (New Delhi, 1961).

3. Debates, Speeches

Hansard Parliamentary Debates, Vols. CXXV, CXXXX, CXL, CXLI, CLXXXIV.

Speeches by Lord Curzon of Kedleston, Viceroy and Governor-General of India (Calcutta, 1906), 4 Vols.

U. S. Department of State Archives, Great Britain Instructions, Vol. 34.

4. Personal Records

Bell, Sir Charles Alfred, *Portrait of the Dalai Lama* (London, 1946).

Bethel, Lt. Col. L. A. ('Pousse Cailloux') 'A footnote', *Blackwoods Magazine* (London), February, 1929.

Candler, Edmund, *The Unveiling of Lhasa* (London, 1905).

Curzon, George Nathaniel (Baron, later Marquess, Curzon of Kedleston)— *British Government in India* (London, 1925), 2 Vols.

——*Leaves from a Viceroy's Notebook* (London, 1926).

Dalai Lama (14th), *My Land and My People* (London, 1962).

Harrer, Heinrich, *Seven Years in Tibet* (London, 1953).

Kawagnchi, Ekai, *Three Years in Tibet* (Benares, 1909)

Landon, Perceval, *The Opening of Tibet* (London, 1905), 2 Vols.

Macdonald, David, *Twenty Years in Tibet* (Philadelphia, 1932).

Markham, Clements R., *Narratives of the Mission of George Bogle to Tibet and of the Journey of Thomas Manning to Lhasa* (London, 1876).

Midleton, Earl of, *Records and Reactions* (London 1939).

Millington, Thomas Powell, *To Lhasa at Last*, 2nd Edn. (London, 1905).

Norbu, Thubton, *Tibet is my country* (London, 1960).

O'Connor, Sir William Fredrick Travers, *Report on Tibet* (Calcutta, 1903).

——*On the Frontier and Beyond,* a record of thirty years' service (London, 1931).

Turner, Samuel, *An Account of an Embassy to the Court of the Teshoo Lama in Tibet containing a Narratiue of a Journey through Bhutan and part of Tibet,* Second Edition (London, 1806).

Younghusband, Sir Francis Edward, 'Geographical Results of the Younghusband Expedition', *Annual Report of the Smithsonian Institution for the year ending June 30, 1905* (Washington, D.C., 1906).

—*India and Tibet* (London, 1910).

—*The Heart of a Continent,* Revised with additional material (London, 1937).

—*The Light of Experience* (London, 1927).

—'Our Position in Tibet', *Central Asian Society* (London, 1910).

B. Secondary Sources

1. Biographies

Seaver, George, *Francis Younghusband* (London, 1952).

Samuel, Viscount, *Man of Acton, Man of the Spirit: Sir Francis Younghusband* (London, 1952).

Harrison, George, "The Great Adventure: A Younghusband Anthology of Divine Fellowship" (in MSS).

Fraser, Lovat, *India Under Curzon and After* (London, 1911).

Leslie, Shane, *Studies in Sublime Failure* (London, 1932).

Moseley, Leonard, *Curzon: the End of an Epoch* (London, 1960).

Nicolson, Harold George, *Curzon, the Last Phase, 2nd Edition* (London, 1939).

Ronaldshay, Earl of, *The Life of Lord Curzon* (London, 1927), 3 Vols.

2. General Works

Aitchison, Sir Charles Umpherton (Compiler) A *Collection of Treaties, Engagements, and Sanads Relating to India and Neighbouring Countries* (Calcutta, 1929-30-31), 14 Vols., XIV.

Bailey, Colonel F. M., *China, Tibet and Assam* (London, 1945)).

—*No Passport to Tibet* (London, 1958).

Balfour, Lady Betty, *History of Lord Lytton's Indian Administration* (London, 1899).

—*Personal and Literary Letters of Robert, First Earl of Lytton* (London, 1906), 2 Vols.

Banerji, Anil Chander, *The Eastern Frontier of India, 1784-1826,* 2nd edition (Calcutta, 1945).

Bell, Charles Alfred, *Tibet, Past and Present* (Oxford, 1924).

—*The People of Tibet* (London, 1928).

—*The Religion of Tibet* (London, 1931).

Black, Charles E. Drummond, *The Marquess of Dufferin and Ava* (London, 1913).

Bower, Captain Hamilton, *Diary of a Journey Across Tibet* (London, 1894).

Brunhes, Jean And Vellau, Camille, *La Geographie de l'Historie* (Paris, 1921).

Buckland, C. E., *Bengal under the Lieutenat Governors* (Calcutta, 1901), 2 Vols.

Cammann, Schuyler, *Trade Through the Himalayas* (Princeton, 1951).

Caroe, Sir Olaf, *The Pathans* (London, 1958).

Carrasco, Pedro, *Land and Polity in Tibet* (Seattle, 1959).

Chamberlain, Austen, *Down the Years* (London, 1935).

Clark, Grover, *Tibet, China and Great Britain* (Peking, 1924).

Cobban, Sir Alfred, *Self Determination,* 2nd edn. (Chicago, 1948).

Collis, Maurice, *The Great Within* (London, 1951).

Combe, G. A., *A Tibetan on Tibetans* (London, 1926).

Cranmer-Byng, J. L. (Editor), *An Embassy to China* (London, 1962).

Cressey, George B., *Asia's Lands and Peoples,* Second Edition (New York, 1950).

Cunningham, Alexander, *Ladakh* (London, 1854).

Curzon, George Nathaniel, *Frontiers, The Romanes Lectures* (Oxford, 1907).

—*Tales of Travel* (London, 1923).

—*Russia in Central Asia in 1889* (London, 1889).

—*Persia and the Persian Question* (London, 1892), 2 Vols.

Dallin, D. J., *The Rise of Russia in Asia* (London, 1950)

Davies. C. C., *Problem of the North-West Frontier 1890-1908* (Cambridge 1932).

Davies, A. Mervyn, *Strange Destiny: A Biography of Warren Hastings* (London, 1935).

Das, Taraknath, *British Expansion in Tibet* (Calcutta, 1927).

Duncan, Marion H., *The Yangtse and the Yak* (London, 1952).

Edwards, H. Sutherland, *Russian Projects Against India: from Czar Peter to General Skobeleff* (London, 1855).

Edwards, Michael, *Asia: the European Age* (London, 1961).

Ekvall, Robert B., *Tibetan Sky-lines* (New York, 1952).

Elwin, Verrier, *India's North-East Frontier* (Oxford, 1959).

Enders, Gordon Bandy, *Nowhere Else in the World* (New York, 1935).

Fairbank, John King and Teng, Ssu-Yu, *Ch'ing Administration: Three Studies* (Harvard, 1961).

Fawcett, C. B., *Frontier, A Study in Political Geography* (Oxford, 1921).

Fraser-Tytler, W. K., *Afghanistan: A Study of Political Developments in Central Asia,* 2nd edn. (Oxford, 1953).

Filchner, Wilhelm, *Sturm uber Asien* (Berlin, 1926).

Fleming, Peter, *Bayonets to Lhasa* (London, 1961).

Florinsky, Michael T., *Russia: A History and an Interpretation* (New York, 1953), 2 Vols.

Ford, Robert W., *Captured in Tibet* (London, 1957).

Furber, Holden, *John Company at Work* (Harvard, 1948).

Gelder, Roma And Sturat, *The Timely Rain* (London, 1948).

Gleig, G. R., *Memoirs of the Life of the Right Hon'ble Warren Hastings* (London, 1841), 3 vols.

Gopal, Ram, *British Rule in India: An Assessment* (Bombay, 1963).

Gould, Sir Basil, *The Jewel in the Lotus* (London. 1957).

Grey Of Fallodon, *Twenty-five Years* (London, 1957).

Gupta, Anirudha, *Politics in Nepal* (Bombay, 1964).

Hedin, Sven, *Trans-Himalayas, Discoveries and Adventures in Tibet* (London, 1909), 2 Vols.

Hertslets, Sir Edward, *China Treatives,* 3rd Edn. (London, 1908).

Holdich, Sir T. H., *The Indian Borderland: 1880-1900* (London, 1901).

—*Tibet, the Mysterious* (London, 1908).

—*Political Frontiers and Boundary-Making* (London, 1894).

(An) Indian Officer, *Russia's March Towards India* (London, 1894). Jain, Girilal, *India Meets China in Nepal* (Bombay, 1959).

Karan, Pradyumna P. and Jenkins, William M., *The Himalayan Kingdoms* (Princeton, 1963).

Khan, Sardar Ali, *Curzon's Administration of India* (Bombay, 1905).

Khan, Sultan Mahomed (Ed.), *The Life of Abdur Rahman* (London, 1900), 2 Vols.

Kingdon-Ward, W.F., *Assam Adventure* (London, 1941).

I. Ya. Korostovets, *Von Cinggis Khan zur Sowjet republik* (Berlin, 1926).

Krausse, Alexis, *Russia in Asia, 1558-1899* (New York, 1899).

Lamb, Alastair, *Britain and Chinese Central Asia* (London, 1960).

Langer, William L., *Diplomacy of Imperialism* (New York, 1935), 2 Vols.

Lattimore, Owen, *Situation in Asia* (Boston, 1949).

—*Sinkiang, Pivot of Asia* (Boston, 1950).

—*Inner Asian Frontiers of China*, 2nd Edn. (New York, 1951).

—*Studies in Frontier History* (Oxford, 1962).

Lattimore, Owen and Eleanor, *The Making of Modern China* (Washington, 1944).

Lha-Mo, Rhin-chen, *We Tibetans* (London, 1903).

Loente'yeu, V.P., *Iostrannaya Ekspansiya v Tibbette, 1888-1919* (Moscow, 1956).

Lyall, Sir Alfred, *The Life of Marquess of Dufferin and Ava* (London, 1905), 2 Vols.

Magnus, Phillip, *Kitchener* (London, 1958).

Majumdar, R. C., *The Age of Imperial Unity* (Bombay, 1951), II, in History and Culture of the Indian People, 10 volumes.

—*The Vedic Age* (London, 1951).

Majumdar, R. C., Raychaudhari, H. C. and Datta, Kalikinkar, *An Advanced History of India*, 2nd edn. (London, 1950).

Mance, Sir Osbert (Brigadier-General), *Frontiers, Peace Treaties and International Organization* (Oxford, 1946).

Marvin, Charles, *Russian Advance Towards India: Conversations with Russian Generals and Statesmen* (London, 1882).

Monger, G. W., *End of Isolation: British Foreign Policy 1900-1907* (London, 1963).

Migot, Andre, *Tibetan Marches* (London, 1959).

Mookerji, Radha Kumud, *Harsha*, 2nd Edition (Delhi, 1959).

Moon, Penderel, *Strangers in India* (London, 1945).

—*Warren Hastings and British India* (New York 1949).

Morse, H. B., *International Relations of the Chinese Empire* (New York, 1918), 3 Vols.

Nicolson, Sir Harold, *Peace-Making* (London, 1919).

—*Some People* (London, 1951).

O'Connor, Sir William Fredrick Travers, *Things Mortal* (London, 1940).

O'Donnel, Charles James, *The Failure of Lord Curzon* (London, 1903).

Ottley, W.J., *With Mounted Infantry in Tibet* (London, 1906).

Pallis, Marco, *Peaks and Lamas* (London, 1940).

Panikkar, K. M., *The Founding of the Kashmir State* (London, 1953).

—*Asia and Western Dominance* (London, 1953).

—*Geographical Factors in Indian History* (Bombay, 1959).

—*Problems of Indian Defence* (Bombay, 1960).

Petech, Luciano, *China and Tibet in the Early 18th Century* (Leiden, 1950).

Pemba, Teswang, *Young Days in Tibet* (London, 1957).

Pribram, A. F., *England and the International Policy of the European Great Powers, 1871-1914* (Oxford, 1931).

Raymond, E. T., *Portraits of the New Century* (New York, 1921).

Reed, Sir Stanley, *The India I Knew, 1897-1947* (London, 1952).

Reeve, A. and Heber, Kathleen M., *In Himalayan Tibet* (Philadelphia, 1926).

Regmi, D. R., *Modern Nepal* (Calcutta, 1961).

Reischauer, Edwin O. and Fairbank, John King, *East Asia: the Great Tradition* (Boston, 1960).

Richard, L. *Comprehensive Geography of the Chinese Empire* (Shanghi, 1908).

Richardson, H. E., *Tibet and Its History* (Oxford, 1962).

Riseley, H. H., *Gazetteer of Sikkim* (Calcutta, 1894).

Rockhill, W. W., *The Life of the Buddha* (London, 1884).

—*Notes on the Ethnology of Tibet* (Washington, 1895).

—*The Dalai Lamas of Lhasa and their Relations with the Manchu Emperors of China* 1644-1908, (Leiden, 1910).

Sandberg, Graham, *The Exploration of Tibet* (London, 1904).

Sanghvi, Romesh, *India's Northern Frontier and China* (Bombay, 1962).

Scott, A. Maccalum, *The Truth About Tibet* (London, 1905).

Shabad, Theodore, *China's Changing Map* (London, 1956).

Shen, Tsung-Lien and Liu, Shen-Chi, *Tibet and Tibetans* (Stanford, 1951).

Sinha, Satyanarian, *The Chinese Aggression* (New Delhi, 1961).

Strausz-Hupe, Robert, *Geopolitics* (New York, 1942).

Sykes, Sir Percy, *Sir Mortimer Durand: A Biography* (London, 1926).

—*A History of Exploration,* Torch Book Edition (New York, 1961).

Teichman, Sir Eric, *Travels of a Consular Officer in Eastern Tibet* (London, 1922).

Thompson, Edward and Garratt, G. T., *Rise and Fulfilment of British Rule in India* (London, 1934).

Toynbee, Arthur J., *From the Jamuna to the Oxus* (London, 1962).

Tyson, Geoffrey, *The Forgotten Frontier* (Calcutta, 1945).

Vernadsky, George, *The Mongols and Russia* (Yale, 1953).

Vinacke, Harold M., *A History of the Far East in Modern Times* (New York 1950).

Waddell, L. A., *The Buddhism of Tibet or Lamaism,* 5th edition (Cambirdge, 1939).

Wang, S. T., *The Margary Affair and the Chefoo Agreement* (Oxford, 1940).

Weitzman, Sophia, *Warren Hasting and Philip Francis* (Machester, 1929).

White, John Claude, *Sikkim and Bhutan* (London, 1909).

Wint, Guy, *The British in Asia* (London, 1947).